Essentials of Treasury Management

FIRST EDITION

FOURTH PRINTING

D.J. Masson, Ph.D., CTP, CertICM
Peggy Weber, P.h.D., CTP, CPA
David A. Wikoff, Ph.D., CTP, CertICM

Association for Financial Professionals®

7315 Wisconsin Avenue
Suite 600 West
Bethesda, Maryland 20814

Tel: 301.907.2862
Fax: 301.907.2864

www.AFPonline.org

Association for Financial Professionals®

Essentials of Treasury Management

First Printing, October 2004
Second Printing, January 2005

All inquiries should be addressed to:

Association for Financial Professionals
7315 Wisconsin Ave., Suite 600 West
Bethesda, MD 20814
Phone: 301.907.2862 Fax: 301.907.2864 E-mail: AFP@AFPonline.org
Web: www.AFPonline.org

ISBN 0-9746708-5-5

Authors' Acknowledgments

The area of treasury management has been evolving rapidly in recent years. As the role of the treasury professional changes, the body of knowledge for treasury professionals must reflect those changes. While this text builds on the ***Essentials of Cash Management, 7th Edition***, it provides a significantly new and expanded body of information for the treasury management profession. The development of this text over the last two years has been both challenging and rewarding to the authors and the reviewers involved in the process.

The CTP Body of Knowledge Committee was a group of dedicated volunteers who shared both their experience and insights to ensure that this new text was both up-to-date and easy to understand. As chair of the committee, Woody Johnson, CTP, Vice President, US Bank NA, kept us all in line and personally reviewed all the chapters. The other committee members are listed at the end of this acknowledgement.

In order to ensure we had the most up-to-date and relevant material in this text, a Treasurer's Panel of current treasury professionals was convened to review all the chapters prior to publication. This panel was chaired by John G. Oros, CTP, Treasurer, Enodis Corporation and a listing of the members of this panel appears at the end of this acknowledgement.

We would like to thank Jacqueline Callahan, Professional Development Consultant, who served as Project Manager for the Body of Knowledge (BOK). We are also grateful to Joseph Tinucci, CTP, Assistant Director of Asset Management, University of Colorado, for his comments and review of both the Electronic Commerce and Information Systems chapters; Michele Allman-Ward, CTP, Cert ICM, President, Allman-Ward Associates, for her comments and contributions in the early stages of this project; and Heather Wikoff, CTP and Laura Wikoff, CTP for their advice and editorial assistance during the final stages of the editing process.

The three authors also want to thank all the many unnamed family members, friends, and clients for their patience, encouragement, and support throughout the course of the creation of this book.

D.J. Masson, President
The Resource Alliance, Inc.

Peggy Weber, Assistant Professor of Accounting
University of Illinois at Chicago

David Wikoff, President
End Results, Inc.

About the Authors

DUBOS J. MASSON, Ph.D., CTP, Cert ICM

D.J. Masson is President of The Resource Alliance, a training/consulting firm specializing in treasury management, electronic commerce, sales management and business process redesign. He is a frequent world-wide conference speaker on treasury and electronic commerce topics and is author of AFP's Treasurer's Handbook of Financial Management, Essentials of Cash Management, 7th Edition and co-author of Essentials of Cash Management 5th Edition. Dr. Masson has an MBA and Ph.D. in finance from Indiana University, is a Certified Treasury Professional and holds the International Cash Management Certification (Cert ICM) from the Association of Corporate Treasurers in the United Kingdom. Dr. Masson is currently serving as a Visiting Professor for the Accounting and Finance Department at the University of West Florida.

PEGGY WEBER, Ph.D., CTP, CPA

Peggy Weber is an Assistant Professor of Accounting at the University of Illinois at Chicago. She has 15 years of banking experience including lending and credit administration, cash management product sales and servicing, and risk management for cash management, investment and payment related products. Peggy has a PhD from the University of Texas at Austin, is a CPA (inactive) and CTP.

DAVID A. WIKOFF, Ph.D., CTP, Cert ICM

David Wikoff is President of End Results, Inc., an independent treasury management training and consulting firm founded in 1985. Among the clients of End Results are prominent domestic and international financial institutions and corporations. David is co-author of Essentials of Cash Management, 5th Edition and an associate editor of the 6th Edition. David's Ph.D. is in English and Irish Literature from the University of Colorado Boulder. David is a Certified Treasury Professional (CTP) and earned the Certificate in International Cash Management (Cert ICM) from the U.K. Association of Corporate Treasurers.

Members of the CTP Body of Knowledge

Woody D. Johnson, CTP, Chair
Executive Vice President
Citizens National Bank of St. Louis
Formerly with U.S. Bank NA

Kathleen J. Collins, CTP
Cash Manager
Cleveland Municipal School District

Timothy T. Hesler, CTP
Principal Consultant
PricewaterhouseCoopers LLP

Heather A. Kelley, CTP
Strategic Analyst-Marketing
Cargill Investor Svcs. Inc.

Jeffrey M. Lewis, AAP, CTP
President & Managing Partner
The Azimuth Group

James F. McCoy, CTP
Director, Business Development
Veritude

William K. Thornton, CTP
Sr. Vice President
Bank of America

Paul Vovchansky, CTP
Senior Treasury Analyst
Hoffmann La Roche Inc.

Members of Treasurer's Panel

John G. Oros, CTP – Chair
Treasurer
Enodis Corporation

Woody Johnson, CTP
Executive Vice President
Citizens National Bank of St. Louis
Formerly with U.S. Bank NA

Ira M. Birns, CTP
Vice President and Treasurer
Arrow Electronics, Inc.

Richard Caloca, CTP
Assistant Treasurer
Adobe Systems Inc

William Doering, CTP
Assistant Treasurer
University of Cincinnati

Mark K. Duckworth, CTP
Treasurer
Greyhound Lines, Inc.

Elizabeth M. Duff, CTP
Assistant Treasurer
Johns Manville

Danielle M. Egerer, CTP
Assistant Treasurer
Occidental Petroleum Corporation

Leanne Evans, CTP
Treasurer
School District of Palm Beach

Ann E. Frattarola, CTP
Assistant Treasurer
Deloitte & Touche

Dianne Greathouse, CTP
Assistant Treasurer
Wendy's International Inc.

Cynthia K. Holmes, CTP
Assistant Treasurer
The Kroger Co.

Randall Landes, CTP
City Treasurer
City of Kansas City

James Loewen, CTP
Assistant Treasurer
CMS Energy

William H. McBain Jr., CTP
Assistant Treasurer
Ocean Spray Cranberries, Inc

Robert J. Pedersen, CTP
Vice President - Treasurer
United States Postal Service

Glenda Probst, CTP, CPA
Deputy Treasurer
West Virginia State Treasurer's Office

Michael J. Smith, CTP
Assistant Treasurer
Los Angeles County Metropolitan
Transportation Authority

William R. Standley, CTP
Assistant Treasurer
New Balance Athletic Shoe, Inc.

Kathryn Thomas, CTP
Treasurer
H. J. Heinz Company

Caroline Walters, CTP
Sr. Vice President and Treasurer
Comdisco Holding Company, Inc.

Darlene G. Williams, CTP
Treasurer
Dallas Independent School District

Table of Contents

Association for
Financial Professionals®

CHAPTER 1
The Role of Treasury Management

I. INTRODUCTION

The area of treasury management has changed significantly in recent years. In some cases, the profession has expanded from traditional cash management to broader working capital and corporate finance issues. In other cases, it has completely embraced new areas of specialization as new tasks have been brought under treasury control. As the role of the treasury professional changes, the body of knowledge for treasury professionals must reflect those changes. While this text builds on the *Essentials of Cash Management, 7th Edition*, it provides a significantly new and expanded body of information for the treasury management profession.

This chapter begins with the recent trends and challenges in treasury management and how the profession has evolved to meet those challenges. It then provides an overview of financial management objectives and the role of treasury and financial managers in an organization. This chapter also introduces a number of terms and concepts that are described in more detail later in this book.

II. TRENDS IN TREASURY MANAGEMENT

A number of important trends in treasury management represent a continuation of former trends and are thus considered evolutionary, while others represent major changes and are considered revolutionary. Electronic commerce and globalization are examples of evolutionary trends, while the impact of legislation such as Sarbanes-Oxley and Check 21 are examples of revolutionary trends. In either case, the following trends, whether evolutionary or revolutionary, represent substantial changes to the treasury profession's body of knowledge and/or significant changes to treasury management practices.

- **Total Working Capital Management:** As the treasury profession has matured there has been a shift away from its original narrow focus on cash management (i.e., the cash account on the balance sheet) to a broader focus on total working capital management. In other words, there is an emphasis on managing all current asset and current liability accounts. This development is reflected in the extensive coverage given to this topic in Chapter 6, Philosophy of Working Capital.

- **Management of the Entire Balance Sheet:** The role of treasury in many organizations involves more than the management of working capital (current assets and current liabilities) to include the management of the entire balance sheet (total assets, total liabilities, and equity). This development is reflected in the extensive coverage given to these topics in Chapter 13, Source of Capital and Leasing, and in Chapter 14, Capital Structure and Dividend Policy.

- **Expanding Role and Responsibilities of Treasury:** The responsibilities of treasury have expanded to areas such as operational risk management, insurance, and pension fund management. These developments are reflected in the extensive coverage given to these topics in Chapter 18, Enterprise Risk Management, and in Chapter 19, Corporate Governance and Ethics.

- **Legal and Regulatory Developments:** New regulations such as Sarbanes-Oxley (SOX), the Patriot Act and Check 21 are having major impacts on the treasury profession and the financial services industry. These developments are reflected in the extensive coverage given to these topics in Chapter 3, U.S. Financial Environment, and in Chapter 19, Corporate Governance and Ethics.

- **Corporate Governance and Ethics:** Though ethics have always been an important issue for treasury professionals, recent corporate scandals and bankruptcies have reinforced the importance of focusing on corporate governance, as well. This development is reflected in the extensive coverage given to this topic in Chapter 19, Corporate Governance and Ethics.

- **International Treasury Management:** As the trend toward globalization continues, especially with the establishment of a unified currency (the euro) in the European region, many companies are establishing either regionalized or centralized international treasury operations using shared service centers (SSCs). Also, the use of derivatives to manage foreign exchange (FX) risk has reached a mature stage of development whereby these products are used not only by multinational corporations (MNCs), but also by many mid-sized companies and even small businesses. These developments are reflected in the extensive coverage given to these topics in Chapter 15, Global Treasury Environment and Chapter 16, Global Treasury Organization and Liquidity Management.

- **Outsourcing:** As the trend toward outsourcing of treasury functions continues, the nature of relationship management has changed. More and more companies are using a wide variety of non-bank financial service providers (FSPs) to perform functions that were formerly managed either in-house or by commercial banks. This development is reflected in the extensive coverage given to this topic in Chapter 21, Relationship Management.

Ultimately, all of these trends are reflected in the decision on the part of the Board of Directors of the Association for Financial Professionals (AFP) to change the title of this book from the *Essentials of Cash Management to the Essentials of Treasury Management*, and to change the industry's professional credential from Certified Cash Manager (CCM) to Certified Treasury Manager (CTP), of which this book represents the new body of knowledge.

III. THE CORPORATE FINANCIAL OBJECTIVE

Classic financial management theory views a company's primary objective as maximizing shareholder value. Shareholders invest in a company to earn a return that exceeds returns available from other investment alternatives. The efficient management of an organization's resources generates profits that enhance value to shareholders. In the short term, treasury professionals perform critical daily tasks that ensure the availability of cash resources necessary to sustain an organization's ongoing operational activities. In the long term, treasury professionals perform critical finance functions that ensure the availability of information necessary to support senior management decision making to attain an organization's strategic objectives.

A. The Finance Function and Financial Decisions

A company's financial policies and practices significantly influence its cash and treasury management operations.

1. The Finance Function

Finance plays a pivotal role in achieving a company's primary objective of maximizing shareholder value. The principal roles of corporate finance include:

- Accounting
- Funding
- Capital budgeting
- Financial planning
- Financial risk management

Accounting: The key role of the accounting function is to record and report a company's financial activity. This includes the recording of assets, liabilities, equity, revenues, expenses and earnings. Most financial statements provided to third parties are prepared in accordance with generally accepted accounting principles (GAAP). The Financial Accounting Standards Board (FASB), the organization that oversees U.S. accounting standards, formulates GAAP principles. A company may also develop various internal financial reports to assist in managing the ongoing operation and control of the business.

The Financial Accounting Foundation (FAF) selects members, provides funds and oversees the Governmental Accounting Standards Board (GASB) and the Financial Accounting Standards Board (FASB). The GASB establishes standards for state and local governments, state universities and other state affiliated agencies, while the FASB establishes standards of financial accounting and reporting for all for-profit entities.

Funding: The funding function involves raising capital to finance a company's operations and capital projects. A critical element in the funding decision is the determination of the proper capital structure (use of debt versus equity capital) and the overall cost of capital for an organization. This capital structure decision is closely linked to the ability to generate and raise necessary funds.

Capital Budgeting: The capital budgeting function involves three key components. The first includes quantitatively evaluating alternative projects in which a company might invest capital resources. Quantitative factors include costs, profits and cash flows. The second involves the estimation of economic returns of projects in relation to one another and in relation to the company's cost of capital must be projected. Finally, the qualitative factors of projects must be evaluated. Qualitative factors include considerations such as how a project fits into a company's core strategy and whether it is an activity in which a company has a competitive advantage.

Financial Planning: The financial planning function involves determining the need for funding in current and future operations. An important part of this function is the forecasting of revenues, income and external financing required in the future in order to support planned growth of the company.

Financial Risk Management: The management of financial risk due to changing currency exchange, commodity prices and interest rates is also a key aspect of the finance function. In some organizations, other types of risk management (operational, enterprise, insurance, etc.) may also be in the finance or treasury area.

2. Corporate Financial Decisions

Among the most critical financial decisions a company must make are those involving capital structure, investments, financing and dividends.

- **Capital Structure:** A company must decide on a desired capital structure, including the relative proportions of debt and equity. The optimal mix of debt and equity financing vary greatly from one company or industry to another.

- **Investment Decisions:** Companies have limited financial resources. Therefore, important decisions include determining what projects are appropriate and how much the company should invest in each venture. This analysis involves estimating both the risks and the returns of a given project. Investment decisions also encompass divestiture decisions such as the sale of a division or a subsidiary or the discontinuance of a product line because a company's capital resources may be utilized more effectively elsewhere.

- **Financing Decisions:** A company weighs several interrelated factors when deciding whether or not to raise additional debt or equity in order to finance projects. For example, a company's capacity to raise different types of capital is influenced by its perceived risk profile, which in turn influences the company's existing capital structure. The projected risk profile of an organization is based upon a proposed debt or equity offering that can influence its ability to market such an offering.

- **Dividend Decisions:** The earnings of a company belong to its stockholders but company management decides how much of the earnings are paid out in the form of dividends versus how much is retained to be reinvested in future operations. This decision is often guided by shareholder expectations, which may be dependent on a company's industry or stage of development. Dividend decisions vary widely by company and industry and payouts may be restricted by covenants contained in a company's debt agreements.

B. Financial Organization

A company's financial organization should be structured to facilitate the achievement of its overall objectives. Therefore, financial organizational structures vary significantly from industry to industry and from company to company. This topic is covered in detail in Chapter 2, Treasury Organizational Structure.

IV. TREASURY MANAGEMENT OBJECTIVES AND THE CASH FLOW TIMELINE

The objectives of treasury management are closely related to the management of the operating cycle. Cash is required to sustain the operating cycle, and treasury managers ensure that a company's operating cycle is adequately financed. This relationship is illustrated in Exhibit 1.1.

EXHIBIT 1.1 – OPERATING CYCLE

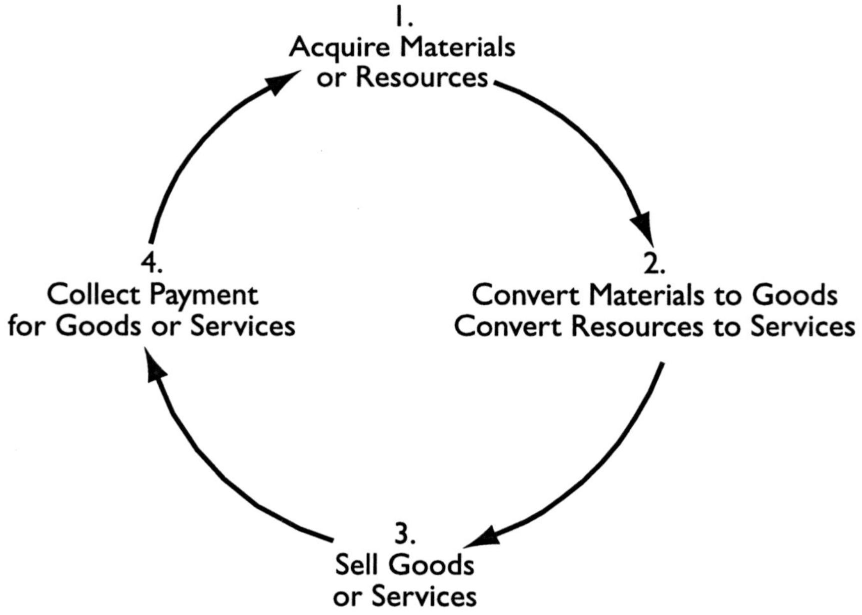

A. Treasury Management Objectives

The primary goal of treasury management is to utilize cash as efficiently as possible in a manner consistent with a company's overall strategic objectives. The major objectives of treasury management include:

- **Maintaining Liquidity:** Treasury managers are responsible for maintaining liquidity. Liquidity refers to a company's ability to meet current and future financial obligations in a manner that is as timely, efficient and cost effective as possible.

- **Optimizing Cash Resources:** Treasury managers are responsible for establishing policies, procedures and systems that minimize holdings of non-earning cash balances while providing adequate liquidity. Excess cash balances are either invested to generate interest income or used to pay down debt in order to reduce interest expense.

- **Establishing and Maintaining Access to Short-Term Financing:** Treasury managers are responsible for establishing and maintaining access to short-term borrowing facilities at the lowest possible cost of funds. Short-term borrowing facilities are used to finance a company's working capital gap, the gap that is created when cash outflows precede cash inflows as a function of the operating cycle.

- **Maintaining Access to Medium:** and Long-Term Financing (Capital Budgeting) – Although capital budgeting is ultimately the responsibility of the Chief Financial Officer (CFO) and senior management, treasury managers are often responsible for maintaining access to medium- and long-term financing alternatives as part of raising capital in the form of either debt (bonds) or equity (stocks).

- **Maintaining Shareholder Relations:** In many organizations, treasury managers are also responsible for maintaining shareholder relations and establishing trust accounts for bondholder interest and shareholder dividend payments.

- **Managing Risk:** Treasury managers are responsible for monitoring and controlling a company's exposure to interest rate risk, foreign exchange risk and other financial risks. In many companies, treasury may also play a major role in enterprise risk management, which focuses on company-wide operational risks.

- **Coordinating Financial Functions and Sharing Financial Information:** Treasury managers are responsible for coordinating financial functions and sharing financial information with other internal divisions and departments (marketing, sales, manufacturing, production, fulfillment, credit and accounts receivable, purchasing, accounts payable, payroll, accounting, management information and systems) for the purpose of ensuring that all of the above objectives of treasury are met.

B. The Operating Cycle and the Cash Flow Timeline

The operating cycle consists of the day-to-day activities in:

- Acquiring resources in the form of raw materials, semi-finished and/or finished goods
- Converting (that is, adding value to) these resources into goods and services that customers will purchase
- Marketing and selling the products or services
- Collecting receipts from sales

From a treasury manager's perspective, the operating cycle translates into a general cash flow timeline as outlined in Exhibit 1.2. The cash inflows and outflows occurring along the cash flow timeline rarely happen at the same time for the same amount. Given both the imbalance and the uncertainty of cash inflows and outflows, the challenge for treasury management is to ensure that sufficient levels of cash are available at each stage of the cycle.

EXHIBIT 1.2 – GENERAL CASH FLOW TIMELINE

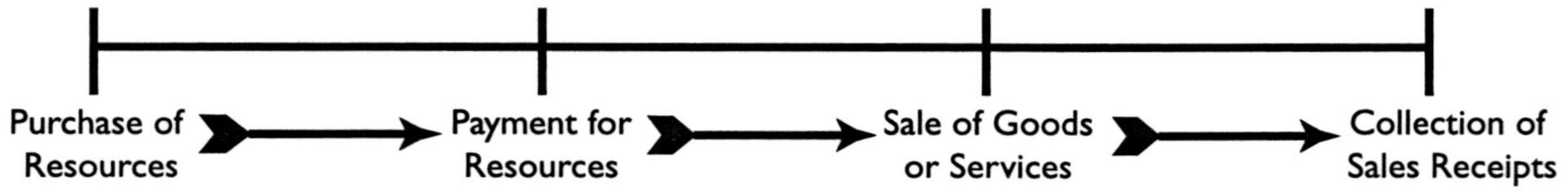

C. Cash Flows

There are three types of cash flows that treasury managers must consider:

- **Cash Inflows:** – Funds collected from customers, obtained from financial sources such as lenders, and/or received from other sources (e.g., a sale of an asset).
- **Concentration and Liquidity-Management Flows:** Internal transfers among operating units of a company and between the company's various bank accounts. The objectives of funds concentration are to:
  1. systematically create a pool of liquid reserves in the form of cash and/or cash equivalents (short-term investments or marketable securities)
  2. pay down short-term borrowings

- **Cash Outflows:** – Funds disbursed to employees, vendors and suppliers, lenders, local, state, and federal tax agencies; bondholders, and shareholders.

D. Cash Flow Timeline and Float

The cash flow timeline comprises the total time interval from the time resources are purchased from vendors and suppliers at the beginning of a company's operating cycle until the time payment is received from customers at the end of a company's operating cycle.

Float refers to the time interval, or delay, between the start and the completion of a specific phase or process occurring along the cash flow timeline. Despite the technological advances of the Internet and automated treasury systems, the majority of business-to-business (B2B) transactions in the U.S. still involve a seller sending invoices by mail and a buyer making payments by check and remitting the payments by mail. The delays inherent in this type of paper-based system result in numerous types of float that a company must manage. These are illustrated in the detailed cash flow timeline in Exhibit 1.3.

EXHIBIT 1.3 – A COMPANY'S CASH FLOW TIMELINE

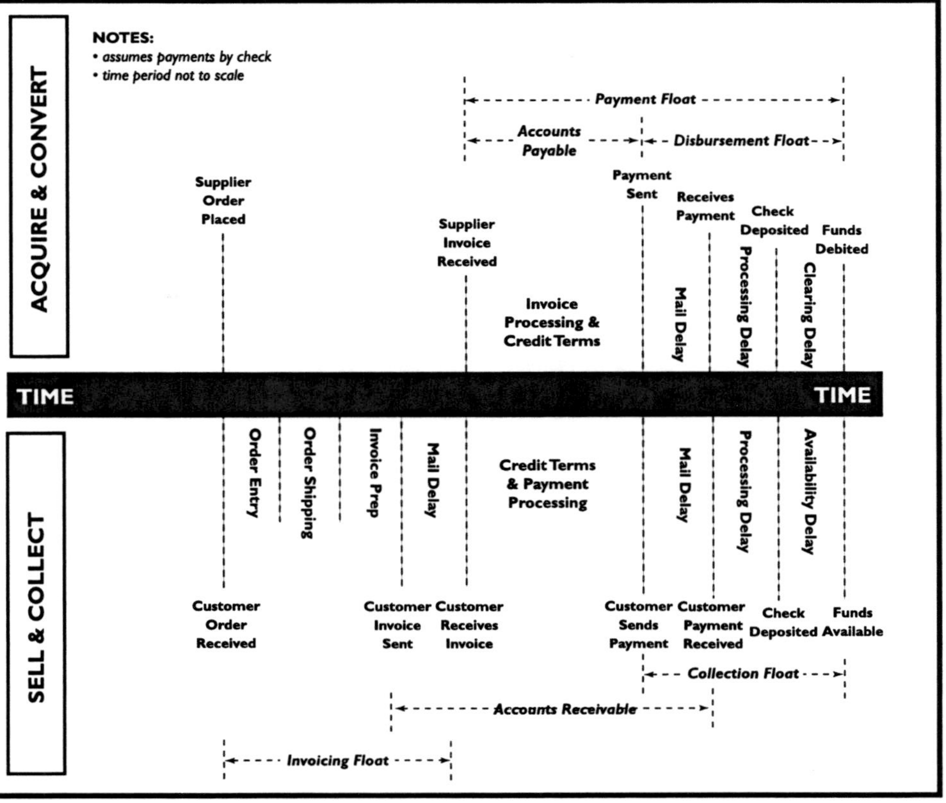

Different float terms may refer to the same (or similar) time intervals, but specific usage varies, depending upon whether or not the time period is viewed from the perspective of the seller/payee or the buyer/payor.

For example, consider the terms "collection float" and "disbursement float" when a check is sent to pay an invoice.

- From the seller's/payee's perspective, collection float (consisting of mail, processing and availability float) represents the delay between the time a check is mailed and the time the seller's/payee's account is credited with available funds.
- From the buyer's/payor's perspective, disbursement float (consisting of mail, processing and clearing float) represents the delay between the time a check is mailed and the time the buyer's/payor's account is debited.

Other types of float that impact the cash flow timeline are invoicing float and payment float. Invoicing float represents the delay between the purchase of goods or services and the receipt of an invoice by the buyer/payor. Payment float represents the delay between the receipt of an invoice by the buyer/payor, including the credit period, and the time the buyer's/payor's account is debited.

A company typically benefits from shortening all types of float associated with paper-based collections and lengthening all types of float associated with paper-based disbursements. However, this is a zero sum game (that is, a game with no real winners) because for every action on the part of a seller/payee to reduce float (e.g., a lockbox) there is an equal and opposite reaction on the part of a buyer/payor to extend float (e.g., controlled disbursement) and vice versa.

Therefore, in many industries, companies have taken a win-win approach by establishing strategic partner relationships. In these industries, the focus has shifted from the end of the operating cycle (sell and collect) to the beginning of the operating cycle (acquire and convert). In other words, the focus has shifted to the areas that represent the greatest possible gains in reducing cycle time such as just-in-time (JIT) inventory and supply chain management. For those industries and companies that have realigned trading partner relationships and reengineered supply chain management, the trend is to replace checks with electronic payment methods (Automated Clearing House [ACH] and wire transfers), thereby eliminating all of the paper-based float delays.

V. THE FUTURE OF TREASURY MANAGEMENT

As discussed earlier in this chapter, the role of treasury managers has been constantly expanding and evolving over the life of the discipline. The changes will continue into the future as both the treasury and overall management functions advance to meet new developments in the global business environment. The continued trend toward use of the Internet as both a communications and delivery mechanism will fuel new (and probably unexpected) changes in many of the basic financial and business practices and procedures. The ongoing evolution and consolidation of the U.S commercial banking industry will also have a significant impact on future treasury operations. Finally, the advent of a true global economy, with the ability to locate or source functions anywhere in the world, will have a dramatic influence on the treasury manager of the future.

Test Your Understanding

These chapter questions are provided to test your understanding of the information in the text. They are neither examples of CTP examination questions nor are they in the examination format.

Answers are on pages 565–566.

1. What are two examples of evolutionary trends and two examples of revolutionary trends in the area of treasury management?

2. What is the primary objective of financial management?

3. What are the principal roles of corporate finance?

4. What are the critical financial decisions a company must make?

5. What are the major objectives of treasury management?

6. What are the three types of cash flows a treasury manager must consider?

7. What are the definitions of cash flow timeline and float?

Association for
Financial Professionals®

CHAPTER 2
Treasury Organizational Structure

I. INTRODUCTION

The structure, role and responsibilities of the treasury function differ widely, depending on the type of organization. Differences include such factors as size, reporting relationships and the role of treasury in corporate governance. Another critical factor is whether or not treasury has responsibility for such areas as risk management, insurance, pension administration and process improvement initiatives such as benchmarking and reengineering. Finally, the structure of treasury functions can range from centralized to decentralized. For multinational companies with global operations, all of these factors are magnified in their complexity.

II. TREASURY OBJECTIVES AND POLICIES

It is important to determine the strategic objectives of the treasury function and to establish policies that outline how the treasury function should operate in order to achieve these objectives. Among the key areas that must be considered are the following:

- Management of cash and working capital management
- Short-, medium- and long-term financing
- Short-, medium- and long-term investing
- Forecasting of cash flows
- Management of banking relationships
- Management reporting
- Management of controls and risk
- Tax reporting and payments
- Accounting for financial instruments
- Management of interest rate exposure
- Management of foreign currency exposure

Treasury Policies

Five key areas for developing treasury policies and clarifying specific roles and responsibilities are:

- Establishing treasury objectives
- Determining funding requirements
- Establishing an investment policy
- Measuring and managing financial exposures
- Evaluating treasury performance

Specific to the operational aspects of the treasury function, policies must outline roles and responsibilities for:

- Calculating a daily cash position
- Initiating and approving internal and external transfers
- Determining methods of short-term funding
- Establishing financial-reporting methods, formats, and timeframes
- Selecting and managing third-party vendor and banking relationships

All treasury policies should be approved by the Board of Directors and documented in a treasury operations manual.

The creation of a treasury operations manual is important for numerous reasons. In addition to providing guidance and legal documentation for the Treasurer and the Board, the manual also provides a written record of treasury policies and procedures for internal and external auditors. A treasury operations manual is an important tool for training, disaster recovery, fraud prevention and system redesign. Because it is vitally important to the daily financial activities of an organization, it should be reviewed and updated on a regular basis.

III. FINANCIAL ORGANIZATION

The structure of a company's financial organization should facilitate the achievement of its strategic objectives. While this section focuses primarily on large corporations, many of the same concepts apply to mid-sized companies, not-for-profit organizations and government entities.

A. Financial Organizational Structure

In any large organization, the Board of Directors serves as the general authority for treasury operations. Ultimately, it is the responsibility of the Board to establish business policies and to approve major undertakings and contracts. For example, the Board grants the authority to:

- Open bank accounts
- Establish borrowing facilities
- Approve investment policies
- Issue securities

The Board also has the responsibility to act in the best interests of shareholders. This is generally interpreted in the U.S. as maximizing shareholder wealth as measured by a company's share price over the long term. (See also Chapter 13, Sources of Capital and Leasing, for a more detailed discussion of stock valuation and shareholder wealth.)

B. Key Roles and Responsibilities

In most large organizations, the senior treasury officer is the Chief Financial Officer (CFO). Some organizations, especially those with international operations, use the title Director of Finance or Finance Director (FD). The Treasurer and Controller typically report to the CFO. Some companies have a flatter organizational structure in which functions such as treasury, accounting, information systems, audit, strategic planning and financial analysis all report directly to the CFO. Exhibit 2.1 illustrates the typical finance reporting structure for a large organization.

EXHIBIT 2.1 – TYPICAL ORGANIZATION OF THE FINANCIAL FUNCTION

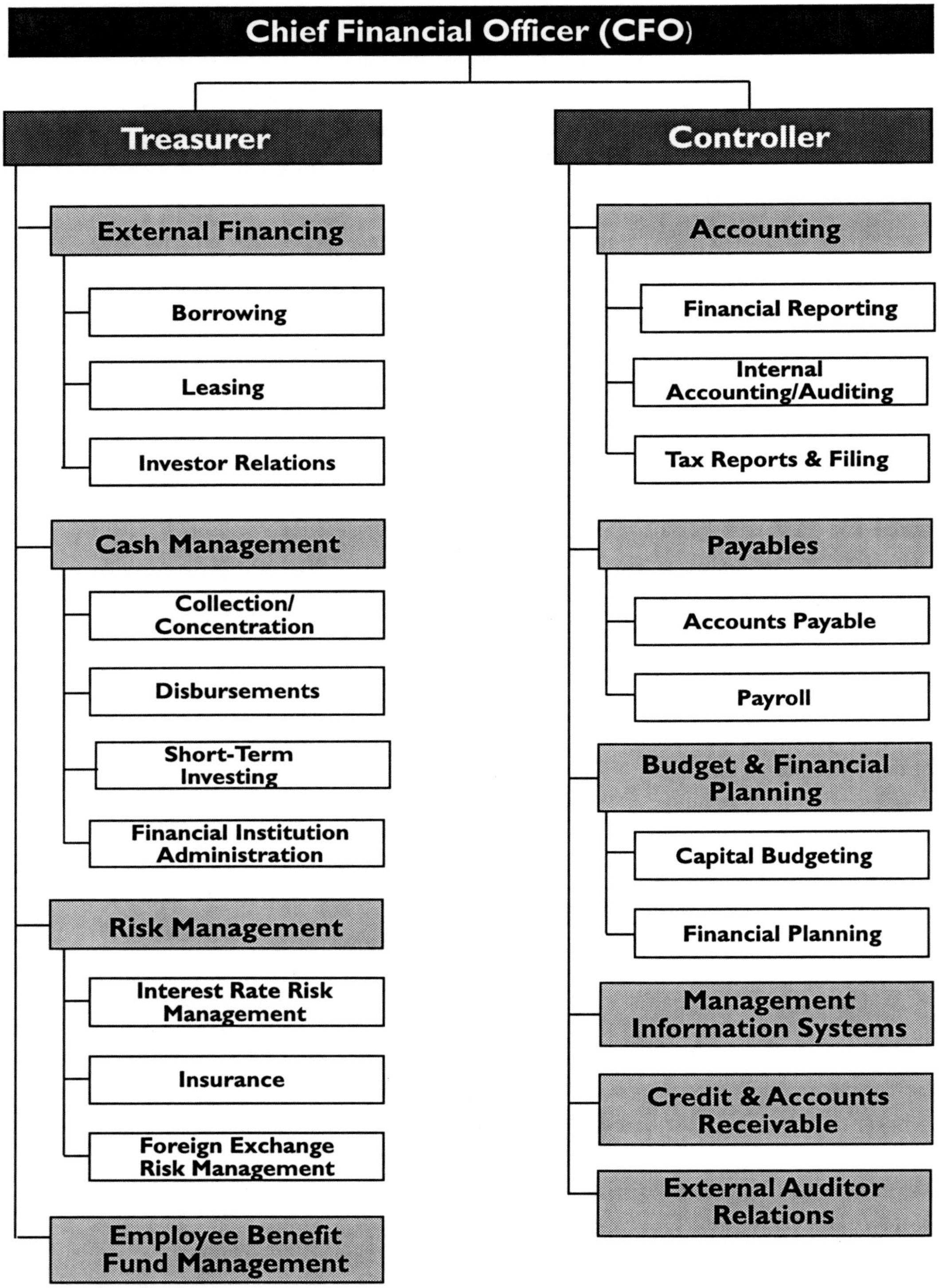

1. Chief Financial Officer (CFO)

The CFO is generally a member of the executive management team and reports to the Chief Executive Officer (CEO). In a large company, the CFO usually oversees both domestic and international treasury, and accounting functions.

The CFO plays an important role in strategic planning as the pivotal person in the capital budgeting process. The capital budgeting function involves establishing financial measures for quantifying alternative investment projects and evaluating both the risks and the outcomes. Selecting from alternative investment projects is one way that a company implements its strategic plan.

For example, the decision regarding whether to build or close a plant, to buy or sell a subsidiary or to develop or discontinue a product line is typically the responsibility of the CEO and the Board of Directors. However, the CFO provides financial information that is critical to these strategic decisions. Since the passage of the Sarbanes-Oxley Act (SOX) in 2002, the CFO also assumes personal responsibility for approving the accuracy of all financial statements.

2. Treasurer

The Treasurer is primarily responsible for:

- Arranging external financing
- Managing relationships with banks and other financial institutions
- Overseeing day-to-day liquidity management

International treasury functions and foreign exchange management may be part of a domestic treasurer's duties or may report to an individual solely responsible for international treasury management.

The Treasurer may be responsible for other functions, including managing dividend disbursements, insurance, pension assets and risk. In a large company, some of these responsibilities may be delegated to an Assistant Treasurer or a Manager of Treasury Operations.

3. Assistant Treasurer (AT) or Manager of Treasury Operations

For those organizations that are large enough to have the position of Assistant Treasurer (AT) or Manager of Treasury Operations, this individual generally handles all of the day-to-day operational aspects of the Treasurer's responsibilities as described above. This enables the Treasurer to deal with issues that are more strategic in scope and with timeframes that are more medium-to-long term.

4. Cash Manager

The Cash Manager, who typically reports to either the Treasurer or the AT/Manager of Treasury Operations, is primarily concerned with the management of day-to-day cash flows and banking relationships. In some companies, the Cash Manager may report to the Controller or the Manager of Accounting.

5. Controller

The Controller is responsible for accounts payable, internal accounting, coordinating with external auditors, preparing financial statements and budgets, tax filings and monitoring budgeted capital expenditures. In some companies, accounts receivable and financial information systems also report to the Controller. In other companies, these functions report to the Treasurer.

6. Risk Manager

While responsibility for financial risk management is a concern of the treasury area, other risk management responsibilities, such as insurance and disaster recovery, may be assigned to the Risk Manager. The Risk Manager typically evaluates and negotiates all insurance policies and coverage, as well as oversees disaster recovery and contingency planning. The Risk Manager usually reports to either the Treasurer or the Controller.

7. Internal Auditor

The Internal Auditor is responsible for ensuring that controls and operating procedures are established to protect a company from losses caused by inefficiency, inaccuracy or fraud. The Internal Auditor typically reports to the Board of Directors but, in some companies, may report to the CEO, the CFO or the Controller.

8. Credit Manager

The Credit Manager is responsible for:

- Preserving and collecting accounts receivable
- Setting corporate credit policies
- Approving the extension of credit terms to customers
- Assisting in setting exposure limits for other counterparties
- Establishing information systems to monitor accounts receivable

The Credit Manager reports to either the Controller or the Treasurer. However, in some companies the Credit Manager reports to the Sales Manager.

9. Accounts Payable Manager

The Accounts Payable Manager is responsible for determining that payments are made to vendors and suppliers based on credit terms. This process involves maintaining lists of authorized vendors and suppliers, reviewing incoming invoices, matching the invoices to approved purchase orders and scheduling payments. In some companies, the Treasurer may review and approve large payments prior to distribution. In other companies, the Accounts Payable Manager has full authority to initiate payments and merely informs the Treasurer of payments as they are made. The Accounts Payable Manager typically reports to the Controller.

C. Daily Cash Management

The primary objective of daily cash management is funds management. Funds management responsibilities vary from organization to organization. They may be the responsibility of a single individual, such as a Cash Manager, or may be divided among several individuals, especially in larger companies. Regardless of how the function is organized, daily funds management involves the following five tasks:

- Preparing a cash-position worksheet
- Monitoring cash balances on deposit at financial institutions
- Mobilizing funds
- Researching and reconciling exception items
- Coordinating functions with other finance areas such as accounts receivable, accounts payable and accounting

Other key responsibilities of daily cash management include banking-system administration, liquidity management and forecasting. Banking system administration involves:

- Managing bank relationships on a daily basis
- Monitoring bank-compensation arrangements on a monthly or quarterly basis
- Conducting bank-service reviews on a semiannual or annual basis

Liquidity management focuses on management of short-term borrowing and investing. Forecasting involves projecting future cash shortages and surpluses and monitoring the accuracy of prior projections

The funds management function may also entail responsibility for systems design and financial risk management. System design includes the development, analysis, implementation and ongoing evaluation of treasury management systems. Financial risk management involves the monitoring and management of currency or foreign exchange (FX) risk, interest rate risk and commodity or price risk.

Coordination with Other Finance Functions: Cash management requires teamwork and cooperation with other internal departments such as purchasing, sales, credit management, accounts receivable, accounts payable, financial planning, auditing and accounting.

The activities of other departments have a direct impact on the cash management function. These departments typically report to managers outside the treasury area, such as the Controller. Therefore, individuals responsible for funds management must interact with these departments on a daily basis to ensure that overall cash management objectives are met. To facilitate this, information from the cash management function may be integrated with the company's enterprise resource planning (ERP) system. ERP systems provide company-wide management information resources.

D. Treasury Management Organization

Treasury operations can be set up as either a cost center or a profit center. A cost center is the most common approach because treasury is usually regarded as a support function. However, in some instances treasury is established as a profit center. This approach is found in companies specializing in global finance, trade or risk management. Companies engaging in these activities have extensive dealings in FX, interest rate or commodities markets that require the use of derivatives and other hedging instruments to increase earnings and/or reduce losses. The rationale for treasury as a profit center is that it should be able to generate income from hedging and/or speculative activities.

1. Centralized Control

In addition to being established as either a cost or profit center, the treasury management function may be centralized, decentralized or a combination. Treasury operations may also be organized in a shared-services arrangement that involves in-house banking services.

Centralized control over treasury management grants either no authority or only minimal authority to field office personnel. For example, a company that operates regional or national sales offices with limited personnel typically centralizes control of treasury functions at the head office. A centralized treasury function is designed with the goal of enhancing administrative services and lowering operating costs.

A centralized treasury selects and manages all banking relationships, working capital management activities, and FX and hedging activities. In centralized arrangements, local banks are typically chosen by local managers and used for depository purposes only. Locally deposited funds are then transferred to a main concentration account, usually controlled at the central treasury level. A centralized treasury also manages short-term investments and negotiates short-term borrowing facilities.

In today's global business environment, the trend is for companies to centralize treasury operations. However, centralization is frequently resisted by managers of local and/or regional field offices because it reduces their authority and autonomy.

2. Decentralized Control

A company with relatively autonomous subsidiaries is more likely to have a decentralized treasury structure, thereby granting local and/or regional field personnel the responsibility for day-to-day treasury functions. The head office typically monitors decentralized treasury activities by requiring frequent and timely management reporting and by making periodic visits to local and regional offices to audit treasury staff. In decentralized treasury organizations, local and regional treasury personnel establish and maintain their own bank accounts, manage all short-term investment and borrowing activities, and manage FX and hedging activities.

3. Combined (Regional)

Some large multinational companies operate regional treasury centers that represent a hybrid of centralized and decentralized structures. Regional treasury centers are responsible for providing treasury services to specific subsidiaries within a designated geographic area. This hybrid or combined structure yields the best results in cases where significant time or cultural differences require local market expertise. Regional treasury centers are typically located in major financial centers of the world such as New York, Miami, London, Frankfurt, Hong Kong and Singapore or in locations that offer significant tax advantages such as the Cayman Islands, Dublin Docks, Luxembourg and the Netherlands.

4. Shared Service Center (SSC)

Many large multinational companies and global financial institutions are utilizing a structure called a shared service center (SSC). The purpose of an SSC is to enhance management and control over the costs associated with a wide range of business-support functions such as treasury, purchasing, accounting, receivables and payables management, payroll, benefits management, legal/tax and human resources.

(A more detailed discussion of SSCs is in Chapter 16, Global Treasury Organization and Liquidity Management.)

5. In-House Banking

Many large multinational companies have established in-house banking structures. In an in-house banking structure, treasury becomes the primary provider of banking services for the organization's operating entities, as well as the coordination center for intracompany lending. In some cases, treasury is the sole provider of banking services. In other cases, treasury may outsource some services to financial institutions or third-party vendors.

The primary benefit of an in-house bank is the overall reduction in bank service charges and FX costs. In the case of the latter, a company benefits by consolidating numerous small FX transactions into a few large FX transactions. An in-house banking structure can also provide a global organization with services such as netting, pooling and reinvoicing, as well as better risk management by centralizing FX exposures.

(A more detailed discussion of in-house banking, netting, pooling and reinvoicing is in Chapter 16, Global Treasury Organization and Liquidity Management.)

E. Treasury Linkages and Interfaces

The treasury function must interface with both internal functions (intracorporate integration) and external entities (intercorporate integration).

Intracorporate integration is oriented toward internal functions such as general ledger, accounts receivable and accounts payable. Relationships among intracorporate's internal functions are illustrated in Exhibit 2.2. Historically, intracorporate integration has been difficult because each business function had its own standalone information systems and software applications. The transfer of information among different business functions required the manual rekeying of data from printed reports, a process that was time consuming and labor intensive. Today, the widespread use of ERP systems allows personnel to enter and retrieve information from diverse business functions in a consistent and structured format. ERP systems have enabled organizations to make considerable progress in realizing the goal of enterprise-wide information integration.

EXHIBIT 2.2 – INTRACORPORATE INTEGRATION

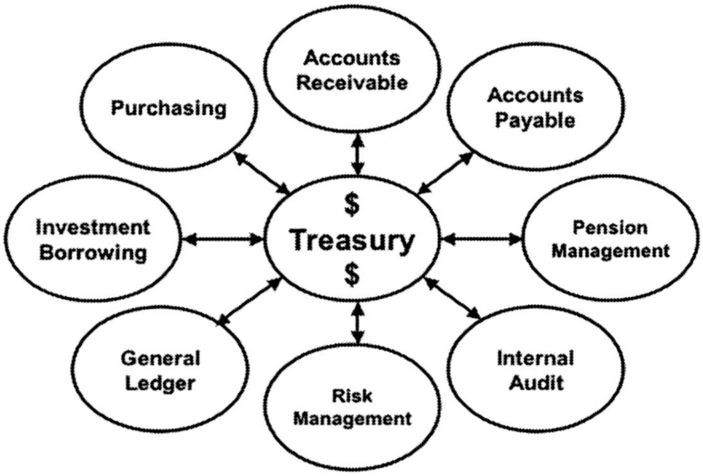

Intercorporate integration is oriented toward external relationships such as financial institutions, financial markets and third-party vendors. These relationships are illustrated in Exhibit 2.3. They play a key role in providing information or services that enable treasury to perform its daily functions.

(Chapter 11, Treasury Systems and Information Management, has a more detailed discussion of external data sources and uses.)

EXHIBIT 2.3 – INTERCORPORATE INTEGRATION

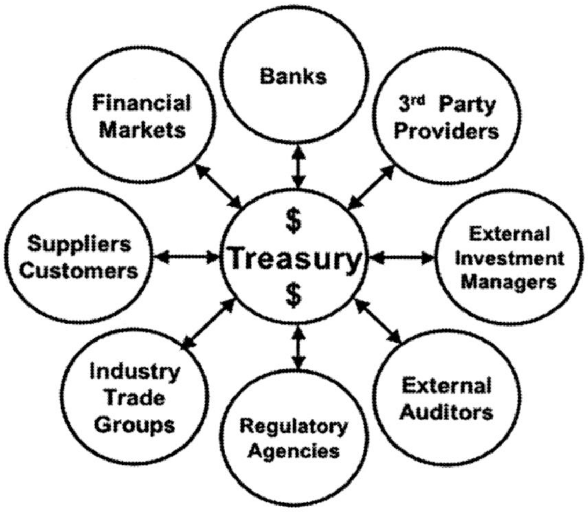

F. Enterprise Treasury Management

One of the newest trends is enterprise treasury management. Facilitated by Web-based technology, enterprise treasury management is a more strategic approach that involves managing a company's entire financial spectrum of activities. Three examples of enterprise treasury management are benchmarking, reengineering and outsourcing.

G. Reorganization of Treasury Operations

As the treasury function has evolved, financial professionals have continually endeavored to use all available resources more effectively. Technological developments have prompted a re-examination of how treasury is organized, how it functions and the efficiency with which it operates. In many cases, improvements in efficiency have resulted in a significant downsizing of treasury personnel and centralizing of treasury operations.

1. Benchmarking

Before making any changes to an existing treasury operation, it is valuable to research other companies that have successfully restructured their treasury functions. This concept is referred to as benchmarking and has been used in virtually all functional areas of business.

Benchmarking involves examining and comparing the core activities either within an industry or cross-industry for the purpose of identifying "best practices." Industry trade associations and consulting firms provide best practices data and benchmarking assistance that can be applied to issues ranging from basic treasury policies and procedures to management of complex global liquidity structures. The key metrics (comparison measures) used in benchmarking are typically either improvements in productivity and cycle times or reductions in costs and error rates.

2. Reengineering

Reengineering involves the radical redesign of a particular business process, with the goal of continuous process improvement. The redesign of treasury operations may include restructuring or eliminating traditional treasury processes. It is important to emphasize the key phrase in the above definition: radical redesign. Reengineering essentially requires the rationalization of all current structures, practices, and procedures.

3. Outsourcing

One possible outcome of treasury reorganization is to arrive at the conclusion that a third party can perform all or part of a given treasury function more efficiently and/or cost effectively. This is referred to as outsourcing. For example, some companies have outsourced their payables processing. These companies periodically send data files containing payment information to either a bank or a third-party processor. The bank or processor then disburses the payments on the company's behalf, using the specific payment method (check, ACH, or wire) requested by the company.

Other frequently outsourced functions are the collection of accounts receivable and the management of investments. In some instances, the entire treasury function may be outsourced to consultants who specialize in treasury management. Benchmarking, reengineering and outsourcing have dramatically altered the role, responsibility and structure of treasury functions over the past two decades and will continue to do so in the future.

Test Your Understanding

These chapter questions are provided to test your understanding of the information in the text. They are neither examples of CTP examination questions nor are they in the examination format.

Answers are on pages 567 and 568.

1. What are the five key areas for developing treasury policies?

2. What is the typical role of a board of directors in the treasury function of an organization?

3. What is the role of the CFO (Chief Financial Officer) in an organization?

4. What is the role of the Treasurer in an organization?

5. What is the objective and primary function of daily cash management?

6. What is the difference between setting up treasury as a cost center versus a profit center and when is the profit-center approach more appropriate?

7. What is a shared service center?

8. What is enterprise treasury management?

9. What is reengineering?

10. What is decentralized control of treasury and when might it be appropriate?

Association for
Financial Professionals®

CHAPTER 3
Financial Environment

I. INTRODUCTION

Historically, the Congress of the United States and federal regulatory agencies have imposed restrictions on financial institutions to protect against a concentration of economic and political power. The legal and regulatory framework has also encouraged institutional segmentation. As a result, from the Glass-Steagall Act of 1933 until the Gramm-Leach-Bliley Act of 1999, U.S. financial institutions served very distinct functions. For a period of 66 years, a legal separation of functions was imposed that resulted in the separation of commercial lending and deposit taking, securities underwriting, mortgage origination and insurance underwriting.

Today, there are still restrictions on the ability of commercial banks to pay interest on corporate demand deposits and for all types of financial institutions to acquire an equity position in industrial enterprises (and vice versa). This makes the U.S. financial system distinct from counterparts elsewhere in the world. In other developed countries, financial institutions have always been segmented and more consolidated. Additionally, some own a major equity stake in industrial enterprises.

Since the Monetary Control Act of 1980, deregulation has changed the financial landscape. Legislation and regulation have fostered consolidation of the financial services industry; today, financial institutions can offer a much wider range of products and services than was possible even a decade ago. There is also increased presence and competition from foreign banks operating in the U.S.

This chapter outlines the history of the development of the current U.S. financial environment in which treasury managers in all types of organizations—publicly traded, privately held, not-for-profit and government—must perform their daily tasks.

II. FINANCIAL MARKETS

Financial markets facilitate all types of financial transactions between individuals and institutions. In a corporate sense, financial markets exist to bring together companies that require cash with individuals and institutions that have excess cash. Financial intermediaries such as commercial banks, investment banks and brokerage firms offer services that bring these parties together, thereby creating the securities market and facilitating the exchange of equity (stocks) and debt (bonds).

A. Different Types of Financial Markets

1. Money Markets and Capital Markets

The main distinction between money markets and capital markets is the maturity of the securities:

- Money market instruments are securities that are short term in nature, generally one year or less until maturity. Money market instruments are generally highly liquid and are issued by borrowers with excellent credit ratings. Examples of money market instruments include Treasury Bills (T-Bills), commercial paper (CP), repurchase agreements (repos) and banker's acceptances (BAs).

- Capital market instruments are securities that are long-term in nature, having more than one year until maturity. Capital market instruments are generally less liquid and are issued by borrowers with various credit ratings. Examples of capital market instruments include term loans, equity instruments and bonds.

(A more detailed discussion of the money and capital markets is in Chapter 10, Liquidity Management and Chapter 13, Sources of Capital and Leasing)

2. Security Exchanges and Markets

Organized stock exchanges facilitate the buying and selling of securities. There are three nationally organized security exchanges:

- The New York Stock Exchange (NYSE)
- The American Stock Exchange (AMEX)
- The National Association of Securities Dealers (NASD)

There is also a nationwide over-the-counter market, the National Association of Securities Dealers Automated Quotations (NASDAQ). Additionally, there are regional exchanges such as the Chicago Stock Exchange and the Pacific Exchange.

The four principal benefits of organized exchanges are that they provide:

- A continuous market with frequent trading executed quickly and with reduced price volatility
- Security prices that are subject to competitive forces of the law of supply and demand
- A market by which companies are able to raise capital through new offerings
- A regulated environment for exchange participants

3. Primary Markets and Secondary Markets

Primary markets are markets in which debt and equity are offered for the first time to investors. An investment banker underwrites and originates an initial public offering (IPO) of a security. New issues represent transactions that increase either the outstanding stock of a publicly traded corporation or the indebtedness of a corporation, a government entity or a not-for-profit organization.

Secondary markets are markets in which previously issued debt and equity are traded by brokers or commercial bankers. All transactions after the IPO occur in the secondary market and do not affect the total outstanding stock of a publicly traded corporation or increase the entity's indebtedness.

B. Initial Public Offerings (IPOs) and Private Placements

When a company decides to raise debt or equity capital, funds can be raised through an IPO or a private (or direct) placement. In an IPO, the managing investment banker or syndicate makes the securities available to the public. Both individual and institutional investors have an opportunity to purchase the securities.

In a private or direct placement, securities are offered and sold to a limited number of investors. The investment banker, acting as a broker to bring the issuer and investors together, will meet with the prospective buyers and confirm the details of the offering. Generally, a private placement is completed more rapidly than a public offering, thereby reducing flotation costs and offering the investment banker flexibility in meeting the needs of the company. However, private placements often incur higher interest rates and have more restrictive covenants than other forms of borrowing.

C. Flotation Costs

Flotation refers to the cost of issuing new stocks and bonds. A company raising long-term capital incurs two types of flotation costs. The primary flotation cost is the underwriter's spread, the difference between the gross and net proceeds of the issue. The issue costs are expenses incurred for the issue, such as printing and engraving, legal fees, accounting fees, trustee fees, and other miscellaneous charges. The underwriter's spread is always greater than the issuing costs.

Flotation costs are highest for common stock issues, followed by preferred stock and bonds. This is based on the concept that common stock inherently has more risk than preferred stock or bonds; therefore, flotation costs increase to compensate the originator for the underwriting risk. Flotation costs also decrease with the increased size of the issue, expressed as a percentage of gross proceeds.

III. FINANCIAL INSTITUTIONS: FUNCTIONS AND SERVICES

This section outlines the key functions and services of the major types of U.S. financial institutions.

A. Commercial Banks

Defined by law as a financial institution that accepts deposits and makes commercial loans, a commercial bank offers a wide range of products and services. Therefore, the term "commercial bank" applies to financial institutions ranging from small, single-site, community banks with ten million dollars in assets to large, multisite, global financial institutions with hundreds of billions in assets.

According to the Federal Deposit Insurance Corporation (FDIC), the number of commercially chartered banks in the U.S. held steady at approximately 13,000 to 14,000 from the 1930s through the mid-1980s, with the number of branches rising from approximately 17,000 in the 1930s to 44,000 in the mid-1980s. By 2002, as a result of significant consolidation in the financial services industry, the number of chartered banks had dropped to under 8,000 while the number of branches had exploded to over 70,000.

Most large commercial banks are owned by bank holding companies that, along with their non-bank subsidiaries, provide a wide range of products and services.

1. Deposit Accounts

The core function of a commercial bank is to serve as a depository for cash. There are two basic types of depository accounts: demand deposit accounts (DDAs) and time deposit accounts (TDAs). There are also interest-bearing accounts that combine features of both demand deposit and time deposit accounts. DDAs and TDAs are insured up to $100,000 per personal or corporate depositor per institution by the FDIC.

Commonly referred to as a checking account, a DDA is a method by which an account holder uses a commercial bank to transfer funds to and receive deposits from a third party. The method of payment can be by check, Automated Clearing House (ACH) or wire transfer. DDAs can be interest bearing for individuals, sole proprietorships, government entities and not-for-profit organizations. However, Regulation Q (see the Glass-Steagall Act later in this chapter) still prohibits payment of interest on demand deposits held by "sub chapter S" and "C" corporations.

Balances are held in DDAs for three purposes:

- Transaction balances are deposits held by companies to facilitate collection and disbursement activity.
- Compensating balances are deposits held by companies in the form of collected balances that are used to compensate for banking services.
- Correspondent balances are deposits held by other banks to facilitate check clearing, securities settlement, negotiation of letters of credit and other transactions.

Time deposits are accounts (TDAs) that must be maintained at a commercial bank for a specified period. One of the primary types of time deposits is the certificate of deposit (CD), which is an obligation of a bank offered at either a fixed or a variable interest rate and which may be either negotiable or non-negotiable. CDs under $100,000 issued to consumers and smaller institutional investors are generally non-negotiable and have a substantial interest penalty for early withdrawal. CDs with values of $100,000 or more are referred to as jumbo CDs and may be offered on a negotiable basis. For larger institutional investors, fully negotiable CDs are generally offered in $1 million blocks with maturities ranging from 14 days to five years. Most are offered with maturities of 12 or fewer months.

Commercial banks also offer other types of TDAs such as savings accounts, money market deposit accounts (MMDAs) and negotiable order of withdrawal (NOW) accounts:

- Savings accounts (or passbook savings accounts) are accounts that pay interest on balances and are mainly owned by individuals and not-for-profit institutions.
- MMDAs pay an unregulated rate of interest determined by each institution and allow limited check writing and electronic withdrawals. MMDAs are available to individuals and all types of businesses.
- NOW accounts offer unrestricted check writing and pay unregulated rates of interest. They are "negotiable" in the sense that, unlike MMDAs, they are interest bearing and allow unlimited check-writing privileges. Because NOW accounts are interest bearing, they are limited to individuals, sole proprietorships, not-for-profit organizations and governmental entities.

2. Credit Services

The primary credit service that commercial banks offer to consumers, businesses, not-for-profit organizations and government entities is a short-term loan with less than one year in maturity. A commercial bank specializes in short-term lending due to the nature of its asset/liability structure. A loan represents an asset of a bank; a deposit represents a liability. Because of the short-term nature of deposits, commercial bank loans tend to be short-term as well.

Short-term loans to businesses are designed to fund working capital gaps that are created when cash outflows precede cash inflows, such as the increase in accounts receivable and inventory that are common in a seasonal business or industry. The source of repayment is the conversion of accounts receivable and inventory into cash through sales. Short-term business borrowing also takes the form of a revolving line of credit (commonly referred to as a "revolver") that allows a company to borrow up to a specified amount, repay and borrow again at any time.

(A more detailed discussion of short-term borrowing is in Chapter 10, Liquidity Management.)

Although commercial banks specialize in short-term lending, some are also involved in medium- and long-term borrowing arrangements designed primarily for capital improvements such as property, plant and equipment. The source of repayment is from earnings of the project being financed. Leasing divisions of banks provide an alternative to medium- and long-term loans for financing capital equipment. Commercial banks also provide mortgage financing for commercial and residential real estate.

3. Investment Banking Services

Commercial banks are an integral part of the investment banking process for the commercial paper (CP) market. CP consists of unsecured, short-term promissory notes issued by companies or commercial bank holding companies. Commercial banks act as agents to place CP with investors and CP is rated for default risk by various rating agencies.

Commercial banks also offer loan sales, private placements and stock/bond underwriting.

- Loan sales involve the structuring of lending facilities so that short-term loans can be sold to other banks and investors.

- Private placements involve the direct sale of long-term loans to institutional investors such as insurance companies.
- Stock and bond underwriting involves originating corporate stocks (equity) and bonds (debt) through investment and brokerage subsidiaries.

4. Payment and Collection Services

Commercial banks assist companies by acting as clearing agents for checks and by originating and receiving ACH transactions and wire transfers. (For a more detailed discussion of payment and collection services, see Chapter 8, Payment Systems, and Chapter 9, Cash Positioning.)

5. Trade Services

Large commercial banks provide a wide range of services to facilitate payment of trade obligations.

- **Trade or commercial letters of credit (L/Cs)** are documents issued by a bank, guaranteeing the payment of a customer's draft up to a stated amount for a specified period, provided that certain conditions are met. In effect, the issuing bank is substituting its good name and credit on behalf of its customer. Likewise, banks issue performance contracts guaranteeing that certain terms and conditions are met by companies involved in large-capital construction projects.

- **A documentary collection** is a trade-services payment method that processes the collection of a draft and accompanying shipping documents through international correspondent banks. Instructions regarding the specifics of the transaction are contained in a collection letter that accompanies the documentation. It is the responsibility of the seller (exporter) to determine the specific instructions used in the collection letter.

- **A banker's acceptance (BA)** is a negotiable short-term instrument used primarily to finance the import/ export of domestic shipments of good, or the storage of readily marketable staples. A BA is created when a bank accepts payment responsibility for a draft issued in connection with an L/C.

(A more detailed discussion of L/Cs, documentary collections and BAs, as well as exhibits that illustrate the role of commercial banks are in Chapter 15, Global Treasury Environment.)

6. Foreign Exchange (FX) Services

Large, global banks are major participants in the FX markets. They offer FX services to customers to facilitate international business and trade. These services allow companies to buy or sell internationally traded currencies for either immediate use (the spot market) or future use (the forward market). In addition, these banks offer risk management services, such as forwards and swaps, that assist international clients in hedging FX exposures.

(A more in-depth discussion of FX and related products are in Chapter 15, Global Treasury Environment and Chapter 17, Financial Risk Management.)

7. Agent or Fiduciary Services

An agent is a bank, bank holding company or trust institution that manages assets whose title remains with the owner. A fiduciary is an individual or institution to which certain property is given to hold in trust according to a trust agreement. Fiduciary services, more commonly referred to as trust services, represent one of the many roles performed by major commercial banks. In this capacity, the trust departments of commercial banks manage the assets and investments for individuals and also act as paying agents for the distribution of proceeds as instructed in wills, trusts and estates.

Trust departments offer a wide range of services to corporate customers. Corporate services include:

- Establishing and managing employee pension plans or qualified employee benefit plans
- Acting as a corporate trustee for corporate bond or preferred stock issues
- Monitoring compliance with bond indenture agreements, which are formal agreements between issuers of bonds and bondholders
- Acting as a transfer agent by keeping records of each sale and purchase of stocks and bonds, including maintaining records of the shareholders of a corporation by name, address, and number of shares
- Acting as a registrar compiling lists of current stockholders and bondholders for the purpose of remitting dividend and interest payments
- Acting as a paying agent, whereby a bank receives funds from an issuer of stocks or bonds to pay dividends to stockholders and principal and interest to bondholders
- Offering custody services, such as providing safekeeping for securities, and buying, selling, receiving, and delivering securities based on terms outlined in a custody agreement

8. Risk Management Services

Fluctuations in exchange rates, interest rates or prices of commodities can significantly impact a company's financial performance. For example, currency movements against the U.S. dollar can impact the profitability of a company that operates in international markets. To control these risks, banks and other financial institutions offer a variety of products such as swaps, forwards, futures, and options. These instruments are known as derivatives because the value of each is derived from, or based on, an underlying asset.

(A more detailed discussion of derivatives is in Chapter 17, Financial Risk Management.)

9. Consulting Services

Banks provide a wide range of consulting services for corporate customers in areas such as treasury management, mergers and acquisitions and corporate financial structure.

10. Other Financial Services

As a result of deregulation, commercial banks can now act as brokers and dealers for certain permissible investment securities and foreign currencies. The Gramm-Leach-Bliley Act of 1999 allows banks to engage in activities previously reserved for securities firms and securities firms to enter areas previously reserved for commercial banks. This Act permits banks to engage in unlimited agency and underwriting activities through a holding company. In addition, insurance companies are able to affiliate with commercial banks.

B. Investment Banking and Brokerage Firms

Investment banks and brokerage firms provide a wide range of financial services. Certain firms specialize in investment banking, others in brokerage. Some firms serve institutional customers while others serve retail customers. Some are full-service firms that fulfill the needs of all types of customers.

1. Investment Banks

An investment bank is a financial intermediary that merchandises securities in the form of either stocks or bonds. An investment bank's intermediation function is often described as having two components: origination and distribution.

- **Origination** is also referred to as underwriting. A significant portion of the underwriting function is related to either corporate stocks or corporate, municipal and federal bonds. To a lesser extent, investment banks also underwrite CP. When an investment bank underwrites a stock or bond offering, it guarantees the issuer a definite sum of money for the issue at a definite time. In purchasing the entire issue, the underwriter assumes two risks: price and marketability. An investment bank is compensated for this risk in the form of fees.

- **Distribution** involves the initial sale of securities to investors. An investment bank may choose to form a syndicate to share in the distribution responsibilities. A syndicate is a group of investment bankers who participate in buying and reselling issues of securities. The investment bank that leads the syndicate is considered the lead underwriter and typically receives more than half of the total fees associated with the issue. Once the underwriting syndicate owns the new securities, each member investment bank uses a distribution system to sell the issue to customers. The syndicate is often referred to as a security wholesaler while the dealer organization is referred to as the security retailer.

Investment banks serve as advisors to issuers of stocks and bonds. In this role, an investment bank has the responsibility for advising the issuer about the prevailing and future market conditions in an effort to raise the most funds at the least cost. Additionally, investment banks help to analyze a firm's capital structure and advise an issuer regarding what source of capital best suits the organization. An investment bank may also offer derivatives such as interest rate and FX swaps, forwards, options, and futures.

2. Institutional and Retail Brokerage Firms

Brokerage firms specialize in the sale of securities to institutional and retail customers. Brokerage is the distribution side of an investment bank's intermediation function. Brokerage firms can be either discount or full-service. Discount brokerages offer investors the opportunity to make trades at reduced prices but do not provide investment advice. Full-service brokerages have research analysts who are industry specialists and who provide investment advice to institutions and individual investors. Some full-service brokerages also manage investment portfolios for institutions and individuals.

C. Thrift Institutions

Thrift institutions were traditionally depository institutions that accepted consumer deposits and lent money, primarily in the form of home mortgage loans. The Depository Institutions Deregulation and Monetary Control Act of 1980 (DIDMCA) provided for a phase-out of interest rate ceilings for thrift institutions and commercial banks, and allowed savings institutions to make commercial and consumer loans. As a result of the savings and loan (S&L) liquidity crisis in the 1980s, many S&Ls were declared insolvent and taken over by the FDIC. During the 1960s, there were approximately 5,000 S&Ls in the U.S. In 2002, there were only 1,500. There are two types of thrift institutions: S&L associations and savings or mutual savings banks.

S&Ls are either federally or state chartered and owned by either shareholders or depositors. Just as with commercial banks, S&L deposits are federally insured by the FDIC. The Office of Thrift Supervision (OTS) supervises and regulates all federally chartered and many state-chartered thrifts.

Another thrift institution is known as either a savings bank or a mutual savings bank. Historically, such banks have been state chartered and owned by depositors. Under the Garn-St. Germain Depository Institutions Act of 1982, these institutions were converted to federal charters and to stock ownership. This Act also allowed expansion into a wider range of investment and lending activities, which ultimately hastened the S&L crisis in the late 1980s and early 1990s.

D. Credit Unions

Credit unions are not-for-profit financial corporations chartered by federal or state agencies. Membership in a credit union is restricted to individuals with a common affiliation such as an employer, an association or a community organization. Credit unions can provide retail financial services similar to those offered by other types of financial institutions. Members/owners often enjoy higher savings and lower lending rates. The National Credit Union Share Insurance Fund (NCUSIF) insures deposits in the majority of the 10,000 credit unions operating in the U.S.

E. Mutual Fund Companies

Mutual funds are pooled investments that sell shares, offering investors diversification and professional portfolio management. Mutual fund providers include commercial banks, brokerage firms and investment companies. Money market mutual funds invest in short-term securities such as T-Bills, CDs and CP. The value of shares fluctuates with the performance of underlying securities. Shares may be redeemed through the provider that insures liquidity. Mutual fund shares are not insured.

F. Other Types of Non-Bank Financial Institutions

There are a variety of other so-called "non-bank" financial institutions that serve specialized areas of the economy. Industrial credit and capital companies are subsidiaries of large industrial corporations that raise funds in the CP market and lend to companies and individuals. A captive finance company solely finances purchases of the company's products. Automobile finance companies such as the General Motors Acceptance Corporation (GMAC) and Ford Motor Credit (FMC) are examples of captive finance companies.

Another type of non-bank financial intermediary is a factor, a company that provides short-term financing to companies by purchasing accounts receivable at a discount. (For more information about factors and factoring, see Chapter 7, Working Capital Tools.)

Insurance companies are also considered non-bank financial institutions. From a corporate perspective, they are primarily long-term lenders to companies. Insurance companies have started to compete with banks for short-term and medium-term loans. They provide mortgage funding, leasing services, guaranteed investment contracts and universal life insurance policies with long-term savings features.

Other examples of non-bank financial institutions include pension funds and consumer finance companies. A consumer finance company extends credit to individuals and businesses but does not accept deposits.

IV. REGULATORY AGENCIES

The United States has a dual banking system. Dual refers to the fact that banks are either federally or state chartered. At the federal level, bank supervision is shared primarily by three agencies: the Board of Governors of the Federal Reserve System, the Federal Deposit Insurance Corporation (FDIC) and the Office of the Comptroller of the Currency (OCC). At the state level, banks are regulated by state banking boards and commissions.

A. Federal Reserve System (Fed)

From the perspective of monetary policy, the Fed acts as the central bank of the United States. It is an independent agency of the U.S. government created by the Federal Reserve Act of 1913 in response to a series of major banking crises in the late 1890s and early 1900s. The Federal Reserve Act was intended to provide the nation with a safe, flexible, and stable monetary and financial system. The Fed is organized into three primary components:

- The Board of Governors
- The Federal Open Market Committee (FOMC)
- The 12 banks and 25 branches of the Federal Reserve

1. Board of Governors

Each of the seven members of the Board of Governors is appointed to a 14-year term by the President of the United States and confirmed by the Senate. Primary functions include formulation of credit and monetary policy, as well as supervision of the Federal Reserve banks, state chartered member banks and bank holding companies. The President of the U.S. appoints one governor as chairperson and another as vice chair. Each serves a four-year term and may be reappointed.

The Board has three key committees that provide advice:

1. The Federal Advisory Council, consisting of 12 members, each of whom is traditionally a commercial banker from each Federal Reserve Districts
2. The Consumer Advisory Council, which represents the interests of consumers
3. The Thrift Institutions Advisory Council, whose members represent the interests of S&Ls, mutual savings banks and credit unions

2. Federal Open Market Committee (FOMC)

The FOMC sets and implements monetary policy by conducting open market operations. There are 12 committee members, including the seven members of the Board of Governors, the president of the Federal Reserve Bank of New York and presidents of four other Federal Reserve banks who serve on a rotating basis.

3. Federal Reserve District Banks

There are 12 Federal Reserve districts, with one Federal Reserve Bank serving each district. In addition to the district banks there are a total of 25 branch banks in various cities. The Fed also has regional check processing centers (RCPCs) to expedite the collection of checks. Commercial banks in each district own the stock in the Federal Reserve banks and serve on the Boards but do not maintain stockholder control. The Board of Governors appoints members and the chairman to each Reserve Board. A map illustrating the Federal Reserve districts is shown in Exhibit 3.1.

EXHIBIT 3.1 – FEDERAL RESERVE CHECK PROCESSING REGIONS

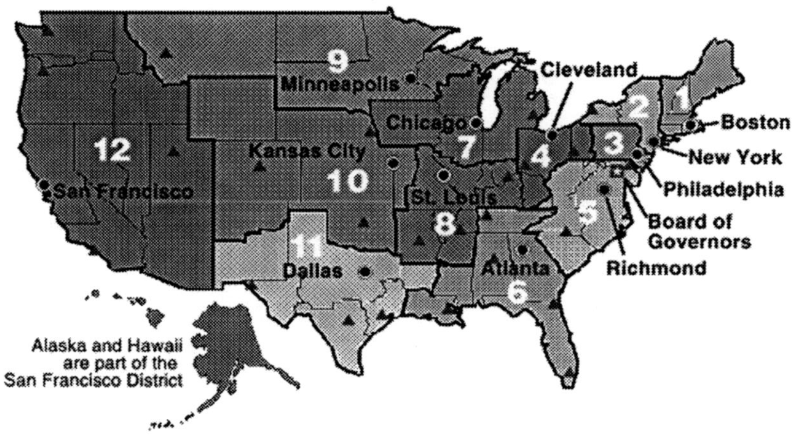

Region 1: Boston
RCPC — Windsor Locks, CT

Region 2: New York
Branches — Buffalo, NY
RCPC — East Rutherford Operations Center (EROC), East Rutherford, NJ; Utica, Oriskany, NY

Region 3: Philadelphia

Region 4: Cleveland
Branches — Cincinnati, OH & Pittsburgh, PA
RCPC — Columbus, OH

Region 5: Richmond
Branches — Baltimore, MD & Charlotte, NC

Region 6: Atlanta
Branches — Birmingham, AL; Jacksonville, FL; Miami, FL; Nashville, TN & New Orleans, LA

Region 7: Chicago
Branches — Detroit, MI
RCPC — Indianapolis, IN; Des Moines, IA & Peoria, IL

Region 8: St. Louis
Branches — Little Rock, AR; Louisville, KY & Memphis, TN

Region 9: Minneapolis
Branches — Helena, MT

Region 10: Kansas City
Branches — Denver, CO; Oklahoma City, OK & Omaha, NE

Region 11: Dallas
Branches — El Paso, TX; Houston, TX & San Antonio, TX

Region 12: San Francisco
Branches — Los Angeles, CA; Portland, OR; Salt Lake City, UT & Seattle, WA

4. Key Roles of the Federal Reserve

The Fed has five principal roles, as follows:

- Supervisor and regulator of member financial institutions
- Manager of U.S. monetary policy
- Wholesaler of banking services (checks, ACH, and wire transfers)
- Fiscal agent of the U.S. Treasury
- Consumer protection advocate for financial services

In the supervisory and regulatory role, the Fed has primary responsibility for the following:

- All bank holding companies, non-bank subsidiaries, and foreign subsidiaries
- State-chartered banks that are members of the Federal Reserve system (state member banks), as well as foreign branches and subsidiaries
- Edge Act Agreement corporations, through which U.S. banks conduct operations abroad

With respect to management of U.S. monetary policy, the Federal Reserve Act directs the Fed to conduct monetary policy to maximize employment, promote price stability, and maintain moderate long-term interest rates. The Federal Reserve's monetary policies influence the demand for and the supply of money at banks and other depository institutions by means of three tools: the discount rate, the reserve requirement and the FOMC.

The discount rate is the rate that the Fed charges member banks for loans using government securities as collateral. The higher the discount rate, the lower the money supply; the lower the discount rate, the higher the money supply.

The reserve requirement is the percentage (currently 10 percent) of cash and other liquid assets that member banks must keep on reserve at the Fed. As with the discount rate, the higher the reserve percentage, the lower the money supply; the lower the reserve percentage, the higher the money supply. The reserve balance allows the Fed improved control over the flow of money and better monitoring and regulating of the actions of depository institutions. The Fed also uses reserves to transfer value from one institution to another.

The FOMC is the Board of Governors committee that oversees the buying and selling of government securities in the form of T-Bills, Treasury notes and Treasury bonds. The FOMC has the greatest impact on monetary policy because the activities related to the buying and selling of government securities have the greatest influence on money market conditions. The sale of government securities by the FOMC reduces the money supply and credit; the redemption of government securities by the FOMC increases the money supply and credit.

The money supply can also be controlled by setting a desired target for the Federal funds rate. Fed funds represent the interest rate at which depository institutions lend balances to other depository institutions overnight via the Federal Reserve. Banks with surplus reserve balances lend those balances overnight to banks with deficit reserve balances.

The Fed explicitly sets the target level for Fed funds shortly before each of its meetings and most banks follow the Fed guidelines.

The Fed provides a wide range of services:

- Primary clearer of checks between depository institutions: approximately 50 million items on a daily basis from the institution of first deposit to the institution on which the check is drawn (the drawee bank). The Fed's check-processing operations electronically capture payment data from all checks and create digital images of many of these items.
- Principal operator of the ACH: processes and settles high-volume, low-value electronic payments in a batch mode
- Operator of Fedwire, the only domestic Real-Time Gross Settlement System (RTGS) that transfers low-volume, high-value electronic payments on a same-day basis

The reserve banks and branches also function as fiscal agents for the federal government. The reserve banks maintain the Treasury Department's checking accounts, clearing Treasury checks, accepting payments for federal taxes on behalf of the Internal Revenue Service (IRS) and acting as fiscal agent to issue, redeem and transfer ownership of government securities.

Finally, the Fed issues regulations to ensure compliance with federal laws governing consumer credit protection, such as Truth in Lending, Equal Credit Opportunity and Home Mortgage Disclosure. Many of these regulations also apply to various lenders outside the banking industry.

B. Office of the Comptroller of the Currency (OCC) (1863)

The OCC is a bureau of the U.S. Department of Treasury, established by Congress in 1863 to regulate the national banking system. In its operations the OCC:

- Administers nationally-chartered banks, overseeing the execution of laws related to national banks and proposing rules and regulations governing the operations of national banks
- Supervises a nationwide staff of bank examiners whose primary functions are to act as administrators of national banks, to issue rules and regulations governing national bank operations, and to oversee federally-licensed branches and agencies of foreign banks
- Approves and denies applications for national bank charters, branches, capital and other changes in corporate or banking structure
- Examines national banks for asset (loan) quality, capital adequacy, management and other key regulatory issues. The OCC takes supervisory action against banks that do not conform to laws and regulations or those that otherwise engage in unsound banking practices.

C. Federal Deposit Insurance Corporation (FDIC) (1933)

The FDIC, which was established in 1933 as part of the Glass-Steagall Act, is an independent agency of the federal government whose primary role is to protect depositors from losses caused by bank insolvency. FDIC responsibilities include:

- Providing deposit insurance
- Supervising depository institutions
- Acting as a trustee in the event of bank failures

The FDIC insures deposits up to $100,000 on both personal and corporate deposit accounts in all federally chartered banks and in most state-chartered banks. A bank's deposit insurance premium is set by the FDIC on the basis of the institution's risk profile.

The FDIC administers two federal deposit insurance funds: the Bank Insurance Fund (BIF) and the Savings Association Insurance Fund (SAIF).

In 1989, as part of the Financial Institutions Reform, Recovery, and Enforcement Act, Congress created the SAIF to succeed the former Federal Savings and Loan Insurance Corporation (FSLIC). This legislation mandated that deposits in most commercial banks be insured by the BIF, while the SAIF insures deposits up to specified amounts at S&Ls and many savings banks. The FDIC was assigned responsibility for managing both of the funds, and these deposit insurance programs are backed by the full faith and credit of the U.S. government.

The FDIC is also the primary federal regulator of state non-member banks and, for insurance purposes, is the back-up supervisor over the remaining federally insured banks and S&Ls. As part of an examination, the FDIC looks for poor risk management or excessive risk taking by an institution and seeks early remedies. In addition, the FDIC examines state non-member banks to ensure compliance with equal credit and other consumer protection laws such as the Community Reinvestment Act (CRA) and the Truth in Lending Act. The CRA encourages banks and thrifts to help meet the credit needs of communities in which they operate. The Truth in Lending Act requires accurate disclosures of interest rates and finance charges so that loan applicants can accurately compare various financial institution mortgages and consumer loans.

Finally, in the event of the failure of a financial institution, the FDIC is the agency that determines the ultimate course of action. In most cases, the FDIC is appointed as receiver of failed insured institutions. The agency is charged with finding a merger partner or, as bankruptcy trustee, liquidating the bank's remaining assets and paying insured depositors.

D. Office of Thrift Supervision (OTS) (1989)

The OTS is a bureau of the Department of Treasury and the primary regulator of all federal- and many state-chartered thrift institutions, including savings banks and S&Ls. Established by Congress in 1989, the OTS serves as the successor to the Federal Home Loan Bank Board and is the primary regulator of all federal- and state-chartered savings institutions that belong to the SAIF. Key functions of the OTS include:

- Serving as the primary regulator of all federal- and state-chartered savings institutions
- Issuing federal charters for S&Ls and savings banks
- Adopting and enforcing regulations to ensure that both federal- and state-chartered thrift institutions operate in a safe and sound manner

E. Other Regulatory/Supervisory Agencies

In addition to the primary agencies listed above, a variety of other agencies regulate or supervise financial institutions.

1. Federal Financial Institution Examination Council (FFIEC) (1979)

The FFIEC was established as a formal, interagency institution empowered to prescribe uniform principles, standards and report forms. These standards aid in the examination of financial institutions by the Fed, the FDIC, the National Credit Union Administration (NCUA), the OCC and the OTS.

2. Office of Foreign Assets Control (OFAC) (1950)

The OFAC is an office of the Treasury Department that administers and enforces economic and trade sanctions against targeted foreign countries, terrorist-sponsoring organizations and international narcotics traffickers. Based on U.S. foreign policy and national security goals, the OFAC has the authority to impose controls on financial transactions and to freeze foreign assets under U.S. jurisdiction. The role of the OFAC was expanded under the USA Patriot Act, covered later in this chapter.

3. Financial Crimes Enforcement Network (FinCEN) (1990)

FinCEN was established by the U.S. Treasury Department. The original intent was to provide a government-wide intelligence network to support the detection, investigation, and prosecution of both domestic and international money laundering and other financial crimes. In 1994, the mission was broadened to include regulatory responsibilities.

Today, FinCEN is the primary agency that oversees and implements policies to prevent and detect money laundering. This is accomplished primarily through enforcement of counter-money laundering legislation (such as the Bank Secrecy Act), which requires reporting of large and/or suspicious monetary transfers conduct at banks. FinCEN also provides intelligence and analytical support to law enforcement agencies in the form of reports, which are used to build investigations and plan new strategies that combat money laundering. As with OFAC, the USA Patriot Act has expanded the role of FinCEN.

4. Securities and Exchange Commission (SEC)

The SEC, which is governed by the Securities Laws of 1933, 1934, and 1940, is a federal agency designed to maintain a fair and orderly market for investors by regulating and supervising the sale of securities. The responsibilities of the SEC include:

- Registering public offerings of debt or equity securities by banks or bank holding companies and other corporations
- Setting financial disclosure standards for corporations that sell securities to the public
- Requiring filing of quarterly and annual financial statements by companies with publicly owned securities
- Regulating mutual funds and investment advisors
- Monitoring insider trading to enforce related regulations

While the role of most of the agencies that oversee the financial services industry are related to protecting depositors, the SEC focuses on protecting investors (stockholders and bondholders). In general, the SEC requires publicly traded companies to fully disclose all relevant financial information to investors.

(A detailed discussion of disclosure requirements is in Chapter 20, Pension Fund Management.)

5. Department of Justice (DOJ)

The DOJ, as well as the Fed, reviews and approves proposed bank mergers and holding company acquisitions to determine the impact on competition as part of antitrust legislation. The Federal Bureau of Investigation (FBI), a bureau of the DOJ, plays a key role in preventing financial institution fraud and theft, as well as in enforcing key money-laundering legislation.

6. State Banking Boards and Commissions

Due to the dual nature of the U.S. banking system, each state has a separate banking board and commission. The primary responsibilities of these state agencies are to issue charters for new state banks and supervise and examine existing state-chartered banks. State banking boards and commissions also reserve the right to approve the applications of banks operating within state borders to form holding companies, to acquire affiliates or subsidiaries and to establish branch offices. The boards and commissions also have the right to impose liquidity requirements and minimum equity capital requirements on state-chartered banks.

V. FEDERAL LEGISLATION

There is a wide range of federal legislation related to financial institutions, dating from the 1913 Federal Reserve Act that provided the foundation for our current banking system to recent legislation addressing money laundering (USA Patriot Act) and financial disclosure (Sarbanes-Oxley [SOX] Act). Approaching the various laws and acts with respect to the impacts each has had on the financial industry; most federal legislation can be categorized as:

- Providing for the regulation and supervision of financial institutions

- Setting guidelines for the types of businesses in which different financial institutions may engage
- Determining geographic boundaries related to financial-institution operations
- Defining the operations and instruments of the payments system
- Providing consumer protection

Usually, the legislation is implemented through specific regulations of the Federal Reserve. A summary of the key provisions of selected bank legislation and regulations demonstrates how the U.S. banking system has evolved.

A. Legislation Governing Regulation and Supervision

1. Federal Reserve Act (1913)

This historic Act provided the foundation for the current banking system by establishing the Federal Reserve and requiring all national banks to become members and to comply with reserve requirements. The Act also granted the Fed supervisory power over member banks and empowered it to create a national check collection and settlement system through member banks.

2. The Securities Laws

Laws passed in 1933, 1934, and 1940 established the SEC, which governs the issuance of securities. While federal legislation is designed primarily to protect the assets of depositors to financial institutions, these securities laws seek to provide protection to investors by requiring full disclosure of financial information relating to securities issues.

3. Garn-St. Germain Depository Institutions Act (1982)

This Act had a major impact on the banking industry through the following provisions:

- Extended the legal lending limit of banks to 15 percent of capital and surplus for unsecured loans and 25 percent for secured loans
- Allowed the FDIC to arrange mergers of banks across state lines when suitable partners could not be found
- Allowed banks to introduce money market deposit accounts (MMDAs) to compete with money market mutual funds
- Permitted thrift institutions to engage in a wide range of investment and lending activities, which ultimately contributed substantially to the S&L crisis in the late 1980s and early 1990s

4. Financial Institutions Reform, Recovery and Enforcement Act (FIRREA) (1989)

The primary purpose of FIRREA was to restructure thrifts after the crisis that arose during the 1980s. Specifically, the Act:

- Established the Resolution Trust Corporation (RTC) to make timely disposal of approximately $500 billion in assets of failed S&Ls. (Having fulfilled this purpose, the RTC is no longer in existence.)
- Dismantled the Federal Home Loan Bank Board (FHLBB) and established the OTS to assume the FHLBB's supervisory responsibilities
- Consolidated the Federal Savings and Loan Insurance Corporation (FSLIC) resources under the FDIC and gave the FDIC increased flexibility to raise deposit insurance premiums charged to banks and S&Ls

5. Federal Deposit Insurance Corporation Improvement Act (FDICIA) (1991)

This Act established higher standards for financial institution safety and soundness in the wake of several bank failures during the late 1980s. It also declares insolvent any bank or thrift that failed to maintain equity capital equal to two percent of assets and to change deposit insurance premiums from a flat-fee basis to a risk-adjusted basis.

6. Bank Secrecy Act (BSA) (1970) and Money Laundering Control Act (MLCA) (1986)

These Acts seek to control the flow of illegal money through financial institutions. Money is "laundered" to conceal criminal activities, usually related to drug trafficking, tax evasion or terrorist activities. Money laundering is a diverse and very complex process involving three stages:

- Placement: Placement is the physical deposit of cash proceeds from illegal activities into a financial institution.
- Layering: Layering involves a series of complex financial transactions designed to separate the cash proceeds from their criminal or terrorist origins.
- Integration: Integration involves creating what appears to be a legitimate explanation for the source of funds. One common method of integration is to attempt to show that the funds have been donated for a charitable purpose.

For money laundering to be successful, there must be no paper trail to connect the three stages of this process.

The primary intent of the BSA is to deter money laundering and the use of secret foreign bank accounts. By requiring all financial institutions to report any suspicious financial transactions, a paper trail is created to assist in detecting and monitoring illegal activities. Financial institutions are liable for substantial civil and criminal penalties for not complying with the reporting provisions of anti-money laundering regulations. The legislation requires financial institutions to establish effective "know your customer" guidelines, to be aware of parties to large-value funds transfers and to file currency transaction reports and criminal referrals.

Specifically, financial institutions must monitor and report the following:

- Activity inconsistent with a customer's business
- Attempts by customers to avoid reporting or recordkeeping requirements
- Unusual or multiple funds-transfer activities
- Customers who provide insufficient or suspicious information

Financial institutions must also closely monitor employees responsible for large-value funds transfers and report any suspicious deviations from normal transaction patterns.

7. USA Patriot Act (2001)

In response to the September 11, 2001 attacks on the World Trade Center in New York, Congress passed wide-ranging legislation designed to improve overall security and to grant the FBI and the DOJ increased latitude in intelligence gathering activities. This legislation is named the Uniting and Strengthening America by Providing Appropriate Tools Required to Intercept and Obstruct Terrorism Act (the Patriot Act). The primary impact for financial institutions is the substantial number of amendments added to the provisions of existing money laundering legislation such as the BSA. These amendments are intended to make it easier to prevent, detect and prosecute international money laundering and the financing of terrorism.

Among the provisions of the Patriot Act are the following:

- Imposes significant obligations upon non-bank financial institutions, including broker dealers, credit card companies and check cashing services. Non-bank financial institutions had not previously been covered by BSA.
- Makes all foreign banks with accounts in the U.S. subject to U.S. jurisdiction, including the power to obtain records and information regarding customers.
- Prohibits U.S. banks from maintaining, either directly or indirectly, correspondent accounts for any foreign "shell" banks. Shell banks are defined as foreign banks without a physical presence in any country.
- Prevents operators of U.S. credit card systems from authorizing foreign banks to issue or accept U.S. credit cards without taking steps to prevent usage by terrorists.

8. Sarbanes-Oxley Act (SOX) (2002)

The primary purpose of SOX is to improve disclosure and financial reporting in the wake of a series of dramatic financial scandals between the years 2000 and 2002. The Act has resulted in numerous changes to SEC rules and regulations.

Specifically, companies are now required to:

- Disclose in annual reports the code of ethics applicable to senior financial officers. Companies that change or waive the code must disclose the event by filing a Form 8-K or posting a notice on the company Web site.
- Disclose in annual reports whether the audit committee has a financial expert.
- New SEC guidelines also require audit committees to preapprove all audit and non-audit services provided by the auditor and to be briefed by auditors on the company's accounting, including alternative approaches that might be preferable to the company's current methods.

The new SEC Regulation G requires that companies reconcile pro-forma financial information to financial statements and that companies who issue earnings releases must file them on Form 8-Ks. Finally, all off-balance sheet arrangements that may have a material current or future effect on the financial statements or liquidity are required to be included in the Management's Discussion and Analysis (MD&A) section.

B. Legislation Governing Types of Financial Services Offered

1. Edge Act (1918)

This Act permitted U.S. banks to invest in corporations engaging in international banking and finance. It also permitted the establishment of subsidiaries to conduct international banking businesses such as import and export financing, foreign exchange, letters of credit and documentary collection in cities throughout the U.S. and overseas.

2. Glass-Steagall Act (also known as the Banking Act of 1933)

This Act was passed to address major issues and problems with the financial services industry stemming from the Great Depression. Specifically, this Act:

- Prohibited commercial banks from securities underwriting except for government issues
- Prohibited securities firms from engaging in bank-like activities such as deposit gathering
- Required the Fed to establish interest rate ceilings on all types of accounts and to prohibit the payment of interest-on-demand deposits (Provisions of this Act are incorporated in Federal Reserve Regulation Q.)
- Created the FDIC to guarantee deposits up to a stipulated maximum amount, in order to restore faith in the banking system after numerous bank failures during the Great Depression

3. Gramm-Leach-Bliley Act (1999)

This Act eliminated many of the provisions of the Glass-Steagall Act, especially those that created barriers among the functions of commercial banking, investment banking and insurance; specifically it:

- Permits the creation of financial holding companies (FHCs) that can engage in any activity considered "financial in nature, incidental to finance or complementary to it"
- Establishes the Fed as the primary regulator of FHCs. FHCs are subject to consolidated capital requirements at the parent company level and bank-style risk management at all levels.
- Allowed easier entry by foreign banks into the U.S. financial services market

For the consumer, Gramm-Leach-Bliley has two key provisions:

- **Restrictions on Mergers:** The Act prohibits a bank holding company from merging with an insurance firm or a securities firm or embarking on new powers if any banks earned less than a "satisfactory" CRA rating during its most recent exam.

- **Disclosure of Privacy Policy:** The Act requires financial institutions to establish and disclose privacy policies at the start of a customer relationship and once a year thereafter. As part of privacy policies, banks are required to give customers an opportunity to block the sharing of confidential information with third parties except in cases of marketing agreements between financial institutions. In addition, credit card information and account numbers must not be shared with third-party marketers in order to prevent identification (ID) theft.

C. Legislation Governing Geographic Boundaries

1. McFadden Act (1927)

This Act established the state boundary as the primary limit for bank expansion by prohibiting banks from accepting deposits across state lines. Additionally, it prohibited branching across state lines unless approved by affected state governments. States were given the power to decide the extent of bank branching within and outside state borders.

The McFadden Act has been modified by two key pieces of legislation. The Douglas Amendment (1956) allowed banks to merge across state lines if each state permitted it. Since 1956, legislation enacted by individual states allowed bank holding companies to acquire banks and bank holding companies in other states. The Interstate Banking and Branching Efficiency Act (1994) phased out, over a three-year period, the state barriers against branching established by the McFadden Act.

2. Interstate Banking and Branching Efficiency Act (IBBEA) (1994)

This Act is also known as the Riegle-Neal Interstate Banking and Branching Act Its primary provisions include:

- Permitted bank holding companies to acquire a bank located in any state, effective September 1995
- Allowed banks in one state to merge with banks in another state, beginning June 1997, so long as neither state took legislative action to prohibit interstate mergers between the date of enactment and May 1997
- Allows banks to establish new branches in states where they do not maintain branches if the host state passes a law expressly permitting such branches

D. Legislation Governing Payment Systems Operations and Instruments

1. Electronic Funds Transfer Act (EFTA) (1978)

This Act defines the rights and responsibilities of consumers using all EFT services except wire transfers. Further, it limits customer liability for unauthorized banking transactions involving automated teller machines (ATMs) and point-of-sale (POS) terminals, provided that the customer promptly notifies the bank or other institution that issues the card. Provisions of this Act are incorporated in Federal Reserve Regulation E.

2. Depository Institutions Deregulation and Monetary Control Act (DIDMCA) (1980)

This Act had major implications for both financial institutions and treasury managers. For the financial-services industry, it:

- Required all deposit-taking institutions to maintain reserves at the Fed
- Made Fed services such as the discount window and check clearing available to all deposit-taking institutions
- Mandated the Fed to reduce and/or price payment system float and to price previously free Fed services according to the standards of a tax-paying vendor

On the deposit side, it provided for phasing out of Regulation Q interest rate ceilings (with the exception of sub chapter S and C corporations) and permitted banks to offer NOW accounts, which are check writing accounts with an unregulated interest rate for individuals, sole proprietorships, not-for-profit organizations and government entities.

3. Debt Collection Improvement Act (DCIA) (1996)

This Act centralized the government-wide collection of delinquent debt and gave the Treasury significant new responsibilities in this area. The Financial Management Service (FMS) is responsible for the Treasury's implementation of the debt collection provisions of DCIA. This Act required that most federal payments, except for tax refunds, be conducted electronically by 1999. While this requirement has since been eliminated, in fiscal year 2001 approximately 33 percent of federal tax payments were made electronically, and about 76 percent of all other Treasury disbursements were made electronically, representing a total of more than 900 million payments.

4. Electronic Signatures in Global and National Commerce Act (2000)

The purpose of this Act was to grant digital signatures the same legal status as ink signatures. It accomplishes this by ensuring the legal certainty of e-commerce transactions and providing a measure of confidence in the enforceability of electronic transactions.

5. Check Clearing for the 21st Century Act (Check 21) (2003)

Signed into law on October 28, 2003 and effective on October 28, 2004, Check 21 was enacted to enhance efficiency in the payments system by reducing the legal impediments to check truncation. The purposes of the Check 21 Act are to:

- Facilitate check truncation
- Foster innovation in the check-payment system without mandating receipt of checks in electronic format
- Improve the payment system overall

The Act creates a new negotiable instrument, called a "substitute check," also known as an image replacement document (IRD). A substitute check is a Magnetic Ink Character Recognition (MICR)-encoded paper reproduction of an original check that:

- Contains an image of the front and back of the check
- Bears an MICR line containing all of the information appearing on the MICR line of the original check
- Conforms to industry standards that enable the substitute check to be processed in the same manner as the original paper check

If the substitute check meets the Act's requirements, then it is the legal equivalent of the original paper check and can be processed in the same manner as that check. Parties cannot refuse to accept a substitute check that meets the Act's requirements; this includes everyone: other banks, paying customers, depositing customers, consumers, corporations, Federal Reserve, processors, etc.

It is important to understand that the Act provides legal equivalence only for substitute checks. While it does facilitate check truncation and check-image exchanges, it does not provide legal equivalence for check images. Systems and clearing arrangements involving check-image presentment still require agreement of the parties who accept the electronic form of the instrument for value.

The Act encourages the use of electronics by empowering banks to truncate original checks, process them electronically, and, where necessary, provide paper substitute checks. All checks, except foreign checks, are eligible to become substitute checks, including, but not limited to, the following:

- Consumer, business, corporate and U.S. Treasury checks
- Government warrants
- Payable-through drafts (PTDs)
- Money orders
- Travelers cheques

E. Legislation Governing Consumer Protection

1. Community Reinvestment Act (CRA) (1977, 1995)

The CRA was passed by Congress in 1977, implemented by Federal Reserve Regulation BB, and revised in May 1995. It encourages depository institutions to help meet the credit needs of the communities in which they operate, including low- and moderate-income neighborhoods.

Additionally, this Act requires that each depository institution's record in helping to meet the credit needs of the entire community be evaluated periodically. This record is taken into account in considering an institution's application for deposit facilities. CRA examinations are conducted by all of the federal agencies responsible for supervising depository institutions.

2. Expedited Funds Availability Act (1988)

This Act primarily protects consumers by defining the maximum funds withdrawal time periods and establishing return procedures for payable-through drafts and checks. The provisions of this Act are incorporated in Federal Reserve Regulation CC.

3. Gramm-Leach-Bliley Act (1999)

Several provisions for consumer protection within Gramm-Leach-Bliley (GLB) require bank holding companies to maintain satisfactory CRA ratings and to establish and disclose privacy policies for customer information. (See Legislation Governing Types of Financial Services Offered, above, for the impact of the GLB Act on deregulation.)

F. Federal Reserve Regulations

After banking legislation is passed by Congress, the law is implemented through rules and regulations imposed by the regulatory agencies. The Federal Reserve defines and enforces several banking regulations that impact treasury managers.

1. Regulation D

This Regulation implements the reserve requirement provision of the Federal Reserve Act of 1913 and imposes uniform reserve requirements on all depository institutions with different levels of reserves for different types of deposits. The Fed uses this regulation in controlling the supply of money.

2. Regulation E

This Regulation implements the provisions of the Electronic Funds Transfer Act of 1978, which establishes the rights, responsibilities, and liabilities of parties engaging in consumer-related EFTs and protects consumers using systems such as ATMs, the ACH, and credit cards. Regulation E also establishes the guidelines for documentation of electronic transfers.

3. Regulation J

This Regulation implements the check collection and settlement provision of the Federal Reserve Act of 1913 and establishes procedures, duties and responsibilities for check collection and settlement through the Federal Reserve system.

4. Regulation Q

This Regulation implements the interest bearing account restriction of the Glass-Steagall Act of 1933. Interest rate ceilings that had initially been set by this Regulation on all commercial bank deposit accounts were phased out in 1986 by the DIDMCA. However, that one remaining provision of this act still prohibits financial institutions from paying interest on demand deposits held by sub S and C corporate entities.

5. Regulation BB

This Regulation implements the provisions of the Community Reinvestment Acts of 1977 and 1995 and requires banks to help meet the credit needs of the entire community in which they do business.

6. Regulation CC

This Regulation implements the provisions of the Expedited Funds Availability Act of 1988, which establishes rules designed to speed the collection and return of checks and insists that banks return unpaid checks expeditiously. This regulation imposes the same return procedures to payable through drafts that apply to checks, and also establishes endorsement standards for banks and companies to follow in depositing and clearing checks.

VI. THE UNIFORM COMMERCIAL CODE (UCC)

The UCC is a uniform set of laws governing commercial transactions. It defines the rights and duties of the parties in a commercial transaction and provides a statutory definition of commonly accepted business practices. UCC laws are enacted separately; hence, the four articles below may take different forms in each state.

A. Article 3 – Negotiable Instruments

The primary provisions of this Article involve negotiable instruments, accord and satisfaction, and how banks handle unauthorized signatures. Article 3 is especially relevant for companies using automated bank or third-party lockbox processors because it defines exactly what constitutes a negotiable instrument such as a draft, a check, a certificate of deposit and a note. Initially, checks were permitted to constitute payment made in full (accord and satisfaction) when a message to that effect was written on the face of the check and the check was deposited. However, this provision allowed for the possibility of inadvertent accord and satisfaction when the customer wrote "paid in full" on a check for a disputed claim, especially when the check was collected through a lockbox. The revised section of Article 3 prevents inadvertent accord and satisfaction if the payee discovers the error and returns the payment to the payor within 90 days.

Article 3 also clarifies that a bank's failure to examine a forged drawer's signature is not a failure to exercise ordinary care if it does not violate the bank's procedures and the procedures do not unreasonably vary from general banking practices. A bank can charge a customer's account only for checks that are properly payable.

Therefore, items with unauthorized signatures do not pass this test. However, a company may be held liable if it does not exercise ordinary care related to check issuance and does not notify the bank in a timely manner.

B. Article 4 – Bank Deposits and Collections

The provisions of Article 4 include the rights, responsibilities and definitions of the parties involved in the deposit and collection process. Specifically, Article 4 addresses the relationship between a bank and its customers. Article 4 defines:

- When a bank may charge a customer's account
- The bank's liability to a customer for failing to honor a good check
- The customer's right to stop payment
- The bank's option not to pay an item more than six months old (stale dated)
- A customer's duty to report an unauthorized signature or alteration

A company has the duty to examine bank statements within a reasonable time, not to exceed 30 days after the statement has been sent, and to report any unauthorized signatures or alterations. This makes it imperative that companies accurately reconcile bank accounts on a timely basis.

C. Article 4A – Funds Transfers

Article 4A provides a legal framework that outlines the risks, rights and obligations of parties in connection with wholesale ACH credit transfers, Fedwire transfers and transactions that are handled through the Clearing House Interbank Payments System (CHIPS). Two of the primary provisions of Article 4A are security procedures and consequential damages:

1. Security procedures: A bank must make such procedures available to the customer. Further, the bank and the customer must agree that the procedures are commercially reasonable for verifying payment. Some common security measures include the use of personal identification numbers (PINs), callbacks, encryption, and message authentication.

2. Consequential damages: Banks generally are not responsible for consequential damages, which are losses resulting from the action or error made by the bank beyond the actual loss. However, a bank incorrectly executing a payment order remains liable for interest losses or incidental expenses. (A bank is liable for consequential damages only when it agrees to assume this liability in a written agreement with the customer.)

D. Article 5 – Letters of Credit (L/C)

Article 5 covers commercial letters of credit requiring documentary drafts and defines a letter of credit, a documentary draft and documentary demand for payment. It also defines the various roles of the issuer of a letter of credit, the applicant for whom the credit is issued, the beneficiary of the credit, the advising bank and the confirming bank. Article 5 does not cover standby letters of credit.

Test Your Understanding

These chapter questions are provided to test your understanding of the information in the text. They are neither examples of CTP examination questions nor are they in the examination format.

Answers are on pages 569–572.

1. What is the definition of a commercial bank?

2. What are the major products and services offered by commercial banks?

3. Discuss the principal function of an investment banking firm.

4. What is an industrial credit and capital company?

5. Who charters savings banks and mutual savings banks?

6. What are the distinctions between money and capital markets and what are examples of some of the instruments in each market?

7. What are the five major roles of the Federal Reserve?

8. Who grants charters to national banks?

9. What is FinCEN and what does it do?

10. What is FFIEC and what does it do?

11. What is OFAC and what does it do?

12. What are the primary provisions of the Patriot Act?

13. What is SOX and what is its primary purpose?

14. What is the primary purpose of the Check 21 Act and what is a "substitute check"?

15. What legislation mandated the Federal Reserve to reduce and/or price float?

16. What legislation consolidated the two financial institution insurance funds under the FDIC?

17. Discuss the primary provisions of the Interstate Banking and Branching Efficiency Act of 1994.

18. What legislation permitted the creation of financial holding companies (FHCs) and what else does this legislation do?

19. What Federal Reserve regulation established rules for handling return of checks and payable- through drafts?

20. Under UCC Article 4A, is a bank responsible for consequential damages?

CHAPTER 4
Financial Accounting

I. INTRODUCTION

A critical skill for a treasury professional is the ability to read and interpret financial statements. This ability is useful for the purpose of analyzing a company's performance and comparing that performance to the company's historical performance and to other companies within the same industry. The use of ratio analysis of financial statements enables a treasury professional to effectively manage and control the financial operations of a company and to manage credit relationships with banks and other lenders. Conducting a ratio analysis of other companies is also an essential element of the credit, investment, and merger and acquisition decision-making processes.

This chapter provides an overview of the accounting and financial analysis practices of for-profit enterprises in the U.S., as well as a brief discussion of governmental and not-for-profit accounting.

II. ACCOUNTING CONCEPTS AND STANDARDS

Accounting provides the data necessary to measure a company's performance and analyze its financial position. The accounting function includes recording a company's assets, liabilities, shareholder equity, revenues and expenses, and reporting this information according to a detailed set of rules referred to as Generally Accepted Accounting Principles (GAAP). These principles are developed, agreed upon, and published in the form of Financial Accounting Standards (FAS) by the Financial Accounting Standards Board (FASB), an independent, self-regulating organization formed in 1973. Authority for enforcing U.S. accounting principles is the responsibility of the Securities and Exchange Commission (SEC, established in 1934). However, the SEC relies largely on the FASB to develop accounting standards.

The SEC, an independent regulatory agency of the United States government, requires all companies that issue publicly traded securities to file audited financial statements. Annual financial statements are filed using the SEC Form 10-K; quarterly financial information is reported on Form 10-Q. SEC filings on specific companies may be obtained through the Electronic Data Gathering Analysis and Retrieval (EDGAR) database.

The SEC enjoys broad powers with respect to prescribing accounting practices for required financial statement filings. Specific reporting guidance issued by the SEC is contained within its Financial Reporting Releases (FRRs), Regulation S-X and decisions on cases that have come before the Commission. However, the SEC's philosophy is that the private sector retains the initiative for establishing and improving accounting standards. Therefore, the SEC relies on the FASB for this purpose. FR-1 recognizes FAS as the authoritative standard for financial reporting. Thus, financial statements conforming to GAAP are presumed to satisfy the SEC's requirements. Adherence to GAAP is crucial because investors, lenders and trade creditors rely on consistent financial information for decision-making.

The International Accounting Standards Board (IASB), which is based in London, England, is made up of Board members from nine countries. The IASB's mission is to develop a single set of global accounting standards. IASB standards are published as pronouncements called International Financial Reporting Standards (IFRS). IASB has also adopted the International Accounting Standards (IAS) developed by IASB's predecessor, the Board of the

International Accounting Standards Committee. The FASB and the IASB are working cooperatively toward creating accounting standards that are globally consistent.

1. Generally Accepted Accounting Principles (GAAP)

The Conceptual Framework

In the mid-1970s, the FASB developed a conceptual framework for financial accounting and reporting. This framework forms the basis for a series of Statements of Financial Accounting Concepts (SFACs). To date, seven SFACs have been issued that serve as the general framework for subsequent accounting principles to be developed. The key issues addressed by the various SFACs include:

- Defining the basic objectives of financial accounting
- Describing the qualitative characteristics of accounting information and the elements of financial statements
- Providing the basic assumptions and principles to be applied in reporting financial activities
- Providing guidelines for using cash-flow information and present value in accounting measurements

The four basic principles underlying GAAP and their implications are:

- The historical-cost principle
- The full-disclosure principle
- The revenue-recognition principle
- the matching principle.

The **historical cost principle** states that most assets and liabilities are reported at historical cost. An important exception to the historical cost principle is reporting for certain marketable securities. This will be discussed later in the chapter.

The **full disclosure principle** states that any information that may influence the judgment and decisions of a user of financial information should be disclosed.

The **revenue recognition principle** maintains that revenue is reported when cash or a claim for cash is received in exchange for goods or services and the earning process is substantially complete. A claim for cash typically refers to accounts receivable. Accounts receivable are assets that represent revenues from sales that have been recognized but not yet collected. When good funds are collected from the customer, the accounts receivable balance is decreased and the cash balance is increased without any impact on income because the revenue was recognized when the receivable was generated.

The **matching principle** requires that expenses be reported when the revenues with which they are associated are recognized. Because long-lived or fixed assets benefit revenues over many accounting periods, they are capitalized (recorded as assets on the balance sheet), then depreciated over time. This practice matches the cost of an asset to the revenues it produces. Under the revenue recognition and matching principles, sales are reported even though cash has not yet been received and expenses are reported even though cash has not yet been paid out. This forms the basis for accrual accounting.

Accrual accounting conforms to GAAP and is used by most businesses. Alternatively, non-GAAP accounting methods may be used by certain non-public businesses and include strict cash basis accounting and modified cash basis accounting. With strict cash basis accounting, revenues and expenses are reported only when cash is received or disbursed. Modified cash basis accounting adopts some elements of accrual accounting such as reporting accounts receivable as revenues and capitalizing and depreciating fixed assets. Professional service firms use modified cash basis accounting extensively.

If revenues and expenses were reported only when cash is transferred, the timing and amounts could be determined objectively. With accrual accounting, the extensive use of estimates and judgments is required, providing flexibility in choosing the timing and the amounts reported in the financial statements. Accrual-based income is more useful to external decision makers because it provides a better basis for making predictions about a company's future earnings and cash flows. However, accrual accounting may be manipulated. Managers may intentionally distort estimates or make judgments that allow them to time their revenues and expenses in order to report a desired level of income. This process is referred to as earnings management. Smoothing refers to a type of earnings management used to create a consistent pattern of income over time.

2. Financial Accounting Standards (FAS)

The SFACs provide the conceptual framework for the financial reporting process. Specific, detailed guidance is issued as Financial Accounting Standards. The FASB continuously monitors the reporting and business environments to provide relevant and timely guidance for preparing financial statements. The general provisions of selected FAS relevant to a treasury professional are summarized in this section.

Accounting for Cash, Cash Equivalents and Overdrafts

Cash consists of coin, currency and available deposit balances (checking accounts). Many short-term investments are considered cash equivalents, including money market funds and marketable debt securities with original maturities (i.e., at issuance) of fewer than three months.

Cash and cash equivalents are commonly reported as a single line item on the balance sheet. If cash is contractually restricted, such as with a formal compensating balance agreement, it should be reported as a separate line item from unrestricted balances.

(A more detailed discussion of short-term investments and compensating balance requirements are in Chapter 10, Liquidity Management.)

Bank account overdrafts should appear on the balance sheet as current liabilities. These financial statement reporting requirements may influence perceptions regarding a company's liquidity and may also have potential implications for debt covenant compliance.

Accounting for Short-Term Investments (FAS 115)
Marketable investment instruments with original maturities of more than three months, but remaining maturities of one year or less, are carried on the balance sheet as short-term investments. For valuation and reporting purposes, short-term investments are classified in three different ways:

- **Trading Securities:** Securities that are purchased for a short time prior to sale are classified as trading securities. This classification is typically reserved for securities that are traded with the objective of generating profits. A trading security is carried as a current asset regardless of its maturity and is listed at fair market value. Unrealized holding gains and losses arise when trading securities are marked-to-market and are reported under current income. Marked-to-market means that the current value of the security is adjusted to market value on the reporting date.

- **Held to Maturity (HTM) Securities:** These are debt securities purchased with both the intent and the ability to hold until maturity. HTM investments are the only marketable securities that are carried at cost on the balance sheet. Because these securities are not marked-to-market, no gains or losses are associated with HTMs. HTMs are reported as current assets when the time remaining to maturity is one year or less; otherwise, they are carried as long-term assets. Reclassification of HTMs to other reporting categories, especially when the reclassification results in the reporting of gains or losses, is subject to SEC scrutiny. The HTM classification should not be used if there is any potential that the underlying investment will be sold prior to maturity for either liquidity purposes or to capture profits arising from favorable market movements.

- **Available for Sale (AFS) Securities:** Most short-term investments are classified as AFS, which is the default classification for all securities not carried as trading or HTM securities. These securities are classified as long-term or current assets, depending on their remaining maturities. Like trading securities, AFS securities are marked-to-market, but the resulting gains and losses are reported in comprehensive income.

(A more detailed discussion of comprehensive income is in the section on the Income Statement later in this chapter.)

Accounting for Derivative Instruments and Hedging Activities (FAS 133 & 138)
Derivatives, such as forwards, futures, options and swaps, are carried at fair value on the balance sheet as assets or liabilities. Accounting for the gains and losses that arise from changes in the fair value of a derivative depends on the intended use of the instrument.

Gains and losses that arise from revaluation of derivatives are reported in current period income provided that the derivatives do not qualify as hedge instruments. If a derivative is used to hedge fluctuations in the value of a specific asset or liability carried on the balance sheet, the gains and losses of the reevaluation are recognized as income together with the offsetting gains and losses on the item being hedged. This type of hedge is referred to as a fair value hedge.

Hedges that are designed to minimize fluctuation in values of cash flows of forecasted transactions include cash flow hedges and foreign currency (FX) transaction hedges. Gains and losses on cash flow and FX transaction hedges are reported in comprehensive income. The hedged gains and losses are not reported in current income until the related transactions impact current income. Rules for classifying derivative transactions are complex and detailed. A treasurer who is responsible for derivative activities must be well versed in the rules or should seek professional guidance to avoid an unanticipated impact on earnings.

Classification of Debt

Debt is classified as current or non-current, depending on when it must be repaid or it contractually matures. In the case of long-term debt with scheduled installments, the portions that are to be paid within one year are carried in current liabilities as current maturities of long-term debt. Remaining portions are reported in the long-term section of the balance sheet. Any long-term debt currently maturing should also be classified as a current liability unless:

- It is to be repaid by assets accumulated for the purpose of repaying debt not shown as current assets.
- It is to be refinanced or repaid with proceeds of another debt issue.
- It is to be converted into stock.

Similarly, short-term debt that is expected to be refinanced on a long-term basis may be classified as long-term if the obligor has a pending financing arrangement to receive long-term treatment. For example, although commercial paper (CP) maturities are less than one year, CP is often classified as a long-term liability when the issuer has a back-up line of credit that expires in more than one year.

(A more detailed discussion of CP and back-up lines are in Chapter 10, Liquidity Management.)

Other Accounting Issues

In addition to the standards that directly impact treasury, FASB adopted rules for accounting for goodwill and other acquired intangible assets (FAS 142). These often require revaluation of business units, a responsibility typically supported by treasury personnel. (For a discussion of goodwill or intangible assets, see the section on the Balance Sheet later in this chapter.) In mergers, the acquiring company may pay a premium over the net market value of the business acquired. This premium is capitalized on the balance sheet as goodwill. FAS 142 requires that goodwill be evaluated for a decline in value annually, with the carrying value adjusted accordingly.

Finally, under the Sarbanes-Oxley Act (SOX) of 2002, the SEC was mandated to improve rules for reporting off-balance-sheet arrangements (OBSA). OBSA include guarantees, contingent interests in assets, operating leases, guarantees and certain variable interest entities (also referred to as special purpose entities). The final rule issued by the SEC requires that specific disclosures related to OBSA be included in the Management Discussion and Analysis (MD&A) section provided with the company's financial statements. This is required whenever the OBSA have, or are reasonably likely to have, an effect on the financial condition of the business. The impact of SOX on accounting and financial professionals is discussed in detail in Chapter 19, Corporate Governance and Ethics.

III. FINANCIAL STATEMENTS

The form and content of a company's financial statements are determined by the requirements of the end-user. A business with public securities must conform to the SEC reporting requirements outlined in Regulation S-X. Non-public businesses also periodically generate financial statements to meet the needs of private lenders, trade editors, venture capitalists and outside shareholders. Most outside end-users (i.e., non-management) with a significant stake in a business require an audit of the financial statements by an independent auditor.

A. Auditing and Financial Statement Reliability

Typically, either an organization produces its own financial statements or an independent Certified Public Accountant (CPA) or CPA firm produces the statements. Statements may be audited or unaudited. Simply having an independent CPA or CPA firm compile a set of financial statements does not mean that the statements have been audited.

An audit is an examination of the financial statements by an independent accountant in accordance with generally accepted auditing standards (GAAS). The purpose of an audit is to verify the integrity of the financial statements by a party who is independent of the company and its management. A company's managers are primarily responsible for preparing financial statements. Because the interests of managers are not always aligned with those of creditors and shareholders, an independent review helps to assure outside parties that the information provided by management is reflective of a company's true performance. Confidence in the integrity of financial reports is critical to maintaining a market-driven economy.

Oversight of the audits of publicly held businesses is the responsibility of the Public Company Accounting Oversight Board (PCAOB). The PCAOB was established under SOX in response to concerns about audit quality following numerous corporate accounting scandals. The PCAOB is a private, non-profit corporation whose chairman and board members are appointed by the SEC. SOX requires the PCAOB to register, monitor, inspect and discipline public accounting firms that provide audits of publicly held businesses. The PCAOB also assumed responsibility for establishing auditing standards from the Auditing Standards Board (ASB) of the American Institute of Certified Public Accountants (AICPA).

(See Appendix B of Chapter 19, Corporate Governance and Ethics, for more information on the PCAOB.)

Audit Reports: The purpose of conducting an audit is to produce an audit report. This report is a document in which an independent CPA or CPA firm indicates the scope of the audit and sets forth an opinion regarding the financial statements as a whole. Opinions fall into five categories:

- Standard unqualified
- Unqualified with explanatory paragraph or modified unqualified
- Qualified
- Adverse
- Disclaimed

1. Standard Unqualified Opinion: A standard unqualified opinion is given when the auditor concludes that the financial statements fairly represent the activities of the business and the following three conditions are met:

- All required financial statements are provided.
- GAAS are followed in conducting the audit.
- The statements are presented in accordance with GAAP. If a standard unqualified opinion cannot be rendered, the appropriate opinion depends on the nature and materiality (i.e., degree) of the exceptions identified by the auditor.

2. Unqualified With Explanatory Paragraph Or Modified Unqualified: When immaterial deviations in GAAS or GAAP occur, an unqualified with explanatory paragraph, or modified unqualified opinion, is appropriate. This happens when:

- Some information requires special emphasis.
- There has been a change in auditor.
- The auditor questions the ability of a business to continue.

3. Qualified: If exceptions are material, yet do not overshadow the usefulness of the information, a qualified opinion is given.

4. Adverse: When exceptions are so material that the auditor determines that financial statements may be misleading, an adverse opinion is required.

5. Disclaimed: A disclaimer is not an opinion but rather a statement that the auditor cannot render an opinion. A disclaimer is required if the auditor is not independent of the company being audited or if the scope of the audit is so limited that no basis exists for forming an opinion.

Generally, investors and creditors give more credence to audited financial statements with an unqualified opinion versus those that are qualified. However, it is important to understand that an unqualified opinion by an auditor does not necessarily mean that a company is in good financial health. An unqualified opinion only indicates that the financial statements are in conformance with GAAP and provide a fair description of a company's financial condition. An investor or creditor must still carefully analyze the financial information when making decisions. Significant leeway in GAAP principles may result in the statements providing a biased picture of a company's condition. Also, a company's management may deliberately tamper with or withhold important information from auditors in order to make a company's financial condition appear more favorable to investors or creditors.

B. Types of Financial Statements

SEC Regulation S-X requires any issuer of securities to include a balance sheet, an income statement and a statement of cash flows, along with the accompanying notes, in both annual and quarterly filings. In addition, a reconciliation of changes in shareholders' equity is required to be included within the notes or presented as a separate statement.

1. Balance Sheet

A balance sheet reports the financial position of a company at a point in time. Another name for the balance sheet is the statement of financial position. It is a snapshot of a company's assets, liabilities, and stockholders' equity as of a specific date. An example of a balance sheet is presented in Exhibit 4.1.

EXHIBIT 4.1 – SAMPLE BALANCE SHEET

Assets	Current Year	Prior Year	Change
Cash	$1,500,000	$1,000,000	$500,000
Short-Term Investments	1,300,000	1,500,000	(200,000)
Accounts Receivable	1,700,000	1,300,000	400,000
Inventory	2,600,000	2,100,000	500,000
Pre-Paid Expenses	900,000	900,000	0
Total Current Assets	8,000,000	6,800,000	1,200,000
Gross Property, Plant & Equipment	9,000,000	8,100,000	900,000
Less: Accumulated Depreciations	1,500,000	1,300,000	200,000
Net Property, Plant & Equipment	7,500,000	6,800,000	700,000
Intangible Assets	0	0	
Total Assets	$15,500,000	$13,600,000	$1,900,000
Liabilities and Owners' Equity	**Current Year**	**Prior Year**	**Change**
Accounts Payable	$1,600,000	$1,200,000	400,000
Short-Term Notes Payable	1,800,000	1,300,000	500,000
Total Current Liabilities	3,400,000	2,500,000	900,000
Long-Term Debt	3,900,000	3,500,000	400,000
Total Liabilities	7,300,000	6,000,000	1,300,000
Common Stock at Par Value	200,000	200,000	0
Paid-In Capital	3,600,000	3,600,000	0
Retained Earnings	4,400,000	3,800,000	600,000
Total Equity	8,200,000	7,600,000	600,000
Total Liabilities and Equity	$15,500,000	$13,600,000	$1,900,000

Assets

Assets are economic resources owned by a company that are expected to provide future economic benefits. In order to be reported as an asset on the balance sheet, the resource must be objectively quantifiable with a reasonable degree of accuracy. Most non-financial assets are valued based on historic cost. They are listed on the balance sheet in order of decreasing liquidity or convertibility into cash. Current assets are defined as assets that are reasonably expected to be converted to cash within one year or within the operating cycle. Current assets include cash and cash equivalents, marketable securities and any operating assets—accounts receivable, inventories and prepaid expenses such as insurance premiums.

- **Fixed assets** are a company's investment in property, buildings, machinery and equipment. Fixed assets (also known as capital assets) cannot be turned into cash as readily as current assets. Fixed assets are recorded at cost when they are acquired. Depreciable fixed assets—those that are used up or decline in value over time—are depreciated, or expensed, over their useful lives. The book value, or carrying value, of a depreciable asset is its cost minus the accumulated depreciation. Other non-current assets include investments in long-term debt (bonds) and equity (stocks) of other companies and intangible assets.

- **Intangible assets** are assets that lack physical substance. Examples are goodwill, trademarks and patents. There is often a high degree of uncertainty concerning the future value of intangible assets. An intangible asset with a finite useful life is amortized over its legal or useful life. If the intangible asset has an indefinite useful life, it is not amortized. However, it must be evaluated annually for decline in value. Any decline in value must be charged against income when identified.

Liabilities and Shareholders' Equity

Liabilities and Shareholders' Equity are the means by which assets are financed. The following formula, known as the accounting equation, always holds: *Assets = Liabilities + Shareholders' Equity*

- **Liabilities**, which represent the obligations of the business, generally consist of operating liability accounts and financing supplied by creditors, primarily lenders and suppliers. Liabilities are obligations or debts that will be paid with assets or services in the future. In the case of current liabilities, the obligation is expected to be repaid out of current assets or fulfilled within the next year.

- **Current liabilities** include obligations such as accounts payable, short-term loans, wages payable, taxes payable and the current portion of long-term debt. Accounts payable (also referred to as trade payables) are amounts due to vendors for purchased items. Accounts payable, together with operating accruals such as wages payable and taxes payable, are operating liability accounts. Short-term notes payable are typically short-term bank loans or commercial paper (CP). Long-term liabilities are obligations such as term loans, capital lease obligations, mortgages and bonds due beyond one year.

- **Shareholders' equity** is the financing provided by the company's owners and from company operations. Contributed capital is the cash invested by shareholders. Retained earnings represent the changes in shareholders' equity arising from the retention of profits or losses of the company. Dividends paid to shareholders reduce retained earnings. The statement of changes in shareholders' equity summarizes transactions affecting shareholders' equity and reconciles the ending balance to the beginning balance for each shareholder's equity account.

2. Income Statement

The income statement (also called the statement of earnings, the statement of operations or the profit and loss statement) summarizes:

- Revenues earned
- Expenses incurred
- Gains and losses arising from conversions of assets and liabilities over an accounting period.

The order of items on the income statement progresses from activities that are most closely associated with the primary revenue generating activities to those with a less direct relationship. While expenses appearing on the income statement vary from business to business, brief descriptions of the major line items that appear on the typical income statement portrayed in Exhibit 4.2 follow in the ensuing text.

EXHIBIT 4.2 – SAMPLE INCOME STATEMENT

	Current Year	Prior Year	Change
Revenues	$15,000,000	$12,500,000	$2,500,000
Less: Cost of Goods Sold	9,200,000	7,400,000	1,800,000
Gross Profit	5,800,000	5,100,000	700,000
Less: Operating Expenses	4,000,000	3,500,000	500,000
EBITDA (EBIT before Dep. and Amort.)	1,800,000	1,600,000	200,000
Less: Depreciation	200,000	150,000	50,000
Operating Income/EBIT	1,600,000	1,450,000	150,000
Less: Interest Expense	300,000	245,000	55,000
Net Profit Before Taxes	1,300,000	1,205,000	95,000
Less: Provision for Income Taxes	450,000	370,000	80,000
Net Income	$850,000	$835,000	$15,000

Statement of Retained Earning

	Current Year	Prior Year	Change
Beginning Retained Earnings	$3,800,000	$3,215,000	$585,000
Earnings Available for Common Shareholders	850,000	835,000	$15,000
Less: Common Stock Dividends Paid	250,000	250,000	0
Plus/Minus Currency Translation Adjustment	0	0	0
Addition to Retained Earnings	$600,000	$585,000	$15,000
Ending Retained Earnings	$4,400,000	$3,800,000	$600,000
Earnings per Share (100,000 shares outstanding)	$8.50	$8.35	$0.15

Revenues represent amounts earned from the sale of merchandise or services to customers. The cost of goods sold (COGS) is the expense of providing the goods or services whose sale is recognized as revenues. COGS includes labor and material directly used in manufacturing the product sold, as well as any indirect, or allocated, manufacturing expenses. These costs are called product costs. "Gross profit" is usually the term used for revenues less the cost of goods sold. Service companies typically do not have COGS.

Operating expenses, such as selling or administrative expenses, represent general expenses that are incurred in the course of running a business but are not directly associated with the production of goods and services. Most operating expenses are considered period expenses because they occur over a period of time and cannot be attributed to specific units of goods or services sold.

One of the common measures for operating profitability is EBITDA or earnings before interest, taxes, depreciation and amortization. Once depreciation and amortization have been subtracted, the remaining amount is usually referred to as earnings before interest and taxes or EBIT. The term "operating income" typically refers to EBIT, but some analysts may use EBITDA for operating income measures.

The income statement may also include other income and expenses such as interest income and expense, or realized currency gains or losses. These income and expenses usually arise from non-operating activities such as financing related activities. Income before taxes is operating income, adjusted for other income and expenses. Net income is income before taxes minus income tax expense.

In addition to net income, GAAP also requires companies to report comprehensive income. Comprehensive income is net income adjusted for three types of gains or losses not reported on the income statement:

- Unrealized gains and losses, such as holding gains and losses on AFS (available for sale) securities or gains and losses on cash flow hedges
- Minimum pension liability adjustments
- Foreign currency translation adjustments. Comprehensive income must be reported as part of the income statement, in the statement of changes in shareholders' equity, or in a separate statement of comprehensive income.

All elements of comprehensive income capture economic activities or flows that occur over a period of time. In contrast, the balance sheet presents the financial position of accounts at a point in time. These economic activities or flows explain the differences between the beginning-of-the-period and the end-of-the-period balance sheet account levels. This interrelationship between the financial statements is referred to as articulation. The statement of cash flows details transactions that explain changes in the cash balance from the beginning of the accounting period to the end of the accounting period.

3. Statement of Cash Flows

Under accrual accounting, the reporting period when a revenue or an expense item is recognized is often different from the reporting period when the corresponding cash transaction occurs. An income statement based on accrual accounting is a useful indication of a company's performance; however, lenders, creditors and investors are concerned with a company's cash flow because cash, not earnings, repays debt, pays bills and may be distributed as dividends. The statement of cash flows provides a detailed picture of the sources of a company's cash flows and how these sources are utilized.

The statement of cash flows is divided into three sections: operating, investing and financing activities. Exhibit 4.3 shows how a statement of cash flows can be derived from information on the balance sheet (Exhibit 4.1) and the income statement (Exhibit 4.2).

EXHIBIT 4.3 – SAMPLE STATEMENT OF CASH FLOWS

Cash Flows from Operating Activities		
Net Income	$850,000	
Adjustments to Reconcile Net Income to Net Cash		
Depreciation	200,000	
Increase in Accounts Receivable	(400,000)	
Increase in Inventory	(500,000)	
Increase in Accounts Payable	400,000	
Net Cash Provided (Used) in Operating Activities		$550,000
Cash Flows from Investing Activities		
Capital Expenditures	$(900,000)	
Decrease in Short-Term Investments	200,000	
Net Cash Provided (Used) in Investing Activities		$(700,000)
Cash Flows from Financing Activities		
Net Short-Term Borrowing (Notes Payable)	$500,000	
Proceeds from Issuance of Long-Term Debt	400,000	
Dividends Paid	(250,000)	
Net Cash Provided by Financing Activities		$650,000
Net Cash Increase (Decrease)		$500,000
Net Change in Cash From Balance Sheet		$500,000

To calculate cash flow from operating activities, depreciation and any other non-cash charges (gains) reported on the income statement are added to (deducted from) net income. Then, changes in accounts receivable, inventories and accounts payable, and changes in other operating accruals are added or subtracted. These items represent cash inflows and outflows, related to the daily operations of a company that must be taken into account in order to determine cash flow. The total is net cash provided (or used) by operating activities.

Other corporate actions affecting a company's cash flow include investing activities, such as buying and selling plant or equipment and/or financial instruments and financing activities, such as issuing or retiring equity or debt.

The statement of cash flows in Exhibit 4.3 shows that the sample company generated a cash flow from operations of $550,000. Net income provided $850,000 and depreciation was $200,000. Net changes in balance sheet amounts absorbed $500,000 because inventory and receivables increased by $900,000 while payables increased by only $400,000.

Investing activities during the period used $700,000, comprised of $900,000 in gross capital expenditures (before depreciation) offset by a $200,000 decrease in short-term investments. The sample company had a net inflow of $650,000 of cash from financing activities. In total, cash increased by $500,000.

IV. FINANCIAL STATEMENT ANALYSIS

Financial statements provide information to existing and potential stakeholders who must make informed decisions about allocating economic resources:

- Suppliers need to determine whether to make sales on credit.
- Trading partners need to assess the financial ability of a counterparty to meet contractual obligations.
- Lenders need to determine whether or not to enter into or maintain a credit relationship.
- Rating agencies need to assess the credit risk of issues.
- Investors need to make decisions about purchasing and selling corporate debt and equity securities.

A great deal of the information required for making these decisions is provided in financial statements, assuming that decision-makers accurately analyze and interpret them.

Ratio analysis and cash flow analysis are two of the most commonly used tools for analyzing financial statements. Cash flow analysis entails developing pro forma financial statements and using the statement of cash flows to assess expected future liquidity needs and resources. Ratio analysis is useful in evaluating past and present performance, efficiency, liquidity and leverage, and serves as a foundation for financial forecasting. Forecasting is used for budgeting, credit evaluation and valuation purposes.

By themselves, ratios do not provide much information. Instead, ratios must be compared to a benchmark. Ratios may be used to:

- Analyze trends over time
- Compare one company with competitors or other companies in the same industry
- Compare the ratio for a company to an absolute standard, such as a debt covenant.

All of the sample calculations below use the data from the financial statements in Exhibits 4.1, 4.2, and 4.3 (dollars expressed in thousands).

The calculations in this text will use period end figures for all balance sheet items. An alternative approach is to use the average figure (beginning balance plus ending balance divided by two) for many of the balance sheet items. Using the average figures will help to smooth out balance sheet fluctuations but may not be relevant if the company's financial position has undergone a major change.

A. Common-Size Ratios

The most basic type of ratio analysis uses common-size financial statements. A common-size income statement expresses every line item on the statement as a percentage of revenues. These common-size percentages are referred to as margins. The gross profit margin is calculated as follows:

$$\text{Gross Profit Margin} = \frac{\text{Gross Profit}}{\text{Revenues}} \times 100 = \frac{\$5{,}800}{\$15{,}000} \times 100 = 38.7\%$$

Common-size ratios may also be calculated for the balance sheet, where total assets are used as the denominator. Common-size financial statements facilitate evaluation of how effectively a company generates profits from revenues and identifies trends over time when several years of statements are considered concurrently.

Common-size ratios compare amounts within a financial statement. Other ratio calculations may involve only flow (income statement) or level (balance sheet) accounts, or may use elements from both the income statement and the balance sheet. When only level measures are required, end-of-the-period balances are used. If the ratio contains a balance sheet number and an income statement number, the average of the beginning and the ending balance sheet amounts maybe used. The beginning balance for a balance sheet account is obtained by taking the ending balance of the prior period.

B. Liquidity or Working Capital Ratios

A company's liquidity (i.e., its ability to meet present obligations when they come due) is measured using liquidity or working capital ratios and related calculations. Working capital refers to a company's current asset accounts – namely cash, accounts receivable and inventory. These are the accounts through which cash flows during a company's cash conversion cycle. Net working capital is equal to total current assets minus total current liabilities.

Liquidity or working capital ratios are standardized and widely used formulas that allow a company's management to:

- Determine adequate liquidity levels
- Establish liquidity policy and guidelines
- Continually monitor liquidity

Banks, other creditors, investors, analysts and ratings agencies use the same working capital and liquidity measures to assess a company's creditworthiness and short-term financial soundness. The principal methods of measuring corporate liquidity are included in the calculations that follow.

1. Current Ratio

The current ratio is defined as total current assets divided by total current liabilities. This ratio measures a company's ability to meet its current obligations or the degree to which current obligations are covered by current assets.

$$\text{Current Ratio}=\frac{\text{Total Current Assets}}{\text{Total Current Liabilities}}=\frac{\$8{,}000}{\$3{,}400}=2.4$$

2. Quick Ratio

The quick ratio is defined as cash plus short-term investments and accounts receivable divided by total current liabilities. It is also known as the "acid test" ratio and is considered a more conservative measure of liquidity than the current ratio. The quick ratio measures the degree to which a company's current liabilities are covered by its most liquid current assets.

$$\text{Quick Ratio}=\frac{\text{Cash + Short-Term Investments + Accounts Receivable}}{\text{Total Current Liabilities}}$$

$$=\frac{\$1{,}500+\$1{,}300+\$1{,}700}{\$3{,}400}=1.3$$

Note that inventory and prepaid expenses are not included in the quick ratio because they are the least liquid of the current assets.

3. Cash Flow to Total Debt Ratio

Cash flow to total debt is defined as net income plus depreciation divided by total long-term and short-term debt. Short-term debt consists of short-term notes, commercial paper or other short-term debt obligations. A relatively low ratio indicates an inability to repay debt. Studies of failed companies have found this ratio to be accurate in predicting financial failure. This ratio includes income statement and balance sheet amounts. The first step in the calculation involves averaging the balance sheet amounts as follows:

$$\text{Cash Flow to Total Debt Ratio}=\frac{\text{Net Income + Depreciation}}{\text{Short-Term Debt + Long-Term Debt}}$$

$$=\frac{\$850+\$200}{\$1{,}800+\$3{,}900}=\frac{\$1{,}050}{\$5{,}700}=0.2$$

4. Cash Conversion Cycle

The cash conversion cycle measures liquidity from another perspective. It calculates the time required to convert cash outflows (necessary to produce goods) into cash inflows (through collection of accounts receivable). By adding the average age of the inventory (measured by days' inventory) and the average age of accounts receivable (measured by days' receivables), and subtracting the average age of the accounts payable (measured by days' payables), the cash conversion cycle indicates how efficiently a company is using its current assets and liabilities.

Days' Inventory

Days' inventory is calculated as a function of the inventory value and the cost of goods sold. The inventory value used here is the ending inventory, though some forms of this ratio may use an average inventory figure. The cost of goods sold, rather than sales, is used in this formula because inventory is valued at its purchase cost rather than its selling price.

$$\text{Days' Inventory} = \frac{\text{Inventory}}{\text{Cost of Goods Sold}} \times 365 = \frac{\$2{,}600}{\$9{,}200} \times 365 = 103.2 \text{ Days}$$

Days' Receivables

Days' receivables are calculated as a function of the accounts receivable value and the level of sales. This figure is also known as average collection period or days' sales outstanding and represents the number of days required to convert a sale into a cash inflow. Ending accounts receivable are used in this example.

$$\text{Days' Receivables} = \frac{\text{Accounts Receivable}}{\text{Annual Sales}} \times 365 = \frac{\$1{,}700}{\$15{,}000} \times 365 = 41.4 \text{ Days}$$

Days' Payables

In this example days' payables are calculated as a function of the ending accounts payable and the cost of goods sold.

$$\text{Days' Payables} = \frac{\text{Accounts Payable}}{\text{Cost of Goods Sold}} \times 365 = \frac{\$1{,}600}{\$9{,}200} \times 365 = 63.5 \text{ Days}$$

Now, the cash conversion cycle can be determined using the three time periods to calculate the average number of days required from: The beginning of the production cycle through the sales and credit and accounts receivable cycle including the receipt of collected funds offset by the number of days of accounts payable.

The net result is the time that a company uses to convert a cash outflow (a payment to a supplier) into a cash inflow (a collection from a customer for the goods sold). This is also commonly referred to as the working capital gap because it expresses the gap between a cash outflow and a cash inflow. In this example, a company has cash invested in its operating cycle for an average of 81.1 days.

$$\begin{aligned}\text{Cash Conversion Cycle} &= \text{Days' Inventory} + \text{Days' Receivables} - \text{Days' Payables}\\ &= 103.2 \text{ Days} + 41.4 \text{ Days} - 63.5 \text{ Days} = 81.1 \text{ Days}\end{aligned}$$

5. Cash Turnover Ratio

The cash turnover ratio is a measure of the number of cash conversion cycles that a company experiences in a single year. The cash conversion cycle and cash turnover ratio are measures of efficiency used to compare companies in the same or similar industries.

$$\text{Cash Turnover} = \frac{365}{\text{Cash Conversion Cycle}} = \frac{365}{81.1} = 4.5 \text{ Times}$$

C. Debt Management Ratios

In addition to liquidity ratios, other standard and widely employed coverage or debt management ratios are used to determine a company's creditworthiness. Several common measures are illustrated below.

1. Times Interest Earned (TIE) Ratio

The times interest earned (TIE) ratio measures how many times a company's earnings before interest and taxes (EBIT) exceed its interest obligations. The higher this ratio, the greater the ability of a company to pay down debt.

$$\text{TIE} = \frac{\text{Operating Profit}}{\text{Interest Expense}} = \frac{\$1{,}600}{\$300} = 5.3 \text{ Times}$$

2. Long-Term Debt to Capital

Most frequently used by financial analysts and credit rating agencies, long-term debt to capital measures what percentage of a company's capitalization is provided by long-term debt. Capitalization consists of long-term debt and equity. Long-term debt includes liabilities such as long-term notes and bonds, term loans, and capitalized lease obligations. Equity capital consists of all preferred and common equity accounts, including retained earnings. The higher the long-term debt to capital ratio, the greater the percentage of debt a company is using to support its long-term capital structure; hence, the greater the extent to which a company is leveraged.

(A more detailed discussion of capital structure is in Chapter 14, Capital Structure and Dividend Policy.)

$$\text{L/T Debt to Capital} = \frac{\text{Long-Term Debt}}{\text{Long-Term Debt + Equity}} = \frac{\$3{,}900}{\$3{,}900 + \$8{,}200} = 32.2\%$$

3. Debt to Tangible Net Worth

Most frequently used by commercial banks as a leverage measure, debt to tangible net worth measures a company's debt as a percentage of its tangible net worth. Tangible net worth equals total equity minus intangible balances such as goodwill, trademarks and patents. As with the long-term debt to capital ratio, the higher the debt to tangible net worth ratio, the greater the percentage of debt a company is using to support its long-term capital structure; hence, the greater the extent to which a company is leveraged.

$$\text{Debt to Tangible Net Worth} = \frac{\text{Total Debt}}{(\text{Total Equity} - \text{Intangible Assets})}$$

$$= \frac{\$1{,}800 + \$3{,}900}{\$8{,}200 - \$0} = 69.5\%$$

4. Total Liabilities to Total Assets

Total liabilities to total assets measures the percentage of all liabilities relative to the total asset base of a company. The higher this ratio, the greater the percentage of liabilities (as opposed to equity) a company uses to finance its asset base.

$$\text{Total Liabilities to Total Assets} = \frac{\text{Total Liabilities}}{\text{Total Assets}} = \frac{\$7{,}300}{\$15{,}500} = 47.1\%$$

D. Performance and Efficiency Ratios

Performance ratios are used to evaluate the income generating capabilities of a company. There are two types of performance measures:

- **Profitability:** These ratios summarize how much profit is generated on revenues, equity and assets. The most commonly used profitability ratios are profit- margin measures, return on assets and return on equity.
- **Efficiency:** These ratios, also called turnover ratios, evaluate how effectively balance sheet accounts are utilized in the income generating process. Days' inventory, days' receivables, days' payables and cash turnover, which are liquidity or working capital ratios, are all examples of efficiency ratios.

Profitability ratios and four additional efficiency ratios—total asset turnover, fixed asset turnover, cash conversion efficiency, and working capital turnover—are presented below.

1. Return on Common Equity

Return on common equity measures the earnings available to common shareholders (net income less any preferred stock dividends) expressed as a percentage of the common equity. The higher this ratio, the greater the potential return to a company's common shareholders. In the example of a company with no preferred stock, the earnings available to common shareholders are equal to net income. In the following example, the return on equity is 10.4 percent.

$$\text{Return on Equity} = \frac{\text{Earnings Available to Common Shareholders}}{\text{Common Equity}}$$

$$= \frac{\$850}{\$8{,}200} = 10.4\%$$

2. Return on Sales

Return on sales, also called the profit margin, measures the net income of a company as a percentage of sales. The higher this ratio, the more after-tax profits a company generates. In the following example, every $1 in revenue returns $ .057 in net income.

$$\text{Return on Sales} = \frac{\text{Net Income}}{\text{Total Revenues}} = \frac{\$850}{\$15{,}000} = 5.7\%$$

3. Return on Total Assets

Return on total assets measures the net income of a company as a percentage of total assets. The higher this ratio, the more after-tax profits a company is generating from its asset base. In the following example, every $1 in total assets generates $ 0.055 in net income.

$$\text{Return on Total Assets} = \frac{\text{Net Income}}{\text{Total Assets}} = \frac{\$850}{\$15{,}500} = 5.5\%$$

4. Total Asset Turnover

Total asset turnover measures how much revenue is generated on all of the company's assets. The higher this ratio, the more productively a company uses its total asset base. In the following example, every $1 in total assets generates $0.97 in revenue.

$$\text{Total Asset Turnover} = \frac{\text{Revenues}}{\text{Total Assets}} = \frac{\$15{,}000}{\$15{,}500} = 0.97$$

5. Fixed Asset Turnover

Fixed asset turnover measures how much revenue is generated on productive or fixed assets. The higher this ratio, the more productively a company uses its assets. In the following example, every $1 in net property, plant, and equipment generates $2.00 in revenue.

$$\text{Fixed Asset Turnover} = \frac{\text{Revenues}}{\text{Net Property, Plant Equipment}} = \frac{\$15{,}000}{\$7{,}500} = 2.0$$

6. Cash Conversion Efficiency

Cash conversion efficiency measures how effectively a company converts sales into cash. The higher the cash conversion efficiency, the greater the net cash generated per dollar of revenue. Commonly referred to as the cash profit margin, it is calculated by using information from the statement of cash flows.

$$\text{Cash Conversion Efficiency} = \frac{\text{Cash Flow From Operations}}{\text{Sales}} = \frac{\$550}{\$15{,}000} = 3.7\%$$

7. Working Capital Turnover

Working capital turnover measures how many times per year a company converts average working capital into sales. The higher this ratio, the more efficiently a company converts working capital into sales. It establishes a relationship for the amount of working capital used to support a given level of sales.

$$\text{Working Capital Turnover} = \frac{\text{Sales}}{\text{Net Working Capital}} = \frac{\$15{,}000}{\$8{,}000 - \$3{,}400} = 3.3 \text{ Times}$$

E. Use of Financial Ratios and Performance Measurements

While financial ratios and performance measurement calculations reveal a great deal about a company's financial and operating condition, there are certain limitations. The major advantages of using ratios for financial analysis are as follows:

- They are easily computed and widely used.
- The information necessary for calculations is easily obtained.
- They facilitate comparisons between companies.

On the other hand, the major disadvantages of using ratios for financial analysis are as follows:

- Ratios assess historical performance at fixed points in time; thus, they do not capture intraperiod variations or are they necessarily indicative of future performance.
- Ratios summarize accounting information; therefore, they may not reflect economic value.
- They do not reflect qualitative value such as business strategy or managerial talent.
- Use of different accounting methods may reduce the validity of comparisons between firms.

V. ACCOUNTING FOR GOVERNMENTAL AND NOT-FOR-PROFIT (G/NFP) ORGANIZATIONS

Governmental and not-for-profit organizations (G/NFP) do not have shareholders or other owners; rather, they are organized to serve a collective group. Governmental agencies provide goods or services that benefit the public. These organizations raise cash primarily through taxes that must be paid by all members of the community regardless of whether they derive any benefit from the goods or services.

Non-governmental not-for-profits serve specific constituencies who pay for some or all of the benefits provided. For example, private colleges charge students tuition and fees; however, some portion of the costs of providing these services is usually funded through grants, endowments and other private donations. Other non-governmental not-for-profits, such as many United Way agencies, rely entirely on altruism and grants to fund their operations. The key feature distinguishing G/NFPs from profit-oriented businesses is that they provide as many goods or services as their resources allow. As a consequence, the financial accounting system of G/NFPs varies from that of for-profit enterprises. G/NFP reporting is focused on compliance and accountability.

The Governmental Accounting Standards Board (GASB) is the authoritative standard-setting body for state and local governments, as well as for public schools, state universities, and other government affiliated agencies. The Financial Accounting Foundation (FAF) is responsible for selecting members, providing funds, and exercising general oversight for both GASB and FASB. FASB has been issuing guidance for non-governmental not-for-profits such as private colleges, universities, and health care organizations since the early 1990s. GAAP accounting standards also apply to non-government entities. Many standards have specific provisions directed at these entities; therefore, their financial reports closely resemble those of for-profit organizations.

Test Your Understanding

These chapter questions are provided to test your understanding of the information in the text. They are neither examples of CTP examination questions nor are they in the examination format.

Answers are on pages 573–575.

1. What is GAAP?

2. Explain the difference between cash and accrual accounting.

3. Discuss the methods a company can use in its reporting of a negative cash balance.

4. What are the basic financial statements?

5. What are different types of opinions that an auditor can render for financial statements?

6. What are common size ratios?

7. What are performance and efficiency ratios?

8. Discuss the impact of leverage on financial results.

9. What are the three classifications of short-term investments according to FAS 115?

10. List the ratios commonly used to measure working capital.

11. Discuss the cash conversion cycle.

12. What is the primary body that sets accounting and reporting standards for government and not-for-profit entities?

13. What are the advantages and disadvantages of using ratios for financial analysis?

14. What are the basic guidelines for accounting for derivatives?

15. What is the impact of Sarbanes-Oxley on the accounting for off-balance-sheet arrangements?

CHAPTER 5
Financial Planning and Analysis

I. INTRODUCTION

Treasury often plays a number of crucial roles in the planning and decision-making processes within an organization. A treasurer must not only develop and implement plans for the treasury area but also incorporate the plans of all other departments in order to forecast the requirements for enterprise-wide liquidity. As part of this role, a treasurer must identify and arrange sources of financing. Also, treasury is often responsible for the financial analysis function.

This chapter discusses the use of financial information for internal planning, decision-making and measuring performance. The chapter begins by introducing the fundamental financial concept of time value of money, as well as the related concepts of opportunity cost, cost of capital and cost behavior. It illustrates how these concepts are put to use in capital budgeting, financial planning and other decision processes. The chapter concludes by introducing commonly used internal performance measures such as return on investment (ROI) and economic value added (EVA). Many of the formulae in this chapter are available in generic spreadsheet software, treasury management system programs and financial calculator functions.

II. BASIC FINANCIAL CONCEPTS

A. Time Value of Money

Most financial decisions involve a trade-off between present and future cash flows. The time value of money, a fundamental principle of finance, establishes the relationship between cash flows received at different times. Time value means that a dollar received today is worth more than a dollar received tomorrow because today's dollar can be invested to earn a return. Conversely, a dollar received tomorrow is worth less than a dollar received today because the opportunity to earn interest is foregone. The value of a cash flow at any point in time may be determined with an appropriate interest rate and the number of time periods involved.

The future value of an investment is the value at some point in the future of a sum of money invested today. Calculation of future value requires compounding. Compounding assumes that any periodic payments received from an investment are reinvested at the same rate. The formula for calculating future value is as follows:

$$\mathbf{FV = PV \times (1 + i)^n}$$

Where:

FV = Future Value

PV = Present Value or Value Today

i = Periodic Interest Rate

n = Number of Periods

The future value of \$100 for two years at four percent compounded annually is:

$$\text{Future Value} = \$100 \times (1 + .04)^2 = \$100 \times (1 + .04) \times (1 + .04)$$
$$= \$100 \times (1.082) = \$108.20$$

Present value is today's value of any sum that is expected to be received in the future. Present value can be determined by applying an appropriate discount rate to a future cash flow stream. This process is called discounting. Discounting facilitates comparison of alternative transactions with cash flows that are expected to be received at a future date or dates. Present value may be used to determine how much an investor would be willing to pay for an investment that provides a particular future stream of cash flows.

The present value formula is obtained by rearranging the terms in the future value formula as follows:

$$PV = \frac{FV}{(1 + i)^n}$$

Where:
PV = Present Value
FV = Future Value
i = Periodic Interest Rate
n = Number of Periods

For example, assume that a company can make an investment that pays $100 in three years. What is the present value of that future payment if the appropriate rate of interest is ten percent? This is determined to be $75.13, as follows:

$$PV = \frac{\$100}{(1 + .10)^3} = \$75.13$$

The present value formula may also be expanded to compute present values for investments that yield periodic cash flows at different points in time:

$$PV = \sum_{t=1}^{n} \frac{C_t}{(1+i)^t} = \frac{C_1}{(1+i)^1} + \frac{C_2}{(1+i)^2} + \ldots + \frac{C_n}{(1+i)^n}$$

Where:
C_t = Cash Flow at time t
PV = Present Value
i = Periodic Interest Rate
n = Number of Periods

When the cash outflows and the cash inflows of an investment are included, the amount computed using the above formula is called the net present value (NPV). A sample calculation using the above formula appears in the section on NPV later in this chapter.

The interest rate used in computing present value is generally referred to as the discount rate or opportunity cost. An opportunity cost reflects the profit that could be earned or the costs that could be avoided if a particular investment is not made. The appropriate opportunity cost depends on the nature of the decision under consideration.

B. Opportunity Cost

All organizations face constraints on resources. Often, a company must choose between multiple opportunities when allocating scarce resources. An opportunity cost is the foregone benefit of an alternative use of funds.

For example, if a treasurer chooses to make a short-term investment rather than to repay borrowings, the opportunity cost is the cost of the interest on the portion of debt that could have been repaid. Conversely, if the treasurer chooses to repay debt, the opportunity cost is the income that could have been earned on the investment. Low-risk, short-term business decisions are typically evaluated using a short-term opportunity cost such as the company's short-term borrowing rate or the return on its short-term investments. The opportunity cost of capital is generally preferred for evaluating long-term investments.

C. Cost of Capital

Cost of capital refers to the cost of the financial resources, or capital, that a company uses to fund long-term investments. In practice, the term "capital" is used to describe only the more permanent sources of funding used by a company, such as long-term debt, preferred stock and common equity, which includes both the money contributed by stockholders and the earnings retained in the business. The opportunity cost of capital is a measure of the costs that could be avoided if a company did not have to raise capital or commit capital to a project.

The overall cost of capital for a company is a function of the mix of the capital components and the individual costs of each component. The mix of capital components is called the capital structure of a company. The individual cost of each component is determined by the perceived riskiness of the business. The primary cost associated with debt is interest while the primary cost of equity is the return expected by stockholders.

Companies try to minimize their cost of capital, which can be calculated based on the cost of equity and after-tax cost of debt. Many companies consider the weighted average cost of capital (WACC) to be an appropriate discount rate for evaluating projects whose risk profiles are consistent with the overall risk profile of the company. The formula for determining WACC is as follows:

$$\text{WACC} = (\text{After Tax Cost of Debt} \times \% \text{ of Debt}) + (\text{Cost of Equity} \times \% \text{ of Equity})$$

Assuming that a company's long-term capital structure is 60 percent equity and 40 percent debt, its cost of equity is 10 percent, its average cost of debt is 6 percent, and the marginal tax rate is 34 percent, the WACC is calculated as follows:

$$\text{WACC} = (0.0396 \times .40) + (.10 \times .60)$$
$$= 0.01584 + 0.06 = 0.07584 \text{ or } 7.584\%$$

where 0.0396 is the after-tax cost of debt:
$6\% \times (1 - 0.34) = 3.96\%$

To evaluate projects with higher or lower risk than the overall risk profile of the company, most firms use a risk-adjusted rate. High-risk projects are typically evaluated using a risk-adjusted discount rate that is greater than the company's WACC. Evaluating a given project with a higher discount rate lowers its net present value because each future cash flow is discounted more deeply due to the additional risk. Conversely, lower risk projects would be evaluated at a lower discount rate, which would increase the NPV.

(A more detailed discussion of capital structure and cost of capital are in Chapter 13, Sources of Capital and Leasing and Chapter 14, Capital Structure and Dividend Policy.)

D. Cost Behavior

Product planning, capital budgeting, cost/benefit analyses and financial plan development all require an understanding of cost behavior. Cost behavior describes the relationship between costs and business activities. Costs can be classified into three categories: fixed, variable and mixed. The behavior of a cost is based on how the cost varies with changes in the cost driver, which is a factor or event that causes a cost to be incurred. For example, borrowing activity is a cost driver for interest expense.

1. Cost Types

Fixed costs are costs that either do not vary in total over a wide range of activity or are not immediately impacted by changes in the cost driver. One example of a fixed cost is a monthly account maintenance fee charged by a bank on a deposit account. The fee remains the same regardless of the number of transactions on the account. A fixed cost is treated as a lump sum when used in decision analysis; however, as the level of activity increases, the fixed cost per unit of activity decreases. The account maintenance fee will be the same regardless of the number of deposits made to an account, but the per deposit cost of a $100 maintenance fee will be $10 if ten deposits are made, yet only $1 if a hundred deposits are made during the statement cycle.

Variable costs are costs that change in total in direct proportion to the level of activity. Cost of goods sold (COGS) is a variable cost. As sales and production levels increase, so do the total COGS. If revenues and production levels decrease, COGS likewise decrease. In many companies, COGS can be expressed as a cost per unit produced; while total variable costs change with activity, per unit variable costs do not.

A mixed cost has both fixed and variable elements. The monthly bank charge on a deposit account is a mixed cost—the account maintenance fee is fixed while the per-transaction fees are variable. The level of analysis affects cost classification. When comparing account analysis charges for two different banks, a treasurer will view itemized account charges as both fixed and variable expenses. However, for corporate level budgetary purposes, the total bank charges are analyzed as mixed costs.

2. Operating Leverage

The relative levels of fixed and variable costs define the cost structure of a company. Two financial concepts that are closely related to cost structure are operating leverage and economies of scale. Operating leverage is the extent to which fixed costs are used in a company's cost structure. The higher the proportion of fixed costs, the higher the operating leverage of the company. A company with high operating leverage is able to achieve a large percentage increase in income from a small increase in revenues. However, the opposite is also true because a small decrease in sales leads to a large decline in income. Companies with high operating leverage also have relatively high breakeven sales, the level of sales at which net income equals zero. Consequently, operating leverage is viewed as a source of business risk.

3. Economies of Scale

Economies of scale occur when an increase in sales results in a lower average cost per unit of sale. If a business has mostly variable costs, the average cost remains fairly stable when sales increase. On the other hand, companies with high operating leverage, or high levels of fixed costs, experience declining average costs on increasing revenues because the fixed costs are distributed over more unit sales. The majority of the fixed costs of a business relate to fixed asset usage. These include items such as lease payments, interest payments, taxes, property insurance, plant and equipment. Thus, economies of scale reflect the extent to which additional sales may be generated on the existing asset base.

III. DECISION EVALUATION

The decision-making process of most organizations centers on financial comparisons among available options. Financial comparisons focus on the costs and benefits for each proposed course of action. While many qualitative factors enter into a business decision, the discussion in this section is restricted to quantitative elements (i.e., those that can be expressed in numerical terms). Treasury often plays a key role in the financial analysis of decisions such as product line changes, selection of banking relationships and third-party providers, and decisions to acquire or divest business units.

A. Identifying Relevant Costs and Benefits

The financial information that is relevant in evaluating decisions is the expected future cash costs and cash benefits among the alternatives. There are two key criteria that a cost or benefit must meet in order to be relevant: They must affect future cash flows, and they must differ among the alternatives.

First, a relevant economic cost or benefit must affect future cash flows. For example, if a company is considering a project that would use a previously purchased piece of equipment, the equipment cost is not relevant to the current decision because it does not affect future cash flows. Instead, this is referred to as a sunk cost or a cost that has already been incurred. Sunk costs are never relevant in decision analysis because they do not affect the future.

Second, a relevant economic cost or benefit must differ among the alternatives. When a treasurer is evaluating proposals from two competing banks for treasury management services, if the charges for demand deposit accounts are the same for both banks, this information has no influence on the decision even though it affects future cash flows. On the other hand, if lockbox service fees differ, these are relevant to the selection process. Costs that vary among options are called differential costs. Only the incremental difference in the costs is relevant. If the lockbox charges are expected to be $3,600 per month for one bank and $3,400 per month for another, then only the $200 difference is relevant to the decision.

Opportunity costs must also be considered when making choices. If a treasurer decides to pay down debt that is not due, the opportunity to invest the cash used for the payment is foregone. If this opportunity cost is not considered, the treasurer may repay debt that costs less than the interest that could be earned from an available investment.

B. Cost/Benefit (CB) Analysis

Nearly all business decisions are based on a cost/benefit (CB) analysis, which is an analysis of whether the relevant economic benefits of a given course of action exceed the relevant economic costs. A breakeven analysis is a type of CB analysis that establishes the level of activity at which the benefits are equal to the costs.

A CB analysis typically attempts to measure the net benefit (benefit minus costs) of an option at the forecast level of activity. An example of a net benefit analysis would be a capital budgeting decision based on net present value. Other treasury decisions requiring CB analysis include ascertaining the minimum issue size for commercial paper, establishing optimal locations for lockboxes and determining whether to outsource a given business process or to perform it in-house.

1. Breakeven Analysis

The breakeven point is the level of activity for an operation at which costs exactly equal benefits. A breakeven analysis is often used by businesses in product decisions to determine what level of sales, at a given price, is required to cover costs. The general formula for a breakeven analysis is as follows:

$$\text{Breakeven Point in Units} = \frac{\text{Fixed Costs}}{\text{Per Unit Benefit} - \text{Per Unit Variable Cost}}$$

There are numerous applications for breakeven analysis in treasury. One example is the calculation of the breakeven amount of funds required to justify a wire transfer. Consider a company that usually uses an ACH (automated clearing house) transfer—sometimes referred to as electronic depository transfers (EDTs)—to move funds from local field depository banks to its principal concentration bank. (In this case, the local field depository banks and the principal concentration bank are different institutions.) A treasurer may want to calculate the breakeven point at which using a wire transfer, which is a more expensive but faster transfer method than EDT, is cost justified.

This calculation is based on the assumption that the funds will be invested one day faster if they are transferred by wire Monday through Thursday and three days faster if they are transferred by wire on Friday. Funds transferred by wire are immediately available whereas funds transferred by EDT are not available until the next business day. Therefore, when using an EDT on a Friday, a treasurer does not have use of the funds for investment purposes for three days (Friday, Saturday and Sunday).

Assuming that the cost of the ACH transaction is \$0.75, the charges for a wire transfer are \$25.00, and the company earns interest at an annual rate of 1.825 percent (0.005 percent per day on a 365-day-per-year basis) on an overnight investment, the breakeven point (i.e., the amount at which the interest earned overnight offsets the incremental cost of the wire), is \$485,000. This is calculated as follows:

$$\text{Breakeven Wire Transfer} = \frac{\text{Wire Cost} - \text{ACH Cost}}{\text{Overnight Investment Rate}}$$

$$= \frac{25.00 - \$0.75}{0.00005} = \$485{,}000$$

It is useful to compare this formula to the general breakeven formula:

$$\text{Breakeven Point in Units} = \frac{\text{Fixed Costs}}{\text{Per Unit Benefit} - \text{Per Unit Variable Cost}}$$

In the wire transfer breakeven formula, the numerator represents the differential or incremental fixed cost between the two alternatives (wire vs. EDT); the denominator represents the rate at which interest can be earned if the funds are invested for the extra day. In other words, the formula determines the opportunity cost if the wire is not sent. In the wire-transfer example, the wire cost is considered to be fixed because it does not vary with the cost driver, which is the dollar amount of the wire transfer. The per unit benefit is the interest that can be earned overnight on the funds. No variable costs are associated with this decision.

2. Capital Budgeting

Capital budgeting is the process by which strategic plans are developed to determine a company's investment in capital assets. Examples of capital budgeting include the replacement of existing equipment, the expansion of existing facilities, the purchase of new equipment and/or the introduction of new product lines. Capital budget decision-making is another form of cost/benefit analysis. Because capital investments involve potentially large sums of money and multiple time periods, several decision models have been developed specifically for capital budgeting analysis. Four commonly used models are discussed below:

- Payback period
- Net present value
- Internal rate of return
- Profitability index

Each of these models is illustrated using the information on the projects presented in Exhibit 5.1.

EXHIBIT 5.1 – CAPITAL INVESTMENT PROJECTS

Projected Cash Flows

	Project A	**Project B**
Year 0	($1,000)	($1,000)
Year 1	$300	$300
Year 2	$300	$300
Year 3	$400	$400
Year 4	$100	$1,000
Year 5	$100	$1,000

3. Payback Period

A payback period decision model determines the number of years before the cash flows from a given project equal the company's initial investment. The decision rule for the payback model is to compare the calculated time with the company's required payback period. In a payback analysis, the decision maker uses either discounted or undiscounted cash flows. In practice, discounted cash flows are preferable because they reflect the opportunity cost of funds invested in the project over time.

For example, if a business, which has a payback requirement of three years and uses undiscounted cash flows, is considering whether to invest in Project A or B, it would find the two projects equally acceptable because the $1 million investment would be "paid back" in three years for both (i.e., $300,000 + $300,000 + $400,000 = $1 million).

However, there are two drawbacks to the payback period model: It ignores cash flows that occur after the payback period and the determination of what constitutes the required payback period is often made arbitrarily.

4. Net Present Value (NPV)

The NPV decision model entails scheduling all relevant cash flows (both inflows and outflows) associated with a project. The present value of each cash flow for each period is calculated using the marginal cost of capital as the discount rate. Then, all of the present values are totaled. The formula for NPV is as follows:

$$NPV = \sum_{t=1}^{n} \frac{C_t}{(1+i)^t} = C_0 \frac{C_1}{(1+i)^1} + \frac{C_2}{(1+i)^2} + \ldots + \frac{C_n}{(1+i)^n}$$

Where:

C_t = Net Cash Flow at time t
NPV = Net Present Value
i = Interest Discount Rate
n = Number of Periods

In calculating NPV, the initial investment and any subsequent investments (cash outflows) are negative values while the benefits generated from the investment (cash inflows) are positive values.

The NPVs of the projects are calculated as follows:

$$NPV_A = -\$1{,}000 + \frac{\$300}{(1.10)} + \frac{\$300}{(1.10)^2} + \frac{\$400}{(1.10)^3} + \frac{\$100}{(1.10)^4} + \frac{\$100}{(1.10)^5}$$

$$= (\$48.42)$$

$$NPV_B = -\$1{,}000 + \frac{\$300}{(1.10)} + \frac{\$300}{(1.10)^2} + \frac{\$400}{(1.10)^3} + \frac{\$100}{(1.10)^4} + \frac{\$100}{(1.10)^5}$$

$$= \$1{,}125.12$$

The decision rule for the NPV model is to accept a project if the NPV is greater than or equal to zero. If the NPV is negative, the project should be rejected. Thus, Project A should be rejected and Project B accepted.

5. Internal Rate of Return (IRR)

The IRR is the discount rate (denoted i) at which the NPV equals zero. This is equivalent to the discount rate at which the present value of a project's cash inflows equals the present value of a project's outflows. In other words, the IRR reflects the expected profit on the investment expressed as an annual rate. The formula is expressed as follows:

$$NPV = \sum_{t=1}^{n} \frac{C_t}{(1+i)^t} = 0$$

The decision rule for the IRR model is that if the IRR is greater than or equal to the required rate of return for the project, the project is acceptable. If the IRR is less than the required rate, the project is unacceptable. The following calculations require a financial calculator or computer program.

Project A:

$$NPV_A = -\$1{,}000 + \frac{\$300}{(1+i)} + \frac{\$300}{(1+i)^2} + \frac{\$400}{(1+i)^3} + \frac{\$100}{(1+i)^4} + \frac{\$100}{(1+i)^5} = 0$$

Project B:

$$NPV_B = -\$1{,}000 + \frac{\$300}{(1+i)} + \frac{\$300}{(1+i)^2} + \frac{\$400}{(1+i)^3} + \frac{\$1000}{(1+i)^4} + \frac{\$1000}{(1+i)^5} = 0$$

The IRR for Project A is 7.7 percent and the IRR for Project B is 38.1 percent. Because the assumed cost of capital is 10 percent, Project A would be rejected and Project B would be accepted.

6. Profitability Index (PI)

The profitability index (PI) decision model is virtually identical to the NPV and IRR models. The only difference is that NPV and IRR are based on sums of benefits and costs whereas the profitability index is a ratio of the benefits to the costs as follows:

$$PI = \frac{\text{PV of Inflows}}{\text{PV of Outflows}}$$

where PV = Present Value

$$PI_A = \frac{\left[\frac{\$300}{(1+i)} + \frac{\$300}{(1+i)^2} + \frac{\$400}{(1+i)^3} + \frac{\$100}{(1+i)^4} + \frac{\$100}{(1+i)^5}\right]}{\$1{,}000} = 0.95$$

$$PI_B = \frac{\left[\frac{\$300}{(1+i)} + \frac{\$300}{(1+i)^2} + \frac{\$400}{(1+i)^3} + \frac{\$1{,}000}{(1+i)^4} + \frac{\$1{,}000}{(1+i)^5}\right]}{\$1{,}000} = 2.13$$

The decision rule for the PI model is that if the PI is greater than or equal to 1, the project is acceptable. In the above example, Project A would be rejected and Project B accepted.

7. Risk Analysis

Most financial decisions involve uncertainty and, therefore, some degree of risk. In fact, all decisions have future outcomes that can usually be predicted but not known with certainty. The longer the time horizon used in analyzing the decision, the greater the likelihood of unanticipated variation in forecasted cash flows, discount rates and other assumptions. Three tools, scenario analysis, sensitivity analysis and simulation, enable decision-makers to assess the impact of risk.

8. Scenario Analysis

Scenario analysis is a type of "what-if" analysis that assesses the outcomes that are realistically possible under a range of circumstances. Often, scenario analysis is used to establish the lower bound of outcomes (the worst case) and the upper bound of outcomes (the best case).

To illustrate, consider Project B in the previous example. Assume that the decision-maker determines that the cost of capital may vary over the life of the project by as much as ±5.0 percent and that the forecasted cash inflows may be 25 percent lower or 10 percent higher than predicted, depending on market conditions. The best case and worst case NPVs are calculated as follows:

$$NPV_{Best} = -\$1{,}000 + \frac{\$330}{(1.05)} + \frac{\$330}{(1.05)^2} + \frac{\$440}{(1.05)^3} + \frac{\$1{,}100}{(1.05)^4} + \frac{\$1{,}100}{(1.05)^5}$$

$$= \$1{,}760.54$$

$$NPV_{Worst} = -\$1{,}000 + \frac{\$225}{(1.15)} + \frac{\$225}{(1.15)^2} + \frac{\$300}{(1.15)^3} + \frac{\$750}{(1.15)^4} + \frac{\$750}{(1.15)^5}$$

$$= \$364.74$$

While the analyst projects $1,125.12 as the most likely NPV for the project, the range of probable outcomes is between $1,760.54 (the best case) and $364.74 (the worst case).

9. Sensitivity Analysis

Often, a decision maker is more concerned about how a specific assumption may influence the results of the analysis. Sensitivity analysis is used to determine how vulnerable the expected outcome is to changes in an individual assumption. A sensitivity analysis can identify and evaluate the areas of greatest vulnerability and allows the decision maker to determine the likelihood of reaching critical levels.

In the previous example for Project B, assume that the decision-maker evaluating the capital expenditure has little confidence in the estimated cost of capital because of high leverage in a rising interest rate environment. A sensitivity analysis can reveal the effect of varying the discount rate while holding all other values constant at their expected levels. Given the previous possible range for the cost of capital of ±5.0 percent, a sensitivity analysis would project the NPV to be between $1,509.59 and $819.65. The calculations are as follows:

$$NPV_{B\ -5.0\%} = -\$1{,}000 + \frac{\$300}{(1.05)} + \frac{\$300}{(1.05)^2} + \frac{\$400}{(1.05)^3} + \frac{\$1{,}000}{(1.05)^4} + \frac{\$1{,}000}{(1.05)^5}$$

$$= \$1{,}509.59$$

$$NPV_{B\ +5.0\%} = -\$1{,}000 + \frac{\$300}{(1.15)} + \frac{\$300}{(1.15)^2} + \frac{\$400}{(1.15)^3} + \frac{\$1{,}000}{(1.15)^4} + \frac{\$1{,}000}{(1.15)^5}$$

$$= \$819.65$$

Sensitivity analysis may also be combined with breakeven analysis to provide an estimate of the extreme value that a given variable could reach before generating an economic loss. Computing a breakeven point for the discount rate is the same as calculating the IRR. For example, by definition the sum of the breakeven investment (a cash outflow) and the present value of the projected cash inflows equals zero. Note that the maximum amount that could be paid for the investment illustrated above is the amount equal to the present value of the projected cash inflows as follows:

$$\text{Breakeven Investment} = \frac{\$300}{(1.10)} + \frac{\$300}{(1.10)^2} + \frac{\$400}{(1.10)^3} + \frac{\$1{,}000}{(1.10)^4} + \frac{\$1{,}000}{(1.10)^5}$$

$$= \$2{,}125.12$$

10. Simulation

Simulation combines scenario and sensitivity analysis, allowing certain assumptions in a decision model to fluctuate simultaneously. Decision models with multiple variables require significant computing resources. The most commonly used model is the Monte Carlo simulation.

A Monte Carlo simulation is an analytical technique in which a large number of simulations are run using random quantities for specified variables and then the distribution of results is analyzed to infer which values are most likely to occur. A Monte Carlo simulation requires estimation of the probability distributions for all of the variables, except the decision variable in the model. Information about the distributions—in particular, the shape of the distribution and the expected parameter values (minimum, maximum, mean, variance, etc.)—is input into the simulation program that randomly combines variable values to generate a distribution for the decision variable. The information generated about the decision variable provides a quantitative assessment of risk.

IV. DEVELOPING A FINANCIAL PLAN

Long-term planning is essential for both for-profit and not-for-profit organizations. A strategic plan establishes the overall goals and objectives of an organization and charts a course of action for achieving objectives over a period of time. Strategic plans are important because they establish the framework necessary for developing detailed financial plans.

Long-range plans quantify the elements of the strategic plan in the form of forecasted financial statements over a five- to ten-year period. These financial statements incorporate major debt and equity activities, as well as high level business activities such as acquisitions and/or divestitures of assets, products, services, divisions or business lines. Because long-range plans quantify the strategic plan, projected balance sheets reflect the target capital structure and projected income statements reflect the expected revenues and expenses. These pro forma financial statements serve as the basis for operating and financial budgets.

Budgets: A budget is an in-depth plan that details how economic resources will be procured and deployed over a specific time period. Budgets may cover periods ranging from one month to several years. A long-range financial plan is essentially a budget. Most organizations use an annual budget for planning and control purposes. An annual budget provides the detail underlying the first year of the long-range plan. It is usually further organized into shorter time divisions such as months or quarters. An annual budget for an entire organization is called the master budget.

1. The Budgeting Process

The master budget has two chief components: the operating budget and the financial budget. The operating budget, or profit plan, focuses on day-to-day operations. The financial budget addresses the financing and investing activities of an organization. The planning process begins with the construction of the elements of the operating budget: a sales budget, a production or a purchases budget and an operating expenses budget.

Because the costs that must be budgeted depend on the expected level of sales, the first and most critical step in developing an operating budget is generating a sales budget. If a business sells goods or services on credit, another critical step in developing the sales budget is the cash collections schedule, which details cash sales, accounts receivable balances and cash collections of accounts receivable. Once the sales budget is established, the expenses necessary to support the expected level of operating activity can be forecast.

After the operating budget is complete, the financial budget can be constructed. The first step in constructing the financial budget is generating the capital budget. The capital budget details the forecast costs for investing activities. Capital investments may be necessary to acquire new facilities, to replace aging or obsolescent equipment, or to initiate longer-term projects required under the long-range plan.

The second step in constructing a financial budget is the development of the cash budget, which translates information from the operating and capital budgets into sources and uses of cash. The final step is the identification of financing sources for any forecast cash needs. If the cash budget projects a surplus, management must decide, based on the strategic objectives of the company, whether to use the cash for future investments, to pay down debt, or to distribute the cash to shareholders through dividends or stock repurchases. If the cash budget projects a deficit, management must decide how to finance the deficit and/or how to reduce costs.

The operating budget and the financial budget are combined to form the master budget, which constitutes a set of pro forma financial statements for the budget period. Exhibit 5.2 illustrates how the information from the operating and financial budgets is used to construct financial statements.

EXHIBIT 5.2 – CONSTRUCTING PRO FORMA FINANCIAL STATEMENTS FROM BUDGETS

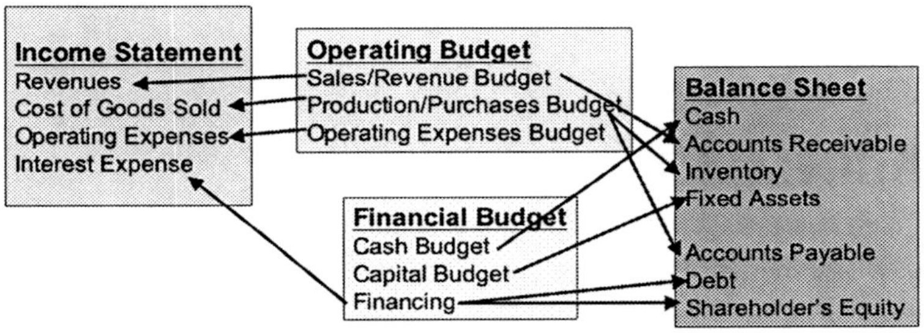

2. Treasury's Role in Budgeting

Treasury is either directly or indirectly responsible for many portions of the planning and budgeting process, as well as for managing the impact on cash flows. As plans and budgets change the cash flow stream, a treasurer must manage short-term assets and liabilities to ensure that a company has adequate funds and liquidity. In addition, a treasurer may be required to assess the impact of plans on debt covenants and credit ratings. A treasurer must also manage the financing of the company's long-term assets through debt and equity issues.

3. Uses of Budgets

Budgets are used for a variety of purposes. However, most budgets are either planning or control related. Budgets discipline managers to plan, requiring an assessment of what resources are needed and how they will be funded. Because managers are often evaluated based on their ability to manage their budgets within plan, the budgeting process also requires managers to anticipate changing conditions and contingencies.

Another use of budgets is resource allocation. All organizations encounter constraints on their resources. Budgets are often used as a tool to assist in allocation decisions. For example, local, state, and federal government agencies use budgets to allocate funds raised from taxes and other sources, as well as to provide the requisite authority for the use of funds. Finally, a budget serves as a communication and coordination tool, informing all areas of an organization of each department's plans during a given budget period.

While the planning aspects of budgeting are forward-looking, the control aspects of budgeting are retrospective. A budget serves as the primary benchmark against which actual results are compared. Any difference between actual results and the budgeted figure is called a variance. The process of identifying and analyzing budget variances is referred to as variance analysis.

While small variances are expected in the course of running a business, large variances may be an early indication of more serious problems such as a change in economic conditions, in the competitive environment or in customer buying patterns. Variances may also indicate a flaw in the forecasting method used. A company's optimal performance can be maintained only if the nature of the variances is identified by management and addressed quickly.

V. PERFORMANCE MEASUREMENT

Once planning is complete and decisions have been made, the ongoing performance of a company's operations must be monitored and evaluated. Budgets provide one benchmark against which performance is often assessed. There are also several other measures that are frequently used for evaluation of projects, divisions, subsidiaries or business units. Three of the common measures are return on investment, residual income and economic value added.

A. Return on Investment (ROI)

Return on investment (ROI) is calculated as the profit generated by a project or an operating unit, divided by the amount of capital invested in the asset or the unit.

$$\text{Return on Investment} = \frac{\text{Profit}}{\text{Invested Capital}}$$

There are three major drawbacks in using ROI as a performance measure:

- If the ROI calculation does not include the full period being measured, it may provide a misleading indication of performance in cases where cash flows are not evenly distributed over time.
- ROI does not include a charge for the cost of the capital invested in the project. (Note that the cost of capital is implicitly included in the NPV calculation by discounting the cash flows.)
- The greatest limitation of ROI as a performance measure is that it may lead management to reject a

positive NPV project if the project results in the decline of a given business unit's ROI.

B. Residual Income (RI)

Residual income (RI) overcomes two of the limitations of ROI by assigning a charge for the invested capital. Also, because RI is a dollar amount, any project that generates profits after deducting the cost of capital will increase RI. The formula for RI is as follows:

Residual Income = Profit – (Invested Capital **x** Cost of Capital)

C. Economic Value Added (EVA)

Economic value added (EVA), defined as after-tax operating profit minus an appropriate charge for the opportunity cost of all capital, is a refinement of RI. EVA measures to what extent profits exceed the cost of invested capital. For an operating unit, EVA increases whenever the following occur:

- The rate of return earned on the existing base of capital improves.
- Additional capital is invested in projects where the return is more than the cost of new capital.
- Capital is liquidated from substandard operations.

Many companies implement EVA as a management tool to provide a practical periodic performance measure for the overall company and for individual divisions and/or operating units. When used at the divisional and/or operating unit level, the parent company acts as a "bank" for the individual units. EVA is used by the parent to determine the difference between the unit's net operating profit and a charge for capital. Managers are typically encouraged to increase EVA relative to a target.

The general formula for EVA is as follows:

EVA = Operating Profit **x** (1-Tax Rate) – (WACC **x** Total Capital)

EVA is also useful for company valuation because it can be linked to a company's stock price through a measure called market value added (MVA). MVA represents the market value of a company's debt and equity less the book value of debt and equity. MVA is the sum of two components:

- The discounted present value of expected EVA for existing assets
- The discounted present value of expected EVA from future investment.

Test Your Understanding

These chapter questions are provided to test your understanding of the information in the text. They are neither examples of CTP examination questions nor are they in the examination format.

Answers are on pages 576 and 577.

1. What is time value of money?

2. Discuss the difference between opportunity cost and cost of capital.

3. When would a risk-adjusted discount rate be used?

4. What are the different types of costs?

5. Explain the concepts of operating leverage and economies of scale.

6. How is a breakeven analysis done and what would be an example of an application in the treasury area?

7. What is capital budgeting and what are the most commonly used capital budgeting models?

8. What are the basic tools used in risk analysis?

9. Describe a master budget and the budgeting process.

10. What is performance measurement, and what are the three most often used measures?

11. What is EVA, and under what circumstances will it increase for an operating unit?

CHAPTER 6
Philosophy of Working Capital

I. **INTRODUCTION**

II. **OVERVIEW OF WORKING CAPITAL MANAGEMENT**
   A. Working Capital Cash Flow Cycle
   B. How Changes in Current Accounts Impact External Financing

III. **WORKING CAPITAL INVESTMENT AND FINANCING STRATEGIES**
   A. Current Asset Investment Strategies
   B. Current Asset Financing Strategies

IV. **BASICS OF SHORT-TERM CREDIT**
   A. Operational Advantages of Short-Term Credit
   B. Operational Disadvantages of Short-Term Credit
   C. Sources of Short-Term Credit

V. **COSTS AND RISKS OF ALTERNATIVE DEBT MATURITIES**

VI. **FINANCING STRATEGIES OF MULTIDIVISIONAL AND MULTINATIONAL COMPANIES**

VII. **CASH DISCOUNT CALCULATIONS**
   A. Cost for a Buyer of Not Taking the Cash Discount
   B. The Benefit for a Seller of Offering a Cash Discount

I. INTRODUCTION

A company's daily operating activities may result in dramatic fluctuations in working capital accounts. It is important for a treasurer to understand the causes of these fluctuations and the interrelationships among working capital accounts. These accounts are critical to a company's short-term liquidity and long-term success and even survival. Working capital strategies affect many of the financial ratios used to evaluate financial conditions, especially the current and quick ratios.

(A more detailed discussion of financial ratios is in Chapter 5, Financial Planning and Analysis.)

In addition, the risks associated with various working capital decisions may influence the company's cost of capital. Working capital may also be positively or negatively impacted by a company's credit and cash management practices. (For a more detailed discussion of basic cash management practices, see Chapter 9, Cash Positioning.)

This chapter defines the terms involved in working capital management and illustrates, through the cash flow cycle, the important interrelationships. The sources, costs and risks of alternative current asset investment and financing strategies are discussed, along with primary examples of short-term credit.

II. OVERVIEW OF WORKING CAPITAL MANAGEMENT

The daily activities of a company result in a flow of cash through the working capital accounts. Working capital management refers to the decisions and strategies concerning the amounts and types of investments for current assets as well as the amounts and types of financing for current liabilities. Therefore, working capital management involves the analysis of the risk/reward relationship in choosing among different strategies.

Working capital is generally defined as current assets. Current assets consist of accounts such as cash, marketable securities, accounts receivable, inventory and pre-paid expenses. Net working capital is defined as total current assets minus total current liabilities, where current liabilities are represented by accounts payable, notes payable and accrued liabilities.

A high value for the current ratio (current assets divided by current liabilities) suggests a strong liquidity position and relatively low risk. However, current assets typically have lower rates of return while current liabilities have relatively higher interest costs. Therefore, a high cost is associated with having too much liquidity. Working capital management involves the determination of what level of liquidity is appropriate for a particular business or industry. For most organizations, investing in cash generates a lower return than investing in capital projects that generate future sales and revenues.

A. Working Capital Cash Flow Cycle

The flow of cash through the working capital accounts is best illustrated with the cash flow cycle. This cycle shows how the strategies concerning inventory, receivables and payables all interact to affect the flow of cash through the company. A diagram of the cash flow cycle appears in Exhibit 6.1.

EXHIBIT 6.1 – THE CASH FLOW CYCLE OF A BUSINESS

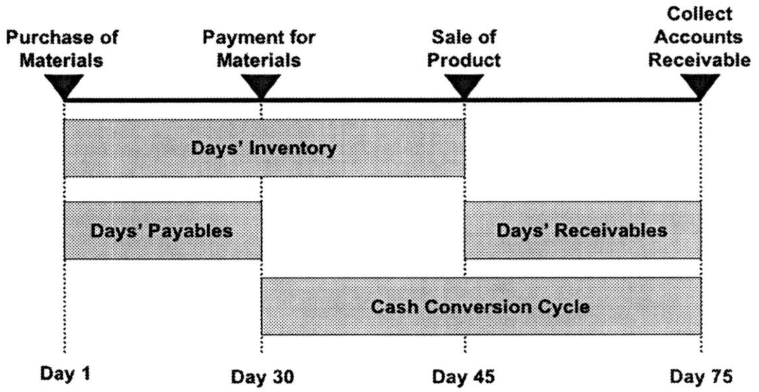

1. Days' Inventory or Inventory Conversion Period

For a manufacturing company, the days' inventory or inventory conversion period is the average number of days from the acquisition of raw materials until the sale of the finished goods. This period of time is the sum of the following factors:

- The average number of days that raw materials remain in inventory
- The average number of days that are necessary to convert these raw materials into finished goods
- The average number of days that the finished goods remain in inventory

Any decision that affects the raw materials, the work in progress or the finished goods held in inventory will impact the inventory conversion period.

For a service company, the days' inventory period is determined by the average length of time that materials are held in inventory until they are used to provide services.

Inventory management techniques such as just-in-time (JIT) may help to significantly reduce inventory levels. (For a more detailed discussion of inventory management, see Chapter 7, Working Capital Tools.)

2. Days' Receivables or Receivables Conversion Period

For both manufacturing and service companies, the days' receivables or receivables conversion period is the average number of days that are required to convert a sale (i.e., accounts receivable) into cash. Changes in accounts receivable policies, such as credit standards, credit terms or collection efforts, impact the receivables conversion period. Any changes in the competitive marketplace or general business conditions may also impact days' receivables. (The days' receivables period is also referred to as Days' Sales Outstanding or average collection period and is covered in greater detail in Chapter 7, Working Capital Tools.)

3. Days' Payables or Payables Conversion Period

Again, for both manufacturing and service companies, the days' payables or payables conversion period is the average number of days between the purchase of materials or supplies and payment for them. Days' payables represent the trade credit period. The ability to purchase materials on deferred payment allows a company to delay the outflow of cash. Any strategy that affects payables, such as stretching payables (sometimes referred to as "riding the trade") or taking cash discounts, impacts the payables conversion period. Stretching payables enables a company to:

- Use cash to reduce debt, thus reducing interest expense
- Invest cash on a short-term basis, thus increasing interest income
- Purchase other assets

However, stretching payables can also have a negative impact on vendor and supplier relationships; hence, this strategy must be used judiciously.

4. Cash Conversion Cycle

The cash conversion cycle is the average number of days between the cash outflow for the acquisition of materials and supplies and the cash inflow from the sale of products or services. The cash conversion cycle is expressed by the following formula:

Cash Conversion Cycle = Days' Inventory + Days' Receivables – Days' Payables

The cash conversion cycle is a method for calculating how long, on average, a company must finance a cash outflow before receiving a cash inflow. (For an example of the cash conversion cycle calculation and how it relates to financial ratio analysis, see Chapter 4, Financial Accounting.)

This cycle may be considered in the framework of net present value (NPV). A treasurer should examine how the timing of cash inflows and outflows relates to the conversion of raw materials into finished goods, sales and the receipt of available funds. Each of the events outlined above can be placed on a timeline. Because the NPV of inflows minus the NPV of outflows can be computed, a treasurer can determine the precise cost of the cash conversion cycle.

Assuming, for example, that a company with $1.75 million in annual sales must finance approximately 66 days of sales and the cost of capital is 12 percent, the NPV cost of the conversion cycle is as follows:

$$\text{NPV Cost} = 66 \text{ days} \times (\text{Average Daily Sales} / 365) \times \text{Cost of Capital}$$
$$= 66 \times (\$1{,}750{,}000 / 365) \times .12 = \$37{,}972.60$$

This represents the cost of financing the net investment in inventory and accounts receivable, minus accounts payable.

5. Shortening the Cash Conversion Cycle

The cash conversion cycle can be shortened by:

- Reducing the inventory conversion period
- Reducing the receivables conversion period
- Lengthening the payables deferral period

When a company is able to shorten the cash conversion cycle, profits may improve as financing costs are reduced. However, these savings must be compared with the costs associated with strategies that lengthen the cash conversion cycle.

Examples of costs related to shortening the cash conversion cycle include:

- Sales lost due to strict credit and collection standards
- Costs of having to stop production due to depletion of materials
- Costs of stretching payables beyond the due date, such as lost discount opportunities or late charges
- Higher prices charged by vendors and suppliers to slow or delinquent payers
- Lost sales from not selling to slow-paying customers for fear of non-payment
- Liberal extension of open credit terms to slow-paying customers

The benefits of lower cash financing cost strategies should be compared with the increased costs and lost sales that may result from shortening the cash conversion cycle. If benefits exceed costs of the strategies, including foregoing the profit from lost sales, the strategies should be implemented. In analyzing working capital strategies, it is important to determine how all decisions regarding inventory, receivables or payables impact the cash conversion cycle.

B. How Changes in Current Accounts Impact External Financing

Many current asset and current liability accounts vary whenever sales activity occurs. These accounts are referred to as being spontaneous. That is, no specific working capital management decisions are involved in increasing these accounts; the changes occur spontaneously with a change in sales. The magnitude of spontaneous changes has a significant impact in determining the amount of external financing necessary for working capital.

1. Changes in Current Assets

Generally, as the volume of sales activity increases, credit sales also increase, resulting in larger dollar amounts invested in accounts receivable, even when no change occurs in working capital policy. Additional sales may also require raw materials to be expanded to support production of finished goods, thereby increasing both inventory and accounts payable. An increase in accounts receivable and inventory may cause the cash account to decrease, or borrowing to increase in order to fund the working capital requirement. If the increased level of sales activity is permanent, it may necessitate larger cash and/or marketable securities balances in order to cover the increase in current assets. Increases in non-cash current assets must be supported by reducing cash, increasing liabilities or increasing debt.

On the other hand, a decrease in sales should cause a corresponding decrease in current asset accounts. However, in the short term, inventories may increase while production continues and sales decline.

2. Changes in Current Liabilities

A decrease in accounts payable results in either a decrease in cash or an increase in debt to pay off the accounts because decreases in current liabilities must be offset by decreases in an asset account or increases in other liability accounts.

For instance, a larger volume of sales activity would typically require a higher volume of materials purchased. If these materials are purchased on credit, the accounts payable account increases. Likewise, the additional labor expenses associated with increased production would cause the accrued wages account to increase. The increase in taxes due to a higher level of taxable income would cause the accrued taxes account to increase. On the other hand, a decrease in sales activity should cause corresponding decreases in these accounts.

3. External Financing Requirements

The total of net increases in the current-asset accounts (excluding cash) represents the total amount of financing necessary to fund working capital, assuming that there are no impacts in cash flows from changes in long-term assets or liabilities.

Current liabilities, such as accounts payable and accrual items, may be considered spontaneous in that they generally will increase automatically with increasing sales. For example, as a company increases its sales, purchases and production rise, thus increasing the amount of accounts payable, accrued wages and taxes. In addition, as the company generates additional profits, the retained earnings account increases. If the need for working capital exceeds increases in funds generated, the difference must be financed.

If current assets (excluding net cash) decrease, this represents funds that have been "freed up" or no longer need to be financed (i.e., lower inventory or lower accounts receivable due to increased sales results in increased liquidity for the company). If current liabilities decrease, this represents the reduction in funds available to support current assets. A company then has to utilize external sources (such as long-term debt or other capital) to support the working capital investment.

III. WORKING CAPITAL INVESTMENT AND FINANCING STRATEGIES

A treasurer must establish the framework for the risk/return trade-off analysis involved in working capital management. Three considerations for developing a framework are as follows:

- The level of current assets and whether or not the level is appropriate to the business or industry
- The current asset investment strategy
- The current asset financing strategy

A. Current Asset Investment Strategies

The current asset investment decision is important due to uncertainties associated with sales levels, costs, production time, lead times for inventory replenishment, quality of customer service, collection periods and payment periods. The normal range of ratios of current assets to sales varies by industry and by the size of the company.

The extent of the uncertainty and the company's risk tolerance determines the investments in current asset accounts. If uncertainty were not a factor, a company would need to have only minimal levels of current assets. However, because suppliers are unpredictable in their delivery patterns and customers are unpredictable in their buying patterns, a large "safety cushion" of raw materials or finished goods may be necessary. For some organizations, greater uncertainty in cash flows or the lack of available credit lines may result in a decision to extend the payables period, or to retain funds in cash or marketable securities as a "safety cushion."

A company may choose between alternative strategies, restrictive or relaxed, regarding the total amount of current assets to support a given level of sales. The following sections examine the trade-offs involved in pursuing restrictive and relaxed current asset investment strategies.

1. Restrictive Current Asset Investment Strategy

Under a restricted current asset investment strategy, a company maintains low levels of current assets relative to sales. The investment in raw materials is managed as tightly as possible using JIT inventory techniques and outstanding accounts receivable balances are kept low, reflecting a restrictive credit policy.

A restrictive current asset investment strategy may entail relatively higher risks associated with the tighter management of credit and inventory and the lack of cash available for accounts payable. In particular, a restricted credit policy may have a negative impact on sales. Likewise, a restrictive inventory policy may have a negative impact on the selection of goods available to meet consumer demand.

On the other hand, a restrictive strategy can sometimes be the most profitable strategy. Because fewer funds are invested in current assets, the total amount of funds invested in the company may also be relatively smaller. A restrictive strategy may, therefore, result in a larger return on investment, so long as the resulting savings from the tighter credit and inventory policies exceed lost sales.

2. Relaxed Current Asset Investment Strategy

Under an relaxed current asset investment strategy, a company maintains high levels of current assets relative to sales. Typically, these current assets consist of high levels of accounts receivable, usually resulting from a liberal credit policy, and/or high levels of inventory, usually resulting from concerns about the ability to replenish raw materials. With a larger investment in current assets, companies using liberal credit policies may have a relatively lower return on investment. However, the larger investment in current assets, combined with a relaxed strategy, may result in a larger current ratio and a lower risk of lost sales due to inventory depletion.

3. Selecting a Current Asset Investment Strategy

Management's choice of a specific current asset investment strategy depends upon the risk/return trade-off characteristics. One characteristic is the viewpoint of the company's creditors in the management of current assets. The current asset strategy of a company is an important consideration for banks and institutional creditors relying on current assets as security for short-term lending, as is the quality of the current assets pledged as security (accounts receivable and inventories).

Many companies, especially smaller ones, have no choice in selecting a strategy and are forced to pursue a restrictive strategy due to limited availability of short-term credit or limited overall capitalization. Likewise, a company's current asset strategy may also be a function of the industry. In industries with high gross profit margins on sales, a liberal credit policy may offer substantial benefits, especially if the potential for additional profit greatly outweighs potential costs—assuming, of course, that the profits gained from the additional sales are greater than the costs of carrying the additional receivables and any additional bad debt costs.

Another factor in determining a current asset strategy depends on which decision makers influence the company's policies. Financial managers often take a different view of current asset management from that of operations or sales managers. Operations managers typically prefer a large inventory of raw materials or partially finished goods to meet production quotas. Sales managers, likewise, typically prefer a large inventory of finished goods to meet consumer demand and a liberal credit policy to stimulate sales. Financial managers, on the other hand, typically prefer to minimize inventory and accounts receivable in order to minimize the cost of financing these assets.

B. Current Asset Financing Strategies

A company's need for current assets will typically fluctuate with variations in sales. While any company may have a sales cycle with major fluctuations over time, it is rare for sales to fall below a set minimum level. There is usually a need for a base level of current assets at all times during the sales cycle, generally referred to as the company's permanent current asset level. The level of permanent current asset investment may be determined by the average of the current asset investments at the low point of several sales cycles. This pattern may be used as an estimate for the necessary permanent current asset level.

Another approach to determine permanent current assets is to monitor the relationships between individual current asset accounts (cash, accounts receivable, and inventory) and the sales cycle over time in order to find a minimum level for each type of current asset. Sudden increases in temporary current assets represent the additional dollars necessary to support the sales increases that may occur at certain times in the cycle (i.e., retailers during the holiday season). Decisions regarding financing both temporary and permanent current assets define a company's working capital financing strategy.

The basic decision in the financing of a company's current assets is whether to use short- or long-term sources of funding. Because the source of funds used to finance current assets is generally debt, the basic question is whether it is less expensive to continuously borrow from the money markets or to lock in a long-term rate in the capital markets. Generally, the yield curve is upward-sloping, indicating that short-term funds are obtained at a lower cost than long-term funds. There are times, however, when the yield curve is downward-sloping or inverted. In these instances, long-term rates may be more attractive.

Before a funding decision is made, it is important for a treasurer to accurately forecast the following:

- The movements in interest rates
- The shape of the yield curve in the future
- The future availability of credit for the company

(A more detailed discussion of yields and the yield curve are in Chapter 10, Liquidity Management.)

The basic approaches to the financing of a company's permanent assets may be classified as maturity matching, aggressive, and conservative. (These policy approaches are shown in Figure 6.2.) Depending on the shape of the yield curve, the movement of interest rates, the forecast of future rates and management's risk tolerance, any of these approaches may be appropriate at any given point.

EXHIBIT 6.2 – ALTERNATIVE CURRENT ASSET FINANCING POLICIES

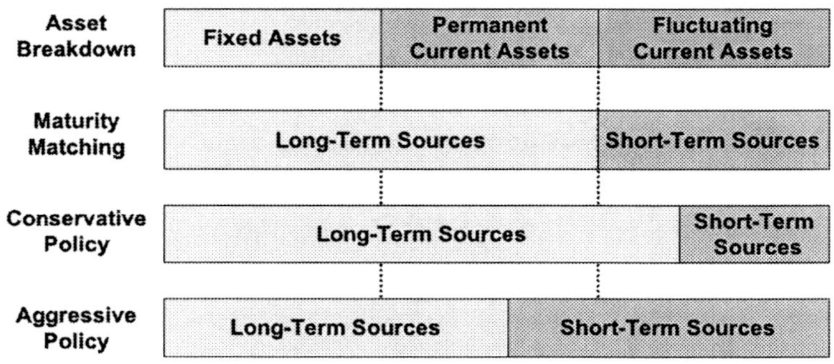

A company may also try to smooth out the use of short-term debt over time, borrowing on a regular basis whether or not funds are needed at a particular time. This approach may yield more stable borrowing rates, especially if more favorable rates can be negotiated with a financial institution.

1. Maturity Matching Financing Strategy

Under a maturity matching financing strategy, the total permanent assets, defined as fixed assets plus permanent current assets, are financed with long-term financing. Short-term financing is used to finance the temporary current assets, as evidenced by the fact that the need for short-term financing follows exactly the same pattern of fluctuation of the temporary current assets.

2. Conservative Financing Strategy

Under a conservative financing strategy, long-term financing supports fixed assets, permanent current assets and some portion of temporary current assets. A company usually tries to finance the average level of temporary current assets with long-term sources. Short-term financing is used for the remainder of the temporary current assets. Because short-term financing is used for only a portion of the temporary current assets, this strategy generally involves the least use of short-term financing and, therefore, has higher financing costs than other approaches.

The relatively more infrequent use of short-term financing results in a higher current ratio but may also result in lower profits for the company. There may, however, be less interest rate risk if long-term debt is on a fixed-rate basis and the short-term financing is on a floating- or variable-rate basis. The risk/return trade-off must be analyzed for decisions involving current asset investment and current asset financing.

3. Aggressive Financing Strategy

Under an aggressive financing strategy, a company finances all fixed assets with long-term debt or equity but finances only a portion of permanent current assets with long-term financing. Short-term financing supports the remainder of the permanent current assets and all temporary current assets. This strategy utilizes more ongoing short-term financing than other financing strategies.

Because short-term financing typically costs less than long-term financing, this strategy is often less costly. However, greater use of short-term financing results in a lower current ratio and greater risk. This risk arises from both interest rate risk (changing rates) and the risk that a line of credit may not be renewed. There are certain types of multi-year (usually three to five years) revolving credit agreements that allow a company to borrow on a short-term basis, yet classify the loan as long-term for accounting purposes. This type of borrowing arrangement does not reduce the current ratio, as does borrowing under a traditional short-term loan.

A restrictive investment strategy will have a higher expected return on investment (ROI) and a higher risk because of the lower current ratio. The use of derivative financing products may enable a treasurer to shift, or hedge, some of the risk from a restrictive investment policy. If a restrictive investment strategy is combined with an aggressive financing strategy, both policies lead to increased profitability and increased risk. That is, the expected ROI increases through the relatively cheaper financing costs, but risk also increases because of the smaller current ratio associated with a larger use of short-term financing. It is important for a company to analyze the risk/return impact from a combination of investment and financing decisions.

IV. BASICS OF SHORT-TERM CREDIT

For organizations planning to utilize short-term credit, there are many advantages and disadvantages to be considered. One of the key advantages generally attributed to the use of short-term credit is that it can be arranged quickly and the terms are usually fairly flexible. This section examines the advantages, disadvantages and sources of short-term credit.

A. Operational Advantages of Short-Term Credit

It is important to understand the advantages and disadvantages of short-term credit (facilities of 365 days or less) and long-term credit (facilities of a year or more). Aside from differences due to cost and risk, there are also operational differences between using short-term versus long-term debt to finance current assets.

The primary operational advantages of short-term credit are the ease of access, flexibility and the ability to efficiently finance seasonal credit needs. Short-term loans are typically easier to obtain than long-term loans. In fact, certain sources of short-term financing, such as accounts payable and accrued expenses, occur spontaneously with sales. This creates synchronization between when financing is required and when it is obtained.

In addition, short-term loans generally have less restrictive covenants than long-term loans. If funds are necessary for only a short time, borrowing on a short-term basis can enable a company to maintain flexibility for future borrowing decisions. Such flexibility tends not to apply when a company has a long-term borrowing arrangement with restrictive covenants, substantial pre-payment costs and/or initial fees for the credit placement.

One major use of short-term credit is the financing of current assets for seasonal industries. In order to meet increased needs, a seasonal company must increase inventory and/or accounts receivable. Short-term loans are the primary option for financing temporary, seasonal increases in current assets.

B. Operational Disadvantages of Short-Term Credit

An operational disadvantage of short-term debt is the continuing need to renegotiate or "roll over" the debt. A lender may decide not to roll over the loan or renew the credit line at maturity due to changing financial variables in the company or changes in general economic conditions. In addition, some lenders who provide lines of credit require that loans used to finance short-term working capital deficits be paid in full for a minimum period each year (known as a clean-up period).

Many companies find that the use of short-term loans for the financing of permanent asset requirements involves significant risk. However, one approach to continued use of short-term debt that carries lower risk involves revolving loans, secured by either accounts receivable or inventory.

C. Sources of Short-Term Credit

The five major types of short-term credit—accounts payable, accrued expenses, short-term bank loans, asset-based loans, and commercial paper—each have different speeds of acquisition, flexibility, cost and risk.

1. Accounts Payable (Trade Credit)

Typically, suppliers and vendors of goods and services allow business customers to purchase on trade credit. Trade credit is the period of time allowed by a supplier or vendor between when a purchase is made and when payment must be received to avoid a late charge or penalty. Accounts payable often represent a major source of short-term credit for companies that are regarded as being creditworthy. Increases or decreases in the current liability account are spontaneous and often quickly accessed.

Increased sales activity usually results in larger orders from suppliers, which leads to larger accounts payable balances. So long as the obligation is paid within the credit period allowed by the supplier, there is no direct cost associated with trade credit. In a sense, it is an interest-free loan from the supplier.

However, if a supplier offers a discount for payment in cash (cash discount), there is a cost associated with not taking the discount. The cost of not taking the discount represents the approximate interest rate of any alternative uses of a company's funds. Therefore, the cash discount interest rate should be compared with the cost of obtaining funds from other sources.

Ideally, if funds can be obtained more cheaply, a company should borrow at the cheaper cost and then take the discount by paying for the goods and services on the discount date. The discount formula and a sample calculation from both the buyer's and the seller's perspectives are provided at the end of this chapter.

The cost of the average collection period for the supplier is already built into the price of the product or service. If the buyer has a less expensive source of funds, a lower price with a shorter payment period (cash discount) will be more beneficial for both the buyer and the seller. Accounts payable are generally not flexible unless a company is willing to pay penalties for late payment and possibly to risk losing the privilege of trade credit. Payment dates for accounts payable are negotiated with the supplier. This source of short-term credit can exist only when goods and services are purchased because a supplier will not generally lend dollars for purposes other than purchases.

However, where the market for supplies is highly competitive, the buyer may be able to dictate or influence the terms of the sale. In order to make a sale, a seller may lend money to the buyer for purposes other than the purchase of supplies, or may offer more flexible terms to a creditworthy buyer purchasing a large volume of supplies in order to gain a volume discount. Some industries also dictate that the terms be flexible or negotiable between supplier and buyer.

2. Accrued Expenses

Wages are generally paid on a weekly, biweekly or monthly basis; taxes are generally paid on a weekly, monthly or quarterly basis. These are referred to as accrued expenses because, until these payments are actually made, the company has use of these wages and taxes. These current liabilities are spontaneous and will typically increase in relation to increases in sales, expenditures or inventories.

Rarely are costs associated with the deferral of wages and taxes. For example, a company does not pay interest to wage earners in order to compensate them for being paid at the end of the month instead of daily. Accrued expenses, however, are not considered flexible and are generally static. A company usually does not have the ability to change the due dates for taxes, and many wage payment patterns are dictated by industry practice or labor negotiations. Within these constraints, a company should utilize these cost-free sources of working capital whenever possible.

3. Short-Term Bank Loans

Loans from banks or other financial institutions appear in the liabilities section of a company's balance sheet as loans payable, notes payable, promissory notes or lines of credit. This short-term source of financing is not spontaneous. Specific decisions to borrow and lend must accompany any increase in the company's short-term borrowing position. Still, increases must be negotiated and approved by the lender. Often, lines of credit are arranged in advance and may be accessed up to the specified limit. While these bank loans all have associated costs, the fact that they are negotiated provides flexibility regarding both pricing and maturity.

In addition, repayment patterns, collateral, compensating balances, credit limits and commitment fees on lines of credit can also be negotiated. Therefore, this source of financing is not as spontaneous as accruals and accounts payable. Also, other costs frequently are involved in establishing bank credit facilities, such as those related to outside counsel, internal administration, accounts receivable, and inventory auditing and reporting.

4. Asset-Based Loans

Short-term bank loans are often secured by some form of collateral, usually accounts receivable, inventory or securitized assets. This practice is referred to as asset-based lending. These types of loans are generally formula-based, meaning that the amount of the loan is usually based on a percentage of eligible receivables or inventory, depending upon the age and/or dollar amount of the asset(s). In effect, a lender agrees to advance some percentage of the value of the receivables or inventory (the advance rate), with certain assets pledged as security, as part of the lending arrangement.

Secured loans have explicit costs, particularly auditing and reporting costs that are higher than the all-in borrowing cost of unsecured lines of credit. While asset-based loans are flexible, considerable time is involved in negotiating terms and receiving loan approval.

One of the most common types of asset-based loans requires the pledging of accounts receivable to provide security on a short-term loan or line of credit. This type of arrangement may be made through a bank or through a third-party financial intermediary such as a non-bank commercial finance company.

- An **inventory loan** is a loan secured by providing the lender with a claim on the company's inventory. This claim on inventory may be general (an inventory blanket lien) or it can identify specific items of inventory as collateral (a trust receipt loan). Inventory loans are also formula-based.

- **Factoring** involves the outright sale of a company's accounts receivable to a third party, referred to as a factor. The sale of accounts receivable is, in effect, a proxy for a short-term loan. With factoring, receivables are not pledged to a lender. Instead, the receivables are sold at a discount to a factor. Factoring arrangements are made either with or without recourse to the originating company in the event of default (non-collection) of receivables. "With recourse" means that the company must collect past dues and bad debts. "Without recourse" means that the factor assumes the responsibility for past dues and bad debts, a more expensive form of factoring.

- **Securitization** is the term used for the creation of new securities based on financial assets such as accounts receivable. In essence, the receivables are bundled into packages and resold to other investors, providing a lending institution with increased liquidity. Common examples of securitized receivables are mortgages, credit card portfolios, equipment loans and student loans.

5. Commercial Paper

Commercial paper is an unsecured promissory note issued by a corporation that is willing to pay a competitive market rate and typically offers maturities of up to 270 days. Commercial paper is normally issued at a discount through dealers. For large companies active in the market, it provides a quick source of low-cost, short-term financing. The cost of commercial paper for the issuer is based on the company's credit rating on the issue, which is a function of the estimated default risk.

(A more detailed discussion of commercial paper is in Chapter 10, Liquidity Management.)

V. COSTS AND RISKS OF ALTERNATIVE DEBT MATURITIES

Economic conditions and yield curves determine the general levels of interest rates and, therefore, the basic cost of borrowing, such as London Interbank Offered Rate (LIBOR) or prime rate. Risk or creditworthiness impacts the costs of borrowing for individual companies. Under normal financial market conditions, yield curves are upward-sloping, meaning that short-term interest rates are lower than long-term interest rates. This implies that there is usually a cost advantage to using short-term credit. There are also several short-term financing sources, such as accounts payable and accruals that have little or no interest costs.

A significant responsibility for treasury management is the monitoring of interest rate cycles and the yield curve in order to make the proper decision on short-term versus long-term financing. Depending on interest rate cycles and the prevailing yield curve of interest rates, a company may be able to secure long-term, low-rate bank or institutional financing and/or to obtain fixed versus floating rate financing.

Borrowing on a short-term basis carries two types of risk that are avoided in longer-term borrowing. The first risk relates to fluctuations in market interest rates. If a company borrows on a short-term floating rate basis, it will borrow at whatever the interest rate is at that time, taking the chance that interest rates may change dramatically in either direction. Many companies utilize short-term borrowing risk reduction techniques such as interest rate caps, collars, swaps and floors to protect themselves against interest rate fluctuations.

(Detailed information about these risk reduction techniques are in Chapter 17, Financial Risk Management.)

The second risk of short-term financing concerns the availability of funds. If a company relies heavily on short-term borrowing, eventually the short-term funds may not be available due to a tightening of credit standards on the part of lenders. Also, a company's credit quality may decline, thus endangering the future rollover of the credit arrangement. Some companies counter this risk by utilizing multi-year credit line commitments, which guarantee the availability of funds over a longer term.

Both fluctuations in market interest rates and the availability of funds are especially relevant risks for a company that relies on short-term borrowing for long-term uses. One way of mitigating these risks is to roll over short-term borrowing at each maturity in order to make short-term borrowing take on the characteristics of long-term borrowing. However, this practice involves the risk that each time a rollover occurs, the company faces whatever interest rate and availability conditions exist at the time of the rollover.

In contrast to short-term borrowing, long-term borrowing on a fixed rate basis stabilizes interest costs, or in the case of a limited variable rate basis, provides a narrow range for fluctuation in interest costs.

VI. FINANCING STRATEGIES OF MULTIDIVISIONAL AND MULTINATIONAL COMPANIES

In a wider context, the current assets and liabilities of a multidivisional company may be regarded as a portfolio of investments. Some divisions have high levels of current assets that can be financed or offset by current liabilities in other divisions.

To the extent that corporate headquarters is granted authority to direct the working capital policy of divisions, the overall working capital position of a consolidated company may be more easily managed. For example, in a multidivisional company it may be possible to use intrasubsidiary transfers or netting to better manage a company's overall liquidity.

To the extent that a company can efficiently mobilize funds between various subsidiaries, there may be more flexibility in terms of overall cash and liquidity management. Also, subsidiaries with excess funds can often lend these funds to other subsidiaries with a shortage of funds. Using intracompany lending, sometimes referred to as internal borrowing, generally results in lower overall cost of short-term funds for a company.

For multinational companies, there may also be some advantages to the following:

- Sourcing debt in different countries or currencies
- Maintaining cash positions in specific currencies
- Hedging the company's exposures on a global basis

(A detailed discussion of these techniques is in Chapter 16, Global Treasury Organization and Liquidity Management.)

VII. CASH DISCOUNT CALCULATIONS

A. Cost for a Buyer of Not Taking the Cash Discount

From the point of view of an accounts payable manager (i.e., a buyer) who receives an invoice from a vendor or supplier that offers discount terms of 2/10, net 90, this means that the buyer is being offered a two-percent discount to pay the invoice by the 10th day. If the buyer pays day 11 through day 90 ("net" means the payment is due on the 90th day), the discount is no longer available and the full amount is due. Assuming that the company's cost of short-term funds is 8 percent, should the buyer take the discount? The formula and a sample calculation are demonstrated below:

$$\text{Effective Cost of Discount} = \frac{D}{(100 - D)} \times \frac{365}{(N - T)}$$

Where:

D = Discount Percentage = 2%

N = Net Period = 90 Days

T = Discount Period = 10 Days

$$\text{Effective Cost of Discount} = \frac{2}{98} \times \frac{365}{(90 - 10)} = 9.31\%$$

The purpose of performing this calculation is to compare the cost of not taking the discount with the opportunity cost for investing short-term funds. In this case, the company should take the discount because the cost of not taking the discount is 9.31 percent versus the company's short-term borrowing rate of 8 percent. The company would, in effect, realize a benefit of 1.31%. If, however, the company's short-term cost of funds were 11 percent, the company should pay the net amount on day 90 because 9.31 percent is less expensive than borrowing the funds at 11 percent to pay the invoice by the 10th day.

B. The Benefit for a Seller of Offering a Cash Discount

From the point of view of an accounts receivable manager (i.e., a seller), the benefit of offering a discount is that it represents an incentive to the buyer to remit the funds earlier, thereby reducing the borrowing costs associated with financing accounts receivable. However, because there is also a cost involved with offering a discount to a buyer for earlier payment, the net seller's benefit must be calculated.

Assume that the seller has a cost of capital of 15 percent, the average credit sale to the buyer is $100,000, and the credit terms are 2/10, net 90.

The present value of receiving the discounted payment on Day 10 is as follows:

$$PV_{\text{Receive on Day 10}} = \frac{[\$100{,}000 \times (1-.02)]}{\left\{1 + \left[10 \times \left(\frac{.15}{365}\right)\right]\right\}} \quad \$97{,}598.96$$

The present value of receiving full payment on Day 90 is as follows:

$$PV_{\text{Receive on Day 90}} = \frac{[\$100{,}000]}{\left\{1 + \left[90 \times \left(\frac{.15}{365}\right)\right]\right\}} \quad \$96{,}433.78$$

$$NPV = PV_{\text{Day 10}} - PV_{\text{Day 90}} = \$97{,}598.96 - \$96{,}433.78 = \$1{,}165.18$$

Thus, the seller's net benefit is $1,165.18 per payment if the buyer takes the discount and pays by day 10 rather than waiting to pay the full amount on day 90. The $1,165.18 represents the amount that the seller gains by not having to finance the receivable for an additional 80 days.

Test Your Understanding

These chapter questions are provided to test your understanding of the information in the text. They are neither examples of CTP examination questions nor are they in the examination format.

Answers are on pages 578–580.

1. What is the difference between working capital and net working capital?

2. Discuss the concepts of the cash flow timeline and cash conversion cycle.

3. What are spontaneous asset and liability accounts?

4. What is the difference between a relaxed and a restrictive strategy in managing the investment in current assets?

5. What are the three basic approaches to financing a company's permanent current-asset base?

6. Discuss the operational advantages and disadvantages of using short-term credit.

7. What are the five major sources of short-term credit?

8. What is asset-based lending?

9. What is commercial paper and how is it issued?

10. What are the risks of borrowing on a short-term basis, and how does borrowing long term reduce these risks?

Association for
Financial Professionals®

CHAPTER 7
Working Capital Tools

I. INTRODUCTION

While working capital management encompasses all of the current assets and current liabilities of a company, three of the accounts on the balance sheet typically represent the bulk of the activity: Accounts receivable (A/R) and inventory comprise the principal asset accounts while accounts payable (A/P) is the principal liability account. These three accounts have a major impact on a company's liquidity.

A/R management is closely linked to the credit, billing and collection policies of a company. Efficient A/R management requires careful monitoring and control of accounts at both the individual and the aggregate levels. A treasury manager generally has responsibility for the collections function, the final stage of the A/R process. A treasury manager may also have either direct or indirect responsibility for arranging the financing of a company's A/R.

With respect to inventory, though treasury managers may not directly manage inventory, they are often responsible for its financing. Finally, because A/P provides a major source of funds for many companies, the treasury area is generally responsible for the funding of disbursement accounts and may also manage the actual disbursement of payments. This chapter covers the primary tools of working capital management as they relate to A/R, inventory, and A/P.

II. CREDIT AND A/R

A/R represents an asset of the company that arises from the extension of trade credit to customers. Effective credit management generally entails four steps:

- Establishing and communicating a company's credit policies
- Setting terms of sale consistent with overall company objectives
- Evaluating customer creditworthiness in order to grant customer credit lines
- Ensuring prompt and accurate customer billing in conjunction with customer service or billing departments

The proper management of A/R includes:

- Creating, preserving, and collecting A/R
- Maintaining up-to-date customer records
- Initiating collection procedures on past-due accounts

Sales, accounting, and finance personnel all become involved in credit and A/R management activity.

A. Organization of the Credit and A/R Management Function

In most companies, the credit management and treasury management responsibilities reside in different departments. While treasury management is typically the responsibility of the treasurer, credit management is typically the responsibility of the controller. However, maintaining a good working relationship with departments and employees involved in credit management is important for a treasury manager—especially because credit policy and collection of A/R have a significant impact on the timing of cash inflows.

A company's credit manager administers policies that establish credit standards, define terms of credit extension, approve customers for credit sales, and set individual and aggregate credit limits. Because credit extension is a method used to increase sales, the credit manager usually works closely with the sales manager.

Once a sale has been made and credit has been extended, an A/R is created. A/R management entails billing and processing payments, monitoring payment patterns and collecting delinquent accounts. In most companies, the management of A/R is generally the responsibility of the credit manager, although other finance personnel may also be directly or indirectly involved. Some companies outsource the management of credit and A/R through captive finance companies and/or factors.

B. Credit Policies

To ensure consistent application and fairness, it is important for a company to have written credit policies and procedures that clearly define its credit standards, credit terms and collection practices. Establishing credit standards is a two-stage process: determining both the risk profile of the type of customer who is granted credit and each individual customer's credit limit.

Establishing credit terms involves designing sales contracts or agreements that clearly specify under what conditions credit terms are granted. Establishing collection policies involves determining the steps involved in collecting delinquent accounts or bad debts. Finally, a company needs to develop an information system or to purchase software that monitors A/R to ensure compliance with credit terms and detects changes in customer payment patterns at aggregate and individual customer levels.

1. Reasons for Offering Trade Credit

The primary reason for offering credit is to increase the level of sales, thereby generating additional revenues. Because the bulk of business is conducted on an open-account basis and many customers do not have access to other sources of financing, competition for customers requires a company to grant trade credit. This is especially true in industries where credit extension is the norm. Credit terms are designed to lure customers away from competitors and to encourage existing customers to increase purchases.

2. Credit Policy Constraints

A number of factors may constrain or influence a company's credit policies. In many industries, credit terms and policies have become standard practices. As a result, it is difficult for a seller to vary from industry practices. A company must also consider the impact that offering trade credit has on existing loan covenants. A change in A/R balances can affect working capital ratios, potentially resulting in being out of compliance with covenants. There are also legal constraints, such as the Robinson-Patman Act, that prohibit various forms of price discrimination. Likewise, many states have usury laws that limit the amount of interest that can be charged or that ban certain unfair credit practices.

3. Financing Implications

A company's credit terms, along with sales and collection patterns, determine the level of A/R. Because receivables are assets that must be financed, a company's ability to extend credit is directly related to its ability to borrow. Mismanagement of receivables can cause liquidity problems due to delayed customer payments. However, receivables may also be a source of liquidity when used as collateral for asset-based loans or when sold for cash to third parties, referred to as factors.

4. Income and Expenses Related to Granting Credit

Trade credit may increase a company's income. The primary income opportunity arises from the increase in sales because offering credit terms generates additional sales volume. Additional volume may, in turn, result in increased profitability. The other potential source of income is from interest on installment payment arrangements. This can be a significant source of profit, especially for retail industries.

There are also costs associated with offering trade credit. On the expense side, the primary costs of A/R are carrying costs. Typically, a company determines this cost by using the marginal cost of short-term borrowings or the weighted average cost of capital (WACC). Another major cost is the expense of operating and maintaining a credit department. These costs typically include personnel costs, data and payments processing, and costs related to credit evaluation or, if a third-party credit bureau is used, to obtaining credit information.

If a company offers discount terms, then the "cost" of discounted payments also impacts income. When customers take advantage of a discount, but sales volumes do not increase, total net revenue is reduced. This loss of revenue may be fully or partially offset by a reduction in A/R carrying costs. While a liberal credit policy may increase sales, it also increases administrative costs as the volume of bad debt losses increases.

In a typical business-to-business (B2B) environment there are often discrepancies in payments. These differences arise from the usual practice of customers paying multiple invoices, each with possible adjustments, in a single check. The costs associated with monitoring, investigating and resolving discrepancies between invoices and customer payments can be substantial. Discrepancies must be researched, the legitimacy of shortfalls and deductions must be ascertained, and all related bookkeeping, invoicing, and payment adjustments must be recorded.

Costs related to delinquent account monitoring and bad debt collection impact a company's income. According to Generally Accepted Accounting Principles (GAAP), A/R that are determined to be uncollectible must be charged off as bad debt. Most companies use historic collection patterns to estimate the level of losses and create a reserve account through periodic charges to bad debt expense. The timing and volume of bad debt expense and charge-offs are important aspects of credit policy.

Generally, the cost of collecting delinquent accounts can be significant. Companies can reduce the impact of bad debts by purchasing various types of insurance that are designed to cover receivables losses. Companies must include insurance premiums in the cost/benefit analysis when assessing the potential profitability of credit sales.

C. Credit Standards

It is important for a company to set and maintain credit standards that encompass credit extension, billing, and collection. In determining credit extension policies, there are two key risk considerations:

- If a company implements credit standards that are too strict, it may decline trade credit to customers who represent an acceptable credit risk, thereby resulting in lost sales opportunities.
- If a company implements credit standards that are too lenient, it may grant trade credit to customers who represent an unacceptable credit risk, thereby resulting in an increase in late payment and bad debt expenses.

In practice, the costs of these two risk considerations are difficult to quantify. However, credit is a sales tool and a zero default rate probably means that a company's credit terms are too strict.

1. Information Sources

A company must consider the type, quantity and cost of information when establishing a method of analyzing credit requests. Credit information is typically gathered in stages from internal and external sources; at each stage, costs are weighed against the expected benefits. The most important sources of internally generated credit information are a credit application/agreement completed by the applicant and a company's own records regarding an applicant's actual payment history.

A company can use a wide variety of external sources to assist in determining the creditworthiness of a credit applicant. One of the key sources is an applicant's financial statements. Both audited and unaudited financial statements provide important information on corporate credit applicants because these statements and related ratios can be compared to industry averages from sources such as RMA (Risk Management Association, formerly Robert Morris and Associates) or VentureLine. Another useful external source, known as trade references, occurs when other companies are contacted to obtain actual payment experiences regarding credit terms extended to the applicant.

Banks or other financial creditors (commercial finance or leasing companies) also provide standardized credit information about an applicant's financial condition and available credit. Finally, there are various local and nationwide agencies, such as Dun & Bradstreet, that collect, evaluate, and report information on the credit history of most companies. These credit reports include information such as payment history, financial information, maximum outstanding credit amounts, the length of time credit has been available and any collection actions that may be outstanding.

2. The Five C's of Credit

Credit analysis depends upon the type of information available and the trade-offs between costs and benefits. The traditional factors that companies consider are known as the five C's of credit. The five C's are:

- **Character:** The perceived honesty or integrity of an individual applicant or of the officers of a corporate applicant. Character is seen as being an indication of intent or willingness to pay, as evidenced by personal or corporate payment history. Bankers typically use the term "know your customer" in reference to character.
- **Capacity:** The current and future financial resources that a company or individual is able to use to pay obligations when they come due. Capacity is often assessed using financial-liquidity ratios and cash flow forecasts.
- **Capital:** An individual or corporate customer's short- and long-term financial resources that could be liquidated if the immediate cash flow is insufficient to meet payment obligations.
- **Collateral:** The assets or guarantees available to secure an obligation in the event that payment terms are not met.
- **Conditions:** The general existing economic environment that impacts the ability of a customer to pay or the willingness of a company to grant credit.

3. Quantitative Credit Analysis

The quantitative analysis of business credit information begins with an examination of a credit applicant's financial statements, frequently through ratio analyses that assess a customer's financial condition. The measures most often used include:

- Liquidity and working capital ratios (the current-, quick-, and cash flow-to-total-debt ratios)
- Debt management and -coverage ratios (times interest earned, long-term debt-to-capital, debt-to-total assets and total liabilities-to-total assets ratios)
- Profitability measures (return on equity, return on sales and return on total assets)

Ratios provide valuable insights when evaluated in relation to industry standards published by credit rating agencies and other associations. Some commercial credit analysis involves credit scoring, which is evaluated by purchasing credit reports from companies such as Dun & Bradstreet.

(A more detailed discussion of quantitative credit analysis using ratios is in Chapter 4, Financial Accounting.)

For consumer credit analysis, major issuers of retail credit, such as department stores, use quantitative credit scoring models. Credit scoring involves a four-step process:

- Differentiating standard and high-risk accounts based on monthly income, outstanding obligations and the employment history of the applicant
- Weighting the characteristics of applicants who fit into each category to establish creditworthiness
- Setting cutoff scores for approval and denial of credit
- Applying further analysis to applicants whose scores fall in between the cutoff points

These quantitative approaches are cost effective and also aid in complying with consumer credit legislation. Formal statistical analysis is often used to identify factors that distinguish paying customers from non-paying customers, sometimes on a region-by-region basis. Credit bureaus also assess creditworthiness based on proprietary models.

D. Billing and Collection Methods

The major objective of a collection policy is to speed the conversion of A/R into cash while minimizing collection expense and bad-debt losses. The type of credit a company offers significantly impacts the collection methods employed.

Effective A/R management involves reducing invoicing float, which is the interval between the time goods and services are purchased and the time the customer receives an invoice. The first step in collecting an account is sending accurate and timely invoices with the terms of payment clearly stated. Delays in invoice preparation or errors on an invoice may extend the payment process by days or even weeks. Sometimes, companies send summary statements of outstanding invoices as a reminder that payment is due. Consumer billing typically involves sending statements listing goods or services purchased over a month's period.

When payment is not received by the due date, a company has several options such as sending a duplicate invoice, mailing a form letter or a series of form letters (dunning letters), calling the customer, visiting the customer in person, suspending further shipment of goods or terminating services until past due items are paid, and negotiating with the customer for payment of past due amounts. Often, all of these measures are taken as a company escalates its collection efforts.

Once a company has exhausted all of the above methods, it may pursue more serious actions such as reporting the customer's delinquent status to credit bureaus, repossessing collateral, negotiating additional corporate or personal guarantees, obtaining a lien on specific assets, initiating direct legal action and turning delinquent accounts over to a collection agency.

E. Forms of Credit Extension

There are four forms of credit extension, the open-account or open-book credit, installment credit, revolving credit and letter of credit.

1. **Open Account:** The open account method, sometimes called open book credit, is the most common type of commercial trade credit in the United States. A seller issues an invoice, as formal evidence of the obligation, and records the sale as an A/R. The customer is billed for each transaction by invoice and/or monthly statement. Full payment of invoiced amounts is expected within the specified credit terms unless certain discounts or deductions are available to the customer. A buyer's creditworthiness is reviewed periodically, but the buyer does not need to apply for credit each time an order is placed.

2. **Installment Credit:** Installment credit is a form of credit whereby a company requires a customer to make equal monthly payments, each of which contains a principal and an interest component. Installment credit is frequently used for the purchase of high-value consumer durables such as automobiles. The seller requires the buyer to sign a contract, which specifies the credit terms of the obligation in full, and discloses the interest rate and other costs.

3. **Revolving Credit:** Under revolving credit terms, a company grants credit without requiring specific approval of each transaction provided the account is kept current. The account is usually considered current if the credit outstanding is below an established credit limit and minimum payments have been made on time. If the account is not paid in full by the monthly payment due date, an interest charge is calculated based on the average amount outstanding over the entire period.

4. **Letter of Credit:** The most complex form of credit extension is a commercial letter of credit or L/C. L/Cs are commonly used in import/export transactions. An L/C is an instrument in which a bank guarantees a seller that the bank, not the buyer, will pay for the agreed upon purchase when the seller presents documents conforming to specified conditions pertaining to the sale and delivery of goods or services. Typically, the buyer pays for initiating an L/C. A variant of a commercial L/C is a standby L/C, which serves as a guarantee to secure credit sales to a specific buyer. Whereas a commercial L/C is utilized to complete a transaction, a standby L/C is used only if payment is not made.

(Additional information on L/Cs is in Chapter 15, Global Treasury Environment.)

F. Considerations Pertaining to Terms of Sale

Buyers and sellers have a variety of standard terms of sale from which they can choose. These terms are usually specified in sales agreements, invoices and other legal or commercial documents.

1. Common Terms of Sale

Among the most common credit terms are the following:

- **Cash Before Delivery (CBD):** CBD terms, sometimes referred to as prepayment terms, require the buyer to make full and final payment before shipment or receipt of goods. In business-to-consumer (B2C) sales, CBD is very commonly used for catalog orders or for orders that are processed by telephone or over the Internet. In B2B sales, CBD is used when the seller does not know the buyer or when the seller considers the buyer a greater credit risk than the seller is willing to accept.

- **Cash on Delivery (COD):** The seller ships the goods and the buyer pays upon receipt. If the buyer refuses to pay, the goods are returned, and the seller must pay the shipping and handling costs.

- **Cash Terms:** The buyer generally has seven to ten days to make payment. Cash terms are frequently used in the sale of perishable items.

- **Net Terms:** The seller specifies a net due date by which the buyer must pay in full. For example, terms of Net 30 require the buyer to pay within 30 days from the date of invoice, date of delivery or some other specified date.

- **Discount Terms:** In addition to specifying a net due date, the seller may also offer a discount if payment is made prior to that date. Terms of 2/10 net 30 mean that the total amount is due within 30 days of the invoice date but the buyer can take a two percent discount if payment is made within ten days. (For a calculation of discount terms, see Chapter 6, Philosophy of Working Capital.)

- **Monthly Billing:** The seller issues a monthly statement covering all invoices prior to a cutoff date, typically toward the end of each month. The buyer must pay by a specified date during the following month. The seller may allow the buyer to take a discount for prompt payment. For example, if terms are 1/10, net 30, the buyer may take a discount of one percent if payment is made by the 10th day of the following month. However, the total due must be paid by the 30th day of the following month.

- **Draft/Bill of Lading:** Also known as a documentary collection, the seller collects payments through banking channels. Documentary collection is more common in international trade than in domestic trade. Having shipped goods to the buyer, the seller sends shipping and title documents to a bank that transmits the documents to the buyer's bank. The buyer gains possession of the documents upon paying the bank or upon signing a draft agreeing to pay at a future date. Upon collection, the buyer's bank remits payment to the seller's bank.

- **Seasonal Dating:** The seller agrees to accept payment at the end of the buyer's selling season. This allows manufacturers to provide short-term financing for a buyer's purchases and reduces the manufacturer's inventory costs. It is common in industries with distinct seasonality of sales such as toys, greeting cards, garden supplies, sporting goods or textbooks. In seasonal dating, the seller may offer a series of discounts to encourage the buyer to pay early.

- **Consignment:** Under a consignment agreement, the seller ships the goods to the buyer with no obligation to pay until the goods have been sold or used. The title to the goods remains with the seller until they are sold.

2. Common Credit Practices

In addition to offering credit terms, companies often assess a penalty fee for payments received after the due date. This fee is usually a percentage of the amount past due. The fee should be clearly stated at the time of the sale and disclosed on the invoice.

A company must also determine the aggregate amount of credit (the credit limit) it should grant each customer. Companies usually grant a new customer credit at the lowest limit. After a period of satisfactory payment performance, they raise the credit limit to the next level, and then continuously review a customer's payment history for the purpose of making adjustments as necessary.

Finally, if discounts are offered, the company must determine a benchmark date of eligibility for discounts. This can be the postmark date of the payment remittance or the date that funds are received.

3. Offering Discounts

When offering cash discounts, the seller must evaluate the costs versus the benefits to be gained from receiving a payment early. Standard practice involves using either the gross or the net method for discounted sales. Under the gross method, gross sales revenues are recorded on the income statement and discounts are taken as an expense on the income statement. In the net method, amounts are entered into the receivables and revenue accounts net of the discounts. Any discounts not taken are shown as income. Exhibit 7.1 illustrates how the annualized cost of trade credit is calculated.

G. A/R Monitoring and Control

Monitoring and controlling a company's A/R at both an individual and an aggregate level are important aspects of the overall credit policy. An aging schedule is a useful method for tracking individual receivables, and a report of days' sales outstanding (DSO) is a useful measure of the overall collection rate for A/R.

EXHIBIT 7.1 – ANNUALIZED COST OF TRADE CREDIT

$$\text{Annualized Cost of Trade Credit} = \frac{\text{Early Payment Discount}}{(1 - \text{Early Payment Discount})} \times \frac{365}{(\text{Net Payment Period} - \text{Discount Payment Period})}$$

Example

Given terms 2/10 net 30, the cost of not taking the discount (i.e., paying the net amount on Day 30 rather than the discounted amount on Day 10) can be calculated as:

$$\text{Cost of Trade Credit} = \frac{.02}{(1 - .02)} \times \frac{365}{(30 - 10)} = 37.24\%$$

If a buyer were able to borrow funds at a rate of less than 37.24%, then he should do so and take the discount for early payment. If borrowed funds cost more than 37.24% or if they are not available, then the buyer should delay payment until the net due date.

A company with excess cash reserves must compare this annualized cost to investment rates. If alternative investment rates available to the company exceed the annualized cost of trade credit, then the discount should be delayed until the net due date.

Among the reasons it is important to monitor individual accounts are: (1) There may be errors or delays in the invoicing or payment process; (2) Some customers may intentionally delay payment until follow-up is initiated and (3) A change in financial condition may alter the ability of a customer to make timely payments and may require a curtailment of future credit sales.

Companies should also monitor A/R on an aggregate level because an increase in receivables impacts liquidity and may prompt a need for additional financing. Also, significant changes in the level of overall A/R may be a symptom of a change in business that could affect a company's financing needs and/or cash levels. Management should analyze these changes to determine underlying causes and then take corrective actions. Developments that may prompt significant changes include variations in sales volume, seasonality, modifications of credit standards policy, fluctuations in economic conditions and promotions or other sales initiatives on the part of competitors. Also, analysis of aggregate receivables forms the basis for forecasting the amount and timing of future cash receipts.

1. Days' Sales Outstanding (DSO)

One method of measuring A/R is days' sales outstanding (DSO) or average collection period. DSO is calculated by dividing outstanding A/R at the end of a period by the average daily credit sales for that period. DSO gives a single number that can be compared to stated credit terms, historic trends or industry norms in order to provide an indication of a company's overall collection efficiency. It may, however, be distorted by changing trends in sales volume or by strong seasonality in sales. Exhibit 7.2 illustrates a basic method for calculating DSO. The average daily sales of $3,444.44 are computed without considering the pattern of sales for the period.

EXHIBIT 7.2 – DAYS' SALES OUTSTANDING (DSO) CALCULATION

Assume

Outstanding receivables of $285,000 at the end of Month 3
Credit terms of net 60
DSO averaging period of 3 months (90 days)
Credit sales history:

Month 1 = $ 90,000.00
Month 2 = $ 105,000.00
Month 3 = $ 115,000.00

DSO Calculation

$$\text{Average Daily Credit Sales} = \frac{(\$90{,}000.00 + \$105{,}000.00 + \$115{,}000.00)}{90} = \$3{,}444.44$$

$$\text{Days' Sales} = \frac{\text{Outstanding Accounts Receivable}}{\text{Average Daily Credit Sales}} = \frac{\$285{,}000.00}{} = 82.74 \text{ Days}$$

Average Past Due Calculation

Average Past Due = DSO – Average Days of Credit Terms
= 82.74 Days – 60 Days = 22.74 Days

2. Aging Schedule

Another method of measuring A/R is an aging schedule. An aging schedule separates A/R into current and past due receivables in 30-day increments. Companies then analyze the aging of receivables on an aggregate or customer basis. An aging analysis identifies past-due accounts, which become less collectible as the age of each increases. Assuming credit terms of net 30, the aging schedule in Exhibit 7.3 shows that 30 percent of the A/R is past due.

An aging schedule is more indicative of trends than the DSO calculation because an aging schedule illustrates a pattern of distribution, not just a single number representing an average. However, an aging schedule can send the same potentially misleading signals as DSO when sales vary significantly from month to month.

EXHIBIT 7.3 – EXAMPLE OF AN AGING SCHEDULE

Age of Accounts	Accounts Receivable	% of Account Receivable
0 – 30 days	$1,750,000	70%
31– 60 days	375,000	15%
61–90 days	250,000	10%
91+ days	125,000	5%
Total	$2,500,000	100%

3. A/R Balance Pattern

Aging schedules are used to establish an A/R balance pattern, which is a useful cash forecasting tool. An A/R balance pattern specifies the percentage of credit sales in a time period, usually a month, that remain outstanding at the end of the month and each subsequent time period. A company's collection history determines the normal balance pattern. Management evaluates any shifts by comparing current patterns with historical norms. Companies also use balance patterns to project A/R levels, measure collection efficiency and forecast future cash inflows.

At the end of March, there will still be $50,000 of A/R outstanding (uncollected) from January's sales. This is forecast as follows:

January Sales			=	$ 250,000.00
Collected in: January = (.05 x $250,000)			=	$ 12,500.00
Collected in: February	=	(.40 x $250,000)	=	$ 100,000.00
Collected in: March	=	(.35 x $250,000)	=	$ 87,500.00
Total Collections			=	$ 200,000.00

Total Outstanding Receivables from January Sales

= $ 250,000 – $ 200,000 = $50,000

An alternative method is to multiply the percentage of sales collected three months after sale (.20) by the total amount outstanding ($250,000) as follows: .

.20 x $250,000 = $50,000.

The above example assumes all receivables are collected on a timely basis. In the real world, a certain percentage of the receivables would also be past due or bad debts. An A/R balance pattern may be adjusted to reflect these items.

EXHIBIT 7.4 – EXAMPLE OF A RECEIVABLES BALANCE PATTERN

Month Sales	Sales	Remaining Accounts Receivable from Month Sales at the End of March	Remaining Accounts Receivable as a % of Month Sales
January	$250,000	$50,000	20%
February	$300,000	$165,000	55%
March	$400,000	$380,000	95%
April	$500,000		

The total outstanding accounts receivable balance at the end of March is:
$595,000 = ($50,000 + $165,000 + $380,000)

The estimate of cash inflows for April = 5% of April sales + 40% of March sales + 35% of February sales + 20% of January sales:

Estimated April inflows = (.05 x $500,000)
+ (.40 x $400,000)
+ (.35 x $300,000)
+ (.20 x $250,000)
= $340,000

Exhibit 7.4 gives an example of a company whose sales are collected as follows:

- 5% of sales collected in the current month of sale
- 40% of sales collected in the month after sale
- 35% of sales collected two months after sale
- 20% of sales collected three months after sale

H. Financing A/R

A/R, a major component of current assets, is financed in a variety of ways. A company that offers trade credit can borrow unsecured funds from a financial institution to support A/R if the company has sufficient cash flow to justify an unsecured line. If a company cannot finance A/R with unsecured borrowings, it may pledge A/R as collateral and borrow on a secured basis. Commonly referred to as asset-based lending, this method of financing is based on the quality of the receivables. A lender evaluates the receivables to determine those acceptable as collateral for a loan. The loan is then repaid as the company collects the receivables.

Large companies, particularly those with finance subsidiaries such as automobile and credit card companies, bundle and issue securities backed by the receivables. This is known as securitization. Securitization allows a company to free up capital and enhance creditworthiness by using consumers' installment payments to pay off the securitized instrument's principal and interest.

Some companies establish a wholly owned subsidiary (known as a captive finance subsidiary) to perform credit operations and obtain A/R financing for the sale of products. Because receivables represent a significant proportion of current assets, operating a captive finance subsidiary enhances the parent's liquidity and allows capital to be obtained at a lower cost.

Another approach to financing receivables is to use third-party financing. A company collects the information necessary to complete a credit application from a customer and forwards the information to a financial institution. The financial institution decides whether or not to grant credit.

Because of the administrative costs involved, companies that use third-party financing tend to manufacture and market big-ticket items such as production machinery. Although third-party financing frees up capital, it does mean a company relinquishes control over the credit granting decision, thus foregoing direct marketing opportunities. It also means the company may have to discount the price of the goods sold in order to compensate the third party, thus foregoing potential income.

1. B2B Credit Cards

A company may also take credit cards as payment for goods and services from commercial customers in a B2B environment.

(A detailed discussion about credit cards is in a B2B environment Chapter 8, Payment Systems.)

Typically, a company receives a payment, less the merchant discount, one to two business days following the transaction. The merchant discount is the amount a credit card company charges a seller for the service and varies depending on the average dollar amount of a sale. The higher the average sale, the lower the discount. Per-item transaction charges may also apply.

The advantages of using credit cards rather than maintaining A/R in a B2B setting are as follows:

- The seller bears none of the direct costs of running a credit department.
- The seller does not have to finance A/R.
- The third party usually absorbs bad-debt losses.
- Sales typically increase by making it easier for customers to charge purchases.

The disadvantages of using credit cards for customer financing are as follows:

- The seller relinquishes control over the credit decision.
- The seller loses the promotional opportunity by not having access to a list of credit customers.
- The seller incurs the cost of the discount and transaction fees. Transaction fees vary depending on the method of transmission (terminal, Internet, paper), the average size of the sale, the total volume, the type of card used (a credit card versus a procurement card) and the type of business or industry.

2. Factoring

Factoring involves the outright sale of receivables to a factor, a company that specializes in the financing and management of receivables. In most factoring arrangements, the buyer of the receivables has no recourse to the seller. "No recourse" or "without recourse" means that the factor must absorb the loss if a customer fails to pay. However, in some cases, the factoring arrangement stipulates the factor has recourse, in which case the seller is liable for the bad debts the factor is unable to collect. Most factoring is performed on a notification basis. In other words, the seller must notify customers that the account has been sold because the payment is remitted directly to the factor.

3. Private Label Financing

In private label financing, a third party operates the credit function in the name of the seller rather than the seller administering a credit program in-house. From the customer's perspective, the credit appears to be arranged through the seller. Private label financing allows the seller to retain many of the promotional aspects of conducting credit functions while incurring none of the costs in maintaining a credit operation and/or financing A/R. At the same time, the seller does not receive the full face value of the sale and may lose the authority to decide which customers should receive credit.

I. Cash Application

Cash application is the process of applying a customer's payment against outstanding invoices or receivables. This is typically performed on either an open item system or a balance forward system.

Advantages and Disadvantages of Factoring	
Advantages	**Disadvantages**
■ Cash flow from the sales of receivables grows automatically with an increase in sales. ■ The cost of maintaining a credit department is reduced or eliminated. ■ The uncertainty in the timing of payments is reduced. ■ The range of customers to whom a company can grant credit is extended because the factor can share the risk with the company. ■ The credit-extension process is improved when the factor has access to information that enables more credit to be granted with fewer delinquencies.	■ High fees may be charged, particularly in without recourse agreements, which is a problem for companies in narrow profit margin industries. ■ The seller loses control over who is granted credit, which may require their internal credit department to reevaluate customers rejected by the factor. ■ A perception exists in the market place that factoring conveys a sign of financial weakness. However, factoring is a standard practice in certain industries and countries that have a long cash conversion cycle, such as furniture manufacturing and the garment industry.

1. Open Item

An open item system is most commonly used in B2B sales. Each invoice sent to a customer is recorded in the A/R file. When a payment is received, it is matched with the specific invoices being paid and any payment discrepancies (discounts, allowances, adjustments, returns, etc.) are noted. Remittance information, which typically accompanies payments, indicates which invoices are being paid, as well as any adjustments to the payment. This application process may be manual or automated or a combination of both.

Many companies have automated cash application programs that take the payment and remittance information and, using a series of algorithms, apply the payments by matching each to specific invoices. A high rate of successful automated applications greatly reduces the manual effort required to complete the cash application process. Developments in electronic invoice presentment and payment (EIPP) are discussed later in this chapter.

Lockbox processors may transmit payment and remittance data to a company to facilitate the cash application process. One common service is to capture the data from the magnetic ink character recognition (MICR) line of the check. Elements captured include the drawee bank's transit routing number, the payor's bank account number and the dollar amount of the check. The transit routing number and the bank account number are used to identify the customer through a database maintained by the receiving company. The lockbox processor may also capture additional customer information manually or automatically from the optical character recognition (OCR) line of a pre-encoded payment stub. Additional customer information may include such items as invoice numbers, amounts paid, customer account numbers, remitter's name, discounts and adjustments taken, dates and other pertinent information.

Some lockbox processors access a company's A/R system information during lockbox processing in order to locate an account number. Other processors attempt to match payments and invoices, prior to data transmission, using information provided by the company or encoded on payment stubs. Another recent development is the increased use of imaging to capture and transmit remittance information. Such services are designed to improve the accuracy and timeliness of the cash application process. Imaging is also used in a customer service environment to provide online information for handling customer inquiries and for researching payment disputes.

2. Balance Forward

A balance forward system is used most often by companies selling goods and services to individual consumers. In a balance forward system, a credit limit is established for each individual. As purchases are made or services are provided, the A/R outstanding balance increases. When payments are made, the A/R balance is reduced accordingly.

J. Legislation Affecting Credit and Collections

1. Pricing and Interest Charge Restrictions

The Robinson-Patman Act (1936) specifically prohibits price discrimination among customers where a cost basis cannot be demonstrated as the reason for a price difference. In cases where cost differences can be substantiated (e.g., higher costs for shipping and handling or lower costs for volume discounts), different credit terms for different customers are acceptable. Because the extension of credit is a benefit to the buyer, credit terms are considered part of the price of the product or service being sold. Also, usury laws, which vary significantly from state to state, restrict the interest rates or penalty fees that companies can charge on installment credit.

2. Consumer and Commercial Credit Legislation

A number of laws regulate the statement of terms, the credit analysis and approval process, and the collection practices that can be employed when selling to consumers on a credit basis. Among the most important federal legislation and regulations are the following:

- **Truth in Lending Act (1969):** This Act requires lenders to disclose the annual percentage rate (APR) and the total dollar cost on loans.
- **Fair Credit Reporting Act (1971):** This Act enables consumers to access the information contained in credit reports at little or no cost.

- **Fair Credit Billing Act (1975):** This Act is an amendment to the Truth in Lending Act and protects charge account customers from billing errors. Individuals are permitted to use the same legal defenses against banks or third-party credit card companies that can be used against merchants.

- **Equal Credit Opportunity Act (1975):** This Act prohibits creditors from discriminating against credit applicants on the basis of sex, marital status, race, color, religion, national origin, age or receipt of public assistance.

- **Fair Debt Collection Practices Act (1978):** This Act is designed to eliminate abusive and unfair debt collection practices such as threats of financial ruin, loss of job, damage to reputation and harassing telephone calls.

3. Uniform Commercial Code (UCC)

In general, revolving credit, installment credit, and financed sales transactions are covered under the provisions of the UCC. The UCC is the model for many state laws pertaining to commerce.

4. Bankruptcy and Reorganization

The Federal Bankruptcy Reform Act of 1978 established a federal bankruptcy court system with exclusive jurisdiction over bankruptcy cases. Under this Act, a company may file a petition for liquidation under Chapter 7 or for reorganization under Chapter 11. Court acceptance of the petition protects the debtor from legal actions by creditors.

When a company files for Chapter 7, all remaining assets are liquidated and the company no longer exists. When a company files for Chapter 11, it is allowed to reorganize under court protection, to restructure debts and to emerge from bankruptcy after certain conditions imposed by the court are met. Chapter 13 is the consumer counterpart for individuals that Chapter 11 is for corporations.

K. Developments in Credit and A/R

There have been many new developments in credit and A/R management. These developments include increased use of electronic commerce, electronic invoice or electronic bill presentment and payment via the Internet, and outsourcing of receivables.

- **Electronic Commerce (e-commerce) and Electronic Data Interchange (EDI)**
  Given the increased use of e-commerce and EDI, a company's A/R system must be able to process electronic payments and remittance information

in order to properly apply payments. Because of the increased remittance data accompanying the payment in an e-commerce/EDI environment, the cash application rate may be increased and exception processing may be reduced.

(A more detailed discussion of e-commerce and EDI are in Chapter 12, Electronic Commerce.)

- **Electronic Invoice Presentment and Payment (EIPP)**

Many companies and banks are implementing EIPP systems in a B2B setting that allows electronic statements to be sent to commercial customers and invoices to be paid by electronic means. In most cases, these applications are Web-based and usable by anyone with Internet access. However, current systems still include only a limited number of both billers and customers. The consumer version of EIPP is referred to as electronic bill presentment and payment (EBPP).

- **Outsourcing of A/R**

Companies outsourcing A/R functions have traditionally utilized factoring companies. However, the development of new Internet-based services is rapidly changing the market. Banks and other third parties are able to offer low-cost processing and management of the A/R function. In addition, the increasing use of purchasing or procurement cards is helping to convert many small, manually processed payments into a single large dollar payment with automated remittance information attached.

III. INVENTORY MANAGEMENT

Inventory carried by a company impacts a company's production and sales activities, which are, in turn, responsible for the majority of cash inflows. The manner in which inventory is managed affects the length of the company's cash flow cycle, as well as the type of cash flow forecasting a company employs and the accuracy of estimations.

The timing and accuracy of cash flows also affects a company's liquidity needs and how liquidity is maintained. Although inventory management is generally the direct responsibility of marketing or manufacturing managers, the treasury manager is primarily responsible for the financing of inventory. The ability to use inventory as collateral for a loan is directly related to the type of inventory and how it is managed.

A. Elements of Basic Inventory Policy

The inventory policy of most companies includes elements such as:

- The reasons for holding inventory
- The types of inventory held
- The levels of inventory
- The costs and benefits associated with holding inventory
- The financing of inventory

1. Why Companies Hold Inventory

Two stages of the operating cycle of a business—the acquisition and conversion stages—involve the purchase of raw materials or finished goods and the manufacturing and/or distribution of a final product. These stages often involve time-consuming processing steps and the physical transport and delivery of goods. Inventories enable a company to plan these activities so that they can be scheduled in as seamless a manner as possible. Several specific drivers affect the size of inventories maintained.

One of the primary reasons for holding inventory is to provide the goods required for the expected level of a company's sales activities during its normal operating and production cycles. Inventory may be held because:

- It is not possible to receive delivery during certain periods of production (such as nighttime manufacturing or weekend shifts).
- It is uneconomical to have materials delivered in very small quantities at infrequent intervals.
- Suppliers might not agree to deliver small quantities.
- The economics involved in the manufacturing process may require large production runs, requiring substantial on-hand inventory to insure that a full run is completed without material shortage.

Inventory may also be held for three other reasons as a precautionary measure, for speculative purposes and to meet supplier requirements:

- As a precautionary measure, excess inventory provides a cushion for changing levels of demand and allows a company to more easily provide the level of goods desired by customers.
- Speculative purposes are related to situations where a company holds inventory in anticipation of price increases or product shortages. This occurs most often in companies whose production materials are commodities that experience volatile price swings and/or volatile patterns of availability (e.g., gold or fuel). The downside in holding excessive inventory for speculative purposes is that the prices may also drop rapidly, resulting in a company holding inventory that has declined significantly in value.
- Finally, a company may hold inventory to meet requirements set by suppliers for dealers or franchisees in order to maintain exclusive distribution rights.

2. Types of Inventory

Most inventories are connected with some part of the company's production process. Any item held in stock that links two or more production processes can also be thought of as inventory. The types of inventory are diagrammed in Exhibit 7.5 and are generally catagorized as follows:

- Raw materials
- Work in progress (WIP)
- Finished goods
- Scrap or obsolete items
- Stores and supplies

EXHIBIT 7.5 – TYPES OF INVENTORY

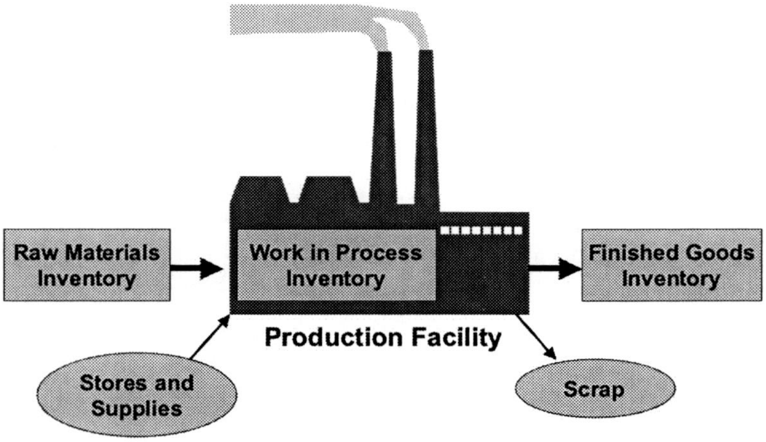

Raw materials inventory represents the basic input to the manufacturing process and allows for arrivals to be separated from production scheduling. Partially completed components, such as sub-assemblies, also fall into this category and give the company more flexibility in the production process.

Work in progress (WIP) inventory represents items or materials that are in the process of being manufactured. This type of inventory allows different phases of the production process to be separated. The use and amount of WIP inventory are generally functions of the production process. A short, continuous process, such as chemical production, may have very little WIP, whereas a long batch-production process, such as furniture manufacture, has a large level of WIP. WIP inventory is also held as a buffer between production stages having different processing speeds.

Another form of inventory is finished goods, which represents completed items or materials available for sale. This type of inventory allows a company to fill orders when received rather than depending upon product completion to satisfy customer demands. Finished goods inventory also enables a company to more easily manage highly variable or unpredictable demand levels. This is extremely valuable in a retail environment because it allows the retailer to maintain a wide variety of goods available for customers. It is important to note a significant difference in the management of finished goods inventory for generic products versus customized products. Due to limited resale value, customized product inventories must be managed much more tightly than more generic, easily sold goods.

In some industries, such as steel and aluminum manufacturing, scrap from production can be reused in later batches or sold to recyclers. Also, a portion of a company's inventories may become obsolete or damaged, especially in environments where there are rapid changes in existing products or introductions of new products. Obsolete or scrap inventories must be identified and dealt with independently. These inventories may be turned into cash through sales to scrap dealers or by taking tax deductions through write-offs.

The final category is represented by stores and supplies inventories, sometimes referred to as indirect purchases. These items are used in support of the production process rather than being used directly. Examples are lubricating oils or maintenance materials for production machinery in a manufacturing business, or paper and other office supplies in a service business.

3. Just-In-Time (JIT) Inventory Management

The just-in-time (JIT) approach to inventory management attempts to minimize the level of inventory by altering the costs or uncertainties that underlie the motives for holding inventory. JIT methodology recognizes that inventory turns from an asset into a liability fairly quickly. JIT is, therefore, not merely an inventory management system but rather a production/business philosophy that treats inventory as being undesirable, a cover-up for poor inventory planning or for inventory location and accuracy problems, inferior supplier quality and/or unbalanced production processes.

JIT systems are often coupled with material planning systems (MPS) that bring together long-range production planning with the current flow of materials through the production process. In today's competitive environment, a company can often negotiate arrangements with suppliers to provide a continuous level of production materials on short notice, resulting in reduced carrying costs for the raw materials used to generate the finished goods. Some retailers link POS (point-of-sale) equipment to suppliers so that sales of specific merchandise can be tracked for automated reordering. JIT and MPS methods allow for better, time-phased methods of planning, which facilitate adjustment to changing costs.

The three basic goals of a JIT system are to:

- Eliminate waste
- Standardize the production process
- Continuously improve quality

JIT offers significant benefits to companies in the form of improved supplier relationships, lower transaction costs and better overall planning. In some cases JIT implementation has resulted in a fundamental restructuring of traditional customer/supplier relationships. Two examples of this restructuring are supplier-managed replenishment programs and paid-on-production processes.

In supplier-managed replenishment programs, the supplier maintains and tracks the inventory of materials that it provides to a customer. As the inventory is used, the supplier bills the customer for the items and replenishes the supply. Title to the product is transferred at the shipping dock. The rationale for this system is that the supplier is better able to track trends in inventory usage and to manage levels of inventory more efficiently, thus reducing costs for both the supplier and the customer.

The paid-on-production process is similar to supplier-managed replenishment programs but has some specific implications for financial managers. Paid-on-production is the process by which a payment record is created for goods and/or services based on usage rather than shipment. It is similar to consignment sales in retail but it is employed in a manufacturing environment. Typically, there is only one supplier, so title to the product is transferred during the manufacturing process rather than at the shipping dock.

The unique demand of the JIT manufacturing environment has a major impact on the treasury and reporting functions of a company, especially with respect to the information system for financial management. JIT implementations often require changes to the accounting methods used for inventory and impact the timing of purchases. Companies using JIT purchase more frequently and in smaller amounts, which increases the number of transactions that need to be monitored and recorded. The process of costing the inventory becomes more difficult for companies using JIT. Most use a rolling average of actual costs rather than traditional transaction-by-transaction cost accounting methods.

4. Benefits and Costs of Inventory

Inventories provide some benefits by separating elements of the purchasing, production, and shipment processes. One of the primary benefits of holding sufficient inventory is in the reduction of stock-out costs; that is, reducing lost sales due to a lack of sufficient inventory on hand. In a more positive sense, inventory (especially of finished goods) may provide a competitive advantage over other companies and result in increased customer goodwill, higher sales levels and increased profits.

There are also costs involved in maintaining varying levels of inventory, such as set-up or order costs and holding costs. Set-up or order costs are transaction costs incurred in obtaining a new batch of inventory, such as supplies for setting up a new production run. Holding costs are those related to carrying the inventory, such as physical storage and handling costs, insurance, taxes and the opportunity cost of funds invested in inventory.

Generally, the objective of inventory management is to minimize the total net costs associated with the inventory while meeting a desired level of production and/or customer service. Several models, called economic order quantity (EOQ) models, calculate the optimal level of inventory, given certain ordering and holding costs. However, EOQ models are somewhat difficult to apply because they do not account for real-world complications such as volume discounts and blanket purchase orders with schedule of receipts.

B. Inventory Financing

When inventory cannot be financed as part of the general working capital requirements, financing alternatives may be tied directly to the amount of inventory. These financing alternatives are likely to be used by companies experiencing rapid growth, by companies with seasonal operations or by companies that are less financially secure. The amount of credit available, as a percentage of the value of the inventory, depends upon the nature of the inventory, the inventory's location, when and where transfer of title occurs, and the existence of a secondary market. Financing is usually not available for WIP inventory, only for raw materials and finished goods.

A significant portion of inventory for many companies is financed by accounts payable (A/P) or trade credit granted by suppliers. This represents a spontaneous source of financing, which increases as the amount of inventory increases due to a higher level of operations and decreases as the inventory declines due to a lower level of operations. Delaying payments to suppliers can sometimes extend the amount of financing provided. The opportunity cost for this form of financing is the cost of lost cash discounts, lost goodwill with suppliers and lost sales due to delayed shipments. In many cases, suppliers refuse to ship additional products unless outstanding invoices are paid promptly. These delays often result in production and sales problems.

Another form of inventory financing is the use of collateralized loans. These loans may be arranged using inventory as collateral for a loan, with the lender providing financing for some predetermined percentage of the inventory's value. The company's cash flows are viewed as the primary repayment source for collateralized loans. The inventory is viewed only as a secondary repayment source or as a means of reducing the amount of loss in the event of default. The claim against the inventory is usually perfected in the form of a lien via a UCC-1 statement filing. The cost of these types of loans might be higher than that of an unsecured loan because of the additional expense incurred by the lender in perfecting and monitoring the claim.

Inventory financing may also involve asset-based loans. Asset-based lending is based on the value of the inventory rather than on the general financial strength of the borrower. To enforce the claim on the inventory, the lender typically takes physical possession of it in the event the company defaults on the loan or files bankruptcy. The lender may store the inventory at a public warehouse or through a field warehouse arrangement. These warehouses are generally secure storage facilities where commodities, raw materials or finished goods are held until a warehouse receipt is presented. In cases where the inventory is directly supporting a loan, a lender may release the materials only after the portion of the loan supported by inventory has been paid.

Floor planning is a type of asset-based lending used for very high-value durable goods such as automobiles, trucks or heavy equipment. Loans are made against each individual item and recorded by serial number. The loan is not repaid until the item is sold. Floor plan lenders typically require periodic inventory audits.

IV. ACCOUNTS PAYABLE (A/P)

The primary responsibility of A/P is to verify incoming invoices and to authorize payments, a process some companies call vouchering. This process generally involves the traditional "three-way match," in which an invoice is matched to both an approved purchase order and receiving information. This ensures that the items being billed to the company are authorized purchases from an approved vendor and that all items are received in satisfactory condition. The A/P function also monitors compliance with trade payment terms. An example of compliance with trade payment terms is paying by a postmark date either to take advantage of a trade discount opportunity or to avoid late-payment charges or interest penalties.

Once the approval process is complete, the invoice is vouchered for payment. In a typical B2B environment, multiple invoices are often combined in a single payment. Once approved, the payments are forwarded to the treasury manager or disbursements area where checks or electronic payments are generated.

There are two critical areas of coordination between treasury management and A/P management. The first is the communication from A/P to treasury regarding the invoices vouchered for payment. The second is the communication from treasury back to A/P regarding the reconciliation of cleared items.

Companies with integrated enterprise resource planning (ERP) or accounting systems with treasury management modules are typically able to integrate these functions easily. However, many companies use either separate systems for disbursement management or treasury information software provided by banks. This software may not interface as easily with the A/P ledger. Customized interfaces or middleware (in a client-server environment) are required to facilitate the transfer of information between applications.

A company's net cost of making payments includes both opportunity costs and the administrative costs of managing the A/P and disbursements process. Opportunity costs include:

- The cost of excess borrowing or lost investment income when idle balances exist in disbursement accounts
- The cost of paying bills late, such as lost discounts or late fees
- The cost of paying bills early, such as short-term investment interest income lost or extra short-term borrowing interest expense incurred

Administrative costs of managing the A/P and disbursement process include:

- Overhead costs of the A/P department
- Fixed costs of the disbursement system, such as account-maintenance and balance reporting
- Variable disbursement costs, including checks paid, account reconciliation, stop payments, fraud prevention, and zero-balance transfers
- Overdraft costs, including the monetary costs of overdrawing disbursement accounts
- The cost of possible damage to a banking relationship

A. Disbursement System Considerations

In designing a disbursement system, an organization must keep three goals in mind:

- The ability to access information: Obtaining access to timely and accurate information regarding the status of disbursement accounts and disbursement clearings enables a company to manage its cash position more effectively.

- The ability to prevent fraud: Preventing fraud means protecting company funds from unauthorized use through written policies and internal controls, prompt bank reconciliation, the use of quality check stock and banking services such as positive pay.
- The ability to maintain good relationships with payees: Maintaining good relationships with payees means ensuring on-time payments to employees, vendors, suppliers, lenders, tax agencies, bondholders and shareholders.

A/P and disbursement systems may be centralized, decentralized, or a combination of both. Each system has distinct advantages and disadvantages in relation to the three goals of a disbursement system: access to information, fraud prevention and payee relationship management.

1. Centralized A/P and Disbursement Systems

- **Advantages:** In a centralized system, the A/P and disbursement functions are located in a single area (either at headquarters or at a centralized processing center). From this centralized location, a company receives all inbound invoices, approves them for payment, issues payments, and funds and reconciles accounts. A centralized disbursement system makes it easier to maintain control, to obtain information, to concentrate excess cash, to provide better access to cash position information and to improve forecasting accuracy.
- **Disadvantages:** The principal disadvantage of a centralized A/P and disbursement system is its potential negative impact on payee relationships. Centralized systems often result in delayed payments to vendors and suppliers and/or lost discount opportunities. Technology developments and improved access to information have helped to reduce some of the problems in this area. There is also a need for coordination between the central A/P department and the company's field offices in order to resolve payment disputes.

2. Decentralized A/P and Disbursement Systems

In a decentralized system, the A/P and disbursement functions are managed at the local or regional level. Field office managers approve invoices for payment, issue payments and reconcile accounts. Additionally, in a decentralized system, checks are often drawn on a local or regional bank.

- **Advantages:** This system gives greater autonomy to field office managers. As a result, the primary advantage is improved relationships with vendors and suppliers because items clear quickly and disputes can be resolved locally. In addition, it is easier to take advantage of discount terms that require payments to be made in a shorter timeframe (typically 10 days).

- **Disadvantages:** The primary disadvantages of a decentralized system are all of the advantages of a centralized system; namely, the loss of control over information, the lost opportunity from concentrating funds to reduce borrowing expense and increase investment returns, and the increased likelihood of unauthorized disbursements. Other disadvantages include the increased possibility of excess or idle balances at the local bank level; the increased difficulty of obtaining information about a company's day-to-day cash position and cash outflows; and increased transfer, reconciliation and administrative costs.

3. Decentralized A/P and Disbursement System with Centralized Clearing

Some companies use a hybrid system whereby local or regional managers oversee the A/P process and issue checks but checks are drawn on a centralized disbursement bank. This provides increased levels of control along with reduced excess balances, improved cash position reporting and forecasting, and increased opportunities for volume discounts on bank disbursement services.

Many banks offer account reconciliation programs designed specifically for hybrid A/P and disbursement systems. These disbursement services are commonly referred to as high order prefix or division sort programs. Using the auxiliary field on a business check, individual field offices, branches, or divisions are assigned a unique identifier. This number allows headquarters to obtain reports that track individual disbursements by location.

4. Control and Fraud Prevention

Disbursement fraud is a significant problem primarily because of technological advances that have increased the frequency, sophistication, and ease of creating fraudulent checks. Such advances include color copiers, high-resolution laser printers and document scanners designed for use with a personal computer. As a result, control and fraud prevention are an important responsibility of both A/P and treasury operations. Control and fraud prevention measures include the following:

- Developing and implementing written policies and procedures for the creation and distribution of checks
- Separating functional authority for collection and disbursement of funds
- Separating expense approval, check-signing authority, and account reconciliation responsibilities
- Using safety paper and watermarks that are difficult to reproduce on check stock
- Using reputable check printing companies
- Storing check stock and signature plates in separate secured areas with controlled access
- Securing canceled checks or switching to check safekeeping with CD-ROM output
- Using either printing processes that do not require preprinted check stock (such as laser printing of checks and MICR lines) or preprinted stock that incorporates micro-print or other safety features
- Using positive pay, a service that matches check serial numbers and dollar amounts against the company's issue file, thereby enabling a financial institution to determine which checks can be paid and which should be returned

- Setting a maximum dollar amount limit on checks issued from each type of account so that checks issued above a limit are returned to the depositor as being unauthorized
- Increasing the use of electronic payment methods and utilizing appropriate security features
- Using an electronic payment authorization service (similar to positive pay for checks) to protect against fraudulent ACH debits
- Reconciling bank accounts on a timely basis
- Monitoring other types of fraud such as fraudulent endorsements and holder in due course
- Imposing strict control over a company's master file of payees

B. Recent A/P Developments

Several relatively new services have an important impact on the operation and management of A/P.

1. Integrated or Comprehensive A/P

An integrated or comprehensive A/P service allows a company to outsource all or part of its A/P and/or disbursements functions. One of the common approaches to integrated or comprehensive A/P occurs when a company sends a single data file to a financial services provider (FSP) containing a list of all payments to be made. The file contains information on when and to whom to issue a payment, as well as instructions on the payment method to be used.

In an alternative approach, an FSP maintains a database of a company's payees that includes detailed information such as preferred payment methods, specific remittance information, and receiving financial institutions. The database is periodically updated as new payees are added or an existing payee's remittance profile changes. In this approach, as a company makes a disbursement, it sends only limited payment information to the FSP.

With either approach, the FSP issues the payments immediately or warehouses them until a future date as instructed by the data file. A company using an integrated or comprehensive payables service is, in effect, outsourcing the disbursement function, thereby potentially reducing the overall cost of A/P operations.

2. Purchasing/Procurement Cards

Many companies are implementing the use of purchasing or procurement cards (P-cards) for the purchase of supplies, inventory, equipment, and service contracts. P-cards differ from corporate travel and entertainment (T&E) cards that do not restrict the use of a card to specific business purposes. P-cards are issued to employees with restrictions on both the types of purchases allowed and individual spending limits. In many cases, employees are even limited to specific vendors or suppliers.

Among the advantages of a P-card are:

- Increased cost savings by eliminating the processing of high-volume, low-dollar purchasing orders and payments
- Improved control over expenditures by applying spending parameters before purchases are made rather than through the expense-reimbursement process
- Improved vendor and supplier relations through earlier payments
- Improved reporting on spending with specific vendors, which aids in the negotiation of more favorable discounts
- More timely access to critical goods and services

3. Imaging Services

Imaging technology is a major component of many disbursement services. Both the front and the back of a check (or any other business document) can be captured and converted into digital information using optical scanning. Check images may be transmitted to a company's computer system for storage or sent to a fax machine. Alternatively, check images are frequently housed in a bank database to which a company is granted access for the purpose of research or customer service inquiries.

Imaging services are particularly useful in conjunction with positive pay. Such services help a company to identify potential unauthorized check activity and to make time-critical pay/no-pay decisions. Images of checks can be obtained in a more timely fashion than photocopies, allowing companies to respond quickly to inquiries from customers, employees, and vendors. Additionally, many financial institutions provide customers with check images on a CD-ROM.

4. Internet Applications

The rapid expansion of Internet services has resulted in a wide variety of A/P and disbursement applications for companies of all sizes. Services are offered either as part of a total accounting and ERP package or as a stand-alone system. The Web offers a mechanism for trading partners to send invoices via a Web page. These invoices can then be paid via an ACH transaction with remittance information returned via the Internet.

(A more detailed discussion of Internet applications is in Chapter 12, Electronic Commerce.)

All of the services discussed above represent major advancements in automating the A/P and disbursements function, the principal objectives of which are to reduce costs by eliminating paper-based manual processes and to improve payee relationships by reducing payment delays.

Test Your Understanding

These chapter questions are provided to test your understanding of the information in the text. They are neither examples of CTP examination questions nor are they in the examination format.

Answers are on pages 581–584.

1. What are the four steps of effective credit management?
2. What are the steps involved in establishing credit standards?
3. Discuss the constraints and/or influences on a company's credit policies.
4. Compare the implications of strict versus lenient credit standards.
5. What are the five C's of credit?
6. Describe the credit scoring process.
7. Discuss the most common type of commercial trade credit used in the U.S.
8. Define the following credit terms: COD, discount, seasonal dating and consignment.
9. Why is it important to monitor individual accounts receivable?
10. What is DSO and how is it calculated?
11. What is the A/R balance pattern and how is it used?
12. What are the primary methods used to finance accounts receivable?
13. What is factoring and what role does recourse play in factoring arrangements?
14. Describe a balance forward system and what types of companies might use it.
15. What are some of the recent developments in credit and A/R management?
16. What is the primary reason for holding inventory?

17 What are the five types of inventory?

18. Describe the just-in-time (JIT) inventory approach.

19. What are the critical areas of coordination between treasury and accounts payable and how might software help in this coordination?

20. What are the primary considerations in designing a disbursement system?

21. What is imaging technology, and how is it used?

CHAPTER 8
Payment Systems

I. INTRODUCTION

A payment system transfers monetary value from one party to another. In the U.S., payments are made using cash, checks, credit or debit cards and electronic systems. While checks are the most widely used non-cash method of payment in the U.S. for small-value transactions, check usage has been declining since the mid-1990s in large part because of credit and debit cards. Measured on a per-item basis (i.e., volume), the majority of U.S. payments are made by check. However, measured on a per-dollar basis (i.e., value), the majority of U.S. payments are made through one of three electronic payment networks: the Automated Clearing House (ACH), Fedwire and the Clearing House for Interbank Payment System (CHIPS). Exhibit 8.1 shows the relative volume and dollar value of transactions by major payment type.

EXHIBIT 8.1 – PROFILE OF U.S. PAYMENTS

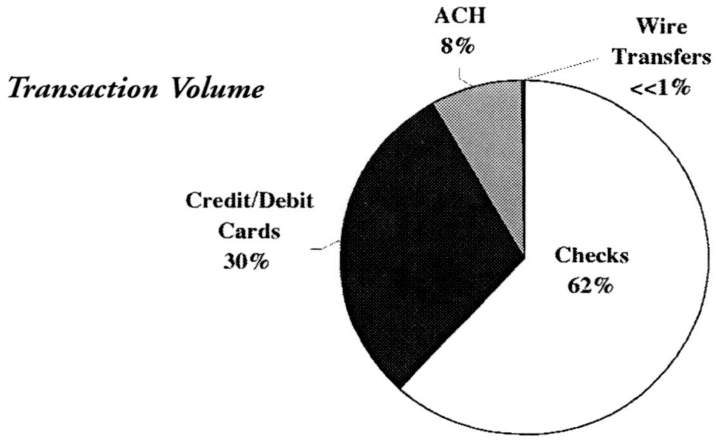

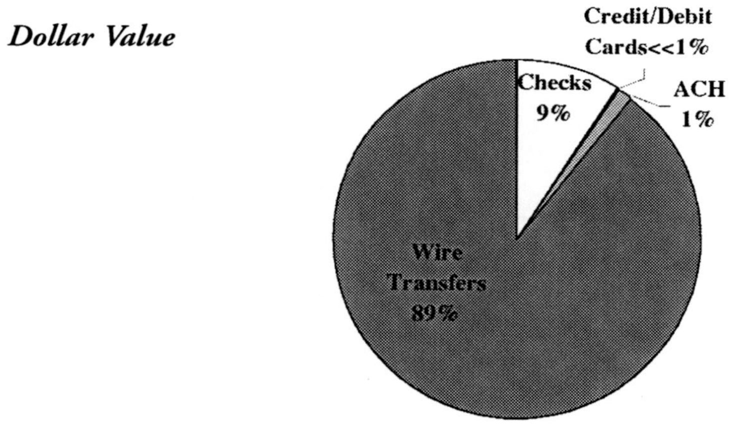

II. OVERVIEW OF PAYMENT METHODS

U.S. payment instruments are cleared and settled through several different mechanisms:

- The first step in the payment process is the issuance of payment instructions. The instructions are captured in a payment instrument (such as a check, payable through draft, money order, travelers check, etc.), which serves as a set of instructions for the transfer of funds between a payor, the party making the payment, and a payee, the recipient of the funds.
- Payment generation is the process by which the actual item is created.
- Clearing is the process by which a payment instrument and the required payment information are transferred from a payor's bank to a payee's bank.
- Settlement is the actual transfer of value from payor to payee.

This combination of a payment instrument, a clearing channel and a settlement mechanism constitutes a payment system. In the U.S., access to clearing and settlement systems is limited to financial institutions.

There are five non-cash payment systems in the U.S.:

- Checks and check-like instruments
- Credit, debit, and other types of cards
- ACH
- Fedwire
- CHIPS

The first three systems are used primarily for high-volume, low-value monetary transactions and are commonly referred to as retail payment systems. Large-dollar, same-day transfer systems such as Fedwire and CHIPS are used for low-volume, high-value monetary and book-entry security transfers and are commonly referred to as wholesale payment systems.

The payment process occurs in two steps, communication and settlement:.

- **Communication** is the transfer of instructions between the payee and payor banks through a clearing system. Using a check as an example of the clearing process, the information on the face of the check moves from the bank of deposit to the bank on which it is written or drawn.
- **Settlement** occurs when the depository bank account is credited and the drawee bank account is debited. At settlement, the payee's and payor's accounts are also credited and debited, respectively. Funds are typically

made available for use (a credit) or withdrawal (a debit) at settlement. Credit for deposited funds is considered provisional until finality. Provisional credit means that the depository institution may reverse a credit posted to an account if the payment instrument is returned or rejected by the drawee institution.

The concepts of settlement and finality are central to an understanding of payment systems. Settlement is final when a payment is unconditional and irrevocable. Finality varies, depending on the payment system and the parties involved in the transaction.

Often, there are provisions for return of payments, so finality is not assured until after the permitted return period has elapsed. Consumer payments made through the electronic retail payment systems (cards and ACH) are governed by Regulation E (Reg E), which provides consumers with considerable return periods for unauthorized charges (generally within 60 days of receipt of the statement with the unauthorized charges but may be longer under extenuating circumstances). However, wire transfer payments such as Fedwire settle in real-time and finality occurs immediately. Therefore, wire transfers are irrevocable and unconditional payment mechanisms.

The distinguishing characteristic of real-time settlement is that each transaction is processed when initiated rather than held for batch processing. There are three types of real-time settlement systems: gross, intraday and net:

- **Gross Settlement:** In a real-time gross settlement system (RTGS), each participating bank's position is adjusted on an item-by-item basis.
- **Intraday Settlement:** In a real-time intraday settlement system, each participating bank's position is adjusted at agreed upon intervals during the day.
- **Net Settlement:** In a real-time net settlement system, a bank's transactions are offset against those of the other system participants without any transfer of funds. As payments are received, they are matched against offsetting payments and released. If a match is not identified, movement of unmatched payments occurs at the end of the day. While net settlement payments are irrevocable, finality does not take place until funds are released. Exhibit 8.2 summarizes the relative properties of the payment systems with regard to payment size, settlement and finality.

III. PAPER-BASED PAYMENTS

The paper check is the oldest non-cash payment instrument in the U.S. and constitutes the largest number of payments. Of all payment systems, the paper-based system is the least efficient and the most susceptible to fraud.

A. The Check Clearing Process

The check clearing process begins with the deposit of a check into a payee's account at a financial institution. The bank of deposit or the payee encodes the check amount on the magnetic ink character recognition (MICR) line. Once encoded with special characters in magnetic ink on the lower portion of the check, the MICR line contains all of the information necessary to process the check through the check clearing system. The American

EXHIBIT 8.2 – CHARACTERISTICS OF THE PAYMENT SYSTEMS

	Average Payment Size (2000)	Typical Settlement Time	Maximum Return Time*	Return Risk	Security
Checks	$925	0 to 4 days	4 days	High	Low
Credit and Debit Cards	$69	0 to 2 days	0 if prior authorization is obtained	Moderate	Moderate
ACH	$1,010	1 to 2 days	2 days (debits) No returns on credits**	Moderate for debits	Moderately High
Wire Transfers	$3,500,000	Immediate	No returns	None	High

** Excluding Regulation E return provision for electronic consumer payments.*
*** Returns on credits may occur if Originating Depository Financial Institution (ODFI) fails on settlement date.*

Bankers Association (ABA) number, also known as the transit routing number (TRN), is preprinted on the MICR line. This nine-digit number identifies the drawee bank and provides the depository bank with the information it requires to route the check back to the drawee bank through the clearing system. Exhibit 8.3 illustrates a sample business check and the elements of the MICR line.

Encoded checks are sent through a reader/sorter that captures the MICR line information and sorts the checks based on the TRN. Checks are sorted according to the clearing channel and enter the clearing system as cash letters. A cash letter is a bundle of checks accompanied by a list of individual items and other control documents. In clearing systems, the bank of first deposit is referred to as the collecting bank; the institution on which the check is drawn is referred to as the paying bank or drawee bank. For settlement to occur, a check must be presented to and accepted by the paying bank. Thus, the key event in the check clearing process is presentment—the physical delivery of a check to the paying bank.

EXHIBIT 8.3 – SAMPLE BUSINESS CHECK

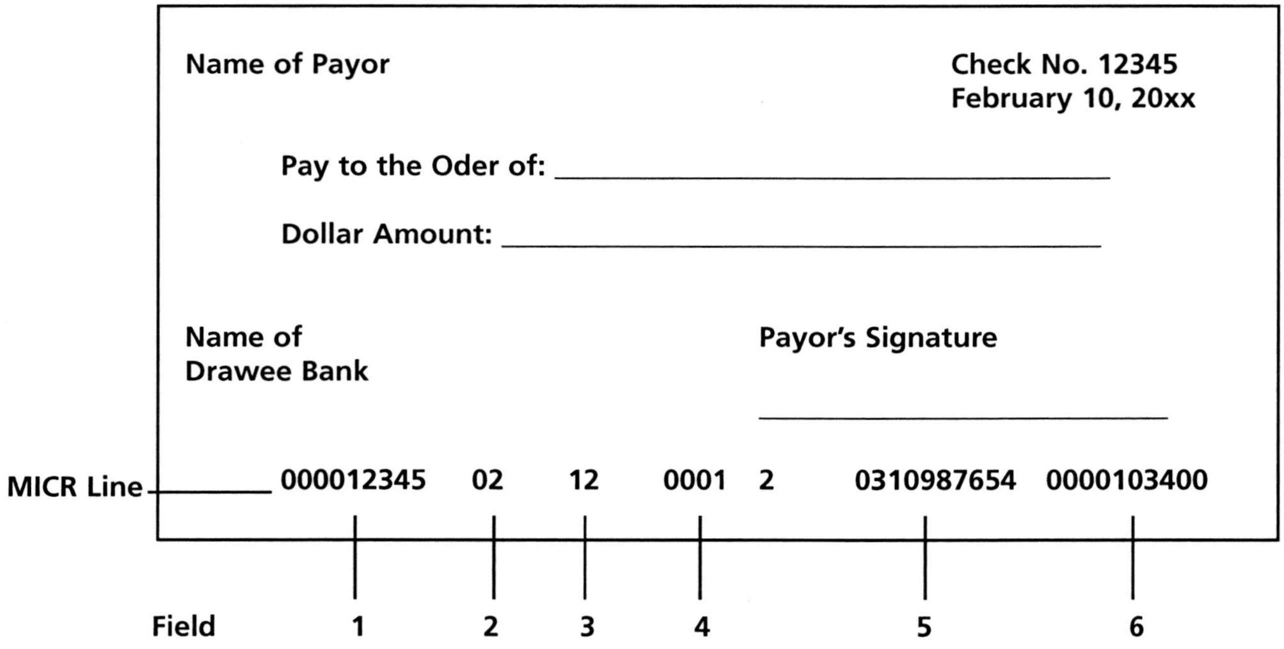

The MICR line contains information in a fixed format that allows the depository bank to route the check back to the drawee bank to identify the account and amount to debit. Fields 2-5 are called the transit routing (TR) number.

1. **Serial Number:** Also called the auxiliary on-us field on a business check
   - This number is frequently the check number.
   - It assists the drawee bank in providing a variety of account reconcilement services, such as sorting the cleared checks before returning them to the payor.
   - It may also be used for identification codes of divisions of subsidiaries.
   - It is a key to providing stop payment and positive pay services.

2. **Federal Reserve Bank Code:** Tow digits (01 to 12) identify the drawee bank's Federal Reserve district. Numbers greater than 12 identify a non-bank depository institution such as theft.

3. **Federal Reserve Office:** The first digit identifies the Fed branch responsible for handling the drawee bank. The second digit is the availability classification.

4. **Bank Identification Number:** Four digits make up the bank's ABA identification number. That number designates the bank location to which the item must be delivered. A number of banks have more than one identification number for the benefit of the automated routing process.

5. **Check Digit:** This digit, when combined with other numbers, enables the computer to verify the accuracy of the routing number for the benefit of the automated routing process.

6. **Payor's Account Number:** This number is assigned to the payor by the drawee bank.

7. **Encoded Amount of Check:** This number should agree with the amount placed on the check by the payor. The amount is typically encoded on the check by the depository bank and appears in the lower right hand corner of the processed check.

As a result of the Check Clearing for the 21st Century Act (Check 21), beginning in October 2004 the bank of first deposit can send a "substitute check" (generally referred to as an image replacement document or IRD) to any other bank in lieu of the original check. However, whether the check is delivered electronically or physically, the process of presentment and acceptance by the paying bank remains the same. The details of this Act are covered in detail in Chapter 3, U.S. Financial Environment.

At the time of presentment, value is subtracted from the paying bank's account with a Federal Reserve Bank, a correspondent bank or some other clearing channel. The amount of the check is also usually subtracted from the payor's account on the same business day. Following presentment, the paying bank reviews the account status and is responsible for inspecting the check for authorized signatures, a proper date, stop payment and positive pay instructions. Paying banks also review accounts for active status and adequate funds.

In practice, most check processing is automated and banks rely on account holders to report fraudulent endorsements and alterations. Stop payment and positive pay instructions are also incorporated into the bank's automated processing systems. Because checks are no longer manually inspected, post-dated and stale dated checks are generally honored.

The bank has until midnight local time on the banking day following presentment to conduct a review of the check and either to authorize final payment or to refuse payment and return the check to the bank of deposit. If the bank elects to return a check that exceeds $2,500, the collecting bank must be notified of the return by 4:00 p.m. on the second banking day following presentment. Returned checks, which are referred to as return items, may be re-deposited or charged back to the depositor's account once received by the collecting bank.

Clearing Channels

Banks utilize various channels for clearing checks back to paying institutions. Selection of a channel is a function of a bank's processing time, geographic location and the clearing agent's availability schedule. Availability, defined as the release of deposited funds for use, is granted to the collecting bank if the check reaches the endpoint (that is, the paying bank or the location established by the clearing agent) prior to a predefined deadline. Availability schedules define the number of days after deposit before funds become available for use by a depositor.

1. On-Us Check Clearing

On-us check clearing involves a single bank and occurs when a payee deposits a check in an account at the same bank on which it is drawn. The bank simultaneously debits the payor's account and credits the payee's account. The depositor receives same-day or immediate availability.

2. Interbank Check Clearing

Four clearing channels are available for clearing of interbank checks, which are checks drawn on institutions other than the bank of deposit. The four channels are a clearing house, a Federal Reserve Bank, a correspondent bank and a direct send.

- **Clearing House:** Clearing houses are either formal or informal associations formed by banks in a geographic area to permit the exchange of items drawn on the member participants. Representatives from member banks make daily, or sometimes more frequent, presentments at the clearing house. The net value (dollar amount of items submitted less items received, calculated on a bank-by-bank basis) is transferred between the banks by debiting and crediting correspondent accounts or through reserve accounts that each bank maintains with the local Federal Reserve Bank. The National Clearing House Association (NACHA) provides member banks nationwide access to many local clearing houses located across the country.

- **Federal Reserve Bank (Fed):** Among its many roles, the Fed also acts as a check-clearing agent. Each bank deposits checks received throughout the banking day into an account at a Federal Reserve Bank and receives a credit for the amount of the checks to the account it maintains at the local Fed. The Fed then transports the checks to the paying banks. Upon presentment, the Fed subtracts the amount of the checks from the paying bank's reserve account.

  In the process of clearing checks, banks sometimes receive availability from the Fed before the Fed generates the offsetting debit. The difference in timing between the availability granted a clearing bank and the actual presentment of the item to the drawee bank is called Fed float. Fed float represents interest-free loans to banks and, indirectly, to companies. The 1980 Depository Institutions Deregulation and Monetary Control Act (DIDMCA) mandated both the reduction of and the pricing for this benefit.

- **Correspondent Bank:** With correspondent bank clearing, the collecting bank maintains a depository account with another bank. The collecting bank sends checks to the correspondent bank, which presents the items to the paying bank through a local clearing house or the local Fed. The collecting bank's depository account at the correspondent bank is then credited with the proceeds of the checks.

- **Direct Send:** As an alternative to using the clearing channels above, banks may make arrangements to send cash letters directly to a paying bank or to a non-local Federal Reserve Bank. These arrangements enable banks to meet various deposit deadlines and achieve faster clearing times. The collecting bank maintains a depository account with the paying bank or non-local Fed, which is credited with the proceeds of the checks.

3. Other Check Clearing Considerations

- **Same-Day Settlement**

  A Federal Reserve rule requires that if a check is presented to a paying bank by 8:00 a.m. local time, the paying bank must settle in same-day funds by the close of Fedwire (6:30 p.m. EST). No presentment fee can be charged. This rule is intended to expedite check collection services.

- **Electronic Check Presentment (ECP)**

  With ECP, the MICR line data captured by the reader/sorter (the check number, TRN, account number and dollar amount of the item) is electronically transmitted to the paying bank. The paying bank uses this data, not the physical check, to debit funds from the payor's demand deposit account. The actual check may be sent to the paying bank for subsequent handling or the check may be truncated (retained) by the clearing bank. The clearing bank may store the check or an image of the check. ECP accelerates clearing and the notification of checks being returned by the paying bank.

  Check 21 has facilitated ECP by creating a new payment instrument, called the substitute check. The substitute check, also referred to as an image replacement document (IRD), is an image copy of the front and back of the check that serves as a legal equivalent of the original check. (Additional details on the requirements of Check 21 are provided in Chapter 3, U.S. Financial Environment.)

  Banks, along with the support of organizations such as the Electronic Check Clearing House Organization (ECCHO), are developing programs for the electronic exchange of check information. Electronic exchange of information enables verification of the availability of funds prior to physical presentment of the check. This expedites the return of non-sufficient funds (NSF) checks.

- **MICR Capture at Point-of-Sale (POS)**

  Many retail outlets have systems that allow customers to have checks scanned, capturing the account information from the MICR line at the point-of-sale (POS). The MICR line data is converted into an ACH debit, and the check is voided and given back to the customer. POS check conversion is permitted only for consumer checks.

B. Settlement and Funds Availability

When funds from a check become available for use by a depositor depends on four factors:

- The drawee bank endpoint
- The time of deposit relative to the depository bank's ledger cutoff time and deposit deadline
- The day the check is deposited
- The bank's availability schedule. An availability schedule specifies an item's deposit deadline and defines the duration before deposited funds are available for withdrawal.

1. Endpoints

An endpoint is the location of the paying bank where final settlement occurs. The endpoint is the TRN on the check. There are four general classifications of endpoints:

- **City items:** checks drawn on banks located in Federal Reserve cities—either the 12 district banks or the 25 branches.

- **Regional check-processing centers:** checks drawn on banks serviced by a Federal Reserve regional check-processing center (RCPC).

- **Country items:** checks drawn on banks located outside a Federal Reserve city or RCPC. In general, clearing times increase as the geographic distance between the collecting bank and the paying bank increase, and as the endpoint of the paying bank moves from city to RCPC to country.

- **High-dollar group sort (HDGS):** HDGS endpoints are identified by the Fed as specific RCPC endpoints that receive, on average, $10 million or more per day in presentments from banks outside their respective Federal Reserve districts. HDGS banks typically receive two daily Fed presentments, instead of the usual single presentment per day. Collecting banks receive expedited availability from the Fed on HDGS items. HDGS endpoints are reviewed and updated twice a year by the Fed.

2. Deadlines and Deposit Timing

There are two deposit-related deadlines established by banks that determine when funds become available – the ledger cutoff time and the deposit deadline. Each bank sets deadlines based on competitive and operational considerations.

A bank's ledger cutoff is the time of day when a deposit must be received in order to be posted to the ledger balance of the depositor's account. Items deposited after the ledger cutoff time are considered to be received by the bank on the next banking day. For example, if a bank has a published ledger cutoff time of 3:00 p.m., a deposit made at 2:00 p.m. on a Friday will be credited to the ledger balance on Friday. However, a deposit made to the same bank after 3:00 p.m. on Friday will not be credited to the ledger balance until Monday. Ledger balances are granted provisional credit on the settlement and finality of the item.

It is important to note that deposits made via automated teller machines (ATMs) typically have earlier ledger cutoff deadlines than deposits made at teller windows. The reason for this is the additional time required to pick up and transport the ATM deposits to a teller line or a check processing facility.

The ledger cutoff is important in determining availability because it defines when a banking day begins and ends. A banking day extends from the ledger cutoff time of the preceding business day until the cutoff time of the present business day. Consider a bank with a ledger cutoff of 3:00 p.m. A Tuesday banking day begins immediately after 3:00 p.m. on Monday and ends at 3:00 p.m. on Tuesday. However, a Monday banking day begins immediately after 3:00 p.m. on Friday and ends at 3:00 p.m. on Monday. The deposit deadline is the time, within the banking day, by which an item must be at the depository bank's processing center, ready for transit, in order to qualify for the availability stated on the availability schedule.

3. Availability Schedules

Availability schedules specify, for each drawee endpoint, when a bank grants available credit or collected balances for deposited items. In order to receive the availability stated on the schedule, the deposited item must have been received by the assigned deposit deadline. If the deposit deadline is missed, availability is delayed by one banking day. The assignment of availability can be in whole or fractional banking days. Checks are generally assigned somewhere between zero and two days' availability.

Most banks assign availability using the proof of deposit (POD) method. Under the POD method, availability is assigned to each check as it passes through the automated check processing equipment. Availability is determined based on the time and day of deposit and the check's drawee endpoint. Some banks may negotiate special availability for selected high volume customers.

The Fed has availability schedules for banks, correspondent banks have availability schedules for other banks and banks have availability schedules for customers. Many banks have multiple availability schedules depending on the customer and the volume of business. Because the availability schedule impacts float balances, the schedule a bank offers to a particular customer is part of the pricing decision.

4. Balances and Float

Balance measurements and float calculations are determined by the relationship of the time that a check is deposited to the deadlines set by the depository institution where the deposit is made. The times and deadlines discussed in this section are all assumed to be local times at the point of deposit.

- **Ledger Balances**

  Ledger balances are bank balances that reflect all entries to a bank account, regardless of whether the deposited items have been collected and are available for withdrawal. Ledger balances are important for accounting purposes but not for funds availability or bank compensation purposes. A negative ledger balance results in a ledger overdraft. Substantial charges can be assessed for ledger overdrafts.

- **Deposit Float**
  Deposit float has two related definitions. First, deposit float is the dollar amount of deposited items that are in the process of collection. Second, deposit float is the interval between the time an item is deposited and the time the funds are collected. For example, treasury managers often refer to average float as a certain number of days, meaning the average length of time prior to when deposited funds become available.

- **Collected Balances**
  Collected balances reflect the dollar amount in an account for which the bank of deposit has received settlement. Collected balances are the difference between ledger balances and the amount of any deposit float.

- **Available Balances**
  Available balances are the amount of funds available for withdrawal from an account. They are equal to the sum of:
    - The collected balances
    - The balances that are scheduled to be collected by the end of the banking day
    - Those additional amounts for which availability must be granted under Regulation CC (Reg CC).

Consider a $1,000 check deposited on Tuesday into an account with a zero balance that is granted one-day availability, meaning the bank gives the customer use of the funds after one banking day. While the ledger balance increases by $1,000 on Tuesday, the collected balance does not increase until Wednesday. On Tuesday, the deposit float is equal to $1,000 and the collected balance is equal to the ledger balance of $1,000 minus the deposit float of $1,000, or $0. When the collected balance is negative, a collected balance overdraft results, in which case a service and/or interest charge usually is imposed for each day that the customer's account remains in a negative collected funds position.

5. Other Factors That Influence Availability

In addition to the above, several other factors impact funds availability. These factors include pre-encoding, reject items and as-of adjustments.

- **Pre-Encoding**
  A customer may elect to MICR encode (pre-encode) the dollar amount on any checks prior to deposit. Pre-encoded deposits typically receive faster availability, a later cutoff time and/or lower service charges because the customer is, in effect, performing a labor-intensive task for the bank.

- **Reject Items**
  Checks that are rejected by a bank's automated check processing equipment are likely to miss critical

deposit deadlines, resulting in longer availability and additional processing fees. The reason is that reject items must be repaired and reprocessed. Most reject items arise either because of physical defects in the MICR line or because the MICR line does not meet banking industry specifications.

- **As-of Adjustments**
  When a check takes longer to clear than the initial availability that was granted, a bank may add the additional time as part of the collected balance calculation. This practice is referred to as making an as-of adjustment. If a bank originally granted one-day availability but actually cleared the check in two days, one more day of float is added in calculating collected balances. As an alternative to as-of adjustments, a bank may grant fractional availability, which is an adjustment to the stated availability to reflect average clearing delays. For example, under normal circumstances, a bank may experience an average collection interval of one day for a certain class of checks but may miss availability deadlines five percent of the time. Rather than to make as-of adjustments, the bank may assign a fractional availability of 1.05 days for items.

C. Additional Paper Payment Instruments

A number of other payment instruments have check-like attributes and clear through the same channels as checks.

- **Payable Through Draft (PTD)**
  A PTD is a payment instrument resembling a check that is drawn against the payor, not the bank. A draft is handled like a check through the clearing system, but the responsibility for paying the draft lies with the drawee. The primary reason companies use PTDs is to preserve the right to review the items prior to final payment. Insurance companies often use PTDs for claim reimbursement because PTDs provide insurers an opportunity to verify the signatures and endorsements before honoring the items. Some state and local governments use a form of PTD called a government warrant.

- **Pre-Authorized Draft/Check**
  With a pre-authorized draft/check, the payor authorizes the payee to draw a draft/check against the payor's account. The payee, rather than the payor, initiates the transaction. Mortgage, insurance and other recurring payments are frequently initiated in this manner. Most pre-authorized drafts are now processed electronically using ACH debits.

- **Money Order**
  A money order is a prepaid instrument issued by parties such as companies, banks, or the United States Postal Service. The purchaser is the instrument's payor and the money order is the obligation of the issuer.

- **Travelers Checques**
  Travelers checques are prepaid instruments similar to money orders. Two signatures are usually required by the purchaser—one at issuance and one at the time the check is used to pay for goods or services.

- **Depository Transfer Checks (DTC)**
  DTCs are checks used in moving funds from one account to another account held by the same company, usually as part of a cash concentration system. No signature is required, but for security there is often a payee restriction. Normally the payee can only be an account at the concentration bank. ACH electronic transfers, commonly referred to as electronic depository transfers (EDTs), have largely replaced paper DTCs.

- **Sight and Time Drafts**
  A sight draft is payable on demand and is usually presented in combination with other documents that verify the terms of a transaction have been met. A time draft is the same as a sight draft except it is not payable until a specified future date. Sight and time drafts are used primarily to support international trade. Time drafts are used for transactions that call for delayed payments.

- **Cashier's Check/Certified Check**
  A cashier's check, also known as an official bank check, is a check drawn on a bank's own funds and signed by a bank officer. A certified check is drawn on a depositor's checking account. It carries the signature of a bank officer certifying the check to be genuine and guaranteeing payment. Due to the higher processing costs of certified checks, most banks have replaced them with cashier's checks.

D. Regulation of Paper Payment Instruments

The primary regulations related to paper-based payment instruments are the Uniform Commercial Code (UCC) Article 3 "Negotiable Instruments," UCC Article 4 "Bank Deposits and Collections" and Federal Reserve Regulations CC and J.

(More detailed information related to these regulations is in Chapter 3, Financial Environment.)

IV. ELECTRONIC PAYMENTS

Electronic payments include card-based transactions and payments made through the electronic funds transfer systems—ACH, Fedwire, and CHIPS.

A. Credit Cards

Credit cards are payment cards issued to individuals and businesses for the purchase of goods, payment for services and/or cash advances. Any vendor may issue credit cards; however, bank-issued credit cards are the most widely used.

1. Transaction Participants

The two primary bank-issued credit cards are VISA and MasterCard. VISA and MasterCard are bank owned national credit card associations that maintain communication networks to support credit card transaction activities such as authorization, clearing and settlement. A cardholder receives a credit card from an issuing bank. Issuing banks underwrite and issue cards to individual and business cardholders who meet credit standards. The issuing bank maintains the individual credit card accounts, bills and collects payments from cardholders and monitors the performance of credit card receivable portfolios.

In addition to issuing cards, banks also act as merchant or sponsoring banks for businesses that accept credit card payments. The merchant bank qualifies businesses (referred to as merchants) that accept credit card payments. The merchant bank provides merchants with credit card terminals and maintains deposit accounts through which the credit card payments settle. Many merchants and merchant banks use third-party processors to manage the information flows related to credit card activities.

2. Transaction Clearing and Settlement

The first step in a credit card transaction is authorization. When a customer pays for a purchase with a credit card, the merchant submits an authorization request for the charge amount to the merchant bank (or the third party processor). The request is usually transmitted through a POS terminal or other electronic communication system to the appropriate national credit card network and, subsequently, to the issuing bank. The issuing bank reviews the cardholder's account and approves or declines the charge. If approved, the issuing bank places a hold on the cardholder's credit limit for the amount of the charge and an authorization is routed back through the network to the merchant. If the merchant bank is also the issuing bank, the on-us transaction is handled internally without involving the national credit card company. The credit card payment clearing process is illustrated in Exhibit 8.4.

The second step in a credit card transaction is clearing—the communication of the payment information through the system. Credit card transaction data is electronically submitted by the merchant to the merchant bank (or the third party processor) at the close of the business day. The merchant bank (or third party processor) then forwards the data to the national credit card company. The national credit card company distributes the charge information to the issuing bank within 24 hours of the transaction. When the issuing bank receives the transaction data, it converts the hold on the customer's account to a charge that will appear on the cardholder's monthly billing statement.

The final step in a credit card transaction is settlement, in which the funds are transferred from the issuing bank to the merchant bank. The national credit card company collects funds from the issuing bank and transfers them to the merchant bank through Fedwire. Settlement usually occurs one to two days following submission of the transaction to the national credit card company. On-us transactions settle on the day that the transaction occurs. Therefore, availability of credit card charge deposits ranges from zero to two days.

EXHIBIT 8.4 – CREDIT CARD CLEARING PROCESS

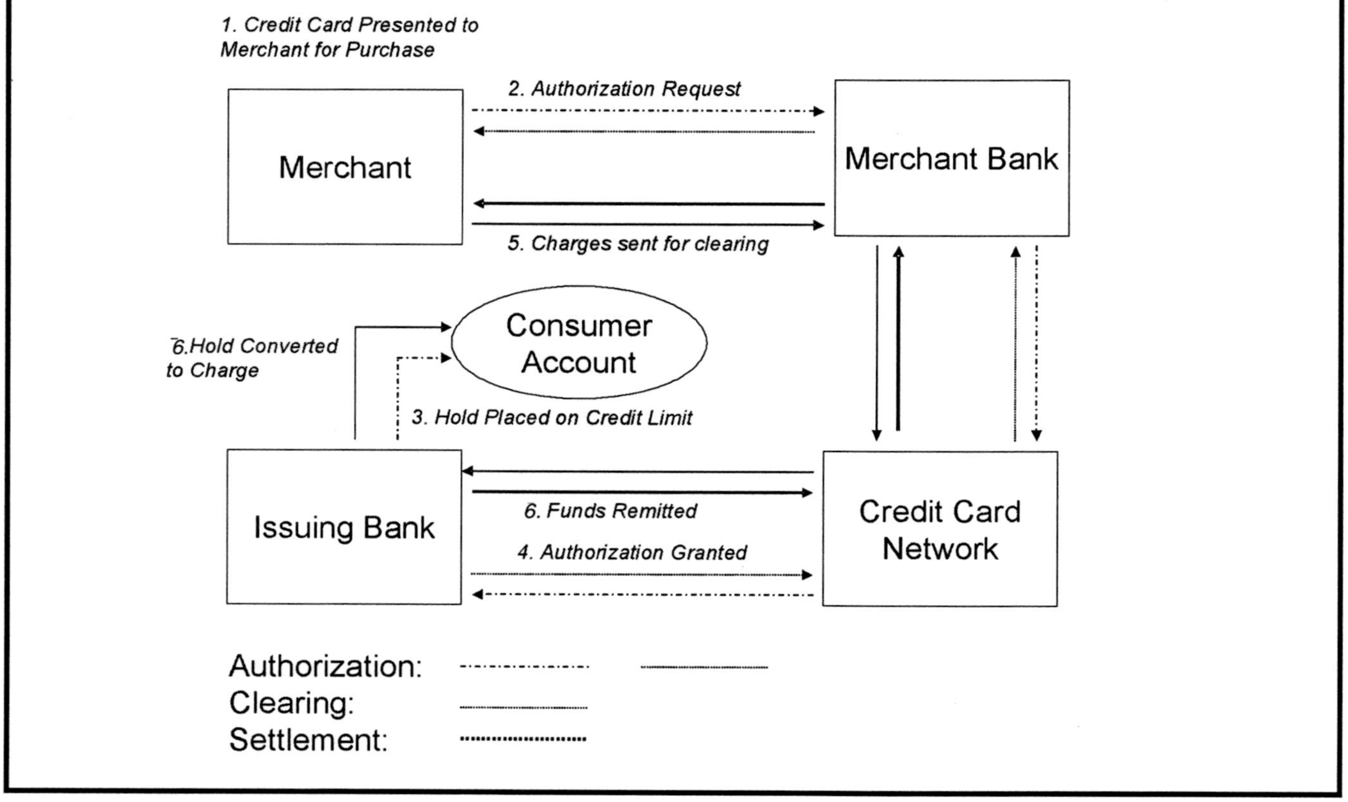

The amount that the merchant receives is the net settlement, that is, the transaction value less the discount. The discount is calculated based on a discount rate negotiated between the merchant and the merchant bank. The discount payment is divided among the merchant bank, the issuing bank, the third party processor (if used) and the national credit card company.

Generally, only errors or unauthorized charges are returned as charge-backs. When the cardholder is a consumer, the return window for charge-backs is potentially greater than 60 days. If charges are legitimate, finality occurs at settlement.

3. Credit Card Regulations

The key regulations pertaining to credit card issuers are the Equal Credit Opportunity Act and the Truth in Lending Act of 1968. Further, Federal Reserve Reg E outlines a consumer cardholder's rights to reject charges.

B. Other Payment Cards

There are four additional major card types: procurement cards, also referred to as purchasing cards, debit cards, smart cards and stored-value cards.

- **Procurement or purchasing cards** (commonly referred to as P-cards) are credit cards used by businesses for the purchase of supplies, inventory, equipment, and service contracts. Typically, P-cards are used for small dollar purchases, with spending limits established on an individual employee basis. Employee purchases can be made only from approved vendors and suppliers. The principal benefit of a P-card for a company is the replacement of the traditional time-consuming, labor-intensive, paper-based requisition process. The principal benefit for an employee is that essential goods and services can be obtained quickly and conveniently.

- **Debit cards** have several features of credit cards; however, debit cards settle by direct deduction of funds from a cardholder's deposit account. Debit cards may be offline or online. The distinguishing feature between the two is the system used for transmittal of transaction information.

    - **Offline debit cards** bear the logos of national credit card companies and are processed in the same manner as credit card transactions using the national networks. These transactions do not require the use of a cardholder personal identification number (PIN), although a hold is placed on the depositor's funds at authorization. Settlement of offline transactions occurs against the cardholder's deposit account one day following the transaction.

    - **Online debit cards** directly access the cardholder's checking account and require the cardholder's authorization through entry of a PIN at the POS terminal. Authorization and clearing are generally immediate or at least same day and may be completed over regional or national POS networks.

- **Smart cards** are payment instruments that look like credit cards but contain an embedded microprocessor. Each transaction made with a smart card updates the card's memory. Smart cards can be used only with special card readers that can read and write to the card. One form of smart card is the stored value card (SVC).

Smart cards are available with varying levels of information and security features. The simplest form is an SVC equipped to carry only monetary value information. The primary security mechanism for this card is data encryption so that any individual with physical possession of the card may use it. This type of SVC is a prepaid card used for the purchase of specific goods or services. Examples include phone cards and gift cards.

More sophisticated smart cards function like small computers and have both read only memory (ROM), which contains the operating system, and random access memory (RAM), which is used for computations and other operations. These cards typically have built-in security features such as PIN access. Some even contain private keys and digital signatures. In addition to carrying monetary value, these cards may internally update and convey information about the cardholder. These cards are often used for multiple applications including stored-value and personal identification to secure physical and systems access.

C. The Automated Clearing House (ACH) System

The ACH system was developed by the financial industry in the early 1970s as an electronic alternative to checks. The ACH system is a batch processing system designed for high-volume, low-value transactions. In an ACH transaction, payment information is processed and settled electronically, thereby increasing reliability, efficiency, and cost-effectiveness. In addition, an ACH transaction is capable of transferring more information about a payment than can be transmitted via check.

1. ACH System Participants

The ACH network is a system that provides clearing and settlement of electronic debits and credits among financial institutions. ACH operators, also called processors, act as intermediaries between financial institutions by receiving, sorting, and distributing ACH transaction files. The Federal Reserve processes the bulk of the ACH transactions, with the remainder being processed by a private operator, the Electronic Payments Network or EPN (formerly the New York Automated Clearing House).

The National Automated Clearing House Association (NACHA), also known as the Electronic Payments Association, is a membership organization that provides marketing and educational assistance and establishes the rules, standards and procedures that enable financial institutions to exchange ACH payments on a national basis. There are also regional ACH associations that provide various support services to members. The majority of financial institutions are members of an ACH association.

ACH transactions may be originated as credits or debits. Consequently, the terms "payor" and "payee" are not used to identify the parties to an ACH transaction. Instead, the terms "originator" and "receiver" are used. Financial institutions that act as intermediaries between the originator and/or the receiver are referred to as the originating depository financial institution (ODFI) and the receiving depository financial institution (RDFI), respectively.

2. Clearing and Settlement of ACH Transactions

An ACH credit transaction is an electronic message that instructs the ODFI to move funds from the originator's account to the receiver's account at the RDFI. An ACH credit is the electronic equivalent of check issuance. ACH credit transactions include direct deposit of payroll, government benefit payments, corporate tax payments and corporate payments to trading partners. Exhibit 8.5 illustrates the clearing process for an ACH credit transaction.

EXHIBIT 8.5 – ACH CREDIT TRANSACTION

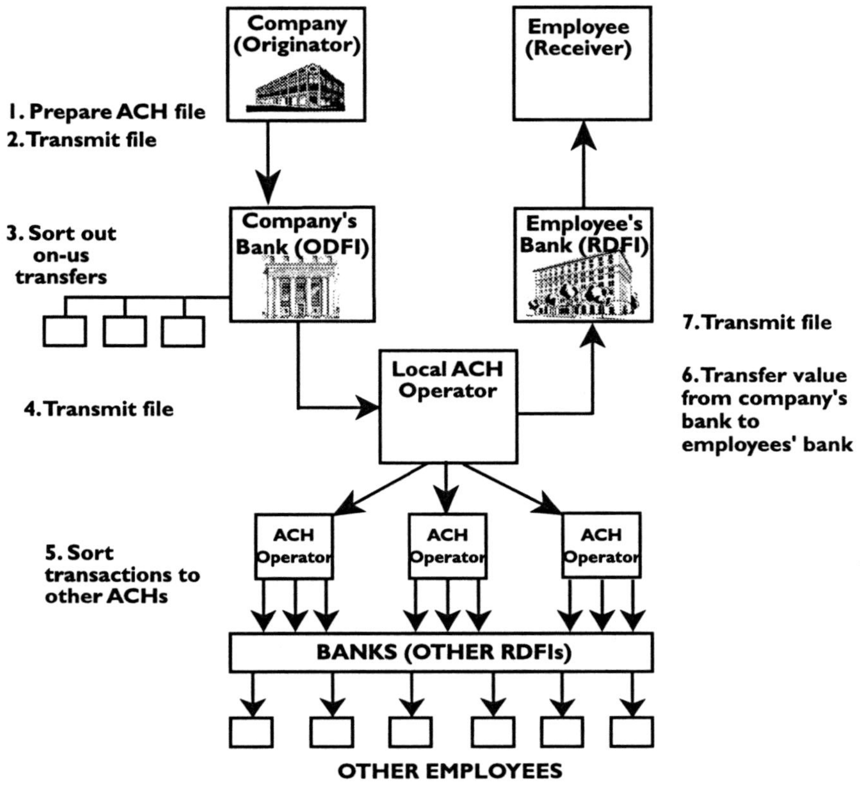

Step 1: A company prepares a file that may contain hundreds of payroll transactions. The file contains each employee's account number, the transit routing number of the employee's bank, the amount of the transfer, the transit routing number of the company's bank, the company's account number and other pertinent information.

Step 2: The company transmits the file to its bank, the originating depository financial institution (ODFI).

Step 3: The company's bank sorts out on-us transactions for employees who have accounts with the bank and credits their accounts on settlement date.

Step 4: The company's bank merges the company's transactions involving other financial institutions with transactions from other firms. A combined file is transmitted to the ACH operator servicing the originating institution.

Step 5: The local ACH operator sorts out those transactions that involve banks in its area and sends the remaining transaction to other ACH operators.

Step 6: Settlement, or transfer of value, occurs when specified in the file. For payroll this is normally after two days.

Step 7: The ACH operator presents a file to the employee's bank containing all transactions pertaining to that bank. The amount the employee receives is credited to the employee's account.

The arrows in Exhibit 8.5 indicate the direction of the flow of information through the ACH system. In the case of a credit transaction, the value transfer moves in the same direction as the arrows.

With an ACH debit transaction, the value transfer is reversed—funds are moved from the receiver's to the originator's account. An ACH debit transaction is identical to the credit transaction (outlined in Exhibit 8.5), except that the file contains a code indicating that the account at the RDFI is to be debited instead of credited and value is transferred from the receiver to the originator. An ACH debit is the electronic equivalent of check collection. An example of an ACH debit application is when an insurance company uses ACH debits to collect pre-authorized premium payments from policyholders.

The ACH system is a batch-process, store-and-forward system. Transactions received by the bank during the day are stored in batches for processing. The batches are then forwarded to the bank's ACH operator for clearing. Cutoff times for receipt of ACH files from the originator vary by ODFI. Some ODFIs accept files over the weekend for Monday settlement.

ACH transactions are value dated, that is, the payment instructions include settlement dates. Transactions are settled one or two business days after the file is released to the ACH operator. Both the receiver and the originator are settled on the same day, so the types of float associated with checks (mail, processing, availability and clearing) do not exist in the ACH system. Credit originations may be entered into the system two banking days prior to settlement. Debit originations may be entered one banking day prior to settlement.

Memo posting is posting of an ACH credit or debit entry early in the day when the actual credit or debit will not be posted to the account until after the close of business. The memo post informs the account holder of the settlement. Funds cleared through the ACH are available on the settlement date.

If an ACH credit file is released by an ODFI, the ODFI is obligated to settle regardless of the status of the originator's account. Thus, ACH credits are considered final to the receiver once the ODFI's account (usually at the Federal Reserve) is debited. One exception to this is a financial institution failure. In this event, the Federal Reserve may reverse a credit no later than the morning following settlement in order to ensure finality.

ACH debit items, like checks, may be returned by the RDFI. Returns must be made so that they will be received by the ODFI no later than the opening of business on the second banking day following settlement. Thus, finality for ACH debits is two days after settlement. An exception to this is debits to consumer accounts, which fall under the return provisions of Reg E.

3. Other ACH Considerations

- **ACH Payment Formats**

  There are standard ACH formats for both consumer and corporate payments. The most appropriate format for a particular payment is determined by the relationship between the parties, the information exchanged and the types of ACH payment services offered by the participating banks. A three-letter standard entry class in the header of the message identifies the format of an ACH payment message. The basic ACH formats are described in Appendix 8.1.

The NACHA operating rules require all financial institutions participating in the ACH to accept all types of ACH entries and to post the dollar amounts to the proper accounts. However, some institutions may not have the capability to process addenda records. Addenda records contain remittance details that follow the standard payment information in ACH payment messages. The Fed sells software that allows smaller financial institutions to extract this data and print it out for customers.

- **Prenotifications**
  Prenotifications (prenotes) are optional zero-dollar entries that are sent through the ACH system prior to live entries. Prenotes provide a verification function at the receiving bank before entries for settlement are processed. For example, when a company adds a new employee to a direct deposit of payroll program, a prenotification ensures that the bank's transit routing number and the employee's personal bank account number(s) are correct. Prenotes are optional but are useful in verifying that all records are correct prior to transaction, especially in consumer applications. While sending a prenote is optional, NACHA rules require receiving financial institutions to provide a response. To ensure acknowledgment of prenotes, many financial institutions advise customers to send some value (usually a penny) instead of initiating a zero-dollar entry.

- **Authorization**
  Companies originating ACH transactions are required by NACHA rules to obtain prior consent from the receiver authorizing the ACH transaction. For ACH debits, consent must be in writing. This authorization is good until terminated by either party. Once terminated or revoked, the originator must be able to produce either the original or a microfilmed copy of the authorization for a period of two years.

- **Consumer Initiations**
  Traditionally, only businesses have had the capability to originate ACH transactions. Thus, any consumer wishing to make payments via ACH had to either allow the payee to initiate a debit or use a bill payment service. In order to support payments for purchases made over the Internet, Project ACTION (ACH Credit Transactions Initiated Online) was instituted by a group of financial institutions in conjunction with NACHA. ACTION payments enable consumers to initiate credits as payment for goods and services purchased over the Internet. This system allows use of ACH without requiring consumers to disclose personal account information to Internet vendors.

4. ACH Regulations

ODFIs and RDFIs are bound by the NACHA Operating Rules and Guidelines, which provide detailed usage guidelines and operating procedures. Regional ACH associations often have supplemental rules that apply to members. Additionally, ACH transactions are covered under UCC Article 4A, and the provisions of Reg E govern consumer debit entries.

(Information related to these regulations, is in Chapter 3, Financial Environment.)

D. Fedwire

The Fedwire funds transfer system is a large-value, real-time, gross settlement transfer system (RTGS) operated by the Fed and is the only true wire transfer system available in the United States. Fedwire hours are 12:30 a.m. to 6:30 p.m. EST, but banks frequently establish earlier cutoff times for customers and other internal departments to allow time to complete processing.

Fedwire funds transfers are settled individually and continuously. Funds are transferred immediately, along with accompanying transaction information, between financial institutions using Federal Reserve accounts. The system is reliable and secure but relatively expensive to use in comparison to checks and ACH transactions. The total price to a user of a wire transfer varies significantly, depending on the type of wire (see classifications below) and frequency of use. Generally, both the sending institution and the receiving institution impose charges.

1. Clearing and Settlement

Except for delays that might result from either a customer or a bank temporarily reaching an overdraft limit, funds are moved almost instantaneously over Fedwire once a request has been received and validated by the originating bank. The entire process generally takes only minutes. Once the Fed notifies the receiving bank of the incoming wire, settlement is final. In the event the sending bank fails to settle, the Federal Reserve guarantees the transferred funds to the receiving bank. Exhibit 8.6 illustrates the steps in the clearing and settlement of a typical wire transfer.

2. Fedwire Format and Types

The Fedwire format is designed to interface with CHIPS and the Society for Worldwide Interbank Financial Telecommunication (S.W.I.F.T.) system. The current format also includes information required by federal authorities to combat illegal money laundering activity.

The Fedwire funds transfer service is both a communications and a settlement system. Information accompanying funds transfers includes the dollar amount, identification of the sender and the receiver, and the date and the description of the transfer. Classification of the type of wire transfer is based on which elements of information may change from wire to wire. These classifications are summarized in Exhibit 8.7.

- **Repetitive Wires:** Repetitive wire transfers are used when a company makes frequent transfers to the same credit parties. The bank maintains a record of the debit and credit parties and accepts instructions either electronically or via telephone to initiate the transfer. A unique identifier is assigned to each instruction template that contains all of the pertinent information. Only the date and the dollar amount may be changed on a repetitive wire.

EXHIBIT 8.6 – CLEARING AND SETTLEMENT OF A WIRE TRANSFER

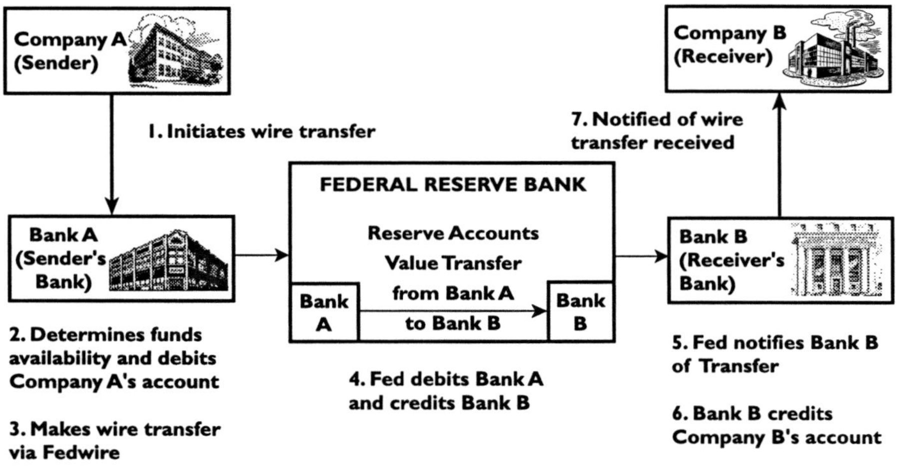

Step 1: Company A initiates a request to transfer funds to Company B. This is typically done through a treasury workstation or by a telephone call. Security procedures may include the use of personal identification numbers (PINs), test key calculations or message authentication algorithms, dual authorization of the transfer or callbacks to verify instructions. Most telephone calls are recorded for security purposes and to resolve disputes.

Step 2: Bank A checks to see if Company A has sufficient funds in its account. If it does, Bank A debits Company A's account. If not, appropriate credit approval must be obtained or the transfer must wait until sufficient funds are available.

Step 3: Bank A uses Fedwire to transfer funds to Company B through the Federal Reserve System.

Step 4: The Federal Reserve (Fed) debits Bank A's reserve account and credits Bank B's reserve account.

Step 5: The Fed notifies Bank B of the transfer, including account information for Company B. If Bank B is in a different Fed district from Bank A, the information is routed through the Fed's communication network to the appropriate receiving Federal Reserve bank.

Step 6: Bank B credits Company B's account.

Step 7: Bank B notifies Company B of receipt of wire transfer.

EXHIBIT 8.7 – WIRE TRANSFER CLASSIFICATIONS		
Wire Classification	**Description**	**Uses**
Repetitive	**The only information that can vary are the date and the amount.**	**Frequent transfers to one receiver for a recurring payment such as dividends**
Semi-Repetitive	**All information may vary except sending and receiving parties.**	**Frequent transfers to one party for various transactions such as vendor payments**
Non-Repetitive or Free-Form	**All information may vary.**	**Any payment**
Drawdown	**Request to a sending bank for an incoming transfer**	**Funds concentration**
Standing	**Request to transfer funds whenever balances reach a designated level**	**Funds concentration**

- **Semi-Repetitive Wires –** With semi-repetitive wire transfers, the debit and credit parties remain the same but the description (e.g., a customer or an invoice number) may be changed along with the date and the dollar amount. Semi-repetitive transfers combine the controls of repetitive transfers with the flexibility of non-repetitive transfers.

- **Non-Repetitive (Free-Form) Wires –** With non-repetitive wire transfers, the debit and credit parties are different each time. As a result, additional security measures are typically required. Examples of such measures are callbacks, secondary levels of approval and segregation of duties.

- **Drawdown Wires –** A drawdown wire transfer is a request sent by a company to a bank in order to initiate a debit wire transfer from either the company's account or another party's account at another financial institution. The party being debited must preauthorize the transfer; therefore, drawdown wires are most frequently conducted as part of a company's concentration system. The vast majority of wire transfers are credit transactions, not drawdown wires.

3. Fedwire Book Entry Securities System

Fedwire also operates a securities safekeeping, transfer, and settlement service known as the National Book-Entry System (NBES). NBES is a real-time gross settlement system used for the transfer of U.S. Treasury, government agency and other securities. Most Fedwire transfers are made delivery-versus-payment (DVP), which entails the simultaneous exchange of securities and funds. Like Fedwire funds transfers, securities settlement is final at the time of transfer. The NBES operating hours are 8:30 a.m. to 3:15 p.m. EST.

4. Wire Transfer Security

Security in wire transfer is critical because procedures are necessary in order to comply with UCC Article 4A. Security procedures are generally outlined in a bank's wire transfer agreement. The types of security procedures most commonly used are as follows:

- Physical security and limited access at both the company and the bank
- Passwords and PINs to identify authorized users
- Test keys or codes to validate wire transfers
- Repetitive wires to limit where and to whom funds can be transferred
- Dual approval (one person enters the wire and another reviews and releases it)
- Electronic security methods such as encryption (the scrambling of a message by the sender and the unscrambling of the message by the receiver), message authentication (a digital signature that prevents an unauthorized person from changing a wire) and digital certificates (a third-party service that ties a user's public and private encryption keys together)
- Security devices or keys to guard against misuse or fraud

(Additional information on electronic security measures is in Chapter 12, Electronic Commerce.)

5. Fedwire Regulation

Fedwire funds transfers are regulated under Federal Reserve Regulation J (Reg J), which adopts UCC Article 4A as the primary law governing Fedwire activity.

E. Clearing House Interbank Payments System (CHIPS)

CHIPS is a bank-owned, large-dollar funds transfer network operated by The Clearing House Association (formerly the New York Clearing House Association). It was established in 1970 to substitute electronic payments for paper checks in international transactions between foreign and American banks. Though not a true wire transfer system in the sense of Fedwire, CHIPS is a real-time, intraday net settlement system that clears and settles transactions in U.S. dollars. It is also used for letters of credit (L/Cs), documentary collection, and third-party transfers.

Any commercial bank with a regulated presence in the United States can become a member of CHIPS and gain access to the system; however, only a limited number of large U.S. and foreign banks participate directly in CHIPS. CHIPS clears over 95 percent of international payments made in U.S. dollars.

1. Clearing and Settlement

Each CHIPS member bank funds a special account maintained by CHIPS at the Federal Reserve Bank of New York. Throughout the day—from shortly after midnight until 5 p.m. EST—transfers between CHIPS member banks are received and authenticated.

CHIPS uses a real-time netting system, providing finality of payments at the time of release. A real-time netting system minimizes the counterparty risk and daylight overdrafts between CHIPS participants, which, in turn, eliminates the need for collateral, bilateral limits and debit caps. Smaller payments are funded directly by member banks' available balances. For larger amounts, the system continuously searches the database for payments and uses bilateral and multilateral netting to match and release payments.

A payment is considered final when CHIPS releases it. At the end of the day, each member bank receives a CHIPS net settlement via Fedwire. CHIPS transfers constitute approximately 80 percent of the daily Fedwire funds transfer dollar volume. In effect, settlement via CHIPS is a viable alternative to Fedwire for transfers between CHIPS member banks.

2. CHIPS Formats

The CHIPS format interfaces with both Fedwire and S.W.I.F.T. In addition, CHIPS is able to transmit significant amounts of remittance information with a payment. Up to 9,000 characters of data in either standard electronic data interchange (EDI) formats (ASC X12 and UN EDIFACT) or new Internet-based formats such as extensible mark-up language (XML) can be transmitted with each CHIPS payment. Invoice numbers, discount details, rebates, bank fees, and data on foreign exchanges can move electronically from remitter to beneficiary. Fedwire does not currently offer this capability.

3. CHIPS Regulation

CHIPS participants are overseen by a federal bank regulator or by the New York State Banking Department. UCC Article 4A governs CHIPS transfers.

4. Society for Worldwide Interbank Financial Telecommunication (S.W.I.F.T.)

S.W.I.F.T. is the major international interbank telecommunication network that transmits international payment instructions as well as other financial messages. It is not a funds transfer network. Messages requesting debits and credits, in addition to other types of messages, are transferred to correspondent accounts. Settlement occurs through Fedwire, CHIPS, correspondent accounts, or other RTGSs such as BACS (Bankers Automated Clearing Service) in the U.K. The formats and uses of the S.W.I.F.T. network are continuously expanded and enhanced.

V. PAYMENT SYSTEM RISK (PSR)

The growth of payment volume and several large bank failures in recent decades have prompted greater attention by the Federal Reserve System to reducing payments system risk. As part of this effort, the Fed instituted an extensive payment system risk (PSR) policy applicable to all Fed member banks. There are four major types of risk in the payments system: systemic, credit, fraud and operational. Actions taken by the Fed to manage these risks have had a tremendous impact on bank participants as well as on end-users of the payments systems.

(A more detailed discussion of operational risk is in Chapter 18, Enterprise Risk Management.)

A. Systemic Risk

Systemic risk is the risk that the failure of one major bank could cause other banks to fail, resulting in a collapse of the entire payment system. One of the primary ways the Fed addresses systemic risk is through setting and monitoring daylight overdraft limits for each institution's Federal Reserve account. A daylight overdraft is an intraday exposure of the Fed occurring when a member bank's Federal Reserve account is in an overdraft position during the business day.

Banks cannot always control the timing of large credits and debits to Fed accounts; hence, daylight overdrafts may arise in a bank's Federal Reserve account for a variety of reasons. For example, if a large file of ACH entries settles early in the day, there may be a daylight overdraft until sufficient credit activity offsets the overdraft. On the other hand, banks may strategically release large-value wire transfers at specific times to avoid deficits.

As part of its PSR policy, the Fed has mandated that all banks using the large-dollar payment systems have a sender net debit cap limiting the intraday overdraft a member bank may incur in each Federal Reserve account. The cap is determined by a Fed schedule based on the bank's capital, the overall creditworthiness as an institution, the bank's credit policies, and operational controls. The Board of Directors must approve the bank's self-evaluation.

Daylight overdrafts are costly to a financial institution because the Fed uses pricing as the primary method of controlling daylight overdraft levels. In effect, this is a market solution rather than a regulatory solution. Daylight overdrafts are measured on a minute-by-minute basis, and fees are assessed based on the magnitude and the duration of the overdraft.

The level of a bank's net debit cap and the frequency with which the cap is reached is of potential concern to any customer who makes sizable funds or securities transfers with critical intraday settlement times. When a bank reaches its net debit cap, the Federal Reserve stops processing debits, such as outgoing wires. Processing resumes when sufficient payments to the account have been received. On the whole, daylight overdraft limits have not been a major obstacle to corporate money transfers, although occasional delays occur.

B. Credit Risk

Credit risk is the risk that the party funding a transaction will default on the settlement obligation. Many payment related activities expose banks to credit risk, which, according to the Fed's PSR policy, must be appropriately measured and managed. Management usually entails approval of customer exposure limits based on a thorough credit analysis. As a result, banks frequently request non-borrowing customers to provide financial statements and other credit information. Payment related activities that generate risk include wire transfers and ACH credit originations. The risk of return items on ACH debit originations and check deposits also give rise to considerable credit risk.

1. Wire Transfer Credit Risk

Wire transfers tend to be for large values and are often time critical. Most financial institutions will release transfers only when the sender's account has sufficient collected balances to fund the wire amount.

Frequently, companies that buy or sell securities in the money markets face a timing problem. For example, a bank customer who issues commercial paper may repay funds to investors in the morning but not receive replacement funds from investors until the afternoon. Account holder daylight overdrafts expose banks to customer credit risk. To accommodate a customer's needs, a bank may establish a daylight overdraft line that permits outgoing wires in excess of collected balances up to a certain limit. Daylight overdraft facilities must be approved in accordance with the bank's credit policy and are intended only for intraday exposures.

2. ACH Origination Credit Risk

An ODFI has credit exposure to the originator of an ACH credit transaction from the time the ODFI releases an ACH file to the ACH processor until settlement occurs. Once a file is released to the ACH operator, it may not be recalled or reversed (reversing entries may be submitted only for correction of errors). If the originator's account has insufficient funds at the time of settlement, an overdraft occurs, resulting in credit exposure. If the originator files for bankruptcy prior to settlement, the ODFI cannot settle against the originator's account. NACHA rules require ODFIs to establish and monitor exposure limits for all ACH originators.

In addition, the Federal Reserve PSR policy recommends that an ODFI take the following actions to reduce ACH credit risk:

- Perform credit assessments on originators generating large dollar volume ACH files
- Establish intraday credit limits for originators
- Act to minimize risk if an originator's financial condition is deteriorating

As a result, more ODFIs now require financial information, credit approval, limit monitoring and/or prefunding for ACH originations.

Because ACH transactions are significantly less expensive than wire transfers, some originators have migrated large value transfers to the ACH system. The technical limit for an ACH transaction is 10 characters or $99,999,999.99. However, ACH system controls are not as extensive as wire transfer controls; hence, ODFI ACH credit risk increases with large payments. Because the exposure related to ACH credit originations may be as long as two days, large value originations result in exposure that a bank may view as a short-term credit extension.

3. Return Item Credit Risk

The main risk to an ODFI that originates ACH debits is return item risk; that is, the risk that return items will exceed the funds remaining in the originator's account. Return items arise when an RDFI is unable to fund a debit request for reasons such as insufficient funds, stop payment or a closed account. The Fed's PSR policy recommends credit assessments of debit originators and the implementation of remedial actions, such as collateralization or delayed availability, for originators with high returns or unacceptable credit risk. Electronic Bill Presentment and Payment (EBPP) initiatives that use high levels of automated ACH debits will likely cause an increase in this type of risk.

Return item risk is also an issue for customers who deposit checks into accounts. Like ACH debit returns, returned checks may exceed the balance in a depositor's account, causing an overdraft. Return times for paper items are much longer than for ACH debits, resulting in potentially greater exposures. The Fed recommends credit evaluation of large-dollar volume check depositors. Return item risk is mitigated by early notification of large-dollar returns and ECP, which shortens the duration for return items.

C. Fraud Risk

Fraud risk is the risk that someone might alter a transaction or enter a false item that could cause a loss for the disbursing party. The greatest fraud risk is associated with checks, followed by credit cards. Access to ACH and wire transfer systems is limited and adherence to reasonable security practices by end-users minimizes the opportunity for fraud with these systems.

(A more detailed discussion of this topic is in Chapter 18, Enterprise Risk Management.)

The availability of sophisticated printing and copying technologies has contributed to the increase in check fraud. Fraud losses are substantial for both banks and bank customers. Check fraud includes:

- **counterfeit checks:** illegitimate facsimiles of genuine checks
- **forged checks:** checks on which either the signer's or the endorser's signature has been forged
- **altered checks:** checks on which some information, usually the amount, has been changed

(A more detailed discussion of measures available to account holders to reduce check fraud risk is in Chapter 9, Cash Positioning.)

Check kiting, which involves multiple deposits and withdrawals between bank accounts in excess of the actual funds underlying the transactions, is another form of check fraud that is perpetrated on banks.

Identity theft is a rapidly growing source of credit card fraud losses for merchants and card issuers. Use of lost, stolen, fraudulent or counterfeit cards and unauthorized use of cardholders' credit card numbers constitutes most credit card fraud. Businesses can avoid bearing losses if they take reasonable precautions in accepting card payments. Specifically, a merchant must obtain an authorization, authentic cardholder signature or electronic imprint of the card. If a merchant performs any one of these actions and fraud is reported, the bank absorbs any losses. Banks reduce this risk by using complex algorithms called neural networks, which monitor cardholder charge patterns for unusual activity.

Merchants who accept mail, phone or Internet orders may mitigate risk by using an Address Verification Service (AVS) that matches the address provided by the cardholder with the account billing address on record with the issuer.

VI. FUTURE OF PAYMENTS

As electronic payment systems continue to evolve, consumers and businesses in the U.S. are gradually migrating from paper-based to electronic-based payment instruments. In recent years, there has been a sharp increase in the use of Financial Electronic Data Interchange (FEDI), PC-based financial transactions, C2B electronic bill presentment and payment (EBPP), B2B electronic invoice presentment and payment (EIPP) and the Internet for C2B and B2B payments. Technology that facilitates consumer-to-consumer (C2C) electronic payments is improving.

Many companies that accept large numbers of checks are implementing new methods to electronically convert paper-based items to the ACH either at the point of sale or at the point of receipt by a lockbox. Technological developments are expected to continue to influence payment methods in the foreseeable future.

(A more detailed discussion of these developments is in Chapter 12, Electronic Commerce.)

APPENDIX 8.1 ACH Payment Formats

There are standard ACH formats for consumer-to-business (C2B), business-to-consumer (B2C) and business-to-business (B2B) payments. All ACH payment formats move funds in essentially the same manner. The most appropriate format for a particular payment is determined by the relationship between the parties, the information exchanged and the types of ACH payment services offered by the participating banks. The basic ACH formats are as follows:

Prearranged Payment or Deposit (PPD): The PPD format is the payment application by which consumers authorize a company or a financial institution to credit or debit (B2C) an account for normally recurring payments in fixed amounts. Examples of consumer PPD credits are payroll, expense reimbursement, dividends, social security, retirement benefits and tax refunds. Examples of consumer PPD debits (C2B) are rent and mortgage payments, subscriptions, dues and memberships, insurance premiums, installment debt payments and utility payments.

Cash Concentration or Disbursement (CCD): CCD is an electronic payment format used for concentration and disbursement of funds within or between companies (B2B). A single 94-character record contains the standard entry class indicating the type of transaction, transit routing numbers for the originating and receiving financial institutions, and the originator and receiver account numbers. CCD is the only corporate ACH format that does not have space for an additional addenda record. However, it does contain space for a reference number.

Cash Concentration or Disbursement Plus Addendum (CCD+) CCD+: is one of the formats used for the U.S. Treasury Vendor Express program and for B2B payments. It is useful when only a limited amount of information must be transmitted. This format is identical to CCD but with an addenda record. The addenda record is 94 characters long and includes a free-form space for up to 80 characters of descriptive data. The CCD+ addenda record is also used to report federal and state tax payment information. The data conforms to the Tax Payment (TXP) banking conventions.

Corporate Trade Exchange (CTX): The CTX format is designed for B2B trade payments. It consists of a standard ACH payment transaction and a variable-length message addendum designed to convey remittance information in the Accredited Standards Committee (ASC) X12 data standard. The addendum can accommodate 9,999 records of 80 characters each. CTX is useful for payments related to multiple invoices and those with substantial invoice detail.

Re-Presented Check (RCK) Entries: The RCK format is utilized to transmit ACH debit entries in place of a paper check after it has been returned for insufficient or uncollected funds. The general requirements are that the item be less than $2,500 and drawn on a consumer account. Originators of re-presented check entries must provide notice to the check writer prior to receiving an item to which the re-presented check entry relates. The notice must inform the check writer that the returned check may be collected electronically if the check is returned for insufficient or uncollected funds. Originators may transmit a re-presented check entry no more than twice after the first return of a paper item, and no more than once after the second return of a paper item.

In addition to the standard ACH entry formats, five new ACH entry formats have been developed in response to the continued widespread use of checks by U.S. consumers and electronic methods of bill payment via the telephone and the Internet.

Accounts Receivable Truncation (ARC): The ARC format is used by retail lockbox providers to convert consumer checks to ACH debits. This format reduces both the cost and the availability float associated with check clearing. It does not, however, reduce the mail or processing float associated with paper-based payments.

Point-of-Purchase (POP): The POP format is used by large, nationwide retailers to truncate checks at the point-of-sale (POS). As with the ARC format, consumer checks are converted to ACH debits. The check is returned to the consumer at the POS.

Customer Initiated Entry (CIE): The CIE format is for used for pre-authorized payments that are initiated by consumers using telephone bill paying services.

Telephone Initiated Entry (TEL): The TEL format is used for payments that are not pre-authorized but are approved by consumers over the phone. TEL entries are single payments used for telephone catalog sales, ticket sales and other one-time purchases.

Internet Initiated Entry (WEB): The WEB format is used for payments that are not pre-authorized but are initiated by consumers using the Internet. WEB entries can be either single payments for one-time purchases or monthly payments made using a financial institution's Web-based bill paying service.

Test Your Understanding

These chapter questions are provided to test your understanding of the information in the text. They are neither examples of CTP examination questions nor are they in the examination format.

Answers are on pages 585–588.

1. Discuss the five non-cash payment methods used in the U.S.
2. What is meant by settlement and finality and why are these concepts important to payment systems?
3. What happens in the encoding stage of the check clearing process and what is the role played by the transit routing number?
4. What is on-us check clearing?
5. What are the four channels used for interbank check clearing?
6. How does electronic check presentment (ECP) work?
7. What factors determine when the funds from a deposited check become available to the depositor?
8. What is an availability schedule?
9. Give two definitions of deposit float.
10. What is a payable through draft and how is it different from a check?
11. What are the primary regulations governing paper-based payments?
12. What are the three steps in the credit card transaction process and how much does the selling merchant get?
13. What are payment or procurement cards and what benefits do they offer?
14. What is the ACH system?

15. What are prenotes and why are they used?

16. Discuss the four categories of Fedwire transfers.

17. What is CHIPS?

18. What is payment system risk and why is the Federal Reserve concerned about it?

19. What is fraud risk as it relates to the payment system?

20. What is the RCK format and how is it used?

CHAPTER 9
Cash Positioning

I. INTRODUCTION

The fundamental treasury responsibility is to determine the daily cash position. Information about the day's opening cash position is obtained through bank balance reporting systems. The opening cash position is the sum of the available balances in a company's bank accounts. The opening position is adjusted for the day's anticipated cash inflows and outflows to arrive at the closing cash position.

The primary objective of establishing the cash position is to plan the day's borrowing or investment decisions based on whether the closing position is projected to be a shortfall or a surplus. This decision process is referred to as liquidity management. Because borrowing rates and alternatives and investment yields and alternatives may be more favorable early in the day, determining the daily cash position is time-critical and requires access to accurate and timely information.

II. CASH MANAGEMENT SYSTEM CONSIDERATIONS

Cash management is a major treasury function and is typically administered by a cash manager, although the title for this responsibility varies from organization to organization.

(For more detailed information on financial titles, functions and responsibilities see Chapter 2, Treasury Organizational Structure.)

Regardless of the title, the individual who performs the daily cash management tasks is responsible for managing external cash inflows and outflows, as well as managing internal cash flows among various bank accounts or subsidiaries. These represent the core daily cash management activities. The primary goal of these activities is to speed up inflows and control outflows while minimizing the net costs of the system. These activities are referred to respectively as collection, disbursement and concentration. They are the focus of this chapter because they relate to enabling a cash manager to determine the daily cash position.

The basic design of a cash management system is determined by many factors. Factors that form a basic framework for cash management system design include: an organization's industry, the legal and regulatory environment, the payments system and available payment instruments.

For example, many existing domestic cash management practices developed based on the predominant use of checks and the large number of financial institutions in the U.S. Practices also evolved in response to changes in the legal and regulatory environment. Interstate banking has consolidated and streamlined cash management for many U.S. companies. Federal Reserve initiatives to reduce float have shifted emphasis from float management to information management.

(A more detailed discussion about the current legal and regulatory environment is in Chapter 3, Financial Environment.)

Industry conventions and standards often dictate acceptable payment instruments or practices that limit collection, concentration and disbursement system options. Some industries almost exclusively use checks. On the other hand, the automotive industry, among others, has pioneered the use of Financial Electronic Data Interchange

(FEDI). In industries using FEDI, payment and payment-related information between buyers and suppliers is predominantly electronic.

(Additional information about FEDI is in Chapter 12, Electronic Commerce.)

An organization's industry, size and structure (centralized, decentralized, global) influence where payments are received and where control of cash resides. An organization's functional role also impacts cash management requirements. The cash management needs of a federal mortgage agency differ from those of a public school district. A retailer with outlets located throughout the U.S. requires a sophisticated cash concentration system, while a payroll service provider may accept only electronic receipts, thus having no need to concentrate funds. Given these constraints and considerations, treasury must design and operate a cash management system that best suits the organization's needs.

III. COLLECTIONS

An efficient collection system minimizes the costs of collection while maintaining the desired level and quality of information regarding customer remittances and other sources of cash inflows. Collection system costs include float costs; the expenditures, such as banking fees, associated with managing the collection system; third-party processor charges and/or in-house processing center expenses.

A. Collection Float

Collection float is the time interval or delay between when payment is initiated and when a company receives available funds. Collection float applies principally to paper-based payment instruments that are subject to three types of float or delays: mail, processing and availability. Converting accounts receivable as quickly as possible into collected funds minimizes float time.

The primary cost associated with collection float is the opportunity cost because uncollected funds cannot be used for investments or debt repayment. The formula for determining the opportunity cost of float and an example are provided at the end of this chapter, along with a number of other core cash management calculations.

Collection Float Components: The components of collection float, are illustrated in Exhibit 9.1., along with the components of disbursement float, which will be covered later in this chapter.

EXHIBIT 9.1 – COMPONENTS OF COLLECTION AND DISBURSEMENT FLOAT

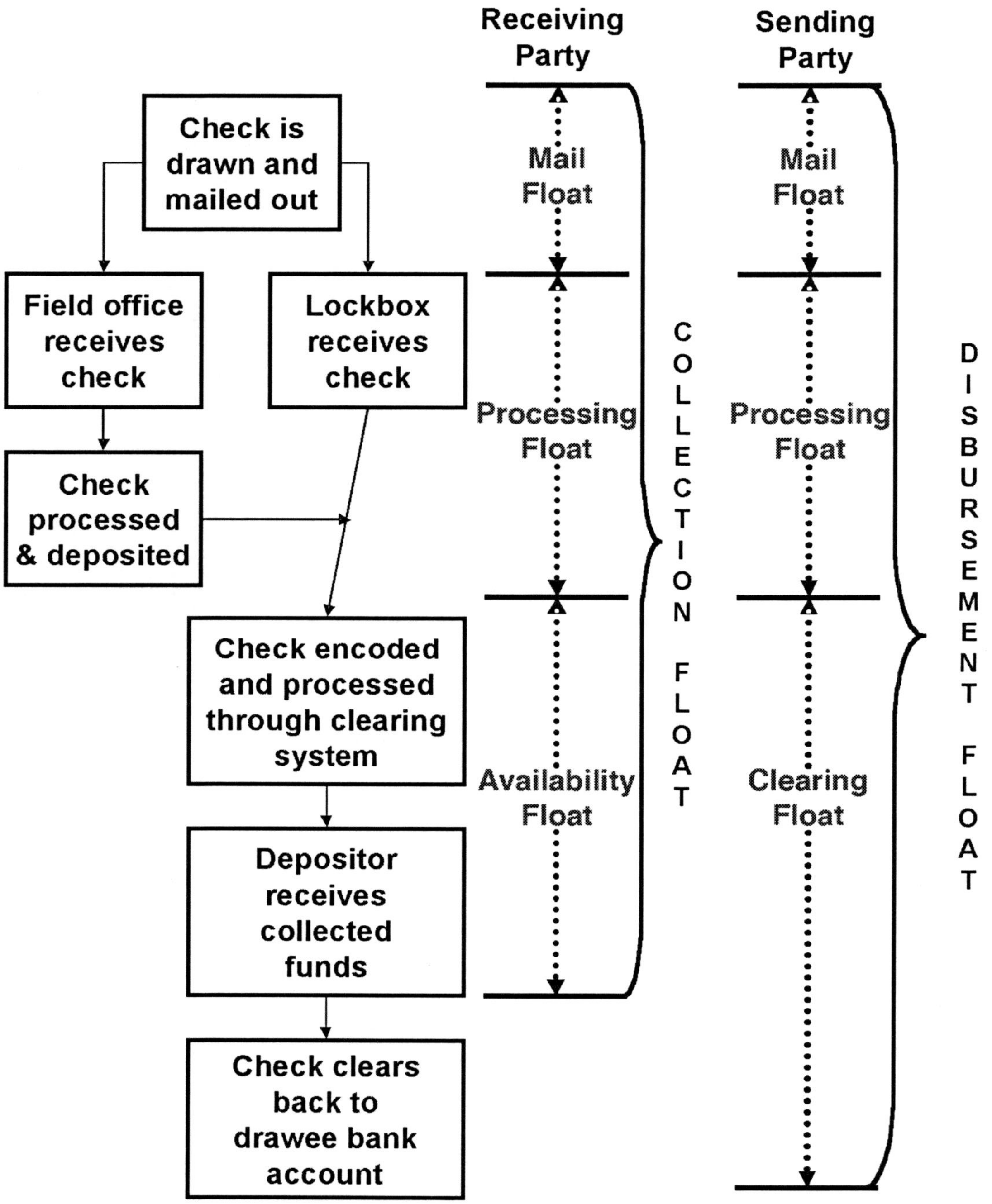

- **Mail Float:** The time interval or delay between the day a check is mailed and the day it is received by a payee or at a payee's processing site. In the U.S., mail float usually ranges from one to five days.

- **Processing Float:** The time interval or delay between the day the payee or the payee's processing site receives the check and the day the check is deposited into the payee's account. Processing time is required to capture remittance and payor information and to prepare the deposit. Processing float is typically one day or less but may extend for more days if the processing system is inefficient.

- **Availability Float:** The time interval or delay between the day a check is deposited and the day a company's account is credited with collected funds. Availability float generally ranges from zero to two business days and is determined by the depository institution's availability schedule.

B. Mail Payment Systems

Paper-based payment collection systems fall into two major categories: over-the-counter/field deposit systems and mail payment systems. Over-the-counter/field deposit systems will be discussed in the section titled Concentration. This section focuses on payment systems in which a company receives checks from consumers and/or from businesses by mail. A company may use either an in-house processing center or a lockbox to receive and process mailed payments. Deciding which of these methods to use depends primarily on two factors: the volume and the dollar amount of the payments.

C. Company Processing Center

With a company processing center, check processing and deposit preparation are performed in-house. This method is typically used by companies in industries with a large volume of relatively small-dollar payments such as utility and insurance companies. The primary advantage of an in-house processing center is control of the operation. This control provides the flexibility to more easily:

- Make changes to the system
- Customize the process to meet a company's needs
- Monitor and maintain customer service quality
- Access information
- Update accounts receivable

Given sufficient volume, internal processing may be less expensive than paying a third-party processor, especially if the company pre-encodes the checks because financial institutions typically charge less for pre-encoded deposits. (Pre-encoding involves using a proof machine to add the dollar amount to the MICR line of the check.)

Several disadvantages to in-house processing include the significant capital investment and ongoing administrative expenses required to staff and operate the center. Also, a company processing center may actually increase three of the collection delays that financial institutions and third-party vendors can reduce: mail, processing and availability float. An in-house processing center may:

- Increase mail float by not being able to receive checks through a unique ZIP code or by not being optimally located near customers
- Increase processing float by not expediting the time between when checks are received and deposited
- Increase availability float by not being able to meet critical check clearing deadlines

In addition, contingency plans for business continuity or disaster recovery may not be established easily.

D. Lockbox Processing Systems

A lockbox is a collection system in which a financial institution or third-party vendor receives payments at a specified lockbox address, processes the remittances and deposits payments in a payee's account. Lockboxes may be paper-based, electronic or a combination of both. In the U.S., lockboxes are one of the most widely used collection methods due to the predominant use of checks.

The major advantage of a lockbox system over a company-processing center is the ability to reduce mail, processing and availability float.

Mail float is reduced because a lockbox processor uses a unique ZIP code to expedite mail processing and makes frequent mail pickups from a postal facility instead of waiting for the mail to be delivered. To further reduce mail float, lockboxes may be part of a nationwide network that enables a company to have a number of collection points optimally located near significant concentrations of customers. Lockbox networks may involve either several processors in different cities or a single processor with multiple locations. If a company uses a single processor, it can obtain consolidated remittance data and concentrate funds faster.

Processing float is reduced with a lockbox because remittances are mailed directly to the lockbox processor, eliminating a company's intermediary role in receiving, processing and delivering checks to the bank. Furthermore, many lockboxes operate 24 hours per day, seven days per week, with maximum staffing during peak periods.

Availability float is reduced because lockbox processors have direct access to clearing systems and are able to meet time-critical clearing system deadlines 24 hours per day.

(A more detailed discussion of availability and clearing deadlines is in Chapter 8, Payment Systems.)

Additional advantages of lockboxes include:

- Efficient processing
- Control and record keeping capabilities
- Uninterrupted service
- Scalability

A lockbox provides efficient processing through economies of scale and potentially lower per-unit processing costs. Typically, dedicated personnel process the remittances for a particular account, with other personnel trained to back up these specialists. A lockbox also establishes an external audit trail for payments received and segregates check processing from other accounts receivable functions. Lockbox operators generally can more readily establish business continuity plans and disaster recovery sites than individual companies. Finally, a lockbox is generally easier to scale up or scale down as business volumes change. This is especially an advantage for a seasonal business.

The two disadvantages of a lockbox are that a company has less control over customized processing and over payments to respond to customer inquiries. However, image processing, which will be discussed under the heading Collection System Information Management, negates the latter disadvantage.

There are four types of lockboxes: wholesale, retail, hybrid (which combines features of a wholesale and retail lockbox) and electronic.

1. Wholesale Lockbox

Wholesale lockbox systems are used primarily to process low-volume, large-dollar business-to-business (B2B) payments that, unlike consumer payments, must often be matched to specific invoices (i.e., several invoices are paid with one check). Detailed information is required about the invoices paid, discounts taken, returns and allowances. Other principal characteristics of wholesale lockbox systems are:

- They focus on float reduction due to the large dollars involved.
- They offer a combination of manual and semiautomated processing of payments.
- They are capable of handling detailed, non-standardized remittance documentation.
- They provide timely access to information about available funds and about the invoices being paid.
- They are customized to meet specific customer requirements.

As an example of customization, a lockbox processor may be required to manually enter remittance data for transmission to the company or may use image technology and optical character recognition (OCR) to capture data. This data assists a company in automating cash applications.

While lockbox processes vary, the typical steps in a wholesale lockbox operation are described and illustrated in Exhibit 9.2.

EXHIBIT 9.2 – WHOLESALE LOCKBOX PROCESSING

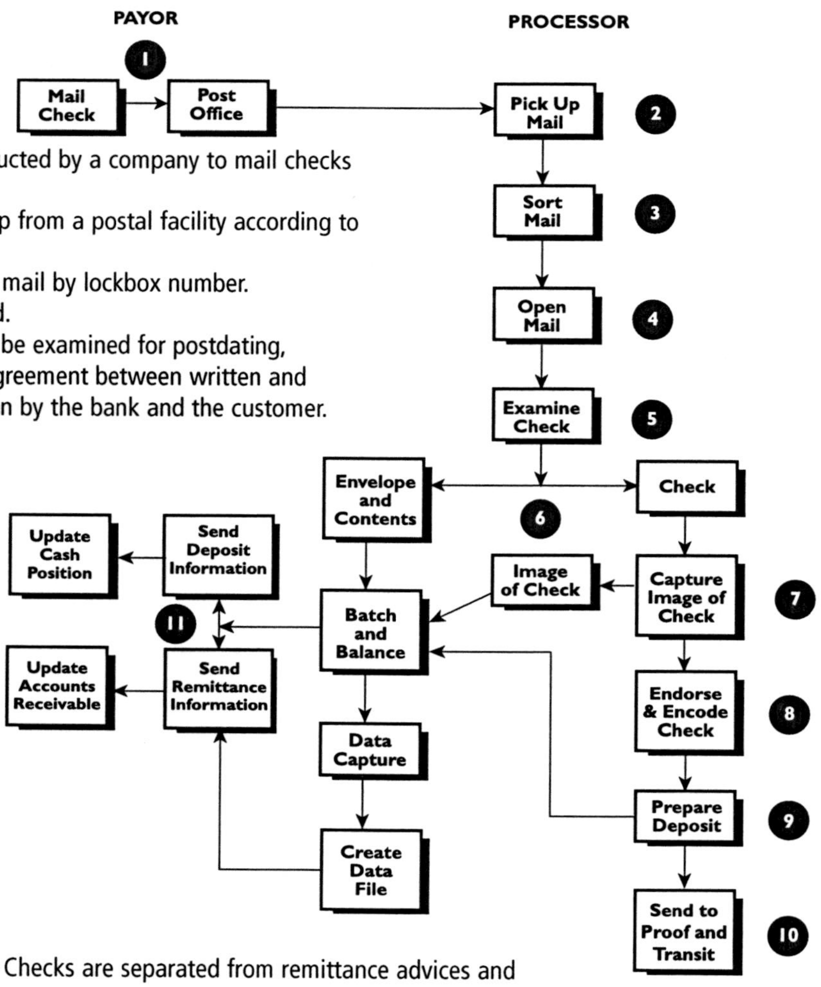

Step 1: Mail Check — The payor is instructed by a company to mail checks to a lockbox address.

Step 2: Pick Up Mail — Mail is picked up from a postal facility according to a predetermined schedule.

Step 3: Sort Mail — The processor sorts mail by lockbox number.

Step 4: Open Mail — The mail is opened.

Step 5: Examine Checks — Checks may be examined for postdating, restrictive legends, payee, and agreement between written and numeric amounts, as agreed upon by the bank and the customer.

Step 6: Separate Checks and Advices — Checks are separated from remittance advices and other contents.

Step 7: Capture Image of Checks — If required, the checks are copied by means of photocopier or imaging technology. In some instances the invoices, envelope or other remittance documents may also be copied.

Step 8: Endorse and Encode Checks — Checks are encoded with a dollar amount and endorsed.

Step 9: Prepare Deposit — Check amounts are added and balanced and deposit tickets are prepared.

Step 10: Clear Checks — Checks are sent to the proof and transit department for clearing.

Step 11: Send Deposit and Remittance Data — The processor provides both deposit information (such as the amount of the deposit and its availability) and remittance information (such as invoices paid and deductions or discounts taken). This information is transmitted daily to the company or to its concentration bank.

2. Retail Lockbox

Retail lockbox systems are used primarily to process high-volume, small-dollar consumer remittances (C2B) that frequently involve recurring, monthly installment payments. The checks are accompanied by standardized, machine-scannable remittance documents enclosed in pre-addressed window envelopes. Because of the large volume of items processed, retail lockboxes focus on cost reduction rather than float reduction.

Retail lockboxes employ highly automated, high-speed equipment that opens envelopes, reads machine-scannable information on checks and remittance documents, automatically encodes the dollar amount of the check during the scanning process and electronically transmits captured data for the purpose of updating accounts receivable. Data capture is enabled through the use of three types of technologies:

- Magnetic ink character recognition (MICR), a process that captures the machine-readable information on a check
- Optical character recognition (OCR), a process that reads pre-printed information on remittance documents
- Intelligent character recognition (ICR), a process that reads handwritten or typed information

In addition to checks, some retail lockboxes also process credit card payments.

3. Hybrid Lockbox

Hybrid lockbox systems combine features of wholesale and retail lockboxes. They are configured, usually on a customized basis, to process both B2B and C2B payments. They are used by companies, such as utilities, whose consumer customers return standardized remittance documents that can be processed automatically and whose business customers remit documents that require manual handling. The processor combines consumer and business remittance data and transmits it to the company.

4. Electronic Lockbox

Electronic lockbox systems are used to process incoming ACH and wire payments. Related remittance information is captured and reported on a consolidated basis, sometimes in combination with wholesale, retail or hybrid lockbox information.

5. Lockbox Selection

Assessing the suitability of using a lockbox system or a lockbox network requires a lockbox cost-benefit analysis to determine whether the net benefit of reduced float and/or elimination of in-house processing outweighs the incremental costs of lockbox processing. The net benefit from a lockbox is equal to the reduction in the opportunity cost of float adjusted for the difference between lockbox charges and internal processing costs. Opportunity cost of float is a function of three factors:

- The dollar amount of the collected items
- The total collection time for items
- A company's current opportunity cost of funds (usually its short-term investment or borrowing rate)

Therefore, the first step in a lockbox cost-benefit analysis is to compare the differences in mail, processing and availability float for a company processing center versus for a lockbox provider. However, in the case of a retail lockbox, float savings may not be as important as improved efficiency and lower per-item costs. An example of a float calculation is provided at the end of this chapter.

A collection study is conducted to estimate the float savings of implementing the lockbox. A collection study uses data from remittance envelopes and photocopies of checks to obtain information such as the location and geographic concentration of customers and the location of the customers making the largest payments. The company's existing depository institutions are often asked to perform an endpoint analysis that provides information about availability on both an aggregate and an item-by-item basis. Additional information necessary for the collection study includes intercity mail times and bank availability schedules.

Treasury consulting companies and major cash management banks perform periodic studies to compare mail times for various combinations of cities. These services generally report mail times between central city post offices for a uniform distribution of mailings throughout the week. If necessary, other adjustments may be made for non-surveyed mail points and day-of-the-week mail experience, especially in areas where the United States Postal Service (USPS) has limited weekend processing.

Availability schedules vary from bank to bank and must be obtained from all banks under consideration. The results of mail time studies are combined with information from availability schedules to compare providers. Banks or consulting firms use this data, in conjunction with an analysis of a company's actual remittances, to determine which cities or combinations of cities are the most effective collection sites. Computer analysis is performed to produce an optimal solution.

The second step in a lockbox cost-benefit analysis is to compare the differences between the fixed and variable costs of a company processing center versus a lockbox provider. Lockbox providers have many different methods of charging for services, but the costs fall into two basic categories: fixed and variable. Fixed monthly costs may include fees for preparing deposits, renting the post office box, sending remittance data to the company, balance reporting and account maintenance. Often, several of these costs are combined into a monthly lockbox maintenance charge. There also may be a charge for transferring funds to a concentration bank.

Variable costs may include charges for deposits, transmission of remittance data, photocopying, imaging and microfilming. These and other customized processing charges are often on a per-item basis. Some costs, such as those for deposit preparation, may be considered either fixed or variable, depending on the lockbox processor.

A sample net benefit lockbox calculation is provided at the end of this chapter.

Lockbox providers also differ in terms of service flexibility and quality. Usually, only those providers meeting a customer's standard service criteria are included in the final lockbox selection process.

E. Collection Process Improvement

Using electronic methods of payment is an example of a collection process improvement. Electronic payments, which include wire transfers, ACH debits and credits, and debit or credit card payments, offer three benefits:

- The predictability of settlement timing and available funds
- The flexibility of directing payments to any account or any financial institution without any manual intervention
- The ease of transmitting customer remittance information that may accompany the payment to facilitate updating of accounts receivable

(A detailed discussion of these electronic payments is in Chapter 8, Payment Systems.)

Migration of customer remittances from paper to electronic methods improves control, reduces or eliminates collection float, reduces costs and improves forecasting accuracy.

ACH payments have become widely used and accepted in B2B settings. On the consumer side, pre-authorized debits are useful for collecting mortgage payments, loan installments, insurance premiums, utility payments and a wide range of other recurring payments of fixed amounts. Variable consumer payments can be paid electronically by means of the telephone and/or the Internet.

As a result of the Check Clearing for the 21st Century Act of 2003 (Check 21), check truncation at the bank of first deposit is being used to enhance collection efficiency. Check truncation converts the information on a business or consumer check into an electronic form or image that is transmitted electronically, thereby avoiding the need for physical presentment of the item. If the drawee bank's customer wants the check returned in a statement, Check 21 allows the drawee bank to create a substitute document called an image replacement document (IRD).

Many retailers now convert checks to ACH debits at the point-of-purchase (POP), and many lockbox processors convert checks to ACH at the lockbox site (ARC).

(Additional information regarding ACH and ACH formats such as POP and ARC is in Chapter 8, Payment Systems.)

Both consumers and businesses can also initiate payments using the Internet by means of a Web-based collection method known alternatively as electronic bill presentment and payment (EBPP) or electronic invoice presentment and payment (EIPP). EBPP and EIPP systems integrate the billing and payment processes, thereby enabling companies to send electronic statements and to receive electronic remittances from customers. EBPP and EIPP may be handled through a company Web site or through a third-party vendor. Third-party Web-based collection services facilitate access to FEDI and ACH payment systems for businesses that want to outsource this function or cannot afford the investment in infrastructure.

(A more detailed discussion of the various electronic payment mechanisms is in Chapter 8, Payment Systems, and Chapter 12, Electronic Commerce.)

F. Collection System Information Management

Imaging technology is used to facilitate processing of both wholesale and retail lockbox payments. This technology allows paper documents, such as checks and remittance advices, to be scanned, converted to a digital image, and stored for subsequent distribution, handling, and processing. Potential benefits of applying image technology to the remittance-processing function include:

- Reduced overall processing costs
- Increased productivity
- Improved accuracy
- Automated updating of accounts receivable
- Improved response time to customer inquiries

In addition to these benefits, imaging technology is useful for delivery and storage of remittance data. A lockbox provider can transmit images of checks and other payment documents, supplying this data on a CD-ROM or archiving the information electronically for online retrieval. This is especially beneficial for companies, such as mortgage, insurance and utility companies, that must research a high volume of customer service inquiries.

An additional information management service used in conjunction with a lockbox collection system is receivables matching. With receivables matching, the lockbox service provider matches processed payments against the company's open invoices, applies the payment and updates the accounts receivable record.

IV. CONCENTRATION

Cash concentration is the transfer of funds from outlying depository locations to a central bank account, commonly referred to as a concentration account. Two major objectives of a cash concentration system are to mobilize funds and to minimize excess bank balances. Pooling funds into a single concentration account enables those funds to be managed more efficiently and effectively and facilitates daily liquidity management. Concentration enables a company to do the following:

- Invest a larger amount of funds, potentially increasing interest income
- Pay down debt faster, potentially reducing interest expense
- Take advantage of supplier and/or vendor discount terms, potentially reducing costs of goods sold or operating expenses

A. Over-the-Counter/Field Deposit Systems

Many businesses collect receipts over-the-counter at field locations, which include local offices or branches and retail stores. Methods retail businesses use to collect at the point-of-sale (POS) include cash, checks, credit cards, debit cards and smart cards. Often, a wholesale customer or its agent may deliver checks or cash to a vendor's office. Alternatively, a payee or a payee's agent may pick up cash or checks directly from a customer when making a delivery.

When a company's field locations receive cash and/or checks drawn on local banks, a depository institution located near each field location offers convenience, increased cash handling security, and expedited clearing of checks. Deposits to field accounts may be delivered by a company employee or through use of an armored courier service. Credit, debit and smart card payments may be captured at a POS terminal and transmitted electronically to the company's concentration bank or processor.

B. Concentration System Configuration

The following are the three key components in the configuration of a company's concentration system:

- The size and geographic distribution of its collection system
- The transfer alternatives for concentrating funds
- The branch footprint of its banking network

In contrast to lockbox systems, which have limited collection points and rely on major cash management banks and/or third-party vendors to process checks and remittance documents, concentration systems have multiple, over-the-counter/field collection points and rely on banks with multiple branch locations to process deposits consisting of coin, currency and checks.

Concentration Methods: The two most frequently used methods for concentration are electronic depository transfers (EDTs) and wire transfers. EDTs are ACH transactions that concentrate funds using the National Automated Clearing House (NACHA) CCD or CCD+ formats. EDTs are inexpensive and are available one business day after origination. An EDT is the most common method of depository transfer in use today, having virtually replaced depository transfer checks (DTCs). DTCs are a special category of check used by a company to transfer funds from its outlying depository locations to its main concentration account.

Field offices, field banks, headquarters offices or concentration banks can originate EDTs. A field office can initiate credit transfers from the depository field account to the concentration account, notifying headquarters of the transfer amounts. In practice, it is more common for the field office to notify either headquarters or the concentration bank of the deposit amount. Then, either headquarters or the concentration bank initiates a debit transfer from the depository field account to the concentration account.

Some large retail networks transmit information on cash receipts from POS terminals to headquarters. Headquarters then transmits the ACH debit instructions to a concentration bank. In addition, some third-party providers specialize in gathering deposit information from field units by phone, POS terminal or computer. After gathering the deposit data, the third party can create an ACH file that is sent directly to the concentration bank for origination. Alternatively, the deposit data can be sent to headquarters to allow it to determine the transfer amounts and to prepare and transmit the ACH debit file. Some concentration banks are also able to receive deposit data reported by phone, e-mail or other electronic communication directly from the field offices. Many of these banks offer online access for headquarters to review deposit-reporting activity and to identify non-reporting units.

Fedwire is an alternative to EDT when a company needs to expedite funds transfers. Typically, these are repetitive wires. Wire transfers provide immediate funds and help to reduce excess balances at deposit banks. However, because wire transfer is the most expensive funds transfer mechanism, it is used primarily to concentrate large dollar amounts when same-day value and finality are critical.

In determining whether to use an EDT or a wire transfer in order to concentrate funds, the first step is to establish the value of funds acceleration. The opportunity cost of funds is typically either a short-term investment rate (e.g., the T-Bill rate) or a short-term borrowing rate. By comparing this value to the incremental cost of the wire, the appropriate transfer mechanism can be selected. The breakeven formula for determining whether to use a wire or an EDT and a sample calculation are provided at the end of this chapter.

Like EDTs, wire transfers may be initiated by either local managers or headquarters staff. Alternatively, a field bank may have standing instructions to transfer funds that exceed a specified balance on a periodic basis. Standing instructions specify the amount, the frequency and the concentration bank. Another option is for headquarters to issue transfer instructions through the concentration bank to wire funds out of a field bank. This is known as a drawdown wire. Alternatively, a company may give instructions to a lockbox or a field bank authorizing a wire transfer of collected funds to the concentration bank.

Concentration is simplified by using branches of the same bank or banks. When a company uses multiple branches of a single bank, two services are available that facilitate deposit or automatic concentration into a single account while retaining separate information trails for accounting and internal audit purposes.

First, zero balance accounts (ZBAs) allow separate units to deposit funds to distinct accounts. These deposits are automatically transferred into a master concentration account at the end of the day's business, thereby maintaining the depository account balance at zero.

(A more detailed discussion of ZBAs is in the section under Disbursements later in this chapter.)

Second, a deposit reconciliation service enables deposits from multiple locations to be credited to a single corporate bank account. The auxiliary-on-us field of the deposit ticket MICR line carries a unique identifier for each company location, thereby enabling the bank to produce deposit reports on a daily, weekly or monthly basis.

C. Concentration System Costs

The number of banking relationships a company has will impact the transfer and administrative costs of a concentration system. If branches of a single bank are used, the number and cost of concentration transfers can be reduced and administrative tasks such as cash application and account reconciliation can be simplified. The growth in interstate branch banking has benefited companies by reducing concentration costs, including the opportunity costs of maintaining excess balances, transfer costs, bank charges and administrative overhead.

1. Excess Balances

An account has an excess balance when its average collected balance is greater than either the amount that a financial institution requires for compensation or the target level that a company has chosen to maintain. Excess balances may result from deposit reporting delays, clearing delays and transfer initiation delays:

- Deposit reporting delays may arise at field locations or in the deposit information gathering system.
- Clearing delays of one or more business days may result when using EDTs or DTCs. EDT delays occur when immediately available funds, such as cash, are deposited into a field account. EDTs do not move these funds until the next business day. DTC delays occur when checks deposited in field banks are collected before the DTC clears back to the deposit account.
- Transfer initiation delays occur if concentration entries are submitted to the originating bank late or if they contain reporting errors.

2. Bank Charges

Deposit and concentration banks may assess charges for each deposit, deposited items, inbound and outbound wires, EDT clearings, deposit reports, overdrafts, negative collected balances and account maintenance. A company using other vendors to assist in concentration must also pay vendor charges for collecting deposit information from field units and for transmitting data to a concentration bank and/or company.

3. Administrative Costs and Responsibilities

The administrative costs of operating a concentration system include the costs of:

- Managing deposit reporting
- Scheduling of cash transfers
- Preparing debit files
- Reconciliation of deposit reports
- Monitoring transfers to prevent internal fraud.

Cash transfer scheduling involves deciding when and what amounts to transfer. These are routine activities if a company's policy is to transfer the entire amount of the daily deposit. Otherwise, a cost is associated with deposit monitoring and decision-making. Receiving and monitoring daily deposit reports from local managers and concentration banks are major administrative responsibilities. Automatic software and/or systems also are available to calculate and generate ACH drafts for concentration purposes.

4. Reducing Concentration System Costs

Companies attempt to enhance concentration system efficiency, improve transfer timing and reduce transfer costs. Excess balances may be reduced by anticipating availability, anticipating deposits or using a faster transfer mechanism.

Availability anticipation involves the initiation of a transfer after a deposit has been made but before all of the items have been granted availability by the depository bank. The transfer is initiated based on the projected availability. This method risks drawing on uncollected funds because potential delays in the clearing system and return items can cause collected balances to be unpredictable. Sometimes, availability anticipation can even lead to a ledger overdraft if there are a significant number of return items. In addition, if wire transfers are used as a method of concentration and the amounts transferred are significant, there can even be intraday overdrafts.

Deposit anticipation involves the initiation of a transfer before the items to be deposited have been received from customers. The transfer is initiated on the basis of historical cash flows over a given period. Because there is a substantial risk of ledger overdraft, this is considered an aggressive cash management technique and should be used only with the full knowledge and consent of the depository bank. Deposit anticipation is often employed by retailers to transfer weekend receipts.

Companies can reduce the costs of operating cash concentration systems by using less expensive transfer mechanisms and by transferring funds less frequently. For companies whose deposits are mostly checks with delayed availability, it is more advantageous to transfer funds using an EDT on the day of deposit rather than to initiate a wire transfer on the day funds become available. If a wire must be used, repetitive transfers are usually less expensive than non-repetitive transfers.

Threshold concentration may be used to minimize the number of transfers from an account. With threshold concentration, a company allows account balances to build to a predetermined level (a ceiling) before transferring funds to the concentration bank. A cash manager can monitor average balances and adjust the threshold as necessary over time.

Target concentration involves frequent, often daily, transfers and is used primarily when field or lockbox banks are compensated in balances. Target concentration requires establishing a target balance. All funds above the target balance level (a floor) are transferred to the concentration bank. This system maintains constant balances in depository banks at the desired level.

V. DISBURSEMENTS

The basic goal of managing an accounts payable and disbursement system is to disburse funds to vendors, suppliers, employees and other payees in a timely, accurate and cost-effective manner. Typically, the accounts payable and payroll functions are responsible for scheduling and initiating vendor and employee payments, respectively. Information regarding these payments is communicated to the cash manager for use in cash forecasting and position management. In most cases, the treasury area is directly responsible for debt and dividend payments, in addition to the funding of disbursement accounts.

Disbursement Float: Disbursement float is the time interval or delay between the day a payment is mailed and the day funds are debited from the payor's account. Disbursement float applies principally to paper-based payment instruments that are subject to three types of delays or float: mail, processing and clearing. Disbursement float is analogous to collection float, except that it is viewed from the payor's perspective. As illustrated in Exhibit 9.1, the mail and processing float components of disbursement float are the same as in collection float. The primary difference between collection and disbursement float is availability versus clearing float.

Float Components: To reiterate, mail float is the time interval or delay between the day a check is mailed and the day it is received by a payee or at a payee's processing site. Processing float is the time interval or delay between the day the payee or the processing site receives the check and the day the check is deposited into the payee's account. Clearing float is the time interval or delay between the day a check is deposited by the payee and the day the payor's account is debited. In most cases, the payee's account is credited with collected funds at the same time the payor's account is debited.

A. Disbursement Products

A basic disbursement system consists of a single bank account from which all payments are made. Most organizations have more complex systems that utilize a variety of payment methods and products.

1. Controlled Disbursement

Controlled disbursement is a bank service that provides same-day notification to a company of the dollar amount of checks that will clear against the account. The controlled disbursement account is not funded until after this notification is received. The daily clearings are usually available by early or mid-morning, allowing the cash manager to determine the day's funding needs at a time when investment and borrowing alternatives are more favorable. The disbursement bank must receive its final cash letter of the day from the local Federal Reserve Bank (Fed) early in the morning so that the checks can be sorted and the company can be notified of its funding requirement for the account. The company must then provide adequate funds to the account to cover the value of the checks presented that day.

A controlled disbursement account is usually funded from a company's concentration account, in which case an automatic internal bank transfer is made. In situations where a company negotiates the funding of a controlled disbursement account from other sources, typically a wire transfer is used. However, in some cases funding by ACH is negotiated. When the funding account for the controlled disbursement is not at the controlled disbursement bank, the typical requirement is that a balance equivalent to an average day's clearing be maintained to reduce the bank's risk.

Major cash management banks use Payor Bank Services, an information service of the Fed that electronically notifies controlled disbursement banks early in the morning of all checks that will be physically presented later that day.

Another Fed program impacting controlled disbursement services is the High-Dollar Group Sort (HDGS) program. Under HDGS, the local Fed automatically makes a second presentment to banks with more than $10 million in daily presentments from financial institutions outside the banks' Fed district. This second presentment delays the communication of final clearing totals until mid-morning, hence, there are two notifications of presentments to controlled disbursement clients.

One of the principal advantages of a controlled disbursement account is that it allows a company to calculate the daily cash position early enough to take advantage of better market rates for investing or borrowing. However, there are instances where discrepancies arise between the reported disbursement clearings and the actual amount of checks presented for payment. These discrepancies arise from same-day presentment, over-the-counter and reject items. Some banks carry over these adjustments until the following business day.

According to Fed regulations, checks directly presented to a drawee bank by 8:00 a.m. must be paid on the same day that they are presented. These same-day presentment items are handled separately from the bulk of the controlled disbursement checks.

Banks also have the option to designate the local Fed as the clearing point for same-day presentment items, thereby eliminating the challenge of combining presentment totals. Presentment after the morning notification arises when a check that was missed by the Fed in the Payor Bank Services notification is discovered on the same morning. Checks may also be presented for payment at the disbursement bank by the payee. These checks, commonly known as over-the-counter items, may also cause discrepancies in clearing totals. Finally, checks may be mis-encoded or unreadable and become exception items. These items have to be handled separately and may arrive at the bank after the usual presentment times.

2. Zero Balance Account (ZBA)

A ZBA is a disbursement account on which a company issues checks, initiates ACH debits or initiates wire transfers. The balance in the account is maintained at zero. A transfer of funds from a master account located in the same bank covers all debits against a ZBA. Funding of the ZBA is generally automatic and involves only an accounting entry by the bank. As noted before, a ZBA can also be a depository account from which funds are debited and transferred into a master account at the end of each day.

Some ZBAs are used for both collections and disbursements. Credits and debits that post to the ZBA are netted at the close of each business day. If there is a credit balance in the ZBA, the ZBA will be debited and the master account will be credited. This brings the balance in the ZBA back to zero. If there is a debit balance in the ZBA, the ZBA will be credited and the master account will be debited. Again, this end-of-day transaction returns the balance in the ZBA to zero.

Multi-tiered ZBAs may be used to allow companies with multiple divisions or subsidiaries to write checks on separate accounts or to segregate different types of payments such as accounts payable, payroll, dividends and taxes. A cash manager can control the balances and funding of a master account and that account's associated ZBAs as if they were all one account. This reduces excess balances and the need for multiple manual transfers while maintaining distinct information and audit trails.

3. Payable Through Draft (PTD)

A payable through draft (PTD) is a payment instrument resembling a check that is drawn against the payor, not the bank, and for which the payor has a period of time to honor or refuse payment. The deadline under Federal Reserve Regulation CC for approval or rejection of a PTD is the same as for a check (one business day).

PTDs are frequently used for insurance claims and other field office disbursements that have multiple signers and require headquarters' approval. They allow a company the time to ensure that all terms have been met or expenditures authorized. PTDs may also be issued in electronic form and are essentially ACH debits to a company's account in which the company makes the final determination regarding whether to pay or return each item.

4. Positive Pay

Positive pay is a disbursement service used to combat check fraud. With this service, the company transmits a file of issued check information to the disbursement bank either at or before the time of the physical distribution of checks. The bank matches check serial numbers and dollar amounts of checks presented for payment against the issue file and pays only those checks that match the file. Any exceptions are conveyed to the company for decision to pay or return the item.

Some positive pay services match against the payee field, as well as the serial number and the amount, in an effort to detect altered payees. Also, many banks offer imaging services with positive pay, enabling faster identification and research of fraudulent items. The Internet is being increasingly used for notification due to the time-critical nature of returning the items.

A similar service, known as reverse positive pay, occurs when the bank transmits a file of the checks presented for payment to the company on a daily or intra day basis. The company matches this file to a list of checks issued and notifies the bank of any items to be returned. This service, however, does not prevent fraudulent checks from being cashed at the payor bank teller line since the bank does not have access to the issue file.

It is important to note that neither of the above services protects against certain types of fraud, such as fraudulent endorsement; nor can such efforts prevent losses arising from a holder in due course defense. Fraudulent endorsements occur when an authorized check is stolen or intercepted by a third party and then is endorsed and cashed by that party. So long as the check amount and the check number are not altered, this type of fraud is not usually detected by positive pay.

The holder in due course defense arises when a financial institution or a company accepts or cashes a fraudulent item in good faith. An example might be when a check cashing store that regularly accepts payroll checks from a company now accepts a fraudulent item that is virtually identical to the company's regular payroll checks. Positive pay is designed to reject the item, but the company may ultimately be held liable if the check cashing store is deemed to be a holder in due course. In other words, the check cashing store took the check in good faith, with the understanding that the check was bona fide and contained no defects. In addition, some companies encounter significant problems with exception items as a result of repeat check numbers or large numbers of manual checks.

5. Multiple Drawee Check

Multiple drawee checks, also known as payable-if-desired (PID), are checks that can be presented for payment at a bank other than the drawee bank. Typically, both bank names appear on the check. Uses for multiple drawee checks include payroll in states that require employees to be paid by checks payable locally, payroll for employees on assignments away from the company office and dividend checks. Companies maintain balances and/or pay a fee at an alternate payment bank to compensate the bank for cashing multiple drawee checks. The alternate bank requires indemnity from the paying company for any loss related to the checks, including fraud. Not all banks provide this service.

6. Imprest Account

An imprest account, sometimes referred to as a petty cash account, is an account maintained at a prescribed level for a particular purpose or activity. For example, a field office may have an imprest account for local disbursements, with a balance sufficient for one or two months' expenses. Based on either an established time frame or a designated level of imprest account balances, the field office submits expenses to headquarters for approval, and headquarters reimburses the imprest account.

B. Electronic Disbursement Methods

Electronic disbursements via Fedwire and ACH are used for payments from businesses to individuals (B2C), from individuals to businesses (C2B), and from businesses to businesses (B2B). The volume of electronic payments is still low when compared to checks. However, electronic disbursements continue to increase as the value of float declines, the emphasis on expense control increases, and the impact of Check 21 becomes more widespread.

The increasing use of EBPP or EIPP is also stimulating the growth of electronic disbursements. In addition to the long-standing use of direct deposit, three recent electronic methods that are gaining increasing acceptance are purchasing/ procurement cards, federal and state tax payments, and electronic benefit transfers and payroll cards.

1. Direct Deposit

Direct deposit payments have been widely used since the early 1980s. Direct deposits are transfers made from a company's account to the accounts of employees, shareholders, vendors and trading partners using ACH credit transactions. While direct deposit of payroll is the most common form of ACH payment, direct deposit is also used for employee expense reimbursements, interest payments, tax payments, dividend distributions and B2B transactions. In addition, local, state and federal tax agencies use direct deposit for tax refunds and Social Security benefit distributions. Two advantages of direct deposit are the low cost of the transactions and the certainty of timing.

2. Purchasing/Procurement Cards (P-Cards)

Many companies use purchasing or procurement cards (P-cards) for small-dollar purchases of supplies and service contracts. However, as the acceptance has increased, the dollar amounts of the purchases have grown larger and the types of purchases have expanded to include even inventory and equipment.

Purchasing cards are not to be confused with corporate credit cards used for travel and entertainment expenses. Purchasing cards are issued to designated employees with spending limits and are authorized only for pre-specified types of purchases. Purchasing cards save costs by eliminating the processing of high-volume, low-dollar purchase orders and payments and by enabling companies to negotiate better pricing or payment terms with preferred suppliers. Finally, many purchasing card providers now offer rebate programs as an added incentive.

3. Tax Payments

The Electronic Federal Tax Payment System (EFTPS) is the primary method for collecting and accounting for federal taxes withheld by employers from individuals' salaries and wages, as well as corporate business and excise taxes.

In addition, many states require companies with tax payments above certain amounts to remit taxes electronically. This is accomplished either by initiating an ACH credit or authorizing an ACH debit. The standard NACHA payment format for state tax payments via ACH is known as TXP, yet usage and specific formats vary from state to state. Some states also accept tax payments by wire transfer. Many bank systems can support and maintain multiple, diverse tax formats.

4. Electronic Benefit Transfers and Payroll Cards

Most state governments now use electronic benefit transfer systems for the disbursement of benefits under food stamp programs. These systems allow recipients of government transfer payments to receive benefit payments through automated teller machines (ATMs) and point-of-sale (POS) terminals. Also, many companies with large numbers of low-income or temporary workers, who frequently do not have bank accounts, have introduced payroll cards that work in a manner similar to electronic benefit transfer systems.

C. Outsourcing Products

Because of the complexity of many payment types and the need for extensive controls over disbursement activities, outsourcing of the accounts payable functions is quite common. Outsourcing products include freight payment services, payroll services, and integrated or comprehensive accounts payable.

1. Freight Payments

Some banks and third parties offer a payment service called freight payment in which specialists pay all of a shipper's freight bills, audit bills for possible overcharges and duplicate payments, and provide reports that assist a company to compare costs for different routes and carriers. Manufacturers and wholesale distributors typically use this service.

2. Payroll Services

Numerous vendors offer payroll services that handle many payroll functions including check and direct deposit file issuance, payroll tax filing and payment and 401K administration. Payroll services also provide employees with the required withholding forms. Many small- to medium-sized businesses find outsourcing of payroll to be cost effective and convenient.

3. Integrated or Comprehensive Accounts Payable

An integrated or comprehensive accounts payable service allows a company to outsource all or part of the company's accounts payable and/or disbursements functions. There are two common approaches to managing an integrated or comprehensive accounts payable service.

First, a company may periodically send a data file, containing a list of all payments to be made, to a financial services provider (FSP). The file contains information on when to issue a disbursement and to whom, as well as instructions on the payment method to be used (check, wire, ACH, foreign drafts, or foreign currency).

Alternatively, the FSP may maintain a database of a company's payees that includes detailed information such as preferred payment methods, specific remittance information and the names of receiving financial institutions. The database is periodically updated as new payees are added or an existing payee's remittance profile changes. Under this method, when a company needs a disbursement it sends only limited payment information to the FSP.

With either approach, the FSP issues the payments immediately or "warehouses" the items according to the future date in the data file.

D. Managing Disbursement Information

Accurate and comprehensive information management is central to an effective disbursement system. Obtaining timely and accurate information about the status of disbursement accounts and disbursement clearings enables a company to manage its cash position more effectively. In addition, information must be provided to the accounts payable function regarding the status of outstanding items.

1. Interface with Accounts Payable (A/P)

Two critical areas of interface between cash management and A/P relate to disbursements. The first is the communication from A/P regarding the invoices vouchered for payment and the second is the communication from cash management back to A/P regarding the reconciled payments. Companies with integrated Enterprise Resource Planning (ERP) accounting systems that include treasury management modules typically are able to integrate these functions. However, many companies must use either separate systems for disbursement management or bank-provided treasury information software that may not interface with the A/P ledger. In these cases, customized "patches" or middleware (in a client-server environment) are required to facilitate the transfer of information between applications.

2. Account Reconciliation Services (ARP)

Banks provide account reconciliation services to meet companies' information and control requirements. In a partial reconciliation service, a bank lists all checks paid in numerical order by check serial number or in chronological order by date paid. For each item, the paid report generally shows the check serial number, dollar amount and date paid. The listing is available as a paper report, on CD-ROM, via a direct data transmission or through a Web site.

With a full reconciliation service, a company supplies an electronic file of checks issued to the bank and the bank matches checks paid against the file. Again, the bank delivers a listing of checks issued, paid, and outstanding in check serial number order via a paper report, CD-ROM, direct data transmission or through a Web site.

Related bank services that are important for disbursement activities include stop payments and high-order prefix sorting. Stop payments may be initiated by voice, electronically or in writing. Written confirmation may be required by the bank for telephone instructions. Stop payments usually remain in place for only six months and must be renewed, if necessary. A high-order prefix (divisional) sort is the disbursement counterpart to deposit reconciliation services. Divisional sorting allows a single account to be used by a company with multiple units. Codes identifying the various units are included in the check serial number field. This method is used to facilitate the identification and sorting of payments by operating unit.

3. Image Technology

Just as image technology is an important enhancement to a collection service such as a lockbox, image technology is also an important enhancement to disbursement services.

Both the front and the back of a check may be captured and converted into digital information using optical scanning. Check images (either all or selected ones) may be transmitted to a company via fax, Internet, or direct transmission. The check images may also be stored in a bank database that a company can access online for viewing or retrieving the images. Imaging allows a company faster access to disbursement check information and is particularly beneficial when used in conjunction with controlled disbursement, payable through drafts and/or positive pay services.

VI. NET SETTLEMENT SYSTEMS

Net settlement is a mechanism whereby debits or credits (in the case of financial institutions) or receivables and payables (in the case of companies) are offset between parties and only the net remaining balance is settled through funds transfers. A bank clearing house exchange is an example of the former; an intra- or intercompany settlement system between business units or trading partners is an example of the latter. Industries that employ intercompany net settlement systems include airlines, oil and gas, telecommunications and securities.

At the end of a specified period of time, all of the participants in a netting system determine the net flows that are required to balance the system. These clearing systems process transaction information and allow participants to make periodic net settlements with each other. Net settlement benefits participants by requiring only a single transfer of the net amount due to other parties, thereby significantly reducing the volume and cost of what would otherwise be multiple transfers.

VII. THE PROJECTED CLOSING CASH POSITION

The various cash management tools and techniques discussed in this chapter serve the dual purpose of mobilizing funds to arrive at the closing cash position and providing timely and accurate reporting to optimize use of the available funds.

To arrive at the projected closing cash position, a cash manager adjusts the opening bank available balance by adding the expected settlements in the collection (lockbox, wire and ACH) and concentration accounts (depository banks) and by deducting the projected disbursement totals. Information about checks in the process of collection and ACH credits is available from the prior day's balance reports. Lockbox and controlled disbursement totals are reported to a cash manager on a same-day basis.

However, clearings of disbursements issued on accounts other than controlled disbursement accounts must be estimated. Because wire transfers are real-time transactions, notice of incoming and outgoing wires is often available on an intraday basis from all major cash management banks. The estimated closing position is then used to determine whether there will be a cash surplus or a cash deficit.

VIII. CASH MANAGEMENT SYSTEM RISKS AND CONTROLS

Cash resources are critical for the operation of any organization. Appropriate controls should be in place to protect funds from operational, fraud and other risks that compromise cash assets.

(A detailed discussion of operational risks, system security, and disaster recovery, is in Chapter 18, Enterprise Risk Management.)

A. Internal Control Issues

Internal control primarily involves checks and balances and the monitoring of transactions, cash flows and information within an organization. Appropriate use of controls such as matching, verification and separation of duties helps to protect against employee error and fraud.

The matching process looks for possible errors in amounts, prices and other provisions. Matching of an invoice to the original purchase order may help to confirm the order was indeed placed, and the invoice complies with the agreed terms. A further match against receiving records ensures the order has been fulfilled. Another application of matching is comparison of amounts deposited with reported sales. Verification determines whether transactions are authorized in accordance with established policies and procedures prior to their implementation. This process is often used to determine whether a purchase order should be sent or a request for a wire transfer request should be released.

Segregation of duties is a particularly important treasury control issue. At the management level, it is important that functional authority for collection and disbursement of funds remains independent. At an operational level, responsibilities such as approval, authorization, and verification functions, including expense approval, check-signing authority and account reconciliation, should be separated. Internal control guidelines recommend separation of responsibility for each step of a transaction. In many organizations, personnel limitations prevent sufficient division of responsibilities. In these situations, outsourcing may the best solution for protecting a company's assets.

B. External Fraud

Disbursement fraud is a significant problem. Technological advances have increased the frequency, sophistication and ease of creating fraudulent checks. These advances include color copiers, high-resolution laser printers and document scanners designed for use with a personal computer. Fraudulent endorsements and alterations of legitimate checks also result in substantial losses. As a result, control and fraud prevention are an important responsibility of accounts payable and treasury operations.

(A more detailed discussion of control and fraud prevention is in Chapter 7, Working Capital Tools.)

C. Bank Failure

Field deposit systems typically have many banks, and a company may be at risk if one fails. To reduce the risk of bank failure, a cash manager needs to monitor the creditworthiness of each bank in a company's concentration system. Timely concentration also limits this risk. A greater risk is presented if a company's main cash management bank fails.

(A more detailed discussion of the criteria used to evaluate a bank's condition is in Chapter 21, Relationship Management.)

APPENDIX 9.1 CALCULATIONS AND EXAMPLES

1. Float Calculation

Collection float is usually measured in dollar-days and is a function of a transaction's dollar amount and the number of days of delay. The dollar-days of float on an individual check are calculated by multiplying the dollar amount of the check by the number of days between the time when the payor mails the check and the payee is granted credit for collected funds. Average daily float is calculated by dividing the sum of the dollar days of float for all items received in a certain period by the number of days in the period. The cost of float is a product of the opportunity cost of funds and the average daily float.

Assume that ABC Corporation has annual sales of $400 million, 90 percent of which are sold on credit and the remaining 10 percent of which are received in cash. All credit sales are paid by check with an average collection float time of three days. ABC is a net borrower with an average borrowing cost of 4 percent. Average daily float and annual cost of float are calculated as follows (assuming 365 days per year):

$$\text{Average Daily Float} = \text{Average Daily Receivables Collected} \times \text{Average Days of Float}$$

$$= \left(\frac{\$400{,}000{,}000 \times 0.90}{365}\right) \times 3 \text{ days}$$

$$= \$986{,}301 \times 3 \text{ days}$$

$$= \$2{,}958{,}903$$

$$\text{Average Cost of Float} = \text{Average Daily Float} \times \text{Opportunity Cost of Funds}$$

$$= \$2{,}958{,}903 \times 0.04$$

$$= \$118{,}356$$

2. Lockbox Cost Benefit Calculation

Assume that ABC Corporation had an annual opportunity cost of float in the amount of $118,356. This figure represents three days of float due to delays in the collection process or a cost per day of float of $39,452 ($118,356 / 3). Currently, ABC has an in-house remittance processing center. The cash manager has determined that if a lockbox can reduce the average collection float by one day, the company might consider outsourcing remittance processing to a lockbox provider. In order for ABC to justify outsourcing, the lockbox must cost less than $39,452—the opportunity cost of one day's collection float.

Assume that ABC has received a proposal to implement a lockbox that is expected to reduce average collection float by one day. ABC estimates it currently spends

$35,000 to internally process the 52,500 payments received annually from customers. The bank has proposed to provide the lockbox for a monthly fixed service fee of $500 plus a charge of $0.75 for each item processed.

$$
\begin{aligned}
\text{Annual Cost of Lockbox} &= \text{Fixed Costs} + \text{Variable Costs} \\
&= [\$500 \times 12] + [\$0.75 \times 52{,}500] \\
&= \$6{,}000 + \$39{,}375 \\
&= \$45{,}375 \\
\text{Incremental Cost of Lockbox} &= \text{Cost of Lockbox} - \text{Current Processing Cost} \\
&= \$45{,}375 - \$35{,}000 = \$10{,}375 \\
\text{Net Benefit of Lockbox} &= \text{Value of Reduced Float} - \text{Incremental Cost} \\
&= \$39{,}452 - \$10{,}375 = \$29{,}077
\end{aligned}
$$

Because the net benefit is positive, ABC would convert from an in-house processing center to a lockbox, assuming that the decision is based strictly on a cost-benefit analysis.

3. Cash Concentration Breakeven Calculation

In determining whether to use an EDT or a wire transfer to concentrate funds, it is important to establish the value of funds acceleration. Comparing this value to the costs of the alternative transfer method, the most beneficial transfer mechanism can be selected. The opportunity cost of funds is typically either a short-term investment rate or a short-term borrowing rate.

For example, assume the following:

- Total costs for an EDT are $1.00.
- Total costs for a wire transfer are $10.00.
- Transfer amount is $100,000.
- The opportunity cost of funds is 3.5 percent.
- A wire transfer accelerates funds one day faster than an EDT.

The formula for computing the breakeven wire transfer amount is as follows:

$$
\text{Minimum Transfer} = \frac{\text{Wire Cost} - \text{EDT Cost}}{\text{Days Accelerated} \times \dfrac{\text{Opportunity Cost}}{\text{365 Days}}}
$$

$$
= \frac{\$10.00 - \$1.00}{\text{1 Day} \times \dfrac{.035}{\text{365 Days}}} = \$93{,}857
$$

So long as the wire transfer amount is larger than $93,857, the additional cost of the wire transfer is justified.

Test Your Understanding

These chapter questions are provided to test your understanding of the information in the text. They are neither examples of CTP examination questions nor are they in the examination format.

Answers are on pages 589–592.

1. Discuss collection float.

2. What are the two types of paper-based collection systems?

3. What is a lockbox collection system and what is its primary advantage?

4. Discuss the four types of lockboxes currently used in the U.S.

5. What are the typical types of electronic payments, and what benefits do they offer over paper-based payments?

6. What is cash concentration and what are its major objectives?

7. What are the most frequently used methods for concentrating cash?

8. What is availability anticipation, and how is it used?

9. What is the basic goal of managing an accounts payable and -disbursement system and what role does the treasury area play?

10. What is disbursement float and how is it different from collection float?

11. What is a ZBA?

12. Discuss positive pay.

13. What are direct deposits and what benefits do they offer?

14. What is an integrated or comprehensive accounts payable service and what are the two common approaches used in implementing this service?

15. What are the two primary account reconciliation services offered by banks?

16. What is net settlement and how is it used?

17. What process used to determine a projected cash closing position?

18. What is involved in internal controls for cash management?

19. What is segregation of duties in cash management and why is it important?

CHAPTER 10
Liquidity Management

I. INTRODUCTION

Liquidity management is the process of maintaining an optimal cash position through short-term investing and short-term borrowing activities. The primary objective of liquidity management is to maintain a cash position that allows a company to meet daily obligations without incurring the opportunity costs that arise from having excess cash. An organization will quickly become insolvent if it does not have sufficient resources to meet its day-to-day obligations, so liquidity management is critical to the success of any business.

(A more detailed discussion of the concept of a daily cash position is in Chapter 9, Cash Positioning.)

The need for liquidity management arises from the fact that daily cash inflows seldom equal daily cash outflows. When outflows exceed inflows, liquidity is maintained by means of the sale of short-term investments or by a drawdown on short-term borrowing facilities. When inflows exceed outflows, short-term borrowings are repaid or funds are invested in short-term instruments. This process is summarized in Exhibit 10.1.

EXHIBIT 10.1 – CASH FLOW DIAGRAM

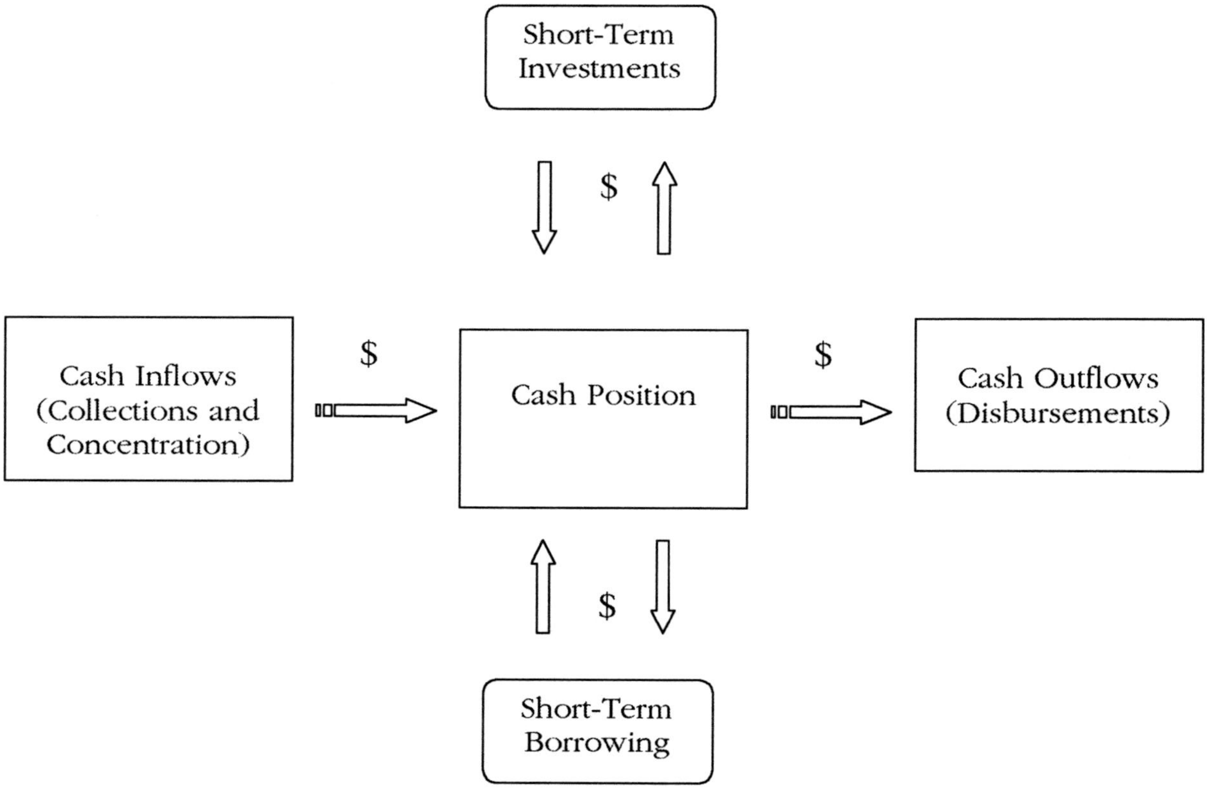

This chapter begins with a discussion of the concept of operating liquidity and how cash forecasting is used to measure and manage it. The chapter also presents the most commonly used short-term investing and borrowing instruments along with a series of calculations used for decision-making.

II. LIQUIDITY MANAGEMENT

Liquidity is the ability to meet short-term obligations when they come due. Short-term obligations include payments to employees (payroll), vendors and suppliers, lenders and tax agencies. Management of liquidity is the treasurer's responsibility. This daily task necessitates careful measurement and continual monitoring of net working capital to ensure an organization has sufficient financial resources to pay current and upcoming obligations while, at the same time, taking advantage of opportunities to invest and/or to pay down debt when there is a cash surplus. Liquidity must be maintained to cover both expected and unexpected demands for cash.

The three reasons that an organization must maintain liquidity are:

- **Transaction Requirements:** arise because day-to-day cash inflows and outflows are unsynchronized, uneven and uncertain. Unexpected demands for cash may result when inflows are not as expected.
- **Precautionary Requirements:** arise from unplanned expenses. Liquidity reserves for precautionary requirements may be maintained in the form of unused short-term borrowing facilities or short-term investments.
- **Speculative Requirements:** arise from unplanned investment opportunities. Liquidity reserves for speculative requirements are typically maintained in the form of short-term investments but short-term borrowing may be used in some cases.

Determination of the appropriate level of liquidity to hold for transaction, precautionary and speculative requirements is usually based on historical experience and professional judgment. Some companies may maintain a fixed number of days of average cash disbursements or use other methods to estimate an appropriate level. In general, the more unpredictable a company's cash flows are, the higher the required levels of liquidity that must be maintained.

It is important that adequate, but not excessive, liquidity be maintained. Treasurers are concerned with the risk of having insufficient liquidity. However, excess liquidity is also costly. Cash that might otherwise be applied to outstanding debt or invested in income-generating assets carry opportunity costs such as paying more interest than necessary or losing interest earnings. Similarly, securing credit facilities is time consuming and may be expensive because most financial institutions require payment of fees based on the level of available funds kept in reserve.

The starting point for determining required liquidity is estimating the future cash position through short-term cash forecasting. The short-term forecast allows a treasurer to identify anticipated cash surpluses and cash deficits in order to plan investing and borrowing activities that minimize borrowing costs or maximize investment income.

III. CASH FORECASTING

Short-term forecasts predict cash receipts and disbursements and the resulting balances on a daily, weekly or monthly basis. Short-term forecasts assist a treasurer in planning cash management activities such as scheduling cash concentration transfers for field and lockbox accounts, funding disbursement accounts, and making short-term investing and borrowing decisions. Short-term forecasting is also important in establishing and managing target balances for purposes of bank compensation.

(Bank compensation is covered in greater detail in Chapter 21, Relationship Management.)

A forecast requires a treasurer to take three steps:

- Estimate future operating cash inflows and outflows
- Generate a pro forma cash position
- Identify how to cover any cash deficits or how to use any cash surpluses. The shortfall or surplus is measured relative to the predetermined minimum desired liquidity or target balances.

Once developed, a cash forecast should be reviewed and updated periodically.

A. Objectives of Cash Forecasting

The primary objective of cash forecasting is liquidity management. Forecasts are used to schedule investment maturities and anticipate borrowing requirements. This enables a treasurer to maximize short-term investment income while minimizing borrowing costs, as well as the opportunity cost of excess bank balances. Another key objective of forecasting is to support strategic initiatives. The cash forecast is often used to project future funding requirements to support a company's strategic plan. In addition, forecasts facilitate the capital budgeting process.

A third key objective of forecasting is financial control and risk management. Using variance analysis to compare actual cash flows with projected cash flows helps identify problems such as unanticipated inventory changes, delays in accounts receivable collection or missed discount opportunities. Early identification allows a company to initiate corrective measures. Companies conducting business internationally may also use the cash forecast to determine global cash flows and to assess the degree of foreign currency exposure.

B. Forecasting Considerations

In most organizations, the short-term forecast is the treasurer's responsibility. However, compiling the information necessary to prepare a forecast requires the involvement of many different areas of a company such as sales, purchasing, accounts receivable, and accounts payable, among others. Preparation of a short-term forecast involves predicting each source and use of cash that impacts the cash position.

1. Data Identification

Identifying where to obtain the necessary information to be used in the forecast is an important element of the forecasting process. Information must be obtained from external and internal sources, including the company's banks, field managers, sales managers and the accounts payable, accounts receivable and payroll departments. For companies that have an integrated enterprise resource planning (ERP) financial reporting system, gathering the required information is facilitated by the fact that an ERP system is automated. For companies that have stand-alone treasury management information systems (TMIS), gathering the information required to prepare a forecast is semi-automated.

2. Certainty of Cash Flows

The proper forecasting of cash flows requires an understanding of the degrees of certainty for each component. The amount and timing of some outflows are known with accuracy in advance. These are referred to as certain flows and include payments such as principal and interest on debt, dividends and royalties.

Other cash flows may be predictable but the exact timing or amount is unknown. For example, cash collections from credit sales represent a cash flow component that may be predicted with reasonable, but not complete, accuracy. A prediction of future cash flows may be made based on the recent history of past collection experience using an accounts receivable balance pattern. Similarly, the pattern of clearing of vendor checks may be determined on the basis of past clearing times using a distribution forecast.

Less predictable cash flows, such as those related to sales of a new product, unexpected repairs, pending settlement of insurance claims or the cost of settling a strike, are difficult to forecast. In these instances, the experience and judgment of the person responsible for the forecast are important in estimating less predictable cash flows. For less predictable flows, multiple scenarios of the cash forecast may be generated to determine the potential minimum and maximum cash positions.

C. Short-Term Forecasting Techniques

Three techniques used in short-term forecasting are:

- An accounts-receivable balance pattern: to estimate cash inflows
- A distribution forecast: to estimate cash outflows
- A receipts and disbursements forecast: based on the combination of an accounts receivable balance pattern and a distribution forecast

1. Accounts Receivable Balance Pattern

An accounts receivable (A/R) balance pattern is useful in estimating the inflows associated with collection of accounts receivable. The A/R balance pattern specifies the percentage of credit sales that remain uncollected at the end of a specific period, such as a month or a quarter. A company's collection history determines the normal balance pattern. Balance patterns are used to forecast future cash inflows and to project accounts receivable levels. A treasurer may also use balance patterns for credit decision purposes by comparing current patterns with historical norms.

EXHIBIT 10.2 – SAMPLE A/R BALANCE PATTERN FOR THE MONTH OF MARCH

Month Sales	Sales	Remaining Accounts Receivable from Month Sales at the End of March	Remaining Accounts Receivable as a % of Month Sales
January	$250,000	$50,000	20%
February	$300,000	$165,000	55%
March	$400,000	$380,000	95%
April	$500,000		

The total outstanding accounts receivable balance at the end of March is:
$595,000 = ($50,000 + $165,000 + $380,000)

The estimate of cash inflows for April = 5% of April sales + 40% of March sales + 35% of February sales + 20% of January sales:

Estimated April inflows = (.05 x $500,000)
+ (.40 x $400,000)
+ (.35 x $300,000)
+ (.20 x $250,000)
= $340,000

Exhibit 10.2 demonstrates how an A/R balance pattern is used to estimate the monthly cash inflows from accounts receivable in the month of April for a company whose sales are collected as follows:

5%	of sales collected in the current month of sale
40%	of sales collected in the month after sale
35%	of sales collected two months after sale
20%	of sales collected three months after sale

At the end of March, there will still be $50,000 of accounts receivable outstanding (uncollected) from January's sales. This can be forecast as follows:

January Sales			=	$ 250,000.00
Collected in: January	=	(.05 x $250,000)	=	$ 12,500.00
Collected in: February	=	(.40 x $250,000)	=	$ 100,000.00
Collected in: March	=	(.35 x $250,000)	=	$ 87,500.00
Total Collections			=	$ 200,000.00

Total Outstanding Receivables from Jan. Sales = $ 250,000 – $ 200,000 = $50,000

2. Distribution Forecast

A distribution forecast estimates the effect a single event has on cash outflows over a specified interval based on historical patterns. Distribution forecasts are useful in estimating individual line items that appear on a receipts or disbursements schedule. For example, the expected daily clearing of payroll checks may be estimated using a distribution forecast.

Distribution percentages may be derived with a simple moving average or by regression analysis. For example, a forecaster may sample past clearings of payroll checks and discover that, on average, 40 percent of the payroll checks clear on the day checks are issued, 50 percent on the day after, and 10 percent two days after issuance. This is known as a simple moving average. These percentages may then be applied to the dollar value of subsequent payrolls to forecast the funding requirements for a given day after issuance. Exhibit 10.3 provides an example of a distribution forecast.

The problem with using a simple moving average is that more factors than just the number of days after check issuance may affect the check clearing delay. It is quite possible that the day of the week of check issuance, the day of the month of check issuance, or the proximity of holidays may affect the distribution of check clearings.

EXHIBIT 10.3 – FORECASTING USING THE DISTRIBUTION METHOD

A company has used regression analysis based on historical data to estimate the proportion of dollars that will clear on a given business day. It has determined that this proportion depends on the number of business days since the checks were distributed. The estimated proportions are given below.

Business Days Since Distribution	Percentage of Dollars Expected to Clear
1	13%
2	38%
3	28%
4	13%
5	8%
Total	100%

Therefore, if $100,000 in checks are distributed on Wednesday, May 1, the checks are estimated to clear according to the schedule below.

Date	Business Days After Distribution	Day of the Week	Percentage of Dollars Clearing	Forecast of Dollars Clearing
May 2	1	Thursday	13%	$ 13,000
May 3	2	Friday	38%	$ 38,000
May 6	3	Monday	28%	$ 28,000
May 7	4	Tuesday	13%	$ 13,000
May 8	5	Wednesday	8%	$ 8,000
		TOTAL	100%	$100,000

If more than one factor affects the distribution of an item's expected cash flow pattern, a statistical estimation technique, such as regression analysis, can be helpful in obtaining a more accurate forecast. Regression analysis allows seasonality and other trends to be incorporated into forecasts. However, this method requires large amounts of data and may need to be revised as business conditions change.

3. Receipts and Disbursements (R&D) Forecast

A receipts and disbursement (R&D) forecast is a fundamental liquidity planning tool. Construction of the forecast begins with the creation of separate schedules of cash inflows and cash outflows using A/R balance patterns and distribution forecasts.

A receipts schedule includes projected cash collections from customers (cash sales or payments from accounts receivable), other recurring cash inflows such as interest or dividends received from investments, as well as expected non-recurring cash inflows such as the proceeds from asset sales. A disbursements schedule involves forecasting the cash disbursements for purchases and other cash outflows, such as payroll, taxes, interest, dividends, rent and debt repayments.

Completing the forecast involves combining the R&D schedules to determine the net cash flow for the period. The cash position is determined by adding cash balances from the beginning of the period to the net cash flow. This total is compared with the minimum cash position required to meet transaction, precautionary and speculative requirements.

EXHIBIT 10.4 – R&D FORECAST

$ Amounts in $1,000	Week 1	Week 2	Week 3
Cash Receipts	$ 1,000	$ 1,000	$ 950
Cash Disbursements	(870)	(1,450)	(1,000)
Net Cash Flow	130	(350)	(50)
Beginning Cash Balance	100	230	(120)
Ending Cash Balance	230	(120)	(170)
Minimum Cash Req. (Target Balance)	(50)	(50)	(50)
Financing Needed (Deficit)		$ 170	$ 220
Investable Funds (Surplus)	$180		

In Exhibit 10.4, a company has determined its minimum cash requirement to be $50,000 to protect against unexpected expenses and to be able to take advantage of unanticipated opportunities. The beginning cash balance for each week is the ending cash balance from the prior week. The last two line items represent the anticipated surplus or deficit cash position each week. In this example, the forecast shows a surplus of funds in Week 1 that could be invested to earn interest. In Weeks 2 and 3 the forecast shows shortages of cash that would need to be managed by liquidating short-term investments or borrowing funds on a short-term basis. With an R&D forecast, a company can now better manage its investing and borrowing activities.

IV. SHORT-TERM INVESTMENTS

Companies require access to cash in order to meet ongoing obligations in a timely manner. However, the opportunity cost of maintaining cash balances in non-interest earning checking accounts can be significant. In order to minimize foregone interest income, companies invest in short-term instruments such as money market investments. Money market investments are highly marketable, interest-earning securities with stable market values and maturities of one year or less. These short-term investments provide an important source of liquidity whenever cash outflows exceed cash inflows.

Temporary surplus funds arise when a company receives cash for which it has no immediate use. Excess cash may arise from a variety of sources including ongoing operations, asset sales and debt or equity issuance. Often, cash surpluses arise from seasonal businesses that have uneven sales patterns throughout the year. For example, businesses such as retailers generate a large portion of the cash required to finance the year's operations during a brief period of time. The excess funds are temporarily invested until required to fund future operations.

On the other hand, a company may need to accumulate or temporarily house permanent surplus funds for debt or equity distributions or until they are required for capital investments. A company may also gradually accumulate excess cash from asset sales or securities issuance. Because most capital investments, equity distributions and debt reductions occur in specific amounts at specific times, excess cash may have to be held until needed.

A. Short-Term Investment Considerations

Deciding among short-term investment alternatives involves a trade-off between risk and higher returns. Some degree of risk is inherent in all investments, with those that offer higher returns carrying greater degrees of risk. Preservation of principal is the primary objective in choosing among short-term investment alternatives. As a result, the investment policies of many organizations limit short-term portfolios to money market instruments in order to reduce risk and ensure liquidity. Viewing short-term investment management as a profit center is not considered to be sound financial management. To address these issues, a company must implement a clearly defined written investment policy that governs management of short-term investments.

B. Short-Term Investment Policy

A company may incur substantial losses by making poor investment choices, assuming unnecessary risks or assigning investment responsibilities to unqualified personnel.

An investment policy should do four things:

- Establish the criteria for instrument suitability and portfolio configuration
- Delineate specific individual responsibilities for developing the policy
- Implement the policy on a day-to-day basis
- Require periodic review of investment performance

These are the key factors in constructing an investment policy, whether a company manages its own portfolio or outsources it to a third-party investment manager or a money market mutual fund. A sample of an excerpt from an investment policy is provided in Appendix 10.1 at the end of this chapter.

C. Investment Risk Considerations

Controlling investment risk involves preserving principal or ensuring against loss. The formulation of a short-term investment policy requires an organization to determine its risk tolerance. The primary risks associated with investments include credit or default risk, liquidity risk and price or market risk. Guidelines for each of these types of risk should be developed as part of a comprehensive investment policy.

1. Credit or Default Risk

Credit risk or default risk is the risk that payments on a security will not be made under the original terms. Credit evaluation of a security assesses the likelihood of the issuer defaulting on the obligation.

Most acceptable investment securities (other than U.S. Treasuries, which are considered risk free because they are backed by the "full faith and credit of the U.S. government") carry credit ratings that are assigned by credit rating agencies, such as Moody's or Standard and Poor's (S&P). Credit ratings are assigned to specific securities based on the default risk and seniority of the issue, also taking into consideration any collateral, back-up lines of credit or credit enhancement provided to support the obligation. If a financial intermediary provides credit enhancement by issuing an instrument such as a standby letter of credit or a surety bond to guarantee the obligation of the borrower, the obligation then assumes the credit rating of the institution providing the credit enhancement.

Exhibit 10.5 gives examples of the different ratings that selected rating agencies assign to short-term financial instruments.

EXHIBIT 10.5 – SELECTED SHORT-TERM CREDIT RATINGS

Moody's Ratings

Prime-1 (P1)	Superior ability for short-term debt repayment
Prime-2 (P2)	Strong ability for short-term debt repayment
Prime-3 (P3)	Acceptable ability for short-term debt repayment
Not Prime	Rated below the first three categories

Standard & Poor's Ratings

A-1+	Top degree of safety for short-term debt repayment
A-1	Strong degree of safety for short-term debt repayment
A-2	High degree of safety for short-term debt repayment
A-3	Acceptable degree of safety for short-term debt repayment
B	Below investment grade

2. Liquidity Risk

Liquidity risk is the risk that a security cannot be sold quickly without taking a significant loss. By definition, a liquid security is one that can be converted quickly and easily into cash at a known price and for a small transaction cost. The primary determinants of a security's liquidity are its marketability and maturity. The existence of an active secondary market ensures securities are readily marketable, regardless of the maturity.

Most financial instruments other than money market funds have a maturity date on which the obligation they represent is settled. Maturities for short-term investments may be as short as one day or a few days, so that quick conversion to cash is almost certain. By definition, however, short-term securities have maturities of up to one year.

Investors employing certain strategies may also use longer-term investments in a short-term portfolio. If active secondary markets do not exist, these investments may take considerable time to liquidate and, in some cases, may have to be held until maturity. Even with active secondary markets, holding investments over longer periods of time increases exposure to price risk.

A major drawback of investing in securities that are unrated, such as loan participations, is the risk that they cannot be resold. This exposes the holder of the securities to liquidity risk. If unrated securities are included in a company's short-term portfolio, the investor must perform a credit analysis to evaluate the credit quality of the borrower prior to making the investment.

3. Market Risk or Price Risk

Market risk or price risk is the uncertainty over the price at which a security can be sold prior to maturity. Securities with longer maturities are generally subject to more price risk than similar securities with shorter maturities. An investment's market risk typically takes one of two forms, interest rate risk and foreign exchange rate risk.

Interest rate risk arises from the threat that interest rates will rise during the holding period of a fixed-rate security, coupled with the necessity or intent to sell the security prior to maturity. In this case, the investment may have to be sold at a loss in order to induce a buyer to accept the below market face rate (i.e., a yield that is competitive with other similar investments).

Foreign exchange (FX) rate risk arises when foreign securities are held in the short-term investment portfolio. FX rate risk is the risk that there is a change in the rate of exchange between the currency in which a security is denominated and the company's home currency. If the issue's currency depreciates relative to the investor's home currency, the value of the investment declines. This risk is present whether the investment is sold prior to or at maturity. In order to limit this risk, most companies only allow investment in foreign securities issued in economically and politically stable countries.

(FX risk is discussed in greater detail in Chapter 17, Financial Risk Management.)

Another type of risk exposure arises in a declining rate environment when an issuer pays off a security prior to the stated maturity. This is referred to as reinvestment risk. A mortgage-backed security (MBS) is an example of an investment frequently held in short-term portfolios that is subject to reinvestment risk. Falling interest rates result in mortgages in the security pool being prepaid, causing a premature cash flow to the investor. These cash flows must then be reinvested at lower interest rates.

D. Factors Influencing Investment Pricing

Yield is a measure of the gain an investor derives from a financial instrument. Typically, it is stated as an annual percentage rate of return. In general, higher risk is associated with higher yields. In other words, there is a tradeoff between risk and return. Investors typically require a higher yield to compensate for higher risk. The greater the likelihood of default, the higher the risk premium and the higher the expected yield. A risk premium is the extra yield above that of a comparable risk-free security that investors require as compensation for assuming the additional risk.

Most money market instruments have low default, liquidity and price risk, thereby making them ideal for short-term portfolios. However, these low levels of risk also imply relatively low investment yields. U.S. government treasury securities, which are "backed by the full faith and credit of the U.S. government," have no default risk; therefore, other short-term securities are evaluated in comparison to them.

Liquidity risk is also associated with yield. The marketability of securities affects their yield because investors require a higher return for holding securities that are more difficult to sell. Similarly, an investment's length of time to maturity also influences yield. How the market values a debt instrument in comparison with similar securities that have longer or shorter maturities is revealed by the yield curve, which describes the term structure of interest rates. A yield curve depicts the differences in yield of securities that are identical except for their dates of maturity.

The liquidity preference theory of term structure states that investors demand a premium as a tradeoff for the lack of liquidity. Thus, higher yields may be earned by investing in longer-term securities versus shorter-term securities. Under these conditions, the yield curve is upward sloping and is referred to as a normal yield curve. This "normal" relationship may be modified by market expectations regarding future economic conditions.

An inverted yield curve slopes downward, reflecting higher short-term yields than long-term yields. Yield curve inversion happens infrequently. One theory explaining an inverted yield curve is that short-term uncertainties, such as an anticipated recession, shift investor preferences away from short-term instruments to those carrying longer maturities, thus driving down long-term rates. Exhibit 10.6 illustrates the relationship between market yield and maturity.

EXHIBIT 10.6 – SAMPLE YIELD CURVES

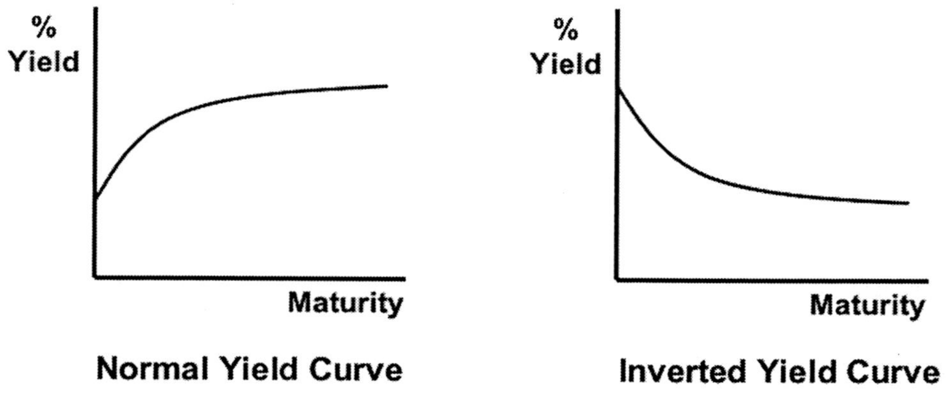

The price risk associated with longer maturities is an important contributing factor to the normal term structure of interest rates. Consistent with the relationship between risk and return, securities that are vulnerable to prepayment in a declining rate environment tend to have higher yields than similar securities with lower reinvestment risk. (For a detailed discussion of tools available for hedging of price and prepayment risk, see Chapter 17, Financial Risk Management.)

The tax status of an investment also affects yield. Tax-exempt securities, such as Treasury Bills (T-Bills) (which are exempt from local and state taxes) and municipal bonds (which are exempt from federal taxes) provide a lower pre-tax yield than taxable securities of similar maturity and default risk because of their tax advantage. When comparing taxable and tax-exempt instruments, the tax-exempt yield is usually converted to a taxable equivalent yield as follows:

$$\text{Taxable Equivalent Yield} = \frac{\text{Tax-Exempt Yield}}{(1 - \text{Marginal Tax Rate of Investor})}$$

This taxable equivalent yield can then be used to compare the tax-exempt instrument with other taxable investments. An example of a calculation of taxable equivalent yield is included in Appendix 10.2.

E. Yield Calculations for Short-Term Investments

Yield calculations for short-term investments are usually made on a simple interest basis, while yields on long-term investments are typically made on a compounded net present value (NPV) basis. The quoted yield for most short-term investments is a simple annual rate, called a nominal yield, which does not reflect compounding.

(The following section only discusses the calculations related to short-term investments. The valuation and yield calculations on long-term investments are covered in Chapter 13, Sources of Capital and Leasing.)

The yield on any instrument is a function of:

- The cash flows received from the investment
- The amount paid for that investment
- The maturity or holding period

The holding period yield is the yield for the time that a security is held. However, yields are quoted on an annualized basis that is obtained by adjusting the holding period yield for the number of days to maturity. The two commonly quoted yields that are calculated using the annual yield formula are the money market yield and the bond equivalent yield. The money market yield uses a 360-day year basis and the bond equivalent yield uses a 365-day year basis. The formulas for these basic yield calculations are as follows:

$$\text{Holding Period Yield} = \frac{\text{Cash Received at Maturity} - \text{Amount Invested}}{\text{Amount Invested}}$$

$$\text{Annual Yield} = \text{Holding Period Yield} \times \frac{\text{Days in Year}}{\text{Days to Maturity}}$$

$$\text{Money Market Yield} = \frac{\text{Dollar Discount}}{\text{Purchase Price}} \times \frac{360}{\text{Days to Maturity}}$$

The "days in year" appearing in the numerator of the annual yield calculation is called the year basis. The year basis underlying a quote given by an issuer determines the interest received by the investor. Rate quotes and interest payments on money market investments are computed on a 360-day-per-year basis. However, an investor's yield is computed using a 365-day-per-year basis. The convention for conversion from a 360-day to a 365-day basis is as follows:

$$\text{365-Day Basis Yield} = \text{60-Day Basis Yield} \times \frac{365}{360}$$

Debt investment securities are issued as either discount instruments or interest-bearing instruments. T-Bills, commercial paper and banker's acceptances are discount instruments. The amount invested in a discounted investment equals the face (par) value minus the interest that will be earned over the holding period. The cash received at maturity is the face value. The interest payment, or discount, is calculated using the following formula:

$$\text{Discount} = \text{Discount Rate} \times \text{Face Amount} \times \frac{\text{Days to Maturity}}{360}$$

Interest-bearing instruments, such as certificates of deposit (CDs) and Eurodollar deposits, pay interest in arrears at maturity or at periodic intervals. The cash received at maturity from an interest-bearing security is the face value plus the interest payment. The amount invested is the face value if the security is purchased in the primary market at issuance. If, on the other hand, the security is purchased on a secondary market, the amount invested is the total amount paid, including any interest or premium paid to, or discount received from, the seller.

The most reliable way to compare rates between instruments is to use effective annual yields. Effective annual yields assume compounding and are calculated on a 365-day-per-year basis. Because of compounding, an effective annual yield assumes that the investor always has the opportunity to reinvest funds at the same rate. The effective annual yield formula is as follows:

$$\text{Effective Annual Yield} = \left[1 + \frac{\text{Interest Received at Maturity}}{\text{Amount Invested}}\right]^{\frac{365}{\text{Days to Maturity}}} - 1$$

Examples of all yield calculations are provided in Appendix 10.2.

V. SHORT-TERM INVESTMENT MARKETS AND INSTRUMENTS

The market for debt and equity instruments has two major components:

- The money markets on which short-term debt securities are traded
- The capital markets on which longer-term debt and equity instruments (i.e., stocks and bonds) are traded

Generally, a company invests short-term by purchasing the debt securities offered through the money market. Rather than a single integrated entity or a particular exchange, the money market is a group of over-the-counter markets conducted among brokers, dealers, investors and borrowers. The money market is very large and efficient, with no single participant being large enough to impact prices. Certain capital market investments are also sometimes included in a short-term investment portfolio either directly or through mutual funds.

Nearly all short-term securities are issued in book-entry form. Book-entry securities are registered and transferred electronically either by the U.S. Treasury (treasury securities only) or through the commercial book entry system. Participants in the commercial book-entry system include the Treasury, the Federal Reserve System, banks, brokers, dealers and other financial institutions. The chief advantage of book-entry securities is the ease and speed of transaction clearing without the need for movement of physical certificates. Prior to book-entry, securities were issued in bearer and registered form. Both bearer and registered securities are certificated, but they are no longer used for new issues of money market securities in the U.S.

A. Money Market Participants

Issuers of money market instruments include the U.S. Treasury, federal agencies and government-sponsored enterprises (GSEs), securities dealers, banks, thrifts, and other corporations that raise funds by borrowing in the money market. Except for the U.S. Treasury, investors in the market include many of the same entities that are issuers.

Individuals also invest in this market directly through purchases of money market investments and indirectly through the investment in money market mutual funds. Investors purchasing money market instruments are making short-term loans to the issuers. In the money markets, investors are lenders while issuers are borrowers.

A broker acts as a transaction intermediary, matching buyers and sellers of money market securities. Brokers are compensated by the fees and/or commissions they charge for their services. Brokers and dealers play key roles in the money markets by placing the majority of new issues in the primary market and providing the secondary markets with the liquidity necessary for outstanding issues.

(For a detailed discussion of primary and secondary markets, see Chapter 3, Financial Environment.)

Dealers serve a dual role in the money market. Like brokers, dealers act as transaction intermediaries but they also take positions in securities so they are able to act as the counterparty in the purchase and sale of transactions. The price or yield at which the dealer will sell a security is known as the ask price; the price or yield at which the dealer will purchase a security is known as the bid price. Dealers also issue repurchase agreements, which are money market instruments used to finance their securities inventories.

Money market activities fall under the jurisdiction of a variety of regulators, depending on the parties to a transaction, the securities involved and the markets or exchanges on which the instruments are traded.

The Federal Reserve plays three important roles in the money markets:

- The settlement of most book-entry security sales and purchases is accomplished through the Federal Reserve accounts of member institutions using Fedwire as the primary transfer mechanism.
- The Fed's Open Market Committee implements its monetary policy through purchases and sales of treasury securities in the secondary markets, often using repurchase agreements.
- The Fed buys, sells and redeems treasury securities in its role as fiscal agent for the U.S. Treasury.

B. Money Market Instruments

Money market securities are debt instruments with remaining maturities of up to one year, although most mature in three months or less. Some debt securities, issued by the U.S. government and GSEs with longer maturities, are often treated as money market securities due to the existence of large, active secondary markets for these issues.

Money market securities have differing credit quality, yields, maturities and marketability. In general, however, money market instruments have low credit risk, may be readily converted to cash at low cost due to active secondary markets, and have minimal price risk due to their shorter maturities.

1. U.S. Treasury Bills (T-Bills)

The U.S. Treasury is the largest issuer of money market securities. Treasury issues include T-Bills, notes and bonds. Because of the low liquidity risk and no default risk associated with these issues, U.S. Treasury rates are considered to be risk-free and serve as the benchmark against which rates and prices on other debt securities are compared. Other investment alternatives generally trade at yields above those of government securities. Interest income on U.S. Treasuries is exempt from state income tax. However, some states do charge corporations a franchise tax from which U.S. Treasury securities are not exempt.

T-Bills are money market discount instruments issued in maturities of one year or less. Primary treasury offerings are sold through a multiple-price, sealed-bid auction. For those submitting competitive bids, the bids are accepted starting with the highest price (lowest yield) offered, down to the lowest price necessary to sell the entire issue. Non-competitive bids may also be submitted, with the bidder being guaranteed to receive the desired amount of bills, at the average price from the competitive bid process. Eligible banks, broker/dealers, and other private and governmental entities tender bids for specific amounts of the offered securities. Again, all Treasury securities are registered and issued in book-entry form.

The secondary market for U.S. Treasury securities is one of the largest in the world and has low transaction costs. Therefore, T-Bills can be readily bought and sold in significant volumes with negligible, if any, impact on market prices. Hence, they are considered to be highly marketable. Dealer bid and ask yield quotes for T-Bills are published daily. A sample of daily T-Bills quotations that appear in the financial press is provided in Appendix 10.2.

2. Federal Agency and Government Sponsored Enterprise (GSE) Securities

Government National Mortgage Association (GNMA or Ginnie Mae), a wholly owned agency of the U.S., provides liquidity for government sponsored mortgage programs through its mortgage-backed securities (MBS) program. Individual mortgages that are insured or guaranteed by certain government agencies are pooled and interests in them are sold, either as MBSs or as Real Estate Mortgage Investment Conduits (REMICs), supported by Ginnie Mae's guarantee. The Ginnie Mae guarantee is backed by the full faith and credit of the U.S. government, so yields on Ginnie Mae issues are lower than those for most other MBSs.

The primary risks associated with Ginnie Mae MBSs are interest rate related price and prepayment risks. REMICs allow some control over these risks by allocating principal and interest payments from pools of mortgages to classes (tranches) with differing maturity, prepayment and interest characteristics that appeal to a variety of investment risk profiles.

The U.S. Department of Veterans Affairs (VA) also guarantees REMICs issued through the Vendee Mortgage Trust. Like Ginnie Mae, the VA guarantees timely payment of principal and interest to the REMIC investor and this guarantee is backed by the full faith and credit of the federal government.

GSEs are private companies that act as financial intermediaries to provide funds for loans made in the housing, education and agriculture sectors. GSEs do not carry the credit backing of the U.S. government though there is a strong implication that in a crisis the federal government would intervene to help repay investors because of the importance of the GSEs to public welfare.

GSE securities are issued by the Federal National Mortgage Association (Fannie Mae), the Federal Farm Credit Banks Funding Corporation, the Federal Home Loan Mortgage Corporation (Freddie Mac), the Federal Home Loan Banks Office of Finance and the Student Loan Marketing Association (Sallie Mae) to provide liquidity in support of their loan programs. At the time of this publication, issues by GSEs were not required to be rated by rating agencies.

3. Bank Issues

Banks raise funds in the money markets through time deposits, repurchase agreements, banker's acceptances and fed funds. Examples of time deposits include savings accounts, CDs and Negotiable CDs. Negotiable CDs are domestic large dollar time deposits issued by banks and thrift institutions that are bought and sold on the open market. Negotiable CDs are usually traded in $1 million blocks. While all CDs have a fixed maturity, there is an active secondary market for negotiable CDs. Non-negotiable CDs or retail CDs, which are issued in many different denominations to consumers and businesses, cannot be redeemed prior to maturity without a penalty.

Foreign banks and foreign branches of U.S. banks raise funds in the money market through Eurodollar deposits (Eurodollars). Eurodollars are dollar denominated deposits held outside the U.S. and may be issued as Eurodollar CDs, which are negotiable, or as Eurodollar time deposits, which are non-negotiable. Both Eurodollar CDs and Eurodollar time deposits are interest-bearing.

Banks, as well as securities dealers, raise large volumes of short-term funds by selling investment securities under repurchase agreements (repos). An investor in a repurchase agreement buys government securities from the bank or dealer who simultaneously agrees to repurchase them for a slightly higher price at a future date. Most repos are overnight, but some may be arranged for longer periods. Repos over 30 days are called term repurchase agreements.

A banker's acceptance (BA) arises out of commercial trade. A BA represents a time draft, issued by a purchaser of goods to pay a supplier, that has been "accepted" by the bank on which the draft is drawn. The bank's acceptance constitutes its unconditional promise to pay the draft. In a typical transaction the drawee bank discounts (i.e., pays cash for) the acceptance, which it may hold in its own portfolio or sell (rediscount) in the secondary market.

(A more detailed discussion of BAs, is in the short-term borrowing section of the current chapter, as well as Chapter 16, Treasury Organization and Liquidity Management.)

Banks borrow and lend on an overnight basis to maintain adequate reserve positions with the Fed using Fed funds. While Fed funds activity constitutes a significant portion of the daily money market transaction volume, it is limited to financial institutions, not open to other investors.

4. Corporate Commercial Paper (CP)

Bank holding companies, non-bank finance companies and non-financial businesses such as utilities, manufacturers and service companies sell CP directly to investors or through dealers. The key characteristic of CP is that it is an unsecured promissory note. CP that is issued in the public market must have maturities of 270 days or less in order to be exempt from Securities and Exchange Commission (SEC) registration requirements. Private placements of CP may have maturities of up to 360 days. CP issuers can tailor maturities to match large investors' needs, so the secondary market for CP is limited.

CP is evaluated by rating agencies and may be credit enhanced. While unrated CP is available, most investors limit their CP holdings to the most highly rated issues. CP has among the highest yields of all money market investments due to its default risk and the limited secondary market.

5. Municipal Notes and CP

State and local governments, their agencies, authorities and subdivisions raise funds in the money market through municipal notes and CP. Many municipal issues are exempt from federal income taxes and/or state income taxes in the state of issue, making these attractive for investors seeking tax-sheltered income. Maturities of three months to one year are typical for municipal notes and range up to 270 days for CP. Most of these short-term municipal issues are used by local governments to provide interim financing for general obligation bond projects or to provide short-term working capital in anticipation of future (tax) revenues. Dealers provide an active secondary market for short-term municipal obligations.

6. Money Market Mutual Funds

Money market mutual funds (MMMFs) – not to be confused with either non-money market mutual funds (see discussion below) or money market accounts offered by banks—are commingled funds of money market instruments in which fund investors have an ownership interest. MMMFs are sold in shares. Because minimum investments in MMMFs tend to be substantially smaller than those required for direct investments in money market securities, treasurers can more easily tailor their short-term portfolios to meet diversification and maturity requirements.

MMMFs are an increasingly important component of corporate short-term investment portfolios and may offer advantages over other securities under changing interest rate conditions. For example, when interest rates are falling, fund managers may extend maturities to lock in a yield. Thus, investors in the fund get the greater return of longer-term instruments while enjoying the liquidity and stability of principal associated with investments with shorter maturities.

MMMFs can provide a company with a professionally managed marketable securities portfolio at a low management cost. For many companies, using MMMFs may be less expensive than managing a short-term investment portfolio. Using MMMFs rather than in-house investment management may also free up valuable treasury resources for other tasks.

MMMFs are configured to report a net asset value (NAV) of $1.00 per share. They generate different yields and have slightly different risk thresholds. MMMFs charge management fees or service charges based on the investor's balance, level of activity and services provided.

7. Short-Term Mutual Funds

Mutual funds are available to suit most short-term investment needs. Funds place the majority of their holdings in specific types of instruments such as U.S. Treasuries, CDs, CP or municipal issues. Some companies offer a variety of short-term funds based on differing average maturities or duration. In most cases, the longer maturity funds offer not only higher average returns but also a higher risk of losing some NAV. Unlike MMMFs, these funds are not configured to maintain a stable $1.00-per-share NAV. Using these funds, a treasurer can place some portion of short-term investment funds in a low-risk, short-term fund to meet near-term needs, and other portions in longer-term funds to meet needs further in the future. This approach facilitates an investment strategy known as matching, whereby investment needs are matched with forecasted cash flows.

C. Investment Strategies

A variety of short-term investment strategies are available to a company, depending on its strategic objectives:

- A conservative investor may prefer a matching strategy.
- A more aggressive investor may prefer riding the yield curve.
- A high-tax-bracket investor may favor tax-based strategies.
- Alternatively, any of these types of investors may choose to outsource investment management, using their strategy as the guidelines for the investment manager.

1. Matching

Matching involves purchasing securities that mature when funds are required to meet an expected obligation or obligations. Matching allows companies to invest for extended periods and potentially increase yields. To be effective, this strategy requires careful forecasting of future cash flows and capital requirements. If cash is needed sooner than expected, the securities purchased to match a specific cash outflow may have to be sold prematurely, perhaps at a loss. Companies that match tend to do so conservatively, covering a portion, but not the entire amount, of the expected capital need.

2. Riding the Yield Curve

Riding the yield curve involves buying highly liquid marketable securities, such as T-Bills, that mature on a different day from the day the investor intends to sell the securities. There are two strategies; the appropriate one to use depends on the shape of the yield curve:

- When the yield curve is upward-sloping or normal, an investor purchases securities that mature beyond the time period when funds are needed. Then, the securities are sold prior to maturity. At the time of sale, the security has a shorter remaining time to maturity than it did when it was purchased, providing a return that exceeds that which could be achieved using maturity matching. The risk of this strategy is that interest rates may increase more than had been anticipated, thereby reducing the value of the security at the time it is sold.

- When the yield curve is inverted or downward sloping, an investor purchases securities for shorter than the time period when funds are needed, reinvesting the funds when the first set of securities mature. The risk of this strategy is that interest rates may fall further than expected or the yield curve may shift.

3. Tax-Based Strategies

With a wide variety of tax-favored securities available, many investors are able to realize superior tax-equivalent yields by including these tax-exempt or tax-advantaged instruments in short-term portfolios.

Besides investing in specific municipal issues, investors have the option of buying shares in tax-advantaged mutual funds tailored to their states of domicile. The yield advantage of tax-favored investment is directly related to an investor's marginal tax rate. See a sample calculation in Appendix 10.2.

Dividend capture is a tax-motivated, short-term investment strategy available to tax-paying corporations. An investor purchases common stock just before the ex-dividend date and sells it after "capturing" the dividend. However, in order to take advantage of the 70 percent intercorporate dividend tax exclusion, the investor must hold the shares for more than 45 days. Even when investments are limited to high quality blue chip stocks, this strategy exposes the investor to a high degree of market or price risk. Many events may adversely impact the security price during the holding period.

VI. SHORT-TERM FINANCING

Because daily cash flows are unsynchronized, uneven and uncertain, companies may face short-term, temporary cash needs that must be met through borrowing. Available short-term credit is a key source of liquidity for many companies, particularly growing and seasonal businesses. A key responsibility of a treasurer is to obtain the most cost effective sources of short-term financing available.

A. Short-Term Financing Considerations

Short-term financing is used to meet temporary cash needs for periods of one year or less. While short-term financing is often equated with debt, there are actually three primary sources of short-term funds: (1) spontaneous financing such as trade credit, (2) sale or factoring of accounts receivable and (3) borrowing arrangements with banks, finance companies or in the money markets. In addition, multi-divisional businesses may allow internal borrowing from subsidiaries. Selecting the best short-term financing plan requires consideration of a number of factors.

B. Planning Credit Needs

Credit is an important source of liquidity for many companies but it does require planning to obtain the best terms and rates. Negotiating arrangements with suppliers or lenders, or issuing CP, is not accomplished overnight. It is critical that sources of funds be established well in advance of the borrowing need. Cash forecasting helps to identify future short-term credit needs.

C. Short-Term Financing Objectives

The objective of short-term financing is to ensure adequate credit availability at minimum cost and minimum risk and with maximum flexibility. The amount and timing of short-term credit requirements are identified through cash forecasting. The cost of borrowing funds depends on the type of credit facility used, with the least costly funds usually provided through spontaneous financing. Major costs of formal credit arrangements include interest, fees and underwriter or dealer costs.

The manner in which a company's credit is structured may expose it to varying degrees and types of risk. Standard provisions customarily used in lending agreements influence default risk, and the consequences of default. Payment default risk, which is the risk that future cash flow will not be sufficient to service debt, may increase when a company is over-leveraged (i.e., takes on too much debt). When a payment default occurs, lenders are less willing to provide funds. As a result, borrowing costs increase, and credit terms may be tightened or additional funds may be withheld and payment demanded, potentially leading to bankruptcy. The same consequences exist if there is a technical default.

A technical default occurs when a borrower continues to make required payments but violates some other term, frequently a financial covenant such as a liquidity, coverage or performance ratio. The risk of technical default increases with the degree of constraint imposed through covenants. It is important that a treasurer negotiate covenants that accommodate business plans and allow for a reasonable margin of variance.

Nearly all creditors include cross-default provisions in their agreements. If a default occurs under any borrowing, then all credit facilities with cross-default provisions are in default and subject to the remedies discussed above. Another common provision is a material adverse change (MAC) clause, also referred to as a discretionary clause. A MAC clause allows a lender to refuse funding or to declare a default even if all agreements are in full compliance if, in the lender's opinion, a MAC has occurred in the borrower's condition. Cross-default provisions and MAC clauses severely limit financial flexibility. A treasurer must carefully consider agreeing to a MAC clause when negotiating with lenders.

Maintaining a variety of sources for credit with differing degrees of structure enhances flexibility by allowing a treasurer to choose the least expensive alternative and to maintain funding resources under differing circumstances. In addition, a bank's willingness to fund on uncommitted facilities may depend on its appetite for credit at a given time or on Fed-induced credit supply pressures.

D. Strategic Objectives

The need for and use of short-term funds is often determined by a company's strategic plan. The strategic objectives determine future courses of action that have an impact on borrowing requirements. Credit needs may increase in order to support sales growth, for a planned capital investment or other major expenditures. Management must determine and plan for:

- The level of debt
- The mix of debt among short-term, intermediate- and long-term sources
- The appropriate mix of debt and equity

(A more detailed discussion of this topic is in Chapter 14, Capital Structure and Dividend Policy.)

The impact of short-term borrowing on the financial structure of the company must be considered at all times. Most organizations control their levels of liabilities in order to conform to strategic plans, industry conventions and provisions in agreements because these may all impose constraints on financial leverage. In addition, levels of debt directly influence a company's marginal cost of capital and negatively affect credit ratings.

E. Factors Influencing Financing Costs

Financing issues represent an investment for the lender or counterparty to the transaction. As a consequence, the factors that influence investment yield are the determinants of credit pricing. Pricing and fees on loans increase with default risk, price risk, liquidity and length of maturity. Factors that enter into borrowing costs, yet do not impact investor's yields, include dealer and placement fees, credit enhancement and backup credit costs.

F. Short-Term Funding Alternatives

Short-term debt instruments mature within one year. They are generally used to finance current assets such as accounts receivable and inventory. Any type of loan or credit arrangement can be referred to as a credit facility. In addition to debt, trade financing and the sale of receivables are potential sources of liquidity that should be considered.

1. Trade Credit

Trade credit arises when a buyer receives goods but payment is not made until some later date. Trade credit is the primary source of short-term financing used by many businesses. While the supplier does not advance cash to the buyer, trade credit allows a buyer to use the supplier's goods while using the cash it would otherwise have had to pay in advance or upon delivery. Trade credit provides a tangible economic benefit because the buyer may avoid liquidating investments or incurring debt over the credit period. A company buyer who pays its suppliers before the invoice due date (assuming no discount for early payment) may be foregoing an inexpensive source of working capital.

In addition to terms offered in the ordinary course of business, suppliers may also provide special financing under certain circumstances. Suppliers, to assist buyers through periods when cash is particularly constrained, commonly grant occasional payment deferrals and seasonal dating terms. Because trade credit impacts supplier relationships, and credit ratings depend on timely payments, stretching of payables (i.e. deliberately paying late) is usually not an advisable practice. However, a business should fully utilize the terms offered and consider suppliers as an option when seeking short-term financing. (For a more detailed discussion of trade credit, see Chapter 7, Working Capital Tools.)

2. Internal Borrowing

Multiple units of an organization may borrow and lend among themselves through an in-house bank or internal borrowing. Often, these arrangements are formal and priced at market rate; however, the entity as a whole retains the money and, therefore, the benefits. Many laws and regulations affect domestic and cross-border intra-company transfers. For example, the length of time that intracorporate loans are outstanding can affect whether repayment of principal is treated as return of capital or as a dividend for tax purposes. Policies related to intra-company transactions should be designed based on advice from legal and tax professionals in order to avoid possible problems.

3. Asset Sales

Receivables may be sold or discounted to raise cash in two ways. First, receivables may be factored. Factoring is the sale or transfer of title to accounts receivable to a third party called a factor. A factor is a financing institution that discounts acceptable accounts receivable with or without recourse to the borrower. Factors charge a percentage commission (i.e., a discount) on the amount of receivables, depending on the quality of the receivables. The advantage of factoring is that the factor pays on the basis of the quality of the company's customers and is not, therefore, dependent on the company's financial statements. A factoring arrangement is also able to respond more quickly than a typical lending facility to changes in sales level (hence, in receivables).

(More detailed information about factoring, is in Chapter 7, Working Capital Tools.)

The second method by which receivables may be sold is through securitization, a financing technique by which a company issues debt securities backed by a pool of receivables. Assets that are suitable for debt securitization usually have a predictable cash flow stream to retire the issue and a low level of historical loss experience.

4. Commercial Bank Credit

Bank credit is an important source of short-term funds for businesses. Bank borrowings are the chief source of working capital for middle market and smaller companies. Larger organizations often find bank credit attractive because banks are able to customize debt structures and to use private information to underwrite the debt. Bank loans may be offered on a secured basis or an unsecured basis. Security, provided in the form of collateral or guarantees, may be used to obtain more favorable rates by some borrowers or to make credit available to businesses that are unable to access unsecured credit facilities. In addition, use of private information (i.e., information that is not publicly disclosed) by a lender may also result in lower borrowing costs.

Banks are able to extend large credit facilities through loan syndications and participations. In a loan syndication, multiple financial institutions share a single credit facility. The syndicate, or group of lenders, is led by an agent who acts as the intermediary between the company and the syndicate for purposes of negotiating the credit terms and documentation, making advances and payments on the loan and disseminating information. All of the syndicate members share common documentation, but each lender has a promissory note, making it a direct lending relationship.

With a loan participation, a financial institution purchases an interest in another lender's credit facility. This purchaser is called a participant, and the seller is commonly referred to as the lead institution. The participant does not have a separate note and has only an indirect relationship with the borrower. A participation agreement specifies the rights and the obligations of both the participant and the lead institution. In the case of a blind participation, the participation is not disclosed to the borrower, and the participant may not directly contact the borrower or disclose the participant's role in the credit facility.

5. Single Payment Notes

Single payment notes are usually granted for a short period of time for a specific purpose, with both principal and interest paid at maturity. Because of the limited duration and precise maturity of a single payment note, a specific cash flow event is frequently identified as the repayment source at the time the funds are advanced.

6. Reverse Repurchase Agreement

Another source of short-term funds available through commercial banks is a reverse repurchase agreement (reverse repo). Securities are sold to the bank, providing the seller with cash until the securities are repurchased. This is also referred to as securities lending. Reverse repos enable companies to tap into the liquidity of their investment portfolios without having to dispose of investments in the money markets. An equivalent transaction may be structured by using a single payment note secured by marketable securities.

7. Line of Credit

A line of credit is an agreement in which the lender gives the borrower access to funds up to a maximum amount over a specific period of time. Lines of credit are usually revolving, meaning the borrower may borrow, repay and re-borrow funds up to the established limit during the commitment period. A line of credit may be used to provide short-term financing, to back up CP or to provide temporary liquidity.

Requirements and conditions frequently associated with lines of credit include clean-up periods, credit sub-limits and MAC clauses. To ensure a line is used for temporary, not permanent, financing, a lender may require a clean-up period consisting of 30 to 60 consecutive days without any outstanding borrowings on the line. This requirement is used mostly for middle market and small companies. A lender may also establish sub-limits under the line for specific uses such as letter of credit issuance, drafts under BAs, or for advances against certain types of collateral. Finally, a MAC clause gives the lender the flexibility to refuse funding if there has been an adverse change in the borrower's credit profile.

Lines of credit may be unsecured or secured, uncommitted or committed. Secured lines require the borrower to pledge some form of collateral, typically current assets such as accounts receivable and inventory. The availability under some secured lines is limited by a borrowing base (sometimes referred to as loan value) that is negotiated as a percentage of the value of the collateral securing the line. (The concept of a borrowing base is discussed under the Asset-Based Borrowing section later in this chapter.)

An uncommitted line is usually made available for a one-year period; however, funding may be refused at the lender's discretion or canceled outright. Hence, an uncommitted line is often referred to as a discretionary line. A committed line usually involves a formal loan agreement that specifies the terms and conditions of the credit facility and typically requires compensation in the form of balances or fees because the lender is obligated to provide funding up to the credit limit stipulated in the agreement so long as the borrower is not in default. A commitment fee may be assessed based on either the total amount or the unused portion of the commitment. Payment is usually made quarterly. Fees vary depending on the creditworthiness of the company, the stated purpose of the line and the term of the commitment.

Another type of line is referred to as a guidance line. Examples of guidance lines include money market and demand lines of credit. Guidance lines are also often used by banks to accommodate credit exposure arising from non-borrowing activities such as daylight overdrafts, ACH credit exposure and FX exposure. However, banks do not always make borrowers aware of guidance lines.

Compensating balances are balances that are maintained in the company's deposit accounts at the bank and generally do not earn interest or offset depository service charges. In a compensating balance arrangement, the balance requirement can be specified as a percentage of:

- The total commitment
- The unused amount of the commitment
- The outstanding borrowings

If compensating balances are required, their effect is to reduce the amount of the borrowed funds that can be used by the borrower, thereby increasing the effective annual interest rate. The practice of requiring compensating balances is becoming less and less common due to the competition for credit among commercial banks.

Pricing for a line of credit is usually negotiable. The lender may take into account various aspects of the overall lender/borrower relationship in pricing the line. There are three basic cost components for lines of credit:

- The all-in rate of interest
- Commitment fees
- Compensating balances (Compensating balances are less common than they were in the past due to the competition among lenders for creditworthy borrowers.)

The all-in rate consists of a base rate, such as LIBOR, prime or the Fed funds rate, plus a spread that is added to the base rate. Rates on lines are normally variable and adjust immediately to changes in the base rate.

The effective borrowing rate for a line of credit is computed using the following formula:

$$\text{Effective Annual Borrowing Rate} = \frac{\text{Total Interest} + \text{Total Commitment Fees Paid}}{\text{Average Usable Funds Borrowed}}$$

The total interest paid is calculated as the all-in rate times the average loan amount outstanding for the year. Total fees paid include all commitment fees, placement fees and any issuance costs. Average usable funds borrowed is the average outstanding loan for the year less the required compensating balances. A sample effective annual borrowing rate calculation is provided in Appendix 10.2.

8. Revolving Credit Agreement

A revolving credit agreement, also known as a revolver, is a committed line of credit that is established for a specified period of time, often on a multiyear basis. Revolving credits are formal contractual commitments with loan agreements, including covenants. Usually, there is a commitment fee on the unused portion, as well as a fee for use of the borrowing facility. While often used for short-term borrowing, the commitment term typically ranges from two to five years and may be followed by a period in which the principal is systematically repaid. If more than a year is left on a multiyear revolver, current GAAP guidelines allow balances on this agreement to be carried as a long-term liability on the borrower's balance sheet.

All of the features of committed lines may be found in revolvers. In addition, revolvers often feature short-term fixed rate funding options that offer fixed rate loans for specified periods with penalties imposed for prepayments. An example would be a funding option for 90-day advances fixed at a rate equal to some pre-established spread over the 90-day CD rate. The amount of the spread varies depending on the credit risk.

9. Commercial Paper (CP) Issuance

CP is a short-term, unsecured promissory note issued in the money markets. CP is often the least expensive available source of short-term debt for creditworthy companies with large, ongoing short-term funding requirements. CP maturities are limited to a maximum of 270 days. In practice, many issuers of CP roll over the outstanding balances at maturity into a new CP issue. In this way, CP may also be used for longer-term financing. CP backup lines of credit are maintained with banks in order to repay CP in the event that it cannot be rolled over.

In order to ensure a publicly issued CP's marketability, it must carry a strong credit rating. The rating must be solicited and paid for by the issuer. Rating agencies require extensive information from the issuer in order to conduct a thorough credit analysis. If the issuer's rating is below investment grade, a higher rating may be attained through credit enhancement.

The most common form of enhancement is a standby letter of credit (L/C) issued by a highly rated bank. The L/C constitutes a commitment by the bank to repay the CP if the issuer fails to do so. A CP issue backed by an L/C assumes the rating of the L/C bank, resulting in more favorable pricing for the issue. However, the fees charged by the bank for the L/C may offset the pricing advantage.

CP is issued at a discount; therefore the proceeds to the issuer are less than the issue amount. The discount on a CP issue represents the interest paid by the borrower at maturity. Other costs associated with a CP program include dealer fees, backup credit facility fees, rating agency charges and credit enhancement costs. Most CP is placed in the market through dealers. The dealers, who are selected by the issuer, charge a fee for their services, usually a fractional percentage of the issue amount.

The effective annual interest cost for CP takes into account the discount rate, the dealer fee, and the fee on the backup line or standby L/C and is calculated as follows:

$$\text{Effective Annual Interest} = \frac{\text{Discount} + \text{Dealer Fee} + \text{Backup Fee}}{\text{Usable Funds}} \times \frac{365}{\text{Days to Maturity}}$$

$$\text{Usable Funds} = \text{Face Value} - \text{Discount}$$

$$\text{Discount} = \text{Discount Rate} \times \text{Face Amount} \times \frac{\text{Days to Maturity}}{360}$$

A sample effective annual interest CP calculation is provided in Appendix 10.2.

Because of the effort and cost involved in establishing a CP program, CP financing is desirable only when ongoing funding needs are large. Few companies consider CP for issue amounts of less than $50 million. In addition, companies that do not have excellent credit ratings often find commercial bank credit to be more attractive than CP because banks have more flexibility in structuring credit to mitigate risk.

10. Asset-Based Borrowing

Commercial finance companies and some commercial banks specialize in asset-based lending. Asset-based lines of credit are secured by accounts receivable and inventory. They are often used to support temporary working capital needs. Because availability of an asset-based line is closely tied to the level of the collateral, advances are made as additional collateral is generated and are liquidated as the underlying receivables are collected or as inventories are sold. Because the collateral serves as the primary source of repayment, a lender closely evaluates and monitors the asset.

When receivables secure the credit, the lender evaluates the type of customers who buy from the borrower by analyzing the volume of customer purchases, delinquency rates and the level of bad debt write-offs. A loan secured by receivables normally requires the borrower's customers to remit payments directly to the lender. These payments are then applied to the outstanding loan balance.

The lender also monitors the borrower's accounts receivable aging schedule to determine the timeliness of customer payments. Based on this evaluation, an advance rate is established for the receivables. The advance rate is stated as a percentage of accounts receivable outstanding. This percentage, when applied to the amount of pledged accounts receivable, determines the maximum amount of debt that can be supported by the collateral, which is called the borrowing base. The borrowing base is recalculated at specified times or when an advance under the line is requested. The funds available under the line vary as the borrowing base changes.

Inventory may also collateralize asset-based lines. As with accounts receivable financing, borrowing is limited by an advance rate that is calculated as a percentage of inventory. Generally, inventory lenders are more willing to advance against finished goods and raw materials than work in progress. Sometimes, different advance rates are determined for different types of inventories. However, the advance rate is typically much less than it is for accounts receivable, reflecting the less liquid nature of inventory.

Asset-based inventory lines, referred to as floor plan lines, are extended to dealers who sell major purchase items such as automobiles, trucks, farm equipment and major appliances. The lender advances funds to pay for specific inventory purchases. To secure the amount owed to it by the dealer, the lender retains legal title to the goods until they are sold. The proceeds from the sale are then used to repay the loan.

11. Banker's Acceptance (BA)

A banker's acceptance (BA) is a negotiable short-term instrument used primarily to finance the import/export or domestic shipment of goods or the storage of readily marketable staples. A BA is considered a debt obligation and is evidenced by a time draft drawn by the borrower that is accepted by the bank on which it is drawn. By accepting the draft, the bank becomes directly obligated for payment of the draft on the maturity date.

Acceptance financing is often provided to a buyer or seller in connection with a letter of credit, but acceptances can be created to finance open account transactions as well. The pricing on a BA compares favorably with other short-term borrowing rates. The all-in rate for acceptance financing includes the discount rate plus the BA commission paid to the accepting bank.

(A more detailed discussion of BAs is in Chapter 16, Global Treasury Organization and Liquidity Management.)

VII. OUTSOURCING OF LIQUIDITY MANAGEMENT

Complete delegation of liquidity management to an outside provider may not be desirable. There are, however, several products that enable companies to comfortably and efficiently outsource some aspects of the liquidity management process.

A. Outsourcing of Investment Management

Some organizations outsource investment management in order to increase yield and provide fiduciary oversight. For example, an investor may purchase shares in mutual funds, thereby capitalizing on the investment management expertise of the fund manager. The wide range of options available allows a company to easily tailor its investments to risk/return objectives.

Hiring registered investment advisors is another outsourcing alternative. Outsourcing of investment management is often cost effective and allows treasury personnel to focus on more time-critical daily tasks. However, it is important to establish clear risk/return objectives and to monitor investment management performance on a regular basis.

B. Sweep Accounts

A company may have its depository institution sweep any excess, end-of-day funds into an investment account. Investment sweep options are diverse, including repos or other money market instruments, managed accounts and mutual funds. Some sweeps offer offshore investments that are tax-exempt. Such strategies entail minimal risk, time and effort and they typically produce lower, but extremely safe, returns. Sweep arrangements are often used in conjunction with controlled disbursement so that funding requirements are known early in the day.

It is becoming increasingly common for a company to outsource daily position management by combining loan and investment sweeps at the same bank that also provides the company with collection, concentration, and disbursement services.

Loan sweeps are also available for a business with a line or revolver at its main depository bank. With a loan sweep, advances are automatically made to fund deposit accounts or, alternatively, collected balances are automatically applied to reduce the debt.

APPENDIX 10.1 – Sample Excerpt from an Investment Policy

Investment Objectives

To invest in high-quality, short-term debt obligations in order to achieve the maximum yield consistent with safety of principal and maintenance of liquidity. Liquidity and preservation of capital are the primary considerations. Yield is important but secondary to these objectives.

Responsibilities

The Treasurer shall have the responsibility to manage the short-term investments within the terms of the policy set by the Board of Directors, maintain a reasonable relationship between short-term borrowings and short-term investments, and maintain a level of liquidity adequate to meet the company's financial obligations.

Approved Instruments

The following are approved investment vehicles with attached limitations:

- U.S. Government and Agency Securities – no limits
- Money Market Funds – up to $1 million may be invested in any one fund
- Banker's Acceptances – may be up to 40 percent of the portfolio
- Repurchase Agreements – may be up to 20 percent of the portfolio
- Commercial Paper – may be up to $2 million per issuer. Commercial paper holdings may not exceed 50 percent of the portfolio.
- Certificates of Deposit – may be up to 50 percent of the portfolio and further limited to an approved schedule of banks

Constraints

- **Diversification:** Foreign-denominated securities may not exceed 10% of the portfolio. Options and futures contracts may be used only to hedge underlying exposures.
- **Credit Quality:** All domestic commercial paper purchased must be rated A-1/P-1. All domestic CDs must be rated the equivalent of AA or higher.
- **Maturity:** The portfolio should have an appropriate mix, with 65% of the portfolio having no longer than a two-month maturity. The remaining maturities may not exceed two years.
- **Safekeeping:** Securities purchased by the company are to be delivered against payment and held in a custodian account by one of the company's principal banks.

APPENDIX 10.2 Calculation Examples

1. Taxable Equivalent Yield

$$\text{Taxable Equivalent Yield} = \frac{\text{Tax-Exempt Yield}}{(1 - \text{Marginal Tax Rate of Investor})}$$

Assuming a marginal tax rate of 34 percent, the taxable equivalent yield for an investment with a tax-exempt yield of 4 percent is determined as follows:

$$\text{Taxable Equivalent Yield} = \frac{0.04}{(1 - 0.34)} = 6.06\%$$

2. Holding Period Yield

$$\text{Holding Period Yield} = \frac{\text{Cash Received at Maturity} - \text{Amount Invested}}{\text{Amount Invested}}$$

Assuming a 182-day, $100,000 T-Bill purchased for $96,486.39, the holding period yield is calculated as follows:

$$\text{Holding Period Yield} = \frac{\$100{,}000 - \$96{,}486.39}{\$96{,}486.39} = 0.0364$$

The numerator of the holding period yield is the dollar discount:

$$\begin{aligned} \text{Discount} &= \text{Face Amount} - \text{Purchase Price} \\ &= \text{Cash Received at Maturity} - \text{Amount Invested} \\ \text{Discount} &= \$100{,}000 - \$96{,}486.39 = \$3{,}513.61 \end{aligned}$$

3. Discount Rate

An alternative formula for calculating the dollar discount is as follows:

$$\text{Discount} = \text{Discount Rate} \times \text{Face Amount} \times \frac{\text{Days to Maturity}}{360}$$

Because the dollar discount, face amount and days to maturity for the T-Bill used in the holding period yield calculation are known, the discount formula given above can be rearranged to solve for the discount rate as follows:

$$\textbf{Discount} = \textbf{Discount Rate} \times \textbf{Face Amount} \times \frac{\textbf{Days to Maturity}}{\textbf{360}}$$

$$\textbf{Discount Rate} = \frac{\$3{,}513.61}{\$100{,}000} \times \frac{360}{182} = 6.95\%$$

4. Annual Yield

$$\textbf{Annual Yield} = \textbf{Holding Period Yield} \times \frac{\textbf{365}}{\textbf{Days to Maturity}}$$

Using the T-Bill from the holding period yield calculation, the annual yield formula is as follows:

$$\textbf{Annual Yield} = 3.64\% \times \frac{365}{182} = 7.30\%$$

5. Money Market Yield

The money market yield on the T-Bill is calculated using the annual yield formula with a 360-day-per-year basis as follows:

$$\textbf{Money Market Yield} = \frac{\textbf{Dollar Discount}}{\textbf{Purchase Price}} \times \frac{\textbf{360}}{\textbf{Days to Maturity}}$$

$$\textbf{Money Market Yield} = \frac{\$3{,}513.61}{\$96{,}486.39} \times \frac{360}{182} = 7.20\%$$

6. Bond Equivalent Yield

The bond equivalent yield on the T-Bill is calculated using the annual yield formula and a 365-day-per-year basis as follows:

$$\text{Bond Equivalent Yield} = \frac{\text{Dollar Discount}}{\text{Purchase Price}} \times \frac{365}{\text{Days to Maturity}}$$

$$\text{Bond Equivalent Yield} = \frac{\$3{,}513.61}{\$96{,}486.39} \times \frac{365}{182} = 7.30\%$$

Alternatively, the bond equivalent yield may be calculated by converting the money market yield as follows:

$$\text{Bond Equivalent Yield} = \text{Money Market Yield} \times \frac{365}{360}$$

$$\text{Bond Equivalent Yield} = 7.20\% \times \frac{365}{350} = 7.30\%$$

Note that the bond equivalent yield is greater than the money market yield, which is greater than the discount rate. This relationship always holds true among these three rates.

7. Treasury Bill Quotes

Dealers buy and sell T-Bills in the secondary markets. The bid quote is given as the discount at which the dealer will buy a T-Bill. The ask quote is the discount at which the dealer will sell the T-Bill. Both the bid and the ask quotes are based on a 360-day-per-year basis because they are given in terms of a discount.

In addition to the bid and ask discounts, the ask yield is provided. The ask yield is the yield to an investor purchasing a T-Bill at the ask discount. This yield is calculated on a 365-day-per-year basis. Sample quotes and calculations are as follows:

Maturity Date	Days to Maturity	Bid	Ask	Ask Yield
Feb 20	29	1.14	1.13	1.15
Feb 27	36	1.14	1.13	1.15
Mar 06	43	1.13	1.12	1.14

The following two formulas are used to calculate the purchase price that must be paid by an investor to the dealer (or that the dealer would pay to an investor selling a T-Bill):

$$\text{Discount Rate} = \frac{\text{Dollar Discount}}{\text{Face Amount}} \times \frac{360}{\text{Days to Maturity}}$$

Discount = Face Amount – Purchase Price, which can be rearranged to give:
Purchase Price = Face Amount – Discount

The purchase price an investor would pay for a $1,000,000 T-Bill maturing February 27 is calculated as follows:

$$\text{Discount} = 0.0113 \times \$1{,}000{,}000 \times \frac{36}{360} = \$1{,}130$$

Purchase Price = $1,000,000 – $1,130 = $998,870

The sale price paid to the investor would be based on the 1.14-percent bid discount.

The ask yield, or annual yield to the investor, is calculated as follows:

$$\text{Annual Yield} = \text{Holding Period Yield} \times \frac{\text{Days in Year}}{\text{Days to Maturity}}$$

$$\text{Annual Yield} = \left[\frac{\$1{,}000{,}000 - \$998{,}870}{\$998{,}870}\right] \times \frac{365}{36} = 1.15\%$$

$$\text{Holding Period Yield} = \frac{\text{Cash Received at Maturity} - \text{Amount Invested}}{\text{Amount Invested}}$$

8. Effective Annual Yield (EAY)*

$$\text{Effective Annual Yield} = \left[1 + \frac{\text{Interest Received at Maturity}}{\text{Amount Invested}}\right]^{\frac{365}{\text{Days to Maturity}}} - 1$$

Assume a company receives $500 in interest on an investment of $10,000 and the investment matures in 150 days. The calculation is as follows:

$$\text{EAY} = \left[1 + \frac{\$500}{\$10{,}000}\right]^{\frac{365}{150}} - 1 = 12.6\%$$

*Solution of this equation requires the use of a financial calculator

9. Effective Annual Borrowing Rate for a Line of Credit

$$\text{Effective Annual Borrowing Rate} = \frac{\text{Total Interest Paid + Total Commitment Fees Paid}}{\text{Average Usable Funds Borrowed}}$$

Assume that a company is considering a $3,000,000 line of credit for liquidity purposes. Borrowings over the commitment period are expected to average $1,000,000. The bank will charge a commitment fee of 0.25 percent (25 basis points or 25BP) of the unused portion and advances will bear interest at prime plus 2 percent. Prime is currently 5 percent. The effective annual borrowing rate is calculated as follows:

Total Interest Paid = Average Borrowing x All-In Rate = $1,000,000 x 0.07 = $70,000.

Total Fees Paid = $2,000,000 x 0.0025 = $5,000

$$\text{Effective Annual Borrowing Rate} = \frac{\$70,000 + \$5,000}{\$1,000,000} = 7.5\%$$

If the bank also proposes a compensating balance requirement equal to 10 percent of the commitment amount, the average usable funds borrowed need to be adjusted as follows.

$$\text{Effective Annual Borrowing Rate} = \frac{\$70,000 + \$5,000}{\$1,000,000 - \$300,000} = 10.71\%$$

Alternatively, if the company still requires $1,000,000 in usable funds, the average borrowing would be adjusted upward, causing an increase in the interest paid and a decrease in the fee paid.

10. Effective Annual Interest Cost for Commercial Paper (CP)

The effective annual interest cost for CP takes into account the discount rate, the dealer fee, and the fee on the backup line or standby letter of credit and is calculated as follows:

$$\text{Discount} = \text{Discount Rate} \times \text{Face Amount} \times \frac{\text{Days to Maturity}}{360}$$

Usable Funds = Face Value – Discount

$$\text{Effective Annual Interest} = \frac{\text{Discount + Dealer Fee + Backup Fee}}{\text{Usable Funds}} \times \frac{365}{\text{Days to Maturity}}$$

A company issues $20,000,000 of CP with a 30-day maturity at a discount of 3.4 percent. The fees associated with the issue are an annual dealer fee of 0.125 percent (12.5BP) and a back-up line of credit fee of 0.25 percent (25BP). Because the fees are assessed on an annual basis, they must be prorated for this particular 30-day CP issue as follows:

$$\textbf{Prorated Dealer Fee} = 0.00125 \times \$20{,}000{,}000 \times \frac{30}{360} = \$2{,}083$$

$$\textbf{Prorated Backup Credit Fee} = 0.0025 \times \$20{,}000{,}000 \times \frac{30}{360} = \$4{,}167$$

The effective annual interest rate on the CP issue and supporting calculations are as follows:

$$\textbf{Discount} = 0.034 \times \$20{,}000{,}000 \times \frac{30}{360} = \$56.667$$

$$\textbf{Usuable Funds} = \$20{,}000{,}000 - \$56{,}667 = \$19{,}943{,}333$$

$$\textbf{Effective Annual Interest} = \frac{\$56{,}667 + \$2{,}083 + \$4{,}167}{\$19{,}943{,}333} \times \frac{365}{30} = 3.84\%$$

The CP nominal yield to the investor in this issue is as follows:

$$\textbf{Commercial Paper Nominal Yield} = \frac{\textbf{Dollar Discount}}{\textbf{Puchase Price}} \times \frac{365}{\textbf{Days to Maturity}}$$

$$\textbf{Commercial Paper Nominal Yield} = \frac{\$56{,}667}{\$19{,}943{,}333} \times \frac{365}{30} = 3.46\%$$

Test Your Understanding

These chapter questions are provided to test your understanding of the information in the text. They are neither examples of CTP examination questions nor are they in the examination format.

Answers are on pages 593–597.

1. What is liquidity, and why is managing it an important part of treasury responsibility?
2. Is it possible for a company to have too much liquidity?
3. What does a cash forecast require a treasurer to do?
4. What are the objectives of cash forecasting?
5. Discuss the receipts and disbursement forecast.
6. What are the primary considerations in short-term investment management?
7. Discuss the concept of credit or default risk for short-term investments and how it is measured.
8. What is yield and how is it related to risk?
9. What is the difference between discount and interest-bearing short-term securities?
10. How are most short-term securities issued in the U.S. and what benefits does this approach have?
11. What are the roles of brokers and dealers in the money market?
12. Why are U.S. Treasuries considered to be the benchmark investment?
13. What are GSEs?
14. Discuss corporate commercial paper, including its characteristics, ratings, and the role of credit enhancements.
15. Describe the matching investment strategy and when it might be used.
16. What are the three primary sources of short-term funding?

17. What is the primary objective of short-term financing?

18. What primary factors influence financing costs?

19. Discuss the use of commercial bank credit.

20. What is a revolving credit agreement and how is it used?

21. What is asset-based borrowing?

22. Discuss the outsourcing of investment management.

Association for
Financial Professionals®

CHAPTER 11
Treasury Systems and Information Management

VII. USE OF THE INTERNET IN TREASURY

A. Benefits of Using the Internet in Treasury

B. Challenges of Using the Internet in Treasury

VIII. FUTURE ISSUES IN TREASURY MANAGEMENT SYSTEMS

I. INTRODUCTION

Information management, technology and treasury systems are used by treasury professionals to perform a variety of tasks on a daily basis. This chapter covers the objectives of information management, the gathering of information from banks and other external sources, the different types of treasury systems and software available, as well as the security, database management, and disaster recovery issues involved with their use. This chapter also covers the impact of the Internet on treasury management systems.

II. A BRIEF HISTORY OF TREASURY MANAGEMENT SYSTEMS

A. Early Systems

The first treasury systems were custom developed in the early 1980s. They were designed to provide manual capture, manipulation and analysis of data. There was minimal or, in most instances, no interface to other systems and little automation of tasks. These systems relied on manual entry of data from telephone, spreadsheet, fax sources and mailed bank statements. They required a great deal of paper-intensive, labor-intensive and time-consuming re-entry of information from one system to another.

B. First Commercial Systems

In the mid to late 1980s, U.S. treasury systems focused on daily cash management activities and were often bank-provided or designed to link to bank databases. Outside the U.S., the first treasury systems focused on foreign exchange (FX) and interest rate risk management. Most of these systems were standalone, character-based or spreadsheet systems with limited external interfaces. Though there were a few non-bank providers of software, most were typically independent of the major business software providers. Many large companies developed their own proprietary, in-house treasury solutions.

C. PC-Based and Client Servers with Windows

The advent of Microsoft Windows® in the early 1990s allowed for the development of user-friendly interfaces to treasury workstations. Though systems still lacked full integration with other intra company systems, most represented a significant improvement over earlier versions. Many major cash management banks and third-party providers began to provide treasury applications for a wide range of hardware requirements for companies of different sizes across a wide range of industries.

D. Modern Treasury Management Systems

Today, companies have a variety of system choices, from standalone cash and risk management software to fully integrated treasury modules for large ERP (Enterprise Resource Planning) systems. Many of these systems take advantage of the Internet and browser technology for easier access to data by multiple users.

III. OBJECTIVES OF INFORMATION MANAGEMENT AND TECHNOLOGY

Information management is an integral part of treasury management. Many companies view the finance area as the clearinghouse for a wide variety of intracompany information flows. Therefore, one of the major responsibilities of treasury is the integration of treasury operations with other operational areas of an organization.

Treasury is typically responsible for compiling, integrating, reporting and, occasionally, accounting for external data. This data includes bank balance and transaction activity with internal data such as general ledger (GL), accounts receivable and accounts payable activity. In larger companies, treasury may also be responsible for gathering data from such areas as purchasing or procurement, production management, supply chain management, commodity management, risk management, pension administration, FX trading, and long-term investment and debt management.

Typically, ERP systems are required to integrate such vast amounts of data. ERP systems are sophisticated management information and accounting software packages that link different areas and divisions of a company on an enterprise-wide basis. A diagram of typical ERP system and treasury-management system interfaces is provided in Exhibit 11.1.

The primary, time-critical treasury responsibilities are to reconcile the prior day cash balance and to prepare a daily cash position worksheet. These tasks require access to timely and accurate information such as ledger, collected and available bank balances, cash inflows and cash outflows, maturity status of short-term investments, maturity status of short-term debt and FX rates.

Daily Information Management

It is the cash manager who typically prepares a daily cash position worksheet in order to:

- Reconcile the prior-day cash balance
- Determine cash requirements
- Track activity
- Identify opportunities
- Update cash forecasts
- Update management information

EXHIBIT 11.1 – DIAGRAM OF TYPICAL ERP/TREASURY MANAGEMENT SYSTEM

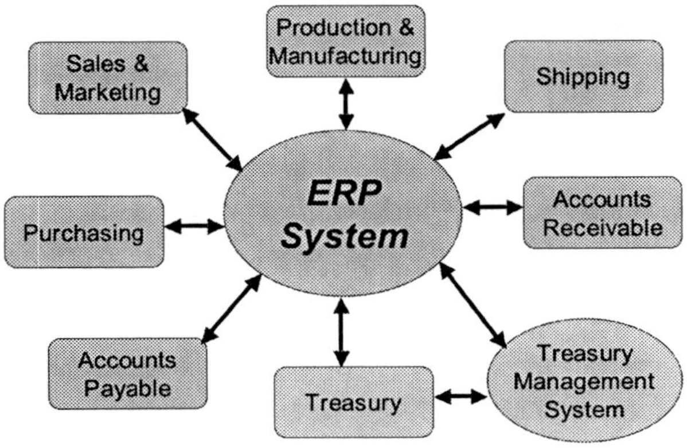

1. Reconciling the Prior Day Cash Balance – The first step in determining a daily cash position is to reconcile the prior day close-of-business collected balance with the current day opening-of-business available balance. Transactions are subject to errors and adjustments. For example, an encoding error may impact the amount of a check that was credited to or debited from an account. Any out-of-balance situation especially if it is large, needs to be researched and reconciled.

2. Determining Cash Requirements – A daily cash position assists a cash manager in determining a company's cash and liquidity needs. If additional cash is required to meet short-term obligations, it may be necessary to access lines of credit or to sell marketable securities. If excess cash is available, it may be invested or used to pay down debt.

3. Tracking Activity – As part of preparing a daily cash position, a cash manager obtains information about a wide variety of individual transactions such as incoming and outgoing wire transfers, same-day items that are collected through a lockbox, same-day clearing of disbursement items by means of controlled disbursement, and Automated Clearing House (ACH) credits and debits. This information is typically used to update accounts receivable, reconcile disbursement accounts, identify exception items, resolve mismatches, identify potential fraud and post to GL.

4. Identifying Opportunities – Knowing a daily cash position early in the day enables a cash manager to take advantage of the best financial rates and potential trade discount, as well as short-term investment and short-term debt repayment opportunities.

5. Updating Forecasts – A daily cash position facilitates comparison of short-term forecasted cash flows with actual cash flows. This is important in detecting and preventing cash shortfalls. If necessary, variances are used to update forecasts. As part of this process, a cash manager may also adjust target or compensating balances at financial institutions.

6. Updating Management Information – The daily cash position is compared to financial data compiled from a wide range of sources. The treasury function and other areas of a company use information from the cash position report to update performance metrics and cash forecasting. While operational information is gathered daily, it is usually reported weekly, monthly or quarterly, depending on the size and needs of an organization.

IV. THE ROLE OF INFORMATION MANAGEMENT IN TREASURY

To add real value to a company, treasury must expand information management beyond the narrow focus of the daily cash position. The benefits of an information-enhanced treasury area are numerous, especially for larger, global companies.

A. Treasury Management Systems Benefits

The primary benefits of implementing treasury management systems generally include improved productivity and expedited data gathering, compilation and analysis. Faster access to treasury data also often results in increased forecasting accuracy, reduced borrowing expenses, improved short-term investment returns and improved management reporting.

The ability to provide a consistent treasury infrastructure for the entire company assures the application of best practices in treasury management and results in increased quality of services, better control and lower costs. This is especially true when treasury is linked to other areas of the company through an ERP system. ERP systems allow companies to eliminate manual processing and rekeying of information, thereby allowing treasury and other areas of the company to exchange financial data in a seamless manner.

B. Benefits of Treasury Information Management for a Global Company

For a global company, treasury information management systems centralize reporting and transaction initiation on a worldwide basis, resulting in increased control, more accurate data for decision-making and reduced expenses. Treasury information management is also necessary to accomplish the pooling of subsidiary funds either regionally or globally. It also allows a company to maximize overall liquidity, increase control and optimize interest earnings. The implementation of global payment and netting systems enables a global enterprise to reduce overall FX costs, minimize transaction costs and better manage a worldwide cash position.

(The details of many of these practices, such as pooling and netting systems, are discussed in greater detail in Chapter 16, Global Treasury Organization and Liquidity Management.)

C. Treasury Management Systems Costs

The initial costs of implementing treasury management systems include hardware and software selection, purchase, installation, start-up and personnel training expenses. On an ongoing basis, fixed costs include administration, overhead, software maintenance, licensing and upgrades; variable costs include telecommunications charges, transaction service charges and system security expenses.

D. Cash Management Processing Tasks and Responsibilities

Treasury acts as a clearinghouse for financial information. The cash manager is specifically responsible for:

- Compiling information from a wide range of internal and external sources
- Sorting, storing, and analyzing the information
- Reporting information to management

On a daily basis, the cash manager is generally responsible for:

- Obtaining account balances and transaction detail from external sources
- Obtaining internal information that affects the cash-flow timeline
- Consolidating the information into the cash-position worksheet

Once the cash position is determined, the cash manager must initiate required funds transfers, which may entail concentrating funds from other sources, making decisions to purchase or redeem short-term investments, and making decisions to drawdown or repay short-term borrowing facilities. The cash position worksheet and short-term forecast should also be updated regularly, revising new projections based on actual cash flows.

E. Cash Management Processing Timeframes

The timeframes for cash management reporting vary, depending on:

- A company's operating and cash-conversion cycles
- The type of company (e.g., retail vs. wholesale)
- The industry
- The size of the company
- The degree to which management relies on financial information for decision-making

It is also important to note that senior management often relies on these reports to make long-term decisions. The following are examples of possible timeframes and reports:

- Daily – Cash position
- Weekly – Cash scheduling
- Monthly – Short-term cash forecast
- Quarterly – Investment and debt maturity schedule
- Annually – Funding and investment liquidity plan.

F. Cash Management Internal Data

Cash managers utilize a wide variety of internal information gathered from other areas of the company. One of the primary uses for internal data is to prepare a cash receipts and disbursements (R&D) forecast. The key sources for generating this forecast are the sales summary reports (information on actual and projected weekly or monthly sales) and purchasing summary reports (information on actual and projected weekly or monthly purchases). An aging schedule, which provides information on the aggregate status of accounts receivable, as well as information on large collection items still outstanding, is also useful for preparing the forecast. Ultimately, the R&D forecast is linked to the company's investment and debt repayment schedules.

(Additional information on an R&D forecast is in Chapter 10, Liquidity Management.)

The data gathered internally is also used in the preparation of a cash journal, which is the recording of individual debits and credits affecting the cash account. The information may also be used to update GL through the posting of transactions to the proper internal accounts. Finally, the data is useful for the tracking of cash flows between different operating units or between different subsidiaries of a company, as well as for the comparison of budgeted to actual financial performance.

G. Cash Management External Data

Information gathered from external sources is generally categorized into three types: (1) current day, (2) prior day and (3) historical. In addition to these three categories, some information is provided on an intraday basis or a real-time basis such as wire transfers and money market and FX rates. ACH transactions, which settle one or two business days after they are initiated, are also often calculated by a cash manager as part of current day activity, especially if the items memo post (i.e. the ACH items are posted on a memo, or non-value basis, the day prior to their settlement). Examples of the three types of data are provided in Exhibit 11.2.

H. Multibank Reporting

Companies that have relationships with two or more financial service providers (FSPs) may establish an arrangement in which one of the company's FSPs or a third-party reporting service gathers and consolidates the account balances and transaction activity from each of the company's financial institutions. This arrangement is commonly referred to as multibank reporting or data exchange. Many FSPs offer this type of service via the Internet.

EXHIBIT 11.2 – TABLE OF CASH MANAGEMENT EXTERNAL DATA

Current/IntraDay	Prior Day	Historical
Available balance	Balance and transaction activity, current ledger and collected balances	Average balances and balance history
Lockbox deposits and remittance detail	One-day and two + days' float	Target balance activity
Controlled disbursement clearings	Debit and credit detail	Exception item inquiries
Positive pay reporting	Adjustment items	Account analysis
Wire transfers	Returned items	Cash concentration transfer history
Investment activity (e.g., overnight sweeps)	Stop payments	Investment and borrowing activity
Payable-through-drafts	International transactions	Custody activity
ACH transactions		
Money market and FX rates		

I. External Information Formats

There are three major standardized formats for transmission of external data: BAI, ASC X12 821 and S.W.I.F.T. MT940. The first two are used primarily by U.S. financial institutions for domestic transactions. They include the Bank Administration Institute (BAI) format and the Accredited Standards Committee (ASC) X12 821 Financial Information Reporting transaction set. The BAI format is more established and more commonly used; however, an enhanced BAI-2 format is replacing the original BAI format. In addition, there is a migration toward ASC X12 821, which is an Electronic Data Interchange (EDI) transaction set. For international transactions, financial institutions use the S.W.I.F.T. (Society for Worldwide Interbank Financial Telecommunications) MT940 format (statement with detail).

As the Internet gains acceptance for the transmission of external data, other formats and languages such as XML (eXtensible Markup Language), FSML (Financial Services Markup Language) and XBRL (Business Reporting Language) are experiencing wider use.

(These concepts are discussed in greater detail in Chapter 12, Electronic Commerce.)

V. INFORMATION EXCHANGE BETWEEN FSPs AND TREASURY

While some companies still utilize methods such as mail, telephone and fax to exchange information with financial institutions and FSPs, a wide array of more direct electronic communication methods is now available. When implementing electronic communications with FSPs, treasury managers must consider cost limitations, security concerns and, for global companies, the telecommunications infrastructures of different countries. The manner in which FSP information is linked to the company's other applications or ERP system must also be considered.

A. Basic Choices in Linking Treasury to an FSP

There are several ways to link internal treasury systems to an FSP.

1. Dial-Up Connection

Due to security concerns and the continued existence of some older legacy systems, a dial-up connection is still a fairly common mechanism used today. A dial-up allows a user to make a connection via a modem to the FSP's computer in order to access account information and to initiate a variety of treasury related instructions. Access may be granted via server or PC-based software at the company or through terminal access to software residing at the FSP. Dial-up is a relatively inexpensive way for a company to link internal treasury systems to an external FSP.

2. Host-to-Host Link

A host-to-host link is an approach that provides a direct, two-way link between FSP's systems and a company's computers. It is generally a dedicated, full-time, leased line that handles high volumes of automated data. While more expensive to set up and maintain than the dial-up method, a host-to-host link allows multiple users access to an FSP's full suite of services.

3. Internet

Many FSPs offer a wide range of services via the Internet. These include cash balance, transaction initiation and reporting, and trade financing support. In addition, FSPs are also focusing less on server or PC-based solutions (referred to in the trade as "fat clients" because the application software resides on the customer's desktop computer) and more on Internet-based solutions (referred to as "thin clients" because the application software resides at the FSP's central client server site). The advantage of the thin client approach is that software is easier to update and maintain.

B. Treasury Workstations

A treasury workstation, sometimes referred to as a treasury management system (TMS), is typically PC- or client server-based and has software that gathers information from both internal and external sources. A TMS compiles financial data for the purposes of analysis and decision-making, thereby automating a number of manual tasks.

These systems also enable a treasury department to prepare and distribute financial information in a variety of customized spreadsheets and management reports and to be either stand-alone part of a company's computer network. TMS may be purchased from an FSP, a third-party vendor or be developed in-house. Treasury systems generally have three primary attributes: modularity, data integration and database management.

1. Modularity

TMS software is modular in design. In other words, different modules offer different applications. There are three basic choices:

- **Standalone:** Allows users to select the applications they need based on their business requirements
- **Prepackaged:** Requires users to purchase the entire range of business applications
- **Semi-Customized:** Basic modules are pre-packaged but users are able to customize the software by selecting from a range of applications

The basic TMS modules are:

- Balance reporting
- Cash positioning
- Cash forecasting
- Bank administration
- Investment-portfolio management
- Payment initiation
- Debt-service scheduling

Additional modules offer clients choices such as the GL interface, FX trading, commercial paper issue/pay, custody activity and letter of credit initiation capabilities. Typical TMS modules and related applications are shown in Exhibit 11.3.

2. Data Integration and Database Management

A TMS is capable of integrating a wide range of information from both internal and external sources. The data is downloaded and organized into various reporting formats. These systems provide users with database management capabilities. This capability allows users to determine how to store, retrieve, share and organize information. Users are also able to produce formatted financial reports.

C. Transaction Initiation

Increasingly, treasury departments are using automated methods available through a TMS to initiate transactions. Once a treasury area has compiled and analyzed data and completed the daily decision-making process, transactions are initiated to make payments, manage liquidity and fund international trade. Examples of the different types of transactions are outlined in Exhibit 11.4.

EXHIBIT 11.3 – TREASURY WORKSTATION MODULES

Treasury Workstation Module	Treasury Application
Account Balance Report	Monitor Ledger and Collected Balances
Target Balance Report	Manage Compensating Balances
Cash Position Worksheet	Manage Cash Position
Transaction Detail Report	Monitor Individual Debits and Credits
Investment Portfolio Management	Manage Short-Term Investments
Debt Scheduling	Monitor Debt Repayment
Letters of Credit	Issue Letters of Credit

EXHIBIT 11.4 – EXAMPLES OF DIFFERENT TYPES OF TRANSACTION INITIATIONS

Payment Related	Liquidity Management	International Trade
Wire transfers	Investment purchases and sales	International wires
ACH debits and credits	Loan drawdowns	Letters of credit
Positive pay administration	Loan payments	FX transactions
Stop payments		

D. Straight Through Processing (STP)

STP is an initiative being considered by many financial institutions to streamline transactions by maintaining contact throughout all stages of the processing of those transactions. It is presently in discussion and early development, and represents a major shift from present day T+3 trading (settlement within three business days after a transaction) toward same day settlement by removing redundant operations and utilizing electronic transfers.

VI. TREASURY MANAGEMENT SYSTEMS AND SOFTWARE

The most common type of treasury platform is a TMS, which may be purchased from a FSP, a third-party or developed in-house. A TMS provides financial reporting templates and database tools, thereby enabling a cash manager to prepare an electronic spreadsheet that is used to collect, manage and report data from a variety of sources. Spreadsheets and other analytical tools are used for basic balance and transaction reporting, cash position reporting, investment and debt scheduling, and forecasting.

Often, middleware (software that links two different applications) is used to integrate information between a TMS and other company-wide software applications. Treasury may also utilize special software for financial risk management, such as managing and monitoring:

- FX exposures
- Interest-rate risk
- Commodity risk
- Counter-party exposures
- Market rates and conditions

(The topic of financial risk management is covered in greater detail in Chapter 17, Financial Risk Management.)

A. Basic Choices in TMS

TMSs are generally classified as a treasury module of ERP software, third-party treasury management software or customized treasury systems developed in-house. Many of these systems are beginning to utilize the Internet for communications and browser technology to provide a user-friendly interface.

1. Treasury Modules of ERP Software

Some of the large ERP software providers offer integrated treasury modules for their systems. Companies that implement corporate-wide ERP systems are better able to link information technology to corporate strategy and to daily operational functions on a standardized and timely basis. Generally, however, the current offering of ERP treasury modules do not provide the same level of functionality as stand-alone offerings.

2. Stand-Alone Treasury Systems

Stand-alone TMS and other treasury software offered by FSPs or third-parties are often tailored to specific needs of individual treasury departments. Most of the larger systems also provide access to multibank reporting and interfaces to major ERP systems. The more sophisticated of these systems address treasury-specific issues such as financial risk management and support for FAS133, none of which are available on most ERP systems.

3. Customized Treasury Systems

Some companies have developed their own customized treasury systems. Customized solutions are often the only option for global treasury departments with special needs such as multicurrency environments, foreign tax and regulatory constraints and widely dispersed operations or for treasury departments that perform highly sophisticated financial modeling for strategic purposes.

B. Selecting a Treasury Management System

In purchasing or developing a customized TMS, a company must have a well-defined selection criteria process with detailed business and technical requirements. Requirements should include a detailed project and implementation plan developed by a cross-functional team of key individuals from other departments that use financial data on a daily basis. Many companies utilize a formal RFP process managed by a selection/implementation team of key stakeholders.

C. Treasury Management Systems Security

1. Database Management Issues

Treasury data files contain confidential information that, if improperly disseminated or misused, can leave organizations vulnerable to everything from breaches of confidentiality to internal fraud. Consequently, it is vital to control access to treasury information. Proper internal control requires separation of duties pertaining to data access and use. For example, the same individual should not initiate, approve and release a wire transfer. Determining who has access to information entails not only consideration of technical competency but also of appropriate designation of responsibilities within the company.

2. Basic Security Risks

The three most common types of risks involved with TMS are data loss, unauthorized user access and computer viruses.

- **Data Loss –** The risk of loss or compromise is often precipitated by unforeseen external factors such as power surges/failures or telecommunications system failure. Data loss can also result from computer system failure, software defects or from misplaced or lost storage devices such as disks, CDs or tapes. Finally, data can be compromised by intentional tampering or an unintentional user error. The degree of risk depends on the nature of the information that is lost and the amount of time and costs involved in restoring it – if it can be restored at all.

- **Unauthorized User Access –** This type of risk is a major security issue. There are two different types of unauthorized user access. The first occurs when unauthorized individuals within the company are able to access information by logging on to a computer in the treasury area or by means of a company's local area network (LAN). The second type is when unauthorized users outside the company access information either accidentally or intentionally. In either case, if an unauthorized user has access to confidential information, data may be intentionally or unintentionally altered or destroyed and/or unauthorized or fraudulent transactions may be initiated.

- **Computer Viruses –** A computer virus is a software program that is designed to corrupt or destroy data. This type of risk is becoming increasingly common, especially because many treasury workstations are now networked on the same servers that enable employees to access e-mail and word processing programs.

Some viruses are relatively harmless and may affect only a small portion of a software program. Other viruses can catastrophically sabotage an entire information system. Even if anti-virus protection programs are employed, these programs are not always fail-safe. Other computer viruses known as "worms" and "Trojans" (short for Trojan Horse) may also cause serious problems for computer users. Worms are self-contained programs that can spread without human intervention. Trojans are programs that masquerade as useful or entertaining software, but contain instructions that allow an outside party to access and gain control over the infected computer for the purpose of stealing data or passwords.

3. Security Safeguards

Companies must take measures to prevent either authorized or unauthorized users from executing fraudulent financial transactions. Companies can safeguard the security of TMS by assigning this duty to a security officer/system administrator. This individual is responsible for developing, monitoring and enforcing TMS security policies and procedures.

Companies should also establish formal policies that specify procedures for approval of access levels and protection of passwords. Such written policies are effective only if they are implemented, enforced and updated. To further ensure the ongoing integrity of the system, periodic system tests/audits should be performed by internal auditors.

Physical security, which includes protection of both hardware and software, includes:

- Storing computer systems and software in a secure place to restricting access to certain areas
- Instituting basic access requirements such as use of passwords

- Monitoring log-on activity
- Limiting sign-on attempts
- Using smart-card and/or biometric controls
- Enforcing periodic password changes
- Establishing different levels of access and segregation of duties so that, for example, a transaction is not approved by the same person who entered it
- Using backup storage methods
- Scanning information at both the overall system-wide and the individual workstation levels to ensure that data has not been compromised
- Employing electronic security, such as encryption and message authentication by means of electronic signatures or certificates, where necessary

The degree of physical security, as with all safeguards, depends upon the risks involved, the costs, personnel constraints and the practicality of imposing such controls.

(See Chapter 12, Electronic Commerce for more information on encryption and message authentication.)

4. Disaster Recovery

All TMS and other electronic communications systems are vulnerable to disasters or catastrophic events. As a result, all organizations should have disaster recovery plans that include identifying internal and external threats, assessing general business risks and monitoring for corporate espionage. It is important to determine the requirements for performing critical tasks and to develop backup or alternative systems and sites. To be effective, disaster recovery plans should be approved by top management, tested at least every six months and be kept as current as possible.

Disaster recovery is especially important because treasury has become increasingly reliant on both technology and outsourcing for basic treasury functions. Disaster recovery plans should encompass all forms of automation used by the treasury area, including workstations, electronic banking systems, spreadsheet programs and e-mail systems. Whenever treasury outsources to third-party providers, these providers should be required to submit detailed disaster recovery plans. These external plans should be coordinated with a company's own internal plans.

D. Integrating Treasury Systems in Merged Companies

One of the greatest challenges for treasury is to integrate dissimilar TMS and accounting systems in a recently merged company. In most cases, each company has different systems and procedures prior to the merger. Normally, the acquiring company will control the post-merger environment and convert the merger partner to its existing systems. Occasionally, the acquired company's systems will be deemed superior and will be utilized for the newly merged entity. The same issues arise in the case of bank mergers, but the conversion has an even greater impact because either the acquiring or the acquired bank's entire customer base may be affected by a shift to a new common platform.

VII. USE OF THE INTERNET IN TREASURY

As TMSs have developed, they have migrated from mainframe and PC-based platforms to Internet and browser-based systems. This migration to the Internet has significantly changed the treasury environment.

A. Benefits of Using the Internet in Treasury

One of the primary benefits of using the Internet is the easy access to services and applications. In an Internet/browser environment, the software typically resides on a server rather than locally on a user's PC. This allows access to a wide range of applications with greater flexibility from multiple, non-traditional remote locations and business units outside treasury. This ease of access may also simplify restoring a system after a computer failure or another type of disaster.

Using the Internet in treasury also allows for easier implementation and version control. For many applications, software does not have to be installed at the user's site. Instead, initial installations and upgrades can be executed from a remote location for multiple users in multiple sites. It is also possible to utilize the Internet or an intranet for project management and collaborative work on projects and documents. For example, many financial institutions use browser-based technology to implement intranet-based proposal development and customer quality service programs. The Internet or an extranet can also be used for presentations and virtual meetings to share information with a large number of both internal and external users.

(Intranets and extranets are covered in detail in Chapter 12, Electronic Commerce.)

Finally, the Internet is proving to be an extremely inexpensive communications vehicle. This is a major benefit for large, global companies with widely dispersed operating units.

B. Challenges of Using the Internet in Treasury

1. Security Issues

Though best practices such as 128- or 256-bit encryption are standard on business Internet communications, many companies have not fully implemented these technologies for e-commerce applications. Likewise, many financial institutions have not fully implemented proper security practices and procedures for transaction initiation and funds transfers.

(Security issues are also discussed in Chapter 12, Electronic Commerce.)

2. Identity Problems

One of the significant risks in using the Internet is the counter-party risk associated with trading partners and customers. While the risks of trading with known suppliers and customers can be substantial, the risk of trading with unknown companies and individuals can be disastrous. Counter-party risk is greatest in auction markets, in which a company may be bidding to buy or sell products and services with many unknown trading partners, or in dealing environments, in which a company may be working with unknown dealers or portals to dealers to buy or sell FX or financial instruments. Many companies are exploring the use of certificate authorities or closed trading communities to reduce counter-party risk. (This topic is discussed in greater detail in Chapter 12, Electronic Commerce, and in Chapter 18, Enterprise Risk Management.)

VIII. FUTURE ISSUES IN TREASURY MANAGEMENT SYSTEMS

Three forces are driving the TMS of the future

- The consolidation of providers in the FSP and third-party TMS markets
- The ability of ERP treasury modules to offer a wider range of functionality for more and more applications
- The increasing volume of more complex financial transactions moving both funds and information at faster speeds

Straight through processing (STP) is the key to enabling treasurers to deal with these challenges. STP offers the promise of freeing up resources currently devoted to daily, repetitive, tactical tasks and of devoting them to long-term, value added, strategic activities.

Finally, the Internet has already had a significant impact on treasury systems and information management and will continue to do so in the future. The treasurer of the future will be able to employ improved techniques for forecasting, financial analysis and funds management and will have greater responsibility for enterprise-wide corporate finance, risk management and global liquidity management.

Test Your Understanding

These chapter questions are provided to test your understanding of the information in the text. They are neither examples of CTP examination questions nor are they in the examination format.

Answers are on pages 598–600.

1. Who typically prepares the daily cash position worksheet and what are the six requirements?

2. What are the benefits of implementing a treasury management system?

3. Discuss the benefits of a treasury management information system for a global company.

4. What are the costs involved in implementing a treasury management system?

5. How do cash managers typically use internal data?

6. What is multibank reporting?

7. Discuss the major standardized formats for transmission of external data.

8. What are some of the issues involved when implementing electronic communications with financial service providers?

9. What is a treasury workstation and how is it used?

10. What is straight through processing, and how is it used?

11. Discuss the difference between a treasury module of an ERP program and a stand alone treasury system.

12. What are the most common types of risks involved with treasury management systems?

13. What is a disaster recovery plan and why does an organization need one?

14. What are the benefits of using the Internet in the treasury area?

Association for
Financial Professionals®

CHAPTER 12
Electronic Commerce

I. INTRODUCTION

The majority of business documents and payments exchanged among companies in the U.S. are paper-based and move through the check clearing and postal systems. E-commerce is an alternative to these traditional paper-based systems. Since the 1970s, individual companies and entire industries have implemented e-commerce for the purpose of eliminating the delays that result from time-consuming, manual, paper-based processes. They have formed strategic alliances with trading partners, facilitated just-in-time (JIT) inventory management and offered customers alternative methods of ordering and paying for goods and services. All of these practices have had a significant impact on treasury and, in particular, on reducing the three components of the cash conversion cycle: inventory, accounts receivable and accounts payable.

(A discussion of the cash conversion cycle is in Chapter 4, Financial Accounting.)

This chapter focuses on the different types, benefits, costs and barriers to e-commerce. It also discusses the standards for sending and receiving electronic messages and the role of software and service providers in facilitating e-commerce.

II. BASICS OF ELECTRONIC COMMERCE (E-COMMERCE)

E-commerce is defined as the application of information and secure network technology for the purpose of facilitating business relationships among trading partners. E-commerce encompasses many types of formats and communications protocols, including traditional Electronic Data Interchange (EDI), Financial Electronic Data Interchange (FEDI) and World Wide Web-based commerce. E-commerce may be conducted by means of three applications: the Internet, an intranet or an extranet.

The Internet is an unrestricted, worldwide network that allows access to anyone with the appropriate hardware and software. In essence, the Internet is a collection of many computer networks linked together to form a global communications pathway. Communication on the Internet is made possible due to the open standards and common protocols.

Users operate browser software over an inexpensive Internet service connection that is commonly available. A browser is software that allows a user to access Web-based sites on the Internet, an intranet or an extranet. Advanced browsers, such as Microsoft Internet Explorer or Netscape Navigator, offer a wide range of options and features that provide users a means to obtain, organize and utilize data from all three types of networks. Advanced browsers also incorporate built-in security features such as Secured Socket Layer (SSL).

Many companies also use intranets. Intranets are internal networks ("intra" meaning internal or within a company) that utilize commonly available browser technology to provide data and applications for employees or other authorized internal users. An intranet uses the open standards of the Internet, rather than proprietary software, for communications among a company's computers.

In addition to the Internet and intranets, many companies also use extranets. Extranets are external networks ("extra" meaning external or outside a company). Extranets are most commonly used by trading partners (suppliers) and customers. A typical example would be a bank that provides an extranet for customers to access account information. The bank would generally place only static copies of the information on the extranet to prevent unauthorized tampering with financial records. As is the case with the Internet and intranets, extranets utilize browser technology and servers to provide access to applications and data. For security purposes, companies typically establish a "firewall" between the extranet and internal applications. (A diagram of a typical setup for these arrangements is provided in Exhibit 12.1.)

EXHIBIT 12.1 – DIAGRAM OF INTRANET, EXTRANET AND INTERNET RELATIONSHIP

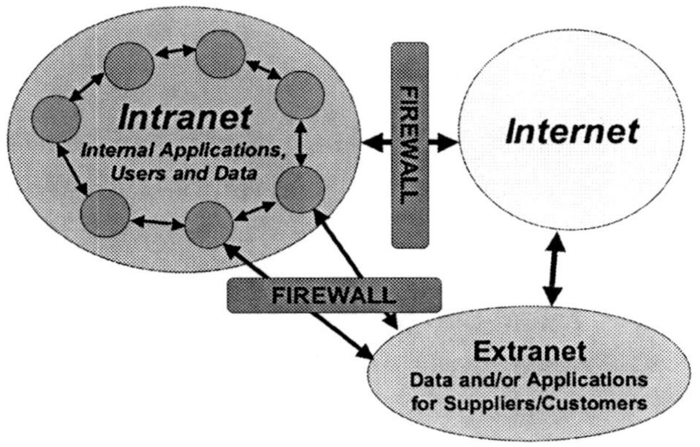

A. Electronic Data Interchange (EDI)

Electronic Data Interchange (EDI) is a traditional form of e-commerce that utilizes structured electronic transactions within established standards to exchange data from one company's business application system to another company's business application system. Transactions that impact business application systems for a buyer are purchasing or order placement, receiving and accounts payable; while those that impact a seller are sales or order processing, shipping and accounts receivable. EDI allows senders to generate secure messages directly from business applications, thereby allowing receivers to bring data into business applications without the need to reenter any of the information.

Specific EDI standards may be used in multiple industries, a single industry or among selected trading partners. Proprietary EDI is developed by companies for the exclusive use of trading partners and was the standard initially used by the retail, transportation and automotive industries.

Cross-industry EDI, such as ASC X12 (the Accredited Standards Committee [ASC] of the American National Standards Institute [ANSI] or EDIFACT (EDI for Administration, Commerce, and Transportation), is a set of format standards that address the needs of many different users in many industries. If a company sends a cross-industry EDI purchase order to another company that conforms to the same standard, the receiving company can capture the purchase order data directly without reentering data.

Industry convention EDI is a specific format standard, or a subset of the more generic cross-industry EDI standards, used within a particular industry. Examples of industries that utilize these types of EDI standards include:

- Grocery
- Retail
- Automotive
- Electrical
- Manufacturing
- Chemical production and distribution

Most e-commerce and EDI is executed by a trading community of suppliers, customers, employees and agents through distribution and logistical systems. These trading communities may be vertical, such as a supply chain, or horizontal, such as a trade group or an association.

B. Financial EDI (FEDI) and Electronic Funds Transfer

Financial EDI (FEDI) and electronic funds transfer (EFT) refer to the area of electronic commerce related to payments and/or payment information. FEDI and EFT are subsets of EDI. FEDI is the electronic transmission of payments and/or payment-related information in a standard format between trading partners and/or the company's banks. FEDI includes such business applications as invoices, payment initiations, lockbox deposit reports and remittance information sent directly to a trading partner and processed through a financial institution or third-party communications intermediary. EFT is the exchange of value associated with an FEDI application. EFT requires the involvement of financial intermediaries, such as banks and the Federal Reserve, to send and receive electronic payments.

Examples of EFT include:

- Fedwire
- Automated Clearing House (ACH) payments
- CHIPS (Clearing House for Interbank Payments Systems) in the U.S.
- CHAPS (Clearing House Automated Payment System) in the U.K.
- TARGET (Trans-European Automated Real-Time Gross-Settlement Express Transfer System) in the Economic Monetary Union. (For more information on TARGET, see Chapter 15, Global Treasury Environment.)

C. Relationship Among EDI, FEDI and EFT

To explain the relationship among these various methods, take the example of a supplier (seller) sending an EDI invoice to a customer. The customer (buyer) sends a FEDI payment instruction to the bank. The buyer's bank then sends an electronic payment and associated information to the supplier's bank through the ACH system (i.e., EFT). The supplier's bank notifies the supplier of the receipt of payment through an electronic deposit report.

The payment-related information transmission is FEDI, whereas EFT (ACH) involves a transfer of value and typically occurs only between financial institutions. Therefore, FEDI is any EDI transaction set that either: (1) results in a transfer of value, such as instructions to send funds via wire or ACH or (2) results from a transfer of value when a bank notifies a payee that funds have been received, such as in electronic transmission of lockbox information. Exhibit 12.2 shows an example of the relationship among companies and financial and communications intermediaries using EDI, FEDI and EFT.

EXHIBIT 12.2 – RELATIONSHIP AMONG EDI, FEDI AND EFT

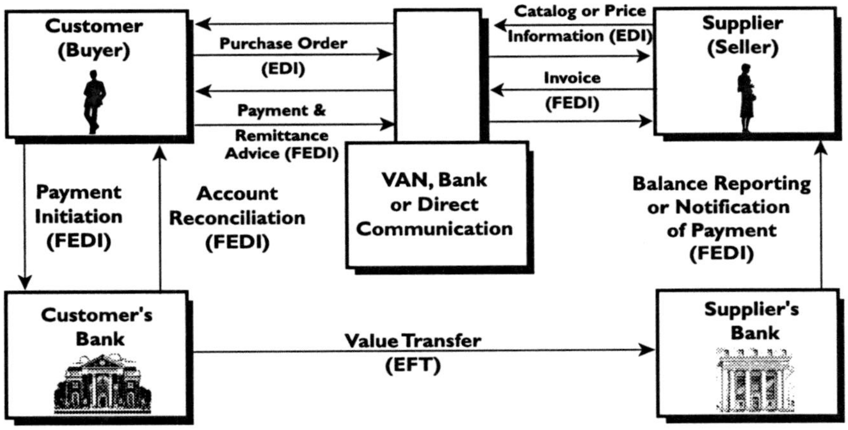

Mode	EDI Electronic Data Interchange	FEDI Financial EDI	EFT Electronic Funds Transfer
Parties Involved	Company-to-Company Company-to-VAN/Bank VAN/Bank-to-VAN/Bank VAN/Bank-to-Company	Company-to-Company Company-to-Bank Bank-to-Bank Bank-to-Company	Bank-to-Bank (Value Transfer)
Applications	Catalog Price Information Request for Quote Purchase Order PO Acknowledgement Production Schedule Shipping Information	Invoice Payment & Remittance Advice Payment Initiation Lockbox Information Balance Information Account Information Reconcilement Analysis	ACH Debits ACH Credits Wire Transfers CHIPS

D. Different Types of E-Commerce

E-commerce is generally described as either business-to-consumer (B2C) or business-to-business (B2B).

1. Business-to-Consumer (B2C) E-Commerce

The initial development of Internet-based e-commerce was primarily targeted toward B2C applications. Companies quickly realized that the Internet was a cost-effective way to advertise and sell products and services to consumers, as well as to provide enhanced customer service. With Internet-based e-commerce, the consumer does most of the work in the process, including reviewing available products and services, filling out forms online and providing shipping and billing information.

2. Business-to-Business (B2B) E-Commerce

B2B e-commerce began with EDI but has expanded into a wide array of formats and protocols for conducting business electronically. The earliest B2B applications were in the areas of sales to customers and purchasing from suppliers. Applications later extended into logistics and supply chain management, as well as billing and payment. Newer e-commerce developments are continuing in the areas of Web-based e-commerce and auction marketplaces.

E. Factors Influencing the Use of EDI

The structure of EDI systems among different companies varies widely, depending on the number of trading partners, the volume and type of EDI transactions used, and whether the company is an originator or a receiver of EDI transactions.

Companies implement EDI for many reasons:

- Requested by key customers/suppliers
- To reduce costs and increase efficiency
- As part of a redesign or reengineering process
- To reduce the cash-conversion cycle
- To benefit from the cost reductions associated with improved productivity, shorter order lead times, just-in-time (JIT) inventory and faster accounts-receivable turnover

One of the most common reasons for EDI implementation is in reaction to a request (or mandate) from a key customer or supplier. These companies are generally suppliers to a customer that is already a major user of EDI. To avoid expensive upfront costs, this type of EDI implementation is initially conducted on a small scale using only a personal computer (PC) and off-the-shelf software. Such companies, which are referred to as EDI spokes, implement EDI with only one or more major customers.

The companies that mandate suppliers to implement EDI are referred to as EDI hubs. Although hubs often start as EDI originators (sending EDI purchase orders to suppliers), they tend to become EDI recipients as trading partners send EDI invoices in response to purchase orders. One of the major challenges for a large EDI hub is to provide the necessary support and training for the many related EDI spokes.

While a mandate from a customer is a common reason for implementing EDI, some companies may implement EDI to reduce costs and increase efficiency. These companies usually implement EDI after performing a cost/benefit analysis and surveying potential trading partners. EDI facilitates the outsourcing of financial functions to a third-party provider. Another justification for EDI is to include it as part of a redesign or re-engineering process.

Historically, large manufacturers and retailers implement EDI on a large scale to reduce the cash conversion cycle and to benefit from the cost reductions associated with improved productivity, shorter order lead times, just-in-time (JIT) inventory and faster accounts receivable turnover. In many cases, companies are migrating from traditional EDI into more generic forms of e-commerce in order to maintain competitiveness.

F. Use of the Internet and Web for E-Commerce and EDI

The Internet is utilized for both Web-based e-commerce and EDI. Although there are many similarities in these applications, there are also several key differences between Web-based e-commerce and Web EDI.

1. Web-Based E-Commerce

This approach utilizes the Internet and Web technology to link business applications between trading partners. The primary difference between this type of e-commerce and Web-enabled EDI is that the data transfer is in a non-EDI format. The format may be proprietary between two users or a more general standard used within an industry. One of the key objectives is to move data entry and other tasks toward a company's trading partners resulting in the transfer of data required to complete an electronic transaction.

2. Web EDI

The World Wide Web (commonly referred to as "the Web" or "Web" and seen as "www" in Web addresses, such as www.afponline.org) is often used by large EDI hubs to encourage smaller trading partners to begin using EDI. Transactions are Web-based to enable smaller trading partners to receive information or to create business documents using forms completed online. The large hub still utilizes standard EDI transaction sets to send or receive information from the smaller trading partners. This approach is useful for low transaction volumes within limited trading communities.

G. Key Issues in the Development of E-Commerce

Two of the initial factors impeding the development and rapid growth of EDI were technology and communications capabilities (often referred to as "bandwidth"). However, with the rapid increase in technology, this is much less an issue than in the past. Today, the technological and communications capabilities needed for e-commerce are readily available and already deployed.

Another factor impeding the development and rapid growth of EDI has been the delay in enacting legislation that supports e-commerce initiatives. The U.S. legal and business environment is still based on the Uniform Commercial Code (UCC), which provides the guidelines for contracts, business transactions and payment instruments that are paper-based. In 2000, the passage of the Electronic Signatures in Global and National Commerce Act (the "E-Sign Law") gave digital signatures the same authority as ink signatures. This legislation ensures the legal certainty of e-commerce transactions and provides a measure of confidence in the enforceability of electronic transactions.

Yet another factor impeding the development and rapid growth of e-commerce has been the lack of social acceptance of the technology and the hesitancy of business users to alter existing processes. As demonstrated by the rapid development of the B2C segment of e-commerce, consumers are often the first to adopt new technology while businesses lag behind. Also, legislation generally lags behind the adoption of e-commerce practices by businesses.

The future development of B2B e-commerce will depend on the development of trading communities that emphasize the purchase of direct materials (raw materials for manufacturing) and indirect materials (such as office supplies). The development of the direct materials market will require greater integration with Enterprise Resource Planning (ERP) systems, working capital management and expertise in supply chain planning and execution.

ERP systems are generally fully integrated, company-wide accounting and management information systems that utilize sophisticated database software to provide reports and information in a timely manner to management. Most modern ERP systems provide interfaces to EDI and e-commerce formats, and protocols that allow organizations to easily implement e-commerce practices.

(The integration of ERP systems with treasury operations is in Chapter 11, Treasury Systems and Information Management.)

H. Benefits of E-Commerce

E-commerce presents several key benefits:

- Improves productivity, thereby enhancing working-capital management
- Makes data reentry unnecessary, thereby reducing error rates and enabling faster data processing
- Eliminates mail time, thereby enhancing cash-flow processes
- Offers improved communication capabilities

One of the key benefits of e-commerce is improved productivity. Once data is entered at the beginning of a transaction, the same data can move from one business application system to another without manual intervention. E-commerce eliminates manual processes such as filing, matching, sorting and retrieving material, as well as envelope stuffing, stamping and mailing. It also significantly reduces cycle time because e-commerce transactions have no mail-time delays, involve minimal processing time and facilitate JIT inventory management in many companies, all of which are key objectives of working capital management.

Because e-commerce makes data reentry unnecessary, it reduces error rates and enables faster data processing. For example, using e-commerce for the receipt of remittance information allows for greater accuracy in the posting of payments to the accounts receivable ledger. E-commerce eliminates mail time, thereby reducing uncertainty in cash flow timing, enabling more accurate cash flow forecasting and improving management of working capital. It also offers improved communication capabilities. For example, acknowledgment that a customer has received an invoice (which is not available in a mail-based system) helps to resolve issues of payment timing between the buyer and the seller.

I. Costs of E-Commerce

A number of costs are associated with e-commerce and must also be considered:

- Hardware and communications technology upgrades
- Training
- Maintaining economies of scale
- Effect of implementation on payments and credit terms

Most companies have hardware and communications technology already established but these systems may need to be upgraded to handle the requirements of an e-commerce implementation. Additional software is almost always required because data from electronic transactions must be integrated with data from existing applications. This integration often requires modification of current business software applications before data can be translated from the company's current format into a recognizable e-commerce format.

Commercially available software packages are capable of performing translation processes for standard e-commerce formats. Encryption and message authentication, as well as security measures to ensure the integrity of the system, are required in implementing e-commerce and often entail significant expenses. Other expenses in implementing e-commerce arise when a company must train both internal personnel and trading partners.

In addition, many of the benefits of traditional e-commerce depend on economies of scale, which are realized only when a significant number of transactions are involved. (One of the principal benefits of Web-enabled e-commerce is that even low levels of trading partner activity can be managed in a cost effective manner.) Finally, implementing e-commerce may affect the timing of payments and require renegotiation of credit terms. Such negotiations can be costly and protracted, particularly when legal, compliance or audit issues are involved.

J. Barriers to E-Commerce

In addition to the costs of implementing e-commerce systems, there are other barriers and drawbacks to implementation. One of the primary barriers is the convenience and efficiency of current U.S. paper-based systems. The U.S. Postal Service (USPS) delivers to all addresses in the U.S. for a uniform postage fee and provides low cost delivery of paper-based correspondence and payments. Virtually all companies and individuals, as well as banks or other financial intermediaries, have access to the postal delivery system and rely on the USPS to handle the payment part of the cycle.

In addition, the legal, audit and processing structures supporting paper-based systems in the U.S. are highly developed. Most articles of the UCC and most accounting and legal standards are based on paper-based contracts and business conventions requiring signatures for control purposes. Attempts to address the regulatory, legal and audit issues surrounding e-commerce remain a significant challenge.

Another drawback that many companies encounter in implementing e-commerce and/or electronic payments is the need to continue to use dual systems (both paper and electronic) after implementation. Banks and other financial intermediaries have only recently been required to pass remittance information from the receiving bank to the receiving company. Companies attempting to make electronic payments to suppliers find that many financial service providers are not yet fully capable of complying with this mandate.

III. EDI INFRASTRUCTURE

EDI is a traditional form of e-commerce that is based on four primary infrastructure components: EDI standard formats, EDI software, communication networks and standards and computer hardware.

A. EDI Standard Formats

To send information electronically, companies must agree on a specific format and structure for electronic messages and data. In the early years of the development of EDI, companies designed proprietary formats and communication interfaces and either encouraged or mandated trading partners to participate. Proprietary data formats and technical requirements are utilized when a company deals with a small number of partners. However, when a company has many EDI partners, a common standard becomes necessary. EDI standards have evolved from proprietary standards to the current cross-industry and international standards.

1. ASC X12 Standards

The Accredited Standards Committee (ASC) of the American National Standards Institute (ANSI) is the coordinating body that develops cross-industry EDI standards in the U.S. The development of the current U.S.

standards for EDI began in 1968 with an initiative by the transportation industry to establish communications standards between and among railroads, ocean carriers, air carriers and motor carriers. Following this lead, the grocery and retail industries also developed EDI standards. In 1979, ASC X12 was formed to develop general EDI standards that could be used cross-industry.

2. ASC X12 Financial Transaction Sets

By convention, numbers and names are used to identify ASC X12 transaction sets. Transaction sets are generally defined as the electronic equivalent of a paper business document or form, with specific rules governing formats. As defined by NACHA (National Automated Clearing House Association), the common EDI transaction sets used in the finance arena include the following:

- 810 Invoice – This transaction set allows the user to convey invoice data, such as the unit price, quantities purchased and terms of sale, from a seller to a buyer.

- 820 Payment Order/Remittance Advice – This transaction set has two purposes. An 820 initiates an ACH transfer to a payee and/or provides the payee with information describing the purpose of the associated payment. Thus, the 820 not only allows multiple invoices to be paid in a single payment but also includes the amount of discounts and other payment adjustments.

- 821 Financial Information Reporting – This transaction set facilitates bank-to-corporate account reporting. An 821 provides for the reporting of multiple levels of financial information, including balances, transaction summaries and individual transactions. Financial Information Reporting may be used for balance and transaction reporting, account reconciliation and bank account statements.

- 822 Customer Account Analysis – This transaction set allows banks to transmit account analysis information (e.g., balances, volumes, service charges) to corporate customers. AFP service codes are used in the 822 transaction set to identify bank balances, services and associated charges.

- 823 Lockbox Information – This transaction set conveys lockbox check data including remittance detail, such as payors, invoices, amounts being paid, deposit totals and available funds.

- 824 Application Advice – This transaction set conveys acceptance of data, acceptance of data with change or rejection of data received from another transaction set. An 824 is often used to notify a payor of changes in information received in an 820 Payment Order/Remittance Advice.

- 828 Debit Authorization – This transaction set can be used to provide information to a financial institution regarding electronic debits when, for example, in a B2B scenario, Company A (a buyer) authorizes Company B (a seller) to debit Company A's bank account for payment of an invoice. An 828 enables a buyer to have greater control over the payment because it restricts the debit to authorized sellers, time periods, dollar limits and even the types of transactions allowed. This transaction set can also be used to convey check issue files for positive pay or reconciliation applications.

- 835 Health Care Claim Payment/Advice – This transaction set is used by the health care industry to transmit medical claim payment and remittance information.

- 997 Functional Acknowledgment – This transaction set is used by a recipient to confirm to an originator that the transmitted sets have been received and are in compliance with ASC X12 standards.

3. Issues in Using CCD+ and CTX Formats for B2B Payments

There are several issues in the use of the CCD+ (Cash Concentration or Disbursement, Plus Addenda) and the CTX (Corporate Trade Exchange) in a B2B environment. The key decision in using CCD+ and CTX formats for B2B payments is whether to keep the payment and remittance information together or to separate the two.

Using CCD+ and CTX formats to keep the "dollars and data" together means that many financial institutions receiving these formats cannot process remittance information in order to forward it on to customers. Payors who follow the approach to separate the "dollars and data" send payments through the banking system (i.e., the ACH system) while the remittance information is transmitted via a third-party information service or the Internet.

The advantage of the latter approach is that the payment and remittance advice can be sent to almost any payee, regardless of the ability of the payee's financial institution to process remittance information. However, the challenge with separating "dollars and data" is that the payment and remittance information must be matched up by the payee in order to complete the payment application process. (For more detailed information on ACH formats, see Appendix 1 in Chapter 8, Payment Systems.)

4. UN/EDIFACT Standards

Many countries have become involved in developing EDI standards, which has led to the development of United Nations EDI for Administration, Commerce, and Transportation (UN/EDIFACT) rules. UN/EDIFACT is a set of internationally agreed-upon standards, directories and guidelines for the electronic interchange of structured data relating to the trade of goods and services between independent computerized information systems. UN/EDIFACT standards are widely used in Europe and some Asian countries.

5. Changing Standards and Recent Developments

As information needs change and companies gain experience in EDI, the standards also evolve. Each year, most organizations involved with establishing standards publish revisions. While this process is necessary to adapt the standards to changing needs, it poses problems for EDI users. A company's trading partners may be using different versions of the standard; hence, an EDI user often must support multiple versions of EDI standards. EDI software, as well as financial institutions, often assists users in reconciling the issues related to supporting different versions.

B. EDI Software

EDI systems rely on specialized software or ERP systems that are able to interpret EDI messages. The software or system converts the data into standard formats for transmission between trading partners.

1. Functions Performed by EDI Software

EDI software assembles information into transaction sets for electronic transmission. Transaction sets are either created by a company or provided by a third party. Additionally, transaction sets can be provided by a single integrated software package or by several software programs that exchange information. This process, which is illustrated in Exhibit 12.3, is for an outgoing EDI message; for an incoming message the process is reversed.

EXHIBIT 12.3 – STEPS PERFORMED BY EDI SOFTWARE

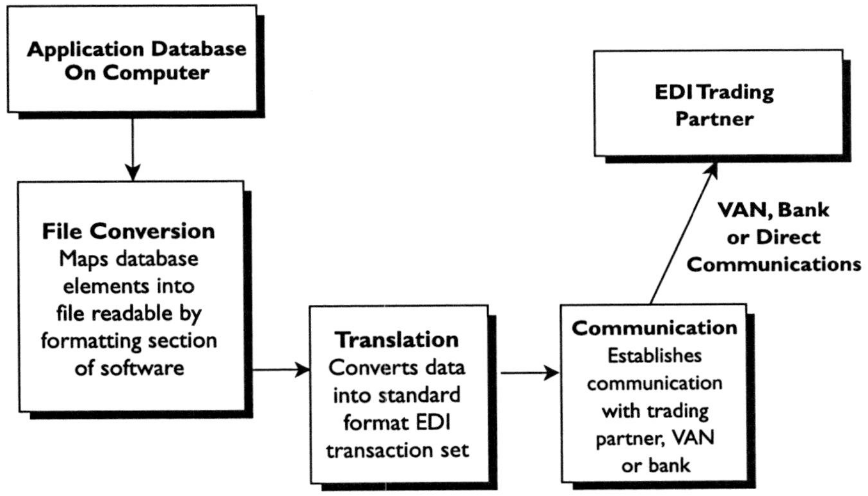

- **File Conversion:** – The first step is to convert paper-based information from the company's records into an electronic file that is readable by the formatting component of the EDI software.

- **Translation/Mapping:** – This stage, also known as formatting or mapping, takes the data input from the file conversion and translates it into the desired EDI standard format. Most software is capable of mapping data into any accepted cross-industry standard or industry convention, thereby creating EDI transaction sets according to required formats and protocols. Some banks perform these EDI translation services for customers.

- **Communication:** – This software application establishes communications directly with a trading partner, with a third-party communications service or with a bank for the purpose of sending (or receiving) the EDI-formatted data to (or from) another party using mutually acceptable communication protocols. If the Internet is used as a communications channel, this process must include software for encrypting and establishing a secure communication session for both parties. Secure file transfer protocol (FTP) should also accompany the file transmission.

2. Availability of EDI Software

EDI software packages with mapping utilities are available for most computer platforms and operating systems. Most EDI software is table-driven, meaning that all of the requirements and formats for EDI transaction sets are stored in easy-to-change tables. Thus, the software can produce any desired transaction set and can be updated easily as standards evolve.

C. Value Added Networks (VANs)

A VAN is a communication intermediary that provides various services to the users of e-commerce. VANs were developed during the inception of EDI to help resolve interface problems between two companies with different computer systems, different format needs and different protocols. VANs make it easier for companies to implement EDI and to add new EDI trading partners. VANs also offer implementation assistance in the form of consulting, software and training of trading partners. Finally, because a VAN is essentially a private network, it can provide enhanced security for commercial transactions.

D. E-Banking Services (Electronic Banking)

Some banks provide VAN-related services for B2B payment information to support the translation of electronic payment and remittance data between trading partners who use different communication protocols. Some of these banks also provide EDI information services not directly related to payments or FEDI.

1. E-Banking Payment Services

E-banks provide integrated payables in two different ways. One approach is to have a company send a single data file to a bank that contains a list of all payments to be made. The file contains information on when to issue a payment and to whom, as well as instructions on the payment method to be used (i.e., check, wire, ACH, foreign currency draft). These instructions may be in a proprietary format or in an ASC X12 820 transaction set (820 Payment Order/Remittance Advice).

Alternatively, a bank maintains a database of a company's payees that includes detailed information, such as preferred payment methods, specific remittance information and receiving financial institutions. The database is periodically updated as new payees are added or as an existing payee's remittance profile changes (e.g., a payee switches from check to ACH as the standard payment type). In these instances, a company making payments sends only limited information to the third party.

Regardless of which approach is employed, the bank either issues the payments immediately or warehouses the payments until a future date as instructed by the data file. A company utilizing these types of services is outsourcing much of the disbursement functions and potentially reducing the overall costs of accounts payable operations.

(Additional information on integrated payables is in Chapter 7, Working Capital Tools.)

2. E-Banking Collection Services

Some banks offer collection services that record the receipt of incoming payments (such as checks, ACHs and wires), reformat the data and transmit the data to a company. This service is referred to as an electronic lockbox. An electronic lockbox provides the information to a company in a proprietary format, a BAI lockbox format or an ASC X12 format.

3. Electronic Clearing House Services

Several national and regional electronic clearing house services are operated by member banks or third parties, such as the Financial Services Technology Consortium (FSTC), that specialize in providing various types of EDI services to members and/or customers. These clearing houses allow member banks to offer a wider range of EDI services than was formerly possible.

E. Computer Hardware

A variety of computer systems, ranging from single-user PCs to large server systems, can accommodate EDI. Some companies, particularly those new to EDI, may initially choose the PC-based method because of the low cost and ease of implementation. Then, as EDI transaction volumes increase, companies shift EDI to in-house mainframes or to a client-server environment.

IV. THE INTERNET AND E-COMMERCE

Companies are increasingly using the Internet as a payment and financial information channel. Because the Internet is accessible by virtually anyone with a

PC nearly everywhere in the world, it is attractive to many businesses as a means to reach more customers and to facilitate sales and service. However, the openness and accessibility of the Internet make security a major concern. Many Internet-based systems are proprietary intranets that have sophisticated security systems that ensure confidentiality of information, protect company networks and databases from unauthorized access and prevent fraud. Properly secured systems are able to handle B2B or B2C transmissions or a combination of both.

A company must trust e-commerce partners more than paper-trading partners because of three factors:

- A trading partner's access to the company's internal systems
- The speed with which errors can be made and propagated through the trading channel
- The consequences of security breaches to a company's system

A. Key Terms and Definitions

There are two types of providers in the Internet/e-commerce arena. The first is an Internet service provider (ISP), which is a communications intermediary that provides Internet service to individuals and small businesses, typically over telephone lines (T-1 or T-3 lines), cable, satellite or wireless. The other provider is an application service provider (ASP), which offers individuals or organizations access via the Internet to application programs and related services that would otherwise have to be located on individual personal computers or on a company's computer network. Many companies fully integrate Internet systems with existing business ERP and application systems. This is known as enterprise application integration (EAI).

Several protocols are used on the Internet:

- **FTP:** The file-transfer protocol (FTP) is a standard protocol that is the simplest way to exchange files between computers on the Internet.
- **HTTP:** The hypertext-transfer protocol (HTTP) is a set of rules for exchanging files (text, graphic images, sound/video and other multimedia files) on the World Wide Web (www).
- **URL:** The uniform resource locator (URL) is an address format utilized on the Web—for example, www.afponline.org, which is the Web site of the Association for Financial Professionals.

B. The Languages of E-Commerce

In order for the many different types of systems to communicate with one another, standard languages must be used. These languages include:

- EDI
- Hypertext markup language (HTML)
- eXtensible markup language (XML)
- eXtensible business-reporting language (XBRL)
- Financial-services markup language (FSML).

1. Electronic Data Interchange (EDI)

This is a highly structured method of sending e-commerce information in standardized electronic transactions. EDI languages are designed to be machine-readable. They are not intended to be human-readable except by a highly trained expert.

2. Hypertext Markup Language (HTML)

HTML is the language used to create Web pages on the Internet and other browser-based delivery formats. HTML is human-readable. The information, text and graphic content can be presented in a consistent format, independent of the browser used to view the data.

3. eXtensible Markup Language (XML)

XML is an extension of HTML that allows the content and the structure to be defined. In essence, while HTML provides a consistent format for displaying information, XML adds "tags" that specifically define the information. For example, HTML ensures that the price of an item on a Web page appears on a certain place on the page and in a specific font, size, and color. XML further ensures that a specific field is the price of a specific item. Once a data element has been clearly identified, it is easy to transfer this information from the Web page to an application within the company.

4. eXtensible Business Reporting Language (XBRL)

XBRL provides a common platform for critical business reporting processes and improves the reliability and ease of communicating financial data between both internal and external users to the reporting enterprise. XBRL is an XML-based, royalty-free, open standard being developed by XBRL International Inc., which is a not-for-profit consortium of approximately 200 companies and agencies delivering benefits to investors, accountants, regulators, executives, financial analysts and information providers.

5. Financial Services Markup Language (FSML)

FSML is a language developed to implement e-checks and other secure financial documents. FSML is designed to include encryption and digital signatures necessary to create electronic checks. Developed and supported by a group of financial institutions, FSML is not directly compatible with XML standards.

C. Security Issues

When using e-commerce, a treasurer must also consider the security issues and initiatives involved.

1. Basics of Security

Security is the assurance that transactions are safe from intrusion, detection and modification. Security must provide four key factors:

- **Privacy:** the assurance that the message is readable only to the intended recipient and that data will not be used for unintended purposes

- **Authentication:** the ability to know, with a reasonable amount of certainty, who sent or received a message
- **Integrity:** the ability to ensure that a message was not modified in transit, which is especially important for financial transactions
- **Non-repudiation:** the inability of the sender or the receiver of a message to deny having sent or received the message.

2. Firewalls

Wherever external users are allowed access to internal applications or data, it is important to utilize a "firewall" to protect the internal systems. The purpose of a firewall is to ensure that only authorized users are allowed access data or data systems. They also help to protect against viruses and other system compromises. Firewalls may be software based, hardware based or a combination.

3. Solving Security Issues

The use of encryption technology with public/private keys can help to resolve many of the security issues on the Internet. Most e-commerce Web sites have already implemented a form of encryption/authentication technology known as SSL (secure sockets layer) to ensure privacy, integrity and authentication of data moving between clients and servers. SSL is built into most major browsers and is part of the basic World Wide Web infrastructure.

4. Shared-Secret Key System

In a shared-secret key (symmetric key) system, both the sending and the receiving parties have a private key to encrypt/read messages. Because both parties must have the same private key, the distribution and management of shared-secret keys may be difficult and complex. This type of arrangement is most often used between two established trading partners.

5. Public Key Infrastructure (PKI) System

A public key infrastructure (PKI) system enables e-commerce and file exchange over a public network. The encryption technology is based on ANSI X.500 and X.509 standards for Public Key Certificates and Directory services, and can be used for virtually all secure EDI Web transactions. One of the key features of PKI is the use of public/private key pairs based on standard encryption technology known as RSA (named after the developers: Rivest, Shamir and Adleman).

The private key is held in a secret, secure file that is protected with a password or a personal identification number (PIN). The corresponding public key is freely distributed to trading partners. Anyone can use public keys to encrypt messages while only the receiver with the proper private key can open and read the message. The main advantage of PKI is that it definitely identifies a person or an organization and allows for privacy. PKI is most often used in the form of digital signatures and digital certificates.

6. Digital Signatures

A digital signature is a message encoded with the sender's secret private key. The receiver can identify the source using the sender's public key. So long as the private key is never shared with anyone, forgery of a digital signature is impossible. A digital signature is tied to a document and to the signer; the signer's digital signature will be different for each document signed. A digital signature serves four purposes:

- Data integrity, which verifies that the message has not been altered
- Origin authentication, which verifies where the message came from
- User authentication, which verifies who sent the message
- Non-repudiation, which ensures that the message/transaction cannot be denied as sent or received

Note that a digital signature is different from a "digitized signature," which is used as a facsimile signature on laser printed checks.

7. Digital Certificates

Digital certificates tie the identity of the user (private key) to the user's public key. The identification information is secured by a trusted third-party's digital signature on the certificate. The trusted third-party is known as the certificate authority.

8. Authentication Devices

Smart card authentication devices, also known as "tokens," look like a credit card and contain circuitry that encodes personal information to ensure password protection. One device contains a clock in the smart card synchronized to the clock on the computer. When the user wants to log onto the computer, the card will provide a unique code that, when entered with the user's PIN or password, will ensure that the user is authorized to access the system.

Biometric devices provide authentication through electronic recognition of personal characteristics such as fingerprints, retinal patterns, voiceprints, and hand or face geometry. The advantage to this approach is that it is based on a biometric "key" that is unique to each individual. Biometric keys cannot be lost, stolen or copied, which is not the case with passwords, encryption keys or smart cards.

9. Other Security Initiatives

Banks and other third parties are forming partnerships with security companies, certificate authorities, software providers, and other technology firms to administer the public/private key infrastructure and to issue electronic certificates. These initiatives serve as virtual passports to subscribers.

The key objective of this type of partnership is for corporations to trust the identity of digital partners through real-time authentication and validation of the transmission under legally binding contracts. These associations also allow users to verify unknown buyers through a trusted financial institution and can establish multilateral trust through a single bilateral customer agreement. Finally, certificates are often stored in a smart card with dual authentication. A combination of the smart card and an assigned PIN "unlock" the card.

V. CREDIT TERMS AND E-COMMERCE TRANSACTIONS

Most credit terms assume the use of a paper-based system involving mailed invoices and checks. Today, credit terms are often renegotiated by companies that implement e-commerce.

A. B2B Financial Impact of E-Commerce and EFT

E-commerce enables companies to complete processing more rapidly. EFT also removes much of the payment float resulting from mail, processing, availability and clearing delays. Therefore, many trading partners are forced to re-examine conventional credit terms because faster payments are viewed as a disadvantage to buyers and an advantage to sellers. To compensate buyers for the shortening of the cash flow timeline (i.e., shortening of days' payables), sellers often must negotiate new e-commerce-based credit terms. This is frequently referred to as "float neutralization."

B. Negotiating Shared Benefits

By changing the terms of transactions, buyers and sellers can transfer value. It is important to note that some companies negotiate terms separately with each trading partner while other companies may decide to unilaterally adjust terms for all trading partners. Two common approaches to negotiating terms are to adjust the price through a discount or to change the payment timing.

In the price change or discount approach, the seller offers the buyer a cash discount to compensate for earlier payment. For example, a seller offers a 1.5 percent discount to customers who allow the seller to electronically debit bank accounts on the day the product or service is delivered. This compares to the normal payment timing under the paper system of 30 days or more.

In the change of payment timing approach, the buyer delays payment to take advantage of the shorter interval of electronic payments, compared with the time required for paper checks. For example, a customer initiates an ACH payment to a supplier three days later than a check payment would have been mailed. This offsets or mitigates the loss of float resulting from the switch to EFT.

In an e-commerce environment, the amount of the discount that is required to renegotiate credit terms successfully depends on the present value impact of changing the payment timing and any transaction cost savings resulting from electronic versus paper-based payments. Companies using a discount approach set the discount for electronic payments approximately equal to the equivalent benefits or cost reductions derived from receiving earlier payments. Companies that change the timing of the payment often determine a "float-neutral" solution to payment timing, which simply makes the electronic payment date equal to the paper payment date, plus any normal collection float. With either approach, a successful solution is one that provides benefits to both the buyer and the seller.

C. Single Sourcing Arrangements

Many companies are utilizing e-commerce to negotiate single sourcing arrangements with suppliers. The buyer receives the benefits of e-commerce and a lower price on raw materials. The seller typically receives a much larger order with e-commerce, which may also result in faster collections and a shortened cash flow cycle.

D. B2C Financial Impact of E-Commerce and EFT

Many retailers are utilizing e-commerce/EFT initiatives such as check truncation at point-of-sale to process the large volumes of consumer checks in a more timely and cost effective manner. A new NACHA point-of-purchase (POP) e-commerce format has been developed for check truncation.

(Additional information on POP and other recent NACHA e-commerce formats are in Chapter 8, Payment Systems.)

VI. E-COMMERCE IMPLEMENTATION

E-commerce plays an integral part in the redesign of finance functions and processes. Two important integration techniques and primary examples of treasury re-engineering are the implementation of Evaluated Receipts Settlement (ERS) and Paid-on-Production.

A. Evaluated Receipts Settlement (ERS)

ERS is a payment method designed to eliminate the need for a supplier to provide an invoice to a customer. The transfer of value amount for an ERS payment is based not on an invoice but rather on a calculation of the quantity actually received by a customer multiplied by a pre-determined price. The supplier does not send an invoice but instead is simply paid by the customer on an agreed-upon date after receipt of the shipment. The use of ERS allows a buyer to automate the accounts payable process and a seller to automate the accounts receivable and payment application processes.

ERS is most commonly used in a retail environment where the cash conversion cycle is typically short, large volumes are involved, inventory turns over rapidly and JIT inventory is required to meet consumer demand.

B. Paid-on-Production

Paid-on-production is the process by which a payment record is created for goods and/or services when they are used rather than when they are shipped or delivered. The reason for this is that in a manufacturing environment, unlike a retail environment, there are multiple legal concerns related to liability, potential bankruptcy and use of inventory assets for supporting loans.

- In a retail environment, the title to merchandise transfers from the supplier to the buyer when the merchandise is delivered to the buyer's receiving dock.
- In a manufacturing environment, the title to raw materials or finished goods transfers when the product is used in the manufacturing process.

Therefore, it is critical to determine exactly when and where the transfer of title takes place.

Paid-on-production is most commonly used in a manufacturing environment where the cash conversion cycle is typically long, the manufacturer has formed a strategic partnership with a single supplier, turnover of raw materials or finished goods depends on the cycle time of the manufacturing process itself, and JIT inventory is required to meet production demands.

C. Future of E-Commerce

The Internet and e-commerce have dramatically changed business practices and are expected to continue to impact how companies are developed and managed in the future.

The ability of the Internet and the Web to provide easy access for all divisions and functional areas of a company on a global basis results in major changes in the way that information is gathered and disseminated.

The latest concept in distributed computing is known as peer-to-peer or P2P, where each computer linked to the Internet can be linked directly to another computer in order to share information. Applications that perform P2P computing are essentially automating the machine-to-machine communication process.

As companies and treasury departments consider ways to take advantage of Internet technology, the expansion of internal network capabilities and connections will be required. Information management is the most challenging problem facing companies in the coming years.

Test Your Understanding

These chapter questions are provided to test your understanding of the information in the text. They are neither examples of CTP examination questions nor are they in the examination format.

Answers are on pages 601–604.

1. What is electronic commerce and how is it conducted?
2. Discuss the concepts of the Internet, intranet and extranet.
3. What is EDI?
4. Compare and contrast FEDI and EFT.
5. What are some of the benefits of e-commerce?
6. What are the common EDI transaction sets used in the finance area?
7. What are the functions of EDI software?
8. What is a VAN?
9. What are electronic banking services?
10. What is the difference between an ISP and an ASP?
11. What is XML?
12. What is a firewall and how is it used?
13. What is a digital signature and how is it different from a digitized signature?
14. What is the impact of e-commerce on trade and credit terms?
15. What is "paid on production" and how is it implemented?

Association for
Financial Professionals®

CHAPTER 13
Sources of Capital and Leasing

D. Shelf Registration
E. Due Diligence

IX. INITIAL PUBLIC OFFERING (IPO)

A. Advantages of Going Public
B. Disadvantages of Going Public

X. THE DECISION TO LIST SECURITIES

A. Advantages of Listing Securities
B. Disadvantages of Listing Securities
C. Choice of Exchanges

APPENDIX 13.1 FINANCIAL MANAGEMENT MBA-LEVEL TEXTBOOK REFERENCES

I. INTRODUCTION

The general concept of securities valuation builds on theories of the time value of money and the analysis of cash flows. A corporate treasury manager must recognize the impact that valuation concepts and an investor's rate of return requirements have on a company's value. The key issue for a treasury manager is to obtain the required capital at the best cost and mix to meet operational opportunities and to analyze those opportunities for a company. The two questions that a treasury manager continually needs to ask are:

- "How do a company's operational risks and expected returns impact the available cost and mix of capital?"
- "What is the best combination for maximizing a company's capital market value?"

The primary purpose of this chapter is to explore the role of a treasurer in determining and managing the costs of long-term capital for an organization. To this end, the chapter provides an overview of the sources of long-term capital including the use of leasing as an alternative financing technique. The chapter also discusses valuation techniques for corporate securities, the relationship between risk and return (including measuring and adjusting for risk) and outlines the investment banking process as it relates to initial public offerings (IPOs).

II. ROLE OF TREASURY IN DETERMINING AND MANAGING COSTS OF LONG-TERM CAPITAL

The treasury area of a company plays a very important role in both the determination and the management of a company's cost of capital. The treasurer, along with the Chief Financial Officer (CFO) and the Board of Directors, is typically responsible for determining the type and the amount of various forms of capital that are raised. In addition, the treasurer is often responsible for the management of a company's issued securities. The mix of different types of securities, the timing of the issues and the perceptions of a company by analysts and investors ultimately determine the overall availability and cost of capital for a company.

A. Raising Capital

For any company, the ability to raise capital at a reasonable price is often one of the primary determinants of long-term success. While small companies primarily use personal capital and borrowed funds from banks, most middle to large companies issue some type of debt or equity securities in addition to using borrowed funds. Many government entities and some not-for-profits utilize bond issues to raise needed capital in the private or public markets.

Other companies sell debt instruments and equity instruments, such as preferred stock and common stock, in the private market rather than to the general public. The purchaser in a private sale is usually an institutional investor such as a pension fund, an insurance company, a bank or a trust company.

The reasons that private placement is preferred over public issuance includes:

- Less-restrictive covenants
- The size of the issue
- The reduced time and number of parties involved
- The complexity of the securities
- A desire for minimal reporting, agency ratings, or public disclosure
- Lower costs
- Control over who holds the debt

There are advantages and disadvantages to raising capital through public offerings. One of the principal advantages is that access to capital markets offers the potential to raise large amounts of debt and equity at prevailing rates. One of the primary disadvantages is the significant costs involved in managing the reporting, disclosure and rating agency requirements for public security issues.

Initial public offerings (IPOs) require significant disclosure of a company's ownership, business activities and financial statements. Publicly-held companies are required by the Securities and Exchange Commission (SEC) to file a wide variety of forms and reports, such as 10-K's, 8-K's, 10-Q's, on a regular basis.

(A more detailed discussion of the role of the SEC is in Chapter 3, Financial Environment; a more detailed discussion of the required SEC reporting is in Chapter 4, Financial Accounting.)

In addition, the price of capital for a company may fluctuate widely due to factors over which a company has no control. Among these factors are the general economic environment, new technologies, government regulations and public perceptions of a company's future prospects.

In both the raising and the management of capital, an organization must deal with a wide variety of different parties, including investment bankers, corporate bankers, regulatory agencies, Wall Street analysts, rating agencies, external auditors, shareholders, and bondholders. Each of these parties requires different types and degrees of information, and each views a corporation from a different perspective. In order to successfully raise the needed capital for a company, a treasurer must be able to respond to the needs and expectations of all parties.

B. Managing Outstanding Capital

Once a company has issued stocks, bonds or other securities, a treasurer must manage the information, legal and payment requirements for each type of security. A treasurer may have to manage trustee relationships and responsibilities relative to a company's securities, as well as to act as disbursing agent for shareholder or bondholder payments. Shareholders must receive dividends as declared for preferred and common stock. Bondholders must receive interest payments. Also, any sinking fund obligations (funds accumulated in a custodial account to retire debt instruments according to a predetermined schedule) or covenants on bond issues must be met. Financial reports must be completed and sent to interested parties in a timely manner, and various reports must be prepared and sent to regulatory agencies such as the SEC. Management must also plan for the future retirement of maturing issues and manage bank credit relationships.

In addition to the trustee and disbursing responsibilities, a treasurer may often be responsible for investor relations, including participating in presentations to potential investors to raise capital (commonly known as "road shows"). These responsibilities include:

- Maintaining shareholder lists
- Sending out reports
- Communicating with shareholders and bondholders
- Addressing investors' questions

C. Cost of Capital

The overall cost of capital for a company is a function of the mix of capital components used and the individual costs of the components. In the simplest model of corporate long-term capital, there is a combination of debt (short- or long-term borrowing) and equity as the primary sources of capital. Debt is usually less expensive due to the lower rate of return required by investors and the tax-deductibility of interest payments on the debt. (This topic is covered in detail later in this chapter as part of a discussion of the use of debt and equity capital, including the impact of the cost and mix of these capital components on the capital structure of a company, how the mix is determined and who is responsible for the capital structure.)

The other primary source of long-term capital for a company is the ability to generate and retain profits for reinvestment in a company (i.e., retained earnings). The dividend policy of a company has a major impact on the ability to retain capital, as opposed to paying all earnings out to shareholders.

(A more detailed discussion of dividend policy is in Chapter 14, Capital Structure and Dividend Policy.)

The ultimate mix of debt and equity and other forms of capital for a particular company is primarily a function of a company's ability to generate earnings, the ability to minimize risks, and both acquisition and dividend policies.

III. DEBT (BOND) CAPITAL MARKETS

Organizations can raise debt capital in either the short-term money market or the long-term capital market. (For a detailed discussion of the money and capital markets, see Chapter 3, Financial Environment.) In either case, debt capital typically imposes a fixed payment requirement on a company. The interest portion of these payments is usually tax deductible and must be paid prior to any payments to equity holders. In addition, debt holders have priority claims on a company's assets in the event of financial distress. Debt that is senior has a higher priority than debt that is junior or subordinate. Finally, given the fixed nature and tax deductibility of debt payments, the use of debt provides financial leverage for a company.

In order to properly utilize debt in a company's capital structure, a treasurer must understand the basic concept of debt, the lender's perspective and the credit process. Most debt issues that are sold to investors, with the exception of Federal Treasuries and most Federal agencies, are rated for credit risk by one or more rating agencies.

In addition, a treasurer must be aware of the advantages and disadvantages of using both short- and long-term debt. Under most conditions, the use of short- and long-term debt by a company results in a lower overall cost of capital and an increase in cash flows (that is, a higher value) per dollar of equity. This advantage results from:

- The generally lower cost of debt (versus equity)
- The tax deductibility of interest payments
- The fixed nature of debt payments

If a company is profitable, debt represents an attractive source of funds because the payments are limited to principal and interest, and the profits after principal and interest expenses are either retained for investment purposes or distributed to a company's owners as dividends.

Use of debt carries the risk that a company's cash flows may not be sufficient to service the debt, causing a company to borrow additional funds or raising the possibility of default or bankruptcy.

Another consideration in utilizing debt is the intended use of the funds. A very common and important reason for the use of debt is to meet obligations when other funds are not available or to finance working capital needs. For many businesses, cash flows are unsynchronized due to such factors as seasonality or because cash outflows related to accounts payable precede cash inflows derived from accounts receivable.

If funds are used to purchase an asset or to buy a security, the major justification for borrowing may be that the asset or other investment generates funds for repayment of the loan. It is also important to consider the maturities of assets versus the maturities of liabilities funding those assets. Although matching the duration of the assets to the liabilities is a common practice, there are other approaches used by treasurers.

(A detailed discussion of other approaches is in Chapter 6, Philosophy of Working Capital.)

The relationship between a borrower and a lender is intended to be mutually beneficial. A borrower receives needed funds while a lender realizes a return on investment in the form of fees, interest and/or other considerations such as warrants that allow the purchase of a company's stock at a predetermined price:

- To a lender, a loan is an investment. The interest and fees received represent the yield.

- To a borrower, a loan allows immediate access to funds that can be repaid at a future date. The fees and interest paid is the cost of using the funds.

A lender wants to be certain that a borrower can repay both the principal of the loan and the interest. In the credit process, a borrower usually develops a business plan that demonstrates a company's ability to repay the loan according to the terms of the loan agreement.

A general rule for successful use of debt is that management understands the operating and cash flow cycles of a particular business, industry, organization or government entity. Generally, an organization with stable cash flows and large amounts of assets does not significantly increase overall risk with the use of debt. On the other hand, an organization or industry with high uncertainty in cash flows or high operating risk may find that debt magnifies the risk.

Because the use of debt may have an impact on the risk profile of an organization, it is necessary to consider how debt affects the willingness of investors to purchase the organization's securities. For companies, investors generally gravitate toward stocks that provide a cash flow stream and a risk/return profile that fits their investment strategies. This is referred to as the clientele effect.

The use of debt potentially impacts the amount and timing of dividends, as well as the overall risk of a company, thereby potentially changing the mix of investors in a company's stock and the price that investors are willing to pay for the stock.

(A detailed discussion of the clientele effect is in Chapter 14, Capital Structure and Dividend Policy.)

A. Short-Term Borrowing

The use of short-term sources of funds is often determined by:

- A company's business and/or industry
- Factors such as seasonality of sales
- Timing of collections and disbursements
- Economic conditions and trends

Many organizations (including government entities and not-for-profits) use short-term or money market borrowing as a temporary source of funds until short-term obligations can be rolled over into medium and long-term debt such as notes or bonds. Many government entities also issue short-term tax anticipation notes (TANs) or bond anticipation notes (BANs) to cover differences in timing between expenditures and expected tax collections or proceeds from bond issues.

Short-term borrowing is, therefore, an important part of an organization's long-term strategic plan. Failure to incorporate short-term borrowing into long-term strategic planning may result in inappropriate levels of borrowing or inadequate levels of liquidity.

Many organizations find that short-term borrowing is an important source of financing, for several reasons:

1. It is often more flexible and easier to access in comparison to long-term financing. Therefore, it is often used in increasing amounts until refinancing for a longer term is economically justified.
2. It may also provide a temporary source of financing to support a temporary need for funds, such as seasonal increases in accounts receivable and/or inventory.
3. It affords the use of maturity matching for an organization's short-term debt. This involves matching the maturity of the debt to the specific financing needs of an organization. An example would be a company that borrows to purchase inventory, then pays off the loan as the inventory is sold.

   (A detailed discussion of the specific sources of short-term credit is in Chapter 10, Liquidity Management.)

4. It is offered at a fixed or variable interest rate. The choice between either fixed or variable rates is affected by the spread between the two, expected future changes in interest rates, yield curve and the effect of potential changes in interest rates on an organization's cash flows. Because short-term borrowing involves a lower interest rate than long-term financing, it is often used on a continuing basis to provide an ongoing source of lower-cost debt.

The disadvantage of short-term borrowing in contrast to long-term borrowing is that, in times of economic distress, the availability of short-term borrowing may decrease and costs may increase. Economic distress can be caused by any one or more of the following:

- Deterioration of an organization's financial condition
- Tightening of credit standards by a lender
- Changes in lending practices
- Reduction in the availability of credit due to poor economic conditions
- Increases in short-term interest rates

B. Medium- and Long-Term Borrowing

A wide range of different sources exists for medium- and long-term borrowing. Primary sources are term loans, intermediate-term notes and bonds, and long-term bonds. In using debt, it is also important to understand the role of seniority of claims for that debt. In the event of bankruptcy, there is a specific order of claims for each type of debt. In some cases, such as secured debt, there are designated assets that are used to satisfy the debt. For unsecured debt, the priority of claims is generally determined by the indenture agreement and covenants related to each debt issue. For example, senior debt has priority over junior or subordinated debt.

1. Term Loan

A term loan is a loan with a fixed maturity, usually greater than one year, which can be repaid either in installments or in a single payment. Frequently, a term loan is issued for a specific financing need such as the purchase of a new plant or new equipment or for general expansion. Interest is usually paid at periodic intervals and may be fixed or variable. A term loan is usually secured by the asset being financed and its maturity is related to the useful life of the asset.

For many organizations, leasing of equipment is an alternative to term loans, especially in instances when the seller/manufacturer of the equipment provides specialized leasing arrangements. (See the section titled Lease Financing, later in this chapter.)

2. Medium- or Intermediate-Term Notes and Bonds

Companies or government entities issue medium- or intermediate-term notes and bonds with terms in the two- to 10-year range. In most cases, these bonds are coupon bearing (i.e., interest payments are made at periodic intervals) and are very similar to long-term bonds except for the shorter maturity.

3. Long-Term Bonds

Long-term bonds, which are typically issued for periods of 10 to 30 years, represent a major source of long-term debt financing for many organizations. Bonds are a long-term contract in which the issuer of the bond (the borrower) agrees to make specific payments of interest (usually semiannually) and principal (at maturity) to the holders (lenders/investors) of the bonds. In the event of bankruptcy, bonds have different priority claims, depending on the seniority of the bonds and liens or pledges on any assets. Bonds are available in a wide variety of structures. The primary types of bonds are as follows.

- **Mortgage Bonds –** Used to finance specific assets that are pledged as security against the issue, mortgage bonds usually include substantial financial covenants or indenture agreements. These covenants outline:
    - The assets involved
    - The ability of an organization to issue additional bonds
    - The use of second or junior mortgages
    - Sinking-fund requirements
    - Reporting requirements
    - Restrictions involving key financial ratios
    - Prepayment terms

  Indenture agreements serve to protect the interests of the bondholders by restricting the actions of managers, which may reduce the value of the bonds.

- **Unsecured Bonds (Debentures) –** Typically unsecured bonds that represent general claims against the assets and/or cash flows of an organization, debentures may carry a higher cost than secured bonds. Large, financially secure organizations issue debentures based on their reputations in the marketplace. Organizations that do not have easily mortgaged assets must utilize unsecured borrowing through the use of debentures. The claim of debentures on the assets of a company is generally junior to that of bonds but senior to equity. Debentures may be issued on a subordinated basis, indicating that the claim on assets is subordinate to designated notes payable, bank loans or other specified debt.

- **Callable Bonds –** Issued with a call provision that allows the issuer to call or retire the bonds prior to maturity, callable bonds are typically issued during high interest rate periods with the intent to retire the bonds when the opportunity arises to refinance in a lower interest rate environment. In some cases, these types of bonds may have a "trigger price," or a pre-specified market price or an interest rate at which the bonds are callable.

- **Convertible Bonds and Warrants –** Corporate securities that can be converted by the holder, or sometimes the issuer, into shares of common or preferred stock at a fixed price, these bonds provide the holder with a potential for capital growth in return for a lower interest rate. Bonds issued with warrants are similar in nature to convertible bonds.

  Warrants are options to buy stock at a stated price for a stated period of time. Warrants have the advantage of enabling an investor to assume an ownership position if a company grows and prospers while, at the same time, enabling an investor to receive interest payments even if the bonds never convert to equities.

- **Government Bonds –** Bonds issued by government entities are usually in the form of general obligation or revenue bonds. General obligation bonds are paid from the proceeds of general tax revenues while the repayment of revenue bonds is directly linked to the revenues generated from specific assets (i.e., airport or stadium construction bonds or toll road/bridge bonds). Many non-federal government bonds (municipals) have some type of tax-advantaged status and are thus exempt from federal and, in some cases, state and local income taxes.

- **Industrial Revenue Bonds –** These are tax-exempt bonds, sometimes referred to as industrial development bonds, issued by a state or local government agency to finance industrial or commercial projects that serve a public good. The bond is not usually backed by the full faith and credit of the government that issues the bond but rather is backed by the company that sponsors the project or in some cases by a bank letter of credit. These types of bonds should not be confused with the government revenue bonds discussed above.

- **Zero (or Low) Coupon Bonds –** These bonds typically pay no or very low interest during the life of the bond and pay just the face value (par value) at maturity. As a result, zero coupon bonds are issued at a substantial discount from par value. There are two advantages for the issuer: first, there is no cash outflow until maturity and, second, the company receives an annual tax deduction until maturity.

There are, however, two major disadvantages relative to traditional bonds: first, zero coupon bonds are generally not callable or refundable and, second, current IRS tax codes make these bonds unattractive to non-institutional investors. Taxable investors are required to pay taxes on the estimated interest earnings each year, even though the interest is not received until maturity. Thus, for non-institutional investors, there is a negative cash flow stream (tax outflows) during the life of the bond.

- **High-Yield Bonds –** Also referred to as junk bonds or below investment grade (rating of BB or less), high yield bonds usually come from one of two sources. First, some junk bonds are originally sound but become high-risk when a company issuing the bond experiences financial trouble or files for bankruptcy. Though these bonds may have reasonable coupon payments, the riskiness of the company's financial position causes a deep discount at sale (thus providing a high yield-to-maturity). Second, some high-yield bonds are originally sold as high-risk instruments, in which case they are sold by companies either to finance a leveraged buyout or to relieve financial distress.

- **Other Types of Bonds –** Many other types of bonds are used for special purposes or related to specific types of assets. Among them are the following:
    - Income bonds pay interest only if a company has profits, thus reducing some of the risk of issuing debt from a company's viewpoint.
    - Collateral trust bonds are backed by securities, such as other companies' stocks and bonds, held by the issuing company.
    - Equipment trust certificates are bonds that are secured by movable equipment, such as a fleet of trucks or railroad equipment.
    - Indexed bonds' interest rates are tied to an economic index and are used in countries with high inflation.
    - Economic development bonds are typically issued by underdeveloped countries or sponsoring organizations such as the World Bank or the International Monetary Fund (IMF)
    - Tax Increment Financing (TIF) bonds are used primarily for local financing in which a municipality may use all, or a portion of, new property taxes within a designated district to assist in the project's financing.

A variety of other special purpose bonds are continually being developed to meet specialized needs.

4. Other Forms of Debt Capital

There are many other types of debt-like instruments that can be utilized in raising capital. Among some of the current products available are the following.

- **Floating (Adjustable) Rate Debt –** This type of debt is especially attractive to investors during periods of rising interest rates.
    - Some investors prefer floating-rate debt because it has a stable market value and matches current interest rates.
    - Some borrowers prefer floating-rate debt because it allows the borrower to take advantage of falling interest rates yet still match the maturity of debts to the maturity of assets.

- **Project Financing –** This type of financing applies to large projects, usually related to energy explorations, refineries and utility power plants. The typical project financing arrangement is complex, involving several companies, or sponsors, forming a separate legal entity to operate the project. The lenders are paid from the project cash flows and generally do not have recourse to the individual sponsors or owners of the project.

- **Securitization –** In recent years, many types of debt instruments have been securitized in order to increase liquidity, thus lowering the cost of capital to borrowers. The primary corporate applications of securitization are accounts receivable and inventory. These are bundled together to collateralize the securities, making them more liquid and, therefore, more attractive to investors. Securitization of debt instruments has occurred because certain financial institutions have been willing to form a market in these instruments, in particular, for commercial paper and for high-yield bonds.

  The other type of securitization is called asset securitization or asset-backed securities. The primary example of this type of securitization is in the home mortgage market where many different entities such as the Federal National Mortgage Association (FNMA), the Government National Mortgage Association (GNMA), the Federal Home Loan Mortgage Corporation (FHLMC), and the Collateralized Mortgage Obligations (CMOs) bundle together pools of mortgages into securities and sell the securities to investors. This arrangement provides significant liquidity to the mortgage market, which benefits both borrowers and lenders.

- **Off-Balance Sheet Financing (Leasing) –** This type of financing is typically used by organizations that have high current levels of debt or those that have very restrictive covenants on the use of additional debt. As the name implies, this form of financing does not appear on a company's balance sheet and usually entails the use of some type of leasing arrangements or sale of receivables. There are significant restrictions on the use of this type of financing as outlined in Financial Accounting Standards Board (FASB) Statement 13. FAS 13 requires that companies entering into certain types of leases must capitalize the leases. This means that companies must restate balance sheets to report a leased asset as a fixed asset and the present value of the future lease payments as a liability, which may appear as a footnote to financial statements. This topic is covered in greater detail later in this chapter.

5. Debt Contract Provisions

Although debt generally results in lower costs of capital for a company, it also requires that managers accept some restrictions. The only way that debt holders can effectively protect their interests is to establish, at the time of the initial debt contract, certain provisions (representations, warrants and covenants) that prevent the managers or equity holders from reducing the value of the bonds. These provisions also give debt holders additional rights under certain deteriorating conditions or events of default.

In addition, treasurers may make provisions for early retirement of the debt, repayment of the principal or refinancing of the issue. The debt contract also includes a promissory note that outlines the amount of funds borrowed and the financial terms. Several examples follow.

- **Bond Indentures and Covenants –** An indenture is a legal document that outlines the rights and obligations of both the borrower (bond issuer) and the lender (bondholder). These indentures may be quite lengthy and include various restrictive covenants that impose constraints on the actions of a company's management. These covenants may be negative (i.e., actions the company cannot take, such as double pledging of collateral) or affirmative (i.e., actions the company must take, such as providing regular financial statements or maintaining certain financial ratios).

  The purpose of the document is to protect the bondholders from actions by a company's management that would increase the value of equity holders or other stakeholders at the expense of bondholders. Violation of an indenture agreement is usually sufficient grounds for the bondholders to make the debt immediately due and payable, which may force a company into bankruptcy. In addition, the SEC approves indenture agreements in public offerings and ensures that all indenture provisions are met before allowing a company to sell new securities to the general public.

- **Representations and Warranties –** Representations and warranties are the existing conditions at the time the loan agreement is executed, as attested to by the borrower. Such conditions generally include:
  - Affirmation of the valid legal existence of the borrowing company
  - A resolution by the borrower's Board of Directors authorizing the borrowing
  - The authority of the corporate officers signing the documents
  - The company's confirmation of compliance with the Employee Retirement Income and Security Act (ERISA)
  - An indemnity protecting the lender from environmental liabilities

- **Events of Default –** An event of default may occur if any term or condition under a debt agreement is breached or violated by the borrower. Events of default are incidences such as:
  - Non-payment of interest or principal when due
  - A material adverse change in the condition of the borrower
  - Violation of a specified covenant

The characteristics of events of default include cure periods, remedies and waivers of defaults:
  - Cure periods, often specified in the agreement, are a period of time in which an event of default may be corrected before the lender is allowed to pursue default remedies.
  - Remedies available to a lender normally include an acceleration of all principal and interest on the debt when a default occurs.
  - Waivers of defaults may be given at the lender's discretion.

- **Call Provisions –** These provisions give the issuing entity the right to call in a bond or other issue for redemption prior to the original maturity. As compensation to the investors for early redemption, a call premium is paid when a bond is called. The call premium is usually set on a sliding scale, with larger premiums above par required the earlier an issue is called.

  The call privilege is valuable to a company because it allows redemption of a bond issue if interest rates fall or if excess cash becomes available and refinancing becomes an attractive option. As a result, bonds with call provisions typically require a higher coupon rate than non-callable bonds of similar size, duration and quality in order to attract investors. The primary downside to the investor is that if interest rates fall and the bond is called, the investor is forced to reinvest the call proceeds at a lower rate.

- **Sinking Funds –** The usual format for bond issues is for an organization to pay interest only (coupon payments) for the life of the bond and then to repay the principal (par or face value) at maturity. In other words, most bonds are not amortized. This means a treasurer must plan to make a large lump sum payment at the issue's maturity.

  Typically, sinking fund provisions in the indenture agreement require companies to call, or to repurchase on the open market, a portion of the outstanding bond issue each year. In essence, this amortizes the bond's issue over its life. Other types of sinking funds require a company to make payments into a trust account, which either repurchases bonds on the open market or amasses a lump sum for retirement of the bonds at maturity.

  The existence of some type of sinking fund arrangement, as specified in the bond indenture agreement, generally increases the safety of the bonds and, hence, lowers the required interest rate.

- **Refinancing Operations –** Refinancing operations are often used following periods of high interest rates. During high interest rate periods, many entities that must issue bonds attach call provisions that allow the bonds to be redeemed prior to maturity. When interest rates fall, companies then issue new bonds at a lower interest rate and use the proceeds to call in the older, higher-interest bonds. The primary purpose of these operations is to take advantage of falling interest rates and to reduce the overall cost of debt for a company.

- **Defeasance of Debt –** This is a method for removing debt from an organization's balance sheet without actually retiring the debt issue. In this arrangement, the borrower places sufficient funds in escrow, usually in U.S. government securities, to pay for interest and principal on the debt issue. Because control of both the debt and escrow funds is relinquished, and payment and retirement of the debt issue is now guaranteed, this debt (and the related securities) can be removed from the balance sheet, as well as any restrictive covenants related to the debt. (Defeasance of debt is covered under FAS 140.)

- **Promissory Note –** A promissory note is an unconditional promise to pay a specified amount plus interest at a defined rate either on demand or on a certain date. A promissory note can be issued for each individual borrower or for a total line amount, against which multiple borrowings exist. A master note is a type of promissory note used to simplify the paperwork connected with loans that have a multiple advance feature such as lines of credit and revolvers. A company signs one comprehensive promissory note for the total amount of the line of credit. Any loans or repayments under the note are covered by the terms of the master note.

- **Warrants and Convertibles –** Warrants and convertibles are considered debt/equity and hybrids and will be covered in detail later in this chapter in the section on equity issues.

6. Issues in Secured Lending

For long-term debt that uses some type of asset as security, several issues must be addressed.

- **Collateral –** The assets being used as security for the loan are called collateral. They may include physical assets (plant, equipment, inventory, etc.) or financial assets (receivables, marketable securities, etc.). The condition of the assets must be monitored; in the case of physical assets, insurance is also a requirement.

- **Liens –** In most types of secured lending, the lender has a lien, or legal claim, on the assets used as collateral in the event the lender cannot take physical possession of the asset. This may be in the form of a mortgage (for larger assets) or a blanket lien (against inventory and receivables). In the event the borrower defaults on the loan or bond issue, the lender can seize the assets in lieu of repayment.

In order to ensure this process, the lender files a UCC-1 under Article 9 of the Uniform Commercial Code, with the secretary of state in each state in which the company does business. This filing becomes a matter of public record and establishes the order of priority of secured claims on a company's assets. In addition to the UCC-1 filing, the creditor executes a security agreement outlining the nature of the assets pledged on the loan. These items "perfect" the lien and make it enforceable in a court of law. Lenders often perform a lien search on a potential borrower to determine whether the assets being pledged are already pledged to some other creditor.

- **Guarantee –** When a subsidiary of a larger company is borrowing funds or floating a bond issue, the lenders may require that the parent corporation (or sister subsidiary, supplier, customer or other entity) provide a guarantee of principal for the arrangement. In some cases a subsidiary may even provide a guarantee for the parent. This allows lenders recourse to the parent company (or guaranteeing party) to obtain payment in the event the subsidiary is in default. There are several levels of guarantees that the parent corporation or others (referred to as the guarantee party) can make according to the degree of protection offered to a lender:
  - **Full Guarantee:** The guarantee party fully guarantees any borrowing arrangement by the subsidiary and agrees to take over the loan if the subsidiary fails to make timely payments.
  - **Specific Project Guarantee:** The guarantee party guarantees only loans relating to specific projects of the subsidiary, not all loans.
  - **Guarantee of Payment or Collection:** The guarantee party guarantees to make payment on the loan or to collect payment from the subsidiary, only if the subsidiary formally defaults on the loan. This usually requires the lender to initiate default proceedings on the subsidiary and to initiate collection efforts before the parent becomes involved.
  - **Comfort Letter:** This type of guarantee is generally just a letter from another party stating actions they will or will not take on behalf of the borrower. This type of agreement may not be legally enforceable.
  - **Performance Guarantees:** In some cases, the lender may ask for specific performance guarantees relative to the assets being financed. Under a full guarantee, the parent fully guarantees performance by the subsidiary. Under a best-efforts guarantee, the parent agrees to make best efforts to get the subsidiary to perform but does not guarantee subsidiary performance.
  - **Personal Guarantee:** In some cases, especially for smaller, privately held companies, the lender may require a personal guarantee on the part of the owner or other principals in the business before granting a loan.

- **Bond Ratings –** Bond issues are assigned quality ratings that reflect the probability a company issuing the bonds is likely to default on an issue. Each public bond issue is independently rated by one or more of the accredited rating agencies. The four rating agencies recognized by the SEC are:
    - Moody's Investor Service
    - Standard and Poor's Corporation
    - Fitch Investors Service
    - Dominion Bond Rating Service (based in Canada)

There are several considerations relative to bond ratings. The first consideration is the bond rating criteria used by the agency. Ratings are generally based on both qualitative and quantitative factors but tend to be somewhat subjective. Given the complexity of most large companies, there is no precise mathematical formula that analysts can use to determine the rating; instead, many factors must be taken into account.

The second consideration is the importance of the bond ratings to both investors and company management. Many charters restrict institutional investors to buying investment grade bonds or better, and these investors make up the bulk of the bond market. Also, a company's bond rating is considered a direct measure of the riskiness of a company, and this has an impact on a company's cost of capital (i.e., the rating sets the pricing).

The third consideration is related to changes in bond ratings. Rating agencies review outstanding bonds on a periodic basis and may upgrade or downgrade an issue based on changes in either a company or in the general economic environment. Companies or government entities with downgraded bonds have a more difficult time raising additional capital in the market and have to pay a higher price for bonds issued or other debt incurred.

The basic bond rating scales are provided in the table below:

Long-Term Bond Definitions

Definitions	Moody's	S&P	Fitch	Dominion
Prime – Maximum Safety	Aaa	AAA	AAA	AAA
High Grade – High Quality	Aa1 to Aa3	AA+ to AA-	AA+ to AA-	AA
Upper Medium Grade	A1 to A3	A+ to A-	A+ to A-	A
Lower Medium Grade	Baa1 to Baa3	BBB+ to BBB-	BBB+ to BBB-	BBB
Below Investment Grade	Ba1	BB+	BB+	
Speculative	Ba2 to Ba3	BB to BB-	BB to BB-	BB
Highly Speculative	B1 to B3	B+ to B-	B+ to B-	B
Substantial Risk	Caa	CCC+	CCC	CCC to C
In Poor Standing		CCC to CCC-		
Extremely Speculative	Ca			
May be in Default	C			
Default		D	DDD to D	0

Table Source: Equity Analytics, Ltd.

C. Other Factors Influencing Long-Term Debt Decisions

A variety of other factors influence a company's decisions regarding long-term debt issues.

1. Capital Structure Considerations

Most CFOs and treasurers have some target capital structure in mind for their companies. The target capital structure is a function of a variety of factors:

- The type of company
- The company's financial history
- The industry
- General economic conditions
- The operating risk of a company
- The type of investors holding a company's securities

The availability and choice of debt issues obviously has a major impact on the ultimate capital structure of a company. Because debt issues can usually be planned, many companies are able to direct capital structure in the general direction of the desired target. Additionally, government entities may be limited by either legislation or charter regarding what types of debt and maturities can be issued.

(A detailed discussion of capital structure is in Chapter 14, Capital Structure and Dividend Policy.)

2. Maturity Matching

Maturity matching involves matching the life of a debt issue to the life of any assets being financed. Generally, companies do try to match maturities of debt issues and assets wherever possible in order to reduce the overall risk of a company.

3. Effects of Interest Rate Levels and Forecasts

The general level of interest rates and economic activity has an impact on both the use and the cost of debt for companies. Also, a treasurer's forecast of future interest rates has an impact on both the type of capital raised by a company and the provisions that may be attached to capital issues. Treasurers must consider the issue of "flight to quality" whenever financial market conditions decline. In these times, investors move toward safe or quality investments; hence, the spread between high- and low-risk investments typically increases significantly. In good financial markets, the spread between high- and low-risk investments may be much smaller, so a high-risk borrower may be able to obtain relatively good rates.

4. Availability of Collateral

Companies that have large available assets that can be used as collateral are typically able to borrow at lower rates than companies of the same credit quality and rating that do not have collateral. Companies with lower risk profiles have the financial strength to borrow on an unsecured basis and to obtain funds at lower rates than companies and industries that are more prone to default and, therefore, must resort to secured borrowing in order to obtain funds.

IV. LEASE FINANCING

For many types of equipment acquisitions, leasing may be considered a substitute for debt. The lease-versus-borrow decision is one of the most important types of analysis for companies acquiring capital assets. The leasing decision process has two general stages.

- Acquisition: The process by which a company decides to acquire a particular building or asset, basing the decision on regular capital-budgeting procedures. The decision to acquire the asset is not the issue of an analysis because the decision to proceed with the project has already been made.
- Finance: Once the asset acquisition has been justified, the asset must be financed by either borrowing or leasing. For capital-structure purposes, leasing normally has the same effect on capital structure as borrowing, so the cash flows from leasing are usually compared with the cash flows from borrowing funds to purchase the asset.

A. Why Companies Use Leasing

In leasing, the owner of the asset is called the lessor and receives lease payments from the lessee who has use of the asset. A key reason for leasing is the tax benefit for both the lessor and the lessee. There may be an advantage to using leasing as a source of off-balance-sheet financing or for certain tax incentives. This method of financing and the tax advantages will be explained in the section titled Types of Leases. In most cases, long-term lease arrangements may be considered a direct substitute for debt in a company's capital structure. Also, loan and debt covenants may dictate the form and the structure of leases for many corporations.

Leasing is generally an appealing choice for assets that have a high potential for technological obsolescence, such as computers, medical equipment and communications equipment. Leasing may also be attractive to start-up companies or companies beginning sales in a new area that has a high level of uncertainty about future demand. The cancellation provisions of a lease may offer substantial protection in business ventures of this kind.

A company may also choose to lease assets that are needed to conduct business but fall outside the company's area of expertise (i.e., core competency). For example, a food wholesaler may choose to lease a fleet of delivery trucks rather than purchase the assets. The lessor takes care of the financing and maintenance of the fleet while the wholesaler focuses efforts on what it knows best. In many cases, lease financing may be offered at the same time as the acquisition of the asset, making it an easy, one-stop shopping arrangement.

B. Types of Leases

There are several types of leases whose differences primarily include:

- Length of lease period
- Which party is responsible for maintenance and upkeep of the asset
- The residual value of the asset (the estimated value of the asset at the end of the lease)
- The relevant tax treatment
- The determination of who retains the assets at the end of the lease and under what terms. Different types of leases also have different accounting guidelines, which are outlined in FAS 13.

1. Sale and Leaseback

Under a sale and leaseback arrangement, equipment owned by a company is sold to another party (the lessor) and then immediately leased back by the original owner (lessee). This type of lease arrangement aids companies that need a cash infusion or that cannot take full advantage of the tax advantages from depreciation due to excessive operating losses. The sale and leaseback arrangement can also move the cash flow stream (income or costs) to different periods.

2. Operating or Service Leases

Operating leases, also known as service leases, are established in such a way that the lessor provides maintenance for the equipment and retains ownership of the equipment at the end of the lease. These are often done on an off-balance-sheet basis, meaning that the lease payments are reflected only on the income statement but neither the assets nor the lease appear on the balance sheet.

Operating leases usually run for periods substantially shorter than the life of the equipment. This means that the lease payments usually are not sufficient to amortize the equipment, but the lessor intends to make up the full value of the equipment upon the release or sale at the end of the lease contract. In analyzing operating leases, it is important to carefully consider the flexibility of cancellation policies.

3. Capital or Financial Leases

Capital leases, also known as financial leases, have terms different from those of operating leases. Capital leases have the following characteristics:

- They are typically for a period greater than one year.
- The lessor usually does not provide maintenance for the equipment.
- The lease agreement is not cancelable.
- Accounting guidelines require that a financial lease appear on the balance sheet as a capitalized lease; hence, the payments are set up to fully depreciate the cost of the equipment.
- The lease usually runs for the life of the asset.
- The lessee has the option to renew the contract or to purchase the asset at the end of the original lease contract for an agreed-upon residual value.

The residual value for this type of lease is generally the estimated value of the asset at the end of the lease. The amortization of the asset's value takes the residual value into account in the computation of lease payments. The lessee is generally responsible for maintaining the asset and must pay any applicable taxes and insurance.

Because the lessor receives payment after expenses are paid, a financial lease is sometimes referred to as a net, net lease. When this type of lease is used in real estate, it may be referred to as a triple-net lease because it includes taxes, insurance, and utilities. This type of lease is an alternative to borrowing funds to finance the acquisition of an asset.

Under certain conditions, leases may be considered a source of off-balance-sheet financing, thus avoiding the appearance of additional debt on a company's balance sheet, as well as increasing return on assets. To correct this problem, the FASB issued FAS 13. This requires companies entering into financial leases to capitalize the lease. This process restates a company's balance sheet in order to show the leased asset as a fixed asset and the present value of the lease payments as a liability.

The logic behind the FASB requirement is that when a company signs a financial lease agreement, the obligation to make lease payments is just as binding as in a long-term loan agreement. Thus, for most purposes, capitalized leases are a direct substitute for a company's long-term debt financing. Significant operating lease arrangements must be reported in a footnote to the financial statements, further ensuring that no investor or lender is unaware of leasing arrangements.

C. Estimated Residual Value

The lessor owns the property upon expiration of the lease and has a primary claim on the asset's residual value; that is, the amount remaining after all allowable depreciation charges have been subtracted from a depreciable asset. In most cases, the estimated residual values are built into the leasing arrangements. Assets with potentially high residual values generally have lower lease payments than similar assets with lower residual values.

The setting of the residual value may also have an impact on the tax status of the lease, as well as on requirements for listing the lease as an on- or off-balance-sheet item. In lease analysis it is critical to know the asset's assumed residual value in order to avoid surprises at the end of the lease.

D. Tax Considerations

The full amount of the annual lease payment is a tax-deductible expense for the lessee, provided the IRS agrees that a particular contract is a genuine lease, not simply an installment loan in the guise of a lease. The primary reason for IRS restrictions on lease terms is to prevent a company from setting up a lease arrangement that allows for more rapid write-off of an asset than that allowed by the IRS's Modified Accelerated Cost Recovery Schedule (MACRS) depreciation schedules. The MACRS depreciation schedule provides a listing of how much can be depreciated annually for various types of assets.

V. EQUITY (STOCK) MARKETS

A. Common Stock

Common stock represents ownership in a company. The management of a company acts as an agent for the shareholders to protect their interests. Common equity usually represents a significant portion of a publicly traded company's capital base.

1. Balance Sheet Accounts and Definitions

Treasury managers must be aware of three key terms relating to common stock: par value, retained earnings and paid-in capital. The total amount of stockholders' equity is the sum of these accounts. It is important to realize that these accounts represent only the historical accounting value of the equity, not the current market value.

- **Par Value:** An arbitrary amount (usually stated in the corporate charter) indicates the minimum amount that stockholders have put up (or must put up) in the event of bankruptcy. For many publicly traded companies this is $1.00 or $0 (no par value).

- **Retained Earnings:** This balance sheet account represents the accumulated net earnings of a corporation since its inception, less dividends paid to shareholders. This is part of the stockholders' equity and is an accounting of the money reinvested in a company in lieu of dividends paid out. It is important to understand that retained earnings are simply an accounting concept and are not a pool of funds sitting idle in a company.

- **Paid-in Capital:** This account reflects the difference at the time of issue between the par value and the issuance price (less underwriting costs) of any new stock that is sold by a company. For example, if a company were to sell a new issue of stock with a par value of $1, and a company nets $25 per share, then a $1 per share increase would be shown in the par value account and a $24 increase would be shown in the additional paid-in capital account per share.

- **Book Value per Share:** This is defined as total common stockholders' equity divided by the number of shares outstanding.

- **Market Value per Share:** This is defined as the current price at which a share of the stock is traded. Though this is not technically part of the accounting statements, it is often included in reports issued by a company and various financial reporting services.

- **Treasury Stock:** This is defined as stock issued by a company but later reacquired. It may be held in the company's treasury indefinitely, reissued to the public, or retired. Treasury stock receives no dividends and does not carry voting power while held by the company. It is considered to be issued but not outstanding and is, therefore, deducted from any capital calculations.

2. Types of Common Stock

While most companies have only one class of common stock, more and more companies are beginning to issue multiple levels of stock to different types of investors. Classified stocks are typically referred to as Class A or Class B, but these terms have no standard meaning; rather, they are specific to each company. Generally, the different classes of stock may limit voting privileges, dividends and/or resale.

The use of multiple classes is true for some preferred stock. The general purpose is to raise capital through the issue of new equity while still maintaining control of a company. Different classes of stock may be issued to differentiate returns for various pieces (divisions) of a large, diversified company. Large multinational corporations often issue stock in this manner to offer non-diversified investments to certain classes of stockholders.

Another type of stock is known as tracking stock. A tracking stock is a separate stock created by a parent company to "track" the financial progress of a particular piece of business. Despite being part of a publicly traded entity, tracking stocks trade under unique ticker symbols. These stocks are meant to create opportunities for investors to buy into a fast-growing unit without investing in the whole company. However, tracking stocks neither provide shareholders ownership in the parent company nor do they include voting rights.

Institutional investors—pension funds, insurance companies and mutual funds—own about 60 percent of all common stock. Brokerage firms use different criteria for determining institutional investors, but the most typical designation would be a commercial bank, savings & loan, insurance company, registered investment company or advisor (an individual or mutual fund with total assets of at least $100 million).

3. Convertibles

Convertible securities are usually bonds or preferred stock that may be exchangeable at the holder's or issuer's option for a company's common stock under certain terms and conditions at a pre-stated price. The conversion does not provide any new capital for a company. It simply converts existing debt or preferred stock into common equity. The conversion ratio states the number of shares of stock that one bond may be converted to if the owner so chooses. The maturity value of the bond and the conversion ratio determine the conversion price of the issue. For example, a $1,000 par-value bond with a conversion ratio of 20 (20 shares of common stock per bond) implies a stock conversion price of $50.

Most convertibles contain clauses that protect against the dilution of value due to stock splits, stock dividends or depressed stock prices. The typical provision states that if new common stock is sold at a price below the conversion price, then the conversion ratio must be raised (thus, the conversion price lowered) to the issue price of the new stock. Convertibles have an important advantage for the issuer in that they offer a company a chance to sell debt with lower interest rates and less restrictive covenants in exchange for a chance for the investor to participate in potential capital gains as the value of a company increases.

Convertibles also may have three significant disadvantages for the issuer.

- If a company's stock price increases significantly during the convertible's life, a company may have been better off issuing regular debt, then refunding the debt with a new stock issue.
- If the convertible issue has a low-coupon rate, this is lost if the holders convert the bonds into stock.
- If stock prices do not rise, a company may be locked into the debt issue, although it typically is at a lower coupon rate than regular debt.

4. Warrants

Warrants are options issued by companies that give the warrant's owner the right to buy a stated number of shares of a company's stock at a specified price for a specified period of time. They are often listed on major exchanges and traded like options.

Unlike convertibles, warrants issued with bonds represent additional equity capital for the issuing company. Most warrants are "detachable," meaning they can be traded separately from the bond. When these warrants are exercised, the low-coupon bond issue remains outstanding, so the warrants bring additional funds into a company while keeping debt costs low. Warrants are used extensively by small, rapidly growing companies as "sweeteners" when selling either debt or preferred stock. A bond with warrants has some characteristics of debt and some characteristics of equity, thus creating a hybrid security (sometimes called a bond with an "equity kicker") that provides a company with the ability to expand its mix of securities and to appeal to a broader group of investors.

Warrants may have the effect of diluting the value of the current stockholders' equity and the earnings per share (EPS). Some companies report a fully diluted EPS figure, which assumes that all outstanding warrants have been exercised. The SEC requires that disclosure of EPS include:

- Information on the capital structure
- Explanation of the computation of EPS
- Identification of common-stock equivalents (including convertibles, rights and warrants)
- Number of shares converted
- Assumptions made

B. Preferred Stock

Although preferred stock is considered equity, it is different from common stock both in terms of stockholder rights and in the payment stream. In terms of cash flows, it is more like debt than equity because of the fixed nature of the return. Unlike debt, however, a company does not risk bankruptcy by missing a preferred stock dividend. Another difference is that preferred stock does not have the tax deductibility feature that debt does; therefore, the cost is generally much higher than that of a similar debt issue.

1. Major Provisions of Preferred Stock Issues

Preferred stockholders have priority in both earnings and assets. That is, they are paid their share of the earnings before the common shareholders. In the event of bankruptcy, preferred stockholders' claims on a company's assets are senior to those of common shareholders but behind the creditors' and bondholders' claims. Preferred stock always has a par value, which is typically used as the basis for setting dividends as a percentage or rate of return based on the par value.

Preferred stocks also generally have provisions related to cumulative dividends. In the event that a company is not able to pay required preferred dividends, these dividends become "in arrears." In most cases, preferred stock dividends are cumulative, which means that all arrears dividends owed must be paid in full before any common stock dividends can be paid. Many issues of preferred stock have provisions that, if dividends are in arrears for a certain number of periods, the preferred stockholders may be granted voting rights and/or Board memberships in order to protect their interests.

Many preferred stock issues may be convertible into either common stock or debt under certain conditions. Either of these features offers more flexibility to the issuer of the preferred stock, as well as a unique investment opportunity to purchasers. In recent years, many new provisions have been offered to help make preferred stock more attractive to investors. These include:

- Voting rights
- Participation in earnings
- Sinking funds
- Maturity dates
- Retirement dates
- Exchange or call provisions

2. Evaluation of Preferred Stock

From the viewpoint of the corporate issuer, the main advantage is that a company can lock in financing costs and potentially leverage the return to the common shareholders due to the fixed nature of the dividends. With preferred stock, a company accomplishes this without increasing a company's default risk. Also, large portions of preferred stock issues are private issues to institutional investors. This usually means substantially lower flotation costs and less stringent disclosure requirements for the issue.

From the investor's perspective, preferred stock provides the investor with a steadier and more assured income than common stock, though the pricing may be sensitive to interest rate movements. Also, for most corporate holders of preferred stock, 70 percent of the dividend income may be excluded from federal income tax. This makes preferred stocks especially attractive to institutional investors.

3. Recent Trends

Many companies have found the unique features of preferred stock to be advantageous to raising capital in certain circumstances. Utilities and financial institutions have been heavy users of preferred stock. Money markets have seen the development of adjustable rate preferred stocks (ARPS), which take advantage of the tax exclusion on dividends to offer higher returns to money market investors. ARPS are designed to adjust dividend rates according to some interest rate index, thereby maintaining a more constant price level. This form of investment is attractive to many treasurers for a portion of the short-term portfolio because current tax regulations allow corporate holders of preferred stock to exclude 70 percent of the dividend income received from federal income taxes if the stock is held for at least a 45-day period. This type of instrument is a popular short-term investment vehicle.

There has also been a movement toward offering convertible preferred, especially in the case of recent mergers, where convertible preferred was used to finalize the last portion of financing needed. Another recent development has been the introduction of adjustable rate preferred stock as a money market investment.

(A more detailed discussion of all of the above trends is in Chapter 14, Capital Structure and Dividend Policy.)

VI. VALUATION OF CORPORATE SECURITIES

The valuation of corporate securities by the stock and bond markets includes bonds, preferred stock and common stock. Each of these is covered at a basic level. For more advanced information about this topic, a list of MBA-level financial management textbooks is provided at the end of this chapter. All of these textbooks also have relevant formulas and sample calculations.

In general, a security (or any asset) derives its value from the cash flow stream returned to the investor through the life of the security. The valuation of the asset includes the opportunity cost or required return to the investor; therefore, the valuation must take into account the time value of money. For any asset (including financial assets) the value of the asset is equal to the following:

$$V_0 = \sum_{j=1}^{n} \frac{CF_j}{(1+K_i)^j} = \frac{CF_1}{(1+K_i)^1} + \frac{CF_2}{(1+K_i)^2} + \dots + \frac{CF_n}{(1+K_i)^n}$$

Where:

V_0 = the current value of the asset

CF_j = the cash flow for the asset for periods 1 through n

k_i = the opportunity cost or required rate of return for asset type i

This formula illustrates that the asset's value is equal to the discounted value (present value) of the cash flows (both positive and negative) for the asset, discounted at the required rate of return. This model works for any type of asset or stream of cash flows. The investor estimates the cash flows for the asset and determines the appropriate required rate, then calculates the value of the asset. Asset valuation can be performed either on a financial calculator or with spreadsheet software.

A. Bond or Fixed Income Valuation

Valuation of bonds, otherwise known as fixed-income securities, is straightforward and is based on the present value of the cash flows related to the bond. These cash flows are easy to identify because they are outlined in the indenture agreement. The two cash flows from bonds are the periodic coupon payment (based on the coupon rate) and the return of the principal amount borrowed. The periodic coupons are usually paid semiannually or annually, and the payment dates are given in the indenture. As a result, investors find it easier to estimate the cash flows and the timing of the flows.

B. Preferred Stock Valuation

Preferred stock has many of the features of both debt financing and equity financing. From the investor's perspective, the cash flows are similar to bond cash flows while tax treatment and other features are similar to equity. Preferred stock has preference over common stock in the event of liquidation and has a prior claim on the earnings of a company; hence, the term "preferred stock."

C. Common Stock Valuation

Common stock valuation differs from bond and preferred stock valuation in an important way. The common stock cash flows (dividends) are usually perpetual but are not set by contract, as is the case with preferred stock. Instead, the dividends are set by the Board of Directors on a period-by-period basis. This complicates the analysis because of the difficulty in estimating the dividends. An additional complication in the valuation process arises due to the fact that capital gains (stock price appreciation) is an important consideration and must also be a factor in the equation.

D. Investment Risk and Rates of Return

An integral part of the valuation of corporate securities is the determination of a required rate of return by investors for each type of security. Also accompanying each security is an estimate of the risk related to that security's return.

1. Defining and Measuring Investment Risk

Risk refers to the chance that some unforeseen event may occur. The risk associated with investment in financial assets is the possibility that realized returns may be different from those expected by the investor. In a slightly different example of risk, the investor realizes a return lower than needed to compensate for the risk involved in the investment. Statistical measures provide the capability to measure risk. The statistical concepts of expected value and standard deviation provide measures of expected return and any related risks. In most cases, the stand-alone risk of a single investment can be summarized in terms of the mean (average) and standard deviation or possible returns.

2. Capital Asset Pricing Model (CAPM)

The Capital Asset Pricing Model (CAPM) describes one possible relationship between risk and the required rate of return for equity securities (stocks). The CAPM is based on the concept that the typical investor holds a diversified portfolio of stocks and that the only measure of risk relevant to such an investor is the beta of a stock. Beta is defined as the risk of a particular stock relative to an overall stock market measure, such as the S&P 500 Index. The betas for most major companies are calculated by many different sources and are readily available for interested investors.

The basic model assumes a linear relationship between the return on any particular stock and that stock's beta. The formula is expressed as follows:

$$k_i = k_{RF} + (k_M - k_{RF})B_I$$

Where:

k_i = the required rate of return for asset i

k_{RF} = the expected rate of return on a riskless asset (T-Bill rate)

k_M = the expected return on the market portfolio (S&P 500 Index)

B_I = the beta of asset i, described above

The return on the riskless asset is typically measured by the return on short-term U.S. government securities, such as the T-Bill. Another approach is to use a risk-free rate with a maturity that matches the maturity of the asset. In this case, the long-term government security rate could be used as a risk-free rate for long-term bonds or stocks.

The CAPM essentially represents a linear relationship between risk (beta) and required rate of return. At a beta of 0, the risk-free rate is the required rate of return. This level of beta indicates that the asset is not exposed to systematic risk. As beta increases, the required rate of return also increases. To find the required rate for a specific asset, determine the beta for the asset, and then find the level of y (required rate of return) that corresponds with that level of beta. According to this model, under equilibrium conditions, all assets are properly priced with respect to beta risk.

- If an asset is priced so that the rate is greater than that predicted by the CAPM, it would have an expected return above its required return. This indicates that investors find it desirable to hold, meaning that there is buying pressure on the asset. This pressure drives the price up (and the return down) until the asset is priced correctly relative to its beta.
- If an asset is priced so that the expected return is below that determined by the CAPM, investors do not want to hold the asset, causing downward pressure on the asset price and moving the return upward until it is properly priced.

Therefore, in equilibrium, all assets are priced so that they may be expected to provide the required rate of return.

VII. COST OF CAPITAL

The cost of capital figures in many aspects of decision making, especially capital budgeting. Cost of capital reflects the cost of funds to a company, therefore representing the minimum required rate of return that a company needs to achieve for any capital investment. It is important to recognize that most cost of capital determinations represent only an estimate of the costs. There are many factors that are difficult to incorporate into the analysis. For most companies, the estimation of cost of capital need only be reasonably accurate.

Capital Components and Costs: The primary sources of funds for a company, especially long-term funds, are debt and equity capital in the form of newly issued common stock and retained earnings. It is important for an investor to recognize that the most important item is the marginal cost of these components; that is, what the cost is of raising new amounts of these forms of capital. Using the marginal, or expected, cost of these components provides an investor with the market's current evaluation of a company's risk, and therefore, the required rate of return.

There is an additional consideration, however, as changes in a company's capital structure impact the marginal costs of individual capital components. Trying to determine a specific capital structure is analogous to trying to hit a moving target. It is also important to recognize that some of the funding is repaid with before-tax cash flows (debt) and some with after-tax cash flows (equity). Given the overriding goal of maximizing shareholder wealth, the analysis should be made using the after-tax costs of the financing sources. Therefore, debt costs should be adjusted to an after-tax basis.

1. Cost of Debt

The relevant component in cost of debt is after-tax costs. For any newly issued debt, the cost is the Yield to Maturity (YTM) on the bonds, which is the return that the investor receives if the bond is bought at the current price and held until it matures. The following computation is made to determine the after-tax cost of debt:

$$\mathbf{k_D(after\text{-}tax) = k_D(1 - T)}$$

Where:

k_D(after tax) = the after-tax cost of debt

k_D = the YTM projected for newly issued debt (before tax)

T = a company's marginal state and federal income tax rate

In many companies with complicated tax liabilities, this may be difficult to estimate from standard financial statements. If the analysis is being done internally, a company's tax accounting department may be able to provide an appropriate figure. The analyst could also use, as an estimate, the most recent year's taxes paid divided by the pre-tax earnings. Another approach is to use the average tax rate paid (as a percentage of pre-tax profits) over the last few years.

The cost of debt is adjusted to an after-tax cost because outlays associated with debt financing are an expense for tax purposes. The flotation (issuance) costs associated with debt may be significant for some companies. If so, these costs should be included in the determination of the cost of debt. Companies with minimal issuance costs (usually large, well-established companies) may not have to include these costs because it is necessary only to be reasonably accurate in the estimation. Because of errors inherent in the estimation, it is impossible to determine the exact costs involved for any given component in the cost of capital.

2. Cost of Common Equity

Funds from common equity can be raised from two sources:

- Retaining earnings during the period (instead of paying the earnings out in dividends)
- Issuing new common stock

It is important to realize that a company must apply a cost factor to the use of retained earnings because these are not free funds. This is based on the concept of opportunity cost, which assumes that a company should be able to earn at least the equity rate of return on any retained earnings.

If a company cannot find investment opportunities that meet this criterion, the earnings should be paid out to the shareholders as dividends so that they can find other investments that can fulfill the required rates of return. Applying the required rate of return on equity as a cost factor for retained earnings satisfies the opportunity cost principle. If new common stock is issued, then the flotation costs associated with underwriting and selling the issue must also be considered.

One of the primary methods of determining the costs of common equity is the CAPM. Additional methods for determining the cost of the equity component can be found in the MBA-level financial management textbooks referenced at the end of this chapter.

3. Weighted Average Cost of Capital (WACC)

To determine a company's cost of capital, the investor calculates a weighted average of the component costs of funds for a company. The computation is as follows:

$$WACC = [(W_D)(k_D)(1 - T)] + [(W_S)(k_S)]$$

Where:

WACC = the weighted average cost of capital of a company

W = the weight of the capital structure for each component D (debt) and S (common equity or stock)

$(K_D)(1 - T)$ = the after-tax cost of debt

K_S = the cost of common stock, either retained earnings or newly issued stock

Note that the cost of equity is either the cost of retained earnings or new issues of stock. From a pure cost perspective, the preference would be to use retained earnings because the costs are lower than new issues. However, the dividend policy of a company may restrict the amount of retained earnings available for reinvestment or a company may have limited earnings for the period.

Depending on the size of earnings and a company's dividend policy, there generally is a limited supply of retained earnings. For large capital budgets, or in times of low retained earnings, newly issued common stock has to be used. The exclusive use of retained earnings works only if internal generation of funds exceeds 100 percent of capital needs at the target debt/equity level.

VIII. PROCEDURES FOR SELLING ADDITIONAL COMMON STOCK

Companies that are already publicly traded may, from time to time, offer additional shares of stock in order to raise new equity capital. These are generally classified as primary distributions of authorized, but previously unissued, common shares. Secondary distributions involve stock previously issued that is now being resold, such as the sale of treasury stock.

A. Investment Banking Process

Investment bankers offer many services to a company issuing stock, bonds and other securities. The investment banking process has several levels of decision-making. The sale of new common stock and the operation of secondary markets are primarily regulated by the SEC and, to a lesser extent, by similar agencies in each state. The Federal Reserve has control over the flow of credit into the securities markets through margin requirements, which specify the maximum percentage of a security's purchase price that can be borrowed. This is set forth in Federal Reserve Regulation T, which governs the amount and type of credit that a broker/dealer may extend or maintain if customers purchase, carry or trade corporate securities. The regulation of the securities market is important to maintain stable markets, ensure sound brokerage companies and prevent stock manipulation.

B. Initial Decisions

Five basic decisions need to be made by a company's management and Board of Directors at this stage:

- The amount of money to be raised
- The types of securities to be issued
- The manner in which the deal is to be negotiated
- The selection of an investment bank
- Whether to issue under a best-efforts basis or on a full-underwriting agreement

Best Efforts or Underwritten Issues: Investment bankers typically underwrite new stock issues on either a best efforts or a full-underwriting basis. Under a best-efforts agreement, an investment bank attempts to obtain the best price possible for the securities issued. However, there is no guarantee of either the price or the number of shares eventually sold. The issuing company runs the risk that if the market softens for the issue, the proceeds will be less than originally projected due to a lower than expected selling price. The issuing company may even run the risk of not selling a portion of the offering at all due to a lack of investors or an acceptable price. The investment bank bears no risk in this arrangement and takes a smaller fee.

Under a full-underwriting agreement, an investment bank essentially buys the full issue from a company at an agreed-upon price and then sells the issue to the general public or to other brokerage companies. The investment bank runs the risk that the issue's price will decline before it can be sold or the investment bank may be forced to hold onto the securities for a long period of time, thereby tying up funds because the company has already been paid for the stock. In practice, an investment bank sets the spread between the expected issue price and the proceeds to an issuer, ensuring that the investment bank is compensated for the risk of a full-underwriting agreement.

The underwriting spread is generally defined as the income that is generated by the underwriting investment bank, which is essentially the difference between the amount paid to the issuer of securities in a primary distribution and the public offering price. Total flotation costs related to an issue include the underwriting spread, as well as the accounting, legal, printing and other costs associated with the issue. Gross proceeds represent the total amount of funds raised from the offering while the net proceeds are what the issuer receives after all flotation costs are paid.

C. Selling Procedures

Before any issue can be sold to the general public, it must be filed with and approved by the SEC. For major public offerings, a company's executives may visit financial centers around the country, or even around the world for a globally held company, in order to promote the new issue. In most large issues, the lead investment banker brings in other investment banks to take portions of the issue before it is released to the general public. This achieves three goals:

- Allows for wider distribution of the issue
- Brings more capital into play
- Enables the lead bank to spread the underwriting risk

D. Shelf Registration

A large, well-known corporation that frequently issues securities may file a master registration statement with the SEC and update it with a short-form statement just prior to each of the initial offerings. This form of shelf registration allows a company to bring an issue to market quickly in order to take advantage of market conditions that make rates for particular sources attractive. This form of registration is made available under SEC Rule 415 and can be used by publicly traded companies that are already reporting on a quarterly basis to the SEC.

Securities that are shelf registered may be sold at any time over a two-year period following the registration by a process resembling competitive bidding. Under this rule, a company simply announces the intention to issue all or part of the securities registered under the shelf registration and receives offers from investment banks. Because the stock issue essentially sells at the prevailing market price, the investment bank with the smallest spread generally receives the right to underwrite the issue.

E. Due Diligence

The due diligence process ensures that the financial and other statements provided by a company are accurate and represent the true value of a company according to the current provisions of the Generally Accepted Accounting Practices (GAAP). In addition, due diligence requires the disclosure of all information that may be of interest to any potential investor in a company's securities. Due diligence involves all areas of a company's operations and is required of all companies issuing new securities to the general public.

IX. INITIAL PUBLIC OFFERING (IPO)

The term IPO is used to describe an issuer's first public offering of a security of any class, although the term tends to be limited to common stock. The term is also used to designate an offering of previously authorized, but unissued, securities. For companies with equity securities that are not currently available to the public, or are not listed on one of the various exchanges, the decision to go public and/or to list the company's securities can be critical to a company's future growth.

A. Advantages of Going Public

For a company that is currently privately or closely-held, the decision to go public offers several advantages.

1. Diversification and Increased Liquidity

One of the primary advantages is the diversification offered by going public. Owners of closely held companies usually have most of the wealth tied up in one company and thus are not well diversified. By selling a portion of the stock to the general public, the owners are able to invest the proceeds in other areas and increase personal diversification. An IPO also can provide increased liquidity. For investors in closely held companies, the stock of a company is very illiquid. It can be sold only to certain types of investors; hence, there is no intermediary to help in the sale. As a result, such companies' ability to raise capital when needed is difficult because the stock is generally not as attractive to outside investors.

These problems are less of an issue for publicly traded companies. Making the stock more liquid makes it become a more attractive investment to outsiders with capital. In order to have stock become publicly listed, a company must meet certain levels of disclosure of information and regulatory requirements by the SEC. Disclosure and outside regulation makes investors more willing to purchase the stock of a publicly traded company and greatly facilitates a company's ability to raise new capital.

2. Establishing the Value of a Closely-Held Company

One of the primary problems of the closely held corporation is establishing its value. Making the stock of a company publicly available allows its value to be determined by the market and disclosed as a company's stock price. There are also two major long-term advantages to going public:

- A company "creates" a currency (in common stock) that can be used for future acquisitions of other companies
- A company may be able to buy out a venture capitalist currently involved with a company or current owners who want to sell their interests.

3. Spin-Off of Subsidiary

Another option is to use an IPO to spin-off a portion of a public company's wholly owned subsidiary. This enables a company to realize the potential value of a hidden asset, thus increasing the overall market value of the parent company. Finally, many companies use stock rather than cash to acquire other companies. These include companies that are currently privately held, but decide to issue stock in order to finance an expansion program or acquisition of another company. Companies that are currently publicly held often use stock to finance very large acquisition programs.

B. Disadvantages of Going Public

The decision to publicly trade the stock of a company is not without some disadvantages.

1. SEC Disclosure

Owner/managers of closely held companies may not be comfortable with the level of disclosure required for publicly held corporations for two reasons. First, competitors gain access to greater amounts of information on a company due to the public disclosure requirements. Second, the compensation and net worth of the owners is now more easily determined by outside parties.

2. Managerial Flexibility

When a company's stock is closely held, the owners/managers have great flexibility with respect to how the company is managed. Because the owners of a company and management are one and the same, large salaries or generous "perks" do not produce the kind of management/shareholder conflicts that may occur in a publicly held company.

3. Control

Owners/managers of closely held companies surrender some control by going public, even if majority ownership is retained. In publicly held companies, minority shareholders may have significant rights with respect to the operation of a company and representation on the Board of Directors. Also, there are many examples of publicly held companies being taken private by management in order to increase the level of control. This is especially true when a company is incorporated in a state where cumulative voting is allowed. This type of voting provides minority interests with a better opportunity to gain Board representation. For example, if an investor has 100 shares and five Board seats are available, that investor would gain a total of 500 votes, all of which could be allocated to one candidate. Through cumulative voting, minority shareholders can potentially ensure that one or more persons on the Board represent their interests.

4. Other Factors

Although increased liquidity of a company's stock may be one reason for going public, stocks of smaller companies may not be considerably liquid. If there is a small market for the stock and/or it is not traded often, the market price may not reflect its true value. This is referred to as "not enough float in the stock." Another problem is that due to the increased level of disclosure and reporting, the costs of these requirements are a major consideration. For smaller companies, this may be a costly process compared with current levels of reporting. Finally, a company going public with debt issues may be required to have the debt rated in order to sell it publicly. These costs may be significant, especially for smaller companies first going public.

X. THE DECISION TO LIST SECURITIES

For most companies, the decision to go public with a company's stock coincides with the decision to have the stock (or other securities) listed on one of the organized exchanges, such as the New York Stock Exchange (NYSE) or the American Stock Exchange (AMEX). Increasingly, companies are foregoing the organized exchanges and having the securities listed on the NASDAQ (National Association of Securities Dealers Automated Quotation), which is essentially a computer-based over-the-counter (OTC) market.

A. Advantages of Listing Securities

1. The primary advantage of having a company's stock listed on one of the organized exchanges is that the marketability of the stock increases. In general, listing is advantageous to both a company and the public because a company's stock can be more widely traded and more investors have access to it.
2. Listing can also result in higher sales for a company because of increased public exposure.
3. Due to the increased level of disclosure required, listing may also lower the required rate of return on a company's common stock and, ultimately, the overall cost of capital, thereby increasing a company's value in the market.

B. Disadvantages of Listing Securities

1. Given the additional reporting requirements and restrictions on the types of stocks that can be traded, some companies decide to remain in the OTC market rather than to list stock on an organized exchange.
2. Since the early 1990s, liquidity in the OTC market has increased significantly; hence, many companies have decided to be listed through the NASDAQ rather than to apply for listing on the NYSE or the AMEX.
3. Some smaller companies have decided to voluntarily delist securities rather than to comply with recent increased disclosure requirements under Sarbanes-Oxley (SOX). Delisting is essentially a cost-effective way for a company to go private.

C. Choice of Exchanges

A company must decide on which of the many exchanges the stock is to be listed. There are requirements for joining the various exchanges, and companies must abide by the rules of the exchange if they want their stocks traded. For companies wishing to raise capital globally, there are stock exchanges in most of the world's money centers, such as London, Tokyo, Frankfurt, Paris, Zurich, Singapore, Taiwan and Hong Kong. Stocks of major U.S. companies may be listed and traded on stock exchanges outside the U.S. Similarly, stocks of large, foreign multinational companies may be listed and traded in the U.S. markets.

Foreign companies wishing to raise capital in the U.S. capital markets may do so through the use of American Depository Receipts (ADRs). These are negotiable receipts, registered in the name of the owner, for shares of a foreign corporation held in trust by a foreign branch of a U.S. bank. If the ADRs are sold in the U.S., they are subject to U.S. securities laws. A similar instrument known as a Global Depository Receipt (GDR) is issued in more than one country for shares in a foreign company. The shares, held by a foreign branch of an international bank, trade as domestic shares but are offered for sale globally through various bank branches.

Appendix 13.1 Financial Management MBA-Level Textbook References

The reader who is interested in additional depth of coverage is encouraged to refer to any of the currently available MBA-level financial management textbooks. A bibliography of the most commonly used of these textbooks is provided below.

Contemporary Financial Management, 9th Edition, Moyer, McGuigan and Kretlow, South-Western College Publishing, 2003.

Corporate Finance, Smart, Megginson and Gitman, South-Western College Publishing, 2004.

Corporate Finance, 6th Edition, Ross, Westerfield and Jaffee, McGraw Hill Finance, 2002.

Corporate Finance: A Focused Approach, Ehrhardt and Brigham, South-Western College Publishing, 2003.

Financial Management: Principles and Applications, 9th Edition, Keown, Martin, Petty and Scott, Prentice-Hall, 2002.

Financial Management and Policy, Van Horne, Prentice-Hall, 2002.

Fundamentals of Financial Management, 10th Edition, Brigham and Houston, South-Western College Publishing, 2004.

Principles of Corporate Finance; 7th Edition, Brealey and Myers, McGraw Hill Finance, 2003.

Test Your Understanding

These chapter questions are provided to test your understanding of the information in the text. They are neither examples of CTP examination questions nor are they in the examination format.

Answers are on pages 605–609.

1. What role does the treasury area play in the determination and management of a company's cost of capital?

2. What is the primary advantage and disadvantage of raising capital through public offerings?

3. Discuss the trustee and disbursing issues related to public issues that the treasury area must deal with.

4. What are some of the issues involved in the use of debt financing?

5. Why is short-term borrowing an important source of financing?

6. What is a term loan and how is it used?

7. What are industrial revenue bonds?

8. Discuss bond indentures and covenants.

9. What is defeasance of debt?

10. What is a loan guarantee and when is it used?

11. What are the three key considerations in bond ratings?

12. What is maturity matching and how is it used?

13. What are the two general stages of the leasing decision process?

14. Discuss operating leases.

15. What is treasury stock?

16. What is preferred stock, and how is it similar to or different from common equity and debt?

17. Describe the general model of security valuation.

18. What is the CAPM and how is it used?

19. What are the primary sources of capital for a company and how are their costs determined?

20. What is the difference between a primary and secondary distribution of common stock?

21. What is shelf registration, and how is it used?

22. What is an IPO?

23. What are some of the advantages of listing securities on one of the organized exchanges?

CHAPTER 14
Capital Structure and Dividend Policy

I. INTRODUCTION

This chapter discusses two key topics related to the financial management of a company. Two of the primary financial decisions that must be made are:

1. How to finance the company and its assets
2. How much of the net income stream should be diverted to the shareholders versus retained in the company for future growth.

The capital structure decision involves raising funds for the company, generally in the form of either debt (borrowed funds) or equity (common stock). This decision will have a major impact on the risk and costs of capital for a company.

The dividend decision is also critical because it determines the amount of ongoing funding a company will have available from its net income stream. While dividends may be good for the investor from a cash-flow perspective, it means that a company may have slower growth due to less availability of internal funding.

II. CAPITAL STRUCTURE OF A COMPANY

As a company grows, it needs capital to fund that growth. This capital generally comes from internally generated funds (retained earnings), debt or additional common stock. The capital structure of a company refers to the mix of long-term financing sources used to raise capital. Although there are many possible components of long-term capital, this chapter focuses on the two major categories – debt and common equity (both retained earnings and new common stock). These two components have the greatest impact in determining a company's overall cost of capital. The chapter discusses the concepts of target and optimal capital structure, the theories behind how companies should raise capital in order to maximize value, the different types of dividends and the rationale in setting dividend policy.

A. Target versus Optimal Capital Structure

Although a significant amount of research has been done on the theory of optimal capital structure, most of the findings have little or no bearing on the day-to-day practice of treasury management. However, it is important for treasury professionals to be aware of these theories and how they may influence management decision-making because they may have to implement the capital structure decisions of senior management.

The desirability of debt is due to:

- The effective cost of debt is lower because interest expense is tax deductible.
- Stockholders do not have to share any of the company's profits with debt holders because the debt holders receive a fixed rate of return.

The disadvantages of debt include:

- The more outstanding debt a company has, the riskier it is considered.
- The riskier a company is considered, the higher interest it will have to pay for future debt issuance.
- Bankruptcy may result if the company becomes unable to meet its debt service obligations.

Management tends to behave as if there were an ideal capital structure for a given company. In theory, there is a certain level of debt for each company that minimizes the overall cost of capital and, therefore, maximizes the value of the company. The general consensus is that some use of debt is desirable but too much debt is undesirable. However, there is significant dispute regarding what constitutes the "optimal" level of debt and how to determine that level.

In practice, the weights generally used are the company's target capital structure; that is, the proportion of each component that management has determined is best for the company. In many cases, new capital will be raised according to this target by either employing the target ratio for any new capital or moving toward that ratio over time. (The concept of target ratio for capital structure is discussed later in this chapter under the heading Target Capital Structure.)

B. Capital Structure Theory

Several competing theories have attempted to explain the capital structure of a corporation. The primary theories are the trade-off model, the pecking order theory and the asymmetric information theory.

1. Trade-Off Model

The most common type of theoretical models are known as trade-off models, meaning that the optimal capital structure is found by balancing (trading off) the tax shield benefits of debt (leverage) against bankruptcy costs and agency costs. Because of the tax deductibility of interest payments, debt is generally the lowest cost capital component when used in moderation.

At some point, however, the increased use of debt increases the probability that the company will default, which will drive up the cost of debt. With respect to debt use, agency costs are incurred as a result of placing constraints (known as debt covenants) on the management of a company to protect the interests of the debt holders. With respect to the use of equity, agency costs are associated with monitoring and restricting the decisions of management to ensure that it acts in the best interest of equity holders.

If trade-off theories are correct, one should be able to observe actual companies with debt levels in accordance with the above statements. While there is some evidence that companies with high levels of tangible assets borrow more heavily than companies with low levels, there does not seem to be an empirical relationship between risk and the use of debt. This suggests that factors not included in trade-off models also have an influence. Therefore, trade-off models do not accurately predict optimal capital structure.

2. Pecking Order Theory

The second most common capital structure theory is known as the pecking order model. This theory measures a company's past earnings, dividends and capital expenditures to explain capital structure. The basic premise of this theory is that, whenever possible, companies prefer to raise capital through retained earnings. Accordingly, over the long-term planning horizon, companies schedule dividend payouts in a manner that keeps sufficient retained earnings on hand to fund future projected capital expenditures.

If a company is forced to seek external sources of new capital due to a shortage in retained earnings, it will typically issue the least expensive form of debt first, then issue more expensive forms of debt, if required. If a company issues too much debt, the issuance of new common stock must be considered to maintain a balance between debt and equity. Generally, issuance of new common stock is a last resort because of both the high flotation costs and the negative signal that the issuance of new equity sends to shareholders regarding a company's future prospects. (See the section on asymmetric information)

Thus, instead of a trade-off, there is a pecking order by which new capital is raised. This means that the capital structure of any given company is not necessarily a planned target. Rather, it is the result of past cash flow fluctuations, dividend policy and investment opportunities. Therefore, a major criticism of the pecking order model is that it is based on observations of corporate behavior rather than on a theoretical model.

3. Asymmetric Information Theory

A theoretical basis for the pecking order model may be explained within the context of asymmetric information theory. In this context, the management of a company has access to more accurate information than the stockholders on a company's prospects. In a world with asymmetric information (management has better information than shareholders), corporations would generally issue new shares only if one of the following is true: (1) a company has very profitable investments that cannot be postponed or financed by debt or (2) if management considers the shares of a company to be overvalued.

Most investors are aware of the above facts. Consequently, investors tend to devalue a company's stock when it announces plans to issue new stock. This is especially true when investors believe that management considers the stock to be overvalued or when management places the interests of existing shareholders above those of prospective shareholders. That is, investors view the new stock issue as a negative signal.

C. Business and Financial Risk

In determining a company's capital structure policy, the total risk of the company's operations and financing must be considered. Total risk comprises both business risk and financial risk. These types of risk or leverage are discussed below, along with the ways they are measured.

(A more extensive discussion of risk is in Chapter 17, Financial Risk Management and Chapter 18, Enterprise Risk Management.)

1. Operating Leverage or Risk

Business risk is the risk associated with a company's operating capabilities and policies, as well as the volatility of operating income or earnings before interest and taxes (EBIT). Some companies use other operating profit measures such as EBITDA (Earnings Before Interest, Taxes, Depreciation and Amortization) in calculating business risk. Three of the factors that affect EBIT volatility are:

- Product-demand variability
- Sales-price variability
- Resource cost variability

All three factors must be analyzed to gain a thorough understanding of business risk. One indicator of a company's business risk is the use of operating leverage, which are the fixed costs in the production of a product. The presence of fixed costs magnifies the impact of changes in other factors, such as price and variable costs.

2. Financial Leverage or Risk

Financial risk is best understood in the context of financial leverage. The fixed costs associated with financial leverage increase the impact of operating leverage. Changes in variables such as product demand, sales price and resource costs have more of an impact on companies that use financial leverage than on companies that do not. A company's total risk increases as it utilizes more financial leverage.

Because management's goal should be to maximize shareholder value, management may take actions that will benefit shareholders at the expense of bondholders. The bondholders will protect themselves by introducing (or adding) covenants restricting management actions. These restrictions may cause a company to be less efficient, thereby adding an agency cost to the overall management cost of a company. In other words, there is an issue of agency risk between shareholders and bondholders in a company's use of debt[1].

D. Target Capital Structure

Business risk and financial risk must be balanced in order for a company to operate within acceptable levels of total risk while maximizing capital structure. To compensate for total risk, companies that employ high levels of operating leverage will normally employ lower levels of financial leverage. The reverse is also true. An investor needs to know how much financial risk a company is willing to assume in order to establish a particular capital structure.

If a company can assume a high level of financial risk, then a high level of debt will be used in the capital structure. If, however, a company already uses high levels of operating leverage it may want to use relatively low levels of debt in the capital structure. This concept determines the debt capacity of a company; that is, how much debt it may safely assume before it has a significant impact on total risk. Thus, determining the balance between a company's operating and financial risk is clearly a critical management decision.

Most managers prefer to use internal sources of funds (retained earnings) rather than external sources. This means that during periods of high earnings, managers will tend to finance a company's growth with retained earnings rather than with borrowed funds. As earnings slow, managers prefer to borrow rather than to issue new equity. Over the long term, therefore, a company's capital structure may be based more on earnings history than from any conscious effort on the part of management to maintain a target level of debt.

It is also important to understand that a particular company's use of debt will change over time. As existing long-term debt is repaid, the capital structure of a company will change. Also, financial market perception of acceptable target levels of debt may change. For example, during periods of rapid economic growth, use of large amounts of debt is generally more acceptable to financial markets than during periods of slow growth.

E. Other Considerations in the Capital Structure Decision

While the primary issue in the capital structure decision is the mix of debt versus equity, there are other considerations. These include issues related to using common stock as a source of funds, rating agency and lender restrictions, and the issue of control of ownership.

1. Using New (Additional) Common Stock as a Source of Funds

The advantages of new common stock financing are:

- It does not obligate a company to make fixed payments to investors.
- It has no specific maturity date.
- For creditors, stock offers a cushion against losses and, if a company's future is bright, equity can often be raised on attractive terms.

The disadvantages of new common stock financing are:

- The sale of common stock may extend voting rights and control to more shareholders. This may be problematic for smaller companies where the principal owner and management are one and the same. In the event that a company does well, the profits must be divided among a larger group of stockholders.
- The cost of underwriting common stock is significant when compared with other sources of capital.
- Common-equity financing does not enjoy the tax shield (deductibility of interest expense) that debt financing provides and, hence, costs more than debt.

2. Rating Agency and Lender Restrictions

Because rating agencies and lenders often impose restrictions on the actions of management as part of debt covenants, they have an impact on a company's capital structure. Regardless of what management or equity holders believe is the optimal capital structure, lenders are likely to require a more conservative level of debt to protect their interests. In some companies, the various debt covenants from different lenders may leave management with limited flexibility in establishing a target capital structure. Occasionally, management restricts the use of debt to ensure that borrowing facilities will be available if a future need arises.

3. The Issue of Control

Control of a company is an important issue in determining capital structure. If a company issues too much equity, it dilutes the stock value, resulting in new shareholders taking control. Additionally, it risks a raid on its stock, resulting in new owners taking control through acquisition. On the other hand, if management uses too much debt, it risks bankruptcy, resulting in creditors taking control.

4. Additional Considerations

Several other factors must be considered in determining the capital structure of a company. For instance, the asset structure of a company is often a key consideration. Companies in capital-intensive industries tend to be highly leveraged. Thus, capital-intensive industries such as real estate, utilities or heavy manufacturing typically have more debt than service industry, high technology or professional firms.

The growth rate of a company may also impact capital structure. Many companies with normal growth rates are able to fund needed investments with internally generated operating revenues. Companies with abnormally high growth rates, however, must often rely more heavily on external capital. Given the high flotation costs involved in new equity, high growth companies often use higher than normal levels of debt. In many cases these are young, smaller companies that are in early, fast growth phases that require significant amounts of new outside capital.

Profitability and taxes also affect capital structure. Companies with high levels of profitability generally need to raise less external capital than those with lower levels. Given management's preference for debt over equity, one would expect to find that higher profit companies have less debt than lower profit companies. With respect to taxes, interest may be tax-deductible, while dividends are not deductible. This implies that companies in higher corporate tax brackets have a greater incentive to use debt than those in lower tax brackets.

III. DIVIDEND POLICY

Management decisions regarding dividend policy also have a major impact on capital. Steadily increasing dividends may make a company's stock more attractive to certain institutional investors and, perhaps, increase the stock price. However, increasing dividends reduces the amount of cash flow (in the form of retained earnings) that a company has available for expansion. This may slow a company's growth; hence, its ability to provide capital appreciation for investors. A company may then become less attractive to investors who prefer high levels of capital gains to regular income in the form of dividends. In effect, dividend policy determines the type of investor who may be interested in becoming a shareholder.

A. Setting Dividend Policy

The optimal dividend policy is one that:

- Maximizes shareholder value
- Maintains adequate retained earnings for future expansion
- Distributes corporate income to investors

Dividend policies can vary widely from company to company, depending on a variety of factors and considerations. Companies set dividend policy within the framework of their overall financial plans. The general practice for management in establishing a dividend policy involves the following steps:

Step #1: The first step involves four tasks:

- Projecting the long-term profits for a company
- Estimating the growth rate of these profits
- Determining a company's need for reinvested earnings
- Setting dividends so that a company can meet its need for reinvestment under most economic scenarios

Step #2: The second step also involves four tasks:

- Determining the long-term needs for equity capital or for capital expansion
- Analyzing the ability of a company to raise other forms of capital (debt, preferred stock, new common stock)
- Establishing the target capital structure of a company
- Determining the ability of a company to generate earnings throughout the planning period

Step #3: The third step involves setting dividends at a steady (or steadily increasing) level so that a company can maintain both a targeted level of investment and dividends. Dividends are rarely reduced unless there is a significant reason such as a negative change in a company's financial situation.

B. Constraints on Dividend Policy

Some of the primary constraints on dividend policy are those listed in bond indentures or loan covenants. Most debt contracts limit the ability of a company to pay dividends by imposing protective covenants related to maintaining specific financial ratios. These covenants are intended to prevent stockholders from draining assets from a company at the expense of bondholders and other creditors.

There may also be restrictions related to preferred stock. Preferred stock is often cumulative in nature, which requires all past preferred stock dividends (dividends in arrears) to be paid in full before any common dividend can be paid. However, there are forms of preferred stock that are non-cumulative in nature and, hence, do not have this restriction.

Typically, there are also restrictions related to impairment of capital for a company. Dividend payments usually cannot exceed retained earnings on the balance sheet. This serves as protection for the creditors of a company. Dividends may be paid out of capital, but the source must be indicated as such and must not reduce capital below the limits stated in a company's debt covenants.

A company needs to ensure that adequate cash is available to pay dividends. If not, then the company has to access unused borrowing facilities to raise cash for the dividend. However, borrowing to finance dividends should be done only when absolutely necessary and only on a short-term basis.

There are also several restrictions related to private and closely held companies. To prevent wealthy individuals from using the corporations they own to avoid personal taxes, the tax code provides for a special surtax on improperly accumulated income. Thus, if the IRS can demonstrate that the dividend payout ratio is being deliberately lowered to help owners avoid personal taxes, heavy penalties may be imposed on a company or the individuals.

For a smaller, privately held company, there may also be an issue related to control. Owners of privately held firms are generally reluctant to sell new common stock because doing so dilutes control. As a result, management may decide to pay either very low or no dividends in order to keep as much cash in the company as possible for reinvestment and growth.

The investment opportunities available to a company may also affect the dividend policy. If there are many acceptable investment opportunities, a company may limit the size of dividends in order to increase the amount of available capital. If a company can easily change the timing of investment projects, then it may have more flexibility in delaying projects when earnings are low and accelerating them when earnings are high.

Finally, the availability of alternative sources of capital makes the dividend decision less critical. This is especially true for companies with access to capital markets. If it is easier to raise new equity in the capital markets, a company's ability to pay dividends is greater.

C. Effects of Dividend Policy on the Cost of Capital

Because dividend policy may affect the perception (and ultimately the price) of a company's stock, it impacts a company's cost of capital. Dividend policy can change the ratios of capital components, which, in turn, impacts a company's cost of capital. As the stock price increases, the value of equity increases relative to debt, thereby decreasing a company's market-based debt ratios.

D. Information Content of Dividends

To expand upon the impact dividend policies have on the cost of capital, there is significant evidence that dividends have a signaling effect. Dividends "contain" information for stockholders that "signal" the intentions of the management. It has been noted that for most companies, dividends tend to be fairly stable or to exhibit a constant rate of growth. Even companies that have periods of abnormal dividend growth usually settle into a stable growth pattern.

The general hypothesis is that when a company's management declares an unexpected increase in the upcoming dividends (higher than expected growth), it is signaling good news to the stock market. This positive information translates into a higher price for a company's stock. Management does not announce higher dividends unless it is certain that it is able to maintain the higher level. Similarly, if dividends are announced that are unexpectedly low or if dividends are eliminated, this signals bad news and the price of a company's stock drops. Management can, therefore, use dividends as a signal to investors concerning a company's future earnings potential.

Although the existence of the information content of dividends has been substantiated, the empirical studies have been unable to show a strong link between a change in dividend policy and stock prices. One theory regarding this relationship maintains that while dividend policy may determine the types of investors holding a company's stock (see clientele effect below), it does not necessarily have a significant impact on the overall value of a company.

E. Clientele Effect

The clientele effect theory holds that different groups of investors (or different institutional investors and mutual funds) prefer different payout policies. The implication for management is that making a change in dividend policy may influence the type of investor that holds the company's stock. For example, some investors are attracted to companies that offer preferred dividend payouts. Other investors with low tax rates and a preference for current income (some pension funds, retired persons and endowment funds) tend to purchase stocks with high regular dividends. Finally, investors in higher tax brackets (wealthy individuals) or those looking for a high long-term return tend to purchase stock in companies that regularly reinvest earnings in a company to stimulate growth. Such companies tend to pay low dividends over time, with investors receiving returns from the long-term appreciation of the stock price.

F. Stability of Dividends

Due to both the information content of dividends (signaling effect) and the clientele effect, most companies attempt to maintain a fairly stable dividend policy. Another factor encouraging companies to maintain a stable dividend policy is that many institutional investors with a need for steady income (especially pension funds) may purchase only stocks that maintain stable dividend payments. Managers must weigh the pros and cons of paying stable dividends versus keeping a certain level of retained earnings for reinvestment. This is a challenge for companies with dramatic fluctuations in earnings.

IV. DIVIDEND CONSIDERATIONS

A. Dividend Payment Procedures

Several important dates occur during the payment period of a dividend:

- **Declaration Date:** The date on which the board of directors announces (declares) the dividend.
- **Record Date:** The date specified by the board of directors when the holders-of-record are entitled to receive the declared dividend.
- **Ex-Dividend Date:** The date on which the stock is sold without the upcoming dividend attached. The ex-dividend date is usually four business days prior to the holder-of-record date, thereby enabling brokerage firms to send the updated list of stockholders to a company on time. Theoretically, there is a drop in the price of the stock equivalent to the dividend on the ex-dividend date. However, this is difficult to measure because other factors may influence the market price.
- **Payment Date:** The date on which the dividend is paid.

B. Dividend Reinvestment Plans

During the 1970s, many companies instituted dividend reinvestment plans (DRIPS). These plans enable shareholders to elect to automatically reinvest their dividends in the stock of a company paying dividends. Companies can buy the stock on the open market, use treasury shares or issue new stock.

These plans benefit smaller shareholders because of the low or non-existent transaction (brokerage) costs involved. In addition, when companies issue new stock in this manner, they may offer a discount in the market price to the reinvesting shareholder. From a company's point of view, this method of raising capital is significantly less expensive than issuing new stock to the general public, thus saving cash for the issuing company. One negative aspect of this type of plan is that it may lead to an increase in the number of small shareholders, resulting in more expensive shareholder relations and increasing the cost of maintaining shareholder records.

While some companies do manage their own DRIP programs, most use a financial institution to administer the plan. This administrator will generally be the main point of contact for investors participating in the DRIP. In some cases, however, a company may not sponsor its own DRIP. These companies will have their DRIP programs sponsored by financial institutions; such programs are generally referred to as bank-sponsored plans. From the perspective of the investor, the only real difference in the bank-sponsored plans is a slightly higher fee structure.

C. Different Types of Dividends

Companies may employ many different methods to pay dividends to shareholders. Regular cash dividends are the most common, but there are other types of dividends such as stock dividends, special dividends and liquidating dividends. Although not technically dividends stock splits are often considered part of dividend policy.

1. Cash Dividends

As mentioned above, the most common form of dividend payment is a regular cash dividend. Corporate dividends are usually paid on a quarterly basis.

2. Stock Dividends

With stock dividends, a company pays the shareholders additional shares of stock rather than cash dividends. In actuality, the economic impact of a stock dividend is the same as that of a stock split. That is, the per-share price of the stock is reduced because additional shares are in circulation but there is no real impact on shareholder wealth. However, there may be additional costs to a company for managing the record keeping for the new shares. If a company is in a period of rapid growth and needs to retain all earnings for reinvestment, then stock dividends may be a means of compensating shareholders for their loyalty.

3. Special Dividends

As previously discussed, dividend policy tends to send information to shareholders, especially if dividends change unexpectedly. For this reason, most companies that pay regular dividends attempt to maintain a stable growth rate. In the event that a company has a one-time spike in earnings, the dilemma is that paying a higher dividend for just one period will send mixed signals to shareholders. This may ultimately have a negative impact on the company's stock price. Therefore, a company usually declares a "special" dividend, which, by definition, is meant to be a one-time payment rather than an ongoing dividend increase.

4. Liquidating Dividends

A liquidating dividend is one that is paid out of capital rather than earnings. In some cases this occurs when a company or one of its divisions is going out of business and management may decide to pay off shareholders through a liquidating dividend. As the name implies, the company liquidates the remaining assets (capital) of the failed company or division to pay the dividend.

5. Stock Splits

The basic idea behind a stock split is that an optimal trading range exists for a stock's price. When the per-share price of a stock gets too high, trading may be affected because of the large dollar amount needed to trade an even lot (100 shares). By splitting the stock, the trading price is reduced to a desired trading range. As a result, there is no real impact on value to shareholders; stock splits are generally not a critical consideration in dividend policy because no value is created or lost in stock splits. A variation of this process for a company whose stock price is trending downward is a reverse stock split. The reverse split increases the effective price of the stock and may help to prevent delisting by the stock exchange. A reverse stock split raises the price of the stock to a desired trading range.

D. Stock Repurchases

As an alternative to paying cash dividends, a company can elect to execute a stock repurchase plan with the authorization of the board of directors. By taking some shares out of circulation, a company may increase the price of the stock, and, if earnings are constant, may also increase the earnings per share because fewer shares are outstanding. An added benefit to the remaining shareholders is that any capital gains made from the increase in the stock price will not be taxable until the shareholder elects to sell the stock. Stock repurchases are generally regarded as being a positive signal by shareholders.

Repurchases are useful to a company for accomplishing a large modification of its capital structure or for reducing the number of small holders of the stock. However, IRS and SEC regulations also affect repurchases. Full disclosure of all relevant information is required by the SEC in any type of stock repurchase plan. In general, most companies have found that stock repurchases offer an attractive alternative to dividends as a way to control shareholder demographics and earnings per share. Another disadvantage is that if a company uses stock repurchases on a regular basis, investors may view them as simply an attempt by management to manipulate the stock price. Also, investors may feel that managers are repurchasing stock because they cannot find profitable investment opportunities.

A review of the advantages and disadvantages of stock repurchases leads to two conclusions. First, stock repurchases may not be feasible on a regular basis due to tax consequences and the long-term impact on stock prices. Second, stock repurchases offer some tax deferral advantages over dividends for the stockholders who do not sell their shares. Under some circumstances, such as abnormally high earnings, an undervalued stock price, or temporary shortage of suitable investment opportunities, stock repurchases may be the best option to provide "one-time" earnings to shareholders.

From management's perspective, an advantage to a stock repurchase is that it may increase financial leverage without directly increasing the amount of debt, provided a company has cash on hand. As such, a stock repurchase decision is similar to an internal investment decision. The question is whether or not a company's stock is truly undervalued in the market. If it is, management may want to consider using some funds for the repurchase of stock rather than investing in new capital projects.

Steps in Managing a Repurchase Operation: As discussed earlier, a stock repurchase plan requires full disclosure to the shareholders and SEC notification. There are three ways by which a company may repurchase stock after notifying the SEC:

- A company can purchase its own stock in the open market. This is referred to as a non-targeted repurchase. In this case, no forms are required by the SEC unless the company is purchasing more than 5 percent of the outstanding stock (tender offer).
- A company can make a tender offer to its stockholders. Tender offers must be registered with the SEC because more than five percent of a company's stock is repurchased. An investment banker usually is involved in a tender offer to help persuade stockholders and to manage the stock repurchase.
- A company can negotiate directly with a major stockholder (often an institutional investor such as an insurance company or a pension fund) to repurchase its stock. This is referred to as a targeted repurchase.

Repurchased shares become treasury stock and, as such, offer four different options:

- They can be retired.
- They can be resold at a later date to raise additional capital.
- They can be used for stock option or warrant programs.
- They can be used to fund repurchases or future acquisitions.

E. Intracompany Dividends

Large companies with wholly owned subsidiaries generally use intracompany dividends to transfer profits from the subsidiaries to the parent. Subsidiaries may be required to pay a stated percentage of earnings to the parent. Because intracompany dividends are only a movement of funds within a company, they are not subject to IRS or SEC regulations. However, covenants with lenders and between the subsidiary and the parent may be impacted.

F. Taxes on Dividends

There are numerous tax considerations on the payment for dividends, mainly for the recipients of those dividends. For the average investor, dividends are taxable as income, though recent changes in tax codes have reduced the effective rate for many holders to the same as the capital gains rate. For corporations receiving dividends from another corporation, in most cases 70 percent of dividend payments can be excluded from income for tax purposes. The tax regulations on dividends are constantly changing and the reader is encouraged to consult tax experts for the latest information.

G. Dividend Policy in Multinational Companies (MNCs)

For multinational companies (MNCs), dividend policy may be constrained by foreign government regulations and tax laws. The intent of these regulations is either to prevent repatriation of capital (the transfer of profits from an international subsidiary back to the domestic parent) or to make sure that the MNC pays its fair share of taxes on profits earned within the country. Some governments may restrict, block or tax this movement of funds in order to force the MNC to reinvest the funds locally. In addition, the existence of bilateral or multilateral tax treaties may have significant impacts on dividend policy. (Multinational dividend policy and other methods of capital repatriation are covered in more detail in Chapter 16, Global Treasury Organization and Liquidity Management.)

Endnotes

1 Note that this agency risk is different from the agency issues that exist between the shareholders and managers. The risk in the shareholder/manager agency relationship is that management may take actions that benefit themselves at the expense of the shareholders.

Test Your Understanding

These chapter questions are provided to test your understanding of the information in the text. They are neither examples of CTP examination questions nor are they in the examination format.

Answers are on pages 610–612.

1. What is capital structure?
2. What are the advantages and disadvantages in using debt in a company's capital structure?
3. What is the difference between optimal and target capital structure?
4. Discuss the asymmetric information theory of capital structure.
5. What is business risk?
6. What is financial risk?
7. Discuss the advantages and disadvantages of new common stock financing.
8. What are some of the issues in determining dividend policy?
9. In theory, what is an optimal dividend policy?
10. What are some of the constraints on dividend policy?
11. Is there any evidence that dividends send a "signal" from managers to shareholders?
12. What is the ex-dividend date?
13. What are stock dividends?
14. Discuss dividend policy in multinational corporations.

CHAPTER 15
Global Treasury Environment

I. INTRODUCTION

II. OBJECTIVES OF GLOBAL TREASURY MANAGEMENT
   A. Challenges Unique to International Treasury Management
   B. Foreign Exchange (FX) Rates

III. CHARACTERISTICS OF INTERNATIONAL PAYMENT SYSTEMS
   A. Paper-Based Payment Systems
   B. Electronic Payment Systems

IV. CHARACTERISTICS OF INTERNATIONAL BANKING SYSTEMS
   A. Regulatory Oversight and Clearing Operations
   B. Characteristics of International Banks and Banking Systems

V. INTERNATIONAL TRADE FINANCING METHODS
   A. Open Account
   B. Documentary Collection
   C. Letter of Credit (L/C)
   D. Other Trade Payment Methods
   E. Banker's Acceptance (BA)
   F. Trade Acceptance

VI. FUTURE OF THE GLOBAL TREASURY ENVIRONMENT

I. INTRODUCTION

International treasury management is becoming increasingly important as the global marketplace expands. Most companies in the U.S. are impacted by global events. Even small, local companies often purchase supplies with foreign contents or sell goods that compete with imported products. The World Trade Organization (WTO), in conjunction with agreements such as the North American Free Trade Agreement (NAFTA) and the General Agreement on Trades and Tariffs (GATT), facilitate trade between organizations in different countries, increasing the level of international business activity.

In addition, increased competition in the domestic marketplace has led many companies to seek international markets for sources of additional revenue, either through sales of exported products or by expansion into foreign markets. These same competitive forces and costs also drive many companies to seek non-domestic suppliers for products or raw materials.

This chapter describes how the global treasury financial environment is different from the U.S. environment and addresses the implications of this for daily treasury management. Key topics include: international payment systems and transaction initiation, the characteristics of international banking systems, global risk management, international tax/accounting and trade finance.

II. OBJECTIVES OF GLOBAL TREASURY MANAGEMENT

The objectives of global treasury management are similar to those of U.S. treasury management. The main objective is the efficient utilization of an organization's global cash resources in a manner consistent with its strategic goals. International treasury management, like domestic treasury management, involves daily, time-critical functions such as: collection, concentration, disbursement, liquidity management (short-term investing and borrowing) and information management.

However, unlike domestic treasury management, international treasury management also involves cross-border funds movement, foreign exchange (FX) and liquidity management techniques that are different from those in the U.S. Therefore, the selection of financial service providers who are capable of assisting a company with international operations is a critical aspect of the global treasury management process.

A. Challenges Unique to International Treasury Management

International treasury management involves the same challenges as domestic treasury management, with several unique aspects.

1. Cash Flow Complexity

A multinational company must manage the cash flows from subsidiaries, suppliers and customers in each of the countries in which it operates. As a result of widely differing regulations, banking practices, payment systems and levels of information availability, multinational companies must be prepared to handle treasury transactions in different currencies that cross national boundaries.

(A discussion of the techniques used for cross-border treasury management is in Chapter 16, Global Treasury Organization and Liquidity Management.)

2. Political Risk

Closely related to political risk is sovereign risk. This is the risk a company's operations in a foreign country may be nationalized or expropriated by the government of that country. In nationalization, a government takes over all companies in a specific industry, such as the oil or mining industries. In expropriation, a government takes over a single company. Other types of political risk include:

- Blocked currencies, in which profits cannot be converted from the local currency into a major trading currency.
- Forced reinvestment, in which funds cannot be transferred out of the country in any form.
- Required majority ownership, in which companies must be owned by resident nationals. In The People's Republic of China, for example, foreign subsidiaries or foreign-owned entities encounter all three of these types of sovereign risk.

As they become corporate citizens of different countries, multinational companies are exposed to varying degrees of political risk. A company with operations in foreign countries must be knowledgeable about the laws, regulations, taxes and customs that govern business activities, as well as the overall political and social dynamics of the countries in which capital is invested.

3. Legal and Ethical Issues

In many countries, "commissions" or "fees" that would be considered bribes in the U.S. are deeply ingrained in the commercial culture. However, the Foreign Corrupt Practices Act forbids U.S. companies to engage in such practices. U.S. companies must also consider whether a company's foreign activities may come under the jurisdiction of the Office of Foreign Assets Control (OFAC). The OFAC is an office of the Treasury Department that administers and enforces economic and trade sanctions against targeted foreign countries, terrorist sponsoring organizations, and international narcotics traffickers based on U.S. foreign policy and national security goals. The OFAC has the authority to impose controls on financial transactions and to freeze foreign assets under U.S. jurisdiction.

4. Tax Issues

Multinational companies face a myriad of tax laws and regulations. Global treasury operations are often required to seek expert legal advice to interpret the rules and regulations of different, and sometimes conflicting, tax authorities.

(A more detailed discussion of foreign taxation issues, is in Chapter 16, Global Treasury Organization and Liquidity Management.)

5. Foreign Exchange (FX) Exposure

International companies with cash flows in various foreign currencies are exposed to FX rate risk. A company must assess the volatility of the different types and levels of FX rate fluctuations for each specific currency involved.

(A more detailed discussion of FX risk is in Chapter 17, Financial Risk Management.)

B. Foreign Exchange (FX) Rates

FX rates are quoted in several ways, depending on the currencies and the markets involved. An FX rate is generally expressed as the equivalent unit of one currency per unit of another currency. From a U.S. perspective, there are two ways to quote FX rates: (1) the U.S. dollar equivalent of one unit of the foreign currency (typically used for the British Pound and euro) or (2) the amount of the foreign currency per one U.S. dollar (used for all other currencies). The table below, based on approximate rates in effect in April 2004, displays the two types of quotation formats for selected foreign currencies.

Sample Foreign Currency Quotation Formats

Currency	U.S. $ Equivalent	Currency per U.S. $
British Pound (£)	$1.791/£	£0.5583/$
Canadian Dollar (C$)	$0.7435/C$	C$1.345/$
Euro (€)	$1.197/€	€ 0.8354/$
Japanese Yen (¥)	$0.009205/¥	¥108.64/$

Using this information, some exchange rate calculations can be illustrated:

£250,000 would be equivalent to $447,750 (£250,000 x 1.791)
C$250,000 would be equivalent to $185,874 (C$250,000 / 1.345)
€ 250,000 would be equivalent to $299,250 (€ 250,000 x 1.197)
¥250,000 would be equivalent to $2,301.18 (¥250,000 / 108.64)

Banks and other dealers quote both bid and offer rates for foreign currency. The bid rate is the rate at which a dealer is willing to buy currency. The offer rate is the rate at which a dealer is willing to sell currency. The difference between the bid rate and the offer rate is generally referred to as the bid/offer spread or bid/ask spread. The spread covers the dealer's exposure and provides a source of fee income.

For example, assume a dealer provides a bid-offer quote of ¥108.60–108.70/$. This means the dealer is willing to buy (bid) one U.S. $ at ¥108.60 and to sell (offer) one U.S. $ at ¥108.70.

If a U.S. treasury manager wants to sell a dealer $50,000 in exchange for ¥, the dealer buys (bids) the $50,000 from the treasury manager for ¥5,430,000. This is calculated as $50,000 x 108.60. However, if the same U.S. treasury manager sells the ¥5,430,000 back to the dealer in exchange for $, the dealer sells (offers) the treasury manager only $49,954, calculated as ¥5,430,000 / 108.70. The difference of $46 ($50,000 – $49,954) represents the dealer's spread on this transaction.

1. How Rates Are Obtained

Most companies active in the FX markets subscribe to one of the real-time rate reporting and/or electronic trading services such as Bloomberg, EBS Dealing Resources, Reuters or Telerate. Companies trading in the FX market on a less frequent basis may be able to access FX rates through a bank or FX dealer. Rates are also available on the Internet, though free services generally have a slight time delay.

2. FX Markets

There are two basic FX markets: the spot market and the forward market. A rate quoted in the spot market for currency is called a spot FX rate (spot rate). These rates are generally quoted for delivery one or two business days from the date of the trade. Faster delivery may be possible but at a rate higher than the spot rate.

A forward FX rate (forward rate) is an exchange rate established today for a currency transaction with delivery occurring beyond two business days in the future. Deliveries under most forward FX contracts occur within a year from the trade date. However, delivery dates beyond one year are available for actively traded currencies.

Forward rates are based on the spot exchange rate and the difference in interest rates between two countries. The interest rate differential between two countries determines if respective currencies will trade at par, at a discount or at a premium in the forward market:

- **Par –** If the spot rate and the forward rate are the same, then the forward rate is at par to the spot rate. In theory, this implies that the interest rate structure between the two countries is exactly the same. Because this is extremely rare, currencies generally trade at a discount or premium.
- **Discount –** A currency is at a discount when it is worth less in the forward market than in the spot market. The currency with the higher interest rate will sell at a discount in the forward market against a currency with a lower interest rate.
- **Premium –** A currency is at a premium when it is worth more in the forward market than in the spot market. The currency with the lower interest rate will sell at a premium in the forward market against a currency with a higher interest rate.

Relationship of Spot and Forward Rates

Par	A currency is worth the same in the spot and forward markets (one currency remains constant relative to another currency).
Discount	A currency is worth more in the spot market than in the forward market (one currency is weakening relative to another currency).
Premium	A currency is worth more in the forward market than in the spot market (one currency is strengthening relative to another currency).

The relationship among the spot, forward and money markets is known as interest rate parity. As long as FX and interest rate markets are efficient, it is not possible to take money from one country, invest in another country's money market, return it to the original country, and make a higher rate of return than could have been earned in the original country's money market. Thus, the differences observed between the spot and forward markets are not a prediction of the future movement of the spot rate but rather an adjustment for the differential interest rates between two countries.

III. CHARACTERISTICS OF INTERNATIONAL PAYMENT SYSTEMS

International payments involve two important considerations: different systems or methods are used for intracountry payments versus cross-border payments, and payments may be denominated in a country's local currency or in the currency of another country. Both of these issues have a significant impact on settlement procedures.

A. Paper-Based Payment Systems

International paper-based systems involve the payment and clearing of checks or drafts within and between countries. International check-clearing processes vary significantly from country to country. The clearing of checks may be managed by:

- The central bank
- Several of the major banks acting as clearing agents
- Correspondent relationships between different banks

The clearing of checks between countries (cross-border clearing) is often a slow and complicated process. Cross-border checks generally clear as collection items that must be presented to the bank in the country on which they are drawn. Settlement is typically accomplished through correspondent bank accounts. For smaller value items, the drawee bank may replace the original check for one that can be cleared in the payee's country. In this case, the check is returned to the payee's bank for deposit. Some financial institutions offer specialized international check clearing services that accelerate the process of collecting cross-border payments.

B. Electronic Payment Systems

Many countries offer different types of electronic systems for both corporate and consumer payments.

1. Business-to-Business (B2B) Electronic Payment Systems

Unlike the U.S., where checks are the most common B2B payment method, in all other developed countries of the world, electronic transfer is the predominant B2B payment method. The actual structure and operation of electronic payment systems vary from country to country but all share some common characteristics. Most B2B electronic payments are credit transactions, in which the payor initiates a transfer of funds to the payee. These payments are analogous to Automated Clearing House (ACH) credits or Fedwire transactions in the U.S. The method by which a company accesses a bank to initiate payment varies widely by country, bank and company. Generally, payment initiation systems are provided by banks to customers on a proprietary basis.

The majority of electronic payment systems outside the U.S. are through correspondent balances of the banks involved in the transfers. Between countries, this clearing is usually done bank-to-bank on a bilateral basis. Within a country, the clearing may also be done on a bilateral basis or through a netting system managed by a few clearing banks. These systems differ from the Fedwire system, in which value is transferred by debiting and crediting reserve account balances held at the Fed.

The Society for Worldwide Interbank Financial Telecommunication (S.W.I.F.T.)® is an interbank telecommunication network that enables banks to send authenticated electronic messages in standard formats. Established in the 1970s, S.W.I.F.T. currently has over 7,500 member financial institutions in approximately 200 countries. The communications that are initiated and received by member banks are known as S.W.I.F.T. messages. Messages cover a wide range of international banking services. A company can request a bank to initiate a balance transfer or foreign payment through S.W.I.F.T. S.W.I.F.T. communications contain payment-related information but do not transfer value. The clearing and settlement of S.W.I.F.T. messages are accomplished through correspondent bank balances.

Standardized S.W.I.F.T. messages have also been developed for other international service needs including balance reporting, letters of credit (L/Cs), documentary collections and FX transactions. S.W.I.F.T. has recently offered membership to large corporations on a limited basis and is also migrating toward an Internet-based service called SWIFTNet® that facilitates the movement toward continuous linked settlement (CLS).

Continuous Linked Settlement (CLS)® is a recent development in the global financial community that allows for international currency transactions to be settled on a same-day basis. CLS provides a real-time global settlement system in which settlement risk due to time zones, legal jurisdiction and operating procedures are significantly reduced. CLS is operated by the CLS Bank, which began operations in late 2002 with the goal of eliminating cross-border intraday settlement exposures. CLS Bank has offices in New York, London and Tokyo. It is owned by about 70 of the world's largest financial institutions and has links to all of the major central banks in North America, Europe and Asia. Multinational corporations are allowed to participate as third-party members without having a direct relationship with CLS Bank. Corporations access CLS activity through settlement member banks. With the compatibility offered by SWIFTNet, the migration of most cross-border transactions to CLS is rapidly increasing.

2. Consumer Electronic Payment Systems

Again, unlike the U.S., where checks are the most common consumer payment method, in all other developed countries of the world, electronic transfer is the predominant method used for consumer-to-business (C2B), consumer-to-consumer (C2C) and consumer-to-government payments. As is the case with B2B payments, the structure and operation of consumer electronic payment systems varies from country to country.

The U.K., Switzerland, the Netherlands, France, Belgium, Japan and the majority of the Nordic countries have giro systems that operate through postal and/or banking channels. Giros are consumer-based payment systems that transfer payments from one account to another using direct debits and credits. Consumers use the giro system in place of checks for payment of monthly bills. In many countries, consumers access these systems via PCs, terminals or telephones. Though primarily used for consumer-initiated payments, there is experimental use of giros for B2B and B2C payments in some European countries.

Debit, smart and stored value cards are generally accepted throughout the world.

- **Debit card:** When a consumer uses a debit card to purchase goods or services, funds are deducted from bank or giro accounts on an on-line basis.
- **Smart card:** Smart cards are similar to debit cards but contain a microchip with additional information that offers security protection. Smart cards are used for prepaid value transactions in which the consumer prepays the bank, giro or company issuing the card.
- **Stored value card:** Stored value cards offer no security protection but merely keep track of purchases, along with any remaining balance. They are used for a wide range of small value purchases such as phone charges. They are also becoming increasingly popular as gift cards.

IV. CHARACTERISTICS OF INTERNATIONAL BANKING SYSTEMS

Each country's banking system is structured with different regulations, various capabilities, and unique services.

A. Regulatory Oversight and Clearing Operations

1. Central Bank

The central bank or monetary authority of a country establishes the conditions for both domestic and non-U.S. bank operations. Rapid changes in conditions and restrictions are occurring in many countries. In general, these changes tend to create more competition and to have a positive impact on the efficiency of all financial institutions operating within the country.

In some countries, central banks perform functions that are very similar to those of the U.S. Federal Reserve system. Central banks operate the payment system, regulate banks, act as lenders of last resort and control the money supply. However, more commonly, a group of large clearing banks (as in Canada and the U.K.) or a monetary authority (as in Hong Kong), rather than a central bank, operate the payment system. In addition, many foreign central banks act as issuers of government debt, a function performed by the Treasury Department in the U.S.

2. Bank and Company Relationships

In some countries, such as Austria, Germany and Switzerland, banks are permitted to own a minor or even a controlling ownership position in corporations through equity investments. In the U.S., commercial banks are prevented by law from such corporate stock ownership.

3. Number of Banks

Most banking systems are less fragmented than the U.S. system. In the U.S., there are thousands of independent financial institutions, ranging from those with extensive branch networks to those with single locations. In the majority of other countries, the banking system is characterized by a few large banks operating on a nationwide basis.

4. Restrictions on Corporate Demand Deposit Accounts

In the U.S., one of the remaining provisions of the 1933 Glass-Steagall Act (Reg Q) prevents financial institutions from paying interest on corporate demand deposit accounts. (Current legislative initiatives in the U.S. could change or eliminate this restriction.) In most other countries, banks pay interest on corporate demand deposit accounts when they have surplus balances. Likewise, they charge interest on these accounts when they have deficit balances. Therefore, some of the cash management services offered by U.S. banks, such as overnight investment sweep accounts, are unnecessary in other countries.

5. Overdrafts on Corporate Demand Deposit Accounts

Overdrafts (negative balances) are permissible under the banking regulations of many countries outside the U.S. The use of overdrafts provides a convenient, if somewhat costly, source of short-term funds. Corporations can legally maintain demand deposit accounts that pay interest on positive balances and charge interest on negative balances. This significantly simplifies the task of daily cash position management for companies in a global treasury environment.

6. Value Dating

Outside of the U.S., banks typically use value dating as compensation for services provided to customers. Under a value dating system, a bank sets a forward value date upon which the value of funds credited to an account is determined and establishes a back value date on which the value of funds debited from an account is determined. For example, if a check or an electronic funds transfer is forward valued, the date of the credit to the customer's account is later than the actual date the item is added to the ledger balance. Similarly, if a check or an electronic funds transfer is back valued, the date of the debit to the customer's account is earlier than the actual date the item is deducted from the ledger balance. In effect, the bank is compensated during the value-dating period either by not having to pay interest on positive balances or by earning interest charged on negative balances.

In some countries, value dating is standardized among the major clearing banks, such as three days in the U.K. In other countries, such as Italy, value dating is negotiated on a customer-by-customer or even an item-by-item basis.

B. Characteristics of International Banks and Banking Systems

Banks and banking systems vary widely from country to country. This section provides an overview of four different countries—Canada, Mexico, the U.K. and Japan—and one major region, Europe, all of which are major trading partners of the U.S.

1. Canada[1]

Canada, the U.S. and Mexico are trading partners in the North American Free Trade Agreement (NAFTA). The Bank of Canada, the country's central bank, controls monetary policy, supplies quality bank notes (currency), promotes the safety of Canada's financial system and provides efficient and effective funds-management services.

A handful of major financial institutions in Canada provide nationwide banking through branches. In addition to the major clearing banks, there are approximately 60 other smaller financial institutions that serve a variety of special interests and markets. The Canadian Payments Association (CPA), a non-profit association created by an Act of Parliament in 1980, operates a national system for the clearing and settlement of checks, performs electronic funds transfers and manages the evolution of the national payment system. CPA membership comprises the Bank of Canada and virtually all of Canada's bank and non-bank deposit-taking financial institutions.

The CPA currently operates two systems for the clearing and settlement of payments: the Automated Clearing Settlement System (ACSS) and the Large Value Transfer System (LVTS). In addition, the U.S. Bulk Exchange (USBE), a system parallel to the ACSS, is used for the clearing of payment items denominated in U.S. dollars and for settlement of USBE balances occurring through correspondent banks in New York. Cross-border settlement between U.S. and Canadian banks is available via ACH.

The vast majority of payment items in Canada are cleared through the ACSS. Within the ACSS, 11 CPA member financial institutions, referred to as Direct Clearers, handle the clearing and settlement of payment items for customers, as well as for individuals, known as Indirect Clearers, who maintain accounts at other financial institutions. The ACSS clears both paper-based payment items (such as checks) and electronic items (including Automated Funds Transfer debits or pre-authorized debits and credits, known as direct deposits). Direct Clearers must maintain settlement accounts at The Bank of Canada. At the end of the daily exchange process, the net positions of the Direct Clearers are determined. During the morning of each business day, The Bank of Canada adjusts the financial positions of the individual Direct Clearers by transferring funds among accounts to reflect the net balances of the previous day's ACSS clearing. In turn, Indirect Clearers settle the same day through special accounts maintained with Direct Clearers.

Although 99 percent of the daily transaction volume is cleared through the ACSS, these transactions represent only about 15 percent of the total value cleared because the majority of ACSS items are for relatively small dollar amounts. The remaining 85 percent of the total value is cleared via the LVTS.

LVTS is an electronic wire system introduced by the CPA in February 1999 to facilitate the transfer of irrevocable payments in Canadian dollars in real-time. Through LVTS, funds are transferred between participating financial institutions virtually instantaneously, and the money is credited to the beneficiary's account on a timely basis. Because all LVTS payments are immediately final and irrevocable, the beneficiary may withdraw the money, invest it or use it to make another payment, confident that the incoming payment will not be reversed for any reason. LVTS is the first model in the world that is a hybrid offering the benefits of the two main models for current payment systems:

- Achieving the real-time payment finality provided by a Real Time Gross Settlement (RTGS) system
- Offering the lower collateral costs associated with a netting system. Each payment is final and settlement is assured immediately, even though the actual settlement does not occur until the end of the day at the Bank of Canada.

On average, LVTS is used to clear and settle about $115 billion in Canadian dollar payments each business day, or approximately 85 percent of the total value moving through the Canadian payment system. LVTS is designed as an open and accessible system that is particularly suitable for time-sensitive payments of any value. Approximately 14,000 LVTS payments are processed each day, with the average transaction being $8 million. Currently, 14 members of the CPA, including the Bank of Canada, participate directly in LVTS. CPA members who establish and maintain LVTS settlement accounts at the Bank of Canada are provided an acceptable system interface and may participate directly. There are no minimum payment value or volume requirements. All other CPA members can arrange LVTS payments for customers through LVTS participants; financial institutions may offer LVTS wire payments to customers under various proprietary names.

2. Mexico[2]

Banking in Mexico is still dominated by a few large financial institutions, many of which are now owned to some degree by foreign banks. Mexico's commercial banks offer a full range of financial services within one institution. These services include deposit accounts, consumer and commercial lending, corporate finance, the operation of trusts and mutual funds, foreign exchange and money market trading. In recent years, the Mexican banking system has undergone significant turmoil, and many of Mexico's smaller banks have failed. As a result, there have been significant opportunities within the financial industry for foreign banks. Also, FX controls have been lifted since the major peso devaluation in 1995.

The Secretariat of Finance, the National Banking and Securities Commission and the Bank of Mexico are the principal regulators of the banking system. The Secretariat of Finance is concerned with institutional issues, such as licensing, and sets credit and fiscal policies. The Bank of Mexico, the country's central bank, implements these policies and also operates interbank check clearing and compensation systems. The Institute for the Protection of Bank Savings (IPAB) acts as a deposit insurance institution. The National Banking and Securities Commission, a semi-autonomous government agency, is responsible for supervision and vigilance. The Mexican Banking Association represents the interests of Mexico's banks.

Although electronic banking capabilities are growing rapidly, many Mexican companies still pay invoices in person at the vendor's bank. Some Mexican banks offer a bill presentment system whereby a company sends details of invoices, organized by creditor, to the bank. Due to high levels of check fraud in the system, many banks are offering a version of positive pay to ensure that only legitimate checks are paid. Also, while NACHA initiatives for cross-border ACH transfers are well established between the U.S. and Canada, cross-border ACH to Mexico is still in development.

3. United Kingdom (U.K.)

There are many similarities between the U.K. and U.S. banking and payment systems. The U.K. has a highly developed banking system that provides a full spectrum of financial and transactional services to customers in wholesale and retail markets. London is one of the major financial centers of the world and features one of the largest international RTGS clearing and settlement systems: the Clearing House Automated Payment System (CHAPS). CHAPS-euro is the major clearing system for the euro in the U.K., enabling payments to be made between parties within the U.K. and also cross-border through the Trans-European Automated Real-Time Gross Settlement Express Transfer System (TARGET).

Payment systems in the U.K. parallel those in the U.S., with checks being the primary method of payment. However, use of a wide range of electronic banking services by consumers, such as telephone banking, online banking and an ACH-like system called the Bankers Automated Clearing Service (BACS) is increasing. There are also several aspects of the U.K. banking and payment systems that appear to be similar to those in the U.S. but have subtle differences. The Bank of England performs a regulatory and supervisory role similar to that of the Federal Reserve but, unlike the Fed, the Bank of England does not operate the clearing system. The Bank of England also performs a monetary role with the authority to establish interest rates.

Both the corporate and the consumer banking systems are dominated by a few major U.K. banks that operate the clearing system for England, Northern Ireland, Scotland and Wales. However, a series of mergers among building societies, the U.K. equivalent of the U.S. mutual savings banks, have begun to challenge the dominant status of the major U.K. clearing banks.

4. Europe

The banking systems and financial markets have been dramatically affected by growing economic integration within Europe. In early May 1998, the Council of the European Union finalized the launch of the Economic Monetary Union (EMU). In January 1999, 11 nations joined the union, including Austria, Belgium, Finland, France, Germany, Ireland, Italy, Luxembourg, the Netherlands, Portugal and Spain. Greece joined in 2000, and there are several smaller countries, such as Andorra, Monaco, San Marino and Vatican City, that now recognize the euro as the official currency. In May 2004, 10 additional countries (primarily throughout Eastern Europe) joined the EU. Denmark, Sweden and the U.K. are members of the European Union but have chosen not to participate in the euro at this time.

The European Central Bank (ECB), which was established in July 1998, oversees a single monetary policy for all EMU members. The euro was initially used primarily in capital markets by the central banks, commercial banks and corporations. Smaller companies and consumers converted to the euro over a three-year period. Euro banknotes and coins were introduced on January 1, 2002 and the national currencies of participating countries ceased to be legal tender within six months. Many countries whose currencies had derived their value from the former European currencies, such as the French franc or the German mark, are valued to the euro today.

The primary advantages of switching to the euro have been the elimination of currency exposures between the EMU countries, as well as reduced FX exposure and transaction costs. Another advantage is that the use of the euro in European capital markets has virtually eliminated the possibility of exchange rate crises for member countries.

Such advantages result in the consolidation of banking relationships and the simplification of certain international treasury management techniques such as pooling and netting.

(A more detailed discussion of pooling and netting is in Chapter 16, Global Treasury Organization and Liquidity Management.)

There are four primary mechanisms for the settlement of euro payments and transfers: TARGET, correspondent banking, internal networks and local clearing systems and the Euro Bankers Association:

- **TARGET:** This system provides real-time settlement for cross-border payments, similar to Fedwire in the U.S. The TARGET system is used primarily for urgent, high value payments. An important function of TARGET is to enable central banks to mobilize liquidity around Europe in order to abide by monetary policy objectives determined by the ECB.
- **Correspondent banking:** The use of correspondent banking, a traditional clearing method, remains the most common method of cross-border transactions for low value, bulk payments.
- **Internal networks and local clearing systems:** European banks continue to use internal networks and access local clearing systems directly.
- **Euro Bankers Association (EBA):** This is an association of major clearing banks that operates a net settlement system similar to the CHIPS settlement procedure in the U.S. but is used primarily for financial, rather than commercial, transactions. EBA converted to euro-denominated transactions in January 1999.

Banks in most European countries are efficient and generally offer a full array of electronic services. Banking in Eastern Europe continues to evolve in conjunction with political reform efforts and the trend toward market-driven economies. Traditional European and U.S. cash management services are typically unavailable in Eastern Europe or are in the early stages of development.

5. Japan[3]

The Japanese banking system is highly developed with many banks having extensive international operations or alliances throughout the world. The Bank of Japan (BOJ) is Japan's central bank and performs many of the same activities as the Fed in the U.S. The BOJ is responsible for implementing monetary policy, examining financial institutions and serving as the lender of last resort. It also provides payment settlement, through direct entries, to the deposit accounts maintained by financial institutions.

At the top of the Japanese banking system are four main city banks with a complicated network of smaller and regional banks, as well as other specialized financial institutions. Outside the main city banks, the system is very much oriented toward the domestic market, with many of the standards and systems being unique to Japan. The current system is undergoing changes that are transforming it from a protected domestic system to a more open and competitive one.

In the consumer and retail sectors, cash is still the primary payment method, although smart cards are used extensively. In addition, there is a well-developed ATM system that supports cross-bank withdrawals during business hours. The Japanese post office also provides some financial services, similar to giros in Europe, which include the receipt of funds for postal savings, insurance and pension accounts. For consumers, there is also a system of electronic kiosks that are used for C2B payments.

The clearing of paper-based items in Japan occurs through local and regional clearing houses. The largest is the Tokyo Clearing House, which also facilitates operation of an automated clearing house system. However, unlike the ACH system in the U.S., this system currently conducts only credit transfers.

The Zengin Data Telecommunications System (Zengin System) is the on-line network through which most domestic funds transfers are initiated. In 1990, the Zengin System went to a real-time basis and established a cap on intraday net debit positions for each participating institution. This system is Japanese-based with unique formats that are not S.W.I.F.T. compatible. BOJ Net is the interbank settlement system operated by the BOJ. Financial institutions that maintain accounts with the BOJ are provided on-line access to initiate settlement transfers between accounts. The Foreign Exchange Yen Clearing System (FXYCS) is used to make payments for non-resident yen accounts and can accept messages in S.W.I.F.T. format. Most transactions through FXYCS are settlements for FX transactions or international treasury settlements.

Overall, the banking and financial markets are highly regulated, with both the Ministry of Finance and the BOJ playing major roles. There are efforts underway to deregulate certain aspects of the financial marketplace but involvement of foreign financial institutions remains somewhat limited. In addition, for companies with operations in Japan, dealing with a very complex domestic language can introduce significant cash management problems. Foreign companies doing business in Japan must choose to operate as either a resident or a non-resident entity. For companies choosing non-resident status, the payment system is limited to the FXYCS system, which, while all-English, is also very expensive. For companies operating as resident entities, the less expensive Zengin System is used but because it is in Japanese, the system poses the difficultly of integrating payment information into an English-based ERP system.

V. INTERNATIONAL TRADE FINANCING METHODS

The most frequently used international trade payment mechanisms—open account, documentary collection and letter of credit (L/C)—can be explained in terms of increasing levels of protection, complexity and cost. Open account terms are the simplest and least costly but offer the least protection. Documentary collections are more complex and costly but offer more protection to both parties. L/Cs are the most complex, costly and secure vehicles for international trade. Exhibit 15.1 shows the hierarchy of trade payment mechanisms.

EXHIBIT 15.1 — HIERARCHY OF INTERNATIONAL TRADE PAYMENT METHODS

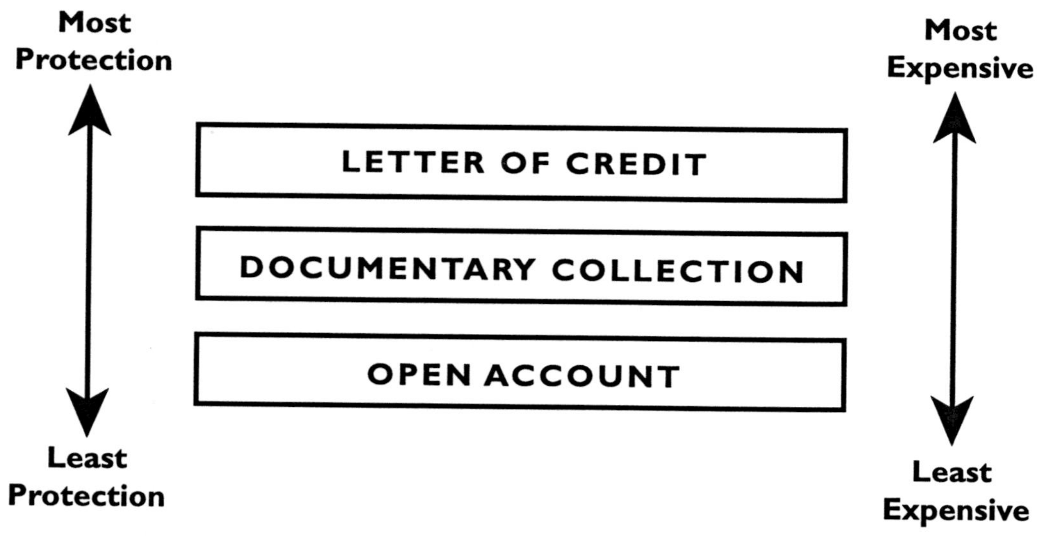

Regardless of the method of trade payment, the used must be agreed upon by the buyer and the seller. Payment is generally specified in either the buyer's or the seller's currency, but it may be in a third currency if acceptable to both parties. The majority of world trade is denominated in a third-party currency, the U.S. dollar.

A. Open Account

In the open account method, the seller checks the creditworthiness of the buyer, establishes credit terms and limits, ships the merchandise and sends an invoice to the buyer. The buyer is responsible for initiating payment to the seller in accordance with any agreed upon credit terms. In the U.S., the open account is the most frequently used method of payment for B2B domestic transactions. An open account is also widely used internationally when two trading partners have an existing relationship; however, exporting goods to a non-domestic buyer, where there is no established relationship, often requires credit risk protection through documentary collection or an L/C.

B. Documentary Collection

Documentary collection is a payment method that processes the collection of a draft and accompanying shipping documents through international correspondent banks. Instructions regarding the transaction specifics are contained in a collection letter that accompanies the documentation. It is the responsibility of the exporter to determine the instructions specified in the collection letter.

Banks that are involved in a documentary collection act only as collecting and paying agents and assume no direct obligation for ensuring that payment is made. Banks involved in these transactions perform different roles:

- **The remitting bank** is the seller's (exporter's) bank that prepares the collection letter and forwards documents to the collecting bank in the buyer's (importer's) country.
- **The collecting bank** is the remitting bank's correspondent responsible for contacting the buyer (importer), collecting the amount due and releasing the documents as instructed.

A collection letter specifies the exact procedures to be followed before shipping documents are released to the importer. The importer usually requires physical possession of the shipping documents in order to obtain the merchandise. Documents are typically released either against payment or acceptance:

- Documents against payment use a sight draft, which is a draft payable on demand that requires the collecting bank to receive full and final payment of the amount owed prior to releasing the documents.
- Documents against acceptance use a time draft, which is a draft payable on a specified future date that must be accepted by the importer before the collecting bank may release documents. Upon maturity of the time draft, it is presented to the importer for payment.
- Once full and final payment is received, the collecting bank transfers funds to the remitting bank, as instructed, for payment to the exporter.

In the event of non-payment or non-acceptance, the exporter has the cost of re-marketing the goods to another buyer or returning the merchandise. The exporter may request the collecting bank to initiate formal action against the importer for non-performance. Exhibit 15.2 illustrates a documentary collection.

EXHIBIT 15.2 — ILLUSTRATION OF A DOCUMENTARY COLLECTION

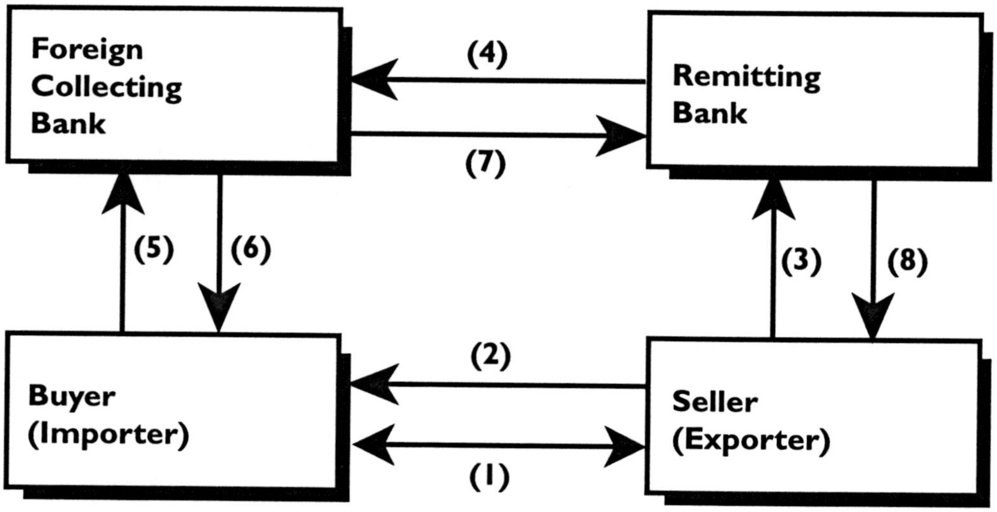

Step 1:	Buyer and Seller agree to a sales contract requiring the use of documentary collection.
Step 2:	The seller/exporter ships merchandise to the buyer/importer.
Step 3:	The seller/exporter delivers the draft documents to the remitting bank.
Step 4:	The remitting bank forwards the documents and collection letter to the buyer/importer's bank, the foreign collecting bank.
Step 5:	The buyer/importer makes payment to the foreign collecting bank in the case of a sight draft, or accepts a time draft.
Step 6:	The foreign collecting bank releases the documents so that the buyer/importer may take delivery of the merchandise.
Step 7:	The forgeign collecting bank transfers funds to the remitting bank.
Step 8:	The remitting bank pays the seller/exporter.

C. Letter of Credit (L/C)

An L/C is a document issued by a bank, guaranteeing the payment of a customer's draft up to a stated amount for a specified period provided certain conditions are met. The L/C substitutes a bank's credit for that of the buyer, virtually eliminating the seller's credit risk. L/Cs are a widely used method of payment for import and export shipments and are also often used as a financing vehicle for international trade transactions.

A commercial L/C is issued by a bank as the intended mechanism of payment in relation to a trade transaction involving the domestic or international shipment of merchandise. An L/C typically requires presentment of a draft, commercial invoice and related shipping documents; hence, it is documentary in nature. Because a bank's role in an L/C transaction is the examination of documents, not the underlying merchandise, it is the responsibility of the importer (buyer) to specify the documentation required prior to payment that reasonably ensures the receipt of the exact merchandise ordered.

Banks may serve a variety of roles in L/C transactions:

- The issuing bank is the buyer's (importer's) bank that issues the L/C in favor of the beneficiary (seller/exporter).

- The advising bank advises the beneficiary of an L/C in its favor.
- Other banks that may be involved in the transaction are the negotiating bank and the confirming bank. The advising and negotiating banks are frequently the same bank, performing dual roles. The advising/negotiating bank examines the documents presented by the beneficiary, receives payment from the issuing bank and pays the beneficiary.

If requested, the advising/negotiating bank may add confirmation (as the confirming bank) to an L/C. In doing so, the confirming bank commits to the beneficiary that payment will be made if documents meet the terms and conditions of the L/C, regardless of the issuing bank's ability to pay. If an L/C is confirmed, the confirming bank will also be the negotiating bank. Most L/Cs are irrevocable, meaning that the L/C cannot be canceled or amended without the agreement of all parties (the buyer, the beneficiary, the issuing bank and, if the L/C is confirmed, the confirming bank) to the transaction. Exhibit 15.3 illustrates a typical international commercial L/C transaction.

Once documentation has been presented, the L/C may provide either immediate (sight draft) or deferred payment (time draft) to the beneficiary (seller/exporter). When the L/C requires the presentment of a sight draft, which is a draft payable on demand, the advising/negotiating bank pays the seller immediately and is reimbursed by the issuing bank. When the L/C requires presentment of a time draft, which provides payment at a future date, the seller is providing credit terms to the buyer. The seller may be able to receive payment prior to maturity by discounting (selling at a discounted value) the time draft to a local bank. A deferred payment L/C provides presentation of one or more sight drafts at specified dates in the future and sometimes extends over several years. When medium-term financing is provided for the export of capital goods, a deferred payment L/C may be used in conjunction with a term loan agreement.

A standby L/C is a variation of a commercial L/C. Standby L/Cs are issued primarily by U.S. banks that are legally prohibited from issuing formal guarantees. Once issued, the standby L/C serves as a vehicle to ensure the financial performance of a bank's customer to a third-party beneficiary. Standby L/Cs typically require presentation of a sight draft and documentation that supports the beneficiary's claim of non-performance on the part of the issuing bank's customer. Standby L/Cs are frequently used as credit enhancement for commercial paper programs or to guarantee a bid tender or financial performance on a contract.

EXHIBIT 15.3 — ILLUSTRATION OF A LETTER OF CREDIT TRANSACTION (SIGHT DRAFT)

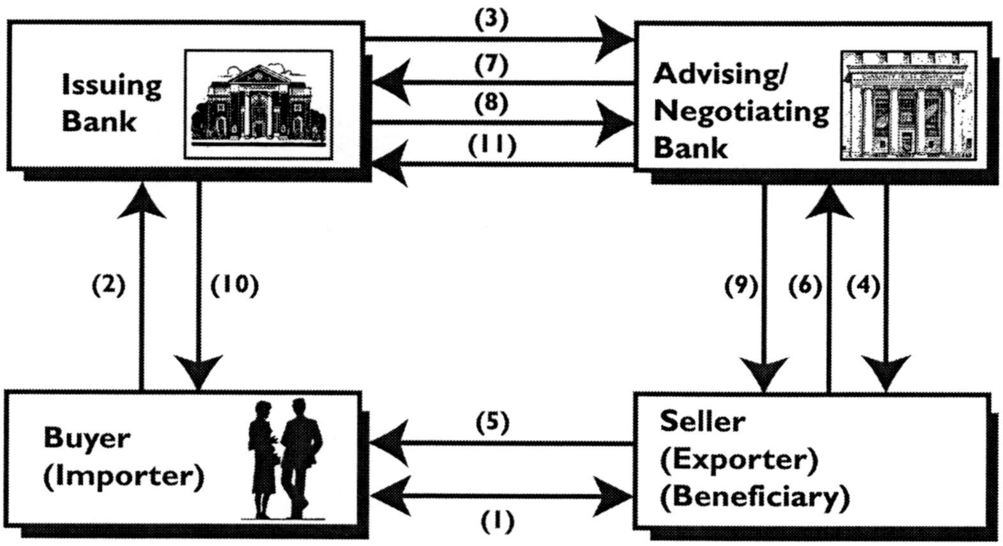

Step 1:	The buyer and the seller agree to a sales contract in which the buyer is required to open an L/C in favor of the seller.
Step 2:	The buyer chooses a bank in its country and opens an L/C in favor of the seller.
Step 3:	The issuing (buyer's) bank send the L/C to a bank in the seller's country. The latter bank becomes the advising bank.
Step 4:	The advising bank sends details of the credit to the seller, who is the beneficiary of the credit.
Step 5:	The seller ships the merchandise to the buyer.
Step 6:	The advising/negotiating bank examines the documents to the advising/negotiating bank.
Step 7:	Separate Checks and Advises — Checks are separated from remittance advises and other contents.
Step 8:	The issuing bank examines the documents, and if everything is in order, accepts the time draft that draws on the L/C. The accepted draft now becomes a banker's acceptance (BA). The BA is returned to the advising/negotiating bank. At this point, the seller may ask their bank to sell the BA at discount so they can receive immediate funds or hold the BA until maturity and receive the full amount at that time.
Step 9:	The seller receives either full payment at the maturity of the BA or a discounted amount immediately.
Step 10:	The issuing bank notifies the buyer it has the documents and, after payment terms are settled, releases the documents to the buyer. With the documents (primarily the bill of lading, which is title to the goods). the buyer is able to claim the merchandise.
Step 11:	At the maturity date of the BA, the holder presents it to the issuing bank, which honors the BA for the face value.

D. Other Trade Payment Methods

Five other less frequently used international trade payment mechanisms include cash before delivery (CBD), consignment, barter, countertrade and trading companies:

- **Cash Before Delivery (CBD):** CBD is when a seller requires the total protection of receiving payment before shipment of goods.
- **Consignment:** Consignment involves the shipment of goods to a foreign agent, where the exporter (seller) retains legal title to the goods. When the goods are sold by the agent, payment is due to the exporter and title transfers to the buyer. For an exporter, regaining possession of unsold goods may be both difficult and costly.
- **Barter:** Barter involves the direct exchange of goods or services between two end users without the exchange of money. It is most frequently used when funds cannot be repatriated. (For a further discussion of repatriation, see Chapter 16, Global Treasury Organization and Liquidity Management.)
- **Countertrade:** Countertrade is a method of payment used by companies that do not have access to sufficient hard currencies (internationally traded currencies) to pay for imports from other countries. For example, a U.S. exporter ships merchandise to the countertrading country and in exchange takes merchandise that may be sold elsewhere in the world.
- **Trading Companies:** Trading companies are used when an exporter (seller) sells products at a discount to an export trading company, which then resells the products internationally.

E. Banker's Acceptance (BA)

A banker's acceptance (BA) is often used to finance the import, export or domestic shipment of goods but can also be used to finance storage of properly titled goods. BAs are frequently used in conjunction with L/Cs requiring a time draft drawn on a bank.

A BA is a time draft on the face of which the drawee bank has written the word "accepted" over the signature. The drawee bank is the bank that issued the L/C and upon which the draft is drawn (or payable). The bank accepting and agreeing unconditionally to pay the draft at the date and place payable is known as the acceptor.

By accepting the draft, the bank creates a BA indicating a commitment to pay the face amount of the draft at maturity. Through the acceptance of payment risk, the bank creates a short-term negotiable instrument. Therefore, a bank can fund the BA transaction by selling it to an investor or by holding the BA in the bank's portfolio.

The cost of acceptance financing has two components: the discount rate (the rate earned by the investor) and the bank's acceptance commission. Most acceptance financing is done with eligible acceptances, which are discounted at the Federal Reserve. To be eligible for discount, the acceptance may not have a maturity of more than 180 days. Eligible underlying transactions include import or export of goods, domestic storage transactions with documents conveying title attached and storage of readily marketable staples secured by warehouse receipts.

F. Trade Acceptance

A trade acceptance is another instrument used in international transactions. It is similar to a BA except it is drawn on and accepted by a buyer (importer). It can be used to evidence a buyer's obligation to pay for purchased merchandise where the seller (exporter) is satisfied with the credit risk. Trade acceptances are often used by importers to secure financing from a bank or, similar to BAs, may even be sold to a bank or an investor at a discount prior to maturity.

VI. FUTURE OF THE GLOBAL TREASURY ENVIRONMENT

The global treasury environment continues to evolve toward automation of key functions and integration with other parts of the organization. Payment systems in different countries continue to migrate toward full integration and straight through processing. The use of the Web (Internet) as a communications and data delivery vehicle will someday become the common standard for global businesses. All of these developments will be supported by the consolidation of global financial institutions that will facilitate the management of treasury operations in a multinational environment. Finally, the maturation of the euro money markets and capital markets will offer an alternative to today's dollar-denominated international financial environment.

Endnotes

1 Information in this section was obtained from the Bank of Canada and Canadian Payments Association (CPA).
2 Information in this section was obtained from the Federal Reserve Bank of Dallas and the Country Commercial Guide published by the U.S. Department of Commerce.
3 Information in this section was obtained from HSBC's Guide to Cash and Treasury Management in Asia, 2003.

Test Your Understanding

These chapter questions are provided to test your understanding of the information in the text. They are neither examples of CTP examination questions nor are they in the examination format.

Answers are on pages 613–615.

1. What are the primary objectives of global treasury management?

2. Discuss political or sovereign risk.

3. What are FX rates and how are they quoted?

4. What is the difference between the spot and forward FX markets?

5. Explain the concepts of par, discount and premium as they relate to FX spot and forward rates.

6. What is S.W.I.F.T., and what does it do?

7. What is CLS and who are the major participants?

8. What are giros and who uses them?

9. How does the U.S. compare to most other countries with respect to the number of financial institutions?

10. In the Canadian banking system, what is the CPA, and what is its role?

11. What have been some of the advantages of the ECU switching to the euro as its currency?

12. Discuss open account trade financing and how it is used internationally.

13. What is a letter of credit and how is it used in international trade?

14. What is countertrade?

Association for
Financial Professionals®

CHAPTER 16
Global Treasury Organization and Liquidity Management

I. INTRODUCTION

II. GLOBAL TREASURY MANAGEMENT ORGANIZATION
- A. Centralized versus Decentralized Control
- B. Shared Service Center
- C. In-House Banking

III. GLOBAL TREASURY MANAGEMENT ISSUES AND TECHNIQUES
- A. Credit and Accounts Receivable Management
- B. Pooling
- C. Overlay Structure
- D. Netting – Bilateral and Multilateral
- E. Leading and Lagging
- F. Reinvoicing
- G. Internal Factoring
- H. Multi-Currency Accounts
- I. Electronic Banking Services

IV. REPATRIATION OF CAPITAL FOR MULTINATIONAL COMPANIES
- A. Multinational Company Dividends
- B. Management Fees
- C. Transfer Pricing
- D. Intracompany Loans

V. OTHER CONSIDERATIONS FOR GLOBAL COMPANIES
- A. Export Financing and Credit Insurance
- B. Offshore Financing and Capital Markets
- C. Tax Considerations
- D. Implementing Global Treasury Operations and Projects

I. INTRODUCTION

Businesses that are truly global in both scope and scale present unique challenges for treasury managers. Treasury structures, systems and solutions that operate efficiently in a domestic financial environment must be adapted or, in some cases, radically redesigned in order to meet the requirements of a wide diversity of international business practices, banking regulations and payment systems. The primary goal of treasury and liquidity management remains the same. However, the tools and techniques for achieving this goal vary from country to country and region to region. This chapter addresses these global treasury tools and techniques.

II. GLOBAL TREASURY MANAGEMENT ORGANIZATION

The organization of the global treasury management function may be centralized, decentralized or a combination of both. This next section offers an overview of these three structures, as well as shared service centers (SSCs) and in-house banks.

A. Centralized versus Decentralized Control

A company that operates overseas sales offices with limited personnel typically centralizes its treasury functions at a head office in the home country. A centralized treasury offers the advantages of control, economies of scale and lower operating costs. However, a centralized treasury gives relatively little autonomy to field office personnel.

A company with autonomous international subsidiaries and/or multiple operational entities (manufacturing, distribution, marketing, sales, finance, etc.) is more likely to operate in a decentralized treasury structure under guidelines and/or policies established by the home country's corporate headquarters. In-country personnel offer the advantages of being familiar with local business and banking practices, as well as the language, customs and culture. In a decentralized structure, field personnel are responsible for all daily treasury functions.

However, for purposes of both information and control, field offices are required to submit periodic financial management reports to the home office. Typically, these reports summarize bank balances and transaction activity, as well as key treasury functions such as borrowing, investment and foreign exchange (FX) trading. In addition, the head office periodically audits local offices to ensure policies, procedures and controls are being adhered to properly.

Finally, some large multinational companies (MNCs) operate regional treasury centers with combined features. These regional centers are responsible for providing treasury services to specific subsidiaries within a designated geographic area (Asia-Pacific, Middle East and Africa, Europe, North America and Latin America). In regional treasury structures, outsourcing daily treasury operations to global banks and other non-bank third-party providers has become common practice.

B. Shared Service Center

Many MNCs and banks utilize a structure called a shared service center (SSC). A SSC is a consolidated operation that supports standardized processes (accounting, payroll, etc.) within an organization. SSCs were initially developed to establish, measure and maintain the cost and contribution of back-office business processes and operations. However, SSCs have expanded to support a wide range of functions such as treasury, accounting, receivables and payables management, human resources, payroll, benefits management, and legal, compliance and tax. In a sense, it is like outsourcing a particular function or process to an in-house provider.

There are many reasons for the popularity of SSCs:

- Many of the recent developments in the treasury area have been a direct result of Internet and browser technology, thereby enabling the re-centralization of database management and maintenance that may have been previously decentralized.
- Many global treasury back office operations do not necessarily require local management and can be centralized into an SSC.
- The development of global treasury management systems (TMS) provides standardization of information and processes that further enhance the benefits of SSCs.
- The European Monetary Union (EMU) and the euro have enabled European and U.S. treasury managers to employ SSC structures in response to the consolidation and rationalization of European banking structures.

Five steps are involved in establishing an SSC:

- Determine the economic contribution of treasury back-office processes.
- Compare an SSC structure to outsourcing solutions.
- Select a location for the SSC in a country that offers tax advantages or tax havens (e.g., the Netherlands, Luxembourg, Ireland, Singapore)
- Choose and implement the technology for the SSC.
- Find and retain quality staff and managers to work at the SSC.

C. In-House Banking

Many large global companies have established their own in-house banks within centralized treasury departments. In these types of arrangements, treasury becomes the main provider of banking services for all of the company's operating entities. Treasury does so by instructing financial institutions to clear transactions and provide services on a bulk basis. The primary benefit is a reduction in overall banking costs by aggregating many small transactions into fewer, larger transactions.

The in-house bank can also manage four of the principal international treasury management solutions: netting, pooling, re-invoicing and centralization of FX exposures. To optimize these benefits, it is critical to link the in-house banking operations to treasury management and ERP systems.

III. GLOBAL TREASURY MANAGEMENT ISSUES AND TECHNIQUES

A. Credit and Accounts Receivable Management

Managing and evaluating credit can be more difficult in countries where unsecured consumer credit is less prevalent and where rating agencies and credit information systems are less evolved. Likewise, lenient laws or standards make past dues and bad debts more difficult to collect. In countries where this is the case, companies typically require stricter credit terms and are more aggressive in managing accounts receivable.

B. Pooling

Companies concentrate cash internationally for the same reasons they do so domestically: to utilize available cash more efficiently, to improve liquidity management by maximizing interest earnings on investments and minimizing interest expense on borrowing and to improve the accuracy of forecasting. In the U.S., concentration of cash involves the physical movement of funds from outlying depository banks into a concentration bank. Outside of the U.S., this physical concentration of funds is usually referred to as "sweeping." (Not to be confused with "sweep accounts" used by treasurers in the U.S. for overnight investment of surplus funds.) In countries where banks are allowed to pay interest on excess demand deposit balances and to charge interest on deficit balances, the typical method of concentration is known as pooling.

The most common form of pooling is practiced in the pan-European region. Any excess funds in the accounts of a company or its subsidiaries are used to offset any deficits in other accounts of the parent or subsidiaries. This type of pooling arrangement is offered for a variety of currencies and is known as notional pooling because no actual funds are transferred.

Pooling requires a company and all subsidiaries to maintain accounts at the same bank. For a given company, all of the balances in subsidiary accounts (excess and deficit) are aggregated each day for the calculation of interest earned or due. In notional pooling, funds are not actually transferred; rather, they are merely totaled for the purpose of calculating interest. Banks usually require credit facilities to support any deficit balances in the pool.

Most pooling is single-currency/one-country pooling in which a company's subsidiaries within a given country are allowed to pool balances in a single country's currency. As the euro becomes more widely adopted across Europe, the instance of single-currency/cross-border pooling will become more prevalent. In this case, a company's subsidiaries throughout Europe can pool euro-denominated funds, even though the subsidiaries may be in different countries. This arrangement is similar to cash concentration practiced in the U.S.

C. Overlay Structure

An approach that combines sweeping and pooling is referred to as an overlay structure. This structure is typically used when a company's primary bank has branches in various countries that do not provide full domestic banking in all countries. A local bank is used, where necessary, to provide domestic transactions and accounts and to sweep surplus funds to the primary bank. The primary bank (called the overlay bank) then notionally pools balances on overlay accounts, providing a multicountry solution. This approach works especially well in Europe where the euro now exists as a common currency among the majority of countries.

D. Netting – Bilateral and Multilateral

Netting is an internal company (intracompany) system that is designed to reduce the number of cross-border payments among units of a company through the elimination or consolidation of funds denominated in different currencies. Many countries impose restrictions on the use of netting systems due to the tax consequences; hence, central bank or government approval is often required.

In a bilateral netting system, purchases between two subsidiaries of the same company are netted against each other so that periodically, typically once a month, only the net difference is transferred. If the payments are in different currencies, the total due each subsidiary is converted to a common currency in order to determine the net amount due. Bilateral netting arrangements tend to use the currency of the receiving company in calculating the net position.

As an example of bilateral netting, if one subsidiary of an MNC is located in France and another is located in the U.K, payments are held until one or two regularly scheduled times during the month. Prior to the settlement date, payment flows in both directions are totaled and the net amount due one of the subsidiaries is made available with a single transfer.

A multilateral netting system is similar to a bilateral system but involves two or more subsidiaries. Each subsidiary informs a central treasury management center of all planned cross-border payments. To determine netting transactions, payments between all subsidiaries are converted into a common currency and combined into a few, larger, transactions. Prior to the settlement date, each unit is informed of the net amount owed or due. The central treasury management center makes the necessary FX conversions. Multilateral netting is used primarily for intracompany transactions, but some companies include third-party payments or receipts, as well. The mechanics of multilateral netting are illustrated in Exhibit 16.1.

EXHIBIT 16.1 — ILLUSTRATION OF MULTILATERAL NETTING

INTERCOMPANY CASH FLOW BEFORE NETTING

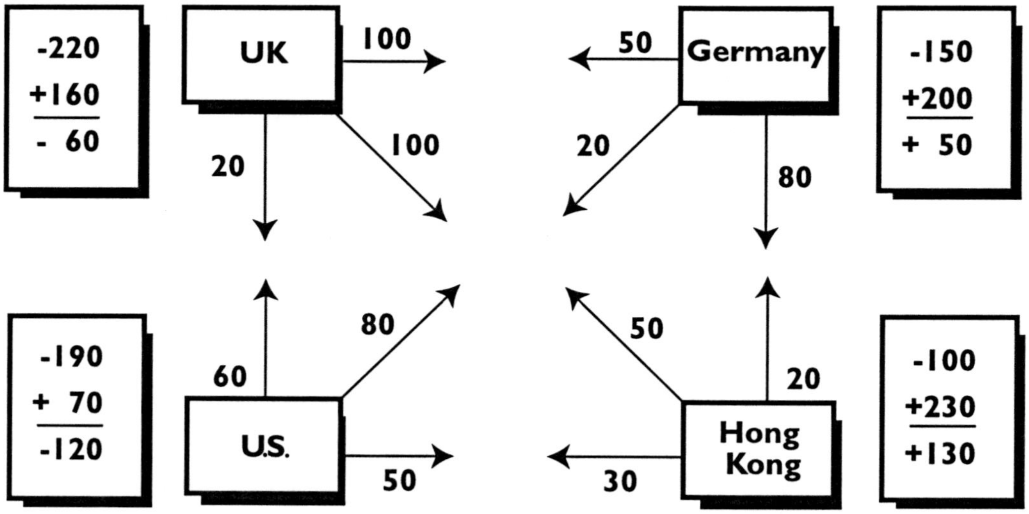

Number of payments = 12
Total cash flows = 660

CASH FLOW WITH MULTILATERAL NETTING CENTER

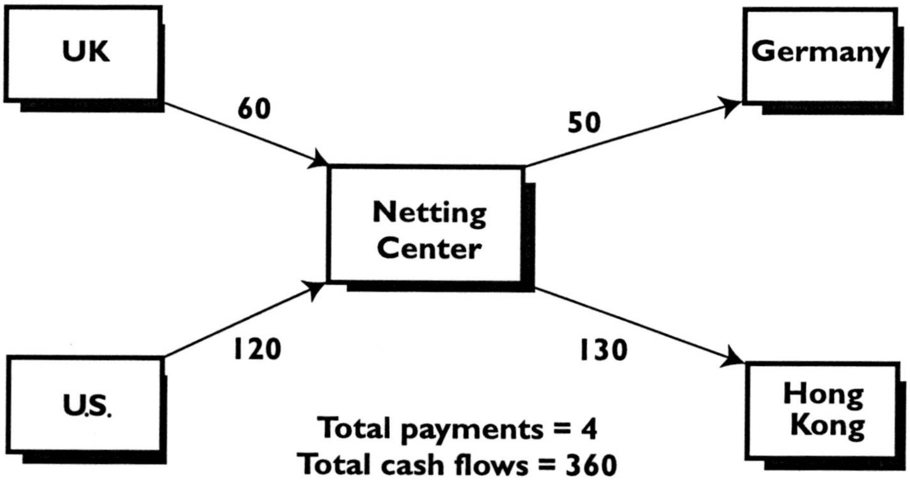

Benefits and Costs of Netting: There are three principal benefits to netting:

- A reduction in the number of FX transactions and cross-border wire transfers
- More favorable FX rates due to the larger FX trades resulting from consolidation
- Improved cash forecasting for both the subsidiary and the parent company as a result of the ability to pre-plan cross-border payments.

On the other hand, the principal costs of netting—which include setup, administration, and maintenance—can be substantial.

E. Leading and Lagging

Netting systems may be used to implement leading and lagging of payments. Leading and lagging involve executing cross-border payments between subsidiaries either ahead of the scheduled payment date (leading) or behind the scheduled payment date (lagging). In both leading and lagging, liquidity is shifted from one subsidiary to another. Leading is employed when a subsidiary country's currency is expected to depreciate relative to the parent company's currency. Lagging is used when a subsidiary country's currency is expected to appreciate relative to the parent company's currency.

F. Reinvoicing

Reinvoicing is an intracompany method of centralizing responsibility for monitoring and collecting international accounts receivable and more effectively managing related FX exposures. A reinvoicing center is a company-owned subsidiary that purchases goods from an exporting subsidiary and sells the goods to an importing subsidiary. The exporting unit invoices and receives funds from the reinvoicing subsidiary in its own currency while the importing unit is invoiced and pays funds to the reinvoicing subsidiary in its own currency. Although the title to the goods passes through the reinvoicing center, usually the actual goods are shipped directly from the exporting subsidiary to the importing subsidiary. Establishing a reinvoicing center requires local government approval and negotiations in determining how the subsidiary is taxed.

Benefits and Costs of Reinvoicing: One of the primary benefits in establishing a reinvoicing center is the centralization of FX exposures so that they are more effectively managed. The reinvoicing center also offers improvement in a company's worldwide short-term liquidity management by providing flexibility in intersubsidiary payments. In addition, reinvoicing:

- Enables leading and lagging arrangements to be implemented easily
- Improves export trade financing and collections
- Reduces bank costs
- Improves FX rates by enabling larger trades.

It is particularly beneficial to have the ability to set worldwide international pricing, but this practice may be heavily regulated by foreign monetary authorities. Major costs include the reinvoicing center expenses, which are incurred primarily when establishing a physical location and budgeting for administration costs. Reinvoicing is illustrated in Exhibit 16.2.

EXHIBIT 16.2 — ILLUSTRATION OF REINVOICING

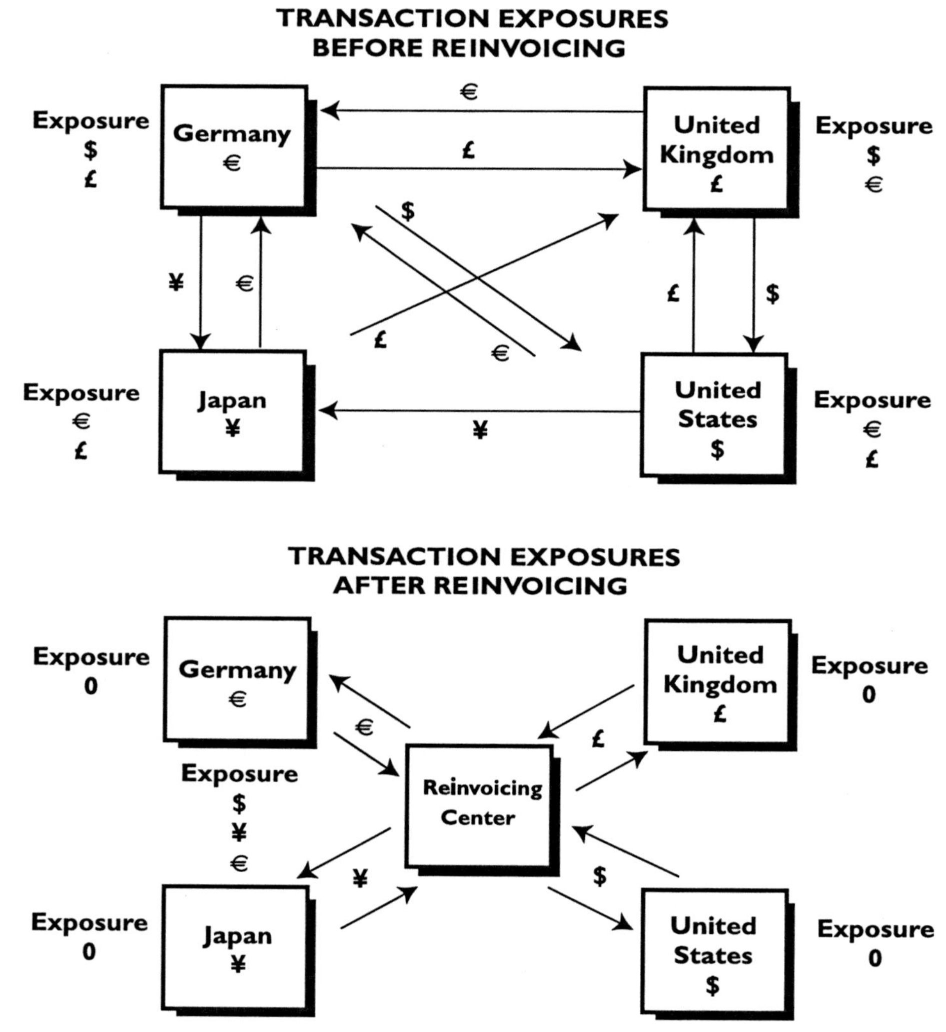

G. Internal Factoring

The benefits of internal factoring are similar to reinvoicing. However, rather than taking actual title to the goods, as is the case with reinvoicing, the internal factoring unit buys accounts receivable from the exporting unit and collects from the importing unit. The benefits of internal factoring are the same as they are for reinvoicing. Most internal factoring is done on a recourse basis, meaning that the factor can return past-due receivables and bad debts to the subsidiary for collection.

H. Multi-Currency Accounts

Multi-currency accounts are a special arrangement between a bank and a company whereby the bank allows the customer to receive or make international payments in a range of currencies from a single account or multiple subsidiary accounts. A multi-currency agreement generally specifies four stipulations:

- The base currency in which the account is denominated
- The portfolio of currencies accepted
- The spread or margin over the spot rate to use in exchanging each currency back to the base currency
- The value date to apply to debits and credits for each transaction type and currency

I. Electronic Banking Services

Major banks in Europe and Asia offer a wide range of electronic banking services. The most widely used electronic banking services are reporting services that provide information on balances and previous day transaction details. Such reporting services allow both domestic and international access. For example, balances, as well as debit and credit details, for a Dutch subsidiary of a U.S. company are reported to local management in the Netherlands and to the U.S. parent company. Major international banks and third-party service providers offer multi-bank reporting that consolidates a company's worldwide banking activity into a single daily report.

Major global banks also provide a range of electronic transaction initiation services. Such services allow companies to collect receivables and disburse payables globally in both paper-based and electronic formats for a variety of foreign currencies.

(Electronic banking services are discussed in more detail in Chapter 10, Liquidity Management.)

IV. REPATRIATION OF CAPITAL FOR MULTINATIONAL COMPANIES

For MNCs, one of the primary issues in treasury is the repatriation of capital from foreign subsidiaries back to the domestic parent's country. Repatriation involves the physical transfer of funds from one country to another. The principal method of repatriation is the use of dividends; however, there may be restrictions on this approach. Therefore, other methods such as management fees, royalties, licensing, transfer pricing and intracompany loans can also be used for repatriation purposes. Most repatriation policies are related to the transfer of funds back to the U.S. parent from wholly- or partially-owned global subsidiaries of U.S. MNCs. The objective is to ensure not only that the MNC is fairly compensated for the foreign investment but also that the host country benefits from the local reinvestment of funds.

A. Multinational Company Dividends

The use of dividends to transfer profits from global subsidiaries is often restricted by host governments. Usually, there are either significant taxes charged on cross-border dividends or outright restrictions on the repatriation of funds through dividends. Host governments view dividend payments to the parent company as a means of taking subsidiary profits out of the country instead of reinvesting the earnings locally.

To counter this problem, the MNCs unbundle the cash flows from subsidiaries into separate items that are more easily justified to foreign governments than outright dividends. The techniques for separating items are management fees, transfer pricing and intracompany loans.

B. Management Fees

Many MNCs charge global subsidiaries licensing and/or management fees in order to justify to host governments the flow of funds from a subsidiary to the parent company. These fees are often negotiated with the host government prior to the MNC's investing in the country.

C. Transfer Pricing

Transfer pricing is the price that subsidiaries of a large corporation charge each other for components sold among themselves. The benefit for MNCs is that transfer pricing can be manipulated to locate profits in subsidiaries in low-tax countries and to move them out of subsidiaries in high-tax countries.

Host governments may resent these actions; hence, they frequently place restrictions on transfer pricing, or changes in transfer pricing, by MNCs within their jurisdictions. The implication for MNC management is that most transfer pricing for global subsidiaries must be done at "arm's length." This means setting transfer prices at the same level at which a company would buy or sell similar products from an unaffiliated company. This assures host governments that the profits from the MNC will be distributed fairly among all of its global subsidiaries. The complexity of transfer pricing is such that MNCs typically seek the advice of highly specialized tax consultants to establish policies and procedures.

D. Intracompany Loans

Another approach to transferring funds between foreign subsidiaries is via intracompany loans. In utilizing this approach, when funds are required by a foreign subsidiary in a country whose government restricts dividends or other transfers from the subsidiary, but permits the transfer of funds for the servicing of a loan, the parent (or another subsidiary) may load funds rather than contribute equity. Should repayment of intercompany loans also be restricted, an MNC can involve a third-party intermediary in the process. Often, companies realize tax advantages because foreign governments do not impose taxes on loan repayments, as would be the practice with dividends paid to a parent company in another country. Intra-company loans may be supported by tax treaties between the countries involved.

V. OTHER CONSIDERATIONS FOR GLOBAL COMPANIES

It is important for a multinational company to also consider export financing including credit insurance, offshore capital markets, financing alternatives and tax implications.

A. Export Financing and Credit Insurance

In many countries, the government provides support for export activities through export loans or guarantees or a combination of both. The advantages of export financing include:

- The interest is generally fixed and at a lower rate and longer term than would otherwise be available from commercial sources.
- The indirect government involvement can provide some protection against government appropriation or interference.

The disadvantages of export financing include:

- Timing necessary to obtain related approvals
- Currency exposures if the currency of the loan is different from that of the cash flow of the project or subsidiary business

B. Offshore Financing and Capital Markets

Offshore financing involves raising funds outside a company's country of origin. There are four primary reasons that an MNC attempts to raise funds in other countries:

- Diversification of funding sources
- Lower borrowing rates
- Possible tax advantages, subsidiary and short-term funding
- Hedging of liabilities or equity obligations

First, offshore financing provides diversification of funding sources rather than depending solely on a company's domestic capital markets. The rationale for diversification is that too much debt or equity raised in a particular market may saturate investors' desire for a company's stocks and bonds, therefore raising the cost of capital for the company. Also, a large company in a small country may be forced to go outside of domestic capital markets to obtain the financing needed to compete in global markets. Especially in times of tight funding, it is helpful to have a presence in several different capital markets.

Second, in the case of borrowed funds, there may be some advantages to using offshore debt markets if a U.S. parent company can borrow in a foreign currency at a lower borrowing rate than the current U.S. borrowing rate. In some cases, a foreign subsidiary may be able to borrow in the local market from a local bank at lower rates than it could obtain through the parent company.

Third, there may be tax advantages available in the subsidiary's country or parent companies may be able to establish offshore financing subsidiaries to obtain funding and benefit from favorable tax regulations. Additionally, a company may choose to fund the needs of a number of subsidiaries in different countries through an offshore finance company, thereby taking advantage of lower rates by borrowing in large amounts. Companies can also invest in short-term foreign financial instruments through offshore subsidiaries.

Fourth, liabilities or equity obligations in a foreign currency can hedge a similar term asset in the same currency. For example, if a U.S. company has accounts receivable denominated in British pounds, it may consider short-term debt denominated in pounds. In this case, if foreign currency-denominated assets depreciate, liabilities denominated in the same foreign currency depreciate, as well, thereby minimizing FX translation exposure. This is also known as a balance sheet hedge or natural hedge.

(A further discussion of hedging is in Chapter 17, Financial Risk Management.)

C. Tax Considerations

Multinational companies must deal with tax codes in all of the countries in which they have operations or sales. Generally, a U.S. company's income derived from its non-U.S. operations is typically included in its tax return to determine the amount of the U.S. income tax due. If foreign source income has already been subject to foreign income taxes, the same income is being taxed twice. To relieve the effect of this double taxation, the U.S. tax law allows a U.S. company a tax credit against its total U.S. income tax liability for those foreign income taxes paid by the parent and its subsidiaries. This credit is called the foreign tax credit. It is allowed only for those foreign taxes that are income taxes and do not exceed U.S. tax rates.

To attract multinational businesses and related employment opportunities, a number of countries offer tax incentives for subsidiaries that perform certain administrative and financial functions. However, the complexity of the laws governing the taxation of non-domestic income makes it important for treasury personnel to consult with tax experts.

1. Capital Tax

In some foreign countries, particularly those experiencing an upsurge in economic growth, companies will be assessed a capital tax on the initial capital used to establish the new venture or on subsequent flows of incoming or repatriated capital. A capital tax is used as a fiscal tool by some countries to augment tax collections. The tax can also be used by a government to slow down foreign direct investment in a country.

2. Asset Tax and Turnover Tax

Despite the fact that a company may not show a profit or owe income tax on an international project, many foreign countries still impose an asset tax. Even though a company may not produce operating profits, it may still owe taxes on the value of accumulated real property or business equipment or on the value of a financial portfolio. There may also be a turnover tax, which is essentially a sales tax on goods and services.

3. Withholding Tax

Companies may be required to pay taxes when moving funds out of a foreign country. The amount can vary from one percent to almost 35 percent of the repatriated flow. Some countries refer to these as lifting fees. Lifting fees are charged whenever funds are transferred from a resident (domestic) account to a non-resident (foreign) account. Depending on the company's overall foreign tax credit position, some offset may be available on the withholding tax.

4. Other Taxes

Another tax commonly used in foreign countries is a value added tax or VAT. This tax is a form of sales tax in which tax is charged at each discrete stage of production and/or distribution on the increased value (value added) occurring at that stage. Other taxes that a company might incur include a transfer tax (in the event of the sale of a company) and perhaps, in the future, an Internet transaction tax on sales.

D. Implementing Global Treasury Operations and Projects

Companies operating in the global marketplace must implement treasury operations and systems on a regional and/or centralized basis. A company also needs to manage the movement of funds for short-term needs between various global subsidiaries to minimize the overall cost of funding. Many global companies utilize SSC and in-house banking to better manage worldwide treasury functions.

A strategic project plan plays an important role in determining the overall success of an international financial project. In addition to a strategic project plan, global operations are further strengthened by devising:

- A strong information technology plan
- A solid accounting package to manage finance and cash management
- A timely and accurate reporting mechanism with banks
- A reliable communications system

Developing a reasonable tolerance for risk is a necessary component of most successful international business ventures and is vital to meeting long-term goals. Because the magnitude of economic change in foreign markets is greater than in the U.S., companies must evaluate their exposures on a regular basis and make appropriate adjustments by utilizing various risk management methods.

(A further discussion of these issues is in Chapter 17, Financial Risk Management.)

To be successful internationally, treasurers of multinational companies must constantly re-evaluate the overall economic stability, political climate and business culture of the country in which a company has foreign operations. Monitoring these factors ultimately determines a company's ability to access sources of start-up capital for new projects, to obtain funds for ongoing operations, to reduce currency exposures and to mitigate tax implications.

Endnotes

1 Portions of this section are excerpts from "Implementing Treasury and Financial Services Projects in the International Arena", Jeff Lewis, Sept/Oct 2001, AFP Exchange.

Test Your Understanding

These chapter questions are provided to test your understanding of the information in the text. They are neither examples of CTP examination questions nor are they in the examination format.

Answers are on pages 616 and 617.

1. What is a shared service center or SSC?

2. What are the five steps in establishing a SSC?

3. Discuss the concept of in-house banking.

4. How do companies manage concentration of funds outside the U.S.?

5. What is netting?

6. Discuss reinvoicing and how it is used.

7. What are multi-currency accounts?

8. What is repatriation and why is it important for multinational companies?

9. Discuss transfer pricing and its implications for an MNC.

10. What is a capital tax and how is it used?

Association for
Financial Professionals®

CHAPTER 17
Financial Risk Management

I. INTRODUCTION

All organizations face a variety of risks. Historically, most businesses focused solely on operational risk, the risk of direct or indirect losses resulting from inadequate internal processes, people and systems or from external events that impact an organization's operations. As such, the traditional concept of risk management was associated with determining and managing insurable risks losses due to accidents, natural disasters and other unforeseen events.

Today, risk management is enterprise wide in scope and includes all of the risks associated with managing a business, including financial risk. While operational and insurance risk managements are important to the overall survival of a company, they do not usually fall under the control of treasury.

Therefore, this chapter focuses on financial risk management, which is typically the responsibility of treasury. (The next chapter, Chapter 18, Enterprise Risk Management, will focus on operational risk management, including insurance, which is typically the responsibility of the risk manager.)

II. OVERVIEW OF FINANCIAL RISK MANAGEMENT

Financial risk is the risk of direct or indirect losses resulting from the uncertainty of the future level of interest rates, foreign exchange (FX) rates and commodity prices or from adverse impacts on a company with a highly leveraged capital structure. The very nature of treasury operations makes many organizations vulnerable to significant financial risks.

Treasurers must make critical decisions that are time sensitive, that typically involve large sums of money and that must be made under volatile financial conditions. Further complicating these decisions is the fact that exposure to financial risk has increased significantly in recent years for two reasons: the speed of business brought about by advances in technology and communications, and the scope of business brought about by the trend toward globalization.

A. Risk Management Process

The risk management process involves five steps:

- Determining an organization's risk attitude
- Identifying the exposure
- Measuring the exposure
- Implementing an appropriate risk management strategy
- Monitoring the exposure to evaluate the strategy

1. Determining Risk Attitude

Organizations assume different attitudes toward risk:

- A new company in a rapidly evolving industry may be more aggressive in taking significant risks in order to gain a competitive advantage.
- An established company in a mature industry may be more cautious about taking risks in order to protect an existing competitive advantage.

- Government entities and not-for-profits may be completely risk averse.

Regardless of an organization's approach to risk, it is important for treasury to have a clearly defined risk management policy endorsed and approved by the highest management level possible, such as the Board of Directors. The policy should contain:

- An overview of the company's attitude toward risk
- The objectives of treasury in regard to risk management functions
- The roles and responsibilities of key treasury individuals
- A list of guidelines for decision making
- The specific performance measurements for results and the frequency with which they are to be reported to senior management.

2. Identifying the Exposure

Financial risks, such as interest rate variations, FX rate changes or fluctuations in commodity prices, will vary, depending on the industry, type of business or government function to which an organization is exposed. Because an organization may be exposed to all three types of financial risks, identification of the specific exposure in each area is critical.

3. Measuring the Exposure

Once an exposure has been identified, measuring and quantifying the exposure is important. Senior management needs to decide whether the organization is in a position to tolerate the risk, or whether it should reduce or eliminate the exposure via an appropriate risk management strategy.

4. Implementing an Appropriate Risk Management Strategy

Once it is determined that an organization needs to manage risk, the appropriate strategy must be implemented. The first step is to examine basic operating procedures to determine where balance sheet hedges can be used. A balance sheet hedge matches exposed liabilities against exposed assets and is frequently referred to as asset and liability management.

Financial institutions commonly employ a balance-sheet strategy of matching interest-sensitive assets with interest-sensitive liabilities in order to eliminate exposure to interest rate fluctuations. Balance sheet hedges are also used by corporations to manage FX translation exposure. In cases where it is not possible to reduce all exposures with a balance sheet-matching strategy, derivatives may be used to hedge remaining exposures.

(A detailed discussion of derivatives is in the section titled Derivative Instruments Used as Risk Management Tools later in this chapter.)

5. Monitoring the Exposure and Evaluating the Strategy

An organization must periodically monitor each financial exposure. The time interval for monitoring exposures is determined on an individual basis and may be shortened or lengthened if volatility of the underlying asset increases or decreases or whenever the risk tolerance of the company changes. An organization must monitor the effectiveness of each strategy it has employed to reduce risk. Evaluation of risk management strategy can be related to the overall risk attitude of an organization.

B. The Risk Profile

The risk profile of a company is the relationship of how the overall value of a company changes as some financial price variables change. A basic risk profile determines the sensitivity of a company to a change in interest rates, FX rates or commodity prices, typically measured by the company's equity value or stock price.

For organizations that are not publicly traded (i.e., privately-held, not-for-profit or governmental), a risk profile determines the impact on cash flows. A risk profile analysis identifies the risks, classifies each risk into clearly defined categories, and quantifies the risks with respect to the probability of occurrence and the impact on a company. Based on this analysis, the effectiveness of the risk reduction measures that are employed can be determined.

1. Value-at-Risk (VAR)

One approach to determining how the value of a company is impacted by changing financial variables is called value-at-risk (VAR). VAR was developed in trading rooms of financial institutions to provide an estimation of the possible losses for an entire trading operation in a one-day period. Specifically designed to handle a wide range of risk factors and to summarize the impacts on the operation into a single measure, the VAR approach determines risk as a function of the probability and monetary impacts of a particular adverse event over a certain period of time.

For instance, VAR is used when a company determines that foreign operations have a five-percent chance of losing over $1 million in the coming month due to exchange-rate fluctuations. Companies utilize historical simulations or scenario analysis, known as Monte Carlo simulations, to determine VAR risk profiles. Numerous treasury-information systems and software providers offer VAR modules and packages.

2. Role of the Treasury Area

As a clearing house for daily financial information, treasury is increasingly becoming a participant in determining the risk profile for a company. The use of derivative instruments for hedging, along with many new external reporting requirements for disclosure (e.g., SOX and FAS 133), have made the role of treasury in financial risk management even more critical. All of these topics are covered later in this chapter.

C. Hedging, Speculation and Arbitrage

A change in the price of an underlying asset can affect the value of a company. Managing the exposure involves hedging, speculation and arbitrage, each of which alters a company's risk profile.

1. Hedging

Hedging is the process by which an organization uses financial instruments to reduce or eliminate risks associated with the uncertainty about the future price of an asset. Hedging is similar to the concept of buying insurance.

2. Speculation

Speculation involves betting on the direction of the market. Speculators are experienced market participants who are willing to assume risks. In speculating that the price of an asset will either decrease or increase, speculators assume either a short position (the assumption that an asset will decrease in value) or a long position (the assumption that an asset will increase in value). Unlike hedgers, speculators are referred to as being "naked" in the sense that there is no underlying asset or exposure to offset; therefore, speculation increases overall financial risk.

3. Arbitrage

Arbitrage is the process by which buying in one market and simultaneously selling in another leads to a riskless profit. A true arbitrage arrangement or transaction has no impact on a company's overall risk profile. Arbitrageurs do not assume any risk; rather, they attempt to profit from market inefficiencies.

It is difficult for the majority of companies to take advantage of arbitrage opportunities. Market inefficiencies that lead to arbitrage opportunities are extremely short-lived and relatively small as measured in basis points. Therefore, only major market participants with large amounts of capital can take advantage of these inefficiencies. For example, the major participants in the FX arbitrage market are large, global banks and third-party dealers.

D. The Benefits of Risk Management

Risk management helps to reduce the variability of a company's future cash flows, which adds value to a company. As a risk management tool, hedging enables a treasurer to smooth uneven cash flows—hence, to forecast with greater confidence. As a result, a company with a lower variability of future cash flows increases value in three ways:

- It is in a better position to assess costs and revenues, which lowers the probability of financial distress.
- It is more attractive to shareholders because shareholders attribute a higher value to companies with less volatile future cash flows.
- It is perceived as being less risky and, therefore, has a borrowing advantage in credit markets.

III. DERIVATIVE INSTRUMENTS USED AS RISK MANAGEMENT TOOLS

A derivative instrument is a financial product that derives its value from an underlying asset. The underlying asset can be a financial instrument, a currency or a commodity. The use of derivates may have an immediate impact on cash that is either favorable or unfavorable. Because derivatives are complex to understand, analyze, apply, account for and report, most treasurers seek the advice of outside experts. There are four basic types of derivative instruments: forwards, futures, swaps and options.

A. Forwards

A forward contract is an agreement between two parties to buy or sell a fixed amount of an asset to be delivered at a future date for an agreed upon price today. The asset involved is referred to as the underlying asset. This underlying asset can be a financial instrument (such as stock index or debt instrument), currency (such as the euro or pound sterling) or a commodity (such as gold or coffee). The future date is referred to as the maturity date of the contract and the price is called the delivery price. A company purchasing a forward contract is one party, while the other party is typically referred to as the counterparty. In forward currency contracts, the counterparty is typically a bank or dealer in the FX markets.

The party who agrees to buy the asset is said to be in a long forward contract (long position) while the counterparty is in a short forward contract (short position). The long position in a forward contract gains value when the underlying asset price rises and loses value when the asset price falls. Conversely, the short position gains value when the underlying asset price falls and loses value when the asset price rises. Exhibit 17.1A and Exhibit 17.1B depict the payoff profiles from a long and a short position, respectively, in a forward contract.

The forward markets are managed and supported by a group of banks, dealers and traders who act as market makers. Market makers are individuals who quote both a bid and an ask price whenever requested to do so. Forward contracts are private contracts between two parties and, hence, are customized to each party's needs. The amount of the underlying asset and the maturity date of the contract are established at the time that the contract is negotiated. Delivery of the underlying asset usually takes place at maturity.

Example of the Use of a Forward Contract: A U.S. importer needs to pay an invoice in GBP 50,000 in 90 days. The importer could purchase a forward contract today for GBP quoted at USD 1.69 per GBP, deliverable in 90 days. At the end of 90 days, the importer would pay USD 84,500 (USD 1.69 x GBP 50,000) and receive GBP 50,000 to pay the invoice. Therefore, no matter what fluctuation occurred in the exchange rate during the next 90-day period, the purchase of the forward contract locks in the exchange rate for GBPs.

EXHIBIT 17.1A — FORWARD CONTRACT – LONG POSITION

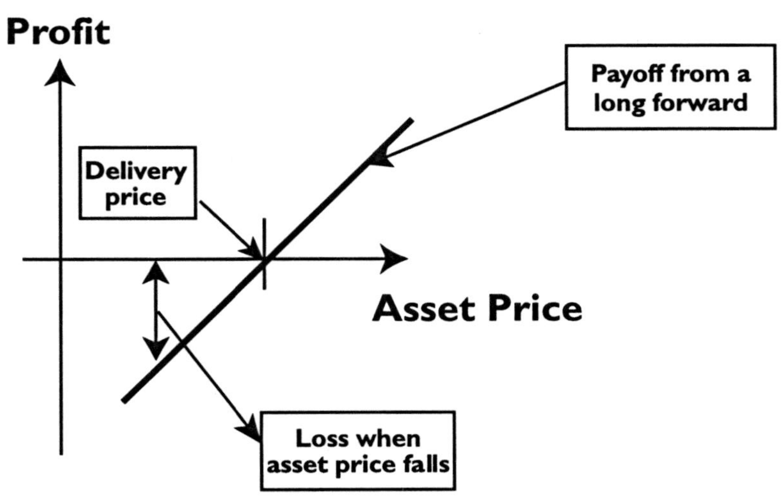

EXHIBIT 17.1B — FORWARD CONTRACT – SHORT POSITION

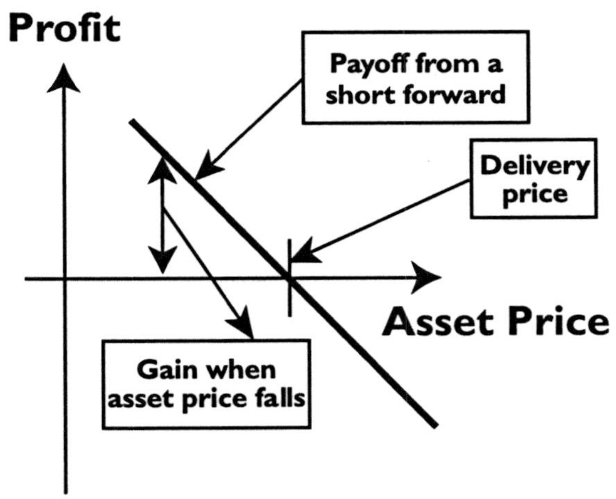

B. Futures

Futures are similar to forwards in intent in the sense that the payoff profile from a long position and a short position in a futures contract looks exactly the same as the payoff from a forward contract (see Exhibit 17.1a and 17.1b). The main difference between futures and forwards is that futures are standardized contracts traded on organized exchanges.

In addition, the counterparty to all future contracts is the exchange itself, which increases liquidity and virtually eliminates counterparty risk. In the U.S., futures contracts are traded on:

- The Chicago Board of Trade (grains, metals, and financials)
- The Chicago Mercantile Exchange (livestock, wood, and meat)
- The International Money Market (foreign currency futures)
- The New York Mercantile Exchange (metals, petroleum, fiber)

Futures contracts are standardized by the exchanges and have a range of delivery dates. Both the size of the contract and the maturity date are not negotiated but rather are set by the exchange. One issue with using futures for hedging purposes is that an underlying position may be difficult to perfectly hedge using a futures contract. For example, the size of a typical euro (EUR) futures contract on the Chicago Mercantile Exchange (CME) is EUR 125,000. If a treasurer has an exposure that is not a multiple of this number, using a futures contract to hedge may either exceed or fall short of the exposure.

Futures trading requires a margin account that is marked-to-market on a daily basis. Marked-to-market means that the hedger's gains or losses on the position are reflected on a daily basis. If the margin account drops below a specified amount (referred to as the maintenance margin), a margin call is issued. The margin call requires the holder of the account to either replenish the account to the initial level or close out the position with the exchange. Therefore, futures contracts are rarely settled by delivery and are usually closed out prior to maturity.

Example of the Use of a Futures Contract: A company buys oil as part of its chemical-production process. The company is uncertain regarding the future price of oil and wishes to prevent exposure due to fluctuations in the commodity price. The company could purchase a futures contract for oil today and hold the contract until oil must be purchased in the commodity market. If the price of oil goes up, causing an increase in the company's raw-material cost, the company could sell the futures contract (the price of which would also rise) for a profit. The profit gained on the futures contract is then used to offset the higher purchase price of the commodity.

For example, assume that a futures contract allows the company to purchase oil for USD 35 a barrel. However, when the company needs to buy oil in the future, the price has risen to USD 40 a barrel. In this scenario, the company could buy the needed oil in the open market, paying USD 40 a barrel. The futures contract that the company holds to buy oil at USD 35 a barrel has a profit of USD 5 per barrel, so the company sells the contract back to the exchange and uses the USD 5-per-barrel profit to offset the purchase price on the spot market, effectively achieving a net price of USD 35 per barrel.

If, instead, the price of oil were to drop to USD 30 per barrel, the company would still buy the needed oil on the open market and close the futures contract at a loss of USD 5 per barrel. In either case, the net cost of oil to the company would still be USD 35 per barrel.

C. Swaps

A swap is an agreement between two parties to exchange (or swap) a set of cash flows at a future point in time. The most common type of swap is an interest rate swap. In this type of swap, party X agrees to pay party Y a stream of cash flows equal to a floating rate of interest on some mutually agreed-upon amount. This amount is referred to as a notional principal because the amount does not exchange hands; instead, only interest payments are exchanged. At the same time, party Y agrees to pay party X a stream of cash flows equal to a fixed rate of interest on the same notional principal at the same future dates. In other words, party X is swapping a fixed-rate loan for a floating-rate loan while party Y is doing exactly the opposite.

Other types of swap arrangements include currency and commodity swaps. Currency swaps are agreements to convert an obligation in one currency to an obligation in another currency. Commodity swaps involve the exchange of a floating price for a commodity at a fixed price.

One of the primary risks in using swaps is that of counterparty risk. The value of the swap depends on the other party fulfilling the obligation to make the agreed-upon payment stream. If the other party (the counterparty) does not make the payments, the first company may still be liable for the original payment stream or cash flow. Using a trusted third party such as a bank or an FX dealer helps to evaluate the credit quality of each party, thereby mitigating counterparty risk.

Example of the Use of a Swap: Two parties, X and Y, wish to borrow USD 20 million for ten years. Assuming that X has a better credit rating than Y, each has been offered the following borrowing rates at the London Interbank Offer Rate (LIBOR):

	Fixed Rate	**Floating Rate**
Party X	10.00%	6-month LIBOR + 0.50%
Party Y	11.00%	6-month LIBOR + 1.00%

Party X wants to borrow at a floating rate while party Y wants to borrow at a fixed rate due to each party's own particular financial strategy. Because party X has a better credit rating than party Y, it pays a lower rate in both fixed and floating markets. Even though party Y pays more in both markets, it pays relatively less in the floating-rate market. So, party X has a comparative borrowing advantage in the fixed-rate market while party Y has a comparative borrowing advantage in the floating-rate market. This provides the basis for an interest rate swap.

An example of an interest rate swap between these two parties would be as follows:

- Party X borrows at a fixed rate of 10 percent and party Y at a floating rate of LIBOR + 1 percent.
- Party X and Y then enter into a swap agreement by which party X agrees to pay for funds at a floating rate and party Y agrees to pay for funds at a fixed rate.
- Parties X and Y negotiate a swap agreement by contacting each other directly or, more commonly, indirectly through a third-party dealer.
- The net advantage to the swap agreement is 50 basis points that, in this example, will be split evenly between the two parties. That is, each will be "better off" by 25 basis points as a result of the swap agreement.

Party X makes payments to a lender at a fixed rate of 10 percent. It makes payments based on LIBOR to party Y and receives payments from party Y at a fixed rate of 9.75 percent to offset the payments to its lender. The rate of 9.75 percent is determined by taking the 10-percent fixed rate and subtracting the 25 basis-point advantage of each party. The net effect of this arrangement for party X is that it ends up paying LIBOR + 0.25 percent, which is 25 basis points less than it would have paid if it had borrowed directly from the floating-rate market.

On the other hand, party Y makes payments to a lender at a fixed rate of LIBOR + 1 percent. Party Y makes payments based on a fixed rate of 9.75 percent to party X and receives payments based on LIBOR from party X. The net effect of this for party Y is that it ends up paying a fixed rate of 10.75 percent, 9.75 percent to party X and 1.00 percent on the LIBOR loan. This is 25 basis points less than what party Y would have paid if it had borrowed directly from the fixed-rate market. See Exhibit 17.2 for an illustration of this transaction.

EXHIBIT 17.2 – A SWAP BETWEEN X AND Y

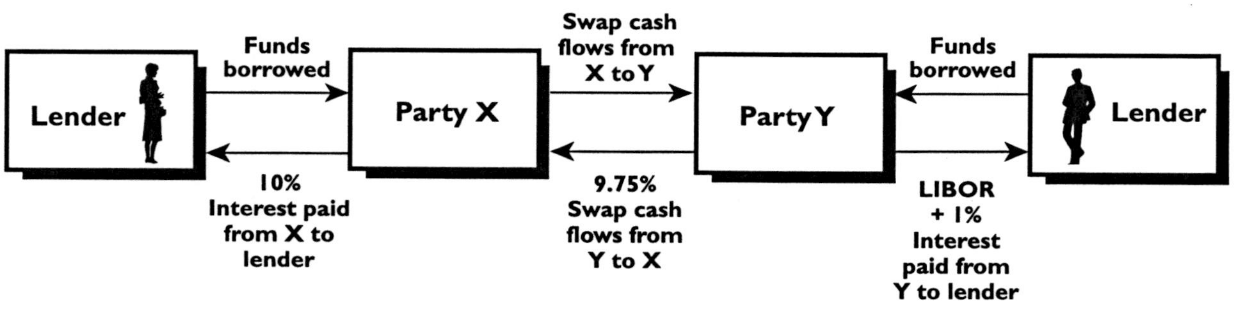

Net Interest Rate Paid by Party X
– 10% fixed paid to Lender
– LIBOR paid to Party Y
+ 9.75% fixed received from Party Y
Net = LIBOR + .25%

Net Interest Rate Paid by Party Y
– LIBOR + 1% paid to Lender
– 9.75% fixed paid to Party X
+ LIBOR received from Party X
Net = 10.75% Fixed

D. Options

An option is a contract between two parties in which the buyer of the contract has the right (but not the obligation) to either buy or sell a fixed amount of some underlying asset at a fixed price on or before a specified date. The party offering the option is called the writer of the option. Options may be either exchange-traded or negotiated with a specific counterparty. Exchange-traded options share many of the same characteristics of futures contracts, with standardized amounts and delivery dates and the exchange serving as the counterparty for all contracts.

A call option gives the owner the right to buy the underlying asset at a fixed price, while a put option gives the owner the right to sell the underlying asset at a fixed price. The fixed price is called the strike price or exercise price of the contract. The specified date is the maturity date or exercise date of the contract. If the contract allows the buyer to exercise (that is, buy or sell the underlying asset) the option only at maturity, the contract is a European option contract. If the contract allows the owner to exercise the option at any time prior to maturity, the contract is an American option contract.

One unique aspect is the premium associated with options. The seller of the option (the writer of the contract) receives a premium from the buyer (the holder of the contract). In return, the writer has the obligation to fulfill the contract (that is, to buy or sell the underlying asset) if the holder chooses to exercise the option. Therefore, American option contracts have a higher premium than European option contracts due to the flexibility in exercising the option prior to maturity.

There are five possible payoff scenarios with options:

- An option is at-the-money if the underlying asset price is equal to the strike price of the option.
- A call option is out-of-the-money if the asset price is less than the strike price of the option.
- A put option is out-of-the-money if the asset price exceeds the strike price of the option.
- A call option is in-the-money if the asset price is greater than the strike price of the option.
- A put option is in-the-money if the asset price is less than the strike price of the option.

In managing financial risk, options allow a hedger to take advantage of favorable market changes. Forwards and futures lock a hedger into a price independent of market changes.

Options are useful for a company that is bidding on a project that may result in financial exposures when the bid is accepted. For example, a U.S. company bids on providing products or services priced in euros to a French company. Due to a large number of other bidders, the company is uncertain whether it will win the bid. However, if the bid is accepted, then the company will have an exposure due to euro-denominated receivables.

A currency option allows the company to lock in a minimum value for euros for a known premium amount. If the company does not win the bid, then the option can be closed out or allowed to expire if it is out-of-the-money. In other words, the company is not obligated to exchange the currencies as with a forward contract, nor is the company exposed to potential losses as with a futures contract. However, the company does forfeit the amount of the premium.

1. Example of the Use of a Call Option

An investor buys a three-month call option on crude oil with a strike or exercise price of USD 40 per barrel and pays a USD 2 premium per barrel. If, at maturity, the market price of crude oil is less than or equal to the strike price of USD 40 per barrel, the investor does not exercise the option because it is cheaper to buy oil at the market price. The investor's loss is limited to USD 2 per barrel, the option premium. When the market price is greater than the strike price (USD 40 per barrel) plus the option premium (USD 2), the investor makes a profit. The payoff, in terms of profit or loss, is illustrated in Exhibit 17.3A.

EXHIBIT 17.3A – PAYOFF FROM A LONG (BUY) CALL

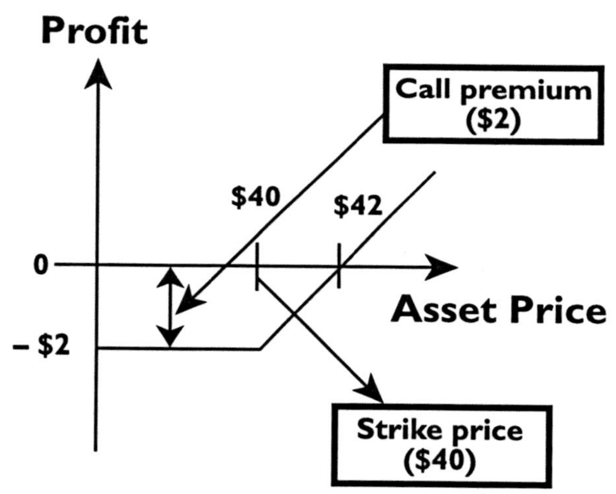

2. Example of the Use of a Put Option

An investor buys a one-month put option on crude oil with a strike or exercise price of USD 35 per barrel and pays a USD 1 premium per barrel.

If, at maturity, the market price of crude oil is greater than or equal to the strike price of USD 35 per barrel, the investor does not exercise the option because the investor will receive more by selling oil at the market price. The investor has a loss of only USD 1 per barrel, the option premium.

If, at maturity, the market price of crude oil is less than the strike price, the investor exercises the option. When the market price is less than the strike price (USD 35 per barrel) minus the option premium (USD 1 per barrel), the investor makes a profit. The payoff, in terms of profit or loss, is illustrated in Exhibit 17.3B.

EXHIBIT 17.3B – PAYOFF FROM A LONG (BUY) PUT

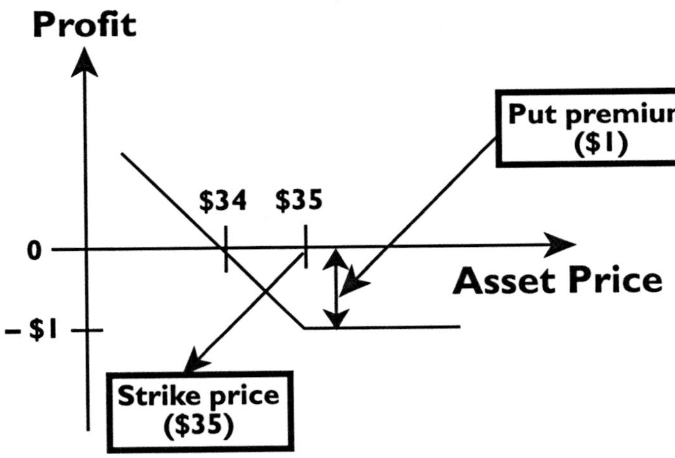

The purchaser of an option contract does not typically take or make delivery of the underlying asset. The actual commodity transaction occurs in the spot market. An option contract is used to offset any losses if the price is higher (call option) or lower (put option) than expected. Essentially, the writer of a call option places a ceiling on the price at which a company is willing to buy crude oil. Conversely, the writer of a put option has placed a floor on the price at which a company is willing to sell crude oil.

IV. INTEREST RATE EXPOSURE

Many organizations face financial risks due to exposure from interest rate changes. The exposure arises from the inherent nature of operations or from financing activities.

Organizations with variable interest rate investments face the possibility of lower earnings when interest rates fall. Organizations with debt tied to variable interest rates face higher borrowing costs when interest rates rise.

Different Types of Interest Rate Derivatives: Four commonly used instruments for interest rate risk management include interest rate swaps, interest rate futures, interest rate options and a forward rate agreement.

- **Interest Rate Swaps**
  The most common type of interest rate swap is the exchange of a fixed interest rate cash flow for a floating interest rate cash flow, with both interest rates in the same currency. This is often referred to as a "vanilla" swap. If both interest rates are floating, then the exchange of cash flows is called a basis-rate swap. An example of a basis-rate swap is the exchange of interest payments based on LIBOR for interest payments based on the prime rate.

- **Interest Rate Futures**
  Interest rate futures are futures contracts on an underlying asset whose price is solely dependent on the level of interest rates. The most popular short-term interest rate contracts are the T-Bill, the Eurodollar contracts traded on the CME and bank certificates of deposit (CD's). In a T-Bill futures contract, the underlying asset is the 90-day T-Bill rate. In a Eurodollar futures contract, the underlying asset is the interest earned on a Eurodollar deposit at the 3-month LIBOR rate. The most actively traded long-term interest rate contracts are the 5-year and 10-year U.S. T-Notes and the 30-year U.S. T-Bonds.

- **Interest Rate Options**
  Interest rate options are options in which the payoff depends on the level of interest rates. There are three basic types of interest rate options: caps, floors and collars.

  - **Interest Rate Cap:** Caps ensure that the borrower of a floating rate loan receives a ceiling rate if interest rates rise above a specified level. This level is known as the cap rate. If rates fall, the borrower is not obligated to exercise the option and can still enjoy the benefits of lower borrowing costs. The price of this "insurance" is the premium paid for the cap.

  - **Interest Rate Floor:** Floors ensure that the owner of a floating rate asset receives a floor rate if interest rates fall below a specified level. If rates fall, the floating rate asset is protected by the put option on interest rates. If interest rates rise, the company can still benefit because it is not obligated to exercise the option. The cost of this "insurance" is the premium paid for the interest rate floor.

- **Interest Rate Collar:** A combination of an interest rate cap and an interest rate floor is called an interest rate collar. A company that buys a cap and sells a floor is effectively locking in a range for borrowing costs. The cap establishes a maximum borrowing rate, thereby protecting the company against higher interest rates while the floor sets a minimum borrowing rate. A collar has no costs when the income received from selling the floor matches the premium paid for the cap. Costless collars are popular hedging vehicles providing some interest rate protection at no cost.

  Besides caps, floors and collars there are several other types of interest rate options. One is an option on an interest rate swap, called a swaption. With a swaption, the buyer of the option has the right to enter into an interest rate swap at a future date.

- **Forward Rate Agreement (FRA)**
  A forward rate agreement (FRA) is a forward contract on interest rates in which two parties agree that a certain interest rate will apply to a certain principal during a specified future period of time. The notional principal amounts are agreed upon but never exchanged. If, at settlement, the actual rate is different from the rate agreed upon in the contract, then one party pays the other a cash amount equal to the difference. The majority of FRAs are based on Eurodollar rates, although other rates are available.

V. FX RATE EXPOSURE

While this section covers FX exposures and derivatives from the perspective of a corporation, the types of exposure and the hedging methods are relevant to any organization that deals in foreign currency.

A. Types of FX Exposures

Companies dealing in foreign currencies face three kinds of exposure: transaction, translation and economic. (For a more detailed discussion of other types of exposure due to foreign operations, see Chapter 15, Global Treasury Environment.)

1. Transaction Exposure

If the receivables or payables on a company's balance sheet are affected by changes in FX rates, then the company has a transaction exposure. Transaction exposure occurs when the receivables and payables are in different currencies. In the case of receivables, adjusting the price of goods and services does not necessarily eliminate transaction exposure.

In the case of a U.S. exporter who sells merchandise to a French buyer agreeing to accept payment in euro three months from now, the exporter records the transaction as an accounts receivable. However, the exporter is exposed to a possible loss in value if the euro depreciates relative to the U.S. dollar in three months.

2. Translation Exposure

Companies with foreign subsidiaries or operations are susceptible to translation exposure. Translation exposure is created when a foreign subsidiary's financial statements are converted—hence, "translated"—into a parent company's home currency as part of the processes of consolidating a company's financial statements. In the U.S., this exposure must be reported on a quarterly basis in accordance with FAS 52.

Using financial instruments to hedge this type of risk is difficult due to the large amounts of funds typically involved. However, using a balance sheet hedge, a company can effectively offset foreign-asset exposures by borrowing funds to finance the assets in the same country and currency. This approach hedges the balance sheet and reduces the net exposure of the parent company.

3. Economic Exposure

Economic exposure is the long-term effect of changes in exchange rates on the present value of future cash flows to a company. Multinational corporations that do business in several different currencies are, in the long run, always subject to fluctuations in cash flows because of exchange-rate changes. Even purely domestic companies are susceptible to economic exposure whenever there is foreign competition within the local market.

For example, a company that purchases supplies locally and sells products locally is clearly not affected by transaction exposure. However, if the local currency appreciates against a competitor's, then the company's earnings in the long run may be impacted when demand shifts towards a less costly foreign competitor's product.

B. Currency Derivatives Used to Hedge FX Exposure

Once a company has identified and quantified exposures to exchange rate changes, it must decide whether or not to hedge each exposure. There are several instruments that a company can use to manage FX-rate risk. The most common type of FX exposure hedged through the use of currency derivatives is transaction exposure.

1. Currency or FX Forwards

A currency or FX forward is a commitment to buy or sell a specified amount of foreign currency on a future date at an exchange rate agreed upon today. FX forwards are traded in major currencies with standard maturities of 1, 2, 3, 6, 9 and 12 months. Because forwards are credit instruments that relate to a company's ability to deliver at the end of the contract, the dealers or counterparties in FX forwards are usually banks. As a result, the documentation concerning FX forwards usually involves credit related risk issues.

2. Currency Futures

Currency futures contracts are similar to currency forwards except that futures are traded on an exchange and are standardized in terms of amount and maturity date. Currency futures are available for only a relatively few major currencies such as the U.S. dollar, the euro and the yen.

3. Currency Swaps

A currency swap involves the exchange of a floating rate cash flow denominated in one currency with a fixed rate cash flow denominated in another currency, as well as an exchange of principal.

4. Currency Options

A currency option gives the buyer the right to buy (call option) or sell (put option) a fixed amount of a foreign currency at a fixed exchange rate (strike price) on or before a specific future date. A foreign-currency put option establishes a floor value (in terms of the domestic currency) for a foreign currency. The floor value is the exercise price less the premium on a put option. Similarly, a foreign-currency call option sets a ceiling cost (in terms of the domestic currency) for a foreign currency. The ceiling cost is the strike price plus the premium paid for the call.

A U.S. importer with an accounts payable due in three months in British pound sterling can ensure a maximum cost for the pounds by going long (buying a call option) on the pound. If, at the time of payment, the spot market price of the pound is less than the strike price of the call option, the importer does not exercise the option and loses only the premium. The net cost of the pounds to the importer is the spot price of the pound plus the option premium. The option acts as insurance against the spot price of the pound rising above a specific level. For this insurance, the importer pays a premium, which is the option price.

VI. COMMODITY PRICE EXPOSURE

Markets exist for several commodities that are used by organizations in either production or operations processes. The most common commodities markets are in the areas of agricultural and meat products, oil and gas, minerals and metals. Examples of commodity price exposure include two types: price exposure and delivery exposure. Different commodity derivatives are used to manage these exposures.

The primary commodity exposure faced by organizations is the potential for changes in the price of a commodity. If an organization utilizes commodities in the production process, rising prices create an exposure for the organization. Conversely, if an organization sells the product, then falling prices create an exposure.

For certain organizations that are heavy users of energy products (e.g., oil, gas, coal), a regular supply of the commodity is crucial. In addition to price exposure, these organizations may also face delivery exposure. Entering into a long-term agreement with an energy producer helps to mitigate this exposure.

Derivative Instruments Used to Hedge Commodity Exposure: As with interest rate risk and FX risk, commodity price risk can also be managed using forwards, futures, swaps and options or even combinations. The following offer two examples. In an oil swap, the parties would agree on a notional principal expressed in barrels of oil (not dollars). Similar to currency or interest rate swaps, the parties make regular settlements on the basis of fixed and floating oil prices. The floating price used in an oil swap is usually the average price of oil over a specified period. To reduce the uncertainty associated with the change in a commodity price, an organization may decide to use a costless collar (a combination of a cap and a floor).

VII. ACCOUNTING AND TAX ISSUES

A. Accounting Issues

Due to the nature of the instruments used in financial risk management, there are special accounting issues to consider. Many of these issues are addressed by the Financial Accounting Standards Board (FASB). Some of the critical FASB pronouncements related to financial risk management are discussed in this section.

1. Financial Instruments Disclosure

A summary of the FAS standards related to financial instruments disclosure is provided in Exhibit 17.4.

EXHIBIT 17.4 SUMMARY OF FAS STANDARDS RELATED TO FINANCIAL INSTRUMENTS

Standard	Description
FAS 105	Disclosure of information about the use of instruments with balance sheet risk and instruments with a concentration of credit risk
FAS 107	Disclosure of fair market value of financial instruments
FAS 114	Accounting by creditors for impairment of a loan
FAS 115	Accounting for certain investments in debt and equity securities
FAS 133	Accounting for derivative instruments and hedging activities
FAS 138	Amendment to FAS 133

Full descriptions and details on FASB statements can be obtained on the Web site: *www.fasb.org/st/*

The pronouncements concerning disclosure have resulted in FAS 105 and FAS 107:

FAS 105 deals with the disclosure and use of off-balance-sheet instruments.

FAS 107 concerns the disclosure of a financial instrument's fair market value.

Additional requirements concerning disclosure are provided in FAS 114, FAS 115, and FAS 133 (Accounting for Derivative Instruments and Hedging Activities).

FAS 133 was amended by FAS 138, which addressed some implementation concerns relative to common, current hedging approaches. FAS 133 and related amendments have significant impact for financial risk management. Some of the key considerations in FAS 133 are as follows:

- The fundamental difference between FAS 133 and prior practice is that FAS 133 does not recognize the principal of off-balance-sheet deferral accounting. FAS 133 requires that all derivatives be marked-to-market and placed on the balance sheet.
- FAS 133 recognizes three types of hedges:
  (1) **Fair value hedges:** hedges of exposures to the changes in value of a recognized asset or liability or an unrecognized firm commitment
  (2) **Cash flow hedges:** hedges of a forecasted transaction, or the variability in the cash flow of a recognized asset or liability
  (3) **Net investment hedges:** hedges of the net investment in a foreign operation
- The key issue for treasury is the impact of FAS 133 on reporting and managing intracompany risk exposure. For a company with centralized treasury and risk management operations, FAS 133 allows the company to hedge intracompany risk, but only if an original risk at the operating-unit level can be identified. Also, a formal agreement between the operating unit and the centralized entity must be in place to execute the hedge.
- The process of preparing for the adoption of FAS 133 and related amendments is a difficult and complex process requiring input and coordination from many areas of a company, including accounting, treasury, risk management, legal, investments and information systems. Outside advisors can also assist with implementation.

2. Other Accounting Issues

Hedge accounting is an accounting technique that is applied to the components of a hedge so that the fair value of the hedged asset and the hedging vehicle are included in earnings for the same period. As a result of the tremendous growth in alternative hedging instruments, no standard accounting guidelines have been established for financial derivatives.

Although hedge accounting has been addressed in FAS 80 (Accounting for Futures Contracts) and FAS 52 (Foreign-Currency Translation), these pronouncements contain certain conceptual inconsistencies. FAS 52 limits hedge accounting for currency transactions to future transactions that are firmly committed. FAS 80 extends hedge accounting to anticipated future transactions that are not firmly committed, provided that certain criteria are met.

B. Tax Issues Related to Hedging

Because the U.S. tax system differentiates between ordinary income and capital gains, the main issue for tax treatment is whether the gains or losses on a hedge should be treated as ordinary gains/losses or capital gains/losses.

As of October 1993, the Internal Revenue Service's Temporary Regulations on Hedging Transactions considers the gains or losses on most business hedges to be ordinary gains/losses. If the loss on the hedge is treated as a capital loss, then the company can deduct the loss only to the extent that it offsets other capital gains in the business. If the gains are not sufficient, then the loss on the hedge cannot be deducted against income.

Due to the complex nature of tax issues and their potential negative impact if they are misinterpreted, most companies seek outside tax and legal advice from firms specializing in these areas.

Test Your Understanding

These chapter questions are provided to test your understanding of the information in the text. They are neither examples of CTP examination questions nor are they in the examination format.

Answers are on pages 618–620.

1. What is financial risk management and why is it important for treasury managers?

2. What are the five steps involved in the risk management process?

3. What is a risk profile and how is it used?

4. Discuss the concepts of hedging, speculation and arbitrage.

5. What is a forward contract?

6. Discuss a futures contract and how it is similar to or different from a forward contract.

7. What is an option?

8. Describe the different types of option contracts.

9. What are caps, collars and floors and how are they used?

10. What is transaction exposure? Provide an example.

11. What are currency options and how are they used?

12. What is hedge accounting and how has it been addressed by the FASB?

Association for
Financial Professionals®

CHAPTER 18
Enterprise Risk Management

I. INTRODUCTION

Companies and financial institutions are moving into the area of enterprise risk management (ERM) in order to better understand credit, price, investment, currency, interest rate and other financial risks. Such risks impact the entire organization's departments, business units, operating or legal entities in a comprehensive manner. Traditionally, risks have been accounted by a single department, subsidiary, division or other organizational segment. With a 360-degree look at all of the risks across the entire enterprise, a company can now assess the full scope of each risk. (For example, the credit risk, based on credit terms extended to a single customer by various independent areas of the company.)

Operational risk can stem from both internal and external sources, so it is one of the key components of risk for many organizations. Regardless of how well operational risk is managed, unforeseen events always occur. The primary means for managing and controlling the impact of these events is through prevention, contingency planning, disaster recovery or business continuity planning, and insurance. This chapter covers these primary areas of operational risk management.

II. OPERATIONAL RISK MANAGEMENT

Operational risk is generally defined as the risk of direct and indirect losses resulting from external events that impact an organization's operations or inadequate and failed internal processes, people and systems. The internal sources of operational risk are usually related to either the lack or failure of controls on people, processes or technology. External events can range from localized events such as momentary communications failures to global events such as terrorism. As treasury relies more and more on complex technology combined with legacy manual processes to generate, store and use information, the potential for operational risk resulting from the use of technology also increases.

Operational risk can be a significant cause of financial loss. Most financial disasters are attributed to a combination of exposure to market risk or credit risk, along with some failure of controls. In many operational risk disasters, a single individual has been responsible for staggering losses, which could have been prevented by appropriate oversight and controls. The problem is often the lack of management involved in establishing financial controls and monitoring the individuals who use financial tools.

A. Internal Risks

Internal risks are risks that involve an organization's employees, processes or technology.

1. Employee Risk

A significant source of internal operational risk is related to employees. In some cases, this risk stems from defalcation, the risk of intentional employee fraud. However, the more significant source of internal risk stems from unintentional actions by employees. Examples include employee errors in data entry or reentry as well as transposition or deletion of numbers. Other potential sources of internal risk are the lack of knowledge or skills and the loss of key personnel. Finally, sources of internal operational risk may be a function of the employer's liability relative to employment law and health and safety regulations.

2. Process Risk

Many organizations experience substantial risk related to the processes employed in day-to-day business operations. One source of process risk is from accounting or financial reporting errors, a potentially serious problem given the penalties introduced under Sarbanes-Oxley (See Chapter 19, Corporate Governance and Ethics). Organizations with high levels of manual processes have significant risks for potential errors in the data entry. The products and services offered by an organization may also contribute to operational risk. For instance, there are risks associated with selling products or services that are unsuitable for the intended use. This often occurs when a salesperson makes false claims of performance that the product or service was not designed to meet.

A related operational risk involves whether an organization can meet the terms of contracts with customers and suppliers.

The final risk related to the production and delivery process is capacity error. Excess capacity increases overhead and fixed costs, which increases the general business and operational risks of an organization. Conversely, insufficient capacity can lead to large backlogs, lost orders, increased errors or unintended interruptions in both the manufacturing and the delivery process due to overtime or extra shifts.

Aside from the normal risk of non-payment for goods or services, there can also be errors in the actual settlement and payment process of financial transactions. On an internal basis, inbound payments may be posted to the wrong account or not properly recorded. Outbound payments may also be misdirected, either unintentionally or as a result of employee fraud. Finally, another risk related to the payment settlement process is valuation risk, which is an issue for transactions denominated in a foreign currency.

(A discussion of foreign exchange risk management is in Chapter 17, Financial Risk Management.)

3. Technology Risk

As the treasury area of an organization relies increasingly on technology, the operational risk related to the use of technology increases:

- There is risk associated with the choice of a particular technological platform or vendor—issues such as after-sale installation and support or even the risk that a vendor may no longer be in business.
- There is also risk associated with the potential failure of vendor-acquired hardware, software and/or communications devices.
- There are issues involving capability, capacity and compatibility.

Another issue for technology is possible security breaches, either from internal sources or from external hackers. For example, a treasury information system vendor may offer a product that is ideal for an organization but the stability and long-run viability of the vendor must be considered. It is not uncommon for an organization to purchase a suboptimal software product from a known provider rather than a superior product from a new and untested provider.

Finally, technology risk may involve the extensive use of computer-based spreadsheets in many parts of an organization's day-to-day operations. While spreadsheets can be extremely useful for many business functions and data management, there are some issues when they are used for "mission-critical" applications that require transactional and information processing. Complex spreadsheet models mixed with formula protection are often difficult to monitor and audit with respect to reliability and may provide an avenue for potential employee fraud.

Though spreadsheets may be appropriate for use in some treasury functions if proper controls are in place, critical treasury functions, especially those related to the payment/settlement process, should be performed on certified treasury systems rather than spreadsheets.

By linking systems, the benefits of straight-through-processing can be achieved, which reduces internal risks and improves efficiencies. When conducting a formal cost/benefit analysis as part of the decision to select a treasury management system it is important to include these considerations.

B. External Risks

There are also numerous external sources of operational risk. These are generally categorized as financial institution, legal/regulatory, supplier, external theft/fraud, physical security, natural disaster and terrorism.

1. Financial Institution Risk

Several key risks are associated with the use of financial institutions. The first is the potential failure of the institution and resulting impact on the company (loss of balances, disrupted services, etc.). Other risks are related to the potential operational failure on the part of the financial institution in performing daily transactions processing or failures in communications between the company and the financial institution.

2. Legal/Regulatory Risk

Given the increasingly litigious environment of business, one of the most significant external operational risks are potential lawsuits or other legal actions. In some cases, insurance may be used to mitigate this risk. Operational risk also stems from the many regulations enforced by federal state and local regulatory agencies that organizations must comply with throughout operations. The recent passage of the USA Patriot Act (see Chapter 3, Financial Environment) has added significant regulatory and compliance overhead for organizations with large numbers of financial transactions, especially those transactions that may be suspected of money laundering. For any organization with operations in foreign countries, the political risk (see Chapter 15, Global Treasury Environment) of expropriation or other loss of foreign asset value is also a significant consideration. Finally, tax risk must be assessed, especially for multinational organizations that deal with a wide variety of tax codes and regulations.

3. Supplier Risk

Risk related to an organization's suppliers and outsourcing arrangements also entails significant operational risks. The more critical the supplier or commodity is in the production process, the more risk an organization faces if the supplier either fails to deliver according to plan or provides substandard products and services that result in customer dissatisfaction. These risks are even more important in today's environment of shortened supply chains and just-in-time inventory management. Supplier failures or shortages quickly impact a company's customers, especially if the process outsourced is critical to day-to-day operations of an organization. Also, the risk of a merger or an acquisition of a particular supplier may result in disruptions in critical supplies or services. The trend toward outsourcing treasury functions has significantly increased this aspect of operational risk.

4. External Theft/Fraud

Traditionally, the primary source of risk in the area of external theft or fraud has been related to the payment process, specifically involving false invoices or check fraud. An accounts payable environment with appropriate controls helps to reduce fraud from false invoices and bank services, such as positive pay, can reduce the risk from check fraud (see Chapter 7, Working Capital Tools).

The trend toward replacing paper-based payments with electronic payments also helps to reduce potential check fraud. There may also be potential risk from malfeasance, the collusion between external criminals and internal employees. Retail environments routinely process large amounts of cash, and organizations dealing with large amounts of cash collections or disbursements run the risk of robbery or theft of those cash balances. The use of armored car services and automated store safes helps to reduce the risk to both the organization and the employees.

5. Physical and Electronic Security

Many organizations also require physical security for premises and employees. This security helps to prevent physical or electronic access to critical information (e.g., identity theft) and ensures the safety of employees. Security measures may also include biometric devices such as handprints, thumbprints and retinal scanning for physical access to facilities or key equipment. Physical security is especially important for industries such as financial institutions, utilities and defense contractors.

6. Natural Disaster

Natural disasters leave organizations open to possible operational risk. These events could range from a temporary power outage to a major earthquake or hurricane. Every organization should have a contingency business resumption plan in place to manage and recover from these events.

7. Terrorism

Terrorism has become a significant threat to the operations of many organizations. Many disaster recovery plans now specifically include recovery from terrorist events in addition to natural disasters. Most organizations try to manage exposure to terrorist activities by increasing physical security on both premises and employees.

C. Fundamental Factors for Operational Risk Management Strategy

The three critical factors in determining a risk management strategy for an organization are: (1) culture, (2) procedures and (3) technology. The importance of each of these varies, depending upon the needs of an organization.

1. Importance of Organizational Culture

Organizational culture plays an important role in managing overall operational risk. Employees who observe improper management behavior or Board members who believe that senior management is not acting in the best interests of shareholders must be free to report these activities without incurring significant personal or career risk. Both federal and state "whistleblower" laws have been enacted to protect employees who report unethical and illegal activities. As will be discussed in more detail in Chapter 19, Corporate Governance and Ethics, a knowledgeable and independent Board of Directors is one of the best protections against managerial malfeasance.

Most risk management experts agree that the best approach is to develop a culture that promotes individual responsibility and is supportive of educated risk taking:

- One of the key characteristics of such a culture is a questioning approach to decision making that encourages anyone to ask legitimate questions or express genuine concerns related to the management of the organization.
- Another important characteristic is the willingness on the part of senior management to admit to a lack of sufficient information where applicable. Often, key decisions need to be made without complete information but decision makers must be aware of the information gaps.
- Finally, the culture must provide all employees with written policies detailing ethical behavior at every level of the organization.

2. Importance of Procedures

As is outlined in more detail in Chapter 19, Corporate Governance and Ethics, procedures for Boards of Directors are especially important for reducing overall operating risk. One example is the restrictions on the number of Board members and key executives who are permitted to travel together in case of an accident. It is also important to address conflicts of interest, clarify personal responsibility, and facilitate the discussion and resolution of difficult or contentious issues. Lines of reporting should be clear, explicit and known to all levels of the organization. The importance of procedures is especially critical to any organization involved in trading activities because of the essential need to monitor and control trading activities relative to both authority and risk limits. Such procedures must be clearly outlined in trading policies and guidelines, as well as subject to regular review.

III. DISASTER RECOVERY AND BUSINESS CONTINUITY[1]

Disaster recovery refers to the restoration of systems and communications after an outage. Business continuity refers to the actions taken with regard to crisis management, alternative operating procedures and communications to staff and customers. Disaster avoidance and recovery equates to revenue preservation and continuation. Despite this, many organizations do not have robust disaster recovery and business continuity plans in place. As a result, these organizations are not able to adequately cope with major incidents that disrupt business.

When organizations implement contingency plans, the focus is often on the business supply chain, ensuring that supplier linkages and production resources are restored and customer service is maintained. While these are important factors, the business supply chain functions only as long as the related cash and information flows of the organization also continue.

The financial supply chain (from purchase to pay and order to receive) is crucial to the financial viability and sustainability following a disaster. Clearly, the treasury area, through working capital management and ensuring adequate sources of liquidity, has a pivotal role in managing the organization's financial supply chain. In conjunction with this role is the responsibility of ensuring that treasury is adequately prepared to respond to a disaster.

The key parties or resources involved in the financial chain are generally classified as either internal resources or external counterparties:

- Internal resources include the treasury staff, computer systems, policies, procedures, processes (both automated and non-automated) and office facilities.
- The external financial counterparties include financial institutions, market- information providers and financial markets.

The infrastructure linking the two must also be considered and should include both internal and external networks such as computers, servers, telecommunications, utilities and vendor support services. An effective disaster recovery program encompasses each of these areas. The specific programs depend upon an organization's business, treasury structure and the specific risks the organization faces.

A. Developing an Effective Treasury Disaster Recovery Plan

In developing an effective treasury disaster recovery program, the key questions to consider are:

- What are the mission-critical functions and activities within the treasury area?
- What are the risks? In other words, what is the worst-case scenario and what would the impact be on the organization if such an event occurred?

An organization should also consider the effectiveness of any current priority contingency measures along with corrective actions that need to be taken.

1. Identify Mission-Critical Functions

An activity or function is mission-critical when an interruption creates significant disruptions in the organization's cash flow/liquidity. Such disruptions have serious repercussions on an organization's ability to continue normal operations and, ultimately, may make it difficult for the company to remain in business. Within the treasury area, mission-critical functions tend to be concentrated in treasury operations, including such time-critical daily tasks as accounts receivable and collection, cash concentration, payroll, accounts payable, interest, bondholder and dividend payments, disbursement funding and the calculation of the daily cash position.

(A more detailed discussion of this topic is in Chapter 9, Cash Positioning.)

Treasury is increasingly reliant on technology. This includes all forms of automation from treasury workstations, electronic bank access systems and spreadsheet programs to e-mail systems. Technology also encompasses an organization's treasury portal, intranet, networks that contain treasury data and programs and the Internet service provider. In an increasingly interconnected world, the potential hazards continue to multiply to include external security threats, such as hackers, as well as threats from inside the organization, such as employee fraud. Despite the financial exposures involved, treasury does not always receive the appropriate degree of attention from an organization's information technology resources. Reviewing the treasury area as part of an overall operational risk assessment is highly recommended.

2. Assess Risks

The next step in building a disaster recovery plan is assessing risk. When conducting a risk assessment, the first question to ask is: What are the treasury area's organizational resources and infrastructure (including people, systems, office facilities and connections), as well as the potential hazards that may result?

The next step is to determine what would happen if the potential hazards actually occurred (for example, if a hacker brings down the treasury system or the organization experiences a computer virus or worm). In calculating the potential losses to an organization, it is important to consider the possibility of individual acts, as well as multiple events caused by a cascading effect. This type of assessment should also consider the impacts on both disaster recovery and business continuity.

Assume, for example, that an organization's treasury information system crashes and, as a result, mission-critical functions cannot be performed (e.g., checking balances, collecting customer receipts, funding disbursement accounts, transferring funds between accounts or between banks, etc.). The impact on the organization may:

- Include direct losses (such as interest charges due to borrowing because cash is inaccessible)
- Extend to a more widespread impact (for example, the organization may be forced to use alternate suppliers)
- Include serious consequential damages such as being out of compliance with financial covenants in loan agreements or the loss of reputation or confidence on the part of customers and suppliers

In gauging risk levels, it is important to assess both the likelihood that something could go wrong and the consequences. Preparing various "what if" scenarios with prioritized steps and procedures is a highly effective method for developing a risk assessment. These scenarios should factor in the duration of the event and establish alternative processes for business continuity.

3. Evaluate Contingency Measures

Once the risks have been assessed, an organization is ready to evaluate the measures already in place to mitigate risks and to provide a contingency in the event of a disaster. However, even in the absence of a formal, documented disaster recovery plan, an organization is likely to have a number of initiatives in place (for example, sending systems backup tapes to a central site or keeping copies of contact lists, operating procedures and secure passwords at an alternate location). The goal is to understand and catalog the measures that are currently in place and to evaluate the effectiveness of the measures considering the mission-critical treasury functions and current risk levels.

4. Prioritize Corrective Action

After a thorough assessment, an organization has identified issues that need to be addressed. To prioritize an action plan for the issues, costs and benefits must be assessed with a judicious mix of qualitative and quantitative analyses. Plotting recovery initiatives on a matrix (such as the one in Exhibit 18-1) helps in the process of prioritization. In actual use, the matrix should have one axis that measures the cost of implementation and another that measures the benefits in terms of risk mitigation. Items plotted in the high-risk mitigation benefit (falling on the top right) call for urgent action. Conversely, items with low-risk mitigation benefit (falling on the bottom left) may merit no more than periodic monitoring.

EXHIBIT 18-1 SAMPLE MATRIX FOR PRIORITIZING CORRECTIVE ACTION

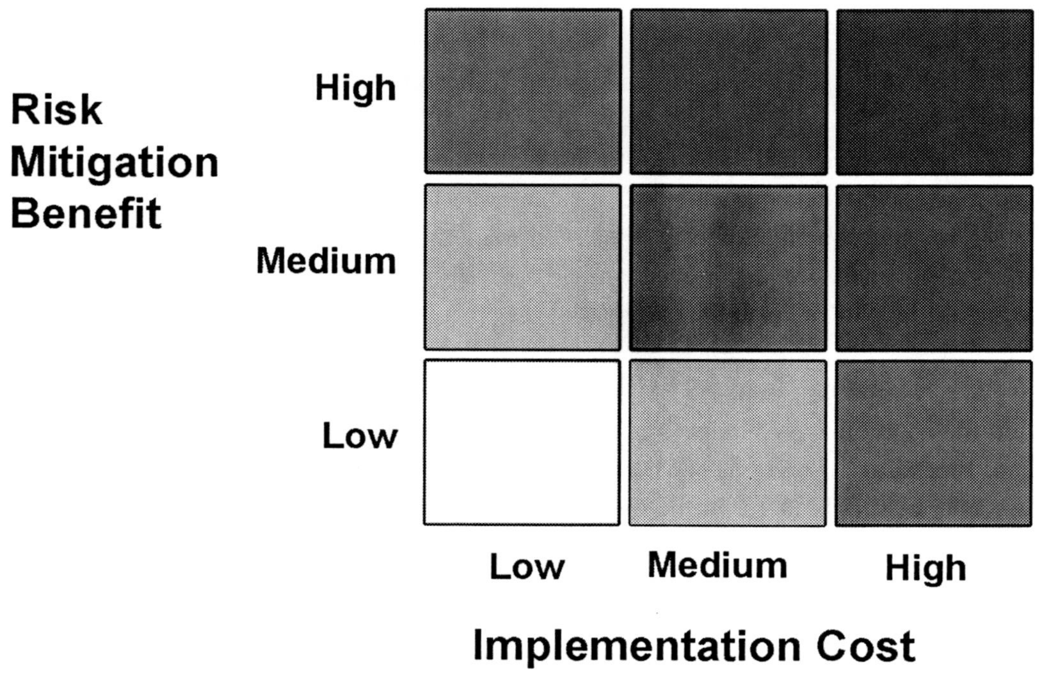

B. Implementing a Disaster Recovery Plan

The final step is to develop a process for implementing the disaster recovery plan. The plan should include detailed information regarding each of the four steps/processes and should include plans for staff training and testing. Once finalized and formally approved, the disaster recovery plan must be distributed to the entire treasury staff so that all parties are aware of their responsibilities and are prepared to take appropriate actions.

C. Making the Plan Work

Disaster recovery and business continuity planning should not be treated as a one-time initiative but rather as an ongoing program with continual review and improvement. This includes:

- Establishing a plan of action for implementing each measure
- Benchmarking the progress on a regular basis
- Periodically testing the disaster plan
- Reviewing the disaster recovery plan annually so that it remains up to date

IV. INSURANCE

One of the traditional approaches to managing and controlling risk is the use of insurance. While enterprise risk management typically seeks to reduce the possibility of losses, insurance is usually designed to compensate for losses, especially accidental losses, after they occur. Accidental losses, even if all are covered by insurance, have broad implications for the treasury area. Management usually finds that accidents tend to reduce the firm's profitability, increase liquidity requirements and impair financial security.

A. Types of Losses

Effective risk management helps to control or prevent losses and adequate insurance helps to finance an organization's recovery when a loss occurs. Events resulting in a major loss generally disrupt an organization's operating and financial plans. Losses may include:

- Property loss (from both internal and external theft)
- Business interruption or net-income loss
- Surety or breach of contract loss (such as a contractor's failure to perform)
- Liability loss (including lawsuits from injured customers)
- Personnel loss (involving the loss of the president or other "key persons")
- Workers' compensation

Even if insurance eventually pays to repair or replace property, damage lowers the projected rate of return on the impaired assets. Any substantial interruption of business is likely to lower profits, because, although an organization has business interruption insurance, cash inflows are slowed, putting pressure on the company's ability to meet debt service obligations.

Not all losses are covered with insurance (such as the loss of market share). In addition, liability losses can drain an organization's cash through payment of uninsured claims, legal defense costs or expenditures in negotiating with the insurers involved. Similarly, contractors' failure to complete projects deprive an organization of anticipated revenues and may impede growth, as can the death, disability or resignation of a valuable, difficult-to-replace employee.

The mere possibility of accidents has a second important implication for any organization's treasury management, beyond the economic losses from accidents that actually occur. Safeguarding against possible accidents imposes added costs (such as outlays to prevent accidents or efforts to reduce the severity of these events) and may include expenditures for fire detection and suppression ("sprinkler") systems, storage of critical records and ongoing safety training.

Many organizations seek to limit these risks by attaining Highly Protected Risk (HPR) status for buildings and plants. This rating entails the installation of appropriate sprinklers, fire gear and other safety equipment, yet provides the organization with a preferred rating status for fire and hazard insurance, resulting in significantly lower insurance premiums. Another major cost in the anticipation and prevention of accidents is risk financing. This involves ensuring the availability of funds either through insurance or the ability to obtain funds from other sources.

In addition to loss prevention and risk financing costs, the possibility of accidental losses imposes administrative costs on an organization. Management must decide where and how to apply loss prevention, select the proper types and amounts of insurance, and collect the insurance reimbursement when a covered loss occurs.

The total of all costs from both actual and potential losses constitutes an organization's cost of risk from losses. The total cost is often difficult to estimate; however, there are experts to assist the treasurers with this process. Experts ideally try to identify the break-even point between the costs of insurance and the costs of uninsured losses for an organization.

B. Responsibilities of the Treasury Area in Risk Management

The treasury area often has diverse but important responsibilities related to the cost of risk. The primary decision is to identify the potential losses for which the organization purchases insurance and those that the organization should either pay for or self-insure. (See the section titled "Risk Retention" later in this chapter for a detailed discussion of self-insurance.) Ultimately, the overall intent is to control the cost of risks associated with a set of loss exposures.

The treasury area may be called upon to identify, measure and allocate the cost of each of the risk elements for a given project (or even for the entire organization) so that the risk factors are analyzed in management decisions. The treasurer often has direct responsibility for managing exposures due to accidental losses that arise from treasury assets or activities managed by treasury. Everything an organization owns or does is a source of potential loss and treasury management activities are no exception.

Loss exposures related to treasury management may include:

- Loss, theft, or destruction of cash or securities by an organization's employees or others
- Loss of the organization's accounts-receivable records, which can cripple revenue collections for substantial periods
- Improper procedures for collecting receivables, which may subject an organization to tort liability for defamation of customers or invasion of privacy
- The inability, or reduced ability, to raise needed capital to prevent a liquidity crisis due to financial and operating difficulties or the loss of key officers.

C. Basic Types of Business Insurance

1. Liability

Liability is generally considered a form of casualty insurance that insures against damage to other parties. The liabilities can arise from product defects, business practices, accidents, actions of the organization's employees, officers or Board of Directors and general negligence in the operation of the organization. Types of liability insurance include:

- Business
- Automobile
- Business owner's liability
- Product liability
- Comprehensive general liability
- Manufacturer's and contractor's liability

2. Difference in Conditions

The primary purpose of difference in conditions (DIC) insurance is to cover the insured's property for perils not covered by basic property insurance policies. Typically used in conjunction with multiple basic policies to make them all uniform, DIC insurance does not provide higher limits of coverage for basic perils, as does an umbrella policy; rather, it provides coverage for conditions and perils not included in the basic policy.

DIC insurance is often purchased to fill voids in policies purchased overseas and to insure property in transit. This type of insurance is not typically standardized because the market for it is limited and DIC insurance is generally written to cover special exposure and circumstances. Often, there are exclusions for important perils such as fire, vandalism, employee dishonesty, machinery losses, etc. because it is assumed that an insured business already has coverage for these losses under standard business property insurance.

3. Excess or Umbrella

Excess or umbrella insurance is designed to supplement basic or primary liability coverage. Policies generally pay after the primary policy's limits have been exhausted. For example, if the primary insurance policy has a limit of $250,000 and claims exceed this amount, an umbrella or excess policy would pay the excess claims up to the limit of the policy. Excess or umbrella policies can also be used to fill gaps in coverage provided by basic liability policies (that is, the difference in coverage between two policies).

4. Property

This type of insurance provides for reimbursement in the event a loss of some type of asset, such as buildings, equipment or inventory, occurs. Insurance often covers the replacement value of the items in question, paying the costs of completely replacing the item at current market prices rather than the historical or book value of the asset.

5. Casualty

This type of insurance is primarily concerned with the legal liability of losses caused by injury to persons or damage to the property of others. It provides specific coverage for losses such as plate glass, crime, robbery, boiler or machinery, and aviation insurance. Many casualty insurers also write surety bonds and other forms of insurance not classified as property.

6. Workers' Compensation

This insurance provides coverage for the four basic types of benefits:

- Medical care
- Death
- Disability
- Rehabilitation

Associated with employee job-related injuries or diseases as a matter of right (without regard to fault), this insurance is usually purchased by the employer from an insurance company, although there are a few monopolistic state funds through which the insurance must be purchased. The premium rates are generally based on a percentage of the employer's payroll and vary according to the employee's occupation.

7. Business Interruption

This insurance provides payments to an organization in the event it is unable to pursue a normal line of business for some period of time due to an unforeseen event, such as fire, hurricane or earthquake. Business interruption insurance generally covers loss of profits and continuing fixed expenses (debt, lease, etc.) while the organization is temporarily out of business for various reasons. For example, if an organization were to suffer a fire at a main production facility, property insurance would pay for the rebuilding of the facility, and business interruption insurance would make payments to compensate the organization for lost profits and increased costs during the rebuilding process.

Other types of business interruption insurance cover a failure of a contingent business (key supplier), extra expenses due to basic loss (such as when the organization can continue to operate only if extra costs are incurred), and loss of profits or commissions due to a loss of inventory.

8. Directors and Officers (D & O)

D & O insurance provides coverage when a director or an officer with an organization commits a negligent act or omission, misstatement or misleading statement and a libel suit is brought against the organization as a result. The policy provides coverage (usually with a large deductible) for directors' and officers' liability exposure if these individuals are sued. Coverage is also provided for the costs of defense, such as legal fees and other court costs.

9. Fidelity and Crime

Fidelity bonds provide coverage that guarantees payment for money or other property lost through dishonest acts of bonded employees, either by name or by position. The bond generally covers all dishonest acts, such as larceny, theft, embezzlement, forgery, misappropriation, wrongful abstraction or willful misapplication, whether employees act alone or in concert. Because a fidelity bond makes up only part of the protection against theft, other crime insurance is mandatory. A blanket bond could be used to cover all employees of an organization while crime insurance provides specific coverage for the perils of burglary, theft and robbery by external parties.

10. Employee Benefits

Many corporations provide certain types of insurance for the benefit of employees. For instance, most organizations pay for a portion of coverage, with the employees being asked to pay the balance. The most common type of insurance offered is medical or health insurance. Disability insurance, which provides coverage for non-work-related disabilities, may be provided for all or some of an organization's employees. For corporations, life insurance coverage for key personnel provides the organization with the resources needed to replace these individuals in the event of death. This is referred to as key-person insurance and is especially useful for smaller firms and partnerships.

11. Other Types of Insurance

A wide variety of other types of insurance are offered for an organization's special needs. The most popular types include:

- Ocean/marine policies to cover ships and cargos
- Special multiperil insurance (SMP), which covers special losses in four basic areas: property, liability, crime, and boilers and machinery (endorsements can be added to cover almost any standard risk in these areas)
- Fiduciary insurance (may be required under ERISA for pension and 401(k) plans) and exclusion policies (also known as gap insurance), which cover losses either not covered or excluded under other policies held by the organization. These policies are intended to "fill in the gaps" or provide higher overall levels of coverage.

D. Steps in Insurance Risk Management

Every organization needs proper insurance risk management due to the possibility of accidental loss (loss exposures) that disrupts operations and lowers overall efficiency and profitability. Risk management reduces the adverse effects of actual and potential accidental losses through cost-effective techniques by either preventing such losses from occurring (risk control) or financing recovery from losses that do occur (risk financing).

The four goals of insurance risk management are as follows:

- Insure against catastrophic loss
- Decide when and what to insure
- Manage the purchase and use of insurance (including brokers)
- Obtain efficient pricing for insurance needs. Insurance risk management is a decision or problem-solving process where the "problem" is exposure to accidental losses.

1. Identify Manageable Risks

Manageable risks are defined as those that an organization can control by managing the risk or the consequences it entails. Risks or loss exposures are usually classified as: (1) Property risks, (2) Business-interruption risks, (3) Workers' compensation risks, (4) Legal-liability risks (including surety risks for failing to carry out contracts) (5) Fidelity risks (from employee dishonesty), (6) Personnel risks (from loss of services performed by especially talented employees who resign, become disabled or retire) are often added as another risk category, (7) In addition, the organization must consider health care and medical insurance for employees.

- **Property Risks –** Property losses are generally characterized as either direct or indirect:
  - Direct losses could include destruction of a facility by fire, theft of inventory or damage to a delivery vehicle in a traffic accident.
  - Indirect (or consequential) damages include the costs of shifting production to another plant, restocking the inventory or renting a replacement delivery vehicle while the damaged one is being repaired.

  To properly identify property risks, a treasurer needs to examine property schedules, appraisals and the process flow of operations from raw materials received through the delivery of finished goods. This helps to identify critical points in the process where property losses could slow down or stop production and delivery of products. As a general rule, property insurance policies should be written for replacement value rather than book value in order to fully protect the organization in the event of loss. However, if an asset insured for replacement value is lost and not actually replaced, the insurance typically pays for only the cash value.

- **Workers' Compensation Risks –** This type of risk stems from potential losses in the form of medical expenses, disability wages and rehabilitation costs for injured workers. In most cases, the schedule of benefits is determined by state law but may be open-ended, especially in the event of organization negligence. To help identify this type of risk, management needs to evaluate safety practices and loss histories at all work locations, the types and distribution of jobs, general hiring practices and the legal and legislative climate in states where the organization has employees.

- **Liability Risks –** These risks arise as a result of any obligations the organization has for the cost of bodily injuries to others or to property other than its own. These obligations could arise from contracts entered into by the organization, accidents by the organization's employees or management or from negligence on the part of the organization.

- **Fidelity Risks** – These risks arise from the theft of money, securities or property by employees, as well as from crime involving employees or outsiders to the organization. To properly deal with these types of risk, management should:
  - Examine amounts and locations of cash and securities holdings
  - Maintain adequate control procedures for cash, securities, property and inventory
  - Implement proper screening and bonding procedures for all employees involved with handling cash, securities or inventory

- **Surety Risks** – These risks are related to contractual obligations on the part of the organization that may not be fulfilled. To identify this type of risk, management should determine the total amount of outstanding surety bonds (or other similar instruments) plus any guarantees that may be attached to contractual obligations.

2. Methods of Identification

The first problem-solving step for a treasurer in identifying the kinds of losses that an organization may suffer (including liability claims and failure to fulfill contracts) is to gather information from many areas of the organization. The treasurer may want to consider using a survey or guide at this stage of the process in order to ensure that all possible areas of potential risk are captured. Many insurance companies and brokers require this type of survey on a regular basis. The documents required for this process may include:

- Property schedules
- Lists of employees
- Loss runs for expired insurance policies
- Flow charts
- Financial statements

When an organization is initially implementing an insurance and risk management process, or if major changes are being made in existing policies, the use of an insurance risk management consultant may be appropriate. This type of consultant can help with interviews, inspections, analysis of risk and selection of required plans.

Proper risk management also requires that the identification of risk be kept as current as possible. This is achieved through good communication with other areas of the organization and the creation of awareness throughout the organization of the importance of risk identification and control.

3. Measure Potential Losses and Financial Impact

The significance of any loss exposure depends on how often actual losses occur (loss frequency) and how large these actual losses are (loss severity). A series of individually small losses may be severe in aggregate if occurring within a brief period. Proper risk management requires that an organization have sufficient resources available (cash, credit or insurance) to finance recovery from any foreseeable accidental loss or series of losses. Some suggested methods for measuring types of loss are presented in the table below.

Methods for Measuring Losses

Property Loss Measurement	Estimate replacement costs of properties and the resulting business interruption costs (including the costs of recovering lost customers) if property is damaged, destroyed or stolen.
Workers' Compensation Loss Measurement	Estimate costs of disability payments, death benefits and lost time, based on payroll, job descriptions and potential injuries. (A loss history report from the last three to five years is useful in developing this estimate.)
Liability Loss Measurement	Estimate probability of loss from potential product liabilities, injuries to customers or visitors to company facilities, accidents and general liability claims on an organization.
Fidelity Loss Measurement	Estimate potential losses from employee theft of cash, securities, organization property or inventory.
General Loss Measurement	Estimate potential losses from any other source, including the impact on personnel, property, finances (administrative costs, taxes or intangible costs) and the future of an organization.

4. Consider Available Control and Financing Techniques

All risk management involves a combination of risk control and risk financing, with the financing options entailing either retention (internally accepting and managing the risk) or transfer (relying on insurance or other external resources). Although risk control is generally considered more important than risk financing, combining the techniques is the best approach. Risk control, without risk financing, may lead to bankruptcy if losses occur despite the best safety measures. Risk financing without risk control wastes money paying for losses that could have been prevented at little cost and may lead to negligence claims. An organization may decide to self-insure small risks but risks with large potential losses should be treated using a broader array or combination of techniques.

5. Select Most Appropriate Techniques

When an organization commits resources to particular assets or activities, it becomes vulnerable to related loss exposures. By properly managing these exposures, an organization can maintain profitability and efficiency at a high level despite threats of accidents. An organization should develop disaster contingency plans in the event of large losses, insurance cancellation or insurance company failure.

6. Monitor the Results

Management should periodically review the entire risk management program to assess the effectiveness of chosen risk management techniques and to adjust to changing conditions. This process includes:

- The regular generation of loss reports
- The review of all losses over a period of time
- Comparison of these losses with both historical data and losses by other firms in the industry. Information may be generated internally or may be obtained from the insurance company holding the organization's policies.

E. Insurance Risk Control Techniques

Several approaches can be used to reduce the frequency or severity of accidental losses that may impact an organization.

1. Safety

Any action that reduces the frequency with which accidents occur, or the amount of harm caused, is a safety measure. The focus of safety is not on the financial consequences of accidents but instead on the frequency and severity of the damage or injury that is caused. Organizations should review examples of accidents within the industry and provide employees with training on accident prevention, including how to cope with accidents.

2. Exposure Avoidance

Exposure avoidance involves refraining from taking on an asset or activity, or eliminating an existing one, when there is no combination of risk control or financing techniques that produces a projected risk-adjusted rate of return that is adequate. This may require an organization to reconsider lines of business or services provided if a particular area is too risky from the standpoint of potential loss.

3. Limiting Contractual Acceptance of Risk

An organization may subcontract with other companies, rather than insurers, to perform certain activities. Thereby, the other companies take on the loss exposures those activities create. Another possibility is for an organization to require others to pay for, indemnify or "hold it harmless" from losses for which it would otherwise have to pay. Banks are generally indemnified from any consequential damages arising from a wire that is either misdirected or that may have failed to send.

(Additional information on UCC regulations related to money transfers is in Chapter 3, U.S. Financial Environment.)

4. Combination of Exposures

Bringing together many isolated loss exposures and placing them under common control makes aggregate losses more predictable and the application of uniform safety measures more effective. One example is the grouping of several diverse production facilities under a single, joint risk management program, such as risk pools formed by airlines to deal with suits from air crashes.

5. Separation of Exposures

Any asset or activity concentrated at one location is subject to being destroyed in a single accident. Physically spreading an asset or activity over two or more locations, or having an available backup, reduces the organization's vulnerability. The procedure of maintaining parallel facilities or assets to reduce exposure is usually known as duplication.

F. Risk Financing Techniques

These techniques involve resources upon which an organization may draw to finance recovery from losses and liabilities for which it is held responsible. Risk financing is only one of the many competing uses to which an organization devotes financial resources. Sound financial management requires integrating the organization's risk financing needs with other, more traditionally "productive" needs. This is necessary because, without proper risk financing, profit-generating activities and assets are almost certain to be impaired (or perhaps ruined) by accidents.

1. Risk Retention

Retention involves the use of an organization's internal financial resources (including credit, if appropriate) to provide funds to finance recovery from accidental losses. In other words, the organization retains the loss rather than paying someone else (an insurance organization) to take it.

- **Non-Insurance:** One approach to risk retention is known as non-insurance. This technique involves relying on normal revenues to pay for small, "normal" losses as current expenses. Non-insurance is appropriate for losses an organization can readily absorb as "costs of doing business" but not for highly disruptive, potentially ruinous accidents. The proper cost of these funds is the rate of return that the organization could have earned in terms of an optimal alternative use.

- **Self-Insurance:** Self-insurance is not technically a form of insurance because it does not involve a transfer of risk to an insurer or another separate entity. Also, the term "self-insurance" is often used to describe any risk retention program, even highly informal unfunded arrangements. Many organizations that practice self-insurance set "cap limits" on self-insurance exposure by purchasing excess coverage (i.e., "real insurance") for claims above some pre-determined limit. Any claims below this limit will be "self-insured," while amounts above the limit (i.e., excess losses) will be covered by the cap limit policy.

Self-insurance can also be used as a risk retention plan. However, as commonly practiced, the term "self-insurance" is actually a misnomer. It generally denotes a retention program that is more formalized than non-insurance. Unlike non-insurance, self-insurance requires real efforts to forecast losses to be retained. In addition, an organization must systematically maintain resources from which to pay losses.

- **Captives:** The last approach to risk retention is the use of captives. A captive is a subsidiary through which a parent firm finances specified types and amounts of the parent's losses in a highly structured form of retention that often resembles insurance but is not insurance.

- **Group Captive:** A group captive, also known as an association captive, resembles a single-parent captive except that it provides risk financing for multiple owners instead of just one. The captive may be jointly owned by each of the individual parents or by an association that the parent companies have formed. This shared ownership makes the group captive arrangement a form of insurance by virtue of the transfer of risk.

- **Risk Retention Group:** A risk retention group is a special type of group captive formed under the terms of a federal law that is designed to more fully enable business firms to work together in jointly financing product liability claims. To the extent that risks are shared, this is considered insurance. These plans are often used in industries with high risk or potential for catastrophic losses, such as the airline industry and certain professional occupations (doctors in high-risk practices, accountants, lawyers, etc).

- **Claims Management:** Many companies who self insure (especially in the area of health insurance) contract out the claims approval and payment process to an insurance company or another third party.

2. Risk Transfer

The essence of any risk transfer is a contract between a transferring organization (transferor) and another entity (the transferee), under which the transferee agrees to pay designated types of the transferor's losses within contractual limits. The transferor may have to pay the transferee a fee (such as an insurance premium) for this promise of indemnity or the transferor may have the bargaining power to secure this promise as a condition for agreeing to do business with the transferee. Such risk transfer arrangements are often made for tax or regulatory reasons and may be accomplished through the purchase of reinsurance, either from a broker or directly from the market. It is important to note that the transfer of risk is only as good as the transferee's, or the insurance company's, ability to pay claims.

- **Contractual Transfer:** Under these contracts, typified by "hold harmless" agreements, the transferee is not an insurer, and the transfer contract may take any form permitted by applicable law. Such contractual transfers may not provide transferors the degree of financial security they could obtain from a true insurer because most "hold harmless" transferees are not in business to bear others' risk of loss, and because the contracts and business activities are not as strictly regulated as insurers.

- **Guaranteed Cost Insurance Program:** In this type of program, the insured pays a fixed premium at the beginning of the policy period and the insurer then takes the risk of paying all losses occurring during the policy period that fall within the scope and amount of the policy. The premium the insured pays cannot be changed until the next policy period, although either the insurer or the insured may be allowed to cancel the coverage in the middle of the policy period under certain conditions. An insured that cancels this type of policy mid-period may not be entitled to a refund of premiums paid.

- **Retrospectively (Retro) Rated Insurance Program:** In this type of program, the insured's cost of coverage for a policy period varies with the insured's losses during that period. Such programs are often used for workers' compensation plans and for product liability insurance. The insured pays a "standard," or "deposit" premium at the beginning of the coverage period. At the end of the period, the insurer computes a final premium based upon an agreed formula that varies with the insured's actual losses (subject to limits) for the policy period. So long as there is an open claim, the retro-rated period continues.

G. Other Concerns in Insurance Programs

In dealing with insurers, many organizations enter the marketplace not so much to buy coverage as to "sell" the company's overall risk management programs to insurance underwriters. In order to "sell" these programs, treasurers must be familiar with the structure of insurance markets and must be equipped to make the rational decisions that transactions in these markets require.

1. Insurance Providers

Legally, most property and liability insurers do not offer insurance; rather, they accept offers to purchase insurance from applicants who make these offers to the insurers' marketing representatives. These representatives may be the insurers' own salaried employees (if the insurer is a direct writer) or, more likely, are independent agents or brokers. Although agents and brokers both receive commissions rather than salaries from insurers, an independent agent is legally an agent of the insurer while a broker is the legal agent of the applicant. Agents and brokers, as well as employees of direct writers, compete for high quality accounts by offering many services to applicants and the insureds without assessing direct charges.

2. Dealing with Insurance Brokers

Insurance brokers present options to an organization and place the organization's insurance business through an insurer, but they may not have the authority to legally bind an insurer. In deciding first whether to use a broker and then in choosing a particular broker, an organization should consider the broker's experience with the types of coverage needed, as well as access to special markets or insurers.

3. Selecting Insurance

When selecting among competing insurers, the crucial factors to consider are:

- Financial strength
- Business integrity
- The extent of coverage offered
- Services available to insureds
- Claims facilities
- Cost

The points to consider in the selection of an insurer include: (1) long-term solvency of the insurer, (2) A.M. Best ratings, (3) service and (4) cost.

- **Long-Term Solvency of the Insurer:** A treasurer should investigate the financial solvency of all insurers for the firm. Generally, state guarantee funds provide only limited protection when an insurer fails and the delays involved in settling claims may be significant. Insurance coverage is only as good as the ability of the insurance company to pay claims, especially those for large losses. Therefore, a firm's credit agreements or loan covenants may stipulate minimum ratings for insurance carriers.

- **A.M. Best Ratings:** A.M. Best Company is the leading provider of ratings and financial information for the global insurance industry and assigns two types of ratings, financial strength and debt. Both are independent opinions, based on the comprehensive quantitative and qualitative evaluation, of a company's balance sheet strength, operating performance and business profile. These opinions are not a warranty of a company's financial strength or a measure of ability to meet obligations to policyholders and other financial obligations. Best's Financial Strength Ratings provide an opinion of an insurer's financial strength and ability to meet ongoing obligations to policyholders. On the other hand, Best's Debt Ratings provide only an opinion for the credit marketplace regarding the issuer's ability to meet financial obligations to security holders when due.

- **Service:** The ability of an insurer to provide good loss control and/or claims service may help to reduce the overall cost of an insurance program. Service levels and specialization or expertise in a particular area of insurance should always be taken into consideration in selecting insurers.

- **Cost:** The cost of an insurer should always be measured in relation to the financial stability, overall coverage and quality of services offered by prospective insurers.

4. Selecting a Deductible

By selecting insurance (particularly property insurance) that has a deductible, an insured can save many premium dollars in comparison to the cost of "first-dollar" coverage. In essence, the deductible forces the insured to share some of the front-end risk from potential losses. The higher the deductible, the lower the cost of the premium for insurance. However, it is important to weigh the many losses that could fall within the deductible and the managerial uncertainty deductible payments impose against the potential savings. Deductibles may also be set on:

- A per-occurrence basis (the deductible applies for each occurrence during the policy period)
- On an aggregate basis (deductible is set on a per-period basis, regardless of the number of occurrences)

5. Selecting a Liability Limit

In selecting a liability limit, the challenge may be made more complex by the unavailability of large amounts of excess liability insurance an organization may wish to purchase. Management must consider the following in determining overall limits for liability: (1) catastrophic event exposure, (2) other catastrophic exposure, (3) cost versus limits and (4) cost versus exposure.

- **Catastrophic Event Exposure:** A company's total assets are only one measure of potential liability. A better measure may be the projected cash flow stream that these assets actually produce over a reasonable horizon.

- **Other Catastrophic Exposure:** Other types of risk may arise from product or service liability claims, suits by competitors, etc.

- **Cost versus Limits:** Purchasing standard policies with high liability limits may become very expensive. Therefore, organizations need to examine the use of excess coverage and self-insurance. Excess coverage can often be purchased in "layers" to provide better overall insurance coverage at a lower cost.

  In some instances, a business cannot obtain the total coverage it requires from a single insurance company or a single high-limit policy may be prohibitively expensive. Thus, an organization may purchase several policies from different insurance companies in order to acquire the total liability needed at an affordable price. Self-insurance can also be used to cover "pockets" or gaps between regular policy limits and excess coverage or between layers of excess coverage when there is a gap.

- **Cost versus Exposure:** Regardless of the insurance cost, the exposure must be managed. Therefore, it may be more important for an organization to have catastrophic protection than primary insurance.

H. Insurance Risk Management Services

Most organizations maintain an in-house risk management information system and a complete set of internal records on insurance and losses. Risk management consultants offer additional expertise, on a fee basis, that is needed to make and carry out risk financing, management and control decisions.

Among the important considerations regarding risk management services are the following:

- Independent audits of an organization's risk-management program are performed on a regular basis (every one to three years).
- Major program reviews of an organization's risk-management procedures are performed at least every five years, or more often if the organization (or the risk structure) is changing rapidly.
- Claims administration (the investigation of losses when a claim is made) is either conducted internally or outsourced as part of purchased risk management services.
- Claims auditors, who are independent consultants, are retained to audit the work of both internal and external claims administrators.
- Loss-control and safety engineering consultants help to identify risks and ways of preventing or reducing losses, especially in areas such as fire protection, industrial safety, environmental risks, computer security and general security concerns.
- Organizations use the services of actuaries who analyze aggregate loss experience (rather than individual claims) and project the ultimate cost of claims over a given period.
- Information systems consultants help to establish or upgrade loss-control and claims handling reporting and record keeping systems.

Endnotes

1 This section is based on an article in the Nov/Dec 2002 issue of AFP Exchange, titled "Treasury Disaster Recovery," by Ron Chakravarti.

Test Your Understanding

These chapter questions are provided to test your understanding of the information in the text. They are neither examples of CTP examination questions nor are they in the examination format.

Answers are on pages 621–623.

1. What is operational risk and where does it come from?

2. Discuss the topic of technology risk.

3. What are the three critical factors in determining a risk management strategy for an organization?

4. What are disaster recovery and business continuity?

5. What are mission critical functions and how do they relate to the treasury area?

6. Why is insurance necessary and what kinds of risks does it protect against?

7. What are the responsibilities of the treasury area in risk management?

8. What is DIC insurance and why is it purchased?

9. What does worker's compensation insurance cover?

10. What are the goals of insurance risk management?

11. What are fidelity risks?

12. What is exposure avoidance?

13. What is the difference between non-insurance and self-insurance?

14. What is risk transfer?

15. Discuss the issues involved in selecting a deductible.

CHAPTER 19
Corporate Governance and Ethics

I. INTRODUCTION

Corporate governance is an especially important subject in light of historic lapses and the resulting loss of investor confidence, such as occurred in 2000-2001. Considerations in governance include the role of independent directors, outside and internal auditors, financial reporting and investor relations. All of these issues are covered in this chapter, along with three topics that have a direct impact on treasury: the 2002 Sarbanes-Oxley Act (SOX), expensing of stock options and the AFP's revised Code of Ethics.

II. CORPORATE GOVERNANCE[1]

Amid corporate accounting scandals that resulted in the "meltdown" of large, once prominent companies due to failures of diligence, ethics and control, the issue of corporate governance has become a major concern for large, publicly traded companies. In July 2002, the U.S. Congress passed SOX, which also imposed corporate governance and reporting guidelines. SOX also created the Public Company Accounting Oversight Board (PCAOB), a private sector, non-profit corporation:

- To oversee the auditors of public companies in order to protect the interests of investors
- To further the public interest in the preparation of informative, fair, and independent audit reports

In August 2002, the NYSE's Board of Directors voted to tighten listing standards, imposing more stringent corporate governance requirements on member companies.

Other key parties in corporate governance are:

- The Securities and Exchange Commission (SEC)
- Large institutional investors
- State attorney general offices (especially New York State)
- Independent organizations such as the Conference Board[2]

It is important to note that for some foreign owned companies operating in the U.S., corporate governance may not be a major issue if the company's stock is not traded in U.S. capital markets.

A. The Issue of Corporate Governance

The issue of corporate governance arises from the separation of ownership and control that exists in most companies. While stockholders own the company, officers (executives) actually control the company. This separation is a potential problem in large, widely held corporations (vs. small, closely-held companies) where management may be able to make decisions with little or no oversight by the owners. In fact, it may be more useful to think of stockholders as investors rather than owners. The difference is subtle but important.

Owners focus on the business performance of the company while investors focus on the risk and return of portfolios. This tends to make most investors passive or inactive shareholders of companies, thereby providing a significant incentive for the management of such companies to take actions that will benefit themselves while reducing the value to the shareholders. This is generally referred to as the "agency problem" between management and stockholders.

To protect the owner/investors, there is an established set of checks and balances, generally referred to as corporate governance. The important components are the Board of Directors (especially independent directors), the independent auditors and the regulatory agencies. Most of the recent failures in corporate governance can be traced back to a failure on the part of one or more these components. An organization should, therefore, have a chief audit executive accountable for the internal audit function that reports directly to the audit committee of the Board of Directors. The Board should provide sufficient funding and resources to the audit function, including periodic private sessions to discuss risk and controls with the chief auditor.

B. Role of Independent Directors

The four purposes of recent SOX and NYSE standards are to:

- Increase the role and authority of independent directors
- Tighten the definition of an independent director
- Give shareholders more opportunity to monitor and participate in the governance of companies
- Establish new control and enforcement mechanisms

Financial professionals at NYSE companies, or those with companies considering listing on the NYSE or other exchanges, must understand these requirements and expectations. Failure to adhere to these standards could cause significant public embarrassment for the company, as well as a significant loss of investor capital. CEOs must certify to the listing exchange(s) that their companies comply with these standards.

1. Tightening the Definition of Independent Directors

Under the new standards, in order for a director to be deemed "independent," the board must determine that the director has no material relationship with the listed company, either directly or as a partner, a shareholder or an officer of an organization. Independent directors must now meet without management in regular executive sessions. Previously, there was no such requirement.

In order to be defined as independent, a director must have a five-year "cooling off" period with the company, meaning that he/she cannot have been an employee with the company or an independent auditor during the past five years. To be considered independent, a director cannot currently be, or in the past five years have been, part of an interlocking directorate in which an executive officer of the listed company serves on the compensation committee or another committee that employs the director. The new standards specify that directors' compensation must be the sole remuneration from the listed company for audit-committee directors. Listed companies must now also adopt a code of business conduct and ethics and must promptly disclose any waivers of the code for directors or executives.

2. Increasing the Role and Authority of Independent Directors

Independent directors must comprise a majority of a board. Companies must have a nominating committee, a compensation committee (or committees of the company's own denomination with the same responsibilities), and an audit committee, each comprised solely of independent directors. Until now, NYSE-listed companies were required to have only a minimum three-person audit committee composed solely of independent directors. There was no requirement for the establishment or composition of nominating or compensation committees.

3. Shareholder Participation in Governance Decisions

Perhaps the most notable and controversial aspect of the NYSE's proposals is that it gives shareholders a greater say in stock option plans and more access to governance information. Under the new requirements, shareholders must be given the opportunity to vote on all stock-option plans, except employment-inducement options, option plans acquired through mergers and tax-qualified plans such as employee stock ownership plans (ESOPs) and 401(k)s.

Brokers may vote customer shares on proposals for such plans only when customers' instructions have been received prior to the vote. The current requirements call for NYSE companies to obtain shareholder approval of stock-option plans in which officers or directors may participate, but broad-based plans and one-time employment inducements are exempt. Brokers can vote customer shares without instructions, so long as the proposal is not contested and the proposal does not cover more than five percent of outstanding stock.

Shareholders also will be able to get more information from companies with the new regulations. Listed companies must publish codes of business conduct and ethics, as well as key committee charters. Waivers for directors or executive officers must be disclosed promptly. Listed foreign private issuers must disclose any significant ways in which current corporate governance practices differ from NYSE rules.

4. New Control and Enforcement Mechanisms

The NYSE is holding CEOs responsible for these new accountability standards. Each listed-company's CEO must certify annually that he/she is not aware of any violation by the company of NYSE corporate governance standards and that the company has established procedures for verifying the accuracy and completeness of the information provided to investors. The NYSE also may issue a public reprimand letter for violation of a corporate governance standard or may delist the company.

While there is clearly a downside for companies that ignore these standards, there are many benefits for companies that meet and exceed these standards. Most notably, companies will be better able to attract and retain shareholders. Many companies are, in fact, already compliant with the standards and, as a result, are benefiting from renewed investor confidence.

C. Independent Auditors and Financial Reporting

In the wake of the failure of several large corporations, one of the issues receiving a great deal of attention is that of auditor independence. The SEC's actions essentially prohibit auditors from providing the following services to corporate clients: tax shelters, legal and management advice and financial-software development. The SEC now requires corporations to disclose annual fees paid to accounting firms for auditing and consulting services. It also requires long-serving audit partners to disengage themselves from accounts to ensure objectivity.

There are ongoing discussions among corporate financial professionals for establishing guidelines for other audit related issues such as the following five:

- Mandatory auditor rotation (i.e., changing auditors after a specified or an unspecified number of years)
- The "revolving door" issue of hiring treasury and financial professionals from an outside audit firm
- Audit-committee chair rotation
- True audit-panel independence
- Financial and accounting expertise on the audit committee

1. Financial Reporting

Recent SEC regulations require companies to assess the effectiveness of financial reporting internal controls in a separate report filed with the annual report on Form 10-K. The external auditor must attest to the company's assessment of internal control effectiveness. The auditor's report is also included with the Form 10-K. In addition, management is required to disclose any "material weakness" and may not conclude that internal controls are effective if there are one or more material breaches.

2. Public Company Accounting Oversight Board (PCAOB)

The PCAOB was created as part of SOX. The primary mission of the PCAOB is to improve the quality and transparency in financial reporting and independent audits, to advance corporate responsibility and to further the public interest. The PCAOB ensures that public company financial statements are audited in accordance with the highest standards of quality, independence and ethics. The SEC appoints the chairman and members of the PCAOB.

III. SARBANES–OXLEY[3] (SOX)

SOX is the most significant business legislation since the Security Acts of 1933 and 1934, which established the modern stock exchanges and created the Securities and Exchange Commission (SEC). SOX similarly brings a whole new regimen for corporate America with respect to auditor oversight, accounting and reporting,, and corporate governance. One significant area of change deals with the increased level of accountability shouldered by corporate officers. Section 302 of the Act requires a public company's principal executive officer (CEO) and principal financial officer (CFO) to personally certify that, to the best of their knowledge, the company's financial statements filed on SEC Forms 10-K (annual) and 10-Q (quarterly) are accurate and complete.

Failure to meet these requirements can lead to significant consequences for a company's CEO and CFO. Section 906 provides penalties for noncompliance as high as $5 million and 20 years in prison. Much of the information included in the financial statements, footnotes, and management discussion and analysis (MD&A) originates in various departments within finance and other parts of the organization. (Detailed information on the impact of Sarbanes-Oxley is provided in Appendix B of this chapter.)

A. Subcertification

Due to the significance and legal implications of SOX, public company CEOs and CFOs have sought to ensure that such information is accurate and complete. One method to help ensure compliance is through subcertification. Subcertification generally consists of a certification of financial information by those who were responsible for providing the information; hence, that may include many employees from the company's treasury and finance departments.

While subcertification is often presented in the form of a signed written statement, it can also be a verbal acknowledgment of the responsibility for certain financial information included in financial statements filed with the SEC.

B. Role of Financial Professionals

Financial professionals play an important role in a company's compliance with SOX, particularly in the role of a company's financial report certifications. In a 2003 AFP survey[4], nearly 60 percent of financial professionals indicated that they provide information used in the company's financial reports. A third of those responding to the survey have been asked by their employers to sign an affidavit vouching for or certifying the accuracy of such information. While treasurers and assistant treasurers represent a majority of the corporate practitioners who have been asked to sign affidavits, financial professionals of all job titles are playing a key role in companies' financial reporting.

The information that most financial professionals (60 percent) indicate that they provide on the company's financial statements is later certified by the company's CFO and CEO, as SOX requires. In turn, many companies are requesting financial staff to certify numbers that are provided to senior management. This certification generally involves information such as specific disclosures in MD&A or footnotes, specific account balances, compliance with company and/or treasury department policies and procedures (P&Ps) and adequacy of internal controls in the department.

C. Section 404 Compliance

One of the other key issues for companies is the cost of complying with Section 404 of SOX. This section requires that managers state their responsibility for establishing and maintaining adequate internal controls for financial repoting. It also requires auditors to attest to and report on management's assessment of corporate perfomance, in accordance with standards established by the PCAOB. Initial estimates project significantly higher audit costs in order to comply with these requirements.

IV. ETHICS[5]

As a result of the well publicized and well documented financial scandals such as Enron, WorldCom, Tyco, Arthur Andersen, Parmalat, and others, long overdue changes to the accounting profession and to corporate governance are now underway. As part of this process, AFP recently updated the Code of Ethics for treasury professionals. (The AFP Code of Ethics is provided in Appendix A of this chapter.) In light of the current environment, treasury professionals should consider the following three essential steps to institutionalize ethical conduct:

- Establish a code of conduct to be pledged and adhered to by all members of the treasury staff
- Develop treasury policies and procedures statements
- Provide training sessions on treasury ethics

A. Code of Conduct for Treasury

A code of conduct establishes rules of behavior for what constitutes appropriate actions and ethical behaviors encountered during normal business activities. It is important to proactively encourage moral conduct through clear statements of what will and will not be tolerated. While a code of conduct cannot prevent the adverse actions of an unethical person, it clearly delineates acceptable behaviors, as well as the consequences for behaviors that are unacceptable. Although each organization must write a code relevant for its particular industry or business, the following general elements are recommended for inclusion.

1. Confidential Information

Confidential information is information that may not be disclosed by employees to parties outside of an organization, such as to vendors, family members, or other third parties. Among confidential information are such matters as:

- Bank-account data
- Names of approved signatories
- Bank contacts
- Credit arrangements
- Bank fees
- System passwords

2. Conflicts of Interest

These include objective managerial actions that require the avoidance of a conflict of interest or the appearance of a conflict. The code should address employee acquisition of stock in companies with which the company does business. In addition, the solicitation and acceptance of gifts and entertainment from current and prospective banks and vendors should be covered, including maximum dollar limits or, as is often the case, absolute prohibition regarding acceptance of any gifts.

3. External Activities

Within limits, corporate staff is often allowed to participate in an external business or professional venture. However, engaging in such activities should not be allowed to interfere with the performance of company duties or to create a conflict of interest with the employee's primary position.

4. Employee Conduct

This includes on-the-job professional behaviors and personal habits of employees that can reflect adversely on a company. On-the-job concerns include:

- Attire and personal grooming
- Work habits and hours
- Personal telephone calls
- E-mail
- Internet use

Personal habits include:

- Failure to financially support one's family
- Excessive gambling
- Use of alcohol or drugs
- Any behavior that could discredit the company or compromise job performance

5. Conformance to Code

Most companies periodically require employees to certify that they have read the code of conduct and are in compliance. Remedies and penalties should be specified for situations that are deemed to be in conflict and cannot be resolved. These elements are not related to employee performance, which is normally handled through performance appraisals based on job descriptions and individual performance evaluations.

B. Treasury Policies and Procedures

Policy and procedure (P&P) statements provide a framework for the design of treasury systems and controls in support of company objectives. Realistically, the behavior of managers cannot be regulated by proclamation. However, assigning specific duties to designated managers establishes the company's position on responsibilities, sets a charter for responsible corporate behavior and assesses penalties should violations occur.

The publication of P&Ps provides a venue by which the corporation can inform employees, agents, contractors and vendors of the disposition of specific treasury activities. Such publication can minimize situations in which unauthorized parties act in the name of the corporation, resulting in potentially detrimental consequences. These standards should be reviewed on a regular basis, with some experts suggesting an annual review. Examples of P&P topics are listed in Exhibit 19-1.

EXHIBIT 19.1 – POSSIBLE TOPICS FOR POLICIES AND PROCEDURES STATEMENTS

Topic	Rationale
Cash and Banking Management	To control the opening/closing of bank accounts and the management of cash balances
Credit Management	To provide oversight for the management of credit facilities including short-term borrowings and the contact with credit rating agencies
Weekly/Monthly Cash Forecast	To direct the content, format, timing, and distribution of periodic cash forecasts
Accounts Receivable (A/R) and Collection Activities	To establish best practices for the invoicing and collection of receivables
Accounts Payable (A/P) and Disbursement Activities	To establish best practices for the management of A/P
Daily Cash Report	To mandate the content, format, timing, and distribution of the daily cash position report
Payroll	To establish best practices for company payroll preparation and distribution
Wire Transfers	To mandate procedures for wire transfers to assure the application of adequate controls
Short-Term Investments	To determine the selection of and responsibility for short-term investments and to limit the use of inappropriate instruments (e.g., certain types of derivatives)
International Treasury	To regulate the management of international banking activities, foreign exchange, and global money transfers

C. Training Sessions in Corporate Treasury Ethics

Corporate ethics are not just words printed on a piece of paper. The most effective way to instill ethical behavior is through formal training sessions. An effective approach is to hold an offsite meeting to remove personnel from daily operations in order to emphasize the importance of the topic. An agenda for such an offsite might include the following:

- Explanation of the company's concern for ethical behavior as expressed in mandates from the Board of Directors, CEO, and/or CFO
- Discussion of recent historical cases involving unethical and/or criminal behavior, including causes, results and impacts on employees or stockholders
- Presentation of hypothetical ethical situations and how they should be resolved
- Description of the code of conduct, explaining the purpose and each employee's obligations
- Review of corporate P&P and, where appropriate, the citing of specific instances in which violations have occurred within the company or at other companies
- Development of a hot-line for reporting ethics violations
- Discussion of insider trading restrictions and reporting requirements

V. INVESTOR RELATIONS[6]

Investor relations (IR) is a strategic management responsibility that integrates finance, communication, marketing, and securities law compliance to enable the most effective two-way communication between a company and the financial community or other constituencies. The goal of investor relations is to ensure that a company's securities achieve a fair valuation in the financial marketplace.

It is now more important than ever for companies to have an effective IR representative in order to attract and retain capital and to restore investor confidence. The establishment of strict separation between the investment banking and investment research divisions of companies has resulted in significant changes in the IR role. In an environment of truly independent research and immediate disclosure, it is extremely important for the IR professional to be perceived by the investment community as having complete access to senior management.

In the area of corporate governance, there is a much higher profile for IR officers. IR professionals must be prepared to report to appropriate company authorities any information that is inaccurate or misleading. The National Investor Relations Institute (NIRI) Guidelines for Earnings Releases urges all public companies to include both a complete income statement and a complete balance sheet, reconcile GAAP earnings to pro forma results and include key management discussion and analysis (MD&A) information in the earnings announcement.

Legal Rights and Privileges of Common Stockholders: The rights and privileges of common stockholders are:

- **Control of Company:** As owners of a company, stockholders have the right to elect a company's directors who, in turn, select the officers who manage the business. There are many state and federal regulations concerning the election of directors and the specific management of the process.

- **Cumulative Voting:** Corporate bylaws typically allow one vote per share of stock and, in some cases, allow for cumulative voting. If, for example, a company has five directors, cumulative voting allows each share of stock to have five votes. If a shareholder wishes, all five of these votes could be made for one director. This is especially attractive to minority shareholders because it may allow them to have at least one or more seats on the Board by pooling votes for one or two candidates.

- **Proxy:** The right to vote at the annual meeting can be assigned to another individual through a proxy. For most companies with satisfied stockholders, the proxies are routinely assigned back to a company. If, however, a group of stockholders are dissatisfied with the management of a company, or other parties try to take control of a company, a proxy battle may occur as each side attempts to accumulate more proxies (votes) than the other side.

- **Staggered Election of Directors:** Another recent practice for maintaining control is the staggered election of directors to multiyear terms so that only a non-majority portion of the Board is elected each year. This prevents a rapid change of directors in the event of an attempted takeover.

- **Pre-Emptive Right:** This is the right that certain (or all) shareholders have to first rights of purchase, on a pro-rata basis, of any new shares of stock issued by a company. This is usually conducted through a rights offering or a "subscription" to any new stock issued by a company. The current shareholders may either purchase additional shares on a pro-rata basis or sell the rights to other parties. Although not a requirement in all states, it offers stockholders protection against dilution of value and protects the power of control for the existing shareholders. Most corporations include this right in charters.

VI. EXPENSING OF STOCK OPTIONS[7]

One of the key issues facing companies is how to treat stock options provided to management and employees. From a shareholder perspective, financial reporting should provide enough information to get a realistic picture of how a company is operating. Responding to requests from investors, financial analysts, and other users of financial information, the Financial Accounting Standards Board (FASB) is currently investigating this issue.

The FASB is currently addressing the issue of whether to require that the cost of employee stock options be treated as an expense. According to the FASB, there is a need for one consistent approach to recognize the costs associated with employee stock options. A move to require an expense treatment is consistent with the FASB's commitment to work toward convergence between U.S. and international accounting standards. While a number of major companies have voluntarily opted to reflect these costs as an expense in reporting the earnings, other companies continue to show these costs in the footnotes of financial statements. In taking all of these factors into consideration, the Board concluded that it was critical that it now revisit this important subject. The Board plans to start issuing guidelines that will become effective in late 2004.

APPENDIX 19.1 AFP CODE OF ETHICS

AFP's Board of Directors passed an updated ethics statement for members at its July 2003 Board meeting. Given current trends in finance and business, it is important for members to be aware of the Association's expectations for ethical conduct and to be well informed should a challenging situation present itself. The conduct of financial professionals has a direct effect on the reputation of the profession. A good reputation is earned on a continuing basis by performing one's business with competence, appropriate confidentiality, integrity, and by complying with applicable laws and regulations. Financial professionals have an obligation to their employers, co-workers, customers, shareholders, the profession, and to themselves to maintain the highest standards of conduct and to encourage their peers to do likewise.

Competence

1. Continue to acquire an appropriate level of professional knowledge and skill in finance.
2. Perform professional duties in good faith and in accordance with technical, legal and regulatory practices, as well as the letter and spirit of the law in the field of finance.

Confidentiality

3. Maintain confidential information acquired in the course of professional activities and disclose such information when legally obligated to do so.
4. Refrain from using or appearing to use confidential information for unethical or illegal advantage either personally or through third parties.

Integrity

5. Practice honesty and accuracy in all dealings without engaging in any activity that would prejudice the ability to carry out professional responsibilities competently and fairly. Avoid conflicts of interest or the appearance thereof.
6. Refrain from abusing the financial systems and markets.
7. Disclose fully all relevant information that could reasonably be expected to influence business dealings.
8. The Certified Cash Manager (CCM) or Certified Treasury Professional (CTP) designation may only be used if the certification is active.

APPENDIX 19.2 IMPACT OF SARBANES-OXLEY ON ACCOUNTING AND FINANCIAL PROFESSIONALS[8]

On July 30, 2002, President Bush signed into law the Sarbanes-Oxley Act of 2002. The Act-which applies in general to publicly held companies and their audit firms-dramatically affects the accounting profession and impacts not just the largest accounting firms, but any CPA actively working as an auditor of, or for, a publicly traded company. The basic implications of the Act for accounting and financial professionals are summarized below.

Public Company Accounting Oversight Board

Moving to a different private sector regulatory structure, a new Public Company Accounting Oversight Board (the Board) will be appointed and overseen by the SEC. The Board, made up of five full-time members, will oversee and investigate the audits and auditors of public companies, and sanction both firms and individuals for violations of laws, regulations and rules.

- **Board Composition:** Two of the five Board members must be or must have been CPAs. The remaining three must not be and cannot have been CPAs. The Chair may be held by one of the CPA members, but he or she must not have practiced accounting during the five years preceding his/her appointment.
- **Funding:** The Board will be funded by public companies through mandatory fees. Accounting firms that audit public companies must register with the Board ("registered firm"), and pay registration and annual fees.
- **Standard Setting:** The Board will issue standards or adopt standards set by other groups or organizations, for audit firm quality controls for the audits of public companies. These standards include: auditing and related attestation, quality control, ethics, independence and "other standards necessary to protect the public interest." The Board has the authority to set and enforce audit and quality control standards for public company audits.
- **Investigative and Disciplinary Authority:** The Board is empowered to regularly inspect registered accounting firms' operations and will investigate potential violations of securities laws, standards, competency and conduct. Sanctions may be imposed for non-cooperation, violations, or failure to supervise a partner or employee in a registered accounting firm. These include revocation or suspension of an accounting firm's registration, prohibition from auditing public companies, and imposition of civil penalties. During investigations, the Board can require testimony or document production from the registered accounting firm, or request information from relevant persons outside the firm. Investigations can be referred to the SEC, or with the SEC's approval, to the Department of Justice, state attorneys general or state boards of accountancy under certain circumstances.
- **International Authority:** Foreign accounting firms that "prepare or furnish" an audit report involving U.S. registrants will be subject to the authority of the Board. Additionally, if a registered U.S. accounting firm relies on the opinion of a foreign accounting firm, the foreign firm's audit workpapers must be supplied upon request to the Board or the Commission.

New Roles for Audit Committees and Auditors

The relationship between accounting firms and their publicly held audit clients is different under the new law. The basic implications are outlined below.

- **Auditors Report to Audit Committee:** Now, auditors will report to and be overseen by a company's audit committee, not management.
- **Audit Committees Must Approve All Services:** Audit committees must preapprove all services (both audit and non-audit services not specifically prohibited) provided by its auditor.
- **Auditor Must Report New Information to Audit Committee:** This information includes: critical accounting policies and practices to be used, alternative treatments of financial information within GAAP that have been discussed with management, accounting disagreements between the auditor and management, and other relevant communications between the auditor and management.
- **Offering Specified Non-Audit Services Prohibited:** The new law statutorily prohibits auditors from offering certain non-audit services to audit clients. These services include: bookkeeping, information systems design and implementation, appraisals or valuation services, actuarial services, internal audits, management and human resources services, broker/dealer and investment banking services, legal or expert services unrelated to audit services and other services the board determines by rule to be impermissible. Other nonaudit services not banned are allowed if preapproved by the audit committee.
- **Audit Partner Rotation:** The lead audit partner and audit review partner must be rotated every five years on public company engagements.
- **Employment Implications:** An accounting firm will not be able to provide audit services to a public company if one of that company's top officials (CEO, Controller, CFO, Chief Accounting Officer, etc.) was employed by the firm and worked on the company's audit during the previous year.

Criminal Penalties and Protection for Whistleblowers

The law creates tough penalties for those who destroy records, commit securities fraud and fail to report fraud.

- **Failure to Maintain Workpapers:** It is now a felony with penalties of up to 10 years to willfully fail to maintain "all audit or review workpapers" for at least five years. The SEC will establish a rule covering the retention of audit records and the Board will issue standards that compel auditors to keep other documentation for seven years.
- **Document Destruction:** It is a felony with penalties of up to 20 years to destroy documents in a federal or bankruptcy investigation.
- **Securities Fraud:** Criminal penalties for securities fraud have been increased to 25 years.
- **Fraud Discovery:** The statute of limitations for the discovery of fraud is

extended to two years from the date of discovery and five years after the act. It was previously one year from discovery and three from the act.

- **Other Provisions:** Other provisions protect corporate whistleblowers, ban personal loans to executives, and prohibit insider trading during blackout periods.

Financial Reporting and Auditing Process Additions

Issuers of public stock and their auditors must now follow new rules and procedures in connection with the financial reporting and auditing process.

- **Second Partner Review and Approval of Audit Reports:** The new regulatory board will issue or adopt standards requiring auditors to have a thorough second partner review and approval of every public company audit report.
- **Management Assessment of Internal Controls:** Management must now assess and make representations about the effectiveness of the internal control structure and procedures of the issuer for financial reporting.
- **Audit Reports Must Contain Description of Internal Controls Testing:** The new regulatory board will also issue or adopt standards that will require every audit report to attest to the assessment made by management on the company's internal control structures, including a specific notation about any significant defects or material noncompliance found on the basis of such testing.

Areas for CPAs to Watch

The ramifications of some of the provisions in the Sarbanes-Oxley Act will become known only as the SEC and the new Public Company Accounting Oversight Board begin implementing the bill.

- **Consulting Services:** The Act lists eight types of services that are "unlawful" if provided to a publicly held company by its auditor: bookkeeping, information systems design and implementation, appraisals or valuation services, actuarial services, internal audits, management and human resources services, broker/dealer and investment banking services, and legal or expert services related to audit services. It also has one catch-all category authorizing the board to determine by regulation any service it wishes to prohibit. Other non-audit services-including tax services-require pre-approval by the audit committee. Pre-approved non-audit services must be disclosed to investors in periodic reports.
- **Implications for CPAs with Tax Practices:** "Expert" services are not defined in the Act and we do not know how broadly the board or the SEC will define this term. It is conceivable that some tax services we view as traditional may be construed as "expert" services, and not permitted by any firm providing audit services to publicly held audit clients. We will encourage the Board or the SEC to understand the importance of auditors providing tax services for publicly held audit clients. In addition, tax services performed by an auditor for a publicly held company would require pre-approval by the client's audit committee.
- **Cascade Effect:** Of particular concern is the cascade effect that the scope of services restrictions could have on small businesses and accounting firms. Our major concern is that the new legislation by Congress may become the template for parallel federal and state legislative or rule changes that directly affect both non-public companies that are subject to other regulations and the CPAs that provide services to them. The AICPA and the state CPA societies are monitoring this situation closely and will continue to keep you informed.

- **Additional Burdens for CPAs in Business and Industry:** CPAs working in the financial management areas of public companies are directly impacted by the Act. These CPAs need to be aware of the new responsibilities of CEOs and CFOs, who are now required to certify company financial statements. They also have a greater duty to communicate and coordinate with corporate audit committees that are now responsible for hiring, compensating and overseeing the independent auditors. There are new requirements regarding enhanced financial disclosures as well. The AICPA is working to develop additional resources specifically tailored for members in corporate practice as they implement these new requirements.

Endnotes

1 This section is adapted from the following sources: (1) "NYSE Raises the Bar on Corporate Governance Standards" by Paul Steidler, AFP Exchange- Nov/Dec 2002; (2) "The Growing Importance of Corporate Governance, an Interview With Pat McGurn, the Institutional Shareholder Services (ISS) Director of Corporate Programs" by Paul Steidler, AFP Exchange – Aug/Sep 2002; and (3) Corporate Governance by Kenneth Kim and John Nofsinger, Pearson/Prentice Hall, 2004.

2 The Conference Board creates and disseminates knowledge about management and the marketplace to help businesses strengthen their performance and better serve society. More information on the Conference Board can be obtained from their Web site at: www.conference-board.org.

3 Content in this section is drawn from, "Subcertification: Financial Professionals Taking the Lead on Sarbanes-Oxley - Report of Survey Results", July 2003, AFP.

4 See Endnote #5.

5 The material in this section is drawn from: "Ethical Behavior and Treasury Governance" by James Sagner, AFP Exchange, Nov/Dec 2002.

6 Content in this section is drawn from: "How Investor Relations is Changing in Light of Corporate Reforms: An Interview With Lou Thompson, President and CEO, NIRI" by Paul F. Steidler, AFP Exchange, Jun/Jul 2003.

7 Information for this section was obtained from the Financial Accounting Standards Board (FASB) Website: http://www.fasb.org/.

8 Information for Appendix 19.2 was obtained from the AICPA (American Institute of Certified Public Accountants) Web site. More detailed and current information on the impact of Sarbanes-Oxley for the accounting and finance area can be obtained at: http://www.aicpa.org/info/sarbanes_oxley_summary.htm.

Test Your Understanding

These chapter questions are provided to test your understanding of the information in the text. They are neither examples of CTP examination questions nor are they in the examination format.

Answers are on pages 624–626.

1. What is corporate governance and why is it important?

2. What are the important components of corporate governance?

3. What are the main purposes of the recent Sarbanes-Oxley and NYSE regulations with respect to corporate governance?

4. What is subcertification?

5. What is a code of conduct and why is it important?

6. Discuss the concept of conflict of interest.

7. Discuss policy and procedure (P&P) statements and why they should be published.

8. What is investor relations and why is it important?

9. What is pre-emptive right?

10. What is the role of financial reporting in expensing of stock options and how is FASB involved?

CHAPTER 20
Pension Fund Management

I. INTRODUCTION[1]

The area of pension fund management is becoming increasingly important for treasury in many organizations, especially with the recent acceleration of downsizing and outsourcing. When a company downsizes or "flattens" its structure, the management of pension funds often becomes the responsibility of the treasurer. Even if a company decides to outsource pension fund management, the treasurer is typically charged with oversight of pension fund managers.

II. ERISA

The Employee Retirement Income Security Act of 1974 (ERISA) is the federal law that established legal guidelines for private pension plan administration and investment practices. ERISA has five major objectives:

- To ensure that employees and beneficiaries receive adequate information about their benefit plans
- To set standards of conduct for individuals who manage employee-benefit plans and plan funds
- To determine that adequate funds are being set aside to pay promised pension benefits
- To ensure that employees receive pension benefits after they have satisfied certain minimum requirements
- To safeguard pension benefits for workers whose pension plans are terminated

ERISA and subsequent legislation (especially the Tax Reform Act of 1986) led to new standards that must be met by all employee benefit plans to qualify for favorable tax treatment and to avoid civil and criminal penalties. Failure to meet these standards can mean disqualification and, in some cases, an excise tax. Penalties on employees who receive benefits above certain limits range from additional taxes to loss of tax exclusion for the benefits. To be qualified under ERISA, a retirement plan must be funded, meaning that contributions by both employer and employees must be placed in a separate fund held by a third party. The third party is usually a trustee or an insurance company.

A. ERISA Regulations

ERISA is the principal legislation governing private pension funds. The Department of Labor (DOL) and the IRS jointly enforce ERISA. ERISA consists of four "Titles":

- **Title I:** Employee rights, including provisions related to reporting and disclosure, participation, vesting, funding and fiduciary liabilities and responsibilities
- **Title II:** Requirements as a condition of qualification for tax deferral under the Internal Revenue Code, and tax provisions administered by the IRS, including those related to the deduction of contributions and taxation of benefits
- **Title III:** Provisions related to administration and enforcement
- **Title IV:** Provisions related only to defined benefit retirement plans

B. ERISA Fiduciary Responsibilities

A fiduciary is an individual or a member of a Board who is given possession of property, such as plan assets, in trust. A fiduciary assumes the legal obligation to administer plan assets solely for the purpose(s) specified. Typically, the employer's Board of Directors designates one or more committees to act as a fiduciary. These committees are charged with administration of the plans and oversight of the management of plan assets.

The cornerstone of ERISA's fiduciary standards is found in Section 404, which explicitly sets forth ERISA's requirements for prudence in asset management. Specifically, Section 404(a)(1) directs a fiduciary to "discharge his duties with respect to the plan solely in the interest of the participants and beneficiaries and for the exclusive purpose of providing benefits to participants and their beneficiaries, and defraying reasonable expenses of administering the plan."

ERISA further requires that a fiduciary act "with the care, skill, prudence and diligence under the circumstances then prevailing that a prudent man acting in a like capacity and familiar with such matters would use in the conduct of an enterprise of like character and with like aims."

The "prudent man" standard has been interpreted and applied as a "prudent expert" standard. It is more stringent than standards contained in most other corporate and securities laws, which merely require that there is not any negligence or gross negligence.

1. Prohibited Transactions under ERISA

A prohibited transaction is an economic transaction directly or indirectly involving plan assets and parties related to the plan. A "party-in-interest" includes:

- Fiduciaries, counsel or employees of the plan
- Individuals providing services to the plan
- An employer whose employees are covered by the plan
- A relative of any of the preceding
- Various other individuals and entities with ties to the employer or the plan [ERISA Section 3(14)]

Prohibited transactions include:

- The sale, exchange or lease of property
- A loan or other extension of credit
- The furnishing of goods, services or facilities
- The transfer or use of plan assets involving a party-in-interest
- The acquisition of employer securities or employer real estate in excess of the limits set by law

ERISA provides three kinds of exemptions from prohibited transaction rules:

- Statutory exemptions have been granted for certain routine transactions, such as payment of benefits to a participant who is also a fiduciary.
- Class exemptions have been granted for certain transactions that are not specifically defined in ERISA, but are considered acceptable by the DOL.
- Individual exemptions have been granted on a case-by-case basis. These exemptions require that the individual or party-in-interest demonstrate that the transaction is in the best interest of the plan participants.

2. ERISA Sanctions on Fiduciaries

Civil liabilities and/or criminal charges can be imposed on a fiduciary that breaches any of the responsibilities, duties or obligations imposed under Title I of ERISA. The fiduciary is liable for any loss resulting from each breach. A fiduciary is also liable to the plan for any profits that the fiduciary or other party-in-interest makes through the use of plan assets. Tax sanctions, in the form of special excise taxes, can be imposed on "disqualified persons" (essentially the same as parties-in-interest) who participate in prohibited transactions. A fiduciary must be aware that if a plan is disqualified, all earnings of the plan are immediately subject to taxation.

C. Impact of ERISA on Corporate Governance

Private pension funds purchase equity securities for investment rather than to gain control of the companies whose securities they buy. With ownership, however, comes the responsibility to exercise ownership rights, including the voting of proxies. In accordance with ERISA, these voting decisions, like investment decisions, must be made solely in the interest of plan participants.

In situations where a change in control of the corporation is at issue, the voting decision must be free of bias toward either the existing management or the prospective acquirer, and must reflect an objective assessment regarding the greatest value to plan participants.

ERISA regulations, as interpreted by the DOL, require that proxy decisions be made by the plan sponsor unless such authority has been fully delegated to an investment manager. If the plan sponsor delegates to an investment manager the right to make voting decisions, the sponsor cannot interfere with the manager's decisions but retains the responsibility to monitor the decisions. In any case, the proxies must be voted solely in the interest of plan participants.

D. ERISA Reporting and Disclosure Requirements

ERISA reporting and disclosure requirements apply to all private pension plans. These requirements are detailed and complex, necessitating filings with several federal agencies. These filings include the following:

- **The Internal Revenue Service:** Annual Report (Form 5500) provides a description of the plan, plan financial statements, insurance, and actuarial information, as well as a summary of plan assets.
- **The Department of Labor:** Summary Plan Description, including the ERISA statement of rights, summarizes the provisions of the plan in language understandable by the average plan participant.

- **The Pension Benefit Guaranty Corporation (PBGC):** The PBGC is a U.S. government agency that insures the pension plans of private U.S. corporations. Quarterly and annual PBGC reports set forth the computation of premiums due.
- **Other Filings:** ERISA requires that plan participants be provided copies of the Summary Plan Description and an annual summary of financial statements. Copies of supporting plan documents, as well as filings with federal agencies, are also provided to plan participants on request.

E. ERISA Nondiscrimination Rule

A retirement plan is qualified under ERISA only if it does not discriminate in favor of Highly Compensated Employees (HCEs). The plan must comply in both form and operation to this rule. To satisfy this basic nondiscrimination rule, there are three requirements:

- The contributions or benefits of the plan must be nondiscriminatory in amount
- The benefits, rights and features provided under the plan must be available ina nondiscriminatory manner.
- The effect of plan amendments and terminations must be nondiscriminatory.

1. Highly Compensated Employees (HCEs)

An HCE is an employee who was a five-percent owner of the sponsoring company at any time during the current or preceding year or who had compensation during the prior year in excess of $90,000. The compensation limit is adjusted for inflation in $5,000 increments. Alternatively, the sponsor may elect to include those employees exceeding the compensation limit only if they are in the top-paid group, generally defined as the top 20 percent of employees, ranked on the basis of compensation.

2. Minimum Coverage Requirements

In order to receive favorable tax treatment, a retirement plan must satisfy one of two coverage tests, either the ratio-percentage test or the average-benefit test:

- Under the ratio-percentage test, the percentage of non-HCEs who benefit under the plan must equal 70 percent of the percentage of HCEs who benefit under the plan.
- Under the average-benefits test, the plan must cover a nondiscriminatory group of non-HCEs and the benefits (expressed as a percentage of compensation) provided to non-HCEs must be at least 70 percent as great as that provided to HCEs.

F. ERISA Plan Termination

ERISA provides for two types of plan termination under the regulatory oversight of the PBGC: distress termination and standard termination with reversion.

1. Distress Termination

In this type of plan termination, the PBGC takes over the plan and pays all guaranteed benefits up to a maximum amount determined by the PBGC. The plan sponsor and any controlled group of companies are liable to the PBGC for any unfunded benefits. Only financially troubled employers, as determined by the PBGC, qualify for distress termination. Typically, these are companies in or near bankruptcy with significantly underfunded pension plans. Prioritization of benefits payable in a distress termination are set forth in detail by ERISA, with benefits attributable to employee contributions taking priority, followed by other PBGC guaranteed benefits.

2. Standard Termination

In standard terminations, benefits are funded through the purchase of annuities or through lump sum payments to participants. The plan administrator must give 60 days' notice to both plan participants and the PBGC and must receive PBGC approval before proceeding.

Plan reversions generally refer to the disposition of assets within a defined benefit plan following standard termination by an employer. In many cases, reversion is not attractive to the employer because any remaining surplus, following termination without a successor plan, is reduced by a confiscatory combination of ordinary federal income tax, excise tax, and termination benefit enhancements totaling 80 percent or more of the residual surplus before the sponsor can recapture the remainder. Plan assets, including income and excise taxes in excess of the insurance premium and other costs of termination, may in certain circumstances "revert" to the employer.

III. FORMATS FOR PENSION PLANS

There are two basic formats for private trusteed pension plans, single- and multi-employer. Single-employer plans are established and maintained by corporations or non-profit organizations for employees while multi-employer plans are maintained pursuant to collective bargaining agreements between a union and two or more employers. The union and the employers share representation on a joint board of trustees that oversees all aspects of plan administration. It is estimated that at the end of 1999, single-employer plans represented 91.5 percent of private trustee plan assets, with multi-employer plans representing the balance.

A. Types of Pension Plans

There are two distinct types of pension plans: defined benefit and defined contribution plans. At the end of 1997, The Committee on the Investment of Employee Assets (CIEBA) estimated that defined benefit plans accounted for 55 percent of private trusteed plan assets, while defined contribution plan assets accounted for the balance. Defined benefit assets represented 62.4 percent of total pension plans assets of CIEBA members as of the end of 2000. This figure is virtually unchanged from 1996, when defined benefit assets represented 63.5 percent of CIEBA member assets.

1. Defined Benefit Plan

In a defined benefit plan, the benefit payment for each participant is calculated (or "defined") by a formula as specified in the plan. The formula is most often based on factors such as the employee's level of pay and length of service at retirement. The projected future benefit payments for all participants are then aggregated and discounted to obtain the plan's liability, also sometimes referred to as the plan's obligation. The plan's liability or obligation is funded by employer contributions (and sometimes employee contributions), as well as cumulative earnings. The value of the assets is measured independently of the liability and is based on fair market value. A defined benefit plan can thus be overfunded or underfunded depending on whether the value of the plan's assets is greater than or less than the amount of the liability.

2. Defined Contribution Plan

A defined contribution plan is a retirement savings vehicle that provides benefits "defined" by contributions to the plan and investment earnings on those contributions. Contributions and the subsequent earnings are credited to an individual account for each participant. The amount owed to participants at retirement is based solely on the account balance at the time of withdrawal.

Participants often bear responsibility for managing the investments in their accounts. For instance, in some cases, participants must choose among investment options that are offered by the employer (plan sponsor). The amount of investment earnings that a participant accumulates is directly related to each participant's investment choices. Unlike the typical defined, in a defined contribution plan the asset and the liability are by definition always equal in value. The typical defined contribution plans offered today are either a 401(k) or a 403(b). In most of these plans, the plan sponsor (employer) chooses a plan provider, typically a mutual fund or insurance company, to offer a set of investment choices for the plan participants (employees).

3. Differences between the Two Types of Plans

The primary difference between defined benefit and defined contribution plans is who bears the risk of a shortfall in investment results. This risk is borne by the employer in the case of defined benefit plans and by the employee in the case of defined contribution plans.

A typical defined benefit plan promises a benefit upon retirement based on the employee's pay and length of service. If contributions and investment earnings on the contributions do not provide enough funds to meet the plan's promise at retirement, then employers must make additional contributions to meet the shortfall. If investment earnings exceed expectations, the employee still receives only the promised benefit. In defined contribution plans, on the other hand, higher than expected investment returns are passed on directly to the employee, who must also accept the risk of a lower asset value if returns are disappointing.

Other important differences between plans include the fact that in the early years of an employee's career, account values in defined benefit plans generally grow slower than in defined contribution plans; however, the reverse is also true in later years. Additionally, defined contribution plan assets are generally more portable than defined benefit plan assets. The general trend is away from defined benefit plans and toward the use of defined contribution plans.

4. Portability

Portability depends on several factors, including the plan type and vesting. Vesting simply defines whether the participant is legally entitled to claim all plan benefits. Normally, the participant is immediately vested in any of his/her own contributions and the earnings on those contributions, but is not otherwise fully vested until the participant has been in the plan for at least three to five years, although this can vary significantly from organization to organization.

Defined contribution plans offer portability of existing asset balances, including employer contributions when vesting requirements have been met. Portability of the participant's benefit value in a defined benefit plan depends upon the design of the particular plan.

B. Risks Borne by Plan Participants

Many defined contribution plans are participant-directed, meaning that participants are responsible for deciding how their individual account assets are invested among a plan's available investment options. Because participants make these investment decisions, they also assume responsibility for the consequences and, therefore, take on any investment risks.

Mortality risk is also transferred to the participant. Mortality risk is the risk that the participant may live longer than average, and thus outlive predicted benefit requirements. In participant-directed plans, the employee has more control over the building of retirement assets through the selection of investments and the ability to specify what portion of the employee's pay is invested in the plan. However, participants have few avenues of recourse if the accumulated assets are insufficient in meeting their retirement needs.

Insufficiency of retirement assets in a defined contribution plan can be ascribed to five factors:

- Failure by employees to set aside enough of current income
- Adverse market results
- Limited investment choices
- Poor investment-fund selection or asset allocation by the employee
- A greater need for retirement assets than was originally anticipated due to changing personal circumstances or mortality assumptions

In a defined benefit plan, on the other hand, the employer is responsible for bearing both investment and mortality risk. The PBGC provides an additional level of security. In the event that the company does not fulfill its obligations, some residual risk of insufficiency of defined benefit plans is borne by the participants to the extent that the PBGC may not cover 100 percent of the promised benefit. For most employees, this risk is generally considered slight.

Also, a portion of the defined benefit may exceed the maximum allowable limit that can be paid out of an ERISA qualified plan. Thus, for the higher-paid employee, the excess benefit can bear long-term corporate credit risk.

C. Risks to the Employer under the Two Types of Plans

The employer's reported expense for a defined contribution plan is closely aligned with employer contributions. In most cases, the amount of employer contributions is far less volatile than contributions to defined benefit plans, which are affected by current interest rates, actuarial assumptions and investment performance. The reported expense of defined benefit plans is not directly tied to employer contributions. Further, the reporting may be less stable than defined contribution plans, which may add to operating income volatility.

The transfer of investment and mortality risk to participants also reduces employers' risk. For the majority of defined contribution plans, employer contributions are directly related to employee contributions and/or to the company's profitability, not to the value of the assets. On the other hand, the opportunity to reduce employer contributions is generally available only in defined benefit plans. If the value of the assets in a defined benefit plan is greater than the promised payments to participants, the required employer contributions may decrease over time. Also, in a defined benefit plan there is a possibility that excess assets could be used to enhance benefits. This opportunity to decrease the level of contributions does not generally exist in a defined contribution plan because contributions are not tied to the value of the assets.

D. Deferred Compensation and Non-Qualified Plans

Employees can obtain significant tax benefits by deferring part of their compensation until a later date when they may be taxed at a lower rate. (The assumption is that overall income, and thus tax rates, will be lower at retirement.) The company recognizes significant tax benefits if this is done in conjunction with a pension or profit-sharing plan. However, to qualify for these benefits, the plan must meet the requirements of section 401(a) of the Internal Revenue Code (IRC). This section requires broad-based employee participation and sets limits on the amount of income that can be deferred.

Also, the IRC prevents qualified plans from discriminating in favor of officers, shareholders, and highly paid employees. If a plan does not meet IRC requirements, the business expense deduction for all contributions to date could be disallowed, and employees could be taxed on the amounts of the contributions in each year in which the contributions were made.

A non-qualified plan can be established to eliminate these requirements but it loses the tax benefits. Such a plan includes only those employees whom the company chooses to include. The employee can still defer the taxability of the income until it is received, but the company cannot take the tax deduction associated with the compensation until the employee receives the income. Other types of plans in this category include the 401(k) plan and the 403(b) or tax-deferred annuity (TDA).

1. 401(k) Plans

These plans are generally referred to as cash-deferred/salary reduction plans and are sanctioned by IRC Section 401(k). Essentially, the employee is given the choice of either receiving an amount, in the form of currently taxable compensation (for federal income tax purposes) or deferring the amount to be taxed at a future date. This amount may be part of normal salary or other compensation such as bonus or profit sharing. Under these plans, employees may divert a portion of their compensation into the deferred-tax 401(k) plans. Employees may also have the choice of making additional contributions into the plans on a before-tax basis, thus avoiding any federal income tax on those amounts until they are received at retirement. This type of plan must meet the same strict guidelines concerning non-discrimination as qualified deferred compensation plans.

The company may also make an additional contribution to the plan on behalf of the employee (typically in cash or company stock). In many cases, the company contribution is based on a matching formula relative to the employee's contribution or, in other cases, the employer's contributions may be made for all eligible employees regardless of their contributions.

2. 403(b) Plans or Tax-Deferred Annuities (TDAs)

TDAs are generally made available to employees of religious, charitable, educational, scientific, and literary organizations that are chartered on a non-profit basis. In these plans, only the employees may make contributions, generally by payroll deductions. The advantage to the employee is that such contributions may be made on a before-tax basis, thus eliminating current income taxes on the deferred amounts.

The funds in the TDA can accrue interest on a non-taxable basis until received at retirement. There are limits to the amount that can be deferred based on the level of annual income and coverage by other types of tax-deferred plans. These limits are essentially the same as 401(k) plans. These plans, both 401(k) and 403(b), offer the employee the right to borrow money from the plan under certain conditions or to withdraw all funds prior to retirement (age 59-1/2) under certain emergencies (medical, hardship, education, etc.).

E. Current Developments in Private Pension Plan Design

Because of the increased complexity of defined benefit plan regulations and the desire on the part of employers to provide a visible and portable benefit, growth has occurred in hybrid plans, whose designs combine defined benefit and defined contribution plan features.

1. Hybrid Plans

Legally, every plan is either a defined benefit plan or a defined contribution plan, regardless of what the various characteristics may appear to be to the participant. However, hybrid plans that offer various blends of defined benefit and defined contribution characteristics have been developed. The increasingly popular cash balance plan, for example, often has a portability feature and reports participant "balances" that look just like defined contribution accounts. However, cash balance plans are actually defined benefit plans. Similarly, pension equity plans, also known as retirement bonus plans, report account balances to participants and look like defined contribution plans but are, in reality, defined benefit plans.

2. Cash Balance versus Pension Equity Plans

The basic difference between the two types of plans is that the cash balance plan is a career-average plan and the pension equity plan is designed as a final-pay plan. In a cash balance plan, benefits increase by a rate applied to eligible compensation for each year of employment, without consideration of future salary inflation. In a pension equity plan, a rate is applied to average final compensation, which generally incorporates the effect of inflation over the service period. The equity plan rate is a cumulative rate based on a participant's age and/or years of service.

3. Floor Plans

Other examples of hybrid plans include various "floor" plans, which are actually two coordinated plans, one of which is a defined benefit plan and the other a defined contribution plan. The defined benefit plan normally sets a floor retirement payment. Investments in the defined contribution plan determine the retirement payment if the value exceeds the value of the floor payment. If the value of the defined contribution account drops below the floor, the defined benefit plan funds the gap and the participant receives the floor payment.

4. Advantages of Hybrid Plans

When an employer decides to change from a traditional defined benefit plan to a plan with defined contribution characteristics, converting the existing plan to a hybrid plan may be the preferred alternative. A hybrid plan may be the more attractive choice when the existing defined benefit plan is substantially overfunded.

Redesigning an existing plan as a hybrid allows the surplus assets in the plan to continue to pre-fund employer contributions, thus controlling costs more effectively than plan terminations allow. The employer may also prefer to retain control of investment decisions in the plan.

The employer may use a hybrid plan designed to improve the workforce recruitment and retention power of the existing plan by giving some user-friendly defined contribution-like characteristics, such as "account" balance reporting and portability. In both cash balance and pension equity plans, the "accounts" reported to participants are the actual balances but are not in any way impacted by actual investment results. The value of the "accounts" is determined by an established formula rather than by a variable investment return, which qualifies the plans as defined benefit in design.

IV. OTHER CONSIDERATIONS IN PENSION MANAGEMENT

Among other considerations in pension management are establishing a pension committee, managing investment managers, understanding tax implications, appointing a custodian and providing education/advice for plan participants.

A. Establishing a Pension Committee

For companies with defined benefit plans and an accompanying pension fund, a pension committee is typically formed to manage and advise the process. In many companies, this responsibility may be under the auspices of the Finance and Pension Committee, which oversees not just pension management but also financial position and policies, financing activities and financial risk management policies and activities. The role of these committees is to provide advice and counsel to the company's senior management.

B. Managing Investment Managers[2]

Financial professionals who want to ensure that plan portfolios are being managed properly must be diligent in their approach to management of investment managers.

A good investment manager is well informed on various economic issues. They frequently evaluate changes in interest rates, economic and political developments, and stock and bond activity. They are adept at analyzing corporate financial statements and monitoring business activities to assess the viability and suitability of a particular investment. High-caliber managers frequently visit corporations in which they currently invest or plan to invest. The purpose is to double-check the facts behind published information in investment research reports, as well as to identify and assess new opportunities, asset allocation policies or investment holdings. Armed with this information, a professional investment manager can execute well-informed and timely investment decisions.

When advising clients, the best investment managers adhere to a formalized process that governs professional service. In essence, the process covers four key components: (1) establishing client objectives and risk tolerance, (2) allocating assets, (3) selecting a mix of investment products that best suit the client's needs and (4) monitoring the portfolio's ongoing progress toward meeting a company's goals.

More specifically, the first step of the process answers three questions:

- What rate of return is necessary to achieve the client/company's investment goals?
- How much time is available to fulfill those financial goals?
- How much risk can the individual and/or the organization tolerate?

This process may have to be repeated if the goals, time, and risk tolerance change.

To develop the optimum asset allocation, an investment manager must:

- Adequately diversify the portfolio
- Maximize returns on investments within the acceptable risk tolerance
- Lower the portfolio's overall volatility
- Position the portfolio for potential investment opportunities. This is accomplished by examining particular asset classes and what proportion each should cover

Identifying the investment manager is the next step. Using the previously noted criteria, due diligence should include understanding the risk and return characteristics of each investment manager's approach. Thereafter, investment managers should be monitored routinely and reevaluated to ensure they are consistently adhering to a professional management style and achieving the desired results.

The review process should encompass a comprehensive quarterly assessment of the manager's progress in meeting the client/company's investment objectives, as evidenced by the portfolio's performance. Ten key questions must be asked of investment managers:

- What are your credentials (education, licenses, certifications, professional recognition, honors, etc.)?
- How long have you been serving as an investment adviser?
- What is your investment philosophy?
- What are your management fees?
- Who are the portfolio managers for this fund and what are their track records?
- Do you have working relationships with other professionals such as accountants and/or tax attorneys?
- Do you participate in industry conferences and continuing education programs?
- What is your current client mix?
- What is the source of your new clients (word of mouth, client/professional referrals, etc.)?
- How do you perform on behalf of your clients, including communications, reporting, and overall due diligence?

C. Understanding Tax Implications

Many tax implications are related to any type of pension plan. The primary implication is that for ERISA-qualified plans, the funds contributed by both employees and the companies are allowed to accumulate on a tax-deferred basis. For defined contribution plans, employee contributions are generally tax-exempt for the employee during the year of contribution while contributions made by the companies are tax-deductible. Also, tax issues in the management of defined benefit plans must be considered. The tax laws are complex and change frequently, so tax experts should be consulted on a regular basis.

D. Appointing a Custodian

The appointment of an independent custodian (often a financial institution) is an effective way to safeguard the physical and legal integrity of the assets in a pension fund. The custodian holds the pension fund assets and, therefore, should be in a position to ensure the safekeeping of the assets. The custodian may provide additional services such as:

- Securities lending
- Cash management
- Investment accounting
- Reporting
- Performance measurement

In some cases, a custodian may also serve as an external audit function with respect to the investment of pension assets.

E. Providing Education/Advice for Plan Participants[3]

One key decision for employers offering defined contribution plans is to what extent the companies offer the employees participating in the plan either investment advice or education. While ERISA does not specifically require that plans offer either investment education or advice, it requires fiduciaries to give appropriate consideration to the relevant facts and circumstances. The failure to address these issues may be a fiduciary breach in and of itself.

Some companies choose to provide only education for plan participants. This is in line with the U.S. Department of Labor's Interpretive Bulletin 96-1, which states that employers can provide investment education to employees without concern about becoming investment advisors. Offering advice could possibly expose employers to potential liability issues if the advice fails to produce the expected financial benefits.

ERISA states that if the following three characteristics are present, the recommendations are considered fiduciary investment advice:

- A fee is charged for the recommendations about investing.
- There is a mutual understanding that the advice is a primary basis for investment decisions.
- The advice is individualized and based on the particular needs of each employee.

A decision by fiduciaries not to offer advice should be reached only through a prudent process. This process consists of analyzing participants' needs and investigating the services available under the plans. Although ERISA regulations do not provide a clear direction that plan sponsors prefer, there is sufficient guidance to meet the law's "prudent expert" standard.

For many plan sponsors, the goal is to provide an investment solution that prudently meets the employees' needs in a cost-effective manner. In some cases, the plan provider may provide education and/or advice solutions. But to protect participants, the DOL states that if a plan provider either owns more than five percent of the adviser or pays more than five percent of the total revenue of the adviser, then the advice is deemed to be conflicted because the adviser is not independent.

The ideal for any plan sponsor is to provide the highest level of benefits to its employees at the lowest cost, which provides a chance for all employees to have the means to retire. Some plan sponsors choose to pay for the advice; other sponsors may want the plan participants to pay. Regardless of who pays, the plan sponsor and the fiduciary must manage plan expenses and ensure that the charges are reasonable. In adding any cost to an ERISA plan, the benefits should warrant the cost.

F. Current Information on Pension Fund Management

The area of pension fund management is in a constant state of change as financial markets and regulations evolve. See the Pensions and Benefits Administration section of the AFP's Web site (http://www.afponline.org) for the most up-to-date information.

Endnotes

1. Significant portions of this chapter are drawn from: The Basics of Pension Plans Regulated by ERISA, Published by The Committee on the Investment of Employee Benefit Assets (CIEBA) of the Association for Financial Professionals, 2003
2. Information in this section is drawn from "Keeping Score – What to Look for in a Professional Investment Manager," by David P. Sobocinski, AFP Exchange, March/April 2004.
3. Information in this section is taken from: "Investment Advice vs. Education: Which Should You Offer?" by C.Frederick Reish, Esq., AFP Exchange, March/April 2004.

Test Your Understanding

These chapter questions are provided to test your understanding of the information in the text. They are neither examples of CTP examination questions nor are they in the examination format.

Answers are on pages 627–629.

1. What is ERISA and what are its primary objectives?
2. According to ERISA, what is a fiduciary?
3. What are prohibited transactions according to ERISA regulations?
4. What are HCEs and how do they impact ERISA nondiscrimination rules?
5. Describe a distress termination of a pension plan.
6. What is a defined benefit pension plan?
7. Discuss the differences between a defined benefit versus a defined contribution pension plan.
8. What is a 401(k) plan?
9. What is a hybrid pension plan?
10. What purpose does an independent custodian serve?

CHAPTER 21
Relationship Management

I. INTRODUCTION

While commercial banks have historically dominated the marketplace for treasury-related products and services, today many different types of non-bank and third-party financial service providers (FSPs) offer treasury-related services. There are two principal reasons for the development of FSPs: first, the deregulation of the financial services industry beginning with the Monetary Control Act of 1980 and, second, the ability of FSPs to provide many products and services at lower costs than commercial banks, especially for smaller and mid-market companies. Therefore, while commercial banks continue to control access to the payment and clearing systems and also remain an important source of commercial credit in the United States, many of the considerations related to bank relationship management apply equally to FSPs.

II. Financial Institution and FSP Selection Process

Consolidation and specialization in the financial services industry have made financial institution and FSP selection a critical decision process for a treasurer. Consolidation reduces the number of providers in certain product areas while specialization raises the importance of matching a given company's needs with a particular provider's strengths.

The selection process may be initiated for a variety of reasons, such as:

- The need for a new product or service
- As part of a reengineering program
- As part of a regular product and service review
- To reduce costs
- To update existing technologies

Regardless of the reason, the process should always begin by identifying the product or service specifications that are critical to achieving both the strategic and the operational objectives of treasury. These specifications form the selection criteria that provide the basis for evaluating financial institution and vendor proposals.

A. Selection Criteria

Evaluating service providers involves assessing each capability based on selection criteria. Selection criteria may be quantitative, such as performance measurements and pricing, or qualitative, such as service quality. Although selection criteria may vary widely from one product or service to another and from one company to another, the criteria often include the following factors:

- Geographic and other convenience considerations
- Ability to fulfill product or service specifications
- Expertise of personnel, including quality of customer service and product support
- Commitment to, or knowledge of, a specific industry or business
- Ability to customize services, develop new services, update technologies and meet future needs of the company
- Adequacy of internal controls, backup systems and disaster-recovery plans
- Pricing
- The cost of switching providers

In addition, a company should also assess the service provider's financial strength, especially in instances when replacing the provider may be difficult or may take considerable time or when the provider holds assets for the company, such as deposits maintained at a financial institution. In selecting a financial institution (versus selecting an FSP), the willingness to provide credit on flexible terms and at competitive rates is also an important consideration.

B. Soliciting Information from Financial Institutions and FSPs

Financial institution or FSP selection often involves a formal process using written proposals. Sometimes, a company may have targeted specific candidates or may already have established a relationship with a particular financial institution or FSP. In such cases, the selection process may not involve a formal written proposal. However, in general, written proposals are preferable because less chance exists for misunderstanding.

In addition, a formal selection process enables a company to review the product and service offerings of multiple providers. The two methods most commonly used to obtain information from potential providers are requests for information (RFIs) and requests for proposals (RFPs).

1. Request for Information (RFI)

In some cases, an RFI may be used in the selection process. An RFI is a letter that requests information regarding a vendor's ability to provide and interest in providing services. An RFI is often employed by a company simply to confirm that the use of a current provider is justified or to narrow the field of potential providers before issuing an RFP. An RFI is also used to solicit ideas from service providers on how to solve a particular business or operational problem. An RFI can speed up the selection process.

2. Request for Proposal (RFP)

An RFP is a formal document prepared by a company that outlines its objectives and service requirements. An RFP may be used to obtain bids for anything ranging from one specific service to a company's entire relationship. By law, some government entities are required to prepare RFPs on a periodic basis, usually every three to five years, to ensure that comparable services are received at competitive prices. Many private sector companies also periodically prepare RFPs for similar reasons. There are now standard formats that allow for electronic submission and comparison of proposals. The Association for Financial Professionals (AFP) and the Bank Administration Institute (BAI) have published standard RFP formats for banking services.

A RFP should address all of the selection criteria that have been identified as being relevant for the products and services under consideration. A typical RFP requests the following 10 items:

- Background information on the provider
- A summary of the proposed solution
- Service descriptions
- Service features and benefits
- A demonstration of the provider's commitment to support and enhance services
- A cost/benefit analysis
- A financial institution's pro forma account analysis statement or an FSP's pricing schedule
- Sample service commitments or agreements
- A timetable for service implementation
- Customer references

In recent years, some companies have also started to send out technical RFPs that stress the level and quality of services rather than pricing. This trend is likely to continue as more and more companies outsource daily treasury functions to financial institutions and FSPs.

C. The Selection Decision

Once all of the responses to an RFP have been submitted, they must be compared in order to choose a provider. The basis for the comparison should be the initial quantitative and qualitative selection criteria. Because many factors are involved, treasury personnel often must rank the selection criteria in order of importance and weight the factors for comparison purposes. By assigning a score to each possible response and applying the predetermined weight to the score, the resulting weighted scores can be used to assist in the selection. An additional consideration in the decision is the responsiveness of the provider during the selection process and the quality of the RFP submitted. The evaluation of responses may be performed either by treasury personnel or by an outside consultant who has been engaged to assist in the selection process.

When the RFP is for banking services, a pro forma account analysis captures most of the pricing and compensation detail. Accurate evaluation and comparison of the pro forma account analysis statements may be critical to making the best selection decision. For a more detailed discussion of this topic, see the section titled Account Analysis, later in this chapter.

III. MONITORING FINANCIAL INSTITUTION AND FSP RISK

Risk management requires ongoing monitoring of bank and FSP practices and creditworthiness. Two particular areas of practice warrant special mention. First, because banks and FSPs often control an organization's information flows, information records and liquid assets, it is critical that banks and FSPs have adequate backup systems and disaster recovery procedures. These procedures should be evaluated at the onset of the relationship and periodically thereafter. In addition, service agreements and contract provisions should indicate specific rights and responsibilities of the parties in the event of an interruption in services.

Second, because banks and FSPs have access to extensive confidential information about an organization's customer base, a treasurer must understand under what conditions, if any, this information may be shared with affiliates or other parties.

Sometimes, a conflict of interest may arise when a bank or an FSP serves in multiple capacities. A bank with a lending relationship may also serve as a bond trustee. If the borrower becomes distressed, there is a risk that the bank might protect its own credit to the detriment of the borrower and/or the bondholders. To prevent such abuses, banks traditionally establish a notional barrier (sometimes referred to as a "Chinese wall") to information flows between different functional areas.

In addition, a recent trend among banks and FSPs is the formation of business alliances with other vendors who have complementary areas of expertise or superior cost efficiencies. Often, these alliances result in the contracted bank or FSP outsourcing some or all of the services to another provider. For example, many banks outsource their credit card merchant processing operations to third-parties. In these cases, information is shared with outside parties to which each task is outsourced.

Finally, a treasurer must closely monitor the credit risk of banks and FSPs. If a bank or an FSP experiences financial problems, it may result in a deterioration of service quality. However, the greatest risk is loss of assets.

Credit ratings are a proxy for creditworthiness. A number of agencies offer rating services. Some agencies only offer ratings, while others also offer detailed backup reports that provide both quantitative financial analyses and qualitative assessments of management. Treasury policy often dictates the minimum credit rating that must be maintained by counterparties and other FSPs.

IV. BANK RELATIONSHIP MANAGEMENT

While there are many similarities between bank and FSP relationship management, bank relationships involve a number of unique considerations due to the type of documentation required, the method of monitoring risk, and the methods of compensation.

Optimal performance by a bank requires an in-depth knowledge of a client's operations, policies, cash flows and financing needs. As a consequence, most bank relationships are long-term. Success in every long-term relationship involves a mutual accommodation of both parties. Among the factors that increase the mutual benefit and profitability of the relationship are:

- Open and frequent two-way communications
- Regular and timely feedback
- Documentation of expectations of both parties in agreements and legal contracts
- Fair compensation of a bank by a company, as well as fair pricing of services by the bank
- Complete and candid disclosure of information by both parties

Treasury is the focal point for bank relationship management. In some organizations, an employee within treasury is assigned primary responsibility for bank relationship management. In other organizations, the oversight of bank relationship management rests directly with the treasurer. In either case, bank relationship management entails many responsibilities, from day-to-day communication regarding transaction inquiries and problem resolution to quarterly, semi-annual, and/or annual performance evaluation and relationship reviews.

A. Number of Bank Relationships

A treasurer must determine how many bank relationships are necessary. Considerations in the determination include the existence of multi-state or international operations, the costs of maintaining multiple relationships, the relative strengths and capabilities of each bank, and the organization's credit needs. Companies in the U.S. with a nationwide over-the-counter/field bank collection and concentration system often deal with many small financial institutions. This is unique to the U.S. since nationwide branch banking is not yet fully available. Companies operating on a global basis may need to have multiple banking relationships to provide product and service coverage in all of the countries where the company has a presence.

The types, sophistication, and geographic location of services needed by a company often require that multiple banking relationships be maintained. In addition, secondary banking relationships allow a treasurer to shift accounts and services if a significant problem develops with the primary provider. In general, however, there is a global trend among large companies toward consolidation of banking relationships.

When a company has multiple bank relationships, one is often designated as a lead institution. There may be different lead institutions for credit and other services. While many companies establish multiple relationships to ensure that they have adequate credit facilities, a company's primary credit bank often facilitates this aspect of relationship management by assuming a lead role and selling excess credit exposure to other institutions or by acting as an agent for a loan syndication. (See Chapter 10, Liquidity Management, for additional information on loan syndication and participations.)

There are internal and external costs for each bank relationship, resulting in incentives for a company to optimize the number of bank relationships. In addition, banks have developed more sophisticated methods for measuring relationship profitability, resulting in lower costs for a company that obtains multiple services from one institution.

For example, pricing of loans is often based on interdependent factors such as:

- The cost of funds
- Risk
- Total loans committed and outstanding
- Service fees
- Deposit balances
- The range of other services used

Likewise, pricing of depository and cash management services is often based on such factors as:

- Volume
- Customization
- Exception handling requirements
- The cost of providing the service
- Operational overhead
- Deposit balances maintained
- Other services used

B. Documentation

Among important documents integral to a bank relationship are service agreements, account resolutions, signature cards, and credit agreements.

(A detailed discussion of credit agreements is in Chapter 13, Sources of Capital and Leasing.)

1. Service Agreements

Service agreements are formal agreements that document the requirements and expectations of both the purchaser and the provider of a specific service or services. The elements of a service agreement often include the following five:

- Operational policies and procedures, including the detailed processing requirements for the service, information needs, and individuals who are authorized to make changes
- Performance standards that define agreed upon levels of service performance and quality
- Compensation policies, including pricing, method of payment, payment frequency, excess/deficit balance arrangements, contract length and adjustments
- Liability clauses defining responsibilities for specified risks
- Other terms and conditions of the relationship

2. An Account Resolution

An account resolution, usually a Board of Directors' resolution, is the basic account or service authorization empowering a representative for a business to enter into agreements for banking services. The resolution specifies what functions can be performed by specific individuals or job titles, authorized signers on an account, and the entire scope and limitations of the relationship.

The account resolution may be general or specific with regard to actions that the financial institution may take on behalf of the company. The resolution may be a standard form used by financial institutions to serve all commercial customers or it can be customized for a given company. Some companies have developed their own standard resolutions for use with all financial institutions; however, a given bank's acceptance of a company's resolution is subject to negotiation.

3. Signature Cards

Financial institutions require companies to furnish signatures of authorized signers or specimens of both facsimile and computerized signatures. These signatures are documented on signature cards. In conjunction with a signature card, financial institutions provide a standardized set of terms and conditions to companies when depository accounts are established. This document, often provided in the form of a brochure, details the responsibilities of the bank and the account holders in the maintenance of accounts. Among the important areas contained in the document include information on funds availability, timeframes during which errors must be reported and a bank's right of offset against accounts related to fees owed. These terms are amended from time to time and notice is generally sent by mail along with account statements.

C. Performance Measurement and Evaluation

Service quality is an important aspect of a company's relationship with a financial institution. A company must clearly determine its performance expectations with regard to quality standards. A company's performance expectations should be based on the service levels stipulated in its agreements with the bank. Two of the most common types of performance measurement techniques are report cards and relationship reviews.

1. Report Card

A report card is a tool companies use to obtain a quantitative rating of a bank's level of service and responsiveness to problems. Criteria commonly found in report cards include number of errors by service, reporting times for information services, responsiveness to inquiries, timeliness of error resolution and the effectiveness of service personnel.

Companies may prepare report cards monthly, quarterly, semi-annually and/or annually. Certain companies that deal with multiple banks and FSPs frequently rank each one by the ability to meet the companies' quality criteria on a service-by-service basis.

2. Relationship Review

A relationship review is another procedure companies use to qualitatively assess service levels and responsiveness. Reviews may be either formal or informal. Formal reviews typically involve a quarterly, semi-annual or annual meeting of the senior management representatives of both parties. Informal reviews typically involve weekly or monthly contacts by individuals responsible for the day-to-day management of the relationship. Financial institutions also initiate relationship reviews by preparing summaries of services, fees, error rates and other relationship information. Relationship reviews enable financial institutions and companies to discuss future strategies and needs.

D. Monitoring Bank Risk

Unique to financial institutions is the CAMELS rating system, a system widely used by regulators to measure financial institution strength. CAMELS is the acronym for Capital Adequacy, Asset Quality, Management Capability, Earnings, Liquidity, and Sensitivity to Market Risk:

- Capital Adequacy – This measures the sufficiency of capital maintained, considering the nature and extent of an institution's risks and the ability of management to identify, measure, monitor, and control these risks.
- Asset Quality – This measures the existing and potential credit risk associated with the loan and investment portfolios, other assets and off balance-sheet items.
- Management Capability – This measures the qualitative expertise and ability of the Board of Directors and management to identify, measure, monitor and control the risks of an institution's activities, as well as the ability to ensure the institution's safe, sound and efficient operation in compliance with applicable laws and regulations.
- Earnings – This measures the level of earnings, earning trends and earnings sustainability. A bank's profitability, asset quality and credit-risk management can affect its earnings ratings.
- Liquidity – This measures the current and future levels of liquidity in comparison with funding needs. It also indicates the adequacy of funds management practices relative to an institution's size, complexity and risk profile.
- Sensitivity to Market Risk – This measures the degree to which changes in interest rates, foreign exchange rates, commodities prices or equities prices might adversely affect a financial institution's earnings or capital.

Although banks are prohibited from disclosing their CAMELS ratings, rating agencies such as Standard & Poor's, Moody's and Bankwatch evaluate the same factors in assessment processes.

E. Bank Compensation Practices

FSPs, and most banks, are compensated by means of a direct payment of fees for services provided. However, there is a form of compensation unique to banks because of the earnings credit typically provided to business account holders. Banks allow companies to pay for services in collected balances as an alternative to direct payment of fees. In some cases, companies pay using a combination of collected balances and fees. Banks may encourage customers to utilize one type of compensation due to their business strategy or desire for either deposits (i.e., balances) or fees. In actual practice, most companies compensate banks with a combination of balances and fees. Necessary transaction balances are maintained for partial compensation purposes and the remainder is paid in fees.

Occasionally, the earnings credit exceeds the service charges. This occurs when a company has collected balances in excess of the amount required for compensation. Regulation Q prohibits banks from paying interest on the excess balances. Policies vary on how financial institutions treat the excess. Institutions may or may not allow these excess balances to be carried forward to future periods. Some, but not all, banks may provide analysis on a combined basis so that excess balances in one account may be used to offset the service charges on another account. If accounts are combined, all balances are averaged together. This approach is helpful for a company that has excess balances in some accounts but deficit balances in others. By combining the balances for purposes of compensation, overall service charges are reduced. Combined analysis clearly provides benefits to companies that maintain most of their accounts at one bank.

F. Fee versus Balance Compensation

The advantages and disadvantages of each method vary, depending on whether they are viewed from a company or a financial institution perspective. There may also be considerations on the tax effects of the alternatives. A company favors fee compensation when it is able to earn more interest on investments than it can obtain in earnings credit on collected balances. The primary reasons for this are the deduction for the reserve requirement when balance compensation is calculated and the fact that the earnings credit rate (ECR) is typically calculated based on short-term investment instruments with low rates. (For a detailed discussion of ECR and related terminology, see the section titled Account Analysis, later in this chapter.)

This is even more compelling when a company is able to use excess balances to pay down short-term debt, which typically has a significantly higher opportunity cost than the ECR. In addition, fees can be budgeted and compared with other costs while balances are not as directly comparable.

Many banks prefer fee compensation because deposit balances increase the liabilities on a financial institution's balance sheet. This may lead to a need for additional capital to meet regulatory or other requirements. A second reason banks often prefer fee compensation is that, in comparison to interest income from loans, fees from services are a recurring and generally lower risk, source of earnings for a financial institution. In effect, services fees are like annuity payments.

On the other hand, from a company's point of view, balance compensation enables a company to take advantage of excess collected balances that arise from unanticipated deposits or precautionary transaction balances. Additional reasons a company may prefer balance compensation are:

- Some financial institutions price loans and other services more favorably if collected balances are maintained.
- Balance compensation is not as visible as fee expenditures for budgeting purposes.
- Some financial institutions' preference for deposit balances is so strong that they charge less if services are paid in balances rather than in fees.

The principal reason a bank prefers balances is that deposits may be used to fund loans and investments at rates in excess of the ECR provided to an account holder.

Comparing Costs Among Banks: Companies usually compare bank service charges both during the initial selection process and during periodic relationship reviews. However, service charge comparisons are difficult to perform due to the differences in analysis practices. Variations in banks' pricing strategies compound this difficulty. For example, service charges may be bundled or unbundled. Again, bundling is the practice of charging for a group of related services while unbundling is charging individually for each service utilized. In order to make valid comparisons, it is necessary to know all of the service charge components included in the bundled amount.

Also, prices may vary, depending on the level of service provided to a company. Some service or agreement provisions can influence bank compensation in ways that do not appear on a schedule of service charges. These include earnings credit for balances, deficient balance charges and availability schedules. Finally, while many institutions require monthly analysis, others may calculate the account analysis quarterly, semi-annually or annually. If an account holder's balances fluctuate from month to month, then quarterly, semi-annual or annual analysis periods allow excess balances in one month to offset charges in other months. Software is available from a variety of vendors to aid in comparing service charges from multiple banks.

V. ACCOUNT ANALYSIS

An account analysis statement is a paper or electronic report that a bank provides to commercial customers specifying:

- Services provided
- Balances maintained
- Volumes processed
- Charges assessed

It is essentially an invoice for services provided, along with detailed information on balances and credit earned for those balances. However, banks often use varying terminology in describing these services and/or varying definitions of identical terms. Services and fees can be bundled into a single line item or flat fee, can be unbundled (that is, detailed and itemized) or, more typically, can be some combination of bundled and unbundled. Fee structures are as varied and complex as the account analysis formats.

A. Account Analysis Standards

The current AFP Account Analysis Standard consists of sections that provide:

- Customer information
- Balance and compensation information
- Rate information
- Service information
- Adjustment detail
- Summary of accounts
- Optional historic balance and compensation information using AFP service codes

AFP service codes are six-character, alphanumeric codes that provide standard, uniform references and terms for identifying, describing and reporting bank services, as well as the associated charges. By simplifying and organizing the often varied and complex terminology used to identify bank services, the codes also help to resolve errors in volume and pricing. Examples of the AFP service code product families, indicated by the first two characters of the service code, are included in Appendix 21.1.

The Accredited Standards Committee of the American National Standards Institute (ANSI) has developed a standardized format (transaction set 822 – Account Analysis) for financial institutions to use in sending account analysis statements to account holders electronically. The ASC X12 822 transaction set accommodates the AFP standard account analysis format and service codes. The AFP Guide To Account Analysis includes a detailed transaction set 822 implementation guide.

B. Account Analysis Terminology

Among the common terms used in account analysis statements are the following:

- **Average Ledger Balance –** This is the sum of the daily ending ledger balances (both positive and negative) divided by the number of days in the analysis period. The balances used in the calculation are net of any current period adjustments.
- **Average Deposit Float –** This is the sum of the daily dollar amount of items in the process of collection divided by the number of days in the analysis period.
- **Average Collected Balance –** This is the sum of the daily ending collected balances (both positive and negative) divided by the number of days in the analysis period. In many account analysis statements, this item is calculated as the average ledger balance minus the average deposit float.
- **Reserve Requirement –** This represents a bank's compensation for the level of idle balances the financial institution is required to maintain at the Fed. The reserve requirement is currently 10 percent. Because a bank must meet the reserve requirement through non-interest-bearing deposits maintained in its Federal Reserve account, each bank passes on to its corporate customers the opportunity cost of maintaining these balances. In some instances, a financial institution may use a reserve percentage other than the 10 percent required by the Federal Reserve.
- **Service Charges –** These are the explicit fees or prices charged for services provided by a financial institution. Service charges are expressed either as a flat monthly fee or as a per-item or per-unit price. In the case of the latter, the unit price is multiplied by the volume to arrive at the analysis period total.
- **Investable Balance –** The investable balance represents the balances in the customer's account that the bank was able to invest in income producing assets during the account analysis period. Some banks calculate the investable balance as the average collected balance reduced by the reserve requirement balance. The investable balance can be either a surplus or a deficit. Some account analysis statements provide the investable balance that is required to compensate the bank for the current level of services.
- **Earning Credit and the Earnings Credit Rate (ECR) –** The earnings credit is the total dollar value of credit that can be used to offset the service charges incurred during the analysis period. It is calculated by multiplying the investable balance by the earnings credit rate (ECR) for the period. The method of determining the ECR varies by financial

institution. The most commonly used ECR is based upon the 90-day T-Bill rate. Other banks reduce the ECR by the reserve requirement (a reserve-adjusted ECR), in which case the average collected balance is used in the earnings credit calculation instead of the investable balance. (Note: The sample calculations below do not use a reserve-adjusted ECR.)

C. Account Analysis Calculations

Integrating these definitions results in the following formula used to measure the earnings credit:

$$EC = CB \times (1 - RR) \times \left(ECR \times \frac{D}{365}\right)$$

Where:

EC = Earnings Credit
CB = Average Collected Balance
RR = Reserve Requirement
ECR = Earnings Credit Rate
D = Number of Days in the Month*

**Some banks use the earnings credit rate divided by 12 to determine this monthly calculation instead of using the actual number of days.*

The earnings credit formula may be rearranged to allow a treasurer to determine the level of average collected balances that are required to offset service charges for the current analysis period. The formula for this computation is as follows:

$$CB = \frac{SC}{\left(ECR \times \frac{D}{365}\right) \times (1 - RR)}$$

Where:

CB = Collected Balances Required for Services
SC = Service Charges
ECR = Earnings Credit Rate
RR = Reserve Requirement
D = Number of Days in the Month*

**Some financial institutions use the earnings credit rate divided by 12 to determine this monthly calculation instead of using the actual number of days.*

Examples of these calculations are provided in Appendix 21.2.

Appendix 21.1 AFP Service Codes

Lockbox Services (05) – This product family includes services associated with wholesale and retail lockbox processing and covers document handling, data capture and programming, as well as lockbox deposit reporting and remittance information delivery.

Depository Services (10) – This product family includes services associated with the processing of coin and currency, encoded and unencoded check deposits, branch and vault deposits, supplies of coin and currency, and services related to domestic collections and return item processing. It also includes deposit reconciliation services, reports and software.

Paper Disbursement Services (15) – This product family includes services associated with the issuance, control, and processing of checks and drafts paid against an account, controlled disbursement, positive pay and payable-through-draft services. It also includes check inquiries and stop payments, returned checks, teller services, check sorting, microfilming and retention, and disbursement information reporting and software.

General ACH Services (25) – This product family includes services associated with the origination and receipt of ACH transactions, ACH input processing, ACH activity reporting, master file maintenance, ACH returns and exception processing and ACH software.

Appendix 21.2 Account Analysis Calculation Examples

EARNING CREDIT AVERAGE CALCULATION EXAMPLE

Assumptions:

Average ledger balance	$250,000
Deposit Float	$30,000
Reserve Requirement	10%
Earning Credit Rate	5%
Service charges for the month	$1,000
Days in month	30

Average Collected Balance Calculation:

Average ledger balance	$250,000
Less: deposit float	($30,000)
Equals: average collected balance	$220,000

$$\text{Earnings Credit} = \text{Collected Balances} \times (1 - \text{Reserve Requirement}) \times \left(\text{Earnings Credit Rate} \times \frac{\text{Days in Month}}{365}\right)$$

$$EC = CB \times (1 - RR) \times \left(ECR \times \frac{D}{365}\right)$$

$$= \$220{,}000 \times (1 - 10) \times \left(.05 \times \frac{30}{365}\right) = \$813.70$$

The answer above assumes that intermediate calculations are rounded as shown.

If the current service charges are $1,000, but the amount of earnings credit is only $ 813.70, the company did not keep sufficient collected balances on deposit to cover the cost of services over the period. In effect, the company has a companion deficit of $188.20, which is owed to the financial institution.

COLLECTED BALANCES REQUIRED CALCULATION

A company uses services with charges that total $10,000 per month. The earnings credit rate is 5%. The reserve requirement is 10%. Assuming a 30-day month the average collected balances required to compensate the financial institution for the services used is as follows:

$$\text{Collected Balances Required} = \frac{\text{Monthly Service Charges}}{\left(\text{Earnings Credit Rate} \times \frac{\text{Days in a Month}}{365}\right) \times (1 - \text{Reserve Requirement})}$$

$$CB = \frac{SC}{\left(ECR \times \frac{D}{365}\right) \times (1 - RR)}$$

$$= \frac{\$10{,}000}{\left(.05 \times \frac{30}{365}\right) \times (1 - .10)} = \$2{,}703{,}703$$

The answer above assumes that intermediate calculations are rounded as shown.

Note: If $1 is used as the service charge in the above formula, the balance multiplier is calculated. This number, 270.38, multiplied by the service charges, gives the collected balances required to pay for services.

Test Your Understanding

These chapter questions are provided to test your understanding of the information in the text. They are neither examples of CTP examination questions nor are they in the examination format.

Answers are on pages 630–632.

1. What impact has consolidation and specialization in the financial services industry had on the FSP selection process?

2. What are some of the key factors to be considered in selecting a financial service provider?

3. What are RFPs and who uses them?

4. Why is it important for an organization to monitor bank and FSP service practices and creditworthiness?

5. What factors are important in a long-term relationship?

6. Describe service agreements and the important factors relating to them.

7. What is a bank report card?

8. What is CAMELS?

9. Discuss bank compensation practices.

10. What is an account analysis statement?

11. Define earnings credit and the earnings credit rate (ECR).

Association for
Financial Professionals®

Exhibits by Chapter

List of Acronyms

Acronym	Description
A/P	accounts payable
A/R	accounts receivable
ABA	American Bankers Association
ACH	automated clearing house
ACSS	Automated Clearing Settlement System
ACTION	ACH Credit Transactions Initiated Online
ADR	American Depository Receipts
AFP	Association for Financial Professionals
AFS	available-for-sale
AICPA	American Institute of Certified Public Accountants
AMEX	American Stock Exchange
ANSI	American National Standards Institute
APR	annual percentage rate
ARC	accounts receivable truncation
ARP	account reconciliation services
ARPS	adjustable-rate preferred stock
ASC	Accredited Standards Committee
ASP	application service provider
ASB	Accounting Standards Board
AT	Assistant Treasurer
ATM	automated teller machine
AVS	Address Verification Service
B2B	business-to-business
B2C	business-to-consumer
BA	banker's acceptance
BACS	Bankers Automated Clearing Service
BAI	Bank Administration Institute
BAN	bond anticipation notes
BIF	Bank Insurance Fund
BOJ	Bank of Japan
BSA	Bank Secrecy Act
C2B	consumer-to-business
C2C	consumer-to-consumer
CAMELS	Capital Adequacy, Asset Quality, Management Capability, Earnings, Liquidity, Sensitivity to Market Risk
CAPM	Capital Asset Pricing Model
CB	collected balance
CBD	cash before delivery

Acronym	Description
CCD	cash concentration or disbursement (ACH format)
CCD+	cash concentration or disbursement plus addendum (ACH format)
CCM	Certified Cash Manager
CD	certificate of deposit
CEO	Chief Executive Officer
CFO	Chief Financial Officer
CHAPS	Clearing House Automated Payment System
CHIPS	Clearing House for Interbank Payment System
CIE	customer-initiated entry
CIEBA	The Committee of the Investment of Employee Benefit Assets
CLS	Continuous Linked Settlement
CME	Chicago Mercantile Exchange
CMO	collateralized mortgage obligations
COD	cash on delivery
COGS	cost of goods sold
CP	commercial paper
CPA (Canada)	Canadian Payments Association
CPA (US)	Certified Public Accountant
CRA	Community Reinvestment Act
CTP	Certified Treasury Professional
CTX	Corporate Trade Exchange
DCIA	Debt Collection Improvement Act
DDA	demand deposit account
DIC	difference in conditions
DIDMCA	The Depository Institutions Deregulation and Monetary Control Act of 1980
DOJ	The Department of Justice
DOL	The Department of Labor
DRIPS	dividend reinvestment plans
DSO	days' sales outstanding
DTC	depository transfer check
DVP	delivery-versus-payment
EAI	enterprise application integration
EBA	Euro Bankers Association
EBIT	earnings before interest and taxes
EBITDA	earnings before interest, taxes, depreciation and amortization
EBPP	electronic bill presentment and payment
EC	earnings credit
ECB	European Central Bank

Acronym	Description
ECCHO	Electronic Check Clearing House Organization
ECP	electronic check presentment
ECR	earnings credit rate
EDGAR	Electronic Data Gathering Analysis and Retrieval
EDI	electronic data interchange
EDT	electronic depository transfers
EFT	electronic funds transfer
EFTA	Electronic Funds Transfer Act
EFTPS	Electronic Federal Tax Payment System
EIPP	electronic invoice presentment and payment
EMH	efficient markets hypothesis
EMU	Economic and Monetary Union or European Monetary Union
EOQ	economic order quantity
EPS	earnings per share
ERISA	The Employee Retirement Income Security Act of 1974
ERM	enterprise risk management
ERP	enterprise resource planning
ERS	evaluated receipts settlement
EVA	economic value added
FAF	Financial Accounting Foundation
FAS	Financial Accounting Standards
FASB	Financial Accounting Standards Board
FBI	Federal Bureau of Investigation
FD	Finance Director
FDIC	Federal Deposit Insurance Corporation
FDICIA	Federal Deposit Insurance Corporation Improvement Act
FEDI	financial electronic data interchange
FFIEC	Federal Financial Institution Examination Council
FHC	financial holding companies
FHLBB	Federal Home Loan Bank Board
FHLMC	Federal Home Loan Mortgage Corporation
FinCen	Financial Crimes Enforcement Network
FIRREA	Financial Institutions Reform, Recovery, and Enforcement Act
FMC	Ford Motor Credit
FMS	The Financial Management Service
FNMA	Federal National Mortgage Association
FOMC	Federal Open Market Committee
FRA	forward rate agreement

Acronym	Description
FRR	Financial Reporting Releases
FSLIC	Federal Savings and Loan Insurance Corporation
FSML	financial services markup language
FSP	financial service provider
FSTC	Financial Services Technology Consortium
FTP	file transfer protocol
FX	foreign exchange
FXYCS	Foreign Exchange Yen Clearing System
G/NFP	governmental and not-for-profit
GAAP	Generally Accepted Accounting Principles
GAAS	Generally Accepted Auditing Standards
GASB	Governmental Accounting Standards Board
GATT	General Agreement on Trades and Tariffs
GDR	Global Depository Receipt
GL	general ledger
GMAC	General Motors Acceptance Corporation
GNMA	Government National Mortgage Association
GSE	government sponsored enterprises
HCE	highly compensated employee
HDGS	High-Dollar Group Sort
HPR	highly protected risk
HTM	held-to-maturity
HTML	hypertext markup language
HTTP	hypertext transfer protocol
IAS	International Accounting Standards
IASB	International Accounting Standards Board
IBBEA	Interstate Banking and Branching Efficiency Act
ICR	intelligent character recognition
IFRS	International Financial Reporting Standards
IMF	International Monetary Fund
IPAB	The Institute for the Protection of Bank Savings
IPO	initial public offering
IR	investor relations
IRC	Internal Revenue Code
IRD	image replacement document
IRR	internal rate of return
IRS	Internal Revenue Service
ISP	Internet service provider

Acronym	Description
JIT	just-in-time inventory
L/C	letter of credit
LAN	local area network
LIBOR	London Interbank Offered Rate
LVTS	Large-Value Transfer System
MAC	material adverse change
MACRS	modified accelerated cost recovery schedule
MBS	mortgage-backed security
MD&A	management discussion and analysis
MICR	magnetic ink character recognition
MMDA	money market deposit account
MMMF	money market mutual fund
MNC	multinational corporation
MPS	material planning system
MVA	market value added
NACHA	National Automated Clearing House Association
NAFTA	North American Free Trade Agreement
NASD	National Association of Securities Dealers
NASDAQ	National Association of Securities Dealers Automated Quotations
NAV	net asset value
NBES	National Book-Entry System
NCUSIF	The National Credit Union Share Insurance Fund
NIRI	National Investor Relations Institute
NOW	negotiable order of withdrawal
NPV	net present value
NSF	non-sufficient funds
NYSE	New York Stock Exchange
OBSA	off-balance-sheet arrangements
OCC	The Office of the Comptroller of the Currency
OCR	optical character recognition
ODFI	originating depository financial institution
OFAC	Office of Foreign Assets Control
OTC	over-the-counter
OTS	The Office of Thrift Supervision
P&P	policies and procedures
P2P	peer-to-peer
PBGC	The Pension Benefit Guaranty Corporation
PCAOB	Public Company Accounting Oversight Board

Acronym	Description
PI	profitability index
PID	payable-if-desired
PIN	personal identification number
PKI	public key infrastructure
POD	proof of deposit
POP	point-of-purchase
POS	point-of-sale
PPD	prearranged payment or deposit
PSR	payment system risk
PTD	payable through draft
PV	present value
R&D	receipts and disbursement
RAM	random-access memory
RCK	re-presented check entries
RCPC	regional check processing center
RDFI	receiving depository financial institution
REMIC	real estate mortgage investment conduits
RFI	request for information
RFP	request for proposal
RI	residual income
RMA	Risk Management Association
ROI	return on investment
ROM	read-only memory
RR	reserve requirement
RSA	Rivest, Shamir, and Adleman
RTC	Resolution Trust Company
RTGS	real-time gross settlement system
S&L	savings and loan
S&P	Standard and Poor's
S.W.I.F.T.	Society for Worldwide Interbank Financial Telecommunications
SAIF	Savings Association Insurance Fund
SOX	Sarbanes-Oxley
SEC	Securities and Exchange Commission
SFAC	Statements of Financial Accounting Concepts
SMP	special multiperil insurance
SSC	shared service center
SSL	secured socket layer
STP	straight through processing

Acronym	Description
SVC	stored value card
TAN	tax anticipation notes
TARGET	Trans-European Automated Real-Time Gross Settlement Express Transfer System
TDA	tax-deferred annuity
TEL	telephone initiated entry
TIE	times interest earned
TIF	tax increment financing bonds
TMIS	treasury management information systems
TMS	Treasury Management System
TRN	transit routing number
TXP	tax payment (format for ACH tax payments)
UCC	Uniform Commercial Code
UN/EDIFACT	United Nations EDI for Administration, Commerce, and Transportation
URL	uniform resource locator
USBE	U.S. Bulk Exchange
VA	U.S. Department of Veterans Affairs
VAN	value added network
VAR	value-at-risk
VAT	value added tax
WACC	weighted average cost of capital
WEB	Internet initiated entry
WIP	work-in-progress
WTO	World Trade Organization
WWW	World Wide Web
XBRL	eXtensible business reporting language
XML	eXtensible markup language
YTM	yield to maturity
ZBA	zero balance accounts

Association for
Financial Professionals®

Glossary Terms

401 (k) plan: These plans are generally referred to as cash-deferred/salary reduction plans and are sanctioned by IRC Section 401(k). Essentially, the employee is given the choice of either receiving an amount, in the form of currently taxable compensation (for federal income tax purposes), or deferring the amount to be taxed at a future date. – Ch20

403 (b) plan: Also called tax-deferred annuities, 403(b)s are generally made available to employees of religious, charitable, educational, scientific and literary organizations that are chartered on a non-profit basis. In these plans, only the employee may make contributions, generally by payroll deduction. – Ch20

accepting bank: A bank accepting and agreeing unconditionally to pay a time draft at the date and place payable is known as the accepting bank or acceptor. – Ch15

account analysis statement: A paper or electronic report that a bank provides to commercial customers specifying services provided, balances maintained, volumes processed and charges assessed. It is essentially an invoice for services provided, along with detailed information on balances and credit earned for those balances. – Ch21

account maintenance fee: One example of a fixed cost is a monthly account maintenance fee charged by a bank on a deposit account. The fee remains the same regardless of the number of transactions on the account. – Ch05

accounts receivable: Accounts receivable are assets that represent revenues from sales that have been recognized but not yet collected. – Ch04

account reconciliation: Banks provide account reconciliation services to meet companies' information and control requirements. Partial or full reconciliation services are available and the information is transmitted to the company as a paper report, on CD-ROM, via a direct data transmission or through a Web site. – Ch09

account resolution: The basic account or service authorization empowering a representative for a business to enter into agreements for banking services. The resolution specifies what functions can be performed by specific individuals or job titles, authorized signers on an account, and the entire scope and limitations of the relationship. – Ch21

accounts payable: Accounts payable (also referred to as trade payables) are amounts due to vendors for purchased items. – Ch04

accounts receivable balance pattern: An accounts receivable (A/R) balance pattern is useful in estimating the inflows associated with collection of accounts receivable. The A/R balance pattern specifies the percentage of credit sales that remain uncollected at the end of a specific period, such as a month or a quarter. A company's collection history determines the normal balance pattern. Balance patterns are used to forecast future cash inflows and to project accounts receivable levels. – Ch10

accounts receivable truncation (ARC): One of the ACH entry formats, the ARC format is used by retail lockbox providers to convert consumer checks to ACH debits. This format reduces both the cost and the availability float associated with check clearing. It does not, however, reduce the mail or processing float associated with paper-based payments. – Ch08

accrual accounting: Sales are reported even though cash has not yet been received and expenses are reported even though cash has not yet been paid out. – Ch04

ACH credit transaction: ACH credit transactions include direct deposit of payroll, government benefit payments, corporate tax payments and corporate payments to trading partners. – Ch08

ACH operators: ACH operators, also called processors, act as intermediaries between financial institutions by receiving, sorting and distributing ACH transaction files. – Ch08

addenda record: Addenda records contain remittance details that follow the standard payment information in ACH payment messages. – Ch08

Address Verification Service (AVS): Merchants who accept mail, phone or Internet orders may mitigate risk by using an Address Verification Service (AVS) that matches the address provided by the cardholder with the account billing address on record with the issuer. – Ch08

adjustable rate preferred stock (ARPS): Money markets have seen the development of adjustable rate preferred stocks (ARPS), which take advantage of the tax exclusion on dividends to offer higher returns to money market investors. ARPS are designed to adjust dividend rates according to some interest rate index, thereby maintaining a more constant price level. – Ch13

advance rate: As part of a lending arrangement, a lender agrees to advance some percentage of the value of the receivables or inventory (the advance rate) with certain assets pledged as security. – Ch06

adverse opinion: An adverse opinion is given by an auditor when exceptions are so material the auditor determines that financial statements may be misleading. – Ch04

advising bank: Banks may serve a variety of roles in L/C transactions. The advising bank advises the beneficiary of an L/C in its favor. The advising and negotiating banks are frequently the same bank performing dual roles. The advising/negotiating bank examines the documents presented by the beneficiary, receives payment from the issuing bank and pays the beneficiary. – Ch15

AFP Account Analysis Standard: The current AFP Account Analysis Standard consists of sections that provide customer information, balance and compensation information, rate information, service information, adjustment detail, summary of accounts, and optional historic balance and compensation information using AFP service codes. – Ch21

AFP service codes: AFP service codes are six-character, alpha-numeric codes that provide standard, uniform references and terms for identifying, describing and reporting bank services as well as the associated charges. – Ch21

after tax cost of debt: The relevant component in cost of debt is after-tax costs. For any newly issued debt, the cost is the Yield to Maturity (YTM) on the bonds, which is the return that the investor receives if the bond is bought at the current price and held until it matures. – Ch13

agency costs: With respect to debt use, agency costs are incurred as a result of placing constraints on the management of a company to protect the interests of the debt holders. With respect to the use of equity, there are agency costs associated with monitoring and restricting the decisions of management to ensure that it acts in the best interest of equity holders. – Ch14

agency problem: Owners focus on the business performance of the company, while investors focus on the risk and return of portfolios. This tends to make most investors passive or inactive shareholders of companies, thereby providing a significant incentive for the management of such companies to take actions that will benefit themselves, while reducing the value to the shareholders. This is generally referred to as the "agency problem" between management and stockholders. – Ch19

agent: An agent is a bank, bank holding company or trust institution that manages assets whose title remains with the owner. – Ch03

aggressive financing strategy: Under an aggressive financing strategy, a company finances all fixed assets with long-term debt or equity but finances only a portion of permanent current assets with long-term financing. – Ch06

aging schedule: An aging schedule separates A/R into current and past due receivables in 30-day increments. Companies then analyze the aging of receivables on an aggregate or customer basis. An aging analysis identifies past-due accounts, which become less collectible as the age of each increases. – Ch07

all-in rate of interest: One of the three basic cost components for lines of credit, the all-in rate consists of a base rate, such as LIBOR, prime or the Fed funds rate plus a spread that is added to the base rate. – Ch10

altered check: Altered checks are those where some information, usually the amount, has been changed. – Ch08

American Bankers Association (ABA) number: The American Bankers Association (ABA) number, also known as the transit routing number (TRN), is pre-printed on the MICR line. This 9-digit number identifies the drawee bank and provides the depository bank the information required to route the check back to the drawee bank through the clearing system. – Ch08

American Depository Receipts (ADRs): Foreign companies wishing to raise capital in the U.S. capital markets may do so through the use of American Depository Receipts (ADRs). These are negotiable receipts, registered in the name of the owner, for shares of a foreign corporation held in trust by a foreign branch of a U.S. bank. – Ch13

American option contract: A contract that allows the owner to exercise (that is buy or sell the underlying asset) the option at any time prior to maturity. – Ch17

application service provider (ASP): A type of Internet/e-commerce provider, an application service provider (ASP) offers individuals or organizations access via the Internet to application programs and related services that would otherwise have to be located on individual personal computers or on a company's computer network. –Ch12

arbitrage: The process of buying in one market and simultaneously selling in another, resulting in a riskless profit. – Ch17

arrears dividends: See dividends in arrears – Ch14

articulation: Economic activities or flows explain the differences between the beginning-of-period and end-of-the-period balance sheet account levels. This interrelationship between the financial statements is referred to as articulation. – Ch04

ask spread: Banks and other dealers quote both bid and offer rates for foreign currency. The difference between the bid rate and the offer rate is generally referred to as the bid/offer spread or bid/ask spread. – Ch15

as-of adjustment: When a check takes longer to clear than the initial availability that was granted, a bank may add the additional time as part of the collected balance calculation. This practice is referred to as making an as-of adjustment. – Ch08

asset tax: On an international project, even though a company may not produce operating profits, it may still owe an asset taxe on the value of accumulated real property or business equipment or on the value of a financial portfolio. – Ch16

asset-backed securities: One type of securitization is called asset securitization or asset-backed securities. The primary example of this type of securitization is in the home mortgage market where many different entities such as the Federal National Mortgage Association (FNMA), the Government National Mortgage Association (GNMA), the Federal Home Loan Mortgage Corporation (FHLMC) and the Collateralized Mortgage Obligations (CMOs) bundle together pools of mortgages into securities and sell the securities to investors. – Ch13

asset-based borrowing/lending: Short-term bank loans are often secured by some form of collateral, usually accounts receivable, inventory or securitized assets. This practice is referred to as asset-based borrowing or lending. – Ch06

assets: Economic resources owned by a company that are expected to provide future economic benefits. – Ch04

association captive: A group captive, also known as an association captive, resembles a single-parent captive except that it provides risk financing for multiple owners instead of just one. – Ch18

asymmetric information theory: A theoretical model based on the context that the management of a company has access to more accurate information on a company's prospects than the stockholders. – Ch14

at-the-money: An option is at-the-money if the underlying asset price is equal to the strike price of the option. – Ch17

authentication: Authentication is the ability to know, with a reasonable amount of certainty, who sent or received a message. – Ch12

automated clearing house (ACH): The ACH system was developed by the financial industry in the early 1970s as an electronic alternative to checks. The ACH system is a batch processing system designed for high volume, low value transactions. In an ACH transaction, payment information is processed and settled electronically, thereby increasing reliability, efficiency and cost-effectiveness. – Ch08

Automated Clearing Settlement System (ACSS): One of the Canadian Payments Association (CPA) systems for the clearing and settlement of payments is the Automated Clearing Settlement System (ACSS). The vast majority of payment items in Canada are cleared through the ACSS. – Ch15

auxiliary-on-us field: The auxiliary-on-us field is a part of a deposit ticket MICR line and carries a unique identifier for each company location, thereby enabling the bank to produce deposit reports on a daily, weekly or monthly basis. – Ch09

availability anticipation: Availability anticipation involves the initiation of a transfer after a deposit has been made but before all of the items have been granted availability by the depository bank. The transfer is initiated based on the projected availability. – Ch09

availability float: The time interval or delay between the day a check is deposited and the day a company's account is credited with collected funds. – Ch09

availability schedule: Availability schedules vary from bank to bank and must be obtained from all banks under consideration. The results of mail time studies are combined with information from availability schedules to compare providers. Banks or consulting firms use this data, in conjunction with an analysis of a company's actual remittances, to determine which cities or combinations of cities are the most effective collection sites. – Ch09

available-for-sale (AFS): AFS is the default classification for all securities not carried as trading or hold-to-maturity (HTM) securities. – Ch04

average collected balance: The sum of the daily ending collected balances (both positive and negative) divided by the number of days in the analysis period. – Ch21

average collection period: The average collection period represents the number of days it takes to convert a sale into a cash inflow. This is also known as days' sales outstanding. – Ch04

average daily float: Average daily float is calculated by dividing the sum of the dollar days of float for all items received in a certain period by the number of days in the period. – Ch09

average deposit float: The sum of the daily dollar amount of items in the process of collection divided by the number of days in the analysis period. – Ch21

average ledger balance: The sum of the daily ending ledger balances (both positive and negative) divided by the number of days in the analysis period. – Ch21

back value date: Outside of the U.S., banks typically use value dating as compensation for services provided to customers. Under a value dating system, a bank establishes a back value date on which the value of funds debited from an account is determined. – Ch15

balance forward system: In a balance forward system, a credit limit is established for each individual. As purchases are made or services are provided, the A/R outstanding balance increases. When payments are made, the A/R balance is reduced accordingly. – Ch07

balance sheet: The balance sheet presents the financial position of asset, liability and equity accounts at a point in time. – Ch04

balance sheet hedge: A balance sheet hedge matches exposed liabilities against exposed assets and is frequently referred to as asset and liability management or a natural hedge. – Ch17

banker's acceptance (BA): A banker's acceptance (BA) is a time draft on the face of which the drawee bank has written the word "accepted" over the signature. A banker's acceptance (BA) is often used to finance the import, export or domestic shipment of goods but can also be used to finance storage of properly titled goods. BAs are frequently used in conjunction with L/Cs requiring a time draft drawn on a bank. – Ch15

Bankers Automated Clearing Service (BACS): The ACH-like system used in the U.K. for high-volume, small value payments. – Ch15

barter: Barter involves the direct exchange of goods or services between two end users without the exchange of money. – Ch15

basis-rate swap: Interest rate swaps where one floating rate basis is swapped for another – i.e. prime for LIBOR. – Ch17

benchmarking: Benchmarking involves examining and comparing the core activities either within an industry or cross-industry for the purpose of identifying "best practices." – Ch02

best efforts guarantee: In some cases a lender may ask for specific performance guarantees relative to the assets being financed. Under a best efforts guarantee, the parent agrees to make best efforts to get the subsidiary to perform but does not guarantee subsidiary performance. – Ch13

beta risk: Beta is defined as the risk of a particular stock relative to an overall stock market measure, such as the S&P 500 Index. The betas for most major companies are calculated by many different sources and are readily available for interested investors. – Ch13

bid/ask spread: Banks and other dealers quote both bid and ask (offer) rates for foreign currency. The difference between the bid rate and the ask rate is generally referred to as the bid/ask spread or bid/offer spread. – Ch15

bilateral clearing: Direct clearing of checks and other payment items between two financial institutions. – Ch15

bilateral netting: Purchases between two subsidiaries of the same company are netted against each other so that periodically – typically once a month – only the net difference is transferred. – Ch16

biometric devices: Biometric devices provide authentication through electronic recognition of personal characteristics such as fingerprints, retinal patterns, voiceprints, and hand or face geometry. –Ch12

blind participation: With a loan participation, a financial institution purchases an interest in another lender's credit facility. In the case of a blind participation, the participation is not disclosed to the borrower and the participant may not directly contact the borrower or disclose the participant's role in the credit facility. – Ch10

blocked currencies: A type of political risk in which profits cannot be converted from the local currency into a major trading currency. – Ch15

bond anticipation notes (BANs): Bond anticipation notes (BANs) are issued by government entities to cover differences in timing between expenditures and proceeds from bond issues. – Ch13

bond equivalent yield: One of the commonly quoted yields that are calculated using the annual yield formula is the bond equivalent yield which uses a 365-day year basis. Note that the bond equivalent yield is greater than the money market yield which is greater than the discount rate. – Ch10

bond indentures: Most debt contracts limit the ability of a company to pay dividends by imposing protective covenants related to maintaining specific financial ratios. These covenants are intended to prevent stockholders from draining assets from a company at the expense of bondholders and other creditors. – Ch13

bond rating: Bond issues are assigned quality ratings that reflect the probability a company issuing the bonds is likely to default on an issue. Each public bond issue is independently rated by one or more of the accredited rating agencies. – Ch13

book value: The book value, or carrying value, of a depreciable asset is its cost minus the accumulated depreciation. – Ch04

book-entry securities: Book-entry securities are registered and transferred electronically either by the U.S. Treasury (treasury securities only) or through the commercial book entry system. – Ch10

breakeven analysis: A type of cost/benefit analysis that establishes the level of activity at which the benefits are equal to the costs. – Ch05

breakeven point: The level of activity for an operation at which costs exactly equal benefits. – Ch05

broker: A broker acts as a transaction intermediary, matching buyers and sellers of money market securities. – Ch10

business continuity: Business continuity refers to the actions taken with regard to crisis management, alternative operating procedures and communications to staff and customers. – Ch18

business risk: The risk associated with a company's operating capabilities and policies, as well as the volatility of operating income or earnings before interest and taxes (EBIT). – Ch14

business-to-business (B2B): B2B e-commerce began with EDI, but has expanded into a wide array of formats and protocols for conducting business electronically. The earliest B2B applications were in the areas of sales to customers and purchasing from suppliers. Applications later extended into logistics and supply chain management, as well as billing and payment. – Ch12

business-to-consumer (B2C): The initial development of Internet-based e-commerce was primarily targeted toward B2C applications. Companies quickly realized that the Internet was a cost-effective way to advertise and sell products and services to consumers, as well as to provide enhanced customer service. With Internet-based e-commerce, the consumer does most of the work in the process, including reviewing available products and services, filling out forms online, and providing shipping and billing information. – Ch12

call option: A call option gives the owner the right to buy an underlying asset at a fixed price. – Ch17

call premium: As compensation to the investors for early redemption, a call premium is paid when a bond is called. The call premium is usually set on a sliding scale, with larger premiums above par required the earlier an issue is called. – Ch13

callable bonds: Issued with a call provision that allows the issuer to call or retire the bonds prior to maturity, callable bonds are typically issued during high interest rate periods with the intent to retire the bonds when the opportunity to refinance in a lower interest rate environment arises. – Ch13

CAMELS rating: A system widely used by regulators to measure financial institution strength based on capital adequacy, asset quality, management capability, earnings, liquidity and sensitivity to market risk. – Ch21

Canadian Payments Association (CPA): The Canadian Payments Association (CPA), which is a non-profit association created by an Act of Parliament in 1980, operates a national system for the clearing and settlement of checks, performs electronic funds transfers and manages the evolution of the national payment system. – Ch15

cap limits: Many organizations that practice self-insurance set "cap limits" on self-insurance exposure by purchasing excess coverage (i.e., "real insurance") for claims above some pre-determined limit. Any claims below this limit will be "self-insured," while amounts above the limit (i.e., excess losses) will by covered by the cap limit policy. – Ch18

cap rate: A ceiling or cap on interest rates in the event that rates rise above a specified level. – Ch17

capital: The permanent and long-term sources of funding used by a company such as long-term debt, preferred stock and common equity. Equity includes both the money contributed by stockholders and the earnings retained in the business. – Ch05

Capital Asset Pricing Model (CAPM): The Capital Asset Pricing Model (CAPM) describes one possible relationship between risk and required rate of return for equity securities (stocks). The CAPM is based on the concept that the typical investor holds a diversified portfolio of stocks and that the only measure of risk relevant to such an investor is the beta of a stock. The CAPM essentially represents a linear relationship between risk (beta) and required rate of return. – Ch13

capital assets: Capital assets, also known as fixed assets, cannot be turned into cash as readily as current assets. Fixed assets are recorded at cost when they are acquired. – Ch04

capital budget: The process by which strategic plans are developed to determine a company's investment in capital assets. The capital budget details the forecast costs for investing activities. – Ch05

capital leases: Capital leases, also known as financial leases, have the following characteristics: (1) They are typically for a period greater than one year; (2) The lessor usually does not provide maintenance for the equipment; (3) The lease agreement is not cancelable; (4) Accounting guidelines require that a financial lease appear on the balance sheet as a capitalized lease, hence the payments are set up to fully depreciate the cost of the equipment; (5) The lease usually runs for the life of the asset and (6) The lessee has the option to renew the contract or purchase the asset at the end of the original lease contract for an agreed-upon residual value. – Ch13

capital market instruments: Securities that are of a long-term in nature, having more than one year until maturity. Capital market instruments are generally less liquid and are issued by borrowers with various credit ratings. Examples of capital market instruments include term loans, equity instruments and bonds. – Ch03

capital markets: The capital markets are where longer-term debt and equity instruments (i.e., stocks and bonds) are traded. – Ch10

capital structure: The mix of capital components of a company, traditionally the mix of long-term debt and equity. – Ch05

captive finance company: A captive finance company solely finances purchases of the company's products. Automobile finance companies such as the General Motors Acceptance Corporation (GMAC) and Ford Motor Credit (FMC) are examples of captive finance companies. – Ch03

cash application: The process of applying a customer's payment against outstanding invoices or receivables. – Ch07

cash balance plans: In a cash balance plan, benefits increase by a rate applied to eligible compensation for each year of employment, without consideration of future salary inflation. – Ch20

cash before delivery (CBD): Cash before delivery (CBD) terms, sometimes referred to as prepayment terms, require the buyer to make full and final payment before shipment or receipt of goods. – Ch07

cash budget: The translation of information from the operating and capital budget into sources and uses of cash. – Ch05

cash concentration: Cash concentration is the transfer of funds from outlying depository locations to a central bank account, commonly referred to as a concentration account. – Ch09

cash concentration or disbursement (CCD): CCD is an electronic payment format used for concentration and disbursement of funds within or between companies (B2B). A single 94-character record contains the standard entry class indicating the type of transaction, transit routing numbers for the originating and receiving financial institutions, and the originator and receiver account numbers. – Ch08

cash concentration or disbursement plus addendum (CCD+): CCD+ is one of the formats used for the U.S. Treasury Vendor Express program and for B2B payments. It is useful when only a limited amount of information must be transmitted. This format is identical to CCD but with an addenda record. The addenda record is 94 characters long and includes a free-form space for up to 80 characters of descriptive data. – Ch08

cash conversion cycle: The cash conversion cycle calculates the time required to convert cash outflows into cash inflows. It indicates how efficiently a company is using its current assets and liabilities. It is the average number of days between the cash outflow for the acquisition of materials and supplies and the cash inflow from the sale of products or services. – Ch06

cash conversion efficiency: Cash conversion efficiency, commonly referred to as the cash profit margin, measures how effectively a company converts sales into cash. – Ch04

cash discount: A discount offered by a supplier for payment in cash or within the cash terms period (typically 7-10 days). – Ch06

cash equivalents: Many short-term investments, including money market funds and marketable debt securities with original maturities of less than three months, are considered cash equivalents. – Ch04

cash flow analysis: Cash flow analysis entails developing pro forma financial statements and using the statement of cash flows to assess expected future liquidity needs and resources. – Ch04

cash flow cycle: This cycle shows how the strategies concerning inventory, receivables and payables all interact to affect the flow of cash through the company. – Ch06

cash flow hedges: Hedges of a forecasted transaction or the variability in the cash flow of a recognized asset or liability. – Ch17

cash flow timeline: The cash flow timeline comprises the total time interval from the time resources are purchased from vendors and suppliers at the beginning of a company's operating cycle until the time payment is received from customers at the end of a company's operating cycle. – Ch01

cash flow to total debt: Net income plus depreciation divided by total long-term and short-term debt. Short-term debt consists of short-term notes, commercial paper or other short-term debt obligations. – Ch04

cash inflow: Inflows are funds collected from customers, obtained from financial sources such as lenders and/or received from other sources (e.g., a sale of an asset). – Ch01

cash letters: A cash letter is a bundle of checks accompanied by a list of individual items and other control documents. – Ch08

cash on delivery (COD): The seller ships the goods and the buyer pays upon receipt. – Ch07

cash outflow: Outflows are funds disbursed to employees, vendors and suppliers, lenders, local, state, and federal tax agencies, bondholders, and shareholders. – Ch01

cash terms: The buyer generally has seven to ten days to make payment. – Ch07

cash turnover ratio: The number of cash conversion cycles a company experiences in a single year. The cash turnover ratio and the cash conversion cycle are measures of efficiency used to compare companies in the same or similar industries. – Ch04

cashiers check: A cashier's check, also known as an official bank check, is a check drawn on a bank's own funds and signed by a bank officer. – Ch08

central bank: The central bank or monetary authority of a country establishes the conditions for both domestic and non-U.S. bank operations. In some countries, central banks perform functions that are very similar to those of the U.S. Federal Reserve system. Central banks operate the payment system, regulate banks, act as lenders of last resort, and control the money supply. In addition, many foreign central banks act as issuers of government debt, a function performed by the Treasury Department in the U.S. – Ch15

centralized treasury: A company that operates overseas sales offices with limited personnel typically centralizes its treasury functions at a head office in the home country. A centralized treasury offers the advantages of control, economies of scale and lower operating costs. – Ch16

certificate authority: Digital certificates tie the identity of the user (private key) to the user's public key. The identification information is secured by a trusted third-party's digital signature on the certificate. The trusted third-party is known as the certificate authority. – Ch12

certificate of deposit (CD): An obligation of a bank offered at either a fixed or variable interest rate and which may be either negotiable or non-negotiable. – Ch03

certified check: A certified check is drawn on a depositor's checking account. It carries the signature of a bank officer certifying the check to be genuine and guaranteeing payment. – Ch08

check kiting: Check kiting, which involves multiple deposits and withdrawals between bank accounts in excess of the actual funds underlying the transactions, is a form of check fraud that is perpetrated on banks. – Ch08

check truncation: Check truncation converts the information on a business or consumer check into an electronic form or image that is transmitted electronically, thereby avoiding the need for physical presentment of the item. – Ch09

city item: City items are checks drawn on banks located in Federal Reserve cities – either the 12 district banks or the 25 branches. – Ch08

claims-occurrences basis: Deductibles may also be set on a per-occurrence basis (the deductible applies for each occurrence during the policy period). – Ch1 8

classified stock: Classified stocks are typically referred to as Class A or Class B, but these terms have no standard meaning; rather, they are specific to each company. – Ch13

clean-up period: Some lenders who provide lines of credit require that loans used to finance short-term working capital deficits be paid in full for a minimum period each year (known as a clean-up period). – Ch06. To ensure a line is used for temporary, not permanent, financing, a lender may require a clean-up period consisting of 30 to 60 consecutive days without any outstanding borrowings on the line. – Ch10

clearing float: The time interval or delay between the day a check is deposited by the payee and the day the payor's account is debited. – Ch09

clearing house: Clearing houses are either formal or informal associations formed by banks in a geographic area to permit the exchange of items drawn on the member participants. – Ch08

Clearing House Automated Payment System (CHAPS) One of the largest international RTGS clearing and settlement systems is the Clearing House Automated Payment System (CHAPS). – Ch15

Clearing House for Interbank Payment System (CHIPS): CHIPS is a bank-owned, large-dollar funds transfer network operated by The Clearing House Association. It was established in 1970 to substitute electronic payments for paper checks in international transactions between foreign and American banks.

Though not a true wire transfer system in the sense of Fedwire, CHIPS is a real-time, intraday net settlement system that clears and settles transactions in U.S. dollars. – Ch08

clientele effect: For companies, investors generally gravitate toward stocks that provide a cash flow stream and a risk/return profile that fits their investment strategy. This is referred to as the clientele effect. – Ch13

closing cash position: To arrive at the projected closing cash position, a cash manager adjusts the opening bank available balance by adding the expected settlements in the collection and concentration accounts and deducting the projected disbursement totals. The estimated closing position is then used to determine whether there will be a cash surplus or cash deficit. – Ch09

code of conduct: A code of conduct establishes rules of behavior for what constitutes appropriate actions and ethical behaviors encountered during normal business activities. – Ch19

collateral: The assets being used as security for the loan are called collateral. They may include physical assets (plant, equipment, inventory, etc.) or financial assets (receivables, marketable securities, etc.). – Ch13

collateral trust bonds: Collateral trust bonds are backed by securities, such as other companies' stocks and bonds, held by the issuing company. – Ch13

collateralized loans: A form of inventory financing is the use of collateralized loans. These loans may be arranged using inventory as collateral for a loan, with the lender providing financing for some predetermined percentage of the inventory's value. The company's cash flows are viewed as the primary repayment source for collateralized loans. The inventory is viewed only as a secondary repayment source or as a means of reducing the amount of loss in the event of default. – Ch07

collected balance: Collected balances reflect the dollar amount in an account for which the bank of deposit has received settlement. Collected balances are the difference between ledger balances and the amount of any deposit float. – Ch08

collecting bank: Banks involved in a documentary collection perform different roles. The collecting bank is the remitting bank's correspondent responsible for contacting the buyer (importer), collecting the amount due and releasing the documents as instructed. – Ch15

collection float: The time interval or delay between when payment is initiated and when a company receives available funds. Collection float applies principally to paper-based payment instruments that are subject to three types of float or delays: mail, processing and availability. – Ch09

comfort letter: A type of guarantee that is generally just a letter from another party stating actions they will or will not take on behalf of the borrower. – Ch13

commercial bank: Defined by law as a financial institution that accepts deposits and makes commercial loans, a commercial bank offers a wide range of products and services. Therefore, the term commercial bank applies to financial institutions ranging from small, single-site, community banks with ten million dollars in assets to large, multi-site, global financial institutions with hundreds of billions in assets. – Ch03

commercial letter of credit: A commercial letter of credit (L/C) is an instrument in which a bank guarantees a seller that the bank, not the buyer, will pay for the agreed upon purchase when the seller presents documents conforming to specified conditions pertaining to the sale and delivery of goods or services. – Ch07

commercial paper (CP): Commercial paper consists of unsecured, short-term promissory notes issued by companies or commercial bank holding companies. CP maturities are generally limited to a maximum of 270 days. – Ch03

commitment fee: For committed lines, the lender may charge a percentage fee based either on the total amount of the commitment or on the unused portion of the commitment. Payment is usually made quarterly. Fees vary depending on the creditworthiness of the company, the stated purpose of the line and the term of the commitment. – Ch10

committed line: A line of credit that usually involves a formal loan agreement that specifies the terms and conditions of the credit facility and typically requires compensation in the form of balances or fees because the lender is obligated to provide funding up to the credit limit stipulated in the agreement as long as the borrower is not in default. – Ch10

commodity swap: The exchange of a floating price for a commodity for a fixed price. – Ch17

common equity: Includes both the money contributed by stockholders and the earnings retained in the business. – Ch05

common-size financial statements: Common-size financial statements facilitate evaluation of how effectively a company generates profits from revenues and identifies trends over time when several years of statements are considered concurrently. A common-size income statement expresses every line item on the statement as a percentage of revenues. – Ch04

compensating balances: Compensating balances are balances that are maintained in the company's deposit accounts at the bank and generally do not earn interest or offset depository service charges. They are often used to provide additional compensation to the bank for services provided. – Ch10

comprehensive accounts payable: An integrated or comprehensive A/P service allows a company to outsource all or part of its A/P and/or disbursements functions. A company using an integrated or comprehensive payables service is, in effect, outsourcing the disbursement function, thereby potentially reducing the overall cost of A/P operations. – Ch07

concentration and liquidity management flows: These include internal transfers among operating units of a company and between the company's various bank accounts. – Ch01

Conference Board: The Conference Board creates and disseminates knowledge about management and the marketplace to help businesses strengthen their performance and better serve society. – Ch19

confirming bank: Banks may serve a variety of roles in L/C transactions. If requested, the advising/negotiating bank may add confirmation (as the confirming bank) to an L/C. In doing so, the confirming bank commits to the beneficiary that payment will be made if documents meet the terms and conditions of the L/C, regardless of the issuing bank's ability to pay. If an L/C is confirmed, the confirming bank will also be the negotiating bank. – Ch15

conservative current asset investment strategy: Under a conservative current asset investment strategy, a company maintains low levels of current assets relative to sales. – Ch06

consignment: Under a consignment agreement, the seller ships the goods to the buyer with no obligation to pay until the goods have been sold or used. The title to the goods remains with the seller until they are sold. – Ch07

consumer finance company: A consumer finance company extends credit to individuals and businesses, but does not accept deposits. – Ch03

Continuous Linked Settlement (CLS): Continuous Linked Settlement (CLS)® is a recent development in the global financial community that allows for international currency transactions to be settled on a same-day basis. CLS provides a real-time global settlement system in which settlement risk due to time zones, legal jurisdiction and operating procedures are significantly reduced. CLS is operated by the CLS Bank which began operations in late 2002 with the goal of eliminating cross-border intraday settlement exposures. – Ch15

controlled disbursement: Controlled disbursement is a bank service that provides same-day notification to a company of the dollar amount of checks that will clear against the account. – Ch09

convertible bonds: Convertible bonds are bonds that are convertible into shares of a company's common stock at a defined price. They generally provide the borrower with a lower interest rate than non-convertible bonds because of the equity conversion option. – Ch13

corporate governance: Considerations in governance include the role of independent directors, outside and internal auditors, financial reporting and investor relations. – Ch19

corporate trade exchange (CTX): The CTX format is designed for B2B trade payments. It consists of a standard ACH payment transaction and a variable-length message addendum designed to convey remittance information in the Accredited Standards Committee (ASC) X12 data standard. The addendum can accommodate 9,999 records of 80 characters each. – Ch08

correspondent balance: Deposits held by other banks to facilitate check clearing, securities settlement, negotiation of letters of credit and other transactions. – Ch03

correspondent bank clearing: With correspondent bank clearing, the collecting bank maintains a depository account with another bank. The collecting bank sends checks to the correspondent bank which presents the items to the paying bank through a local clearing house or the local Fed. The collecting bank's depository account at the correspondent bank is then credited with the proceeds of the checks. – Ch08

cost of capital: Cost of capital reflects the cost of funds to a company, therefore representing the minimum required rate of return a company needs to achieve for any capital investment. – Ch13

cost of goods sold (COGS): The expense of providing the goods or services whose sale is recognized as revenues. COGS include labor and material directly used in manufacturing the product sold, as well as any indirect, or allocated, manufacturing expenses. These costs are called product costs. – Ch04

cost/benefit (CB) analysis: An analysis of whether the relevant economic benefits of a given course of action exceed the relevant economic costs. – Ch05

counterfeit check: Counterfeit checks are illegitimate facsimiles of genuine checks. – Ch08

counterparty: A company purchasing a forward contract is one party; the other party is typically referred to as the counterparty. – Ch17

counterparty risk: The risk that a counterparty may not fulfill its obligation to make the agreed upon payment stream. If the counterparty does not make the payments, the first company may still be liable for the original payment stream or cash flow. – Ch17

countertrade: Countertrade is a method of payment used by companies that do not have access to sufficient hard currencies (internationally traded currencies) to pay for imports from other countries. – Ch15

country item: Country items are checks drawn on banks located outside a Federal Reserve city or RCPC. – Ch08

coupon bearing: Coupon bearing bonds are bonds that make interest payments at periodic intervals. – Ch13

coverage or debt management ratios: Debt management ratios are used to determine a company's creditworthiness. These ratios include: times interest earned (TIE), long-term debt to capital, debt to tangible net worth and total liabilities to total assets. – Ch04

coverage ratios: Coverage ratios provide a measure of a company's ability to "cover" its debt and other fixed payments. These ratios include times interest earned, long-term debt-to-capital, debt-to-total assets, and total liabilities-to-total assets ratios. – Ch04

credit enhancement: A financial intermediary may provide credit enhancement by issuing an instrument such as a standby letter of credit or surety bond to guarantee the obligation of the borrower. – Ch10

credit risk: Credit risk or default risk is the risk that payments on a security will not be made under the original terms. – Ch10

credit scoring: Some commercial credit analysis involves credit scoring which is evaluated by purchasing credit reports from companies such as Dun & Bradstreet. Credit scoring involves a four step process: (1) differentiating standard and high-risk accounts based on monthly income, outstanding obligations and the employment history of the applicant, (2) weighting the characteristics of applicants who fit into each category to establish creditworthiness, (3) setting cut-off scores for approval and denial of credit and (4) applying further analysis to applicants whose scores fall in between the cut-off points. – Ch07

cross-default provisions: Nearly all creditors include cross-default provisions in their agreements. If a default occurs under any borrowing, then all credit facilities with cross-default provisions are in default. – Ch10

cumulative dividends: Preferred stock dividends are cumulative, which means that all arrears dividends owed must be paid in full before any common stock dividends can be paid. – Ch13

cure periods: Cure periods, often specified in the agreement, are a period of time in which an event of default may be corrected before the lender is allowed to pursue default remedies. – Ch13

current assets: Assets that are reasonably expected to be converted to cash within one year or within the operating cycle. Current assets include cash and cash equivalents, marketable securities and any operating assets – accounts receivable, inventories and prepaid expenses such as insurance premiums paid in advance. – Ch04

current liabilities: An obligation that is expected to be repaid out of current assets or fulfilled within the next year. Current liabilities include obligations such as accounts payable, short-term loans, wages payable, taxes payable and the current portion of long-term debt. – Ch04

current ratio: Total current assets divided by total current liabilities. This ratio measures a company's ability to meet its current obligations or the degree to which current obligations are covered by current assets. – Ch04

custody services: Providing safekeeping for securities, and buying, selling, receiving, and delivering securities based on terms outlined in a custody agreement. – Ch03

customer initiated entry (CIE): One of the ACH entry formats, the CIE format is for used for pre-authorized payments that are initiated by consumers using telephone bill paying services. – Ch08

data exchange: Companies that have relationships with two or more financial service providers (FSPs) may establish an arrangement in which one of the company's FSPs or a third-party reporting service gathers and consolidates the account balances and transaction activity from each of the company's financial institutions. This arrangement is commonly referred to as multi-bank reporting or data exchange. – Ch11

daylight overdraft: A daylight overdraft is an intraday exposure of the Fed occurring when a member bank's Federal Reserve account is in an overdraft position during the business day. – Ch08

days' inventory: A part of the cash conversion cycle, days' inventory is calculated as a function of the inventory value and the cost of goods sold. The cost of goods sold, rather than sales, is used in this formula because inventory is valued at its purchase cost rather than its selling price. – Ch04

days' payables: A part of the cash conversion cycle, days' payables is calculated as a function of the average accounts payable and the cost of goods sold. – Ch04

days' receivables: A part of the cash conversion cycle, days' receivables is calculated as a function of the accounts receivable value and the level of sales. This figure is also known as average collection period or days' sales outstanding and represents the number of days it takes to convert a sale into a cash inflow. – Ch04

days' sales outstanding (DSO): Days' sales outstanding (DSO) is calculated by dividing outstanding A/R at the end of a period by the average daily credit sales for that period. DSO gives a single number that can be compared to stated credit terms, historic trends or industry norms to provide an indication of a company's overall collection efficiency. It may, however, be distorted by changing trends in sales volume or by strong seasonality in sales. – Ch07

debentures: Unsecured bonds (debentures) represent general claims against the assets and/or cash flows of an organization. Large, financially secure organizations issue debentures based on their reputation in the marketplace. Organizations that do not have easily mortgaged assets must utilize unsecured borrowing through the use of debentures. – Ch13

debt covenants: Constraints placed on the management of a company to protect the interests of the debt holders. – Ch13

debt to tangible net worth: Most frequently used by commercial banks as a leverage measure, debt to tangible net worth measures a company's debt as a percentage of its tangible net worth. – Ch04

decentralized treasury: Field personnel are responsible for all daily treasury functions. However, for purposes of both information and control, field offices are required to submit periodic financial management reports to the home office. – Ch16

declaration date: The date on which the board of directors of a corporation announces a dividend. – Ch14

defalcation: The risk of intentional employee fraud. – Ch18

default risk: Default risk, also called credit risk, is the risk that payments on a security will not be made under the original terms. – Ch10

defeasance of debt: Defeasance of debt is a method for removing debt from an organization's balance sheet without actually retiring the debt issue. – Ch13

defined benefit plan: In a defined benefit plan, the benefit payment for each participant is calculated (or "defined") by a formula as specified in the plan. The formula is most often based on factors such as the employee's level of pay and length of service at retirement. – Ch20

defined contribution plan: A defined contribution plan is a retirement savings vehicle that provides benefits "defined" by contributors to the plan and investment earnings on those contributions. – Ch20

delivery price: The agreed upon price of a forward contract is called the delivery price. – Ch17

delivery-versus-payment (DVP): Most Fedwire transfers are made delivery-versus-payment (DVP) which entails the simultaneous exchange of securities and funds. – Ch08

demand deposit account (DDA): Commonly referred to as a checking account, a DDA is a method by which an account holder uses a commercial bank to transfer funds to and receive deposits from a third party. – Ch03

deposit anticipation: Deposit anticipation involves the initiation of a transfer before the items to be deposited have been received from customers. The transfer is initiated on the basis of historical cash flows over a given period. – Ch09

deposit deadline: The deposit deadline is the time, within the banking day, by which an item must be at the depository bank's processing center ready for transit in order to qualify for the availability stated on the availability schedule. – Ch08

deposit float: Deposit float has two related definitions. First, deposit float is the dollar amount of deposited items that are in the process of collection. Second, deposit float is the interval between the time an item is deposited and the time the funds are collected. – Ch08

deposit reconciliation service: A deposit reconciliation service enables deposits from multiple locations to be credited to a single corporate bank account. – Ch09

depository transfer checks (DTCs): Depository transfers checks (DTCs) are a special category of check used by a company to transfer funds from its outlying depository locations to its main concentration account. – Ch09

depreciable fixed assets: Assets that are used up or decline in value over time. – Ch04

derivative: A financial product that derives its value from an underlying asset. The underlying asset can be a financial instrument, a currency or a commodity. – Ch17

difference in conditions (DIC) insurance: Difference in conditions (DIC) insurance is often purchased to fill voids in policies purchased overseas and to insure property in transit. – Ch18

digital certificates: Digital certificates tie the identity of the user (private key) to the user's public key. – Ch12

digital signature: A digital signature is a message encoded with the sender's secret private key. The receiver can identify the source using the sender's public key. As long as the private key is never shared with anyone, it is impossible to forge a digital signature. – Ch12

digitized signature: A digitized signature is used as a facsimile signature on laser printed checks. – Ch12

Direct Clearers: The vast majority of payment items in Canada are cleared through the ACSS. Within the ACSS, 11 CPA member financial institutions, referred to as Direct Clearers, handle the clearing and settlement of payment items for customers, as well as for individuals that maintain accounts at other financial institutions, known as Indirect Clearers. Direct Clearers must maintain settlement accounts at The Bank of Canada. – Ch15

direct deposit: Direct deposits are transfers made from a company's account to the accounts of employees, shareholders, vendors, and trading partners using ACH credit transactions. – Ch09

direct placement: In a private or direct placement, securities are offered and sold to a limited number of investors. – Ch03

direct send: Banks may make arrangements to send cash letters directly to a paying bank or to a non-local Federal Reserve Bank, called a direct send. These arrangements enable banks to meet various deposit deadlines and achieve faster clearing times. – Ch08

disaster recovery: The restoration of systems and communications after an outage. – Ch18

disbursement float: Consists of mail, processing, and clearing float and represents the delay between the time a check is mailed and the time the buyer's/payor's account is debited. – Ch01

discount brokerage: Discount brokerages offer investors the opportunity to make trades at reduced prices, but do not provide investment advice. – Ch03

discount instruments: Treasury Bills, commercial paper and banker's acceptances are discount instruments. The amount invested in a discounted investment equals the face (par) value minus the interest that will be earned over the holding period. – Ch10

discount rate: The interest rate used in finding the present value of some future payment. – Ch05

discount terms: In addition to specifying a net due date, the seller may also offer a discount if payment is made prior to that date. Terms of 2/10 net 30 mean that the total amount is due within 30 days of the invoice date, but the buyer can take a two percent discount if payment is made within ten days. – Ch07

discretionary line: A discretionary line, sometimes called an uncommitted line, is usually made available for a one-year period; however, funding may be refused at the lender's discretion or canceled outright. – Ch10

distribution forecast: A distribution forecast estimates the effect a single event has on cash outflows over a specified interval based on historical patterns. Distribution forecasts are useful in estimating individual line items that appear on a receipts or a disbursements schedule. – Ch10

dividend capture: Dividend capture is a tax-motivated short-term investment strategy available to tax paying corporations. An investor purchases common stock just before the ex-dividend date and sells it after "capturing" the dividend. – Ch10

dividend reinvestment plans (DRIPS): These plans enable shareholders to elect to automatically reinvest their dividends in the stock of a company paying dividends. – Ch14

dividends in arrears: Because preferred stock is often cumulative in nature, all past preferred stock dividends (dividends in arrears) are required to be paid in full before any common dividend can be paid. – Ch14

division sort: Also known as high order prefix, division sort uses the auxiliary field on a business check. Individual field offices, branches or divisions are assigned a unique identifier that allows headquarters to obtain reports that track individual disbursements by location. – Ch07

documentary collection: A trade services payment method that processes the collection of a draft and accompanying shipping documents through international correspondent banks. – Ch03

documents against acceptance: Documents against acceptance use a time draft, which is a draft payable on a specified future date that must be accepted by the importer before the collecting bank may release documents. Upon maturity of the time draft, it is presented to the importer for payment. Once full and final payment is received, the collecting bank transfers funds to the remitting bank, as instructed, for payment to the exporter. – Ch15

documents against payment: Documents against payment use a sight draft, which is a draft payable on demand that requires the collecting bank receive full and final payment of the amount owed prior to releasing the documents. – Ch15

dollar-days of float: The dollar-days of float on an individual check are calculated by multiplying the dollar amount of the check by the number of days between the time the payor mails the check and the payee is granted credit for collected funds. – Ch09

draft/bill of lading: Also known as a documentary collection, the seller collects payments through banking channels. Draft/bill of lading is more common in international trade than in domestic trade. Having shipped goods to the buyer, the seller sends shipping and title documents to a bank which transmits the documents to the buyer's bank. The buyer gains possession of the documents upon paying the bank or upon signing a draft agreeing to pay at a future date. Upon collection, the buyer's bank remits payment to the seller's bank. – Ch07

drawdown: A drawdown wire transfer is a request sent by a company to a bank to initiate a debit wire transfer from either the company's account or another party's account at another financial institution. – Ch08

dual approval: A type of security procedure outlined in a bank's wire transfer agreement is dual approval. Dual approval means one person enters the wire and another reviews and releases it. – Ch08

dual banking system: Dual banking refers to the fact that banks are either federally or state chartered. – Ch03

due diligence: The due diligence process ensures that the financial and other statements provided by a company are accurate and represent the true value of a company according to the current provisions of the Generally Accepted Accounting Practices (GAAP). In addition, due diligence requires the disclosure of all information that may be of interest to any potential investor in a company's securities. Due diligence involves all areas of a company's operations and is required of all companies issuing new securities to the general public. – Ch13

earnings before interest and taxes (EBIT): One of the common measures for operating profitability is EBITDA or earnings before interest, taxes, depreciation and amortization. Once depreciation and amortization have been subtracted, the remaining amount is usually referred to as earnings before interest and taxes or EBIT. – Ch04

earnings before interest, taxes, depreciation and amortization (EBITDA): One of the common measures for operating profitability is EBITDA or earnings before interest, taxes, depreciation and amortization. – Ch04

earnings credit: The total dollar value of credit which can be used to offset the service charges incurred during an analysis period. – Ch21

earnings credit rate (ECR): The rate used by a bank to determine the total dollar value of credit to offset a customers service charges. It is calculated by multiplying the investable balance by the earnings credit rate (ECR) for the period. The most commonly used ECR is based upon the 90-day T-Bill rate. – Ch21

e-commerce: See electronic commerce -- Ch12

economic development bonds: Economic development bonds are bonds typically issued by underdeveloped countries or sponsoring organizations such as the World Bank or the International Monetary Fund (IMF). – Ch13

economic distress: Economic distress can be caused by any one or more of the following: (1) deterioration of an organization's financial condition, (2) tightening of credit standards by a lender, (3) changes in lending practices, (4) reduction in the availability of credit due to poor economic conditions and (5) increases in short-term interest rates. – Ch13

economic exposure: The long-term effect of changes in exchange rates on the present value of future cash flows to a company. – Ch17

economic order quantity (EOQ): Economic Order Quantity (EOQ) models calculate the optimal level of inventory, given certain ordering and holding costs. – Ch07

economic value added (EVA): After-tax operating profit minus an appropriate charge for the opportunity cost of all capital. – Ch05

economies of scale: Economies of scale occur when an increase in sales results in a lower average cost per unit of sale. Thus, economies of scale reflect the extent to which additional sales may be generated on the existing asset base. – Ch05

effective annual yield: The most reliable way to compare rates between instruments is to use effective annual yields. Effective annual yields assume compounding and are calculated on a 365-day year basis. Because of compounding, an effective annual yield assumes that the investor always has the opportunity to reinvest funds at the same rate. – Ch10

efficiency ratios: Efficiency ratios, also called turnover ratios, evaluate how effectively balance sheet accounts are utilized in the income generating process. Days' inventory, days' receivables, days' payables, and cash turnover, which are liquidity or working capital ratios, are all examples of efficiency ratios. Additional efficiency ratios include total asset turnover, fixed asset turnover, cash conversion efficiency and working capital turnover ratios. – Ch04

electronic benefit transfers: Electronic benefit transfer systems allow recipients of government transfer payments to receive benefit payments through automated teller machines (ATMs) and point-of-sale (POS) terminals. – Ch09

electronic bill presentment and payment (EBPP): The consumer version of EIPP that allows electronic statements to be sent to customers and invoices to be paid by electronic means. In most cases, these applications are Web-based and usable by anyone with Internet access. – Ch07

electronic certificates: Two of the most common methods of electronic security are encryption and message authentication by means of electronic signatures or certificates. – Ch11

electronic check presentment (ECP): With electronic check presentment (ECP), the MICR line data captured by the reader/sorter (the check number, TRN, account number and dollar amount of the item) is electronically transmitted to the paying bank. The paying bank uses this data, not the physical check, to debit funds from the payor's demand deposit account. The actual check may be sent to the paying bank for subsequent handling or the check may be truncated (retained) by the clearing bank. – Ch08

electronic commerce (e-commerce): The application of information and secure network technology for the purpose of facilitating business relationships among trading partners. E-commerce encompasses many types of formats and communications protocols, including traditional Electronic Data Interchange (EDI), Financial Electronic Data Interchange (FEDI) and Web-based commerce. – Ch12

Electronic Data Gathering Analysis and Retrieval (EDGAR): A database where SEC filings on specific companies may be obtained. – Ch04

electronic data interchange (EDI): Electronic Date Interchange (EDI) is a traditional form of e-commerce that utilizes structured electronic transactions within established standards to exchange data from one company's business application system to another company's business application system. – Ch12

electronic depository transfers (EDTs): EDTs are ACH transactions that concentrate funds using either the National Automated Clearing House (NACHA) CCD or CCD+ formats. EDT is the most common method of depository transfer in use today having virtually replaced depository transfer checks (DTCs). – Ch09

Electronic Federal Tax Payment System (EFTPS): The Electronic Federal Tax Payment System (EFTPS) is the primary method for collecting and accounting for federal taxes withheld by employers from individuals' salaries and wages, as well as corporate business and excise taxes. – Ch09

electronic invoice presentment and payment (EIPP): Many companies and banks are implementing EIPP systems in a B2B setting that allows electronic statements to be sent to commercial customers and invoices to be paid by electronic means. In most cases, these applications are Web-based and usable by anyone with Internet access. – Ch07

electronic lockbox: Some banks offer collection services that record the receipt of incoming payments (such as checks, ACHs and wires), reformat the data and transmit the data to a company. This service is referred to as an electronic lockbox. – Ch12

electronic signatures: Two of the most common methods of electronic security are encryption and message authentication by means of electronic signatures or certificates. – Ch11

encryption: This is the scrambling of a message by the sender and the unscrambling of the message by the receiver. The use of encryption technology with public/private keys can help to resolve many of the security issues on the Internet. Most e-commerce Websites have already implemented a form of encryption/authentication technology known as SSL (Secure Sockets Layer) to ensure privacy, integrity and authentication of data moving between clients and servers. – Ch12

end-point: An endpoint is the location of the paying bank where final settlement occurs. The endpoint is the TRN on the check. There are four general classifications of endpoints: (1) city items, (2) regional check-processing centers, (3) country items and (4) high-dollar group sort (HDGS). – Ch08

enterprise application integration (EAI): Many companies fully integrate Internet systems with existing business ERP and application systems. This is known as enterprise application integration (EAI). – Ch12

enterprise resource planning (ERP): Enterprise resource planning systems are sophisticated management information and accounting software packages that link different areas and divisions of a company on an enterprise-wide basis. – Ch11

enterprise risk management (ERM): The comprehensive analysis and management of all risks that impact an organization's departments, business units, operating or legal entities. – Ch18

equipment trust certificates: Equipment trust certificates are bonds secured by movable equipment, such as a fleet of trucks or railroad equipment. – Ch13

equity "kicker": A bond with warrants has some characteristics of debt and some characteristics of equity, thus creating a hybrid security (sometimes called a bond with an "equity kicker") that provides a company with the ability to expand its mix of securities and to appeal to a broader group of investors. – Ch13

equity capital: Equity capital consists of all preferred and common equity accounts including retained earnings. – Ch04

euro: The euro is the common currency used in the European Monetary Union. -- Ch15

Euro Bankers Association (EBA): One settlement mechanism is the Euro Bankers Association (EBA), an association of major clearing banks that operates a net settlement system similar to the CHIPS settlement procedure in the U.S. but is used primarily for financial, rather than commercial, transactions. – Ch15

Eurodollar deposits (Eurodollars): Eurodollars are dollar denominated deposits held outside the U.S. and may be issued as Eurodollar CDs, which are negotiable or Eurodollar time deposits, which are non-negotiable. Both Eurodollar CDs and Eurodollar time deposits are interest-bearing. – Ch10

European Central Bank (ECB): The European Central Bank (ECB), which was established in July 1998, oversees a single monetary policy for all EMU members. – Ch15

European option contract: A contract that allows the owner to exercise (that is, buy or sell the underlying asset) the option only at maturity. – Ch17

evaluated receipts settlement (ERS): Evaluated receipts settlement (ERS) is a payment method designed to eliminate the need for a supplier to provide an invoice to a customer. ERS is most commonly used in a retail environment where the cash conversion cycle is typically short, large volumes are involved, inventory turns over rapidly, and JIT inventory is required to meet consumer demand. – Ch12

event of default: An event of default may occur if any term or condition under a debt agreement is breached or violated by the borrower. Events of default are incidences such as non-payment of interest or principal when due, a material adverse change in the condition of the borrower or a violation of a specified covenant. – Ch13

excess and umbrella insurance: Excess or umbrella insurance is designed to supplement basic or primary liability coverage. – Ch18

excess balance: An account has an excess balance when its average collected balance is greater than either the amount that a financial institution requires for compensation or the target level that a company has chosen to maintain. Excess balances may result from deposit reporting delays, clearing delays, and transfer initiation delays. – Ch09

exclusion policies: Also known as gap insurance covers losses either not covered or excluded under other policies held by the organization. These policies are intended to "fill in the gaps" or provide higher overall levels of coverage. – Ch18

ex-dividend date: The date on which a stock is sold without the upcoming dividend attached. – Ch14

exercise date: The maturity date of an option contract. – Ch17

exercise price: The fixed price of an option contract. Also known as the strike price. – Ch17

expropriation: Expropriation is a type of sovereign risk wherein a government takes over a single company. – Ch15

eXtensible business reporting language (XBRL): XBRL provides a common platform for critical business reporting processes and improves the reliability and ease of communicating financial data between both internal and external users to the reporting enterprise. – Ch12

eXtensible markup language (XML): XML is an extension of HTML that allows the content as well as the structure to be defined. In essence, while HTML provides a consistent format for displaying information, XML adds "tags" that specifically define the information. – Ch12

extranet: Extranets are external networks ("extra" meaning external or outside a company). – Ch12

factor: A company that provides short-term financing to companies by purchasing accounts receivable at a discount. – Ch03

factoring: Factoring is the sale or transfer of title to accounts receivable to a third party called a factor. – Ch10

fair value hedge: If a derivative is used to hedge fluctuations in the value of a specific asset or liability carried on the balance sheet, the gains and losses of the reevaluation are recognized as income together with the offsetting gains and losses on the item being hedged. This type of hedge is referred to as a fair value hedge. – Ch04

fat client: The application software resides on the customer's desktop computer. – Ch11

Fed float: In the process of clearing checks, banks sometimes receive availability from the Fed before the Fed generates the offsetting debit. The difference in timing between the availability granted a clearing bank and the actual presentment of the item to the drawee bank is Fed float – Ch08

fed funds rate: The interest rate at which depository institutions lend balances to other depository institutions overnight via the Federal Reserve. – Ch03

fidelity bond: Fidelity bonds provide coverage that guarantees payment for money or other property lost through dishonest acts of bonded employees, either by name or by position. The bond generally covers all dishonest acts, such as larceny, theft, embezzlement, forgery, misappropriation, wrongful abstraction or willful misapplication, and whether employees act alone or in concert. – Ch18

fiduciary: An individual or institution to whom certain property is given to hold in trust according to a trust agreement. In pension funds, a fiduciary is an individual or a member of a Board who is given possession of property, such as plan assets, in trust. A fiduciary assumes the legal obligation to administer plan assets solely for the purpose(s) specified. – Ch03 & Ch20

file transfer protocol (FTP): There are several protocols used on the Internet. The file transfer protocol (FTP) is a standard protocol that is the simplest way to exchange files between computers on the Internet. – Ch12

finality: Finality varies depending on the payment system and the parties involved in the transaction. Often, there are provisions for return of payments, so finality is not assured until after the permitted return period has elapsed. – Ch08

Financial Accounting Foundation (FAF): The Financial Accounting Foundation (FAF) selects members, provides funds, and oversees the Governmental Accounting Standards Board (GASB) and the Financial Accounting Standards Board (FASB). – Ch01

Financial Accounting Standards (FAS): Statements of Financial Accounting Concepts (SFACs) provide the conceptual framework for the financial reporting process. Specific, detailed guidance is issued as Financial Accounting Standards. – Ch04

Financial Accounting Standards Board (FASB): Financial Accounting Standards Board (FASB) is an independent, self-regulating organization formed in 1973. The FASB continuously monitors the reporting and business environments to provide relevant and timely guidance for preparing financial statements. – Ch04

financial budget: The financial budget addresses the financing and investing activities of an organization. – Ch05

financial electronic data interchange (FEDI): FEDI is the electronic transmission of payments and/or payment-related information in a standard format between trading partners and/or the company's banks. FEDI includes such business applications as invoices, payment initiations, lockbox deposit reports, and remittance information sent directly to a trading partner and processed through a financial institution or third-party communications intermediary. –Ch12

financial leases: Financial leases, also known as capital leases, have terms that differ from those of operating leases. Capital leases have the following characteristics: (1) They are typically for a period greater than one year; (2) The lessor usually does not provide maintenance for the equipment; (3) The lease agreement is not cancelable; (4) Accounting guidelines require that a financial lease appear on the balance sheet as a capitalized lease; the payments are set up to fully depreciate the cost of the equipment;

(5) the lease usually runs for the life of the asset and (6) the lessee has the option to renew the contract or purchase the asset at the end of the original lease contract for an agreed-upon residual value. – Ch13

financial leverage: Financial leverage is a measure of a company's use of fixed cost financing (such as long-term debt) in its capital structure. In some countries this is also known as "gearing". – Ch14

Financial Reporting Releases (FRRs): Specific reporting guidance issued by the SEC is contained within its Financial Reporting Releases (FRRs). – Ch04

financial risk: The risk related to the use of fixed cost financing such as long-term debt in a company's capital structure. – Ch17

financial risk management: The management of financial risk due to changing currency exchange, commodity prices and interest rates. – Ch01

financial service provider (FSP): A FSP provides financial services to its customers. The most common type of FSP is the commercial bank and banking financial intermediaries. There are also many non-bank financial intermediaries such as commercial finance companies and brokerage firms that can be considered FSPs. – Ch21

financial services markup language (FSML): FSML is a language developed to implement e-checks and other secure financial documents. FSML is designed to include encryption and digital signatures necessary to create electronic checks. –Ch12

Financial Services Technology Consortium (FSTC): There are several national and regional electronic clearinghouse services operated by member banks or third parties that specialize in providing various types of EDI services to members and/or customers such as the Financial Services Technology Consortium (FSTC). These clearinghouses allow member banks to offer a wider range of EDI services than formerly possible. – Ch12

firewall: Wherever external users are allowed access to internal applications or data, it is important to utilize a "firewall" to protect the internal systems. The purpose of a firewall is to ensure that only authorized users are allowed access to data or data systems. – Ch12

fixed asset turnover: Fixed asset turnover measures how much revenue is generated on productive or fixed assets. The higher this ratio, the more productively a company uses its assets. – Ch04

fixed assets: Fixed assets, also known as capital assets, are a company's investment in property, buildings, machinery, and equipment. – Ch04

fixed costs: Costs that either do not vary in total over a wide range of activity or are not immediately impacted by changes in the cost driver. – Ch05

fixed-income securities: Fixed-income securities are primarily debt-type instruments that pay a fixed coupon or interest rate. Technically, preferred stock could also be considered a fixed-income security. – Ch13

float: The time interval, or delay, between the start and the completion of a specific phase or process occurring along the cash flow timeline. – Ch01

float neutralization: With the use of EDI, companies often need to compensate buyers for the shortening of the cash flow timeline (i.e., shortening of days' payables); sellers often must negotiate new e-commerce-based credit terms. This is frequently referred to as float neutralization. – Ch12

floating rate debt: Floating (Adjustable) rate debt is a type of debt that is especially attractive to investors during periods of rising interest rates. Some investors prefer floating rate debt because it has a stable market value and matches current interest rates. Some borrowers prefer floating rate debt because it allows the borrower to take advantage of falling interest rates, yet still match the maturity of debts to the maturity of assets. – Ch13

floor planning: A type of asset-based lending used for very high-value durable goods such as automobiles, trucks or heavy equipment. Loans are made against each individual item and recorded by serial number. The loan is not repaid until the item is sold. – Ch07

flotation cost: The cost of issuing new stocks, bonds or other securities. – Ch03

forced reinvestment: A type of political risk in which funds cannot be transferred out of the country in any form. – Ch15

Foreign Corrupt Practices Act: In many countries, "commissions" or "fees" that would be considered bribes in the U.S. are deeply ingrained in the commercial culture. However, the Foreign Corrupt Practices Act forbids U.S. companies to engage in such practices. – Ch15

foreign exchange (FX) rate risk: Foreign exchange (FX) rate risk arises when foreign securities are held in the short-term investment portfolio. FX rate risk is the risk that there is a change in the rate of exchange between the currency in which a security is denominated and the company's home currency. – Ch10

Foreign Exchange Yen Clearing System (FXYCS): The Foreign Exchange Yen Clearing System (FXYCS) is used to make payments for non-resident yen accounts and can accept messages in S.W.I.F.T. format. Most transactions through FXYCS are settlements for FX transactions or international treasury settlements. – Ch15

foreign tax credit: If foreign source income has already been subject to foreign income taxes, the same income is being taxed twice. To relieve the effect of this double taxation, U.S. tax law allows a U.S. company a tax credit against its total U.S. income tax liability for those foreign income taxes paid by the parent and its subsidiaries. This credit is called the foreign tax credit. – Ch16

forged check: Forged checks are checks on which either the signer's or endorser's signature has been forged. – Ch08

forward contract: An agreement between two parties to buy or sell a fixed amount of an asset to be delivered at a future date for an agreed upon price today. – Ch17

forward rate agreement (FRA): A forward contract on interest rates in which two parties agree that a certain interest rate will apply to a certain principal during a specified future period of time. – Ch17

forward value date: Under a value dating system, a bank sets a forward value date upon which the value of funds credited to an account is determined. – Ch15

fractional availability: A bank may grant fractional availability which is an adjustment to the stated availability to reflect average clearing delays. – Ch08

fraud risk: Fraud risk is the risk that someone might alter a transaction or enter a false item that could cause a loss for the disbursing party. – Ch08

freight payment: Some banks and third parties offer a payment service called freight payment in which specialists pay all of a shipper's freight bills, audit bills for possible overcharges and duplicate payments, and provide reports that help a company compare costs for different routes and carriers. – Ch09

full disclosure principle: The full disclosure principle states that any information that may influence the judgment and decisions of a user of financial information should be disclosed. – Ch04

full guarantee: A lender may ask for specific performance guarantees relative to the assets being financed. Under a full guarantee, the parent fully guarantees performance by the subsidiary. – Ch13

full reconciliation service: With a full reconciliation service, a company supplies an electronic file of checks issued to the bank and the bank matches checks paid against the file. – Ch09

full underwriting agreement: Under a full underwriting agreement, an investment bank essentially buys the full issue from a company at an agreed-upon price and then sells the issue to the general public or to other brokerage companies. – Ch13

full-service brokerage: Full-service brokerages have research analysts who are industry specialists and who provide investment advice to institutions and individual investors. Some full-service brokerages also manage investment portfolios for institutions and individuals. – Ch03

fully negotiable CD: Generally sold to larger institutional investors, fully negotiable CDs are generally offered in $1 million blocks with maturities ranging from 14 days to five years. – Ch03

future contract: Futures are standardized contracts traded on organized exchanges and have a range of delivery dates. Both the size of the contract and the maturity date are not negotiated, but rather are set by the exchange. Futures trading requires a margin account that is marked-to-market on a daily basis. Futures contracts are rarely settled by delivery and are usually closed out prior to maturity. – Ch17

future value: The value at some point in the future of a sum of money invested today. – Ch05

gap insurance: Insurance that covers losses either not covered or excluded under other policies held by the organization. These policies are intended to "fill in the gaps" or provide higher overall levels of coverage. – Ch18

general obligation bonds: General obligation bonds are paid from the proceeds of general tax revenues. – Ch13

Generally Accepted Accounting Principles (GAAP): The accounting function includes recording a company's assets, liabilities, shareholder equity, revenues, and expenses, and reporting this information according to a detailed set of rules referred to as Generally Accepted Accounting Principles (GAAP). – Ch04

giro: Many countries have giro systems that operate through postal and/or banking channels. Giros are consumer based payment systems that transfer payments from one account to another using direct debits and credits. Consumers use the giro system in place of checks for payment of monthly bills. – Ch15

Global Depository Receipt (GDR): A Global Depository Receipt (GDR) is issued in more than one country for shares in a foreign company. The shares, held by a foreign branch of an international bank, trade as domestic shares but are offered for sale globally through various bank branches. – Ch13

Government Sponsored Enterprises (GSEs): Government Sponsored Enterprises (GSEs) are private companies that act as financial intermediaries to provide funds for loans made in the housing, education and agriculture sectors. GSE securities are issued by the Federal National Mortgage Association (Fannie Mae), the Federal Farm Credit Banks Funding Corporation, the Federal Home Loan Mortgage Corporation (Freddie Mac), the Federal Home Loan Banks Office of Finance and the Student Loan Marketing Association (Sallie Mae). – Ch10

Governmental Accounting Standards Board (GASB): Establishes standards for state and local governments, state universities and other state-affiliated agencies. – Ch01

group captive: A group captive, also known as an association captive, resembles a single-parent captive except it provides risk financing for multiple owners instead of just one. – Ch18

guidance line: Examples of guidance lines include money market and demand lines of credit. Guidance lines are often used by banks to accommodate credit exposure arising from non-borrowing activities such as daylight overdrafts, ACH credit exposure and FX exposure. – Ch10

hedge accounting: An accounting technique that is applied to the components of a hedge so that the fair value of the hedged asset and the hedging vehicle are included in earnings for the same period. – Ch17

hedging: The process by which an organization uses financial instruments to reduce or eliminate risks associated with the uncertainty about the future price of an asset. – Ch17

held-to-maturity (HTM): Held-to-maturity (HTM) securities are debt securities purchased with both the intent and ability to hold until maturity. – Ch04

high order prefix: Also known as division sort, high order prefix uses the auxiliary field on a business check. Individual field offices, branches or divisions are assigned a unique identifier that allows headquarters to obtain reports that track individual disbursements by location. – Ch07

high yield bonds: High-Yield Bonds, also referred to as junk bonds or below investment grade (rating of BB or less), usually come from one of two sources. First, some junk bonds are originally sound but become high-risk when a company issuing the bond experiences financial trouble or files for bankruptcy. Second, some high-yield bonds are originally sold as a high-risk instrument, in which case they are sold by companies to either finance a leveraged buyout or to relieve financial distress. – Ch13

High-Dollar Group Sort (HDGS): A Fed program impacting controlled disbursement services is the High-Dollar Group Sort. Under the High-Dollar Group Sort (HDGS) program the local Fed automatically makes a second presentment to banks with more than $10 million in daily presentments from financial institutions outside the banks' Fed district. – Ch09

highly protected risk (HPR): This rating entails the installation of appropriate sprinklers, fire gear and other safety equipment, yet provides the organization with a preferred rating status for fire and hazard insurance, resulting in significantly lower insurance premiums. – Ch18

high-order prefix (divisional) sort: A high-order prefix (divisional) sort is the disbursement counterpart to deposit reconciliation services. Divisional sorting allows a single account to be used by a company with multiple units. Codes identifying the various units are included in the check serial number field. This method is used to facilitate the identification and sorting of payments by operating unit. – Ch09

historical cost principle: The historical cost principle states that most assets and liabilities are reported at historical cost. – Ch04

holder in due course defense: The holder in due course defense arises when a financial institution or a company accepts or cashes a fraudulent item in good faith. – Ch09

holder of record date: The holder of record date is usually four days after the ex-dividend date. It enables brokerage firms to send an updated list of stockholders to a company on time. – Ch14

holding period yield: The holding period yield is the yield for the time that a security is held. However, yields are quoted on an annualized basis that is obtained by adjusting the holding period yield for the number of days to maturity. – Ch10

hub: The companies that mandate suppliers to implement EDI are referred to as EDI hubs. Although hubs often start as EDI originators (sending EDI purchase orders to suppliers), they tend to become EDI recipients as trading partners send EDI invoices in response to purchase orders. – Ch12

hybrid lockbox: Hybrid lockbox systems combine features of both wholesale and retail lockboxes. They are configured, usually on a customized basis, to process both B2B and C2B payments. They are used by companies, such as utilities, whose consumer customers return standardized remittance documents that can be processed automatically and whose business customers remit documents that require manual handling. – Ch09

hypertext markup language (HTML): HTML is the language used to create Web pages on the Internet and other browser-based delivery formats. HTML is human-readable. – Ch12

hypertext transfer protocol (HTTP): One of several protocols used on the Internet, the hypertext transfer protocol (HTTP) is a set of rules for exchanging files (text, graphic images, sound video and other multimedia files) on the World Wide Web (www). – Ch12

image replacement document (IRD): As a result of the Check Clearing for the 21st Century Act of 2003 (Check 21), check truncation converts the information on a business or consumer check into an electronic form or image that is transmitted electronically, thereby avoiding the need for physical presentment of the item. If the drawee bank's customer wants the check returned in a statement, Check 21 allows the drawee bank to create a substitute document called an image replacement document (IRD). – Ch09

imaging: Both the front and the back of a check (or any other business document) can be captured and converted into digital information using optical scanning. Check images may be transmitted to a company's computer system for storage or sent to a fax machine. Alternatively, check images are frequently housed in a bank database to which a company is granted access for the purpose of research or customer service inquiries. – Ch07

imprest account: An imprest account, sometimes referred to as a petty cash account, is an account maintained at a prescribed level for a particular purpose or activity. For example, a field office may have an imprest account for local disbursements with a balance sufficient for one or two months' expenses. – Ch09

income bonds: Income bonds are bonds that pay interest only if a company has profits, thus reducing some of the risk of issuing debt from a company's viewpoint. – Ch13

income statement: The income statement (also called the statement of earnings, the statement of operations or the profit and loss statement) summarizes: (1) revenues earned, (2) expenses incurred and (3) gains and losses arising from conversions of assets and liabilities over an accounting period. – Ch04

indenture agreements: An indenture is a legal document that outlines the rights and obligations of both the borrower (bond issuer) and the lender (bondholder). These indentures may be quite lengthy and include various restrictive covenants that impose constraints on the actions of a company's management. -- Ch13

index bonds: Indexed bonds are bonds in which interest rates are tied to an economic index and are used in countries with high inflation. – Ch13

Indirect Clearers: The vast majority of payment items in Canada are cleared through the ACSS. Within the ACSS, 11 CPA member financial institutions, referred to as Direct Clearers, handle the clearing and settlement of payment items for customers, as well as for individuals that maintain accounts at other financial institutions, known as Indirect Clearers. – Ch15

industrial credit and capital company: Subsidiaries of large industrial corporations that raise funds in the commercial paper market and lend to companies and individuals. – Ch03

industrial revenue bond: Industrial revenue bonds are tax-exempt bonds, sometimes referred to as industrial development bonds, issued by a state or local government agency to finance industrial or commercial projects that serve a public good. – Ch13

industry convention electronic data interchange (EDI): Industry convention EDI is a specific format standard, or a subset of the more generic cross-industry EDI standards, used within a particular industry. Examples of industries that utilize these types of EDI standards include grocery, retail, automotive, electrical manufacturing and chemical production and distribution. – Ch12

in-house banking: In an in-house banking structure, treasury becomes the primary provider of banking services for the organization's operating entities as well as the coordination center for intracompany lending. – Ch02

in-house processing: With a company processing center, check processing and deposit preparation are performed in-house. This method is typically used by companies in industries with a large volume of relatively small-dollar payments such as utility and insurance companies. – Ch09

initial public offering (IPO): The term IPO is used to describe an issuer's first public offering of a security of any class, although the term tends to be limited to common stock. The term is also used to designate an offering of previously authorized, but unissued, securities. – Ch13

installment credit: A form of credit whereby a company requires a customer to make equal monthly payments, each of which contain a principal and interest component. – Ch07

institutional investor: A major stockholder such as an insurance company or pension fund. – Ch14

intangible assets: Intangible assets are assets that lack physical substance. Examples are goodwill, trademarks and patents. – Ch04

integrated accounts payable: An integrated or comprehensive A/P service allows a company to outsource all or part of its A/P and/or disbursements functions. A company using an integrated or comprehensive payables service is, in effect, outsourcing the disbursement function, thereby potentially reducing the overall cost of A/P operations. – Ch07

integration: The third stage of money laundering which involves creating what appears to be a legitimate explanation for the source of funds. One common method of integration is to attempt to show that the funds have been donated for a charitable purpose. – Ch03

integrity: Integrity is the ability to ensure that a message was not modified in transit, which is especially important for financial transactions. – Ch12

intelligent character recognition (ICR): A type of data capture technology that reads handwritten or typed information. – Ch09

interest rate parity: The relationship between the spot, forward and money markets is known as interest rate parity. – Ch15

interest rate risk: Interest rate risk arises from the threat that interest rates will rise during the holding period of a fixed-rate security coupled with the necessity or intent to sell the security prior to maturity. – Ch10

interest rate swap: An agreement between two parties to exchange a fixed rate loan for a floating rate loan. – Ch17

interest-bearing instruments: Interest-bearing issues, such as certificates of deposit (CDs) and Eurodollar deposits, pay interest in arrears at maturity or at periodic intervals. The cash received at maturity from an interest-bearing security is the face value plus the interest payment. – Ch10

internal borrowing: In intracompany lending, sometimes referred to as internal borrowing, subsidiaries with excess funds can lend these funds to other subsidiaries with a shortage of funds. – Ch06

internal factoring: Rather than taking actual title to commercial goods, the internal factoring unit buys accounts receivable from the exporting unit and collects from the importing unit. – Ch16

internal rate of return (IRR): Internal rate of return (IRR) reflects the expected profit on an investment or project expenditure as an annual rate. Specifically, it is the discount rate at which the net present value (NPV) of the project or investment is equal to zero. – Ch05

Internet: The Internet is an unrestricted, worldwide network that allows access to anyone with the appropriate hardware and software. In essence, the Internet is a collection of many computer networks linked together to form a global communications pathway. – Ch12

Internet initiated entry (WEB): One of the ACH entry formats, the WEB format is used for payments that are not pre-authorized but are initiated by consumers using the Internet. – Ch08

Internet service provider (ISP): A type of Internet/e-commerce provider, an Internet service provider (ISP) is a communications intermediary that provides Internet service to individuals and small businesses, typically over telephone lines (T-1 or T-3 lines), cable, satellite or wireless. – Ch12

Internet transaction tax: Sales tax levied on Internet transactions. – Ch16

in-the-money: A call option is in-the-money if the asset price is greater than the strike price of the option. A put option is in-the-money if the asset price is less than the strike price of the option. – Ch17

intracompany dividends: Large companies with wholly-owned subsidiaries generally use intracompany dividends to transfer profits from the subsidiaries to the parent. – Ch14

intracompany lending: In intracompany lending, sometimes referred to as internal borrowing, subsidiaries with excess funds can lend these funds to other subsidiaries with a shortage of funds. – Ch06

intraday exposure: An intraday exposure, also called a daylight overdraft, occurs when a member bank's Federal Reserve account is in an overdraft position during the business day. – Ch08

intranet: Intranets are internal networks ("intra" meaning internal or within a company) that utilize commonly available browser technology to provide data and applications for employees or other authorized internal users. – Ch12

inventory blanket lien: An inventory loan with a general claim on the company's inventory. – Ch06

inventory conversion period: The average number of days from the acquisition of raw materials until the sale of the finished goods. – Ch06

inventory loan: An inventory loan is a loan secured by providing the lender with a claim on the company's inventory. – Ch06

inverted yield curve: An inverted yield curve slopes downward reflecting higher short-term yields than long-term yields. Yield curve inversion happens infrequently. – Ch10

investable balance: The balances in a customer's account that a bank was able to invest in income producing assets during an account analysis period. – Ch21

investment bank: Investment bankers offer many services to a company issuing stock, bonds and other securities. The investment banking process has several levels of decision-making. – Ch13

investor relations (IR): Investor relations is a strategic management responsibility that integrates finance, communication, marketing, and securities law compliance to enable the most effective two-way communication between a company, the financial community and other constituencies. – Ch19

invoicing float: The delay between the purchase of goods or services and the receipt of an invoice by the buyer/payor. – Ch01

issuing bank: Issuing banks underwrite cards to individual and business cardholders that meet credit standards. The issuing bank maintains the individual credit card accounts, bills and collects payments from cardholders and monitors the performance of credit card receivable portfolios. – Ch08 Banks may serve a variety of roles in L/C transactions. The issuing bank is the buyer's (importer's) bank that issues the L/C in favor of the beneficiary (seller/exporter). – Ch15

jumbo CD: CDs with values of $100,000 or more are referred to as jumbo CDs and may be offered on a negotiable basis. – Ch03

junk bonds: High-yield bonds, also referred to as junk bonds or below investment grade (rating of BB or less), usually come from one of two sources. First, some junk bonds are originally sound but become high-risk when a company issuing the bond experiences financial trouble or files for bankruptcy. Second, some high-yield bonds are originally sold as a high-risk instrument, in which case they are sold by companies to either finance a leveraged buyout or to relieve financial distress. – Ch13

just-in-time inventory (JIT): An approach to inventory management that attempts to minimize the level of inventory by altering the costs or uncertainties that underlie the motives for holding inventory. The three basic goals of a JIT system are to eliminate waste, standardize the production process and continuously improve quality. JIT offers significant benefits to companies in the form of improved supplier relationships, lower transaction costs and better overall planning. – Ch07

key-person insurance: For corporations, life insurance coverage for key personnel provides the organization with the resources needed to replace the individuals in the event of death. – Ch18

lagging: Lagging involves executing cross-border payments between subsidiaries behind the scheduled payment date (lagging). Liquidity is shifted from one subsidiary to another. Lagging is used when a subsidiary country's currency is expected to appreciate relative to the parent company's currency. – Ch16

Large Value Transfer System (LVTS): LVTS is an electronic wire system introduced by the CPA in February 1999 to facilitate the transfer of irrevocable payments in Canadian dollars in real-time. Through LVTS, funds are transferred between participating financial institutions virtually instantaneously and the money is credited to the beneficiary's account on a timely basis. Because all LVTS payments are immediately final and irrevocable, the beneficiary may withdraw the money, invest it or use it to make another payment confident that the incoming payment will not be reversed for any reason. LVTS is the first model in the world that is a hybrid which offers the benefits of the two main models for current payment systems: (1) achieving the real-time payment finality provided by a Real Time Gross Settlement (RTGS) system and (2) offering the lower collateral costs associated with a netting system. – Ch15

layering: The second stage of money laundering which involves a series of complex financial transactions designed to separate the cash proceeds from their criminal or terrorist origins. – Ch03

leading: Leading involves executing cross-border payments between subsidiaries ahead of the scheduled payment date. Liquidity is shifted from one subsidiary to another. Leading is employed when a subsidiary country's currency is expected to depreciate relative to the parent company's currency. – Ch16

ledger balances: Ledger balances are bank balances that reflect all entries to a bank account, regardless of whether the deposited items have been collected and are available for withdrawal. – Ch08

ledger cut-off: A bank's ledger cut-off is the time of day when a deposit must be received to be posted to the ledger balance of the depositor's account. Items deposited after the ledger cut-off time are considered to be received by the bank on the next banking day. – Ch08

ledger overdraft: If the ledger balance is negative, there is a ledger overdraft. – Ch08

lessee: In leasing, the owner of the asset receives lease payments from the lessee who has use of the asset. – Ch13

lessor: In leasing, the owner of the asset is called the lessor and receives lease payments from the lessee who has use of the asset. – Ch13

letter of credit (L/C): An L/C is a document issued by a bank, guaranteeing the payment of a customer's draft up to a stated amount for a specified period provided certain conditions are met. The L/C substitutes a bank's credit for that of the buyer, virtually eliminating the seller's credit risk. L/Cs are a widely used method of payment for import and export shipments and are also often used as a financing vehicle for international trade transactions. – Ch15

liabilities: Liabilities represent the obligations of the business and generally consist of operating liability accounts and financing supplied by creditors, primarily lenders and suppliers. Liabilities are obligations or debts that will be paid with assets or services in the future. – Ch04

liability insurance: Liability is generally considered a form of casualty insurance that insures against damage to other parties. The liabilities can arise from product defects, business practices, accidents, actions of the organization's employees, officers or Board of Directors and general negligence in the operation of the organization. – Ch18

liens: In most types of secured lending, the lender has a lien, or legal claim, on the assets used as collateral in the event the lender cannot take physical possession of the asset. This may be in the form of a mortgage (for larger assets) or a blanket lien (against inventory and receivables). In the event the borrower defaults on the loan or bond issue, the lender can seize the assets in lieu of repayment. – Ch13

lifting fees: Companies may be required to pay taxes when moving funds out of a foreign country. Some countries refer to these as lifting fees. Lifting fees are charged whenever funds are transferred from a resident (domestic) account to a non-resident (foreign) account. – Ch16

line of credit: A line of credit is an agreement in which the lender gives the borrower access to funds up to a maximum amount over a specific period of time. – Ch10

liquidating dividends: A dividend that is paid out of capital rather than earnings. – Ch14

liquidity: A company's ability to meet current and future financial obligations when they come due in as timely, efficient and cost-effective manner as possible. – Ch01

liquidity or working capital ratios: Liquidity or working capital ratios are standardized and widely used formulas that allow a company's management to: (1) determine adequate liquidity levels, (2) establish liquidity policy and guidelines and (3) continually monitor liquidity. – Ch04

loan guarantee: When a subsidiary of a larger company is borrowing funds or floating a bond issue, the lenders may require that the parent corporation (or sister subsidiary, supplier, customer or other entity) provide a guarantee of principal for the arrangement. In some cases a subsidiary may even provide a guarantee for the parent. This allows lenders recourse to the parent company (or guaranteeing party) to obtain payment in the event the subsidiary is in default. – Ch13

loan participation: With a loan participation, a financial institution purchases an interest in another lender's credit facility. – Ch10

loan syndication: In a loan syndication, multiple financial institutions share a single credit facility. The syndicate, or group of lenders, is led by an agent who acts as the intermediary between the company and the syndicate for purposes of negotiating the credit terms and documentation, making advances and payments on the loan, and disseminating information. – Ch10

lockbox: A lockbox is a collection system in which a company's customers mail payments to a designated post office box. A third party collects the payments, processes the remittances and deposits the checks directly into the company's account. – Ch03

lockbox network: Lockbox networks may involve either several processors in different cities or a single processor with multiple locations. – Ch09

London InterBank Offer Rate (LIBOR): The London InterBank Offered Rate (LIBOR) is set on a daily basis in London and is the borrowing/lending rate for dollars used between multinational banks. It is also the most commonly used base rate for short-term borrowing. – Ch06

long position: The party that agrees to buy an asset assuming that the asset will increase in value is the holder of a long position. – Ch17

long-term bonds: Long-term bonds, which are typically issued for periods of 10 to 30 years, represent a major source of long-term debt financing for many organizations. Bonds are a long-term contract in which the issuer of the bond (the borrower) agrees to make specific payments of interest (usually semi-annually) and principal (at maturity) to the holders (lenders/investors) of the bonds. – Ch13

long-term debt to capital ratio: Most frequently used by financial analysts and credit rating agencies, long-term debt to capital measures what percentage of a company's capitalization is provided by long-term debt. Capitalization consists of long-term debt and equity. Long-term debt includes liabilities such as long-term notes and bonds, term loans and capitalized lease obligations. – Ch04

long-term liabilities: Long-term liabilities include long-term notes and bonds, term loans and capitalized lease obligations. – Ch04

magnetic ink character recognition (MICR): The information necessary to process checks by machine is contained in the MICR line, which is printed with special characters and magnetic ink on the lower portion of the check. These characters can be read by magnetic or optical scanning equipment. – Ch07

mail float: The time interval or delay between the day a check is mailed and the day it is received by a payee or at a payee's processing site. – Ch09

malfeasance: The collusion between external criminals and internal employees. – Ch18

margin account: Futures trading requires a margin account. The margin account is valued, or marked-to-market on a daily basis, to ensure the party in the futures contract has enough funds to cover the contract. – Ch17

margin call: A margin call occurs in a margin account when the account drops below a predetermined level. The margin call requires the holder of the account to replenish either the account to the initial level or close out the futures position with the exchange. – Ch17

marginal cost: The primary sources of funds for a company, especially long-term funds, are debt and equity capital in the form of newly issued common stock and retained earnings. It is important for an investor to recognize that the most important item is the marginal cost of these components; that is, what the cost is of raising new amounts of these forms of capital. Using the marginal, or expected, cost of these components provides an investor with the market's current evaluation of a company's risk and, therefore, the required rate of return. – Ch13

marked-to-market: The current value of a security is adjusted to market value on the reporting date. – Ch04

market makers: Market-makers are individuals who quote both a bid and ask price whenever requested. – Ch17

market risk: Market risk or price risk is the uncertainty over the price at which a security can be sold prior to maturity. Securities with longer maturities are generally subject to more price risk than similar securities with shorter maturities. An investment's market risk typically takes one of two forms – interest rate risk and foreign exchange rate risk. – Ch10

market value added (MVA): Market value added (MVA) represents the market value of a company's debt and equity less the book value of debt and equity. – Ch05

market value per share: Market value per share is defined as the current price at which a share of the stock is traded. – Ch13

master budget: The annual budget for an entire organization. – Ch05

master note: A master note is a type of promissory note used to simplify the paperwork connected with loans that have a multiple advance feature such as lines of credit and revolvers. A company signs one comprehensive promissory note for the total amount of the line of credit. Any loans or repayments under the note are covered by the terms of the master note. – Ch13

matching principle: The matching principle requires that expenses be reported when the revenues with which they are associated are recognized. – Ch04

material adverse change (MAC) clause: Material adverse change (MAC) clause, also referred to as a discretionary clause, allows a lender to refuse funding or declare a default even if all agreements are in full compliance if, in the lender's opinion, a MAC has occurred in the borrower's condition. – Ch10

material planning systems (MPS): Material planning systems (MPS) are often coupled with JIT systems that bring together long-range production planning with the current flow of materials through the production process. In today's competitive environment, a company can often negotiate arrangements with suppliers to provide a continuous level of production materials on short notice, resulting in reduced carrying costs for the raw materials used to generate the finished goods. – Ch07

maturity matching: Maturity matching involves matching the maturity of the debt to the specific financing needs of an organization. – Ch13

maturity matching financing strategy: Under a maturity matching financing strategy, the total permanent assets, defined as fixed assets plus permanent current assets, are financed with long-term financing. – Ch06

medium- or intermediate-term notes and bonds: Companies or government entities issue medium- or intermediate-term notes and bonds with terms in the 2 to10 year range. In most cases these bonds are coupon bearing (i.e, interest payments are made at periodic intervals) and are very similar to long-term bonds except for the shorter maturity. – Ch13

memo post: Memo posting is posting of an ACH credit or debit entry early in the day even though the actual credit or debit will not be posted to the account until after the close of business. The memo post informs the account holder of the settlement. – Ch08

merchant bank: The merchant bank qualifies businesses (referred to as merchants) that accept credit card payments. The merchant bank provides merchants with credit card terminals and maintains deposit accounts through which the credit card payments settle. – Ch08

message authentication: A digital signature which prevents an unauthorized person from changing a wire. – Ch08

middleware: Software that links two different applications. – Ch11

mixed cost: A cost with both fixed and variable elements. – Ch05

Modified Accelerated Cost Recovery Schedule (MACRS): The Modified Accelerated Cost Recovery Schedule (MACRS) depreciation schedule provides a listing of how much can be depreciated annually for various types of assets. – Ch13

money market demand deposit account (MMDA): Money market demand deposit accounts pay an unregulated rate of interest determined by each institution and allow limited check-writing and electronic withdrawals. MMDAs are available to individuals and all types of businesses. – Ch03

money market funds: Money market mjtual funds invest in short-term securities such as Treasury Bills, CDs and CP. The value of shares fluctuates with the performance of underlying securities. – Ch03

money market instruments: Money market instruments are securities that are short-term in nature, generally one-year or less until maturity. Money market instruments are generally highly liquid and are issued by borrowers with excellent credit ratings. Examples of money market instruments include Treasury Bills (T-Bills), commercial paper (CP), repurchase agreements (repos) and banker's acceptances (BA's). – Ch03

money market mutual funds (MMMFs): Money market mutual funds (MMMFs) are commingled funds of money market instruments in which fund investors have an ownership interest. MMMFs are sold in shares. – Ch10

money market securities: Money market securities are debt instruments with remaining maturities of up to one year although most mature in three months or less. Money market securities have differing credit quality, yields, maturities and marketability. – Ch10

money market yield: One of the commonly quoted yields that are calculated using the annual yield formula is the money market yield which uses a 360-day year basis. – Ch10

money markets: The money markets are where short-term debt securities are traded. – Ch10

money order: A money order is a prepaid instrument issued by parties such as companies, banks or the United States Postal Service. – Ch08

Monte Carlo simulation: The most commonly used decision model that uses an analytical technique in which a large number of simulations are run using random quantities for specified variables, then analyzing the distribution of results to infer which values are most likely to occur. – Ch05

monthly billing: The seller issues a monthly statement covering all invoices prior to a cut-off date, typically toward the end of each month. The buyer must pay by a specified date the following month. – Ch07

Moody's: Moody's is one of the credit rating agencies. Their ratings include Prime-1 (P1), Prime-2 (P2), Prime-3 (P3), and Not Prime. – Ch10

mortgage bonds: Mortgage bonds are used to finance specific assets that are pledged as security against the issue and usually include substantial financial covenants or indenture agreements. – Ch13

Mortgage-Backed Security (MBS): Mortgage-Backed Securities (MBS) are essentially bundles of mortgages that are packaged and resold to investors. Many of these securities are issued by government and quasi government agencies and provide both liquidity to the mortgage market and a government-backed fixed income investment for investors. – Ch10

multi-bank reporting: Companies that have relationships with two or more financial service providers (FSPs) may establish an arrangement in which one of the company's FSPs or a third-party reporting service gathers and consolidates the account balances and transaction activity from each of the company's financial institutions. This arrangement is commonly referred to as multi-bank reporting or data exchange. – Ch11

multi-currency account: A special arrangement between a bank and a company whereby the bank allows the customer to receive or make international payments in a range of currencies from a single account or multiple subsidiary accounts. – Ch16

multilateral netting system: Similar to a bilateral system, multilateral netting involves two or more subsidiaries. Each subsidiary informs a central treasury management center of all planned cross-border payments. Multilateral netting is primarily used for intracompany transactions. – Ch16

multiple drawee checks: Multiple drawee checks, also known as payable-if-desired (PID), are checks that can be presented for payment at a bank other than the drawee bank. Typically, both bank names appear on the check. Uses for multiple drawee checks include payroll in states that require employees to be paid by checks payable locally, payroll for employees on assignments away from the company office and dividend checks. – Ch09

multi-tiered ZBAs: Multi-tiered ZBAs may be used to allow companies with multiple divisions or subsidiaries to write checks on separate accounts or to segregate different types of payments such as accounts payable, payroll, dividends and taxes. – Ch09

municipal notes: State and local governments, their agencies, authorities and subdivisions raise funds in the money market through municipal notes. Many municipal issues are exempt from federal income taxes and/or state income taxes in the state of issue, making these attractive for investors seeking tax-sheltered income. Maturities of three months to one year are typical for municipal notes. – Ch10

mutual funds: Mutual funds are pooled investments that sell shares, offering investors diversification and professional portfolio management. Mutual fund providers include commercial banks, brokerage firms and investment companies. – Ch03 Mutual funds are pooled investments that sell shares to investors, offering these investors diversification and professional portfolio management. Mutual fund providers include brokerage firms, banks and investment companies. Shares may be redeemed through the provider that insures liquidity. Share values fluctuate with the performance of the underlying securities of the fund and mutual fund shares are not insured against losses as deposits are. Money market mutual funds invest in short-term securities such as Treasury Bills, certificates of deposit and commercial paper. – Ch10

National Association of Securities Dealers Automated Quotations (NASDAQ): National Association of Securities Dealers Automated Quotation (NASDAQ), is essentially a computer-based over-the-counter (OTC) market. – Ch13

National Automated Clearing House Association (NACHA): The National Automated Clearing House Association (NACHA), also known as the Electronic Payments Association, is a membership organization that provides marketing and educational assistance and establishes the rules, standards and procedures that enable financial institutions to exchange ACH payments on a national basis. NACHA provides member banks nationwide access to many local clearing houses located across the country. – Ch08

National Book-Entry System (NBES): National Book-Entry System (NBES) is an RTGS used for the transfer of U.S. Treasury, government agency and other securities. – Ch08

National Investor Relations Institute (NIRI): The National Investor Relations Institute (NIRI) Guidelines for Earnings Releases urges all public companies to include both a complete income statement and a complete balance sheet, reconcile GAAP earnings to pro forma results, and include key management discussion and analysis (MD&A) information in the earnings announcement. – Ch19

natural hedge: If a U.S. company has accounts receivable denominated in British pounds, it may consider short-term debt denominated in pounds. In this case, if foreign currency-denominated assets depreciate, liabilities denominated in the same foreign currency depreciate as well, thereby minimizing FX translation exposure. This is also known as a balance sheet hedge or natural hedge. – Ch16

negotiable CDs: Negotiable CDs are domestic large dollar time deposits issued by banks and thrift institutions that are bought and sold on an active open market. Negotiable CDs are usually traded in $1 million blocks. – Ch10

negotiable order of withdrawal (NOW): NOW accounts are accounts that offer unrestricted check writing and pay unregulated rates of interest. – Ch03

negotiating bank: Banks may serve a variety of roles in L/C transactions. The advising and negotiating banks are frequently the same bank, performing dual roles. The advising/negotiating bank examines the documents presented by the beneficiary, receives payment from the issuing bank and pays the beneficiary. – Ch15

net asset value (NAV): This term is typically used for mutual funds to describe the value of a share of the fund. Money market mutual funds are generally configured to report a constant net asset value (NAV) of $1.00/share. Other types of mutual funds may have share values that vary on a daily basis, depending on the performance of the investments in that fund. – Ch10

net discounted sales: Amounts are entered into receivables and revenue accounts net of the discounts. Any discounts not taken are shown as income. – Ch07

net income: Income before taxes minus income tax expense. – Ch04

net investment hedges: Hedges of the net investment in a foreign operation. – Ch17

net present value (NPV): The present value of all inflows for a project or investment, minus the present value of all outflows. – Ch05

net settlement: Net settlement is a mechanism in which debits or credits (in the case of financial institutions) or receivables and payables (in the case of companies) are offset between parties and only the net remaining balance is settled through funds transfers. – Ch09

net terms: The seller specifies a net due date by which the buyer must pay in full. – Ch07

net working capital: Net working capital is equal to total current assets minus total current liabilities. – Ch04

net, net lease: When the lessor receives payment after expenses are paid, a financial lease is sometimes referred to as a net, net lease. – Ch13

netting: An internal company, intracompany, system designed to reduce the number of cross-border payments among units of a company through the elimination or consolidation of funds denominated in different currencies. – Ch16

New York Stock Exchange (NYSE): One of the organized exchanges that list stocks. – Ch13

nominal yield: The quoted yield for most short-term investments is a simple annual rate, called a nominal yield, which does not reflect compounding. – Ch10

non-insurance: This technique involves relying on normal revenues to pay for small, "normal" losses as current expenses. Non-insurance is appropriate for losses an organization can readily absorb as "costs of doing business," but not for highly disruptive, potentially ruinous accidents. – Ch18

non-negotiable CDs: Non-negotiable CDs or retail CDs, are issued in many different denominations to consumers and businesses and cannot be redeemed prior to maturity without a penalty. – Ch10

non-qualified pension plan: A pension plan that is not approved under ERISA guidelines. – Ch20

non-repetitive wire: With non-repetitive wire transfers, the debit and credit parties are different each time. – Ch08

non-repudiation: Non-repudiation is the inability of the sender or receiver of a message to deny having sent or received the message. – Ch12

non-sufficient funds (NSF): This is a situation where there are not enough funds in a checking account to cover a check presented against that account. – Ch08

non-targeted repurchases: A company's purchase of its own stock in the open market. – Ch14

normal balance pattern: A company's collection history determines the normal balance pattern. Balance patterns are used to forecast future cash inflows and to project accounts receivable levels. – Ch10

normal yield curve: When the yield curve is upward-sloping it is referred to as a normal yield curve. – Ch10

North American Free Trade Agreement (NAFTA): The World Trade Organization (WTO), in conjunction with agreements such as the North American Free Trade Agreement (NAFTA) and the General Agreement on Trades and Tariffs (GATT), facilitate trade between organizations in different countries, increasing the level of international business activity. – Ch15

notional pooling: Any excess funds in the accounts of a company or its subsidiaries are used to offset any deficits in other accounts of the parent or subsidiaries. This type of pooling arrangement is offered for a variety of currencies and is known as notional pooling because no actual funds are transferred. – Ch16

off-balance-sheet arrangements (OBSA): Off-balance-sheet arrangements (OBSA) include guarantees, contingent interests in assets, operating leases, guarantees and certain variable interest entities. – Ch04

off-balance sheet financing: Off-balance sheet financing is a type of financing typically used by organizations that have high current levels of debt or those that have very restrictive covenants on the use of additional debt. As the name implies, this form of financing does not appear on a company's balance sheet and usually entails the use of some type of leasing arrangements or sale of receivables. – Ch13

Office of Foreign Assets Control (OFAC): The OFAC is an office of the Treasury Department that administers and enforces economic and trade sanctions against targeted foreign countries, terrorist sponsoring organizations, and international narcotics traffickers based on U.S. foreign policy and national security goals. The OFAC has the authority to impose controls on financial transactions and freeze foreign assets under U.S. jurisdiction. – Ch15

official bank check: A cashier's check, also known as an official bank check, is a check drawn on a bank's own funds and signed by a bank officer. – Ch08

offshore financing: Offshore financing involves raising funds outside a company's country of origin. – Ch16

off-shoring: The movement of processes and/or jobs typically done locally to a foreign country. One example would a U.S.-based company moving its customer service operations or computer programming to India. – Ch01

on-us item: On-us check clearing involves a single bank and occurs when a payee deposits a check in an account at the same bank on which it is drawn. The bank simultaneously debits the payor's account and credits the payee's account. – Ch08

open account: In the open account method, the seller checks the creditworthiness of the buyer, establishes credit terms and limits, ships the merchandise and sends an invoice to the buyer. The buyer is responsible for initiating payment to the seller in accordance with any agreed upon credit terms. In the U.S., the open account is the most frequently used method of payment for B2B domestic transactions. – Ch15

open book credit: The open book credit, more commonly called the open account method, is the most common type of commercial trade credit in the United States. A seller issues an invoice, as formal evidence of the obligation, and records the sale as an A/R. The customer is billed for each transaction by invoice and/or by monthly statement. Full payment of invoiced amounts is expected within the specified credit terms unless certain discounts or deductions are available to the customer. – Ch07

open item system: Most commonly used in B2B sales, each invoice sent to a customer is recorded in the A/R file. When a payment is received, it is matched with the specific invoices being paid and any payment discrepancies (discounts, allowances, adjustments, returns, etc.) are noted. – Ch07

opening cash position: The opening cash position is the sum of the available balances in a company's bank accounts. – Ch09

operating accruals: Operating accruals include such things as wages payable and taxes payable. – Ch04

operating assets: Accounts receivable, inventories and prepaid expenses such as insurance premiums paid in advance. – Ch04

operating budget: The operating budget, or profit plan, focuses on day-to-day operations and includes a sales budget, a production or a purchases budget and an operating expenses budget. – Ch05

operating cycle: The operating cycle consists of the day-to-day activities in acquiring resources in the form of raw materials, semi-finished, and/or finished goods, converting (that is, adding value to) these resources into goods and services that customers will purchase, marketing and selling the products or services, and collecting receipts from sales. – Ch01

operating expenses: Operating expenses, such as selling or administrative expenses, represent general expenses incurred in the course of running a business, but which are not directly associated with the production of goods and services. – Ch04

operating income: The term operating income typically refers to earnings before interest and taxes (EBIT). – Ch04

operating leases: Operating leases, also known as service leases, are established in such a way that the lessor provides maintenance for the equipment and retains ownership of the equipment at the end of the lease. – Ch13

operating leverage: The extent to which fixed costs are used in a company's cost structure. The higher the proportion of fixed costs, the higher the operating leverage of the company. – Ch05

operational risk: Operational risk is generally defined as the risk of direct and indirect losses resulting from external events that impact an organization's operations or inadequate and failed internal processes, people and systems. – Ch18

opportunity cost: The foregone benefit of an alternative use of funds or the profit that could be earned or the costs that could be avoided if a particular investment is not made. – Ch05

optical character recognition (OCR): A type of data capture technology that reads pre-printed information on remittance documents. – Ch09

optimal capital structure: In theory, there is a certain level of debt for each company that minimizes the overall cost of capital and, therefore, maximizes the value of the company. – Ch14

option contract: A contract between two parties in which the buyer of the contract has the right (but not the obligation) to either buy or sell a fixed amount of some underlying asset at a fixed price on or before a specified date. – Ch17

origin authentication: A part of a digital signature which verifies where the message came from. – Ch12

originating depository financial institution (ODFI): ACH transactions may be originated as credits or debits. The financial institution that acts as an intermediary on the part of the originator is referred to as the originating depository financial institution (ODFI). – Ch08

originator: The party in an ACH transaction that originates the credit or debit is known as the originator. – Ch08

out-of-the-money: A call option is out-of-the-money if the asset price is less than the strike price of the option. A put option is out-of-the-money if the asset price exceeds the strike price of the option. – Ch17

outsourcing: Outsourcing is when a company uses an outside provider to perform part, or all, of a business function. – Ch20

overlay structure: An approach that combines sweeping and pooling is referred to as an overlay structure. This structure is typically used when a company's primary bank has branches in various countries that do not provide full domestic banking in all countries. – Ch16

over-the-counter items: Checks that are presented for payment at the disbursement bank by the payee are commonly known as over-the-counter items. – Ch09

over-the-counter/field deposit systems: Many businesses collect receipts over-the-counter at field locations which include local offices or branches and retail stores. Methods retail businesses use to collect at the point-of-sale (POS) include cash, checks, credit cards, debit cards and smart cards. – Ch09

paid-in-capital: Paid-in-capital represents the amounts received from stock (equity) sales by a company that are over and above the par value of the stock. For example if a company receives $10 per share for a stock issue but the par value on the stock is only $1, then the difference ($9) would be reported as paid-in-capital. – Ch13

paid-on-production: Paid-on-production is the process by which a payment record is created for goods and/or services based on usage rather than shipment. It is similar to consignment sales in retail, but it is employed in a manufacturing environment. – Ch07

par value: The face value of an issue. – Ch13

partial reconciliation service: In a partial reconciliation service, a bank lists all checks paid in numerical order by check serial number or in chronological order by date paid. For each item, the paid report generally shows the check serial number, dollar amount and date paid. – Ch09

payable through draft (PTD): A payable through draft (PTD) is a payment instrument resembling a check that is drawn against the payor, not the bank, and for which the payor has a period of time to honor or refuse payment. – Ch09

payable-if-desired (PID): Payable-if-desired (PID), also known as Multiple drawee checks, are checks that can be presented for payment at a bank other than the drawee bank. Typically, both bank names appear on the check. Uses for multiple drawee checks include payroll in states that require employees to be paid by checks payable locally, payroll for employees on assignments away from the company office and dividend checks. – Ch09

payables conversion period: The average number of days between the purchase of materials or supplies and payment for them. – Ch06

payback period: The period of time for an investment to be "paid back." The determination of what constitutes the required payback period is often made arbitrarily. – Ch05

payee: The recipient of funds by check. – Ch08

paying agent: Whereby a bank receives funds from an issuer of stocks or bonds to pay dividends to stockholders and principal and interest to bondholders. – Ch03

paying bank: In clearing systems, the institution on which the check is drawn is referred to as the paying bank or drawee bank. – Ch08

payment default risk: Payment default risk, which is the risk that future cash flow will not be sufficient to service debt, may increase when a company is over-leveraged (i.e., takes on too much debt). – Ch10

payment float: The delay between the receipt of an invoice by the buyer/payor, including the credit period, and the time the buyer's/payor's account is debited. – Ch01

payment instrument: Payment instruments include checks, payable through drafts, money orders, travelers checks, etc. that serve as a set of instructions for the transfer of funds between a payor, the party making the payment and a payee, the recipient of the funds. – Ch08

payment system risk (PSR) policy: There are four major types of risk in the payments system: systemic, credit, fraud and operational. – Ch08

payor: The party making a payment by check. – Ch08

Payor Bank Services: An information service of the Fed that electronically notifies controlled disbursement banks early in the morning of all checks that will be physically presented later that day. – Ch09

payroll cards: Many companies with large numbers of low-income or temporary workers, who frequently do not have bank accounts, have introduced payroll cards that work in a manner similar to electronic benefit transfer systems. – Ch09

pecking order theory: A capital structure theory that measures a company's past earnings, dividends and capital expenditures to explain capital structure. – Ch14

peer-to-peer (P2P): The latest concept in distributed computing is known as peer-to-peer or P2P in which each computer linked to the Internet can be linked directly to another computer to share information. Applications that perform P2P computing are essentially automating the machine-to-machine communication process. – Ch12

pension equity plans: Pension equity plans, also known as retirement bonus plans, report account balances to participants and look like defined contribution plans but are, in reality, defined benefit plans. In a pension equity plan, a rate is applied to average final compensation, which generally incorporates the effect of inflation over the service period. The equity plan rate is a cumulative rate based on a participant's age and/or years of service. – Ch20

performance guarantees: Performance guarantees may be asked for in some cases by the lender relative to the assets being financed. – Ch13

performance ratios: Performance ratios are used to evaluate the income generating capabilities of a company. – Ch04

permanent current asset level: A company's base level of current assets at all times during the sales cycle. – Ch06

personal identification number (PIN): This is a security procedure used to identify authorized users. Typically used with ATM or debit cards to verify the cardholder before processing the transaction. – Ch12

petty cash account: A petty cash account, more commonly referred to as an imprest account, is an account maintained at a prescribed level for a particular purpose or activity. For example, a field office may have an imprest account for local disbursements with a balance sufficient for one or two months' expenses. – Ch09

placement: The first stage of money laundering which refers to the physical deposit of cash proceeds from illegal activities into a financial institution. – Ch03

plan participant: An employee participating in a pension plan. – Ch20

plan provider: The provider of the investments in a pension plan, typically a mutual fund or insurance company. – Ch20

plan sponsor: The employer that offers a pension plan to its employees. – Ch20

pledged accounts receivable: Companies sometimes pledge their accounts receivable to secure a loan. A loan secured by receivables normally requires the borrower's customers to remit payments directly to the lender. These payments are then applied to the outstanding loan balance. – Ch10

point-of-purchase (POP): One of the ACH entry formats, the POP format is used by large, nationwide retailers to truncate checks at the point-of-sale. – Ch08

point-of-sale (POS) collection: Methods retail businesses use to collect at the point-of-sale (POS) include cash, checks, credit cards, debit cards and smart cards. – Ch09

political risk: This is the risk a company's operations in a foreign country may be nationalized or expropriated by the government of that country – Ch16

pooling: In countries where banks are allowed to pay interest on excess demand deposit balances and to charge interest on deficit balances, the typical method of concentration is known as pooling. – Ch16

positive pay: A service that matches check serial numbers and dollar amounts against a company's issue file, thereby enabling a financial institution to determine which checks can be paid and which should be returned. – Ch07

prearranged payment or deposit (PPD): One of the ACH entry formats, the PPD format is the payment application by which consumers authorize a company or financial institution to credit or debit (B2C) an account for normally recurring payments in fixed amounts. – Ch08

pre-authorized draft: With a pre-authorized draft/check, the payor authorizes the payee to draw a draft/check against the payor's account. The payee, rather than the payor, initiates the transaction. – Ch08

precautionary requirements: One of the three reasons it is imperative that an organization maintains liquidity is for precautionary, requirements. Precautionary requirements arise from unplanned expenses. Liquidity reserves for precautionary requirements may be maintained in the form of unused short-term borrowing facilities or short-term investments. – Ch10

pre-emptive right: The right that certain (or all) shareholders have to first rights of purchase, on a pro-rata basis, of any new shares of stock issued by a company. – Ch19

pre-encoding: Pre-encoding involves using a proof machine to add the dollar amount to the MICR line of the check. – Ch09

preferred stock: Preferred stock is a form of equity that offers a fixed rate of return or dividend to the holder. Preferred stock has preference over common stock in the event of liquidation, and has a prior claim on the earnings of a company, hence the term preferred stock. Preferred stock usually does not have voting rights. – Ch13

premium: The seller (writer) of an option receives a payment or premium from the buyer (holder). In return, the seller has the obligation to fulfill the contract (that is, to buy or sell the underlying asset) if the holder chooses to exercise the option. The holder forfeits the premium if the option is not exercised. – Ch17

pre-notification (pre-note): Prenotifications (prenotes) are optional zero-dollar entries that are sent through the ACH system prior to live entries. Prenotes provide a verification function at the receiving bank before entries for settlement are processed. – Ch08

present value: Today's value of any sum expected to be received in the future. – Ch05

presentment: The physical delivery of a check to the paying bank. – Ch08

price exposure: The potential for changes in the price of a commodity. – Ch17

price risk: Market risk or price risk is the uncertainty over the price at which a security can be sold prior to maturity. – Ch10

primary market: Primary markets are markets in which debt and equity are offered for the first time to investors. – Ch03

prime rate: Traditionally, prime was the rate at which commercial banks loaned money to their most creditworthy corporate customers. Prime rates vary by financial institution. Prime based pricing is becoming less common for large corporate borrowers but is widely used for small business and consumer loans. – Ch10

privacy: Privacy is the assurance that a message is readable only to the intended recipient and that data will not be used for unintended purposes. – Ch12

private label financing: In private label financing, a third party operates the credit function in the name of the seller rather than the seller administering a credit program in-house. From the customer's perspective, the credit appears to be arranged through the seller. – Ch07

private placement: In a private or direct placement, securities are offered and sold to a limited number of investors. – Ch03

process risk: Many organizations experience substantial risk related to the processes employed in day-to-day business operations. – Ch18

processing float: The time interval or delay between the day the payee or the payee's processing site receives the check and the day the check is deposited into the payee's account. – Ch09

procurement/purchasing card (P-card): Many companies are implementing the use of purchasing or procurement cards (P-cards) for the purchase of supplies, inventory, equipment and service contracts. P-cards differ from corporate travel and entertainment (T&E) cards that do not restrict the use of a card to specific business purposes. P-cards are issued to employees with restrictions on both the types of purchases allowed as well as individual spending limits. In many cases, employees are even limited to specific vendors or suppliers. – Ch07

profit margin: The profit margin, also called return on sales, measures the net income of a company as a percentage of sales. The higher this ratio, the more after-tax profits a company generates. – Ch04

profit plan: The profit plan, also called the operating budget, focuses on day-to-day operations and includes a sales budget, a production or a purchases budget and an operating expenses budget. – Ch05

profitability index (PI): The profitability index is a ratio of the present value of the benefits to the present value of the costs for an investment or project. – Ch05

profitability ratios: Profitability ratios summarize how much profit is generated on revenues, equity and assets. The most commonly used profitability ratios are profit margin measures, return on assets and return on equity. – Ch04

Project ACTION (ACH Credit Transactions Initiated Online): In order to support payments for purchases made over the Internet, Project ACTION (ACH Credit Transactions Initiated Online) was instituted by a group of financial institutions in conjunction with NACHA. ACTION payments enable consumers to initiate credits as payment for goods and services purchased over the Internet. – Ch08

project financing: Project financing is a type of financing that applies to large projects, usually related to energy explorations, refineries and utility power plants. The typical project financing arrangement is complex, involving several companies, or sponsors, forming a separate legal entity to operate the project. The lenders are paid from the project cash flows and generally do not have recourse to the individual sponsors or owners of the project. – Ch13

promissory note: A promissory note is an unconditional promise to pay a specified amount plus interest at a defined rate either on demand or on a certain date. – Ch13

proof of deposit (POD): Most banks assign availability using the proof of deposit (POD) method. The POD method assigns availability to each check as it passes through the automated check processing equipment. Availability is determined based on the time and day of deposit and the check's drawee endpoint. – Ch08

provisional credit: Provisional credit means the depository institution may reverse a credit posted to an account if the payment instrument is returned or rejected by the drawee institution. – Ch08

proxy: The right to vote at the annual meeting can be assigned to another individual through a proxy. – Ch19

Public Company Accounting Oversight Board (PCAOB): Oversight of the audits of publicly held businesses is the responsibility of the Public Company Accounting Oversight Board (PCAOB). The PCAOB is a private, non-profit corporation whose chairman and board members are appointed by the SEC. The PCAOB was established under SOX in response to concerns about audit quality following numerous corporate accounting scandals. PCAOB also assumed responsibility for establishing auditing standards from the Auditing Standards Board (ASB) of the American Institute of Certified Public Accountants (AICPA). – Ch04

public key infrastructure (PKI): A public key infrastructure (PKI) system enables e-commerce and file exchange over a public network. One of the key features of PKI is the use of public/private key pairs based on standard RSA encryption technology. The private key is held in a secret, secure file that is protected with a password or Personal Identification Number (PIN). The corresponding public key is freely distributed to trading partners. Anyone can use public keys to encrypt a message, while only the receiver with the proper private key can open and read the message. – Ch12

put option: A put option gives the owner the right to sell an underlying asset at a fixed price. – Ch17

qualified opinion: An opinion given by an auditor if exceptions are material, yet do not overshadow the usefulness of the information. – Ch04

qualified plan: A pension plan that is qualified according to ERISA guidelines. For qualified plans any funds contributed by both employees and the company are allowed to accumulate on a tax-deferred basis. – Ch20

quick ratio: Cash plus short-term investments and accounts receivable divided by total current liabilities. The quick ratio is also known as the "acid test" ratio and is considered a more conservative measure of liquidity than the current ratio. The quick ratio measures the degree to which a company's current liabilities are covered by its most liquid current assets. – Ch04

ratio analysis: Ratio analysis is useful in evaluating past and present performance, efficiency, liquidity and leverage, and serves as a foundation for financial forecasting. – Ch04

Real Estate Mortgage Investment Conduits (REMICs): Individual mortgages that are insured or guaranteed by certain government agencies are pooled and interests in them are sold, either as mortgage-backed securities MBSs or as Real Estate Mortgage Investment Conduits (REMICs). REMICs allow some control over interest rate and related price and prepayment risks by allocating principal and interest payments from pools of mortgages to classes (tranches) with differing maturity, prepayment and interest characteristics that appeal to a variety of investment risk profiles. – Ch10

real-time gross settlement system (RTGS): In a real-time gross settlement system (RTGS), each participating bank's position is adjusted on an item-by-item basis. Fedwire is an example of an RTGS. – Ch08

receipts and disbursement (R&D) forecast: A receipts and disbursement (R&D) forecast is a fundamental liquidity planning tool. Construction of the forecast begins with the creation of separate schedules of cash inflows and cash outflows using accounts receivable balance patterns and distribution forecasts. Completing the forecast involves combining the R&D schedules to determine the net cash flow for the period. – Ch10

receivables conversion period: The average number of days required to convert a sale (i.e., accounts receivable) into cash. – Ch06

receiver: The receiver is the party in an ACH transaction that receives the credit or debit is known as the receiver. – Ch08

receiving depository financial institution (RDFI): ACH transactions may be received as credits or debits. The financial institution that acts as an intermediary on the part of the receiver is referred to as the receiving depository financial institution (RDFI). – Ch08

record date: The date specified by the board of directors when the holders-of-record are entitled to receive a declared dividend. – Ch14

recourse: When factoring accounts receivables, with recourse means the company must collect past dues and bad debts. – Ch06

regional check processing center (RCPC) items: Regional check processing items are checks drawn on banks serviced by a Federal Reserve regional check-processing center (RCPC). – Ch08

regional treasury center: These regional centers are responsible for providing treasury services to specific subsidiaries within a designated geographic area (i.e., Asia-Pacific, Middle East and Africa, Europe, North America and Latin America). – Ch16

registrar: The registrar is responsible for compiling lists of current stockholders and bondholders for the purpose of remitting dividend and interest payments. – Ch03

regression analysis: Regression analysis is a statistical technique that systematically identifies the relationship between the variable being predicted (the dependent variable) and selected or appropriate explanatory or independent variables. Though there are many forms of regression analysis, the most basic is a simple linear regression model. This approach essentially determines a line that best represents the relationship between a single dependent variable and a single explanatory variable. – Ch10

reinvestment risk: A type of risk exposure, referred to as reinvestment risk, arises in a declining rate environment when an issuer pays off a security prior to the stated maturity. A mortgage-backed security (MBS) is an example of an investment frequently held in short-term portfolios that is subject to reinvestment risk. – Ch10

reinvoicing center: A company-owned subsidiary that purchases goods from an exporting subsidiary and sells the goods to an importing subsidiary. – Ch16

reject item: Checks rejected by a bank's automated check processing equipment. Most reject items arise either because of physical defects in the MICR line or the MICR line does not meet banking industry specifications. – Ch08

relaxed current asset investment strategy: Under a relaxed current asset investment strategy, a company maintains high levels of current assets relative to sales. – Ch06

relationship review: A procedure companies use to qualitatively assess service levels and responsiveness. Reviews may either be formal or informal. Financial institutions also initiate relationship reviews by preparing summaries of services, fees, error rates and other relationship information. – Ch21

remedies: In the event of default the lender is allowed to pursue default remedies. Remedies available to a lender normally include an acceleration of all principal and interest on the debt when a default occurs. – Ch13

remitting bank: The remitting bank is the seller's (exporter's) bank that prepares the collection letter and forwards documents to the collecting bank in the buyer's (importer's) country. – Ch15

remote disbursement: Remote disbursement was designed to take advantage of the inaccessibility of certain, geographically remote banks. The objective was to increase disbursement float as much as possible. Federal Reserve policies discourage the use of this practice. – Ch03

repatriated capital: Repatriation involves the physical transfer of funds from one country to another. – Ch16

repatriation: The transfer of profits from an international subsidiary back to the domestic parent. – Ch14

repetitive wire transfer: Repetitive wire transfers are used when a company makes frequent transfers to the same credit parties. Only the date and dollar amount may be changed on a repetitive wire. – Ch08

report card: A tool companies use to obtain a quantitative rating of a bank's level of service and responsiveness to problems. – Ch21

representations: Representations and warranties are the existing conditions at the time the loan agreement is executed, as attested to by the borrower. Such conditions generally include: (1) affirmation of the valid legal existence of the borrowing company, (2) a resolution by the borrower's Board of Directors authorizing the borrowing, (3) the authority of the corporate officers signing the documents, (4) the company's confirmation of compliance with Employee Retirement Income and Security Act (ERISA) and (5) an indemnity protecting the lender from environmental liabilities. – Ch13

re-presented check entries (RCK): One of the ACH entry formats, the RCK format is utilized to transmit ACH debit entries in place of a paper check after it has been returned for insufficient or uncollected funds. – Ch08

repurchase agreements (repos): An investor in a repurchase agreement buys government securities from the bank or dealer who simultaneously agrees to repurchase them for a slightly higher price at a future date. Most repos are overnight, but some may be arranged for longer periods. – Ch10

request for information (RFI): A letter that requests information regarding a vendor's ability to, and interest in, providing services. – Ch21

request for proposal (RFP): A formal document prepared by a company that outlines its objectives and service requirements. An RFP may be used to obtain bids for anything ranging from one specific service to a company's entire relationship. – Ch21

required rate of return: Required rate of return represents the minimum a company needs to achieve for any capital investment. – Ch13

reserve requirement: The percentage (currently 10%) of cash and other liquid assets member banks must keep on reserve at the Fed. – Ch03

reserve-adjusted ECR: An earnings credit rate (ECR) that is reduced by the reserve requirement. When using this rate, the average collected balance is used in the earnings credit calculation instead of the investable balance. – Ch21

residual value: The residual value is the estimated value of the asset at the end of the lease. – Ch13

retail CDs: Retil CDs, or non-negotiable CDs, are issued in many different denominations to consumers and businesses and cannot be redeemed prior to maturity without a penalty. – Ch10

retail lockbox: Retail lockbox systems are primarily used to process high volume, small dollar consumer remittances (C2B) that frequently involve recurring, monthly installment payments. The checks are accompanied by standardized, machine-scannable remittance documents enclosed in pre-addressed window envelopes. – Ch09

retail payment system: The three non-cash payment systems in the U.S. primarily used for high volume, low value monetary transactions are commonly referred to as retail payment systems. These payment systems are: (1) checks and check-like instruments, (2) credit, debit and other types of cards and (3) ACH. – Ch08

retained earnings: Retained earnings represent the changes in shareholders' equity arising from the retention of profits or losses of the company. Dividends paid to shareholders reduce retained earnings. – Ch04

retirement bonus plans: Pension equity plans, also known as retirement bonus plans, report account balances to participants and look like defined contribution plans but are, in reality, defined benefit plans.

restrictive financing strategy: Under a restrictive financing strategy, long-term financing supports fixed assets, permanent current assets, and some portion of temporary current assets. – Ch06

retrospectively (Retro) rated insurance program: In this type of program, the insured's cost of coverage for a policy period varies with the insured's losses during that period. Such programs are often used for workers' compensation plans and for product liability insurance. – Ch18

return items: Returned checks, which are referred to as return items. – Ch08

return on investment (ROI): Return on investment (ROI) is a performance measure which is calculated as the profit generated by a project or an operating unit, divided by the amount of capital invested in the asset or the unit. – Ch05

revenue bonds: Repayment of revenue bonds are directly linked to the revenues generated from specific assets (i.e., airport or stadium construction bonds or toll road/bridge bonds). – Ch13

revenue recognition principle: The revenue recognition principle maintains that revenue is reported when cash or a claim for cash is received in exchange for goods or services and the earning process is substantially complete. – Ch04

reverse positive pay: The bank transmits a file of the checks presented for payment to the company on a daily or intraday basis. The company matches this file to a list of checks issued and notifies the bank of any items to be returned. – Ch09

reverse repurchase agreement (reverse repo): A source of short-term funds available through commercial banks is a reverse repurchase agreement (reverse repo). Securities are sold to the bank providing the seller with cash until the securities are repurchased. This is also referred to as securities lending. Reverse repos enable companies to tap into the liquidity of their investment portfolios without having to dispose of investments in the money markets. – Ch10

reverse stock split: A reverse stock split raises the price of a stock to a desired trading range. – Ch14

revolver: See revolving credit agreement. – Ch10

revolving credit: Under revolving credit terms, a company grants credit without requiring specific approval of each transaction provided the account is kept current. The account is usually considered current if the credit outstanding is below an established credit limit and minimum payments have been made on time. If the account is not paid in full by the monthly payment due date, an interest charge is calculated based on the average amount outstanding over the entire period. – Ch07

revolving credit agreement: A revolving credit agreement, also known as a revolver, is a committed line of credit that is established for a specified period of time, often on a multi-year basis. – Ch10

riding the yield curve: Riding the yield curve involves buying highly liquid marketable securities, such as T-Bills, that mature on a different day from the day the investor intends to sell the securities. – Ch10

risk premium: A risk premium is the extra yield above that of a comparable risk-free security which investors require as compensation for assuming the additional risk. – Ch10

risk profile: The risk profile of a company is the relationship of how the overall value of a company changes as some financial price variable changes. A basic risk profile determines the sensitivity of a company to a change in interest rates, FX rates or commodity prices, typically measured by the company's equity value or stock price. – Ch17

risk retention group: A risk retention group is a special type of group captive formed under the terms of a federal law designed to more fully enable business firms to work together in jointly financing product liability claims. – Ch18

risk-adjusted discount rate: Firms use a risk-adjusted rate to evaluate projects with higher or lower risk than the overall risk profile of the company. – Ch05

S&P 500 Index: The Standard and Poor's 500 is a broad-based overall stock market measure. – Ch13

safekeeping bank: Safekeeping banks can provide the institution or organization with added expertise, without the costs of developing and maintaining an in-house investment staff. The safekeeping bank acts as an agent to hold stock certificates or bonds, tracks trades and provides periodic reports. The safekeeping bank can give the institution/organization an international presence through world wide banking affiliates. Safekeeping banks can be an integral part of a cash management system. – Ch03

sale and leaseback: Under a sale and leaseback arrangement, equipment owned by a company is sold to another party (the lessor) and then immediately leased back by the original owner (lessee). – Ch13

same-day settlement: A Federal Reserve rule requires that if a check is presented to a paying bank by 8:00 a.m. local time, the paying bank must settle in same-day funds by the close of Fedwire (6:30 p.m. EST). – Ch08

scenario analysis: Scenario analysis is a type of "what-if" analysis that assesses the outcomes that are realistically possible under a range of circumstances. Used to establish the lower bound of outcomes (the worst case) and the upper bound of outcomes (the best case). – Ch05

seasonal dating: The seller agrees to accept payment at the end of the buyer's selling season. This allows manufacturers to provide short-term financing for a buyer's purchases and reduces the manufacturer's inventory costs. – Ch07

secondary distribution: Secondary distributions involve stock previously issued that is now being resold, such as the sale of treasury stock. – Ch13

secondary market: Secondary markets are markets in which previously issued debt and equity are traded by brokers or commercial bankers. – Ch03

secured lines: Secured lines require the borrower to pledge some form of collateral, typically current assets such as accounts receivable and inventory. – Ch10

Secured Socket Layer (SSL): Most e-commerce websites have already implemented a form of encryption/authentication technology known as SSL to ensure privacy, integrity and authentication of data moving between clients and servers. SSL is built into most major browsers and is part of the basic WWW infrastructure. – Ch12

securities lending: A source of short-term funds available through commercial banks is a reverse repurchase agreement (reverse repo). Securities are sold to the bank providing the seller with cash until the securities are repurchased. This is also referred to as securities lending. Reverse repos enable companies to tap into the liquidity of their investment portfolios without having to dispose of investments in the money markets. – Ch10

securitization: Securitization is the term used for the creation of new securities based on financial assets such as accounts receivable. In essence, the receivables are bundled into packages and resold to other investors, providing a lending institution with increased liquidity. – Ch06

self-insurance: Self-insurance is not technically a form of insurance because it does not involve a transfer of risk to an insurer or other separate entity. Also, the term "self-insurance" is often used to describe any risk retention program, even highly informal unfunded arrangements. – Ch18

semi-repetitive wire: With semi-repetitive wire transfers, the debit and credit parties remain the same but the description (e.g., a customer or invoice number) may be changed along with the date and dollar amount. – Ch08

sender net debit cap: As part of its PSR policy, the Fed has mandated that all banks using the large-dollar payment systems have a sender net debit cap limiting the intraday overdraft a member bank may incur in each Federal Reserve account. The cap is determined by a Fed schedule based on the bank's capital, the overall creditworthiness as an institution, the bank's credit policies and operational controls. – Ch08

sensitivity analysis: Used to determine how vulnerable an expected outcome is to changes in an individual assumption. – Ch05

service agreements: Formal agreements that document the requirements and expectations of both the purchaser and provider of a specific service or services. – Ch21

service leases: Operating leases, also known as service leases, are established in such a way that the lessor provides maintenance for the equipment and retains ownership of the equipment at the end of the lease. – Ch13

settlement: Settlement is the actual transfer of value from payor to payee. – Ch08

shared service center (SSC): A shared service center is a consolidated operation that supports standardized processes (accounting, payroll, etc.) within an organization. The purpose of an SSC is to enhance management and control over the costs associated with a wide range of business support functions such as treasury, purchasing, accounting, receivables and payables management, payroll, benefits management, legal/tax and human resources. – Ch16

shared-secret key (symmetric key): In a shared-secret key (symmetric key) system, both the sending and receiving party have a private key to encrypt/read messages. – Ch12

shareholders' equity: Shareholders' equity is the financing provided by the companies' owners and from company operations. – Ch04

shelf registration: A large, well-known corporation that frequently issues securities may file a master registration statement with the SEC and update it with a short-form statement just prior to each of the initial offerings. This form of shelf registration allows a company to bring an issue to market quickly to take advantage of market conditions that make rates for particular sources attractive. – Ch13

shell bank: Shell banks are defined as foreign banks without a physical presence in any country. – Ch03

short position: The party that agrees to sell an asset assuming that the asset will decrease in value is the holder of a short position. – Ch17

short-term investments: Companies require access to cash to meet ongoing obligations in a timely manner. However, the opportunity cost of maintaining cash balances in non-interest earning checking accounts can be significant. In order to minimize foregone interest income, companies invest in short-term instruments such as money market investments. Money market investments are highly marketable, interest-earning securities with stable market values and maturities of one year or less. These short-term investments provide an important source of liquidity whenever cash outflows exceed cash inflows. – Ch10

short-term tax anticipation notes: Tax anticipation notes (TANs) are issued by government entities to cover differences in timing between expenditures and expected tax collections. – Ch13

sight draft: A sight draft is a draft payable on demand that requires the collecting bank receive full and final payment of the amount owed prior to releasing the documents. – Ch15

signaling effect: The theory that dividends contain information for stockholders that signal the intentions of the management. – Ch14

signature card: Financial institutions require companies to furnish signatures of authorized signers or specimens of both facsimile and computerized signatures. These signatures are documented on signature cards. – Ch21

simple moving average: Simple moving average is a forecasting technique that uses an average of past actual values to predict future values. The length of the moving average determines the amount of smoothing in the process. A long moving average period will produce maximum smoothing, while a short period will produce less smoothing. – Ch10

single payment notes: Single payment notes are usually granted for a short period of time for a specific purpose, with both principal and interest paid at maturity. – Ch10

sinking fund: Sinking fund obligations are funds accumulated in a custodial account to retire debt instruments according to a predetermined schedule. – Ch13

smart card: Smart cards are payment instruments that look like credit cards but contain an embedded microprocessor. Each transaction made with a smart card updates the card's memory. Smart cards are used for prepaid value transactions in which the consumer prepays the bank, giro or company issuing the card. – Ch08

smart card authentication devices: Smart card authentication devices, also known as "tokens," look like a credit card and contain circuitry that encodes personal information to ensure password protection. – Ch12

Society for Worldwide Interbank Financial Telecommunication (S.W.I.F.T.): The Society for Worldwide Interbank Financial Telecommunication (S.W.I.F.T.)® is an interbank telecommunication network that enables banks to send authenticated electronic messages in standard formats. Established in the 1970s, S.W.I.F.T. currently has over 7,500 member financial institutions in approximately 200 countries. – Ch15

sovereign risk: See political risk. – Ch16

special dividend: A one-time dividend payment by a company rather than an ongoing dividend increase. – Ch14

special multi-peril insurance (SMP): Covers special losses in four basic areas: property, liability, crime and boilers and machinery (endorsements can be added to cover almost any standard risk in these areas). – Ch18

special purpose entities: Off-balance-sheet arrangements (OBSA) include guarantees, contingent interests in assets, operating leases, guarantees and certain variable interest entities (also referred to as special purpose entities). – Ch04

specific project guarantee: With a specific project guarantee, the guarantee party guarantees only loans relating to specific projects of the subsidiary, not all loans. – Ch13

speculation: Speculation involves betting on the direction of the market. – Ch17

sponsoring bank: The sponsoring bank, more commonly called the merchant bank, qualifies businesses (referred to as merchants) that accept credit card payments. The merchant bank provides merchants with credit card terminals and maintains deposit accounts through which the credit card payments settle. – Ch08

spontaneous liabilities: These are liabilities such as accounts payable that vary in direct relationship to sales. Thus an given percentage increase in sales would generally result in a similar percentage increase in accounts payable. Other spontaneous liabilities include taxes payable and accrued wages. – Ch06

spot market: One of the two basic FX markets, in the spot market a rate for currency is called a spot FX rate (spot rate). These rates are generally quoted for delivery one or two business days from the date of the trade. – Ch15

stale date: A check or similar item more than six months old. – Ch03

Standard and Poor's (S&P): Standard and Poor's (S&P) is one of the credit rating agencies. Their ratings for long-term debt include A-1+, A-1, A-2, A-3, and B. – Ch10

standard unqualified opinion: A standard unqualified opinion is given when the auditor concludes the financial statements fairly represent the activities of the business and the following three conditions are met: (1) All required financial statements are provided, (2) GAAS are followed in conducting the audit and (3) The statements are presented in accordance with GAAP. – Ch04

standby letter of credit: A standby L/C is a variation of a commercial L/C. Standby L/Cs are issued primarily by U.S. banks which are legally prohibited from issuing formal guarantees. Once issued, the standby L/C serves as a vehicle to ensure the financial performance of a bank's customer to a third-party beneficiary. Standby L/Cs are frequently used as credit enhancement for commercial paper programs or to guarantee a bid tender or financial performance on a contract. – Ch15

statement of cash flows: The statement of cash flows provides a detailed picture of the sources of a company's cash flows and how these sources are utilized. The statement of cash flows is divided into three sections – operating, investing and financing activities. – Ch04

statement of changes in shareholders' equity: The statement of changes in shareholders' equity summarizes transactions affecting shareholders' equity and reconciles the ending balance to the beginning balance for each shareholder's equity account. – Ch04

Statements of Financial Accounting Concepts (SFACs): In the mid-1970s, the FASB developed a conceptual framework for financial accounting and reporting. This framework forms the basis for a series of Statements of Financial Accounting Concepts (SFACs). – Ch04

stock dividends: A dividend paid by a company to its shareholders in additional shares of stock rather than paying out cash dividends. – Ch14

stock repurchase plan: As an alternative to paying cash dividends, a company can elect to take some shares out of circulation by repurchasing them. – Ch14

stock split: The basic idea behind a stock split is that an optimal trading range exists for a stock's price. When the per-share price of a stock gets too high, exchanging multiple shares of new stock for a single share of current stock can help to bring the stock back into the desired trading range. – Ch14

stored value card: One form of smart card is the stored value card (SVC). Smart cards are payment instruments that look like credit cards but contain an embedded microprocessor. – Ch08

straight through processing (STP): Straight through processing is an initiative being considered by many financial institutions to streamline transactions by maintaining contact throughout all stages of the processing of those transactions. – Ch11

strategic plan: A strategic plan establishes the overall goals and objectives of an organization and charts a course of action for achieving objectives over a period of time. – Ch05

stretching payables: Stretching payables (sometimes referred to as "riding the trade") enables a company to: (1) use cash to reduce debt, thus reducing interest expense, (2) invest cash on a short-term basis, thus increasing interest income and/or (3) purchase other assets. – Ch06

strike price: The fixed price of an option contract. Also known as the exercise price. – Ch17

subcertification: Subcertification generally consists of a certification of financial information by those who were responsible for providing the information, hence may include many employees from the company's treasury and finance departments. While subcertification is often presented in the form of a signed written statement, it can also be a verbal acknowledgement of the responsibility for certain financial information included in financial statements filed with the SEC. – Ch19

subordinated debt: Debentures may be issued on a subordinated basis, indicating that the claim on assets is subordinate to designated notes payable, bank loans or other specified debt. – Ch13

substitute check: Check 21 has facilitated ECP by creating a new payment instrument. The substitute check, also referred to as an Image Replacement Document (IRD), is an image copy of the front and back of the check that serves as a legal substitute for the original check. – Ch08

sunk cost: A cost that has already been incurred. – Ch05

supplier-managed replenishment program: In supplier-managed replenishment programs, the supplier maintains and tracks the inventory of materials it provides to a customer. As the inventory is used, the supplier bills the customer for the items and replenishes the supply. – Ch07

surety bond: A form of credit enhancement provided by a financial intermediary to guarantee the obligation of the borrower. The obligation then assumes the credit rating of the institution providing the credit enhancement. – Ch10

swap: An agreement between two parties to exchange (or swap) a set of cash flows at a future point in time. – Ch17

swaption: An option on an interest rate swap in which the buyer of the option has the right to enter into an interest rate swap at a future date. – Ch17

sweep accounts: Banks provide overnight sweep accounts, which automatically transfer excess balances into an interest-earning account. – Ch10

sweeping: Outside of the U.S., this physical concentration of funds is usually referred to as "sweeping." (Not to be confused with "sweep accounts" used by treasurers in the U.S. for overnight investment of surplus funds.) – Ch16

systemic risk: Systemic risk is the risk that the failure of one major bank could cause other banks to fail resulting in a collapse of the entire payments system. – Ch08

target capital structure: The general consensus is that some use of debt is desirable, but too much debt is undesirable. In practice, the weights generally used are the company's target capital structure; that is, the proportion of each component that management has determined is best for the company. – Ch14

target concentration: Target concentration requires establishing a target balance. All funds above the target balance level (a floor) are transferred to the concentration bank. This system maintains constant balances in depository banks at the desired level. – Ch09

targeted repurchases: A negotiation directly with a major stockholder, often an institutional investor, to repurchase a company's stock. – Ch14

tax anticipation notes (TANs): Tax anticipation notes (TANs) are issued by government entities to cover differences in timing between expenditures and expected tax collections. – Ch13

tax increment financing (TIF) bonds: Tax Increment Financing (TIF) bonds are primarily used for local financing where a municipality may use all, or a portion of, new property taxes within a designated district to assist in the project's financing. – Ch13

tax-deferred annuity (TDA): Tax-deferred annuities are generally made available to employees of religious, charitable, educational, scientific and literary organizations that are chartered on a non-profit basis. In these plans, only the employee may make contributions, generally by payroll deduction. – Ch20

tax-exempt: Tax-exempt securities, such as T-Bills, which are exempt from local and state taxes, and municipal bonds, which are exempt from federal taxes, provide a lower pre-tax yield than taxable securities of similar maturity and default risk because of their tax advantage. – Ch10

technical default: A technical default occurs when a borrower continues to make required payments but violates some other term, frequently a financial covenant such as a liquidity, coverage or performance ratio. – Ch10

telephone initiated entry (TEL): One of the ACH entry formats, the TEL format is used for payments that are not pre-authorized but are approved by consumers over the phone. – Ch08

tender offer: A stock repurchase of 5% or more of a company's stock. – Ch14

term loan: A term loan is a loan with a fixed maturity, usually greater than one year, that can be repaid either in installments or in a single payment. Frequently, a term loan is issued for a specific financing need such as the purchase of a new plant, new equipment or for general expansion. – Ch13

term repurchase agreements: Repurchase agreements (repos) over 30 days are called term repurchase agreements. – Ch10

thin client: The application software resides at the FSP's central client server site. – Ch11

third-party financing: A company collects the information necessary to complete a credit application from a customer and forwards the information to a financial institution. The financial institution decides whether or not to grant credit. – Ch07

threshold concentration: With threshold concentration, a company allows account balances to build to a predetermined level (a ceiling) before transferring funds to the concentration bank. – Ch09

thrift institution: There are two types of thrift institutions: savings and loans associations and savings or mutual savings banks. – Ch03

time deposit: Time deposits are accounts that must be maintained at a commercial bank for a specified period of time. – Ch03

time draft: A time draft is a draft payable on a specified future date that must be accepted by the importer before the collecting bank may release documents. – Ch15

time value of money: The time value of money, a fundamental principal of finance, establishes the relationship between cash flows received at different times. The value of a cash flow at any point in time may be determined with an appropriate interest rate and the number of time periods involved. – Ch05

tokens: Smart card authentication devices, also known as "tokens," look like a credit card and contain circuitry that encodes personal information to ensure password protection. – Ch12

total liabilities to total assets: Total liabilities to total assets measures the percentage of all liabilities relative to the total asset base of a company. The higher this ratio, the greater the percentage of liabilities (as opposed to equity) a company uses to finance its asset base. – Ch04

total working capital management: Managing all current asset and current liability accounts. – Ch01

tracking stock: A tracking stock is a separate stock created by a parent company to "track" the financial progress of a particular piece of business. Despite being part of a publicly traded entity, tracking stocks trade under unique ticker symbols. These stocks are meant to create opportunities for investors to buy into a fast-growing unit without investing in the whole company. – Ch13

trade acceptance: A trade acceptance is an instrument used in international transactions. It is similar to a BA except it is drawn on and accepted by a buyer (importer). Trade acceptances are often used by importers to secure financing from a bank or, similar to BAs, may even be sold to a bank or an investor at a discount prior to maturity. – Ch15

trade credit: Trade credit arises when a buyer receives goods but payment is not made until some later date. Trade credit is the primary source of short-term financing used by many businesses. While the supplier does not advance cash to the buyer, trade credit allows a buyer to use the supplier's goods while using the cash it would otherwise have had to pay in advance or upon delivery. – Ch10

trade letter of credit: Trade or commercial letters of credit (L/Cs) are documents issued by a bank, guaranteeing the payment of a customer's draft up to a stated amount for a specified period provided certain conditions are met. – Ch03

trade payables: Trade payables (also referred to as accounts payable) are amounts due to vendors for purchased items. – Ch04

tradeoff models: The most common type of theoretical model in which the optimal capital structure is found by balancing (trading off) the tax shield benefits of debt (leverage) against the costs of bankruptcy and agency costs. – Ch14

trading companies: Trading companies are used when an exporter (seller) sells products at a discount to an export trading company, which then resells the products internationally. – Ch15

transaction balance: Deposits held by companies to facilitate collection and disbursement activity. – Ch03

transaction exposure: If the receivables or payables on a company's balance sheet are affected by changes in FX rates, then the company has a transaction exposure. Transaction exposure occurs when the receivables and payables are in different currencies. – Ch17

transaction set: Transaction sets are generally defined as the electronic equivalent of a paper business document or form, with specific rules governing formats. – Ch12

Trans-European Automated Real-Time Gross Settlement Express Transfer System (TARGET): TARGET provides real-time settlement for cross-border payments, similar to the Fedwire in the U.S. The system is used primarily for urgent, high value payments. An important function of TARGET is to enable central banks to mobilize liquidity around Europe in order to manage monetary policy objectives as determined by the ECB.– Ch15

transfer agent: Keeping records of each sale and purchase of stocks and bonds including maintaining records of the shareholders of a corporation by name, address, and number of shares. – Ch03

transfer initiation delays: Transfer initiation delays occur if concentration entries are submitted to the originating bank late or if they contain reporting errors. – Ch09

transfer pricing: The price that subsidiaries of a large corporation charge each other for components sold among themselves. – Ch16

transfer fax: A tax a company may incur in the event of the sale of a company. – Ch16

transit routing number (TRN): The American Bankers Association (ABA) number, also known as the transit routing number (TRN), is pre-printed on the MICR line. This 9-digit number identifies the drawee bank and provides the depository bank the information required to route the check back to the drawee bank through the clearing system. – Ch08

translation exposure: Translation exposure is created when a foreign subsidiary's financial statements are converted, hence "translated," into a parent company's home currency as part of the processes of consolidating a company's financial statements. – Ch17

travelers checques: Travelers checques are prepaid instruments similar to money orders. Two signatures are usually required by the purchaser – one at issuance and one at the time the check is used to pay for goods or services. – Ch08

Treasury Bills (T-Bills): Treasury Bills (T-Bills) are money market discount instruments issued in maturities of one year or less. – Ch10

Treasury bonds: Treasury bonds are long-term coupon-bearing bonds issued in original maturities of 10 to 30 years. – Ch10

Treasury Management System (TMS): A treasury workstation, sometimes referred to as a Treasury Management System (TMS), is typically PC- or client server-based and has software that gathers information from both internal and external sources. A TMS compiles financial data for the purposes of analysis and decision-making, thereby automating a number of manual tasks. – Ch11

Treasury notes: Treasury notes are intermediate-term bonds issued in original maturities of 1 to 10 years. – Ch03

Treasury securities: The U.S. Treasury is the largest issuer of money market securities. Treasury issues include Treasury Bills, notes and bonds. Because of the low liquidity risk and no default risk associated with these issues, U.S. Treasury rates are considered to be risk-free and serve as the benchmark against which rates and prices on other debt securities are compared. – Ch10

Treasury stock: Treasury stock is defined as stock issued by a company but later reacquired. It may be held in the company's treasury indefinitely, reissued to the public or retired. Treasury stock receives no dividends and does not carry voting power while held by the company. – Ch13

treasury workstations: A treasury workstation, sometimes referred to as a Treasury Management System (TMS), is typically PC- or client server-based and has software that gathers information from both internal and external sources. A TMS compiles financial data for the purposes of analysis and decision-making, thereby automating a number of manual tasks. – Ch11

triple net lease: When the lessor receives payment after expenses are paid, a financial lease is sometimes referred to as a net, net lease. When this type of lease is used in real estate, it may be referred to as a triple net lease because it includes taxes, insurance and utilities. This type of lease is an alternative to borrowing funds to finance the acquisition of an asset. – Ch13

Trojans: Programs that masquerade as useful or entertaining software, but contain instructions that allow an outside party to access and gain control over the infected computer for the purpose of stealing data or passwords. – Ch11

trust receipt loan: An inventory loan with a claim on specific items of inventory as collateral. – Ch06

turnover ratios: Turnover ratios, also called efficiency ratios, evaluate how effectively balance sheet accounts are utilized in the income generating process. Days' inventory, days' receivables, days' payables and cash turnover, which are liquidity or working capital ratios, are all examples of turnover ratios. – Ch04

turnover tax: A sales tax on goods and services imposed by a foreign country. – Ch16

U.S. Bulk Exchange (USBE): The U.S. Bulk Exchange (USBE), a system parallel to the ACSS, is used for the clearing of payment items denominated in U.S. dollars and settlement of USBE balances occurs through correspondent banks in New York. – Ch15

umbrella insurance: Excess or umbrella insurance is designed to supplement basic or primary liability coverage. – Ch18

unbundled: The practice used by banks of charging individually for each service utilized. – Ch21

uncommitted line: An uncommitted line is usually made available for a one-year period; however, funding may be refused at the lender's discretion or canceled outright. Hence, an uncommitted line is often referred to as a discretionary line. – Ch10

underlying asset: The asset to be bought or sold in a contract. This underlying asset can be a financial instrument, currency or a commodity. – Ch17

underwriting: Origination is also referred to as underwriting. – Ch03

underwriting spread: The underwriting spread is generally defined as the income that is generated by the underwriting investment bank, which is essentially the difference between the amount paid to the issuer of securities in a primary distribution and the public offering price. – Ch13

Uniform Commercial Code (UCC): The UCC is a uniform set of laws governing commercial transactions. The UCC defines the rights and duties of the parties in a commercial transaction and provides a statutory definition of commonly accepted business practices. – Ch03

uniform resource locator (URL): A type of Internet protocol, the uniform resource locator (URL) is an address format utilized on the Web. – Ch12

unique ZIP code: A lockbox processor uses a unique ZIP code to expedite mail processing. – Ch09

unsecured bonds: Unsecured bonds (debentures) represent general claims against the assets and/or cash flows of an organization. Large, financially secure organizations issue debentures based on their reputation in the marketplace. Organizations that do not have easily mortgaged assets, must utilize unsecured borrowing through the use of debentures. – Ch13

user authentication: A part of a digital signature that verifies who sent the message. – Ch12

usury laws: Usury laws limit the amount of interest that can be charged or that ban certain unfair credit practices. – Ch07

value added tax (VAT): A form of sales tax in which tax is charged at each discrete stage of production and/or distribution on the increased value occurring at that stage. – Ch16

value date: Under a value dating system, a bank sets a forward value date upon which the value of funds credited to an account is determined, and establishes a back value date on which the value of funds debited from an account is determined. – Ch15

value added network (VAN): A VAN is a communication intermediary that provides various services to the users of e-commerce. VANs were developed during the inception of EDI to help resolve interface problems between two companies with different computer systems, different format needs and different protocols. – Ch12

value-at-risk (VAR): An approach to determining how the value of a company is impacted by changing financial variables. VAR was developed in trading rooms of financial institutions to provide an estimation of the possible losses for an entire trading operation in a one-day period. – Ch17

vanilla swap: The exchange of a fixed interest rate cash flow for a floating interest rate cash flow with both interest rates in the same currency. – Ch17

variable costs: Costs that change in total in direct proportion to the level of activity. – Ch05

variance analysis: A key objective of forecasting is financial control and risk management. Using variance analysis to compare actual cash flows with projected cash flows helps identify problems such as unanticipated inventory changes, delays in accounts receivable collection or missed discount opportunities. Early identification allows a company to initiate corrective measures. – Ch10

vesting: Vesting defines whether the participant is legally entitled to claim all the benefits of a pension plan. Vesting is typically a function of length of employment, – Ch20

vouchering: The verification of incoming invoices and authorization of payments is a process some companies call vouchering. This process generally involves the traditional "three-way match," in which an invoice is matched to both an approved purchase order and receiving information. – Ch07

warranties: Representations and warranties are the existing conditions at the time the loan agreement is executed, as attested to by the borrower. Such conditions generally include: (1) affirmation of the valid legal existence of the borrowing company, (2) a resolution by the borrower's Board of Directors authorizing the borrowing, (3) the authority of the corporate officers signing the documents, (4) the company's confirmation of compliance with Employee Retirement Income and Security Act (ERISA) and (5) an indemnity protecting the lender from environmental liabilities. – Ch13

warrants: Warrants are options to buy stock at a stated price for a stated period of time. Warrants have the advantage of enabling an investor to assume an ownership position if a company grows and prospers, while, at the same time, enabling an investor to receive interest payments even if the bonds never convert to equities. Bonds issued with warrants are similar in nature to convertible bonds. – Ch13

weighted average cost of capital (WACC): The WACC is calculated as an average of the after-tax cost of debt and the cost of equity, each weighted by the proportion of each source of capital in the firm's capital structure. – Ch05

wholesale lockbox: Wholesale lockbox systems are primarily used to process low volume, large dollar business-to-business (B2B) payments which, unlike consumer payments, must often be matched to specific invoices (i.e., several invoices are paid with one check). – Ch09

wholesale payment system: Large dollar, same-day transfer systems such as Fedwire and CHIPS are used for low volume, high-value monetary and book-entry security transfers and are commonly referred to as wholesale payment systems. – Ch08

without recourse: When factoring accounts receivables, without recourse means the factor assumes the responsibility for past dues and bad debts. – Ch06

working capital: Working capital is generally defined as current assets. Current assets consist of accounts such as cash, marketable securities, accounts receivable, inventory and pre-paid expenses. – Ch06

working capital gap: The time it takes a company to convert a cash outflow into a cash inflow is commonly referred to as the working capital gap because it expresses the gap between a cash outflow and a cash inflow. – Ch04

working capital management: Working capital management refers to the decisions and strategies concerning the amounts and types of investments for current assets as well as the amounts and types of financing for current liabilities. Therefore, working capital management involves the analysis of the risk/reward relationship in choosing among different strategies. – Ch06

working capital turnover: Working capital turnover measures how many times per year a company converts average working capital into sales. The higher this ratio, the more efficiently a company converts working capital to sales. – Ch04

work-in-progress (WIP): WIP inventory represents items or materials that are in the process of being manufactured. – Ch07

worms: Worms are self-contained computer programs that can spread without human intervention. – Ch11

year basis: The "days in year" appearing in the numerator of the annual yield calculation is called the year basis. The year basis underlying a quote given by an issuer determines the interest received by the investor. – Ch10

yield: To a lender, a loan is an investment. The interest and fees received represent the yield. – Ch13

yield to maturity (YTM): The yield to maturity (YTM) is the return that the investor receives if the bond is bought at the current price and held until it matures. – Ch13

Zengin Data Telecommunications System (Zengin System): The Zengin Data Telecommunications System (Zengin System) is the on-line network through which most domestic funds transfers are initiated. In 1990, the Zengin System went to a real-time basis and established a cap on intraday net debit positions for each participating institution. – Ch15

zero balance accounts (ZBAs): A ZBA is a disbursement account on which a company issues checks, initiates ACH debits or initiates wire transfers. The balance in the account is maintained at zero. A transfer of funds from a master account located in the same bank covers all debits against a ZBA. Some ZBAs are used for both collections and disbursements. Credits and debits that post to the ZBA are netted at the close of each business day. – Ch09

zero coupon bonds: Zero coupon bonds typically pay no or very low interest during the life of the bond and pay just the face value (par value) at maturity. As a result, these bonds are issued at a substantial discount from par value. – Ch13

Answers

Chapter 1 – The Role of Treasury Management

1. A number of important trends in treasury management represent a continuation of former trends and, therefore, are evolutionary while others represent major changes and are revolutionary. Electronic commerce and globalization are examples of evolutionary trends; the impact of legislation such as Sarbanes-Oxley (SOX) and Check 21 are examples of revolutionary trends.

2. Classic financial management theory views a company's primary objective as maximizing shareholder value. Shareholders invest in a company to earn a return that exceeds returns available from other investment alternatives. The efficient management of an organization's resources generates profits that enhance value to shareholders.

3. Finance plays a pivotal role in achieving a company's primary objective of maximizing shareholder value. The principal roles of corporate finance include accounting, funding, capital budgeting, financial planning and financial risk management.

4. Among the most critical financial decisions a company must make are those involving capital structure, investments, financing and dividends.

5. The major objectives of treasury management include:
   - Maintaining Liquidity
   - Optimizing Cash Resources
   - Establishing and Maintaining Access to Short-Term Financing
   - Maintaining Access to Medium- and Long-Term Financing (Capital Budgeting)
   - Maintaining Shareholder Relations
   - Managing Risk
   - Coordinating Financial Functions and Sharing Financial Information

6. There are three types of cash flows that treasury managers must consider:
   - Cash Inflows – Inflows are funds collected from customers, obtained from financial sources such as lenders and/or received from other sources (e.g., a sale of an asset).
   - Concentration and Liquidity Management Flows – These include internal transfers among operating units of a company and between the company's various bank accounts. The objectives of funds concentration are: (1) to systematically create a pool of liquid reserves in the form of cash and/or cash equivalents (short-term investments or marketable securities) and (2) to pay down short-term borrowings.

- Cash Outflows – Outflows are funds disbursed to employees; vendors and suppliers; lenders; local, state, and federal tax agencies; bondholders and shareholders.

7. The cash flow timeline comprises the total time interval from the time resources are purchased from vendors and suppliers at the beginning of a company's operating cycle until the time payment is received from customers at the end of a company's operating cycle. Float refers to the time interval, or delay, between the start and the completion of a specific phase or process occurring along the cash flow timeline.

Chapter 2 – Treasury Organizational Structure

1. Five key areas for developing treasury policies and clarifying specific roles and responsibilities are: (1) establishing treasury objectives, (2) determining funding requirements, (3) establishing an investment policy, (4) measuring and managing financial exposures and (5) evaluating treasury performance.

2. In any large organization, the Board of Directors serves as the general authority for treasury operations. Ultimately, it is the responsibility of the Board to establish business policies and to approve major undertakings and contracts. For example, the Board grants the authority to: (1) open bank accounts, (2) establish borrowing facilities, (3) approve investment policies and (4) issue securities. The Board also has the responsibility to act in the best interests of shareholders. This is generally interpreted in the U.S. as maximizing shareholder wealth as measured by a company's share price over the long term.

3. The CFO is generally a member of the executive management team and reports to the Chief Executive Officer (CEO). In a large company, the CFO usually oversees both domestic and international treasury and accounting functions. The CFO plays an important role in strategic planning as the pivotal person in the capital budgeting process, providing the financial information that is critical to these strategic decisions. Since the passage of the Sarbanes-Oxley Act (SOX) in 2002, the CFO also assumes personal responsibility for approving the accuracy of all financial statements.

4. The Treasurer is primarily responsible for arranging external financing, managing relationships with banks and other financial institutions, and overseeing day-to-day liquidity management. International treasury functions and foreign exchange management may be part of a domestic treasurer's duties or may report to an individual solely responsible for international treasury management. The Treasurer may be responsible for other functions, including managing dividend disbursements, insurance, pension assets and risk.

5. The primary objective of daily cash management is funds management. Funds management responsibilities vary from organization to organization. They may be the responsibility of a single individual, such as a Cash Manager, or may be divided among several individuals, especially in larger companies. Regardless of how the function is organized, daily funds management involves: (1) preparing a cash position worksheet, (2) monitoring cash balances on deposit at financial institutions, (3) mobilizing funds, (4) researching and reconciling exception items and (5) coordinating functions with other finance areas such as accounts receivable, accounts payable and accounting.

6. Treasury operations can be set up as either a cost center or a profit center. A cost center is the most common approach because treasury is usually regarded as a support function. However, in some instances treasury is established as a profit center. This approach is found in companies specializing in global finance, trade or risk management. Companies engaging in these activities have extensive dealings in FX, interest rate or commodities markets that require the use of derivatives and other hedging instruments to increase earnings and/or reduce losses. The rationale for treasury as a profit center is that it should be able to generate income from hedging and/or speculative activities.

7. Many large multinational companies and global financial institutions are utilizing a structure called a shared service center (SSC). The purpose of a SSC is to enhance management and control over the costs associated with a wide range of business-support functions such as treasury, purchasing, accounting, receivables and payables management, payroll, benefits management, legal/tax and human resources.

8. One of the newest trends is enterprise treasury management. Facilitated by Web-based technology, enterprise treasury management is a more strategic approach that involves managing a company's entire financial spectrum of activities. Three examples of enterprise treasury management are benchmarking, reengineering and outsourcing.

9. Reengineering involves the radical redesign of a particular business process with the goal of continuous process improvement. The redesign of treasury operations may include restructuring or eliminating traditional treasury processes. It is important to emphasize the key phrase in the above definition: radical redesign. Reengineering essentially requires the rationalization of all current structures, practices and procedures.

10. A company with relatively autonomous subsidiaries is more likely to have a decentralized treasury structure, thereby granting local and/or regional field personnel responsibility for day-to-day treasury functions. The head office typically monitors decentralized treasury activities by requiring frequent and timely management reporting and by making periodic visits to local and regional offices to audit treasury staff. In decentralized treasury organizations, local and regional treasury personnel establish and maintain their own bank accounts, manage all short-term investment and borrowing activities, and manage FX and hedging activities.

Chapter 3 – U.S. Financial Environment

1. A commercial bank is defined by law as a financial institution that accepts deposits and makes business loans, offering a wide range of products and services. The term "commercial bank" is used to describe everything from small, single-facility community banks with a few million dollars in assets to large, global institutions with numerous locations and billions in assets.

2. The major products and services of commercial banks are:
   - Deposit Accounts
   - Credit Services
   - Investment Banking Services
   - Payments and Collections
   - Trade Services
   - Credit Enhancement or Payment Guaranty
   - Acting as Agent or Fiduciary
   - Risk-Management Services
   - Consulting Services
   - Broker/Dealer Services

3. Underwriting is one of the primary functions of an investment banking firm. It ensures the issuer of stock or bonds of a definite sum of money for the issue at a definite time. The investment banker assumes the risk of price and marketability.

4. Industrial Credit and Capital Companies are subsidiaries of large industrial corporations that raise funds in the commercial paper market and lend to companies and individuals. A captive finance company solely finances the purchase of its own company's products. Automobile finance companies (i.e., GMAC and Ford Motor Credit Company) are common examples of these.

5. Savings and mutual savings banks have traditionally been state chartered. The Garn-St. Germain Act of 1982 allows mutual savings banks to switch to a federal charter.

6. The main distinction between money markets and capital markets is the maturity of the securities. Money market instruments are securities that are short-term in nature, generally one year or less until maturity. Money market instruments are generally highly liquid and are issued by borrowers with excellent credit ratings. Examples of money market instruments include Treasury Bills (T-Bills), commercial paper (CP), repurchase agreements (repos) and banker's acceptances (BAs). Capital market instruments are securities (BAs) that are long-term in nature, having more than one year until maturity. Capital market instruments are generally less liquid and are issued by borrowers with various credit ratings. Examples of capital market instruments include term loans, equity instruments and bonds.

7. The five major roles of the Federal Reserve are:
   - Supervising and regulating banks
   - Managing monetary policy
   - Providing services for banks
   - Acting as the fiscal agent for the U.S. Treasury
   - Acting as a consumer protection agency

8. National bank charters are granted by the Office of the Comptroller of the Currency (OCC).

9. FinCEN (Financial Crimes Enforcement Network) was established in 1990 by the U.S. Treasury Department. The original intent was to provide a government-wide intelligence network to support the detection, investigation and prosecution of both domestic and international money laundering and other financial crimes. In 1994, the mission was broadened to include regulatory responsibilities. Today, FinCEN is the primary agency that oversees and implements policies to prevent and detect money laundering. This is accomplished primarily through enforcement of counter-money laundering legislation (such as the Bank Secrecy Act), which requires reporting of large and/or suspicious monetary- transfers conduct at banks. FinCEN also provides intelligence and analytical support to law enforcement agencies in the form of reports, which are used to build investigations and plan new strategies that combat money laundering.

10. FFIEC stands for Federal Financial Institution Examination Council. It coordinates the activities of the Fed, the FDIC, the NCUA, the OCC and the OTS to prescribe uniform principles, standards and report forms.

11. OFAC stands for Office of Foreign Assets Control, which is an office of the Treasury Department. It administers and enforces economic and trade sanctions based on U.S. foreign policy and national security goals against targeted foreign countries, terrorist-sponsoring organizations and international narcotics trafficker. The OFAC has the authority to impose controls on financial transactions and to freeze foreign assets under U.S. jurisdiction.

12. In response to the September 11, 2001 attacks on the World Trade Center in New York, Congress passed wide-ranging legislation designed to improve overall security and to grant the FBI and the DOJ increased latitude in intelligence-gathering activities. The primary impact for financial institutions is the substantial number of amendments added to the provisions of existing money laundering legislation such as the BSA. These amendments are intended to make it easier to prevent, detect and prosecute international money laundering and the financing of terrorism. Among the provisions of the Patriot Act are the following:
   - It imposes significant obligations upon non-bank financial institutions including broker dealers, credit card companies and check cashing services. Non-bank financial institutions had not previously been covered by BSA.
   - It makes all foreign banks with accounts in the U.S. subject to U.S. jurisdiction, including the power to obtain records and information regarding customers.

- It prohibits U.S. banks from maintaining, either directly or indirectly, correspondent accounts for any foreign "shell" banks. Shell banks are defined as foreign banks without a physical presence in any country.
- It prevents operators of U.S. credit card systems from authorizing foreign banks to issue or accept U.S. credit cards without taking steps to prevent usage by terrorists.

13. SOX is the acronym for the Sarbanes-Oxley Act, which was passed in 2002 to improve disclosure and financial reporting in the wake of a series of dramatic financial scandals between the years 2000 and 2002. The Act has resulted in numerous changes to SEC rules and regulations. Specifically, companies are now required to disclose in annual reports the code of ethics applicable to senior financial officers. Companies that change or waive the code must disclose the event by filing a Form 8-K or posting a notice on the company Web site. Companies are also required to disclose in annual reports whether the audit committee has a financial expert. New SEC guidelines also require audit committees to pre-approve all audit and non-audit services provided by the auditor and to be briefed by auditors on the company's accounting, including alternative approaches that might be preferable to the company's current methods.

14. Check 21 was enacted to enhance efficiency in the payments system by reducing the legal impediments to check truncation. The purposes of the Check 21 Act are: (1) to facilitate check truncation, (2) to foster innovation in the check-payment system without mandating receipt of checks in electronic format and (3) to improve the payment system overall. The Act creates a new negotiable instrument, called a "substitute check," also known as an image replacement document (IRD). A substitute check is a MICR encoded paper reproduction of an original check that: (1) contains an image of the front and back of the check, (2) bears a MICR line containing all information appearing on the MICR line of the original check and (3) conforms to industry standards that enable the substitute check to be processed in the same manner as the original paper check.

15. The Depository Institutions Deregulation and Monetary Control Act (DIDMCA) of 1980 included mandates that the Federal Reserve reduce and/or price float.

16. The Financial Institutions Reform,Recovery, and Enforcement Act (FIRREA) consolidated the two financial institution insurance funds under the FDIC.

17. The Interstate Bank and Branching Efficiency Act of 1994 has the following primary provisions:
    - Permitted bank holding companies to acquire a bank located in any state, effective September 1995
    - Allowed banks in one state to merge with banks in another state beginning June 1997, so long as neither state had taken legislative action to prohibit interstate mergers between the date of enactment and the end of May 1997
    - Allowed banks to establish new branches in states where they do not maintain a branch if the host state passed a law expressly permitting such branches

18. FHCs are permitted by the Gramm-Leach-Bliley Act of 1999. The Act has the following provisions:
    - Eliminated many of the remaining barriers among the banking, insurance and securities businesses.
    - Permitted the creation of financial holding companies (FHCs) that can engage in any activity considered "financial in nature, incidental to finance or complementary to it."
    - Allowed for easier entry by foreign banks into the U.S. financial services market.
    - Established the Fed as the primary regulator of financial holding companies.
    - Barred a bank holding company from merging with an insurance or securities firm or embarking on new powers if any of its banks earned less than a "satisfactory" Community Reinvestment Act (CRA) rating in its most recent exam.
    - Required financial institutions to establish privacy policies and disclose them at the start of a customer relationship and once a year thereafter.

19. Federal Reserve Regulation CC established rules for handling return of checks and payable through drafts.

20. Under UCC Article 4A, banks are not responsible for consequential damages, which are losses resulting from the action or error made by the bank beyond the simple loss of funds. However, a bank incorrectly executing a payment order remains liable for interest losses or incidental expenses. The bank is liable for consequential damages only when it agrees to assume this liability in a written agreement with the customer.

Chapter 4 – Financial Accounting

1. GAAP (Generally Accepted Accounting Principles) is the detailed rules, developed by the Financial Accounting Standards Board, that govern financial reporting in the U.S.

2. In cash accounting, all accounting entries are directly related to a cash inflow or outflow. In accrual accounting, revenues are recognized as they are earned and expenses as they are incurred, regardless of when the related cash flows occur.

3. A company may avoid reporting a negative cash balance by combining cash and marketable securities on its balance sheet or by reporting checks written but not yet presented as a current liability.

4. The three basic financial statements are the balance sheet, the income statement and the statement of cash flows. In addition, a reconciliation of changes in shareholders' equity is required to be included within the notes or presented as a separate statement.

5. The purpose of conducting an audit is to produce an audit report. This report is a document in which an independent CPA or a CPA firm indicates the scope of the audit and sets forth an opinion regarding the financial statements as a whole. Opinions fall into five categories as follows: (1) standard unqualified, (2) unqualified with explanatory paragraph or modified unqualified, (3) qualified, (4) adverse and (5) disclaimed.

6. Common-size ratios are the most basic type of ratio analysis. A common-size income statement expresses every line item on the statement as a percentage of revenues. These common-size percentages are referred to as margins. Common-size ratios may also be calculated for the balance sheet, where total assets are used as the denominator. Common-size financial statements facilitate evaluation of how effectively a company generates profits from revenues and identifies trends over time when several years of statements are considered concurrently.

7. Performance ratios are used to evaluate the income-generating capabilities of a company. There are two types of performance measures: profitability and efficiency. Profitability ratios summarize how much profit is generated on revenues, equity and assets. The most commonly used profitability ratios are profit margin measures, return on assets and return on equity. Efficiency ratios, also called turnover ratios, evaluate how effectively balance sheet accounts are utilized in the income generating process.

8. If a company is leveraged with high levels of debt or other fixed costs, earnings will change at a more rapid rate than revenues.

9. Marketable investment instruments with original maturities of more than three months, but remaining maturities of one year or less, are carried on the balance sheet as short-term investments. For valuation and reporting purposes, short-term investments are classified in three different ways: Securities that are purchased for a short time prior to sale are classified as trading securities. This classification is typically

reserved for securities that are traded with the objective of generating profits. The second classification is that of held-to-maturity (HTM) securities, which are debt securities purchased with both the intent and ability to hold until maturity. HTM investments are the only marketable securities that are carried at cost on the balance sheet and the third category under which most short-term investments are classified is called available-for-sale (AFS). AFS is the default classification for all securities not carried as trading or HTM securities. These securities are classified as long-term or current assets, depending on their remaining maturities.

10. The ratios typically used to measure liquidity are the current ratio, quick ratio, cash flow to total debt ratio, cash conversion cycle and cash turnover.

11. The cash conversion cycle measures the time it takes a company to convert a cash outflow (for payment of inventory purchases) into a cash inflow (collection of accounts receivable). This measure uses the average age of the inventory, the average days of accounts receivable and the average age of the accounts payable to indicate how efficiently a company is using its current assets and liabilities.

12. The Governmental Accounting Standards Board (GASB) is the authoritative standard-setting body for state and local governments, as well as for public schools, state universities and other government-affiliated agencies. The Financial Accounting Foundation (FAF) is responsible for selecting members, providing funds and exercising general oversight for both GASB and FASB. FASB has also been issuing guidance for non-governmental not-for-profits such as private colleges, universities, and health care organizations since the early 1990s. GAAP accounting standards also apply to non-governmentals. Many standards have specific provisions directed at these entities; therefore, their financial reports closely resemble those of for-profit organizations.

13. The major advantages of using ratios for financial analysis are as follows: (1) They are easily computed and widely used; (2) The information necessary for calculations is easily obtained and (3) They facilitate comparisons between companies. On the other hand, the major disadvantages of using ratios for financial analysis are as follows: (1) Ratios assess historical performance at fixed points in time; thus, they do not capture intra period variations, nor are they necessarily indicative of future performance; (2) Ratios summarize accounting information, therefore, they may not reflect economic value; (3) They do not reflect qualitative value such as business strategy or managerial talent and (4) Use of different accounting methods may reduce the validity of comparisons between firms.

14. Accounting for derivative instruments and hedging activities is governed by FAS 133 & 138. Derivatives, such as forwards, futures, options and swaps, are carried at fair value on the balance sheet as assets or liabilities. Accounting for the gains and losses that arise from changes in the fair value of a derivative depends on the intended use of the instrument. Gains and losses that arise from revaluation of derivatives are reported in current period income provided the derivatives do not qualify as hedge instruments. If a

derivative is used to hedge fluctuations in the value of a specific asset or liability carried on the balance sheet, the gains and losses of the reevaluation are recognized as income together with the offsetting gains and losses on the item being hedged. This type of hedge is referred to as a fair value hedge.

15. Under the SarbanesOxley Act (SOX) of 2002, the SEC was mandated to improve rules for reporting off-balance-sheet arrangements (OBSA). OBSA include guarantees, contingent interests in assets, operating leases, guarantees and certain variable interest entities (also referred to as special purpose entities). The final rule issued by the SEC requires that specific disclosures related to OBSA be included in the Management Discussion and Analysis (MD&A) section provided with the company's financial statements. This is required whenever the OBSA have, or are reasonably likely to have, an effect on the financial condition of the business.

Chapter 5 – Financial Planning and Analysis

1. Most financial decisions involve a trade-off between present and future cash flows. The time value of money, a fundamental principle of finance, establishes the relationship between cash flows received at different times. Time value means a dollar received today is worth more than a dollar received tomorrow because today's dollar can be invested to earn a return. Conversely, a dollar received tomorrow is worth less than a dollar received today because the opportunity to earn interest is foregone. The value of a cash flow at any point in time may be determined with an appropriate interest rate and the number of time periods involved.

2. All organizations face constraints on resources. Often, a company must choose between multiple opportunities when allocating scarce resources. An opportunity cost is the foregone benefit of an alternative use of funds. For example, if a treasurer chooses to make a short-term investment rather than repay borrowings, the opportunity cost is the cost of the interest on the portion of debt that could have been repaid. Conversely, if the treasurer chooses to repay debt, the opportunity cost is the income that could have been earned on the investment. Cost of capital refers to the cost of the financial resources, or capital, a company uses to fund long-term investments. In practice, the term "capital" is used to describe only the more permanent sources of funding used by a company, such as long-term debt, preferred stock and common equity, which includes both the money contributed by stockholders and the earnings retained in the business. For most long-term financing decisions, the appropriate opportunity cost is the cost of capital.

3. To evaluate projects with higher or lower risk than the overall risk profile of the company, most firms use a risk-adjusted rate. High-risk projects are typically evaluated using a risk-adjusted discount rate that is greater than the company's weighted average cost of capital (WACC). Evaluating a given project with a higher discount rate lowers its net present value because each future cash flow is discounted more deeply due to the additional risk. Conversely, lower risk projects would be evaluated at a lower discount rate, which would increase the NPV.

4. Costs are generally classified as fixed, variable or mixed. Fixed costs are costs that either do not vary in total over a wide range of activity or are not immediately impacted by changes in the cost driver. Variable costs are costs that change in total in direct proportion to the level of activity. A mixed cost has both fixed and variable elements.

5. The relative levels of fixed and variable costs define the cost structure of a company. Two financial concepts that are closely related to cost structure are operating leverage and economies of scale. Operating leverage is the extent to which fixed costs are used in a company's cost structure. The higher the proportion of fixed costs, the higher the operating leverage of the company. A company with high operating leverage is able to achieve a large percentage increase in income from a small increase in revenues. Economies of scale occur when an increase in sales results in a lower average cost per unit of sale. If a business has mostly variable costs, the average cost remains fairly stable when sales increase. On the other hand, companies with high operating leverage, or high levels of fixed costs, experience declining average costs on increasing revenues

because the fixed costs are distributed over more unit sales. The majority of the fixed costs of a business relate to fixed asset usage. These include items such as lease payments, interest payments, taxes, property insurance, plant and equipment. Therefore, economies of scale reflect the extent to which additional sales may be generated on the existing asset base.

6. The breakeven point is the level of activity for an operation at which costs exactly equal benefits. A breakeven analysis is often used by businesses in product decisions to determine what level of sales, at a given price, is required to cover costs. There are numerous applications for breakeven analysis in treasury. One example is the calculation of the breakeven amount of funds required to justify a wire transfer versus using an ACH (automated clearing house) transfer – sometimes referred to as electronic depository transfers (EDTs).

7. Capital budgeting is the process by which strategic plans are developed to determine a company's investment in capital assets. Examples of capital budgeting include the replacement of existing equipment, the expansion of existing facilities, the purchase of new equipment and/or the introduction of new product lines. Capital budget decision-making is a form of cost/benefit analysis. Because capital investments involve potentially large sums of money and multiple time periods, several decision models have been developed specifically for capital budgeting analysis. Four commonly used models are: (1) payback period, (2) net present value, (3) internal rate of return and (4) profitability index.

8. Most financial decisions involve uncertainty and, therefore, some degree of risk. In fact, all decisions that have future outcomes can usually be predicted but not known with certainty. The longer the time horizon used in analyzing the decision, the greater the likelihood of unanticipated variation in forecasted cash flows, discount rates and other assumptions. Three tools – scenario analysis, sensitivity analysis and simulation – enable decision-makers to assess the impact of risk.

9. The master budget has two chief components, the operating budget and the financial budget. The operating budget, or profit plan, focuses on day-to-day operations. The financial budget addresses the financing and investing activities of an organization. The operating budget and financial budget are combined to form the master budget, which constitutes a set of pro forma financial statements for the budget period.

10. Once planning is complete and decisions have been made, the ongoing performance of a company's operations must be monitored and evaluated. Budgets provide one benchmark against which performance is often assessed. There are also several other measures that are frequently used for evaluation of projects, divisions, subsidiaries or business units. Three of the common measures are return on investment, residual income and economic value added.

11. Economic value added (EVA) (defined as after-tax operating profit minus an appropriate charge for the opportunity cost of all capital) is a refinement of RI . EVA measures to what extent profits exceed the cost of invested capital. For an operating unit, EVA increases whenever: (1) the rate of return earned on the existing base of capital improves, (2) additional capital is invested in projects where the return is more than the cost of new capital or (3) capital is liquidated from substandard operations.

Chapter 6 – Philosophy of Working Capital

1. Working capital is generally defined as current assets. Current assets consist of accounts such as cash, marketable securities, accounts receivable, inventory and pre-paid expenses. Net working capital is defined as total current assets minus total current liabilities, where current liabilities are represented by accounts payable, notes payable and accrued liabilities.

2. The flow of cash through the working capital accounts is best illustrated with the cash flow cycle. This cycle shows how the strategies concerning inventory, receivables and payables all interact to affect the flow of cash through the company. The cash conversion cycle is the average number of days between the cash outflow for the acquisition of materials and supplies and the cash inflow from the sale of products or services. The cash conversion cycle is a method for calculating how long, on average, a company must finance a cash outflow before receiving a cash inflow and is expressed by the following formula:

   Cash Conversion Cycle = Days' Inventory + Days' Receivables – Days' Payables

3. Many current asset and current liability accounts vary whenever there is sales activity. These accounts are referred to as "spontaneous." That is, there are no specific working capital management decisions involved in increasing these accounts; the changes occur spontaneously with a change in sales. The magnitude of spontaneous changes has a significant impact in determining the amount of external financing necessary for working capital.

4. A company may choose between alternative strategies, restrictive or relaxed, regarding the total amount of current assets to support a given level of sales. Under a restrictive current asset investment strategy, a company maintains low levels of current assets relative to sales. The investment in raw materials is managed as tightly as possible using JIT inventory techniques and outstanding accounts receivable balances are low, reflecting a conservative credit policy. Under a relaxed current-asset investment strategy, a company maintains high levels of current assets relative to sales. Typically, these current assets consist of high levels of accounts receivable, usually resulting from a liberal credit policy, and/or high levels of inventory, usually resulting from concerns about the ability to replenish raw materials.

5. The basic approaches to the financing of a company's permanent assets may be classified as maturity matching, aggressive and conservative. Depending on the shape of the yield curve, the movement of interest rates, the forecast of future rates and management's risk tolerance, any of these approaches may be appropriate at any given point in time. Under a maturity matching financing strategy, the total permanent assets, defined as fixed assets plus permanent current assets, are financed with long-term financing. Short-term financing is used to finance the temporary current assets, as evidenced by the fact that the need for short-term financing follows exactly the same pattern of fluctuation of the temporary current assets. Under a conservative financing strategy, long-term financing supports fixed assets, permanent current assets and some portion of temporary current assets. A company usually tries to finance the average level of

temporary current assets with long-term sources. Short-term financing is used for the remainder of the temporary current assets. Because short-term financing is used for only a portion of the temporary current assets, this strategy generally involves the least use of short-term financing and, therefore, has higher financing costs than other approaches. Under an aggressive financing strategy, a company finances all of fixed assets with long-term debt or equity but finances only a portion of permanent current assets with long-term financing. Short-term financing supports the remainder of the permanent current assets and all temporary current assets. This strategy utilizes more ongoing short-term financing than other financing strategies.

6. The primary operational advantages of short-term credit are the ease of access, flexibility and the ability to efficiently finance seasonal credit needs. Short-term loans are typically easier to obtain than long-term loans. In addition, short-term loans generally have less restrictive covenants than long-term loans. If funds are necessary for only a short time, borrowing on a short-term basis can enable a company to maintain flexibility for future borrowing decisions. An operational disadvantage of short-term debt is the continuing need to renegotiate or "roll over" the debt. A lender may decide not to roll over the loan or renew the credit line at the maturity due to changing financial variables in the company or changes in general economic conditions. In addition, some lenders who provide lines of credit require that loans used to finance short-term working capital deficits be paid in full for a minimum period each year (known as a clean-up period). Many companies find the use of short-term loans for the financing of permanent asset requirements involves significant risk.

7. The five major types of short-term credit – accounts payable, accrued expenses, short-term bank loans, asset-based loans and commercial paper – each have different speeds of acquisition, flexibility, cost and risk.

8. Short-term bank loans are often secured by some form of collateral, usually accounts receivable, inventory or securitized assets. This practice is referred to as asset-based lending. These types of loans are generally formula-based, meaning that the amount of the loan is usually based on a percentage of eligible receivables or inventory, depending upon the age and/or dollar amount of the asset(s). In effect, a lender agrees to advance some percentage of the value of the receivables or inventory (the advance rate), with certain assets pledged as security, as part of the lending arrangement.

9. Commercial paper is an unsecured promissory note issued by a corporation willing to pay a competitive market rate and typically offers maturities of up to 270 days. Commercial paper is normally issued at a discount through dealers. For large companies active in the market, it provides a quick source of low-cost, short-term financing. The cost of commercial paper for the issuer is based on the company's credit rating on the issue, which is a function of the estimated default risk.

10. Borrowing on a short-term basis carries two types of risk avoided in longer-term borrowing. The first risk relates to fluctuations in market interest rates. If a company borrows on a short-term floating rate basis, it will borrow at whatever the interest rate is at that time, taking the chance that interest rates may change dramatically in either direction. The second risk of short-term financing concerns the availability of funds. If a company relies heavily on short-term borrowing, eventually the short-term funds may not be available due to a tightening of credit standards on the part of lenders. Also, a company's credit quality may decline, thus endangering the future rollover of the credit arrangement. Some companies counter this risk by utilizing multiyear credit line commitments, which guarantee the availability of funds over a longer term. In contrast to short-term borrowing, long-term borrowing on a fixed rate basis stabilizes interest costs, or, in the case of a limited variable rate basis, provides a narrow range for fluctuation in interest costs.

Chapter 7 – Working Capital Tools

1. Effective credit management generally entails four steps: (1) establishing and communicating a company's credit policies, (2) setting terms of sale consistent with overall company objectives, (3) evaluating customer creditworthiness in order to grant customer credit lines and (4) ensuring prompt and accurate customer billing in conjunction with customer service or billing departments.

2. Establishing credit standards is a two-stage process: first, determining the risk profile of the type of customer who is granted credit and, second, determining each individual customer's credit limit. Establishing credit terms involves designing sales contracts or agreements that clearly specify under what conditions credit terms are granted. Establishing collection policies involves determining the steps involved in collecting delinquent accounts or bad debts. Finally, a company needs to develop an information system or purchase software that monitors A/R to ensure compliance with credit terms and detects changes in customer payment patterns at both the aggregate and individual customer levels.

3. A number of factors may constrain or influence a company's credit policies. In many industries, credit terms and policies have become standard practices. As a result, it is difficult for a seller to vary from industry practices. A company must also consider the impact that offering trade credit has on existing loan covenants. A change in A/R balances can affect working capital ratios, potentially resulting in being out of compliance with covenants. There are also legal constraints, such as the Robinson-Patman Act, that prohibit various forms of price discrimination. Likewise, many states have usury laws that limit the amount of interest that can be charged or that ban certain unfair credit practices.

4. It is important for a company to set and maintain credit standards that encompass credit extension, billing and collection. In determining credit extension policies, there are two key risk considerations. First, if a company implements credit standards that are too strict, it may decline trade credit to customers who represent an acceptable credit risk, thereby resulting in lost sales opportunities. Second, if a company implements credit standards that are too lenient, it may grant trade credit to customers who represent an unacceptable credit risk, thereby resulting in an increase in late payment and bad debt expenses. In practice, the costs of these two risk considerations are difficult to quantify. However, credit is a sales tool, and a zero default rate probably means that a company's credit terms are too strict.

5. Credit analysis depends upon the type of information available and the trade-offs between costs and benefits. The traditional factors companies consider are known as the five C's of credit: character, capacity, capital, collateral and conditions.

6. Credit scoring involves a four-step process: (1) differentiating standard and high-risk accounts based on monthly income, outstanding obligations and the employment history of the applicant, (2) weighting the characteristics of applicants who fit into each category to establish creditworthiness, (3) setting cut-off scores for approval and denial of credit and (4) applying further analysis to applicants whose scores fall in between the cut-off points.

7. The open account method, sometimes called open book credit, is the most common type of commercial trade credit in the United States. A seller issues an invoice, as formal evidence of the obligation, and records the sale as an A/R. The customer is billed for each transaction by invoice and/or monthly statement. Full payment of invoiced amounts is expected within the specified credit terms unless certain discounts or deductions are available to the customer. A buyer's creditworthiness is reviewed periodically but the buyer does not need to apply for credit each time an order is placed.

8. The definitions are as follows:

Cash on Delivery (COD) – The seller ships the goods and the buyer pays upon receipt. If the buyer refuses to pay, the goods are returned and the seller must pay the shipping and handling costs.

Discount Terms – In addition to specifying a net due date, the seller may also offer a discount if payment is made prior to that date. Terms of 2/10 net 30 mean that the total amount is due within 30 days of the invoice date, but the buyer can take a two percent discount if payment is made within ten days.

Seasonal Dating – The seller agrees to accept payment at the end of the buyer's selling season. This allows manufacturers to provide short-term financing for a buyer's purchases and reduces the manufacturer's inventory costs. It is common in industries with distinct seasonality of sales such as toys, greeting cards, garden supplies, sporting goods or textbooks. In seasonal dating, the seller may offer a series of discounts to encourage the buyer to pay early.

Consignment – Under a consignment agreement, the seller ships the goods to the buyer with no obligation to pay until the goods have been sold or used. The title to the goods remains with the seller until they are sold.

9. It is important to monitor individual accounts receivable because: (1) There may be errors or delays in the invoicing or payment process, (2) Some customers may intentionally delay payment until follow-up is initiated and (3) A change in financial condition may alter the ability of a customer to make timely payments and may require a curtailment of future credit sales.

10. One method of measuring A/R is days' sales outstanding (DSO) or average collection period. DSO is calculated by dividing outstanding A/R at the end of a period by the average daily credit sales for that period. DSO gives a single number that can be compared to stated credit terms, historic trends, or industry norms to provide an indication of a company's overall collection efficiency.

11. An A/R balance pattern specifies the percentage of credit sales in a time period, usually a month, that remain outstanding at the end of the month and each subsequent time period. A company's collection history determines the normal balance pattern. Management evaluates any shifts by comparing current patterns with historical norms. Companies also use balance patterns to project A/R levels, measure collection efficiency and forecast future cash inflows.

12. A/R, a major component of current assets, is financed in a variety of ways. A company that offers trade credit can borrow unsecured funds from a financial institution to support A/R if the company has sufficient cash flow to justify an unsecured line. If a company cannot finance A/R with unsecured borrowings, it may pledge A/R as collateral and borrow on a secured basis. Commonly referred to as asset-based lending, this method of financing is based on the quality of the receivables. A lender evaluates the receivables to determine those acceptable as collateral for a loan. The loan is then repaid as the company collects the receivables.

13. Factoring involves the outright sale of receivables to a factor, a company that specializes in the financing and management of receivables. In most factoring arrangements, the buyer of the receivables has no recourse to the seller. "No recourse" or "without recourse" means that the factor must absorb the loss if a customer fails to pay. However, in some cases, the factoring arrangement stipulates the factor has recourse, in which case the seller is liable for the bad debts the factor is unable to collect. Most factoring is performed on a notification basis. In other words, the seller must notify customers that the account has been sold because the payment is remitted directly to the factor.

14. In a balance forward system, a credit limit is established for each individual. As purchases are made or services are provided, the A/R outstanding balance increases. When payments are made, the A/R balance is reduced accordingly. A balance forward system is used most often by companies selling goods and services to individual consumers.

15. There have been many new developments in credit and A/R management. These developments include increased use of electronic commerce, electronic invoice or electronic bill presentment and payment via the Internet and outsourcing of receivables.

16. One of the primary reasons for holding inventory is to provide the goods required for the expected level of a company's sales activities during its normal operating and production cycle. Inventory may be held because it is not possible to receive delivery during certain periods of production (such as nighttime manufacturing or weekend shifts), because it is uneconomical to have materials delivered in very small quantities at infrequent intervals or suppliers might not agree to deliver small quantities. Also, the economics involved in the manufacturing process may require large production runs, requiring substantial on-hand inventory to insure that a full run is completed without material shortage.

17. Inventories are generally categorized as one of the following: (1) raw materials, (2) work in progress (WIP), (3) finished goods, (4) scrap or obsolete items and (5) stores and supplies.

18. The just-in-time (JIT) approach to inventory management attempts to minimize the level of inventory by altering the costs or uncertainties that underlie the motives for holding inventory. JIT methodology

recognizes that inventory turns from an asset into a liability fairly quickly. JIT is, therefore, not merely an inventory management system but rather a production/business philosophy that treats inventory as being undesirable, a cover-up for poor inventory planning or for inventory location and accuracy problems, inferior supplier quality and/or unbalanced production processes.

19. There are two critical areas of coordination between treasury management and A/P management. The first is the communication from A/P to treasury regarding the invoices vouchered for payment; the second is the communication from treasury back to A/P regarding the reconciliation of cleared items. Companies with integrated enterprise resource planning (ERP) or accounting systems with treasury management modules are typically able to integrate these functions easily. However, many companies use either separate systems for disbursement management or treasury information software provided by banks. This software may not interface as easily with the A/P ledger. Customized interfaces or middleware (in a client-server environment) are required to facilitate the transfer of information between applications.

20. In designing a disbursement system, an organization must keep three goals in mind: the ability to access information, to prevent fraud and to maintain good relationships with payees. Obtaining access to timely and accurate information regarding the status of disbursement accounts and disbursement clearings enables a company to manage its cash position more effectively. Preventing fraud means protecting company funds from unauthorized use through written policies and internal controls, prompt bank reconciliation, the use of quality check stock and banking services such as positive pay. Maintaining good relationships with payees means ensuring on-time payments to employees, vendors, suppliers, lenders, tax agencies, bondholders and shareholders.

21. Imaging technology is a major component of many disbursement services. Both the front and the back of a check (or any other business document) can be captured and converted into digital information using optical scanning. Check images may be transmitted to a company's computer system for storage or sent to a fax machine. Alternatively, check images are frequently housed in a bank database to which a company is granted access for the purpose of research or customer service inquiries. Imaging services are particularly useful in conjunction with positive pay. Such services help a company identify potential unauthorized check activity and make time-critical pay/no-pay decisions. Images of checks can be obtained in a more timely fashion than photocopies, allowing companies to respond quickly to inquiries from customers, employees and vendors. Additionally, many financial institutions provide customers with check images on a CD-ROM.

Chapter 8 – Payment Systems

1. There are five non-cash payment systems in the U.S.: (1) checks and check-like instruments, (2) credit, debit and other types of cards, (3) ACH, (4) Fedwire and (5) CHIPS. The first three systems are used primarily for high-volume, low-value monetary transactions and are commonly referred to as retail payment systems. Large dollar, same-day transfer systems such as Fedwire and CHIPS are used for low-volume, high-value monetary and book-entry security transfers and are commonly referred to as wholesale payment systems.

2. The concepts of settlement and finality are central to an understanding of payment systems. Settlement is the actual transfer of value from the payor to the payee. Settlement is final when the transfer is unconditional and irrevocable. Finality varies depending on the payment system and the parties involved in the transaction. Often, there are provisions for return of payments, so finality is not assured until after the permitted return period has elapsed. Consumer payments made through the electronic retail payment systems (cards and ACH) are governed by Regulation E (Reg E), which provides consumers with considerable return periods for unauthorized charges (generally within 60 days of receipt of the statement with the unauthorized charges but may be longer under extenuating circumstances). However, wire transfer payments such as Fedwire settle in real-time and finality occurs immediately. Therefore, wire transfers are irrevocable and unconditional payment mechanisms.

3. The check clearing process begins with the deposit of a check into a payee's account at a financial institution. The bank of deposit or the payee encodes the check amount on the magnetic ink character recognition (MICR) line. Once encoded with special characters in magnetic ink on the lower portion of the check, the MICR line contains all the information necessary to process the check through the check clearing system. The American Bankers Association (ABA) number, also known as the transit routing number (TRN), is preprinted on the MICR line. This nine-digit number identifies the drawee bank and provides the depository bank with the information required to route the check back to the drawee bank through the clearing system.

4. On-us check clearing involves a single bank and occurs when a payee deposits a check in an account at the same bank on which it is drawn. The bank simultaneously debits the payor's account and credits the payee's account. The depositor receives same-day or immediate availability.

5. Four clearing channels are available for clearing of interbank checks – checks drawn on institutions other than the bank of deposit. The four channels are a clearing house, a Federal Reserve Bank, a correspondent bank and a direct send.

6. With ECP, the MICR line data captured by the reader/sorter (the check number, TRN, account number, and dollar amount of the item) is electronically transmitted to the paying bank. The paying bank uses this data, not the physical check, to debit funds from the payor's demand deposit account. The actual check

may be sent to the paying bank for subsequent handling or the check may be truncated (retained) by the clearing bank. The clearing bank may store the check or an image of the check. ECP accelerates clearing and the notification of checks being returned by the paying bank.

7. When funds from a check become available for use by a depositor depends on: (1) the drawee bank endpoint, (2) the time of deposit relative to the depository bank's ledger cutoff time and deposit deadline, (3) the day the check is deposited and (4) the bank's availability schedule. An availability schedule specifies an item's deposit deadline and defines the duration before deposited funds are available for withdrawal.

8. Availability schedules specify, for each drawee endpoint, when a bank grants available credit or collected balances for deposited items. In order to receive the availability stated on the schedule, the deposited item must have been received by the assigned deposit deadline. If the deposit deadline is missed, availability is delayed by one banking day. The assignment of availability can be in whole or fractional banking days. Checks are generally assigned somewhere between zero and two days' availability.

9. Deposit float has two related definitions. First, deposit float is the dollar amount of deposited items that are in the process of collection. Second, deposit float is the interval between the time an item is deposited and the time the funds are collected. For example, treasury managers often refer to average float as a certain number of days, meaning the average length of time prior to when deposited funds become available.

10. A payable through draft or PTD is a payment instrument resembling a check that is drawn against the payor, not the bank. A draft is handled like a check through the clearing system, but the responsibility for paying the draft lies with the drawee. The primary reason companies use PTDs is to preserve the right to review the items prior to final payment. Insurance companies often use PTDs for claim reimbursement because PTDs provide insurers an opportunity to verify the signature and endorsements before honoring the items. Some state and local governments use a form of PTD called a government warrant.

11. The primary regulations related to paper-based payment instruments are the Uniform Commercial Code (UCC) Article 3 "Negotiable Instruments," UCC Article 4 "Bank Deposits and Collections" and Federal Reserve Regulations CC and J.

12. The first step in a credit card transaction is authorization. When a customer pays for a purchase with a credit card, the merchant submits an authorization request for the charge amount to the merchant bank (or the third party processor). The issuing bank reviews the cardholder's account and approves or declines the charge. The second step in a credit card transaction is clearing – the communication of the payment information through the system. The final step in a credit card transaction is settlement in which the funds are transferred from the issuing bank to the merchant bank. The amount the merchant receives is the net settlement, that is, the transaction value less the discount. The discount is calculated based on a discount rate negotiated between the merchant and the merchant bank. The discount payment is divided among the merchant bank, the issuing bank, the third-party processor (if used) and the national credit card company.

13. Procurement or purchasing cards (commonly referred to as P-cards) are credit cards used by businesses for the purchase of supplies, inventory, equipment and service contracts. Typically, P-cards are used for small dollar purchases with spending limits established on an individual employee basis. Employee purchases can be made only from approved vendors and suppliers. The principal benefit of a P-card for a company is the replacement of the traditional time-consuming, labor-intensive, paper-based requisition process. The principal benefit for an employee is that essential goods and services can be obtained quickly and conveniently.

14. The ACH system was developed by the financial industry in the early 1970s as an electronic alternative to checks. The ACH system is a batch processing system designed for high-volume, low-value transactions. In an ACH transaction, payment information is processed and settled electronically, thereby increasing reliability, efficiency, and cost-effectiveness. In addition, an ACH transaction is capable of transferring more information about a payment than can be transmitted via check.

15. Prenotifications (prenotes) are optional zero-dollar entries that are sent through the ACH system prior to live entries. Prenotes provide a verification function at the receiving bank before entries for settlement are processed. For example, when a company adds a new employee to a direct deposit of payroll program, a prenotification ensures that the bank's transit routing number and the employee's personal bank account number(s) are correct.

16. The four categories of Fedwire transfers are: repetitive, semi-repetitive, non-repetitive and drawdown.
    - Repetitive – Repetitive wire transfers are used when a company makes frequent transfers to the same credit parties. The bank maintains a record of the debit and credit parties and accepts instructions either electronically or via telephone to initiate the transfer. A unique identifier is assigned to each instruction template that contains all the pertinent information. Only the date and the dollar amount may be changed on a repetitive wire.
    - Semi-Repetitive – With semi-repetitive wire transfers, the debit and credit parties remain the same but the description (e.g., a customer or an invoice number) may be changed along with the date and the dollar amount. Semi-repetitive transfers combine the controls of repetitive transfers with the flexibility of non-repetitive transfers.
    - Non-Repetitive (Free-Form) – With non-repetitive wire transfers, the debit and credit parties are different each time. As a result, additional security measures are typically required. Examples of such measures are callbacks, secondary levels of approval and segregation of duties.
    - Drawdown – A drawdown wire transfer is a request sent by a company to a bank in order to initiate a debit wire transfer from either the company's account or another party's account at another financial institution. The party being debited must preauthorize the transfer; therefore, drawdown wires are most frequently conducted as part of a company's concentration system. The vast majority of wire transfers are credit transactions, not drawdown wires.

17. CHIPS is a bank-owned, large-dollar funds transfer network operated by The Clearing House Association. It was established in 1970 to substitute electronic payments for paper checks in international transactions

between foreign and American banks. Though not a true wire transfer system in the sense of Fedwire, CHIPS is a real-time, intraday net settlement system that clears and settles transactions in U.S. dollars. It is also used for letters of credit (L/Cs), documentary collection and third-party transfers. Any commercial bank with a regulated presence in the United States can become a member of CHIPS and gain access to the system; however, only a limited number of large U.S. and foreign banks participate directly in CHIPS. CHIPS clears over 95 percent of the international payments made in U.S. dollars.

18. The growth of payment volume and several large bank failures in recent decades have prompted greater attention by the Federal Reserve System to reducing payments system risk. As part of this effort, the Fed instituted an extensive payment system risk (PSR) policy applicable to all Fed member banks. There are four major types of risk in the payments system: systemic, credit, fraud and operational. Actions taken by the Fed to manage these risks have had a tremendous impact on bank participants, as well as on end-users of the payments systems.

19. Fraud risk is the risk that someone might alter a transaction or enter a false item that could cause a loss for the disbursing party. The greatest fraud risk is associated with checks followed by credit card fraud.. Access to ACH and wire transfer systems is limited, and adherence to reasonable security practices by end-users minimizes the opportunity for fraud with these systems.

20. The Re-Presented Check Entries or RCK format is utilized to transmit ACH debit entries in place of a consumer paper check after it has been returned for insufficient or uncollected funds. Originators of re-presented check entries must provide notice to the check writer prior to receiving an item to which the re-presented check entry relates. The notice must inform the check writer that the returned check may be collected electronically if the check is returned for insufficient or uncollected funds. Originators may transmit a re-presented check entry no more than twice after the first return of a paper item and no more than once after the second return of a paper item.

Chapter 9 – Cash Positioning

1. Collection float is the time interval or delay between when payment is initiated and when a company receives available funds. Collection float applies principally to paper-based payment instruments that are subject to three types of float or delays: mail, processing and availability. Converting accounts receivable as quickly as possible into collected funds minimizes float time. The primary cost associated with collection float is the opportunity cost because uncollected funds cannot be used for investments or debt repayment.

2. Paper-based payment collection systems fall into two major categories: over-the-counter/field deposit systems and mail payment systems. Various businesses collect receipts over the counter at field locations. Field units include local offices and retail stores. Methods used by retail establishments to collect at the point of sale include cash, checks, credit cards, debit cards and smart cards. A wholesale customer or its agent may deliver checks or cash to a vendor's office. Alternatively, a payee or its agent may pick up checks or cash from the customer when making a delivery. A company may use either an in-house processing center or a lockbox to receive and process mailed payments. Deciding which of these methods to use depends primarily on two factors: the volume and the dollar amount of the payments.

3. A lockbox is a collection system in which a financial institution or third-party vendor receives payments at a specified lockbox address, processes the remittances and deposits payments in a payee's account. Lockboxes may be paper-based, electronic or a combination of both. In the U.S., lockboxes are one of the most widely used collection methods due to the predominant use of checks. The major advantage of a lockbox system over a company-processing center is the ability to reduce mail, processing and availability float.

4. There are four types of lockboxes: wholesale, retail, hybrid (which combines features of wholesale and retail lockboxes) and electronic. Wholesale lockbox systems are used primarily to process low-volume, large-dollar business-to-business (B2B) payments, which, unlike consumer payments, must often be matched to specific invoices (i.e., several invoices are paid with one check). Detailed information is required about the invoices paid, discounts taken, returns and allowances. Retail lockbox systems are used primarily to process high-volume, small-dollar consumer remittances (C2B) that frequently involve recurring, monthly installment payments. The checks are accompanied by standardized, machine-scannable remittance documents enclosed in preaddressed window envelopes. Because of the large volume of items processed, retail lockboxes focus on cost reduction rather than float reduction. In addition to checks, some retail lockboxes also process credit card payments. Hybrid lockbox systems combine features of wholesale and retail lockboxes. They are configured, usually on a customized basis, to process both B2B and C2B payments. They are used by companies, such as utilities, whose consumer customers return standardized remittance documents that can be processed automatically and whose business customers remit documents that require manual handling. The processor combines both consumer and business remittance data and transmits it to the company. Electronic lockbox systems are used to process incoming ACH and wire payments. Related remittance information is captured and reported on a consolidated basis, sometimes in combination with wholesale, retail or hybrid lockbox information.

5. Electronic payments include wire transfers, ACH debits and credits, and debit or credit card payments. Electronic payments offer three benefits: (1) the predictability of settlement timing and available funds, (2) the flexibility of directing payments to any account or any financial institution without any manual intervention and (3) the ease of transmitting customer remittance information that may accompany the payment to facilitate updating of accounts receivable.

6. Cash concentration is the transfer of funds from outlying depository locations to a central bank account, commonly referred to as a concentration account. Two major objectives of a cash concentration system are to mobilize funds and to minimize excess bank balances. Pooling funds into a single concentration account enables them to be managed more efficiently and effectively and facilitates daily liquidity management. Concentration enables a company to: (1) invest a larger amount of funds, potentially increasing interest income, (2) pay down debt faster, potentially reducing interest expense and (3) take advantage of supplier and/or vendor discount terms, potentially reducing costs of goods sold or operating expenses.

7. The two most frequently used methods for concentration are electronic depository transfers (EDTs) and wire transfers. EDTs are ACH transactions that concentrate funds using either the National Automated Clearing House (NACHA) CCD or CCD+ formats. EDTs are inexpensive and are available one business day after origination. An EDT is the most common method of depository transfer in use today, having virtually replaced depository transfer checks (DTCs). DTCs are a special category of check used by a company to transfer funds from its outlying depository locations to its main concentration account. Fedwire is an alternative to EDT when a company needs to expedite fund transfers. Typically, these are repetitive wires. Wire transfers provide immediate funds and help reduce excess balances at deposit banks. However, because wire transfer is the most expensive funds transfer mechanism, it is used primarily to concentrate large dollar amounts when same-day value and finality are critical.

8. Availability anticipation involves the initiation of a transfer after a deposit has been made but before all of the items have been granted availability by the depository bank. The transfer is initiated based on the projected availability. This method risks drawing on uncollected funds because potential delays in the clearing system and return items can cause collected balances to be unpredictable. Sometimes, availability anticipation can even lead to a ledger overdraft if there are a significant number of return items. In addition, if wire transfers are used as a method of concentration and the amounts transferred are significant, there can even be intraday overdrafts.

9. The basic goal of managing an accounts payable and disbursement system is to disburse funds to vendors, suppliers, employees and other payees in a timely, accurate and cost-effective manner. Typically, the accounts payable and payroll functions are responsible for scheduling and initiating vendor and employee payments, respectively. Information regarding these payments is communicated to the cash manager for use in cash forecasting and position management. In most cases, the treasury area is directly responsible for debt and dividend payments, in addition to the funding of disbursement accounts.

10. Disbursement float is the time interval or delay between the day a payment is mailed and the day funds are debited from the payor's account. Disbursement float applies principally to paper-based payment

instruments that are subject to three types of delays or float: mail, processing and clearing. Disbursement float is analogous to collection float except that it is viewed from the payor's perspective. As illustrated in Exhibit 9.1, the mail and processing float components of disbursement float are the same as in collection float. The primary difference between collection and disbursement float is availability versus clearing float.

11. A zero balance account or ZBA is a disbursement account on which a company issues checks, initiates ACH debits or initiates wire transfers. The balance in the account is maintained at zero. A transfer of funds from a master account located in the same bank covers all debits against a ZBA. Funding of the ZBA is generally automatic and involves only an accounting entry by the bank. As noted before, a ZBA can also be a depository account from which funds are debited and transferred into a master account at the end of each day.

12. Positive pay is a disbursement service used to combat check fraud. With this service, the company transmits a file of issued check information to the disbursement bank either at or before the time of the physical distribution of checks. The bank matches check serial numbers and dollar amounts of checks presented for payment against the issue file and pays only those checks that match the file. Any exceptions are conveyed to the company for decision to pay or return the item. Some positive pay services match against the payee field, as well as the serial number and the amount in an effort to detect altered payees. Also, many banks offer imaging services with positive pay, enabling faster identification and research of fraudulent items. The Internet is being used increasingly for notification due to the time-critical nature of returning the items.

13. Direct deposit payments have been widely used since the early 1980s. Direct deposits are transfers made from a company's account to the accounts of employees, shareholders, vendors and trading partners using ACH credit transactions. While direct deposit of payroll is the most common form of ACH payment, direct deposit is also used for employee expense reimbursements, interest payments, tax payments, dividend distributions and B2B transactions. In addition, local, state and federal tax agencies use direct deposit for tax refunds and Social Security benefit distributions. Two advantages of direct deposit are the low cost of the transactions and the certainty of timing.

14. An integrated or comprehensive accounts payable service allows a company to outsource all or part of the company's accounts payable and/or disbursements functions. There are two common approaches to managing an integrated or comprehensive accounts payable service. First, a company may periodically send a data file, containing a list of all payments to be made, to a financial service provider (FSP). The file contains information on when to issue a disbursement and to whom, as well as instructions on the payment method to be used (check, wire, ACH, foreign drafts or foreign currency). Alternatively, the FSP may maintain a database of a company's payees that includes detailed information such as preferred payment methods, specific remittance information and the names of receiving financial institutions. The database is periodically updated as new payees are added or an existing payee's remittance profile changes. Under this method, when a company needs a disbursement it sends only limited payment information to the FSP. With either approach, the FSP issues the payments immediately or "warehouses" the items according to the future date in the data file.

15. Banks provide account reconciliation services to meet companies' information and control requirements. The two primary types of services are a partial and full reconciliation. In a partial reconciliation service, a bank lists all checks paid in numerical order by check serial number or in chronological order by date paid. For each item, the paid report generally shows the check serial number, dollar amount and date paid. The listing is available as a paper report, on CD-ROM, via a direct data transmission or through a Web site. With a full reconciliation service, a company supplies an electronic file of checks issued to the bank and the bank matches checks paid against the file. Again, the bank delivers a listing of checks issued, paid and outstanding in check serial-number order via a paper report, CD-ROM, direct data transmission or a Web site.

16. Net settlement is a mechanism whereby debits or credits (in the case of financial institutions) or receivables and payables (in the case of companies) are offset between parties and only the net remaining balance is settled through funds transfers. A bank clearing house exchange is an example of the former; an intra- or intercompany settlement system between business units or trading partners is an example of the latter. Industries that employ intercompany net settlement systems include airlines, oil and gas, telecommunications and securities. At the end of a specified period of time, all of the participants in a netting system determine the net flows required to balance the system. These clearing systems process transaction information and allow participants to make periodic net settlements with each other. Net settlement benefits participants by requiring only a single transfer of the net amount due to other parties, thereby, significantly reducing the volume and cost of what would otherwise be multiple transfers.

17. To arrive at the projected closing cash position, a cash manager adjusts the opening bank available balance by adding the expected settlements in the collection (lockbox, wire and ACH) and concentration accounts (depository banks) and by deducting the projected disbursement totals. Information about checks in the process of collection and ACH credits is available from the prior day's balance reports. Lockbox and controlled disbursement totals are reported to a cash manager on a same-day basis. However, clearings of disbursements issued on accounts other than controlled disbursement accounts must be estimated. Because wire transfers are real-time transactions, notice of incoming and outgoing wires is often available on an intraday basis from all major cash management banks. The estimated closing position is then used to determine whether there will be a cash surplus or a cash deficit.

18. Internal control primarily involves checks and balances and the monitoring of transactions, cash flows and information within an organization. Appropriate use of controls such as matching, verification and separation of duties helps to protect against employee error and fraud.

19. Segregation of duties is a particularly important treasury control issue. At the management level, it is important that functional authority for collection and disbursement of funds remain independent. At an operational level, responsibilities such as approval, authorization and verification functions including expense approval, check-signing authority and account reconciliation should be separated. Internal control guidelines recommend separation of responsibility for each step of a transaction. In many organizations, personnel limitations prevent sufficient division of responsibilities. In these situations, outsourcing may provide the best solution for protecting a company's assets.

Chapter 10 – Liquidity Management

1. Liquidity is the ability to meet short-term obligations when they come due. Short-term obligations include payments to employees (payroll), vendors and suppliers, lenders and tax agencies. Management of liquidity is the treasurer's responsibility. This daily task necessitates careful measurement and continual monitoring of net working capital to ensure an organization has sufficient financial resources to pay current and upcoming obligations while, at the same time, taking advantage of opportunities to invest and/or to pay down debt when there is a cash surplus. Liquidity must be maintained to cover both expected and unexpected demands for cash.

2. It is important that adequate but not excessive, liquidity be maintained. Treasurers are concerned with the risk of having insufficient liquidity. However, excess liquidity is also costly. Cash that might otherwise be applied to outstanding debt or invested in income generating assets carry opportunity costs such as paying more interest than necessary or loss of interest earnings. Similarly, securing credit facilities is time-consuming and may be expensive because most financial institutions require payment of fees based on the level of available funds kept in reserve.

3. A forecast requires a treasurer to: (1) estimate future operating cash inflows and outflows, (2) generate a pro forma cash position and (3) identify how to cover any cash deficits or how to use any cash surpluses. The shortfall or surplus is measured relative to the predetermined minimum desired liquidity or target balances. Once developed, a cash forecast should be reviewed and updated periodically.

4. The objectives of cash forecasting are:
   - Liquidity management
   - Financial control
   - Meeting strategic objectives
   - Capital budgeting
   - Managing costs
   - Managing currency exposure

5. A receipts and disbursement (R&D) forecast is a fundamental liquidity planning tool. Construction of the forecast begins with the creation of separate schedules of cash inflows and cash outflows using accounts receivable balance patterns and distribution forecasts. A receipts schedule includes projected cash collections from customers (cash sales or payments from accounts receivable), other recurring cash inflows such as interest or dividends received from investments, as well as expected non-recurring cash inflows such as the proceeds from asset sales. A disbursements schedule involves forecasting the cash disbursements for purchases and other cash outflows, such as payroll, taxes, interest, dividends, rent and debt repayments. Completing the forecast involves combining the R&D schedules to determine the net cash flow for the period. The cash position is determined by adding cash balances from the beginning of the period to the net cash flow. This total is compared with the minimum cash position that is required to meet transaction, precautionary and speculative requirements.

6. Deciding among short-term investment alternatives involves a trade-off between risk and higher returns. Some degree of risk is inherent in all investments, with those that offer higher yields carrying greater degrees of risk. Preservation of principal is the primary objective in choosing among short-term investment alternatives. As a result, the investment policies of many organizations limit short-term portfolios to money market instruments in order to reduce risk and ensure liquidity.

7. Credit risk or default risk is the risk that payments on a security will not be made under the original terms. Credit evaluation assesses the likelihood of a security's issuer defaulting on the obligation. Most acceptable investment securities (other than U.S. Treasuries which are considered risk free because they are backed by the "full faith and credit of the U.S. government") carry credit ratings that are assigned by credit rating agencies, such as Moody's and Standard and Poor's (S&P). Credit ratings are assigned to specific securities based on the default risk and seniority of the issue, also taking into consideration any collateral, back-up lines of credit or credit enhancement provided to support the obligation. If a financial intermediary provides credit enhancement by issuing an instrument such as a standby letter of credit or surety bond to guarantee the obligation of the borrower, the obligation then assumes the credit rating of the institution providing the credit enhancement.

8. Yield is a measure of the gain an investor derives from a financial instrument. Typically, it is stated as an annual percentage rate of return. In general, higher risk is associated with higher yields. The greater the likelihood of default, the higher the risk premium and the higher the expected yield. A risk premium is the extra yield above that of a comparable risk-free security that investors require as compensation for assuming the additional risk.

9. Debt investment securities are issued as either discount instruments or interest-bearing instruments. Treasury Bills, commercial paper and banker's acceptances are discount instruments. The amount invested in a discounted investment equals the face (par) value minus the interest that will be earned over the holding period. The cash received at maturity is the face value. Interest-bearing instruments, such as certificates of deposit (CDs) and Eurodollar deposits, pay interest in arrears at maturity or at periodic intervals. The cash received at maturity from an interest-bearing security is the face value plus the interest payment. The amount invested is the face value if the security is purchased in the primary market at issuance. If, on the other hand, the security is purchased on a secondary market, the amount invested is the total amount paid, including any interest or premium paid to, or discount received from, the seller.

10. Nearly all short-term securities are issued in book-entry form. Book-entry securities are registered and transferred electronically either by the U.S. Treasury (treasury securities only) or through the commercial book-entry system. Participants in the commercial book-entry system include the Treasury, the Federal Reserve System, banks, brokers, dealers and other financial institutions. The chief advantage of book-entry securities is the ease and speed of transaction clearing without the need for movement of physical certificates. Prior to book-entry, securities were issued in bearer and registered form. Both bearer and registered securities are certificated, but they are no longer used for new issues of money market securities in the U.S.

11. A broker acts as a transaction intermediary, matching buyers and sellers of money market securities. Brokers are compensated by the fees and/or commissions they charge for their services. Brokers and dealers play key roles in the money markets by placing the majority of new issues in the primary market and providing the secondary markets with the liquidity necessary for outstanding issues. Dealers serve a dual role in the money market. Like brokers, dealers act as transaction intermediaries, but they also take positions in securities so they are able to act as the counterparty in the purchase and sale transactions. The price or yield at which the dealer will sell a security is known as the ask price; the price or yield at which the dealer will purchase a security is known as the bid price. Dealers also issue repurchase agreements, which are money market instruments used to finance their securities inventories.

12. The U.S. Treasury is the largest issuer of money market securities. Treasury issues include Treasury Bills, notes and bonds. Because of the low liquidity risk and no default risk associated with these issues, U.S. Treasury rates are considered to be risk free and serve as the benchmark against which rates and prices on other debt securities are compared. Other investment alternatives generally trade at yields above those of government securities. Interest income on U.S. Treasuries is exempt from state income tax. However, some states do charge corporations a franchise tax from which U.S. Treasury securities are not exempt.

13. Government-sponsored enterprises (GSEs) are private companies that act as financial intermediaries to provide funds for loans made in the housing, education and agriculture sectors. GSEs do not carry the credit backing of the U.S. government, though there is a strong implication that in a crisis the federal government would intervene to help repay investors because of the importance of the GSEs to public welfare. GSE securities are issued by the Federal National Mortgage Association (Fannie Mae), the Federal Farm Credit Banks Funding Corporation, the Federal Home Loan Mortgage Corporation (Freddie Mac), the Federal Home Loan Banks Office of Finance and the Student Loan Marketing Association (Sallie Mae) to provide liquidity in support of their loan programs. At the time of this publication, issues by GSEs were not required to be rated by rating agencies.

14. Bank holding companies, non-bank finance companies and non-financial businesses such as utilities, manufacturers and service companies sell CP directly to investors or through dealers. The key characteristic of CP is that it is an unsecured promissory note. CP that is issued in the public market must have maturities of 270 days or less in order to be exempt from Securities and Exchange Commission (SEC) registration requirements. Private placements of CP may have maturities of up to 360 days. CP issuers can tailor maturities to match large investors' needs, so the secondary market for CP is limited. CP is evaluated by rating agencies and may be credit enhanced. While unrated CP is available, most investors limit their CP holdings to the most highly rated issues. CP has among the highest yields of all money market investments due to its default risk and the limited secondary market.

15. Matching involves purchasing securities that mature when funds are required to meet an expected obligation or obligations. Matching allows companies to invest for extended periods and potentially increase yields. To be effective, this strategy requires careful forecasting of future cash flows and capital requirements. If cash is needed sooner than expected, the securities purchased to match a specific cash

outflow may have to be sold prematurely, perhaps at a loss. Companies that match tend to do so conservatively, covering a portion, but not the entire amount, of the expected capital need.

16. Short-term financing is used to meet temporary cash needs for periods of one year or less. While short-term financing is often equated with debt, there are actually three primary sources of short-term funds: (1) spontaneous financing such as trade credit, (2) sale of accounts receivable and (3) borrowing arrangements with banks, finance companies or in the money markets. In addition, multidivisional businesses may allow internal borrowing from subsidiaries.

17. The objective of short-term financing is to ensure adequate credit availability at minimum cost, minimum risk and with maximum flexibility. The amount and timing of short-term credit requirements are identified through cash forecasting. The cost of borrowing funds depends on the type of credit facility used, with the least costly funds usually provided through spontaneous financing. Major costs of formal credit arrangements include interest, fees and underwriter or dealer costs.

18. Financing issues represent an investment for the lender or counterparty to the transaction. As a consequence, the factors that influence investment yield are the determinants of credit pricing. Pricing and fees on loans increase with default risk, price risk, liquidity and length of maturity. Factors that enter into borrowing costs yet do not impact investor's yields include dealer and placement fees, credit enhancement and backup credit costs.

19. Bank credit is an important source of short-term funds for businesses. Bank borrowings are the chief source of working capital for middle market and smaller companies. Larger organizations often find bank credit attractive because banks are able to customize debt structures and use private information to underwrite the debt. Bank loans may be offered on a secured basis or an unsecured basis. Security, provided in the form of collateral or guarantees, may be used to obtain more favorable rates by some borrowers or to make credit available to businesses that are unable to access unsecured credit facilities. In addition, use of private information (i.e., information that is not publicly disclosed) by a lender may also result in lower borrowing costs.

20. A revolving credit agreement, also known as a revolver, is a committed line of credit that is established for a specified period of time, often on a multiyear basis. Revolving credits are formal contractual commitments with loan agreements, including covenants. Usually, there is a commitment fee on the unused portion, as well as a fee for use of the borrowing facility. While often used for short-term borrowing, the commitment term typically ranges from two to five years and may be followed by a period in which the principal is systematically repaid. If more than a year is left on a multiyear revolver, current GAAP guidelines allow balances on this agreement to be carried as a long-term liability on the borrower's balance sheet.

21. Commercial finance companies and some commercial banks specialize in asset-based lending. Asset-based lines of credit are secured by accounts receivable and inventory. They are often used to support temporary

working capital needs. Because availability of an asset-based line is closely tied to the level of the collateral, advances are made as additional collateral is generated and are liquidated as the underlying receivables are collected or as inventories are sold. Because the collateral serves as the primary source of repayment, a lender closely evaluates and monitors the asset.

22. Some organizations outsource investment management in order to increase yield and provide fiduciary oversight. For example, an investor may purchase shares in mutual funds, thereby capitalizing on the investment management expertise of the fund manager. The wide range of mutual fund options that are available allows a company to easily tailor its investments to risk/return objectives. Hiring registered investment advisors is another outsourcing alternative. Outsourcing of investment management is often cost effective and allows treasury personnel to focus on more time-critical daily tasks. However, it is important to establish clear risk/return objectives and to monitor investment management performance on a regular basis.

Chapter 11 – Treasury Systems and Information Management

1. It is the cash manager who typically prepares a daily cash-position worksheet in order to: (1) reconcile the prior day cash balance, (2) determine cash requirements, (3) track activity, (4) identify opportunities, (5) update cash forecasts and (6) update management information.

2. The primary benefits of implementing treasury management systems generally include improved productivity and expedited data gathering, compilation and analysis. Faster access to treasury data also often results in increased forecasting accuracy, reduced borrowing expenses, improved short-term investment returns and improved management reporting.

3. For a global company, treasury information management systems centralize reporting and transaction initiation on a worldwide basis, resulting in increased control, more accurate data for decision making and reduced expenses. Treasury information management is also necessary to accomplish the pooling of subsidiary funds either regionally or globally. It also allows a company to maximize overall liquidity, increase control and optimize interest earnings. The implementation of global payment and netting systems enables a global enterprise to reduce overall foreign exchange (FX) costs, to minimize transaction costs and to better manage a worldwide cash position.

4. The initial costs of implementing treasury management systems include hardware and software selection, purchase, installation, start-up and personnel training expenses. On an ongoing basis, fixed costs include administration, overhead, software maintenance, licensing and upgrades; variable costs include telecommunications charges, transaction service charges and system security expenses.

5. Cash managers utilize a wide variety of internal information gathered from other areas of the company. One of the primary uses for internal data is to prepare a cash receipts and disbursements (R&D) forecast. The key sources for generating this forecast are the sales summary reports (information on actual and projected weekly or monthly sales) and purchasing summary reports (information on actual and projected weekly or monthly purchases). An aging schedule, which provides information on the aggregate status of accounts receivable and on large collection items still outstanding, is also useful for preparing the forecast. Ultimately, the R&D forecast is linked to the company's investment and debt repayment schedules.

6. Companies that have relationships with two or more financial service providers (FSPs) may establish an arrangement in which one of the company's FSPs or a third-party reporting service gathers and consolidates the account balances and transaction activity from each of the company's financial institutions. This arrangement is commonly referred to as multibank reporting or data exchange. Many FSPs offer this type of service via the Internet.

7. There are three major standardized formats for transmission of external data: the BAI, ASC X12 821 and the S.W.I.F.T. MT940. The first two are used primarily by U.S. financial institutions for domestic

transactions. They include the Bank Administration Institute (BAI) format and the Accredited Standards Committee (ASC) X12 821 Financial-Information Reporting transaction set. The BAI format is more established and more commonly used; however, an enhanced BAI-2 format is replacing the original BAI format. In addition, there is a migration toward ASC X12 821, which is an electronic data interchange (EDI) transaction set. For international transactions, financial institutions use the S.W.I.F.T. MT940 format (statement with detail).

8. When implementing electronic communications with FSPs, treasury managers must consider cost limitations, security concerns and, for global companies, the telecommunications infrastructure of different countries. The manner in which FSP information is linked to the company's other applications or ERP system must also be considered.

9. A treasury workstation, sometimes referred to as a Treasury Management System (TMS), is typically PC- or client server-based and has software that gathers information from both internal and external sources. A TMS compiles financial data for the purposes of analysis and decision-making, thereby automating a number of manual tasks. These systems also enable a treasury department to prepare and distribute financial information in a variety of customized spreadsheets and management reports and be either standalone or part of a company's computer network.

10. STP is an initiative being considered by many financial institutions to streamline transactions by maintaining contact throughout all stages of the processing of those transactions. It is presently in discussion and early development, and represents a major shift from present-day T+3 trading (settlement within three business days after a transaction) toward same-day settlement by removing redundant operations and utilizing electronic transfers.

11. Some of the large ERP software providers offer integrated treasury modules for their systems. Companies that implement corporate-wide ERP systems are better able to link information technology to corporate strategy and to daily operational functions on a standardized and timely basis. Generally, however, the current offering of ERP treasury modules does not provide the same level of functionality as standalone offerings. Standalone TMS and other treasury software offered by FSPs or third parties are often tailored to specific needs of individual treasury departments. Most of the larger systems also provide access to multibank reporting and interfaces to major ERP systems. The more sophisticated of these systems address treasury-specific issues such as financial risk management and support for FAS133, none of which are available on most ERP systems.

12. The three most common types of risk involved with treasury management systems are data loss, unauthorized user access and computer viruses.

13. All TMS and other electronic communications systems are vulnerable to disasters or catastrophic events. As a result, all organizations should have disaster recovery plans that include identifying internal and external threats, assessing general business risks and monitoring for corporate espionage. It is important to

determine the requirements for performing critical tasks and to develop backup or alternative systems and sites. To be effective, disaster recovery plans should be approved by top management, tested at least every six months and kept as current as possible.

14. One of the primary benefits of using the Internet is the easy access to services and applications. In an Internet/browser environment, the software typically resides on a server, rather than locally on a user's PC. This allows access to a wide range of applications with greater flexibility from multiple, non-traditional remote locations and business units outside treasury. This ease of access may also simplify restoring a system after a computer failure or another type of disaster. Using the Internet in treasury also allows for easier implementation and version control. For many applications, software does not have to be installed at the user's site. Instead, initial installations and upgrades can be executed from a remote location for multiple users in multiple sites. It is also possible to utilize the Internet or an intranet for project management and collaborative work on projects and documents. For example, many financial institutions use browser-based technology to implement intranet-based proposal development and customer quality service programs. The Internet or an extranet can also be used for presentations and virtual meetings to share information with a large number of both internal and external users. Finally, the Internet is proving to be an extremely inexpensive communications vehicle. This is a major benefit for large, global companies with widely dispersed operating units.

Chapter 12 – Electronic Commerce

1. E-commerce is defined as the application of information and secure network technology for the purpose of facilitating business relationships among trading partners. E-commerce encompasses many types of formats and communications protocols, including traditional electronic data interchange (EDI), financial electronic data interchange (FEDI), and Web-based commerce. E-commerce may be conducted by means of three applications: the Internet, an intranet or an extranet.

2. The Internet is an unrestricted, worldwide network that allows access to anyone with the appropriate hardware and software. In essence, the Internet is a collection of many computer networks linked together to form a global communications pathway. Many companies also use intranets. Intranets are internal networks ("intra" meaning internal or within a company) that utilize commonly available browser technology to provide data and applications for employees or other authorized internal users. An intranet uses the open standards of the Internet, rather than proprietary software, for communications among a company's computers. In addition to the Internet and intranets, many companies also use extranets. Extranets are external networks ("extra" meaning external or outside a company). Extranets are most commonly used by trading partners (suppliers) and customers. A typical example would be a bank that provides an extranet for customers to access account information.

3. Electronic data interchange (EDI) is a traditional form of e-commerce that utilizes structured electronic transactions within established standards to exchange data from one company's business application system to another company's business application system.

4. Financial EDI (FEDI) and electronic funds transfer (EFT) refer to the area of electronic commerce related to payments and/or payment information. FEDI and EFT are subsets of EDI. FEDI is the electronic transmission of payments and/or payment-related information in a standard format between trading partners and/or the company's banks. FEDI includes such business applications as invoices, payment initiations, lockbox deposit reports and remittance information sent directly to a trading partner and processed through a financial institution or third-party communications intermediary. EFT is the exchange of value associated with a FEDI application. EFT requires the involvement of financial intermediaries, such as banks and the Federal Reserve, to send and receive electronic payments. Examples of EFT include wire transfers, automated clearing house (ACH) payments, and other electronic value-transfer systems such as CHIPS in the U.S., CHAPS in the U.K. and TARGET in the European Monetary Union.

5. One of the key benefits of e-commerce is improved productivity. Once data is entered at the beginning of a transaction, the same data can move from one business application system to another without manual intervention. E-commerce eliminates manual processes such as filing, matching, sorting and retrieving material, as well as envelope stuffing, stamping and mailing. It also significantly reduces cycle time because e-commerce transactions have no mail-time delays, involve minimal processing time, and facilitate JIT inventory management in many companies, all of which are key objectives of working capital

management. Because e-commerce makes data reentry unnecessary, it reduces error rates and enables faster data processing. For example, using e-commerce for the receipt of remittance information allows for greater accuracy in the posting of payments to the accounts receivable ledger. E-commerce eliminates mail time, thereby, reducing uncertainty in cash flow timing, enabling more accurate cash flow forecasting and improving management of working capital. It also offers improved communication capabilities. For example, acknowledgment that a customer has received an invoice (which is not available in a mail-based system) helps to resolve issues of payment timing between the buyer and the seller.

6. By convention, numbers and names are used to identify ASC X12 transaction sets. Transaction sets are generally defined as the electronic equivalent of a paper business document or form, with specific rules governing formats. As defined by NACHA (National Automated Clearing House Association), the common EDI transaction sets used in the finance arena include the following:
   - 810 Invoice
   - 820 Payment Order/Remittance Advice
   - 821 Financial Information Reporting
   - 822 Customer Account Analysis
   - 823 Lockbox Information
   - 824 Application Advice
   - 828 Debit Authorization
   - 835 Health Care Claim Payment/Advice
   - 997 Functional Acknowledgment

7. EDI software assembles information into transaction sets for electronic transmission. Transaction sets are either created by a company or provided by a third party. Additionally, transaction sets can be provided by a single integrated software package or by several software programs that exchange information. The basic functions are file conversion, translation/mapping and communication.

8. A VAN is a communication intermediary that provides various services to the users of e-commerce. VANs were developed during the inception of EDI to help resolve interface problems between two companies with different computer systems, different format needs and different protocols. VANs make it easier for companies to implement EDI and to add new EDI trading partners. Value-added networks also offer implementation assistance in the form of consulting, software and training of trading partners. Finally, because a VAN is essentially a private network, it can provide enhanced security for commercial transactions.

9. Some banks provide VAN-related services for B2B payment information to support the translation of electronic payment and remittance data between trading partners that use different communication protocols. Some of these banks also provide EDI information services not directly related to payments or FEDI. Most electronic banking services are related to either the payment or the collection process.

10. There are two types of providers in the Internet/e-commerce arena. The first is an Internet service provider (ISP), which is a communications intermediary that provides Internet service to individuals and small businesses, typically over telephone lines (T-1 or T-3 lines), cable, satellite or wireless. The other provider is an application service provider (ASP), which offers individuals or organizations access via the Internet to application programs and related services that would otherwise have to be located on individual personal computers or on a company's computer network. Many companies fully integrate Internet systems with existing business ERP and application systems. This is known as enterprise application integration (EAI).

11. XML, or eXtensible markup language, is an extension of HTML that allows the content and the structure to be defined. In essence, while HTML provides a consistent format for displaying information, XML adds "tags" that specifically define the information. For example, HTML ensures that the price of an item on a Web page appears on a certain place on the page and in a specific font, size, and color. XML further ensures that a specific field is the price of a specific item. Once a data element has been clearly identified, it is easy to transfer this information from the Web page to an application within the company.

12. Wherever external users are allowed access to internal applications or data, it is important to utilize a "firewall" to protect the internal systems. The purpose of a firewall is to ensure that only authorized users are allowed to access data or data systems. They also help to protect against viruses and other system compromises. Firewalls may be software based, hardware based or a combination of both.

13. A digital signature is a message encoded with the sender's secret private key. The receiver can identify the source using the sender's public key. So long as the private key is never shared with anyone, it is impossible to forge a digital signature. A digital signature is tied to a document and to the signer; the signer's digital signature will be different for each document signed. A digital signature serves four purposes: (1) data integrity, which verifies that the message has not been altered; (2) origin authentication, which verifies where the message came from; (3) user authentication, which verifies who sent the message and (4) non-repudiation, which ensures that the message/transaction cannot be denied as sent or received. Note that a digital signature is different from a "digitized signature," which is used as a facsimile signature on laser-printed checks.

14. E-commerce enables companies to complete processing more rapidly. EFT also removes much of the payment float resulting from mail, processing, availability, and clearing delays. Therefore, many trading partners are forced to reexamine conventional credit terms because faster payments are viewed as a disadvantage to buyers and an advantage to sellers. To compensate buyers for the shortening of the cash flow timeline (i.e., shortening of days' payables), sellers often must negotiate new e-commerce-based credit terms. This is frequently referred to as "float neutralization."

15. Paid-on-production is the process by which a payment record is created for goods and/or services when they are used rather than when they are shipped or delivered. The reason for this is that in a manufacturing environment, unlike a retail environment, there are multiple legal concerns related to liability, potential bankruptcy and use of inventory assets for supporting loans. In a retail environment,

the title to merchandise transfers from the supplier to the buyer when the merchandise is delivered to the buyer's receiving dock. In a manufacturing environment, the title to raw materials or finished goods transfers when the product is used in the manufacturing process. Therefore, it is critical to determine exactly when and where the transfer of title takes place.

Chapter 13 – Sources of Capital and Leasing

1. The treasury area of a company plays a very important role in both the determination and the management of a company's cost of capital. The treasurer, along with the CFO and the Board of Directors, is typically responsible for determining the type and amount of various forms of capital that are raised. In addition, the treasurer is often responsible for the management of a company's issued securities. The mix of different types of securities, the timing of the issues, and the perceptions of a company by analysts and investors ultimately determine the overall availability and cost of capital for a company.

2. There are advantages and disadvantages to raising capital through public offerings. One of the principal advantages is that access to capital markets offers the potential to raise large amounts of debt and equity at prevailing rates. One of the primary disadvantages is the significant costs involved in managing the reporting, disclosure and rating-agency requirements for public security issues.

3. A treasurer may have to manage trustee relationships and responsibilities relative to a company's securities, as well as act as disbursing agent for shareholder or bondholder payments. Shareholders must receive dividends as declared for preferred and common stock. Bondholders must receive interest payments. Also, any sinking fund obligations (funds accumulated in a custodial account to retire debt instruments according to a predetermined schedule) or covenants on bond issues must be met. Financial reports must be completed and sent to interested parties in a timely manner and various reports must be prepared and sent to regulatory agencies such as the SEC. Management must also plan for the future retirement of maturing issues and manage bank credit relationships.

4. Organizations can raise debt capital in either the short-term money market or the long-term capital market. In either case, debt capital typically imposes a fixed payment requirement on a company. The interest portion of these payments is usually tax deductible and must be paid prior to any payments to equity holders. In addition, debt holders have priority claims on a company's assets in the event of financial distress. Debt that is senior has a higher priority than debt that is junior or subordinate. Finally, given the fixed nature and tax deductibility of debt payments, the use of debt provides financial leverage for a company.

5. Many organizations find that short-term borrowing is an important source of financing, for several reasons. Short-term borrowing is often more flexible and easier to access in comparison with long-term financing. Therefore, short-term borrowing is often used in increasing amounts until refinancing for a longer term is economically justified. Short-term borrowing may also provide a temporary source of financing to support a temporary need for funds, such as seasonal increases in accounts receivable and/or inventory. Another important consideration is the use of maturity matching for an organization's short-term debt. This involves matching the maturity of the debt to the specific financing needs of an organization. An example would be a company that borrows to purchase inventory, then pays off the loan as the inventory is sold. Finally, short-term borrowing is offered at a fixed or variable interest rate.

6. A term loan is a loan with a fixed maturity, usually greater than one year, that can be repaid either in installments or in a single payment. Frequently, a term loan is issued for a specific financing need such as the purchase of a new plant new equipment or general expansion. Interest is usually paid at periodic intervals and may be fixed or variable. A term loan is usually secured by the asset being financed, and the maturity is related to the useful life of the asset. For many organizations, leasing of equipment is an alternative to term loans, especially in instances when the seller/manufacturer of the equipment provides specialized leasing arrangements.

7. Industrial revenue bonds are tax-exempt bonds, sometimes referred to as industrial-development bonds, issued by a state or local government agency to finance industrial or commercial projects that serve a public good. The bond is not usually backed by the full faith and credit of the government that issues the bond but rather is backed by the company that sponsors the project or, in some cases, by a bank letter of credit. These types of bonds should not be confused with government revenue bonds.

8. An indenture is a legal document that outlines the rights and obligations of both the borrower (bond issuer) and the lender (bondholder). These indentures may be quite lengthy and include various restrictive covenants that impose constraints on the actions of a company's management. These covenants may be negative (i.e., actions the company cannot take, such as double pledging of collateral) or affirmative (i.e., actions the company must take, such as providing regular financial statements or maintaining certain financial ratios). The purpose of the document is to protect the bondholders from actions by a company's management that would increase the value of equity holders or other stakeholders at the expense of bondholders. Violation of an indenture agreement is usually sufficient grounds for the bondholders to make the debt immediately due and payable, which may force a company into bankruptcy. In addition, the SEC approves indenture agreements in public offerings and ensures that all indenture provisions are met before allowing a company to sell new securities to the general public.

9. Defeasance of debt is a method for removing debt from an organization's balance sheet without actually retiring the debt issue. In this arrangement, the borrower places sufficient funds in escrow, usually in U.S. government securities, to pay for interest and principal on the debt issue. Because control of both the debt and escrow funds is relinquished, and payment and retirement of the debt issue is now guaranteed, this debt (and the related securities) can be removed from the balance sheet, as well as any restrictive covenants related to the debt. (Defeasance of debt is covered under FAS 140.)

10. When a subsidiary of a larger company is borrowing funds or floating a bond issue, the lenders may require that the parent corporation (or sister subsidiary, supplier, customer or other entity) provide a guarantee of principal for the arrangement. In some cases a subsidiary may even provide a guarantee for the parent. This allows lenders recourse to the parent company (or guaranteeing party) to obtain payment in the event the subsidiary is in default.

11. There are several considerations relative to bond ratings. The first consideration is the bond rating criteria used by the agency. Ratings are generally based on both qualitative and quantitative factors but tend to be

somewhat subjective. Given the complexity of most large companies, there is no precise mathematical formula that analysts can use to determine the rating; instead, many factors must be taken into account. The second consideration is the importance of the bond ratings to both investors and company management. Many charters restrict institutional investors to buying investment grade bonds, or better, and these investors make up the bulk of the bond market. Also, a company's bond rating is considered a direct measure of the riskiness of a company, and this has an impact on a company's cost of capital (i.e., the rating sets the pricing). The third consideration is related to changes in bond ratings. Rating agencies review outstanding bonds on a periodic basis and may upgrade or downgrade an issue based on changes either in a company or in the general economic environment. Companies or government entities with downgraded bonds have a more difficult time raising additional capital in the market and have to pay a higher price for bonds issued or other debt incurred.

12. Maturity matching involves matching the life of a debt issue to the life of any assets being financed. Generally, companies do try to match maturities of debt issues and assets wherever possible in order to reduce the overall risk of a company.

13. The leasing decision process has two general stages. First, there is the acquisition decision, a process by which a company decides to acquire a particular building or asset, basing the decision on regular capital budgeting procedures. The decision to acquire the asset is not the issue of an analysis because the decision to proceed with the project has already been made. Second, there is the decision whether to finance the asset by either purchase or lease. For capital structure purposes, leasing normally has the same effect on capital structure as borrowing, so the cash flows from leasing are usually compared with the cash flows from borrowing funds to purchase the asset.

14. Operating leases, also known as service leases, are established in such a way that the lessor provides maintenance for the equipment and retains ownership of the equipment at the end of the lease. These are often done on an off-balance-sheet basis, meaning that the lease payments are reflected only on the income statement, but neither the assets nor the lease appear on the balance sheet. Operating leases usually run for periods substantially shorter than the life of the equipment. This means that the lease payments usually are not sufficient to amortize the equipment, but the lessor intends to make up the full value of the equipment upon the release or sale at the end of the lease contract. In analyzing operating leases, it is important to carefully consider the flexibility of cancellation policies.

15. Treasury stock is defined as stock issued by a company but later reacquired. It may be held in the company's treasury indefinitely, reissued to the public or retired. Treasury stock receives no dividends and does not carry voting power while held by the company. It is considered to be issued but not outstanding and is, therefore deducted, from any capital calculations.

16. Although preferred stock is considered equity, it is different from common stock both in terms of stockholder rights and in the payment stream. In terms of cash flows, it is more like debt than equity because of the fixed nature of the return. Unlike debt, however, a company does not risk bankruptcy by

missing a preferred stock dividend. Another difference is that preferred stock does not have the tax deductibility feature that debt does; therefore, the cost is generally much higher than that of a similar debt issue.

17. In general, a security (or any asset) derives its value from the cash flow stream returned to the investor through the life of the security. The valuation of the asset includes the opportunity cost or required return to the investor; therefore, the valuation must take into account the time value of money. In short, the value of any security is the present value of all the cash flows from the security discounted at an appropriate interest rate.

18. The Capital Asset Pricing Model (CAPM) describes one possible relationship between risk and required rate of return for equity securities (stocks). The CAPM is based on the concept that the typical investor holds a diversified portfolio of stocks and that the only measure of risk relevant to such an investor is the beta of a stock. Beta is defined as the risk of a particular stock relative to an overall stock market measure, such as the S&P 500 Index. The betas for most major companies are calculated by many different sources and are readily available for interested investors. The basic model assumes a linear relationship between the return on any particular stock and that stock's beta.

19. The primary sources of funds for a company, especially long-term funds, are debt and equity capital in the form of newly issued common stock and retained earnings. It is important for an investor to recognize that the most important item is the marginal cost of these components; that is, what the cost is of raising new amounts of these forms of capital. Using the marginal, or expected, cost of these components provides an investor with the market's current evaluation of a company's risk and, therefore, the required rate of return. There is an additional consideration, however, as changes in a company's capital structure impact the marginal costs of individual capital components.

20. Companies that are already publicly traded may, from time to time, offer additional shares of stock in order to raise new equity capital. These are generally classified as primary distributions of authorized, but previously unissued, common shares. Secondary distributions involve stock previously issued that is now being resold, such as the sale of treasury stock.

21. A large, well-known corporation that frequently issues securities may file a master registration statement with the SEC and update it with a short-form statement just prior to each of the initial offerings. This form of shelf registration allows a company to bring an issue to market quickly in order to take advantage of market conditions that make rates for particular sources attractive. This form of registration is made available under SEC Rule 415 and can be used by publicly traded companies that are already reporting on a quarterly basis to the SEC. Securities that are shelf registered may be sold at any time over a two-year period following the registration by a process resembling competitive bidding. Under this rule, a company

simply announces the intention to issue all or part of the securities registered under the shelf registration and receives offers from investment banks. Because the stock issue essentially sells at the prevailing market price, the investment bank with the smallest spread generally receives the right to underwrite the issue.

22. The term IPO is used to describe an issuer's first public offering of a security of any class, although the term tends to be limited to common stock. The term is also used to designate an offering of previously authorized but unissued, securities. For companies with equity securities that are not currently available to the public, or are not listed on one of the various exchanges, the decision to go public and/or to list the company's securities can be critical to a company's future growth.

23. The primary advantage of having a company's stock listed on one of the organized exchanges is that the marketability of the stock increases. In general, listing is advantageous to both a company and the public because a company's stock can be more widely traded and more investors have access to it. Listing can also result in higher sales for a company because of increased public exposure. Due to the increased level of disclosure required, listing may also lower the required rate of return on a company's common stock and, ultimately, the overall cost of capital, thereby increasing a company's value in the market.

Chapter 14 – Capital Structure and Dividend Policy

1. The capital structure of a company refers to the mix of long-term financing sources used to raise capital. Although there are many possible components of long-term capital, the two major categories are debt and common equity (both retained earnings and new common stock). These two components have the greatest impact in determining a company's overall cost of capital.

2. The desirability of debt is due to: (1) The effective cost of debt is lower because interest expense is tax deductible and (2) The stockholders do not have to share any of the company's profits with debt holders because the debt holders receive a fixed rate of return. The disadvantages of debt include: (1) The more outstanding debt a company has, the riskier it is considered; (2) The riskier a company is considered, the higher interest it will have to pay for future debt issuance and (3) Bankruptcy may result if the company becomes unable to meet its debt-service obligations.

3. Management tends to behave as if there were an ideal capital structure for a given company. In theory, there is a certain level of debt for each company that minimizes the overall cost of capital and, therefore, maximizes the value of the company. The general consensus is that some use of debt is desirable but too much debt is undesirable. However, there is significant dispute regarding what constitutes the "optimal" level of debt and how to determine that level. In practice, the weight generally used is the company's target capital structure; that is, the proportion of each component that management has determined is best for the company. In many cases, new capital will be raised according to this target by either employing the target ratio for any new capital or moving toward that ratio over time.

4. In the context of the asymmetric information theory, the management of a company has access to more accurate information than the stockholders on a company's prospects. In a world with asymmetric information (management has better information than shareholders), corporations would generally issue new shares only if one of the following is true: (1) A company has very profitable investments that cannot be postponed or financed by debt or (2) Management considers the shares of a company to be overvalued. Most investors are aware of these facts. Consequently, investors tend to devalue a company's stock when it announces plans to issue new stock. This is especially true when investors believe that management considers the stock to be overvalued or when management places the interests of existing shareholders above those of prospective shareholders. That is, investors view the new stock issue as a negative signal.

5. Business risk is the risk associated with a company's operating capabilities and policies, as well as the volatility of operating income or earnings before interest and taxes (EBIT). Some companies use other operating profit measures such as EBITDA (earnings before interest, taxes, depreciation and amortization) in calculating business risk. Three of the factors that affect EBIT volatility are product demand variability, sales price variability and resource cost variability. All three factors must be analyzed to gain a thorough understanding of business risk. One indicator of a company's business risk is the use of operating leverage, which are the fixed costs in the production of a product. The presence of fixed costs magnifies the impact of changes in other factors, such as price and variable costs.

6. Financial risk is best understood in the context of financial leverage. The fixed costs associated with financial leverage increase the impact of operating leverage. Changes in variables such as product demand, sales price and resource costs have more of an impact on companies that use financial leverage than on companies that do not. A company's total risk increases as it utilizes more financial leverage. Because management's goal should be to maximize shareholder value, management may take actions that will benefit shareholders at the expense of bondholders. The bondholders will protect themselves by introducing (or adding) covenants restricting management actions. These restrictions may cause a company to be less efficient, thereby adding an agency cost to the overall management cost of a company. In other words, there is an issue of agency risk between shareholders and bondholders in a company's use of debt.

7. The main advantage of new common stock financing is that it does not obligate a company to make fixed payments to investors. In addition, it has no specific maturity date. For creditors, stock offers a cushion against losses and, if a company's future is bright, equity can often be raised on attractive terms. The main disadvantage of common stock financing is that the sale of common stock may extend voting rights and control to more shareholders. This may be problematic for smaller companies where the principal owner and management are one and the same. In the event a company does well, the profits must be divided among a larger group of stockholders. Also, the cost of underwriting common stock is significant when compared with other sources of capital. Finally, common equity financing does not enjoy the tax shield (deductibility of interest expense) that debt financing provides and, hence, costs more than debt.

8. Management decisions regarding dividend policy have a major impact on capital costs for a company. Steadily increasing dividends may make a company's stock more attractive to certain institutional investors and, perhaps, increase the stock price. However, increasing dividends reduces the amount of cash flow (in the form of retained earnings) that a company has available for expansion. This may slow a company's growth, hence its ability to provide capital appreciation for investors. A company may then become less attractive to investors who prefer high levels of capital gains to regular income in the form of dividends. In effect, dividend policy determines the type of investor who may be interested in becoming a shareholder.

9. The optimal dividend policy is one that: (1) maximizes shareholder value, (2) maintains adequate retained earnings for future expansion and (3) distributes corporate income to investors.

10. Some of the primary constraints on dividend policy are those listed in bond indentures or loan covenants. Most debt contracts limit the ability of a company to pay dividends by imposing protective covenants related to maintaining specific financial ratios. These covenants are intended to prevent stockholders from draining assets from a company at the expense of bondholders and other creditors. There may also be restrictions related to preferred stock. Preferred stock is often cumulative in nature, which requires all past preferred stock dividends (dividends in arrears) to be paid in full before any common dividend can be paid. Typically, there are also restrictions related to impairment of capital for a company. Dividend payments usually cannot exceed retained earnings on the balance sheet. This serves as protection for the creditors of a company. Dividends may be paid out of capital, but the source must be indicated as such

and must not reduce capital below the limits stated in a company's debt covenants. A company needs to ensure that adequate cash is available to pay dividends. If not, then the company has to access unused borrowing facilities to raise cash for the dividend. However, borrowing to finance dividends should be done only when absolutely necessary and only on a short-term basis.

11. There is significant evidence that dividends have a signaling effect. Dividends "contain" information for stockholders that "signal" the intentions of the management. It has been noted that for most companies, dividends tend to be fairly stable or exhibit a constant rate of growth. Even companies that have periods of abnormal dividend growth usually settle into a stable growth pattern. The general hypothesis is that when a company's management declares an unexpected increase in the upcoming dividends (higher than expected growth), it is signaling good news to the stock market. This positive information translates into a higher price for a company's stock. Management does not announce higher dividends unless it is certain that it is able to maintain the higher level. Similarly, if dividends are announced that are unexpectedly low or if dividends are eliminated, this signals bad news and the price of a company's stock drops. Management can, therefore, use dividends as a signal to investors concerning a company's future earnings potential.

12. The ex-dividend date is the date on which the stock is sold without the upcoming dividend attached. The ex-dividend date is usually four business days prior to the holder-of-record date, thereby enabling brokerage firms to send the updated list of stockholders to a company on time. Theoretically, there is a drop in the price of the stock equivalent to the dividend on the ex-dividend date. However, this is difficult to measure because other factors may influence the market price.

13. With stock dividends, a company pays the shareholders additional shares of stock rather than cash dividends. In actuality, the economic impact of a stock dividend is the same as that of a stock split. That is, the per-share price of the stock is reduced because additional shares are in circulation, but there is no real impact on shareholder wealth. However, there may be additional costs to a company for managing the record keeping for the new shares. If a company is in a period of rapid growth and needs to retain all earnings for reinvestment, then stock dividends may be a means of compensating shareholders for their loyalty.

14. For multinational companies (MNCs), dividend policy may be constrained by foreign government regulations and tax laws. The intent of these regulations is either to prevent repatriation of capital (the transfer of profits from an international subsidiary back to the domestic parent) or to make sure that the MNC pays its fair share of taxes on profits earned within the country. Some governments may restrict, block or tax this movement of funds in order to force the MNC to reinvest the funds locally. In addition, the existence of bilateral or multilateral tax treaties may have significant impacts on dividend policy.

Chapter 15 – Global Treasury Environment

1. The objectives of global treasury management are similar to those of U.S. treasury management. The main objective is the efficient utilization of an organization's global cash resources in a manner consistent with its strategic goals. International treasury management, like domestic treasury management, involves daily, time-critical functions such as collection, concentration, disbursement, liquidity management (short-term investing and borrowing) and information management. However, unlike domestic treasury management, international treasury management also involves cross-border funds movement, foreign exchange (FX), and liquidity management techniques that are different from those in the U.S. Therefore, the selection of financial service providers capable of assisting a company with international operations is a critical aspect of the global treasury-management process.

2. Political or sovereign risk is the risk that a company's operations in a foreign country may be nationalized or expropriated by the government of that country. In nationalization, a government takes over all companies in a specific industry, such as the oil or mining industry. In expropriation, a government takes over a single company. Other types of political risk include: (1) blocked currencies, in which profits cannot be converted from the local currency into a major trading currency, (2) forced reinvestment, in which funds cannot be transferred out of the country in any form and (3) required majority ownership, in which companies must be owned by resident nationals. In The Peoples Republic of China, for example, foreign subsidiaries or foreign-owned entities encounter all three of these types of sovereign risk.

3. Foreign exchange (FX) rates are quoted in several ways, depending on the currencies and the markets involved. An FX rate is generally expressed as the equivalent unit of one currency per unit of another currency. From a U.S. perspective, there are two ways to quote FX rates: (1) the U.S. dollar equivalent of one unit of the foreign currency (typically used for the British Pound and euro) or (2) the amount of the foreign currency per one U.S. dollar (used for all other currencies).

4. There are two basic FX markets: the spot market and the forward market. A rate quoted in the spot market for currency is called a spot FX rate (spot rate). These rates are generally quoted for delivery one or two business days from the date of the trade. Faster delivery may be possible but at a rate higher than the spot rate. A forward FX rate (forward rate) is an exchange rate established today for a currency transaction with delivery occurring beyond two business days in the future. Deliveries under most forward FX contracts occur within a year from the trade date. However, delivery dates beyond one year are available for actively traded currencies.

5. Par – If the spot rate and the forward rate are the same, then the forward rate is at par to the spot rate. In theory, this implies that the interest rate structure between the two countries is exactly the same. Because this is extremely rare, currencies generally trade at a discount or premium.

   Discount – A currency is at a discount when it is worth less in the forward market than in the spot market.

The currency with the higher interest rate will sell at a discount in the forward market against a currency with a lower interest rate.

Premium – A currency is at a premium when it is worth more in the forward market than in the spot market. The currency with the lower interest rate will sell at a premium in the forward market against a currency with a higher interest rate.

6. The Society for Worldwide Interbank Financial Telecommunication (S.W.I.F.T.)® is an interbank telecommunication network that enables banks to send authenticated electronic messages in standard formats. Established in the 1970s, S.W.I.F.T. currently has over 7,500 member financial institutions in approximately 200 countries. The communications initiated and received by member banks are known as S.W.I.F.T. messages. Messages cover a wide range of international banking services. A company can request a bank to initiate a balance transfer or foreign payment through S.W.I.F.T. S.W.I.F.T. communications contain payment-related information but do not transfer value. The clearing and settlement of S.W.I.F.T. messages are accomplished through correspondent bank balances.

7. Continuous Linked Settlement (CLS)® is a recent development in the global financial community that allows for international currency transactions to be settled on a same-day basis. CLS provides a real-time global settlement system in which settlement risk due to time zones, legal jurisdiction and operating procedures are significantly reduced. CLS is operated by the CLS Bank, which began operations in late 2002 with the goal of eliminating cross-border intraday settlement exposures. CLS Bank has offices in New York, London and Tokyo. It is owned by about 70 of the world's largest financial institutions and has links to all of the major central banks in North America, Europe and Asia.

8. The U.K., Switzerland, the Netherlands, France, Belgium, Japan and the majority of the Nordic countries have giro systems that operate through postal and/or banking channels. Giros are consumer-based payment systems that transfer payments from one account to another using direct debits and credits. Consumers use the giro system in place of checks for payment of monthly bills. In many countries, consumers access these systems via PCs, terminals or telephones. Though primarily used for consumer-initiated payments, there is experimental use of giros for B2B and B2C payments in some European countries.

9. Most banking systems are less fragmented than the U.S. system. In the U.S., there are thousands of independent financial institutions, ranging from those with extensive branch networks to those with single locations. In the majority of other countries, the banking system is characterized by a few large banks operating on a nationwide basis.

10. The Canadian Payments Association (CPA), which is a non-profit association created by an Act of Parliament in 1980, operates a national system for the clearing and settlement of checks, performs electronic funds transfers and manages the evolution of the national payment system. CPA membership comprises the Bank of Canada and virtually all of Canada's bank and non-bank deposit-taking financial institutions. The CPA currently operates two systems for the clearing and settlement of payments: the

Automated Clearing Settlement System (ACSS) and the Large Value Transfer System (LVTS). In addition, the U.S. Bulk Exchange (USBE), a system parallel to the ACSS, is used for the clearing of payment items denominated in U.S. dollars and for settlement of USBE balances occurring through correspondent banks in New York. Cross-border settlement between U.S. and Canadian banks is available via ACH.

11. The primary advantages of switching to the euro have been the elimination of currency exposures between the EMU countries, as well as reduced FX exposure and transaction costs. Another advantage is that the use of the euro in European capital markets has virtually eliminated the possibility of exchange rate crises for member countries. Such advantages result in the consolidation of banking relationships and the simplification of certain international treasury-management techniques such as pooling and netting.

12. In the open account method, the seller checks the creditworthiness of the buyer, establishes credit terms and limits, ships the merchandise and sends an invoice to the buyer. The buyer is responsible for initiating payment to the seller in accordance with any agreed upon credit terms. In the U.S., the open account is the most frequently used method of payment for B2B domestic transactions. An open account is also widely used internationally when two trading partners have an existing relationship; however, exporting goods to a non-domestic buyer where there is no established relationship often requires credit risk protection through documentary collection or an L/C.

13. A letter of credit or L/C is a document issued by a bank, guaranteeing the payment of a customer's draft up to a stated amount for a specified period, provided certain conditions are met. The L/C substitutes a bank's credit for that of the buyer, virtually eliminating the seller's credit risk. L/Cs are a widely used method of payment for import and export shipments and are also often used as a financing vehicle for international trade transactions.

14. Countertrade is a method of payment used by companies that do not have access to sufficient hard currencies (internationally traded currencies) to pay for imports from other countries. For example, a U.S. exporter ships merchandise to the countertrading country and in exchange takes merchandise that may be sold elsewhere in the world.

Chapter 16 – Global Treasury Organization & Liquidity Management

1. Many MNCs and banks utilize a structure called shared service centers (SSCs). An SSC is a consolidated operation that supports standardized processes (accounting, payroll, etc.) within an organization. SSCs were initially developed to establish, measure and maintain the cost and contribution of back-office business processes and operations. However, SSCs have expanded to support a wide range of functions such as treasury accounting, receivables and payables management, human resources, payroll, benefits management, legal, compliance and tax. In a sense, it is like outsourcing a particular function or process to an in-house provider.

2. Five steps are involved in establishing an SSC: (1) determine the economic contribution of treasury back office processes, (2) compare an SSC structure to outsourcing solutions, (3) select a location for the SSC in a country that offers tax advantages or tax havens (e.g., the Netherlands, Luxembourg, Ireland, Singapore), (4) choose and implement the technology for the SSC and (5) find and retain quality staff and managers to work at the SSC.

3. Many large global companies have established their own in-house banks within centralized treasury departments. In these types of arrangements, treasury becomes the main provider of banking services for all of the company's operating entities. Treasury does so by instructing financial institutions to clear transactions and provide services on a bulk basis. The primary benefit is a reduction in overall banking costs by aggregating many small transactions into fewer, larger transactions. The in-house bank can also manage four of the principal international treasury-management solutions: netting, pooling, re-invoicing and centralization of FX exposures. To optimize these benefits, it is critical to link the in-house banking operations to treasury management and ERP systems.

4. Companies concentrate cash internationally for the same reasons they do so domestically: to utilize available cash more efficiently, to improve liquidity management by maximizing interest earnings on investments and minimizing interest expense on borrowing and to improve the accuracy of forecasting. In the U.S., concentration of cash involves the physical movement of funds from outlying depository banks into a concentration bank. Outside of the U.S., this physical concentration of funds is usually referred to as "sweeping" (not to be confused with "sweep accounts" used by treasurers in the U.S. for overnight investment of surplus funds). In countries where banks are allowed to pay interest on excess demand deposit balances and to charge interest on deficit balances, the typical method of concentration is known as pooling. The most common form of pooling is practiced in the pan-European region. Any excess funds in the accounts of a company or its subsidiaries are used to offset any deficits in other accounts of the parent or subsidiaries. This type of pooling arrangement is offered for a variety of currencies and is known as notional pooling because no actual funds are transferred.

5. Netting is an internal company (intracompany) system designed to reduce the number of cross-border payments among units of a company through the elimination or consolidation of funds denominated in different currencies. Many countries impose restrictions on the use of netting systems due to the tax consequences; hence, central bank or government approval is often required.

6. Reinvoicing is an intracompany method of centralizing responsibility for monitoring and collecting international accounts receivable and more effectively managing related FX exposures. A reinvoicing center is a company-owned subsidiary that purchases goods from an exporting subsidiary and sells the goods to an importing subsidiary. The exporting unit invoices and receives funds from the reinvoicing subsidiary in its own currency while the importing unit is invoiced and pays funds to the reinvoicing subsidiary in its own currency. Although the title to the goods passes through the reinvoicing center, the actual goods usually are shipped directly from the exporting subsidiary to the importing subsidiary. Establishing a rinvoicing center requires local government approval and negotiations in determining how the subsidiary is taxed.

7. Multicurrency accounts are a special arrangement between a bank and a company whereby the bank allows the customer to receive or make international payments in a range of currencies from a single account or multiple subsidiary accounts. A multicurrency agreement generally specifies: (1) the base currency in which the account is denominated, (2) the portfolio of currencies accepted, (3) the spread or margin over the spot rate to use in exchanging each currency back to the base currency and (4) the value date to apply to debits and credits for each transaction type and currency.

8. For MNCs, one of the primary issues in treasury is the repatriation of capital from foreign subsidiaries back to the domestic parent's country. Repatriation involves the physical transfer of funds from one country to another. The principal method of repatriation is the use of dividends; however, there may be restrictions on this approach. Therefore, other methods such as management fees, royalties, licensing, transfer pricing and intracompany loans may also be used for repatriation purposes. Most repatriation policies are related to the transfer of funds back to the U.S. parent from wholly or partially owned global subsidiaries of U.S. MNCs. The objective is to ensure not only that the MNC is fairly compensated for the foreign investment but also that the host country benefits from the local reinvestment of funds.

9. Transfer pricing is the price that subsidiaries of a large corporation charge each other for components sold among themselves. The benefit for MNCs is that transfer pricing can be manipulated to locate profits in subsidiaries in low-tax countries and move them out of subsidiaries in high- tax countries. Host governments may resent these actions; hence, they frequently place restrictions on transfer pricing or changes in transfer pricing, by MNCs within their jurisdictions. The implication for MNC management is that most transfer pricing for global subsidiaries must be done at "arm's length." This means setting transfer prices at the same level at which a company would buy or sell similar products from an unaffiliated company. This assures host governments that the profits from the MNC will be distributed fairly among all of its global subsidiaries. The complexity of transfer pricing is such that MNCs typically seek the advice of highly specialized tax consultants to establish policies and procedures.

10. In some foreign countries, particularly those experiencing an upsurge in economic growth, companies will be assessed a capital tax on the initial capital used to establish the new venture or on subsequent flows of incoming or repatriated capital. A capital tax is used as a fiscal tool by some countries to augment tax collections. The tax can also be used by a government to slow down foreign direct investment in a country.

Chapter 17 – Financial Risk Management

1. Financial risk is the risk of direct or indirect losses resulting from the uncertainty of the future level of interest rates, foreign exchange (FX) rates and commodity prices or from adverse impacts on a company with a highly leveraged capital structure. The very nature of treasury operations makes many organizations vulnerable to significant financial risks. Treasurers must make critical decisions that are time sensitive, that typically involve large sums of money and that must be made under volatile financial conditions. Further complicating these decisions is the fact that exposure to financial risk has increased significantly in recent years for two reasons: the speed of business brought about by advances in technology and communications and the scope of business brought about by the trend toward globalization.

2. The risk management process involves five steps: (1) determining an organization's risk attitude, (2) identifying the exposure, (3) measuring the exposure, (4) implementing an appropriate risk-management strategy and (5) monitoring the exposure to evaluate the strategy.

3. The risk profile of a company is the relationship of how the overall value of a company changes as some financial price variables change. A basic risk profile determines the sensitivity of a company to a change in interest rates, FX rates or commodity prices, typically measured by the company's equity value or stock price. For organizations that are not publicly traded (i.e., privately held, not-for-profit or governmental), a risk profile determines the impact on cash flows. A risk profile analysis identifies the risks, classifies each risk into clearly defined categories, and quantifies the risks with respect to the probability of occurrence and the impact on a company. Based on this analysis, the effectiveness of the risk reduction measures that are employed can be determined.

4. Hedging is the process by which an organization uses financial instruments to reduce or eliminate risks associated with the uncertainty about the future price of an asset. Hedging is similar to the concept of buying insurance. Speculation involves betting on the direction of the market. Speculators are experienced market participants who are willing to assume risks. Unlike hedgers, speculators are referred to as being "naked" in the sense that there is no underlying asset or exposure to offset; therefore, speculation increases overall financial risk. Arbitrage is the process by which buying in one market and simultaneously selling in another leads to a riskless profit. A true arbitrage arrangement or transaction has no impact on a company's overall risk profile. Arbitrageurs do not assume any risk; rather, they attempt to profit from market inefficiencies. It is difficult for the majority of companies to take advantage of arbitrage opportunities. Market inefficiencies that lead to arbitrage opportunities are extremely short lived and relatively small as measured in basis points. Therefore, only major market participants with large amounts of capital can take advantage of these inefficiencies.

5. A forward contract is an agreement between two parties to buy or sell a fixed amount of an asset to be delivered at a future date for an agreed upon price today. The asset involved is referred to as the underlying asset. This underlying asset can be a financial instrument (such as stock index or debt instrument),

currency (such as the euro or pound sterling) or a commodity (such as gold or coffee). The future date is referred to as the maturity date of the contract and the price is called the delivery price. A company purchasing a forward contract is one party while the other party is typically referred to as the counterparty. In forward currency contracts, the counterparty is typically a bank or dealer in the FX markets.

6. Futures are similar to forwards in intent in the sense that the payoff profile from a long position and a short position in a futures contract looks exactly the same as the payoff from a forward contract. The main difference between futures and forwards is that futures are standardized contracts (standard amounts and delivery dates) that are traded on organized exchanges and require margin accounts. In addition, the counterparty to all futures contracts is the exchange itself, which increases liquidity and virtually eliminates counterparty risk. Finally, futures contracts are rarely settled by delivery and are usually closed out prior to maturity.

7. An option is a contract between two parties in which the buyer of the contract has the right (but not the obligation) to either buy or sell a fixed amount of some underlying asset at a fixed price on or before a specified date. The party offering the option is called the writer of the option. Options may be either exchange-traded or negotiated with a specific counterparty. Exchange-traded options share many of the same characteristics of futures contracts, with standardized amounts and delivery dates, and the exchange serving as the counterparty for all contracts.

8. A call option gives the owner the right to buy the underlying asset at a fixed price while a put option gives the owner the right to sell the underlying asset at a fixed price. The fixed price is called the strike price or exercise price of the contract. The specified date is the maturity date or exercise date of the contract. If the contract allows the buyer to exercise (that is, to buy or sell the underlying asset) the option only at maturity, then the contract is called a European option contract. If the contract allows the owner to exercise the option at any time prior to maturity, the contract is called an American option contract.

9. Caps, collars and floors are interest rate options in which the payoff depends on the level of interest rates. Caps ensure that the borrower of a floating rate loan receives a ceiling rate if interest rates rise above a specified level. This level is known as the cap rate. If rates fall, the borrower is not obligated to exercise the option and can still enjoy the benefits of lower borrowing costs. The price of this "insurance" is the premium paid for the cap. Floors ensure that the owner of a floating rate asset receives a floor rate if interest rates fall below a specified level. If rates fall, the floating rate asset is protected by the put option on interest rates. If interest rates rise, the company can still benefit because it is not obligated to exercise the option. The cost of this "insurance" is the premium paid for the interest rate floor. A combination of an interest rate cap and an interest rate floor is called an interest rate collar. A company that buys a cap and sells a floor is effectively locking in a range for borrowing costs. The cap establishes a maximum borrowing rate, thereby protecting the company against higher interest rates, while the floor sets a minimum borrowing rate. A collar has no costs when the income received from selling the floor matches the premium paid for the cap. Costless collars are popular hedging vehicles providing some interest rate protection at no cost.

10. If the receivables or payables on a company's balance sheet are affected by changes in FX rates, then the company has a transaction exposure. Transaction exposure occurs when the receivables and payables are in different currencies. In the case of receivables, adjusting the price of goods and services does not necessarily eliminate transaction exposure. In the case of a U.S. exporter who sells merchandise to a French buyer agreeing to accept payment in euro three months from now, the exporter records the transaction as an accounts receivable. However, the exporter is exposed to a possible loss in value if the euro depreciates relative to the U.S. dollar in three months.

11. A currency option gives the buyer the right to buy (call option) or sell (put option) a fixed amount of a foreign currency at a fixed exchange rate (strike price) on or before a specific future date. A foreign currency put option establishes a floor value (in terms of the domestic currency) for a foreign currency. The floor value is the exercise price less the premium on a put option. Similarly, a foreign currency call option sets a ceiling cost (in terms of the domestic currency) for a foreign currency. The ceiling cost is the strike price plus the premium paid for the call. An U.S. importer with an accounts payable due in three months in British pound sterling can ensure a maximum cost for the pounds by going long (buying a call option) on the pound. If, at the time of payment, the spot market price of the pound is less than the strike price of the call option, the importer does not exercise the option and loses only the premium. The net cost of the pounds to the importer is the spot price of the pound plus the option premium. The option acts as insurance against the spot price of the pound rising above a specific level. For this insurance, the importer pays a premium, which is the option price.

12. Hedge accounting is an accounting technique that is applied to the components of a hedge so that the fair value of the hedged asset and the hedging vehicle are included in earnings for the same period. As a result of the tremendous growth in alternative hedging instruments, no standard accounting guidelines have been established for financial derivatives. Although hedge accounting has been addressed in FAS 80 (Accounting for Futures Contracts) and FAS 52 (Foreign-Currency Translation), these pronouncements contain certain conceptual inconsistencies. For example, FAS 52 limits hedge accounting for currency transactions to future transactions that are firmly committed. On the other hand, FAS 80 extends hedge accounting to anticipated future transactions that are not firmly committed, provided that certain criteria are met.

Chapter 18 – Enterprise Risk Management

1. Operational risk is generally defined as the risk of direct and indirect losses resulting from external events that impact an organization's operations or inadequate and failed internal processes, people and systems. The internal sources of operational risk are usually related to either the lack or failure of controls on people, processes or technology. External events can range from localized events such as momentary communications failures to global events such as terrorism. The potential for operational risk resulting from the use of technology also increases as treasury relies more and more on complex technology combined with legacy manual processes to generate, store and use information.

2. As the treasury area of an organization relies increasingly more on technology, the operational risk related to the use of technology increases. First, there is risk associated with the choice of a particular technological platform or vendor. Platform and vendor-selection risks include such issues as after-sale installation and support or even the risk that a vendor may no longer be in business. Second, there is also risk associated with the potential failure of vendor acquired hardware, software and/or communications devices. Third, there are issues involving capability, capacity and compatibility. Another issue for technology is possible security breaches, either from internal sources or from external hackers. For example, a treasury information system vendor may offer a product that is ideal for an organization, but the stability and long-run viability of the vendor must be considered. It is not uncommon for an organization to purchase a suboptimal software product from a known provider rather than a superior product from a new and untested provider. Finally, technology risk may involve the extensive use of computer-based spreadsheets in many parts of an organization's day-to-day operations. While spreadsheets can be extremely useful for many business functions and data management, there are some issues when they are used for "mission-critical" applications that require transactional and information processing.

3. The three critical factors in determining a risk management strategy for an organization are: (1) culture, (2) procedures and (3) technology. The importance of each of these varies, depending upon the needs of an organization.

4. Disaster recovery refers to the restoration of systems and communications after an outage. Business continuity refers to the actions taken with regard to crisis management, alternative operating procedures and communications to staff and customers. Disaster avoidance and recovery equates to revenue preservation and continuation. Despite this, many organizations do not have robust disaster recovery and business continuity plans in place. As a result, these organizations are not able to adequately cope with major incidents that disrupt business.

5. An activity or function is mission-critical when an interruption creates significant disruptions in the organization's cash flow/liquidity. Such disruptions have serious repercussions on an organization's ability to continue normal operations and, ultimately, may make it difficult for the company to remain in business. Within the treasury area, mission-critical functions tend to be concentrated in treasury

operations, including such time-critical daily tasks as accounts receivable and collection, cash concentration, payroll, accounts payable, interest, bondholder and dividend payments, disbursement funding and the calculation of the daily cash position.

6. Effective risk management helps control or prevent losses, and adequate insurance helps finance an organization's recovery when a loss occurs. Events resulting in a major loss generally disrupt an organization's operating and financial plans. Losses may include: (1) property loss (from both internal and external theft), (2) business interruption or net income loss, (3) surety or breach of contract loss (such as a contractor's failure to perform), (4) liability loss (including lawsuits from injured customers), (5) personnel loss (involving the loss of the president or other "key persons") and (6) workers' compensation.

7. The treasury area often has diverse but important responsibilities related to the cost of risk. The primary decision is to identify the potential losses for which the organization purchases insurance and those that the organization should either pay for or self-insure. Ultimately, the overall intent is to control the cost of risks associated with a set of loss exposures. The treasuryarea may be called upon to identify, measure, and allocate the cost of each of the risk elements for a given project (or even for the entire organization) so that the risk factors are analyzed in management decisions. The treasurer often has direct responsibility for managing exposures due to accidental losses that arise from treasury assets or activities managed by treasury Everything an organization owns or does is a source of potential loss and treasurymanagement activities are no exception.

8. The primary purpose of difference in conditions (DIC) insurance is to cover the insured's property for perils not covered by the basic property insurance policies. Typically used in conjunction with multiple basic policies to make them all uniform, DIC insurance does not provide higher limits of coverage for basic perils as does an umbrella policy; rather, it provides coverage for conditions and perils not included in the basic policy. DIC insurance is often purchased to fill voids in policies purchased overseas and to insure property in transit. This type of insurance is not typically standardized because the market for it is limited and DIC insurance is generally written to cover special exposure and circumstances. Often there are exclusions for important perils such as fire, vandalism, employee dishonesty, machinery losses, etc., because it is assumed that an insured business already has coverage for these losses under standard business property insurance.

9. This insurance provides coverage for the four basic types of benefits: (1) medical care, (2) death, (3) disability and (4) rehabilitation. Associated with employee job-related injuries or diseases as a matter of right (without regard to fault), this insurance is usually purchased by the employer from an insurance company, although there are a few monopolistic state funds through which the insurance must be purchased. The premium rates are generally based on a percentage of the employer's payroll and vary according to the employee's occupation.

10. The goals of insurance risk management are as follows: (1) insure against catastrophic loss, (2) decide when and what to insure, (3) manage the purchase and use of insurance (including brokers) and (4) obtain efficient pricing for insurance needs. Insurance risk management is a decision or problem-solving process

in which the "problem" is exposure to accidental losses.

11. Fidelity risks arise from the theft of money, securities or property by employees, as well as from crime involving employees or outsiders to the organization. To properly deal with these types of risk, management should examine amounts and locations of cash and securities holdings; maintain adequate control procedures for cash, securities, property, and inventory and implement proper screening and bonding procedures for all employees involved with handling cash, securities or inventory.

12. Exposure avoidance involves refraining from taking on an asset or activity, or eliminating an existing one, when there is no combination of risk control or financing techniques that produces a projected risk-adjusted rate of return that is adequate. This may require an organization to reconsider lines of business or services provided if a particular area is too risky from the standpoint of potential loss.

13. One approach to risk retention is known as non-insurance. This technique involves relying on normal revenues to pay for small, "normal" losses as current expenses. Non-insurance is appropriate for losses an organization can readily absorb as "costs of doing business" but not for highly disruptive, potentially ruinous accidents. The proper cost of these funds is the rate of return the organization could have earned in terms of an optimal alternative use. Self-insurance is not technically a form of insurance because it does not involve a transfer of risk to an insurer or another separate entity. Also, the term "self-insurance" is often used to describe any risk retention program, even highly informal unfunded arrangements. Many organizations that practice self-insurance set "cap limits" on self-insurance exposure by purchasing excess coverage (i.e., "real insurance") for claims above some predetermined limit. Any claims below this limit will be "self-insured" while amounts above the limit (i.e., excess losses) will by covered by the cap limit policy.

14. The essence of any risk transfer is a contract between a transferring organization (transferor) and another entity (the transferee), under which the transferee agrees to pay designated types of the transferor's losses within contractual limits. The transferor may have to pay the transferee a fee (such as an insurance premium) for this promise of indemnity, or the transferor may have the bargaining power to secure this promise as a condition for agreeing to do business with the transferee. Such risk-transfer arrangements are often made for tax or regulatory reasons and may be accomplished through the purchase of reinsurance either from a broker or directly from the market. It is important to note that the transfer of risk is only as good as the transferee's, or the insurance company's, ability to pay claims.

15. By selecting insurance (particularly property insurance) that has a deductible, an insured can save many premium dollars in comparison to the cost of "first-dollar" coverage. In essence, the deductible forces the insured to share some of the front-end risk from potential losses. The higher the deductible, the lower the cost of the premium is for insurance. However, it is important to weigh the many losses that could fall within the deductible and the managerial uncertainty that deductible payments impose against the potential savings. Deductibles may also be set on a per-occurrence basis (the deductible applies for each occurrence during the policy period) or on an aggregate basis (deductible is set on a per-period basis, regardless of the number of occurrences).

Chapter 19 – Corporate Governance and Ethics

1. The issue of corporate governance arises from the separation of ownership and control that exists in most companies. While stockholders own the company, officers (executives) actually control the company. This separation is a potential problem in large, widely-held corporations (vs. small, closely-held companies) where management may be able to make decisions with little or no oversight by the owners. In fact, it may be more useful to think of stockholders as investors rather than owners. The difference is subtle but important. Owners focus on the business performance of the company while investors focus on the risk and return of portfolios. This tends to make most investors passive or inactive shareholders of companies, thereby providing a significant incentive for the management of such companies to take actions that will benefit themselves while reducing the value to the shareholders. This is generally referred to as the "agency problem" between management and stockholders. To protect the owner/investors, there is an established set of checks and balances, generally referred to as corporate governance.

2. The important components of corporate governance are the Board of Directors (especially independent directors), the independent auditors and the regulatory agencies. Most of the recent failures in corporate governance can be traced back to a failure on the part of one or more these components. An organization should, therefore, have a chief audit executive accountable for the internal audit function that reports directly to the audit committee of the Board of Directors. The Board should provide sufficient funding and resources to the audit function, including periodic private sessions to discuss risk and controls with the chief auditor.

3. The purpose of recent Sarbanes-Oxley (SOX) and NYSE standards are to: (1) increase the role and authority of independent directors, (2) tighten the definition of an independent director, (3) give shareholders more opportunity to monitor and participate in the governance of companies and (4) establish new control and enforcement mechanisms. Financial professionals at NYSE companies, or those with companies considering listing on the NYSE or other exchanges, must understand these requirements and expectations. Failure to adhere to these standards could cause significant public embarrassment for the company, as well as a significant loss of investor capital. CEOs must certify to the listing exchange(s) that their companies comply with these standards.

4. Due to the significance and legal implications of SOX, public company CEOs and CFOs have sought to ensure that such information is accurate and complete. One method to help ensure compliance is through subcertification. Subcertification generally consists of a certification of financial information by those who were responsible for providing the information; hence, that may include many employees from the company's treasury and finance departments. While subcertification is often presented in the form of a signed written statement, it can also be a verbal acknowledgment of the responsibility for certain financial information included in financial statements filed with the SEC.

5. A code of conduct establishes rules of behavior for what constitutes appropriate actions and ethical behaviors encountered during normal business activities. It is important to proactively encourage moral conduct through clear statements of what will and will not be tolerated. While a code of conduct cannot prevent the adverse actions of an unethical person, it clearly delineates acceptable behaviors, as well as the consequences for behaviors that are unacceptable. Each organization must write a code relevant for its particular industry or business.

6. Conflicts of interest include objective managerial actions that require the avoidance of a conflict of interest or the appearance of a conflict. The code should address employee acquisition of stock in companies with which the company does business. In addition, the solicitation and acceptance of gifts and entertainment from current and prospective banks and vendors should be covered, including maximum dollar limits or, as is often the case, absolute prohibition regarding acceptance of any gifts.

7. Policy and procedure (P&P) statements provide a framework for the design of treasury systems and controls in support of company objectives. Realistically, the behavior of managers cannot be regulated by proclamation. However, assigning specific duties to designated managers establishes the company's position on responsibilities, sets a charter for responsible corporate behavior and assesses penalties should violations occur. The publication of P&Ps provides a venue by which the corporation can inform employees, agents, contractors and vendors of the disposition of specific treasury activities. Such a publication can minimize situations in which unauthorized parties act in the name of the corporation, resulting in potentially detrimental consequences. These standards should be reviewed on a regular basis; some experts suggest an annual review.

8. Investor relations (IR) is a strategic management responsibility that integrates finance, communication, marketing and securities law compliance to enable the most effective two-way communication between a company and the financial community or other constituencies. The goal of investor relations is to ensure that a company's securities achieve a fair valuation in the financial marketplace. It is now more important than ever for companies to have an effective IR representative in order to attract and retain capital and to restore investor confidence. The establishment of strict separation between the investment banking and investment research divisions of companies has resulted in significant changes in the IR role. In an environment of truly independent research and immediate disclosure, it is extremely important for the IR professional to be perceived by the investment community as having complete access to senior management.

9. Pre-emptive right is the right that certain (or all) shareholders have to first rights of purchase, on a pro-rata basis, of any new shares of stock issued by a company. This is usually conducted through a rights offering or a "subscription" to any new stock issued by a company. The current shareholders may either purchase additional shares on a pro-rata basis or sell the rights to other parties. Although not a requirement in all states, it offers stockholders protection against dilution of value and protects the power of control for the existing shareholders. Most corporations include this right in charters.

10. One of the key issues facing companies is how to treat stock options provided to management and employees. From a shareholder perspective, financial reporting should provide enough information to get a realistic picture of how a company is operating. Responding to requests from investors, financial analysts and other users of financial information, the Financial Accounting Standards Board (FASB) is currently investigating this issue. According to FASB, there is a need for one consistent approach to recognize the costs associated with employee stock options. A move to require an expense treatment is consistent with the FASB's commitment to work toward convergence between U.S. and international accounting standards. The Board plans to start issuing guidelines that will become effective in late 2004.

Chapter 20 – Pension Fund Management

1. The Employee Retirement Income Security Act of 1974 (ERISA) is the federal law that established legal guidelines for private pension plan administration and investment practices. ERISA has five major objectives:
   - To ensure that employees and beneficiaries receive adequate information about their benefit plans
   - To set standards of conduct for individuals who manage employee-benefit plans and plan funds
   - To determine that adequate funds are being set aside to pay promised pension benefits
   - To ensure that employees receive pension benefits after they have satisfied certain minimum requirements
   - To safeguard pension benefits for workers whose pension plans are terminated.

2. A fiduciary is an individual or a member of a Board who is given possession of property, such as plan assets, in trust. A fiduciary assumes the legal obligation to administer plan assets solely for the purpose(s) specified. Typically, the employer's Board of Directors designates one or more committees to act as a fiduciary. These committees are charged with administration of the plans and oversight of the management of plan assets.

3. A prohibited transaction is an economic transaction directly or indirectly involving plan assets and parties related to the plan. A "party-in-interest" includes fiduciaries, counsel or employees of the plan, individuals providing services to the plan, an employer whose employees are covered by the plan, a relative of any of the preceding, or various other individuals and entities with ties to the employer or the plan [ERISA Section 3(14)]. Prohibited transactions include the sale, exchange or lease of property; a loan or other extension of credit; the furnishing of goods, services or facilities and the transfer or use of plan assets involving a party-in-interest. Prohibited transactions also include the acquisition of employer securities or employer real estate in excess of the limits set by law.

4. An HCE is an employee who was a five-percent owner of the sponsoring company at any time during the current or preceding year or who had compensation during the prior year in excess of $90,000. A retirement plan is qualified under ERISA only if it does not discriminate in favor of highly compensated employees (HCEs). The plan must comply in both form and operation to this rule. To satisfy this basic nondiscrimination rule, there are three requirements: (1) The contributions or benefits of the plan must be nondiscriminatory in amount; (2) The benefits, rights and features provided under the plan must be available in a nondiscriminatory manner and (3) The effect of plan amendments and terminations must be nondiscriminatory.

5. In a distress termination, the PBGC takes over the plan and pays all guaranteed benefits up to a maximum amount determined by the PBGC. The plan sponsor and any controlled group of companies are liable to the PBGC for any unfunded benefits. Only financially troubled employers, as determined by the PBGC, qualify for distress termination. Typically, these are companies in or near bankruptcy with significantly

underfunded pension plans. Prioritization of benefits payable in a distress termination are set forth in detail by ERISA, with benefits attributable to employee contributions taking priority, followed by other PBGC-guaranteed benefits.

6. In a defined benefit plan, the benefit payment for each participant is calculated (or "defined") by a formula as specified in the plan. The formula is most often based on factors such as the employee's level of pay and length of service at retirement. The projected future benefit payments for all participants are then aggregated and discounted to obtain the plan's liability, also sometimes referred to as the plan's obligation. The plan's liability or obligation is funded by employer contributions (and sometimes employee contributions) as well as cumulative earnings. The value of the assets is measured independently of the liability and is based on fair market value. A defined benefit plan can thus be overfunded or underfunded, depending on whether the value of the plan's assets is greater than or less than the amount of the liability.

7. The primary difference between defined benefit and defined contribution plans is who bears the risk of a shortfall in investment results. This risk is borne by the employer in the case of defined benefit plans and by the employee in the case of defined contribution plans. A typical defined benefit plan promises a benefit upon retirement based on the employee's pay and length of service. If contributions and investment earnings on the contributions do not provide enough funds to meet the plan's promise at retirement, then employers must make additional contributions to meet the shortfall. If investment earnings exceed expectations, the employee still receives only the promised benefit. In defined contribution plans, on the other hand, higher-than-expected investment returns are passed on directly to the employee, who must also accept the risk of a lower asset value if returns are disappointing. Other important differences between plans include the fact that in the early years of an employee's career, account values in defined benefit plans generally grow slower than in defined contribution plans; however, the reverse is true in later years. Additionally, defined contribution plan assets are generally more portable than defined benefit plan assets. The general trend is away from defined benefit plans and toward the use of defined contribution plans.

8. In a 401(k) plan, the employee is given the choice of either receiving an amount, in the form of currently taxable compensation (for federal income tax purposes) or deferring the amount to be taxed at a future date. This amount may be part of normal salary or other compensation such as bonus or profit sharing. Under these plans, employees may divert a portion of their compensation into the deferred-tax 401(k) plan. Employees may also have the choice of making additional contributions into the plan on a before-tax basis, thus avoiding any federal income tax on these amounts until they are received at retirement. This type of plan must meet the same strict guidelines concerning non-discrimination as qualified deferred compensation plans. The company may also make an additional contribution to the plan on behalf of the employee (typically in cash or company stock). In many cases, the company contribution is based on a matching formula relative to the employee's contribution or, in other cases, the employer's contributions may be made for all eligible employees regardless of their contributions.

9. Legally, every plan is either a defined benefit plan or a defined contribution plan, but hybrid plans offer various blends of defined benefit and defined contribution characteristics. The increasingly popular cash balance plan, for example, often has a portability feature and reports participant "balances" that look just like defined contribution accounts. However, cash balance plans are actually defined benefit plans. Similarly, pension equity plans, also known as retirement bonus plans, report account balances to participants and look like defined contribution plans but are, in reality, defined benefit plans.

10. The appointment of an independent custodian (often a financial institution) is an effective way to safeguard the physical and legal integrity of the assets in a pension fund. The custodian holds the pension fund assets and, therefore, should be in a position to ensure the safekeeping of the assets. The custodian may provide additional services such as securities lending, cash management, investment accounting, and reporting as well as performance measurement. In some cases, a custodian may also serve as an external audit function with respect to the investment of pension assets.

Chapter 21 – Relationship Management

1. Consolidation and specialization in the financial services industry have made financial institution and FSP selection a critical decision process for a treasurer. Consolidation reduces the number of providers in certain product areas, while specialization raises the importance of matching a given company's needs with a particular provider's strengths. The selection process may be initiated for a variety of reasons: such as the need for a new product or service, as part of a re-engineering program, as part of a regular product and service review, to reduce costs or to update existing technologies. Regardless of the reason, the process should always begin by identifying the product or service specifications that are critical to achieving both the strategic and the operational objectives of treasury. These specifications form the selection criteria that provide the basis for evaluating financial institution and vendor proposals.

2. Although selection criteria may vary widely from one product or service to another and from one company to another, the criteria often include the following factors: (1) geographic and other convenience considerations, (2) ability to fulfill product or service specifications. (3) expertise of personnel, including quality of customer service and product support, (4) commitment to, or knowledge of a specific industry or business, (5) ability to customize services, develop new services, update technologies and meet future needs of the company, (6) adequacy of internal controls, backup systems and disaster recovery plans, (7) pricing and (8) the cost of switching providers.

3. A RFP is a formal document prepared by a company that outlines its objectives and service requirements. A RFP may be used to obtain bids for anything ranging from one specific service to a company's entire relationship. By law, some government entities are required to prepare RFPs on a periodic basis, usually every three to five years, to ensure that comparable services are received at competitive prices. Many private sector companies also periodically prepare RFPs for similar reasons.

4. Risk management requires ongoing monitoring of bank and FSP practices and creditworthiness. Two particular areas of practice warrant special mention. First, because banks and FSPs often control an organization's information flows, information records and liquid assets, it is critical that banks and FSPs have adequate backup systems and disaster recovery procedures. These procedures should be evaluated at the onset of the relationship and periodically thereafter. In addition, service agreements and contract provisions should indicate specific rights and responsibilities of the parties in the event of an interruption in services. Second, because banks and FSPs have access to extensive confidential information about an organization's customer base, a treasurer must understand under what conditions, if any, this information may be shared with affiliates or other parties. Sometimes, a conflict of interest may arise when a bank or FSP serves in multiple capacities. A bank with a lending relationship may also serve as a bond trustee. If the borrower becomes distressed, there is a risk that the bank might protect its own credit to the detriment of the borrower and/or the bondholders.

5. Success in every long-term relationship involves a mutual accommodation of both parties. Among the factors that increase the mutual benefit and profitability of the relationship are: (1) open and frequent two-way communications, (2) regular and timely feedback, (3) documentation of expectations of both parties in agreements and legal contracts, (4) fair compensation of a bank by a company, and fair pricing of services by the bank and (5) complete and candid disclosure of information by both parties.

6. Service agreements are formal agreements that document the requirements and expectations of both the purchaser and the provider of a specific service or services. The elements of a service agreement often include the following: (1) operational policies and procedures, including the detailed processing requirements for the service, information needs, and individuals who are authorized to make changes; (2) performance standards that define agreed upon levels of service performance and quality; (3) compensation policies, including pricing, method of payment, payment frequency, excess/deficit balance arrangements, contract length, and adjustments; (4) liability clauses defining responsibilities for specified risks and (5) other terms and conditions of the relationship.

7. A report card is a tool companies use to obtain a quantitative rating of a bank's level of service and responsiveness to problems. Criteria commonly found in report cards include the number of errors by service, reporting times for information services, responsiveness to inquiries, timeliness of error resolution and the effectiveness of service personnel. Companies may prepare report cards monthly, quarterly, semiannually and/or annually. Certain companies that deal with multiple banks and FSPs frequently rank each one by the ability to meet the companies' quality criteria on a service-by-service basis.

8. Unique to financial institutions is the CAMELS rating system, a system widely used by regulators to measure financial institution strength. CAMELS is the acronym for Capital Adequacy, Asset Quality, Management Capability, Earnings, Liquidity and Sensitivity to Market Risk.

9. FSPs, and most banks, are compensated by means of a direct payment of fees for services provided. However, there is a form of compensation unique to banks because of the earnings credit typically provided to business account holders. Banks allow companies to pay for services in collected balances as an alternative to direct payment of fees. In some cases, companies pay using a combination of collected balances and fees. Banks may encourage customers to utilize one type of compensation due to their business strategy or desire for either deposits (i.e., balances) or fees. In actual practice, most companies compensate banks with a combination of balances and fees. Necessary transaction balances are maintained for partial compensation purposes and the remainder is paid in fees.

10. An account analysis statement is a paper or electronic report that a bank provides to commercial customers specifying services provided, balances maintained, volumes processed and charges assessed. It is essentially an invoice for services provided, along with detailed information on balances and credit earned for those balances. However, banks often use varying terminology in describing these services and/or varying definitions of identical terms. Services and fees can be bundled into a single line item or flat fee, unbundled (that is, detailed and itemized) or, more typically, some combination of bundled and unbundled. Fee structures are as varied and complex as the account analysis formats.

11. The earnings credit is the total dollar value of credit that can be used to offset the service charges incurred during the analysis period. It is calculated by multiplying the investable balance by the earnings credit rate (ECR) for the period. The method of determining the ECR varies by financial institution. The most commonly used ECR is based upon the 90-day T-Bill rate. Other banks reduce the ECR by the reserve requirement (a reserve-adjusted ECR) in which case the average collected balance is used in the earnings credit calculation instead of the investable balance.

Index

B

D

E

F

G

H

I

J

K

L

M

N

O

P

S

X

Y

Z

Printed in the United States
77560LV00012B/1-44